Law Enforcement

FLORIDA
BASIC RECRUIT
TRAINING PROGRAM VOL.1 (2026.07)

Florida Basic Recruit Training Program: Law Enforcement, Volume 1

Copyright © 2026 by the Florida Department of Law Enforcement (FDLE)

Disclaimer

FDLE makes a sincere effort to ensure accuracy and quality of its published materials; however, no warranty, expressed or implied, is provided. FDLE disclaims any responsibility or liability for any direct or indirect damages resulting from the use of the information in this course or products described in it. Mention of any product does not constitute an endorsement by FDLE of that product. All referenced persons, places, or situations are intended to be fictional, unless otherwise stated. Any resemblance to real persons, places, or situations is coincidental. The training in this course is provided to familiarize students with issues that may involve high liability and/or high stress. FDLE urges students to ensure that their practices are correct in accordance with their agencies' policies and procedures. Employing agencies are solely responsible for guiding their employees' actions in actual situations.

Published in the United States of America

Illustrations by Rob Bates, FDLE

Table of Contents

Chapter 1 — Introduction to Law Enforcement / 1

UNIT 1 THE LAW ENFORCEMENT OFFICER PROFESSION
- LESSON 1 The Roles of a Law Enforcement Officer / 3
- LESSON 2 Steps to Becoming a Certified Officer / 6
- LESSON 3 The Criminal Justice System / 10
- LESSON 4 Chain of Command / 14
- LESSON 5 Procedural Justice / 16

UNIT 2 OFFICER ETHICS AND CONDUCT
- LESSON 1 Criminal Justice Ethical Concepts / 18
- LESSON 2 Unethical Behavior / 21
- LESSON 3 Fair and Unbiased Policing / 25

UNIT 3 OFFICER WELL-BEING
- LESSON 1 Adjusting to Shiftwork / 28
- LESSON 2 Officer Wellness / 30
- LESSON 3 Stress / 33
- LESSON 4 Substance Abuse Awareness and Suicide Prevention / 38

Chapter 2 — Communication / 43

UNIT 1 FUNDAMENTALS OF COMMUNICATION
- LESSON 1 Communication Basics / 45
- LESSON 2 Verbal and Non-verbal Communication / 48
- LESSON 3 Conflict Resolution and De-escalation / 51

UNIT 2 PROFESSIONAL COMMUNICATION
- LESSON 1 Knowing Your Community and Interacting With the Public / 54
- LESSON 2 Core Communication Competencies / 57

Chapter 3 — Legal / 61

UNIT 1 INTRODUCTION TO LAW
- LESSON 1 Law Systems / 63
- LESSON 2 Constitutional Law / 66

LESSON 3 Classification of Offenses / 69
LESSON 4 Reading and Understanding Statutes / 71

UNIT 2 LEGAL CONCEPTS
LESSON 1 Categories of Criminal Intent / 74
LESSON 2 Standards of Legal Justification / 78
LESSON 3 Search and Seizure / 85
LESSON 4 Weapons and Firearms Possession / 94
LESSON 5 Laws of Arrest / 96
LESSON 6 Use of Force / 99

UNIT 3 LIABILITY
LESSON 1 Types of Liability / 103
LESSON 2 Protecting Officers Against Liability / 108

UNIT 4 COURT BASICS
LESSON 1 The U.S. and Florida Court Systems / 111
LESSON 2 Court Proceedings / 114
LESSON 3 Court Orders / 118

Chapter 4 Interviewing and Report Writing / 121

UNIT 1 BASICS OF INTERVIEWING
LESSON 1 Taking Good Notes / 123
LESSON 2 Preparing for the Interview / 127
LESSON 3 Conducting the Interview / 131
LESSON 4 *Miranda* and Laws of Interrogation / 138

UNIT 2 WRITING A REPORT
LESSON 1 Reports / 142
LESSON 2 Mechanics / 145
LESSON 3 Elements and Principles of Effective Report Writing / 151
LESSON 4 Reviewing a Report Before Submission / 158

Chapter 5 Fundamentals of Patrol / 161

UNIT 1 PATROL BASICS
LESSON 1 Patrolling / 163
LESSON 2 Officer Safety and Survival / 166
LESSON 3 Electronic Communications / 170
LESSON 4 Electronic Sources of Information / 174

UNIT 2 DUTIES ON PATROL

- LESSON 1 Initial Response / 178
- LESSON 2 Approaching and Contacting a Suspect / 182
- LESSON 3 Responding as Backup / 185
- LESSON 4 Behavioral Threat Assessment and Management / 186

UNIT 3 NON-CRIMINAL CALLS FOR SERVICE

- LESSON 1 Assisting Your Community / 189
- LESSON 2 Well-Being and Security Checks / 191
- LESSON 3 Death Notifications / 193
- LESSON 4 Animal Complaints / 195
- LESSON 5 Fire-Related Incidents / 196
- LESSON 6 Lost, Stolen, or Recovered Property / 198
- LESSON 7 Property Disputes / 200
- LESSON 8 Civil Disturbance / 202
- LESSON 9 Crowd Control / 204

UNIT 4 STRUCTURE AND AREA SEARCHES

- LESSON 1 Alarms and Searches / 206
- LESSON 2 Area Searches / 210

UNIT 5 ARREST PROCEDURES

- LESSON 1 Taking Custody of the Suspect / 214
- LESSON 2 Processing the Arrestee / 218

Chapter 6 Serving Your Community / 221

UNIT 1 INTERACTING WITH YOUR COMMUNITY

- LESSON 1 Introduction to Responding to Your Community / 223
- LESSON 2 Serving the Elderly / 225
- LESSON 3 Serving Juveniles / 227
- LESSON 4 Serving Veterans / 229
- LESSON 5 Serving the Homeless / 232
- LESSON 6 Americans With Disabilities Act / 234
- LESSON 7 Serving People With Physical Impairments / 236
- LESSON 8 Serving People With Developmental Disabilities / 240
- LESSON 9 Serving People With Autism / 243
- LESSON 10 Serving People With Mental Illnesses / 245

UNIT 2 RESPONDING TO A PERSON IN CRISIS

- LESSON 1 Crisis Situations / 249
- LESSON 2 The Baker Act / 253
- LESSON 3 Suicide Risk / 256
- LESSON 4 Substance Abuse / 259
- LESSON 5 The Marchman Act / 262
- LESSON 6 Transportation and Documentation / 264

UNIT 3 IDENTIFYING AND RESPONDING TO HIGH-RISK GROUPS

- LESSON 1 Criminal Gangs / 266
- LESSON 2 Extremist Groups / 268

Chapter 7 Crimes Against Persons / 271

UNIT 1 BASIC INVESTIGATIONS

- LESSON 1 The Investigative Sequence / 273
- LESSON 2 Victims' Rights and Brochures / 277

UNIT 2 CRIMES AGAINST PERSONS

- LESSON 1 Assault and Battery / 280
- LESSON 2 Domestic Violence / 284
- LESSON 3 Stalking Crimes / 289
- LESSON 4 Child Abuse / 291
- LESSON 5 Abuse, Neglect, and Exploitation of an Elderly Person or Disabled Adult / 295
- LESSON 6 Interference With Custody, Luring or Enticing of a Child, False Imprisonment, and Kidnapping / 299
- LESSON 7 Missing or Missing Endangered Persons / 302
- LESSON 8 Sexual Offenses / 306
- LESSON 9 Human Trafficking / 310
- LESSON 10 Respond to a Death / 312
- LESSON 11 Robbery / 316

Chapter 8 Crimes Involving Property and Society / 319

UNIT 1 PROPERTY CRIMES

- LESSON 1 Theft / 321
- LESSON 2 Criminal Mischief, Trespassing, and Burglary / 325
- LESSON 3 White-Collar Crimes / 330
- LESSON 4 Crimes Against Animals / 334

UNIT 2 **CRIMES AGAINST SOCIETY**
LESSON 1 Loitering or Prowling, Disorderly Behavior / 338
LESSON 2 Illicit Drugs and Vice Crimes / 342

Chapter 9 Crime Scene Follow-Up Investigations / 347

UNIT 1 **THE CRIME SCENE**
LESSON 1 Evidence Rules and Concepts / 349
LESSON 2 Secure and Protect the Crime Scene / 352
LESSON 3 Manage Victims, Witnesses, and Suspects / 355
LESSON 4 Document the Crime Scene / 358
LESSON 5 Evidence-Handling Procedures / 361

UNIT 2 **FOLLOW-UP INVESTIGATION**
LESSON 1 Review Initial Information and Pursue Leads / 371
LESSON 2 Gather Information on an Unknown Suspect / 374
LESSON 3 Gather Information on a Known Suspect / 376
LESSON 4 Showup, Photographic Array, and Photo Lineup / 378

UNIT 3 **PREPARING FOR COURT**
LESSON 1 Testimony / 382

Chapter 10 Traffic Incidents / 389

UNIT 1 **TRAFFIC BASICS**
LESSON 1 Traffic Law and Legal Terms / 391
LESSON 2 The Florida Driver License, Registration, and Insurance / 394
LESSON 3 The Uniform Traffic Citation / 401

UNIT 2 **RESOLVING TRAFFIC INCIDENTS**
LESSON 1 Parking Violations / 405
LESSON 2 Abandoned, Disabled, or Unattended Vehicles / 406
LESSON 3 Search and Inventory of an Impounded Vehicle / 408
LESSON 4 Directing Traffic / 410

Chapter 11 Traffic Stops / 413

UNIT 1 **UNKNOWN-RISK TRAFFIC STOPS**
LESSON 1 Communication With Drivers / 415
LESSON 2 Initiating the Stop / 417
LESSON 3 Conducting the Stop / 421

UNIT 2 HIGH-RISK TRAFFIC STOPS
- LESSON 1 Initiating the Stop / 429
- LESSON 2 Conducting the Stop / 432

Chapter 12 Traffic Crash Investigations / 437
- LESSON 1 Introduction to Traffic Crash Management / 439
- LESSON 2 Assess a Traffic Crash Scene / 441
- LESSON 3 Secure a Traffic Crash Scene / 444
- LESSON 4 Injuries at a Traffic Crash Scene / 447
- LESSON 5 Gather Traffic Crash Information / 449
- LESSON 6 Gather Traffic Crash Evidence / 452
- LESSON 7 Driver Information Exchange / 459
- LESSON 8 Issue a Traffic Citation / 460
- LESSON 9 Clear the Traffic Crash Scene / 462
- LESSON 10 Complete a Traffic Crash Report / 463
- LESSON 11 Manage Unique Traffic Crashes / 468

Chapter 13 DUI Traffic Stops / 473

UNIT 1 DUI BASICS
- LESSON 1 Effects on Society and Deterrence / 475
- LESSON 2 Alcohol and Drug Impairment / 476
- LESSON 3 Legal Issues / 479
- LESSON 4 DUI Field Notes / 483

UNIT 2 CONDUCTING THE DUI INVESTIGATION
- LESSON 1 DUI Detection Process / 485
- LESSON 2 Phase One—Vehicle in Motion / 486
- LESSON 3 Phase Two—Personal Contact / 489
- LESSON 4 Phase Three—Pre-arrest Screening / 491

UNIT 3 STANDARDIZED FIELD SOBRIETY TESTS
- LESSON 1 Horizontal Gaze Nystagmus / 492
- LESSON 2 Walk and Turn / 496
- LESSON 3 One Leg Stand / 499

UNIT 4 CONCLUDING THE DUI INVESTIGATION
- LESSON 1 Law Enforcement Action / 501
- LESSON 2 DUI Report Writing / 505

Chapter 14 Critical Incidents / 507

UNIT 1 CRITICAL INCIDENT RESPONSE
- LESSON 1 Incident Command System and Response / 509
- LESSON 2 Natural Disasters / 511
- LESSON 3 Active Shooter / 513

UNIT 2 CHEMICAL AND HAZARDOUS MATERIALS
- LESSON 1 Hazardous Materials / 515
- LESSON 2 Methamphetamine and Chemical Suicide / 522

UNIT 3 EXPLOSIVE DEVICES
- LESSON 1 Types of Explosive Devices / 524
- LESSON 2 Responding to a Bomb Threat / 527
- LESSON 3 Searching for an Explosive Device / 530

UNIT 4 POST-CRITICAL INCIDENT CARE
- LESSON 1 Recovery After Disaster / 533

Glossary / 537

Bibliography / 559

Statute and F.A.C. Index / 563

Court Case Index / 573

Index / 575

Preface and Acknowledgments

This project is a collaboration between the Florida Department of Law Enforcement, Criminal Justice Standards and Training Commission Certified Training Schools, other state and local agencies, and volunteers. We extend our sincere appreciation to the agencies of the Florida Criminal Justice System that allowed their members to assist in the development of this training program.

The mission of the Florida Criminal Justice Standards and Training Commission is to ensure that all citizens of Florida are served by criminal justice officers who are ethical, qualified, and well-trained. The Commission certifies officers who complete a Florida basic recruit training program and gain sworn employment through a Florida criminal justice agency, or who are diversely qualified through experience and training and who meet minimum employment standards.

As staff for the Commission, the Florida Department of Law Enforcement (FDLE) Criminal Justice Professionalism, Standards & Training Services division is responsible for establishing and maintaining officer training programs. Criminal Justice officer training is conducted at Commission-certified training schools housed in Florida criminal justice agencies, community and state colleges, and vocational technical schools. By statute, entrance into the basic recruit training programs for law enforcement and correctional officers is limited to those who have passed a basic skills examination and assessment instrument, which is based on a job task analysis in accordance with s. 943.17(1)(g), F.S. The same job analysis process is used to develop job-related training and performance standards for basic recruit training. Hundreds of officers, residents, and instructors have participated in the development of the officer job analysis and training curricula. Through an annual review and revision of basic recruit training curricula, the Commission ensures that basic recruit graduates are prepared for sworn employment with state or local criminal justice agencies in Florida.

DIRECTOR ROBERT C. PIGMAN
MAY 2, 1960 – JULY 5, 2025

This edition of the law enforcement basic recruit training program textbook is dedicated to the memory of Director Robert C. Pigman of the Central Florida Criminal Justice Institute at Valencia College. Director Pigman began his law enforcement career as an officer at the Orlando Police Department after graduating from Florida Atlantic University. He served in a variety of roles over his 28 years with the agency, including working the undercover drugs and drug interdiction units and serving as a member of the SWAT team where he was also the high-risk incident commander. He rose through the ranks and became deputy chief of the Orlando Police Department before retiring in 2016 and joining Valencia College. As a training center director, he supported the mission of the Criminal Justice Standards and Training Commission by contributing to curriculum development and providing time, space, and subject matter experts for a variety of topics. He served on the most recent Law Enforcement Advisory Committee and helped guide program enhancements that will have a positive impact on training in Florida for years to come.

Chapter 1
Introduction to Law Enforcement

UNIT 1 THE LAW ENFORCEMENT OFFICER PROFESSION
- LESSON 1 The Roles of a Law Enforcement Officer / 3
- LESSON 2 Steps to Becoming a Certified Officer / 6
- LESSON 3 The Criminal Justice System / 10
- LESSON 4 Chain of Command / 14
- LESSON 5 Procedural Justice / 16

UNIT 2 OFFICER ETHICS AND CONDUCT
- LESSON 1 Criminal Justice Ethical Concepts / 18
- LESSON 2 Unethical Behavior / 21
- LESSON 3 Fair and Unbiased Policing / 25

UNIT 3 OFFICER WELL-BEING
- LESSON 1 Adjusting to Shiftwork / 28
- LESSON 2 Officer Wellness / 30
- LESSON 3 Stress / 33
- LESSON 4 Substance Abuse Awareness and Suicide Prevention / 38

UNIT 1 THE LAW ENFORCEMENT OFFICER PROFESSION
LESSON 1 The Roles of a Law Enforcement Officer

⊚ Lesson Goal

At the end of this lesson, you will be able to explain your role and commitment to serving your community as a criminal justice officer.

Think About This

You respond to a call about a stolen car. The victim is angry, crying, cursing, and visibly upset. They say they don't have a ride to pick up their children, and the only way you can help them is to get their car back right now. What role (or roles) would you play to calm the situation and help the victim?

Law enforcement is a service-oriented profession. Television and film often portray the life of a law enforcement officer as one of continually responding to burglaries, investigating crimes, or conducting high-speed pursuits. While officers do respond to these calls, most of the job is spent serving the community.

An officer's customer is the public. This means you will likely spend the majority of your time on tasks like assisting a driver with a flat tire on the side of the road, speaking with business owners about crime prevention, or presenting information on spring break safety to a class of high school students.

☑ LE111.1. Describe the services you will provide as a law enforcement officer

Each day, law enforcement officers focus on helping people in the communities they serve, maintaining civil order, and enforcing laws. As a law enforcement officer, you are responsible for protecting the public. This includes maintaining order, enforcing the law, and responding to emergencies. Such emergencies may include being called to a domestic violence situation, a child custody issue, or an active shooter event.

To accomplish all of these tasks, an officer should be service-oriented, dependable, communicative, a problem-solver, and a multitasker. You need to be able to think on your feet and react to challenging situations appropriately while taking care of other people and yourself. Constantly strive to improve your skills, assess your abilities, and ask how you can better serve your community.

DETERMINING YOUR ROLE

A law enforcement officer is expected to perform a variety of duties and adapt to multiple roles. You will take on many roles as a law enforcement officer, but there are three main ones to remember: the supporter, the stabilizer, and the enforcer. The situation will determine which role you assume. They do not have to occur in this order, and your roles may change as the circumstances change.

☑ LE111.2.
Explain the main roles of a law enforcement officer

Supporter

The role of the supporter is the role you should automatically adopt when interacting with your community. As the supporter, you will help people who are grieving, hurt, or experiencing a personal tragedy. For example, you might need to calm a lost child, help a confused person with Alzheimer's, or interview someone who has gone through severe trauma. All of these situations require you to be a compassionate and reassuring presence.

Another important aspect of this role is learning how you can best support your community. This requires that you take time to learn about the community and the people who live there. Reaching out to community members will give you the tools you need to properly fill the role of the supporter. It will also increase the likelihood that community members will reach out to you with their own support.

Stabilizer

When critical incidents occur, you will need to display confidence to calm those around you. Maintaining your composure and displaying confidence in your capabilities are important to this role. As the stabilizer, you will help those who are struggling to remain calm. You will guide them through the confusion and bring order to uncontrolled situations. Examples of situations that might require you to assume the stabilizer role include disaster recovery and responding to the scene of a traffic crash.

Enforcer

The role of the enforcer represents duties that are typically associated with a law enforcement officer. Making arrests and maintaining order by giving lawful commands when deemed necessary are just a few examples of where the enforcer role is appropriate. This is when you need to be assertive and give orders rather than ask questions. While there will be times when you will play the role of the enforcer, the majority of your time will be spent as the supporter and the stabilizer.

SHIFTING ROLES

Moving between different roles is an important skill that you need to develop to be an effective law enforcement officer. For example, if you are responding to a sexual battery case, you might first need to stabilize the situation to preserve evidence and keep the victim and their family or friends calm. While stabilizing the scene is critical, it is also important that you shift into a supporter role when talking to the victim and asking them questions. Putting the victim more at ease will help secure their cooperation during the investigation. However, if circumstances change and the suspect is on the scene or the victim's family wants to take the situation into their own hands, you may need to take on the role of the enforcer. The enforcer role is an essential part of the job. However, incorrect or excessive use of this role may degrade the trust of the community and damage the way people view law enforcement.

Improving your emotional intelligence can help you determine when to assume certain roles. Someone who has *emotional intelligence* has the ability to identify and cope with their own emotions while also doing the same for the people around them. Officers who have greater emotional intelligence more easily recognize when to take on and switch roles. They acknowledge that, during chaotic situations, the ability to manage their own emotions helps manage disorder. Emotional intelligence does not mean you suppress your emotions or the emotions of others; it means you know how to recognize them, cope with them, and view them as assets to your professional life.

☑ LE111.3. Explain the importance of emotional intelligence in the law enforcement profession

Emotional intelligence is a skill that can make you a better officer. It can enhance officer safety by helping you keep your emotions in check when tensions are high. To strengthen your emotional intelligence, engage with community members and genuinely listen to them. Ask your fellow officers and command staff for honest feedback on how they think you deal with tense situations and how approachable you are to community members. You might receive a critical response, but learning from this criticism can help you improve your overall emotional intelligence.

Strengthening your emotional intelligence and recognizing the roles that you assume as an officer will help in your ultimate goal of service. No matter what role the situation calls for, service will be at the center of all that you do. Treat every person you encounter with respect and dignity. This commitment to service should be at the core of who you are. Even outside of your job, you will be regarded as a public servant.

Each time you put on your uniform, you assume the societal position of a law enforcement officer. This is a position that gives you the authority and power to enforce the law. You should understand that this places you in a unique situation within your community. It gives you a level of power that your community members do not share. Being aware of this power imbalance helps you understand why some people may react to your presence with fear, mistrust, or even anger. Acknowledging this power imbalance, remembering that all of your roles are centered on service, and strengthening your emotional intelligence will help improve relations between you and your community.

UNIT 1 THE LAW ENFORCEMENT OFFICER PROFESSION
LESSON 2 Steps to Becoming a Certified Officer

◎ Lesson Goal

At the end of this lesson, you will understand how the Criminal Justice Standards and Training Commission regulates the requirements for obtaining and maintaining your certification as a law enforcement officer.

Think About This

An officer has made false statements during their employment process. Does the Criminal Justice Standards and Training Commission have the ability to take away this officer's certification?

The Florida Statutes define a law enforcement officer as:

> *any person who is elected, appointed, or employed full time by any municipality or the state or any political subdivision thereof; who is vested with authority to bear arms and make arrests; and whose primary responsibility is the prevention and detection of crime or the enforcement of the penal, criminal, traffic, or highway laws of the state. The term includes all certified supervisory and command personnel whose duties include, in whole or in part, the supervision, training, guidance, and management responsibilities of full-time law enforcement officers, part-time law enforcement officers, or auxiliary law enforcement officers but does not include support personnel employed by the employing agency.*

THE CRIMINAL JUSTICE STANDARDS AND TRAINING COMMISSION

The Criminal Justice Standards and Training Commission (CJSTC) was established with the mission to ensure that qualified, competent, and ethical criminal justice officers serve the residents and visitors of Florida. In pursuit of these goals, the CJSTC is committed to delivering quality standards and training as well as increasing the professionalism of officers throughout the state.

☑ LE112.1. Describe the role of the Criminal Justice Standards and Training Commission

The CJSTC is responsible for overseeing the certification, employment, training, maintenance of officer records, and overall conduct of all criminal justice officers in Florida. The Florida Statutes appoint the Criminal Justice Professionalism (CJP) Division within the Florida Department of Law Enforcement (FDLE) to support and assist the work of the CJSTC.

TRAINING REQUIREMENTS

To become a law enforcement officer, you must follow a training and certification process outlined by the Florida Statutes and Florida Administrative Code (F.A.C.).

To complete the Florida Basic Recruit Training Program, recruits must:

- achieve a passing score of 80% on each of the end-of-course examinations
- demonstrate proficiency in DUI Traffic Stops
- demonstrate proficiency in the High Liability courses
- participate in the Physical Fitness Program

You are responsible for your own success in this training course. You must adhere to the requirements and follow all rules and regulations of this training program.

☑ LE112.2. List the requirements for completing the basic recruit training program

STATE OFFICER CERTIFICATION EXAMINATION

After completing a basic recruit training program, you must pass the State Officer Certification Examination (SOCE) within three attempts. If you do not pass the SOCE within three attempts, you will have to retake the entire basic recruit training.

You can find information about the SOCE in the Florida Department of Law Enforcement Candidate Handbook that is available at criminal justice training academies or online at the FDLE website. This website also has information regarding SOCE registration and exam topics.

OFFICER CERTIFICATION

Simply completing the basic recruit training program and passing the SOCE does not mean that you are certified. You must also ensure that you have met all the remaining requirements for certification. To become certified (sworn) as a law enforcement officer, you must complete the following:

☑ LE112.3. List the requirements for becoming a certified law enforcement officer in Florida

- meet all the minimum requirements and standards
- complete the approved basic recruit training
- pass the SOCE
- be actively employed with a law enforcement agency in a full-time, part-time, or auxiliary sworn officer position

You have four years from the starting date of your basic recruit training to complete the certification process, not from the date when you pass the SOCE.

For example, if you begin the basic recruit training on July 1, 2026, you must meet all the minimum requirements and standards, complete the basic recruit training, pass the SOCE, and become actively employed with a law enforcement agency as a sworn officer by June 30, 2030. If you do not meet all of these requirements by June 30, 2030, you will have to repeat the basic recruit training, and a new four-year period will begin.

OFFICER COMPLIANCE AND DISCIPLINE

Before an agency hires you, they will conduct a thorough background investigation to assess your moral character. Florida Statutes defines good moral character as a history of fairness, honesty, and respect for the rights of others as well as the laws of this state and nation. While in the academy, you are subject to the same moral character requirements as active certified officers. If evidence indicates that you do not comply with these standards, the CJSTC may deny your certification.

☑ **LE112.4.** Outline the statutory conditions and penalties of the officer disciplinary process

The CJSTC may also act against an officer's certification if an officer does any of the following (please note that this is not a definitive list and that it is subject to change):

- pleads **nolo contendere** (when a person does not accept or deny responsibility for the charges but agrees to accept punishment) or pleads guilty to, or is found guilty of, any felony
- pleads *nolo contendere* or pleads guilty to, or is found guilty of, a misdemeanor involving perjury or false statement
- fails to maintain good moral character, as defined by the Florida Statutes and described in F.A.C.
- commits any act constituting a felony offense, regardless of criminal prosecution
- commits any act constituting any of the serious misdemeanor offenses specified in F.A.C., regardless of criminal prosecution
- commits or attempts to commit, as a principal or accessory or through solicitation or conspiracy, an act that, according to the Florida Statutes, would have been a felony offense had the crime been completed or committed
- commits any act in any jurisdiction other than the state of Florida that, if committed in the state of Florida, would constitute a felony, any of the serious misdemeanors specified in F.A.C., or a violation of the Florida Statutes
- tests positive for a controlled substance by a urine or blood test, in accordance with the requirements specified in F.A.C.
- commits an act of excessive use of force as explained under F.A.C.
- engages in sexual harassment involving physical contact or misuse of official position
- misuses the official position, as described in the Florida Statutes
- engages in sex while on duty
- has unprofessional relationships with an inmate, detainee, probationer, parolee, or community controlee
- has written or oral communication that is intended to facilitate conduct prohibited by the CJSTC
- engages in any physical contact not required in the performance of official duties that is normally associated with the demonstration of affection or sexual misconduct as defined in the Florida Statutes
- makes false statements during the employment process

- subverts or attempts to subvert the SOCE process, as identified in F.A.C.
- subverts or attempts to subvert the CJSTC-approved training examination process or an employing agency's promotional examination process according to, but not limited to, acts described in F.A.C.

You can read more about the disciplinary process in F.A.C.

Using a set of established penalty guidelines, the CJSTC may discipline an officer who commits any of the above violations. These penalties include:

- a written reprimand
- probation of up to two years (with or without mandatory retraining or counseling, if applicable)
- suspension of up to two years (with or without mandatory retraining or counseling, if applicable)
- revocation of certification

Under Florida law, the CJSTC must revoke your certification if you are convicted of, plead guilty or *nolo contendere* to, or are found guilty of any felony offense, even for a withholding of adjudication or suspension of sentence. When the CJSTC revokes an officer's certification, the officer can no longer work as a certified officer in the state of Florida.

While these guidelines are specific to sworn officers, the CJSTC and the academy will expect you to adhere to the same standards of conduct during basic recruit training. Violating them may result in the denial of your officer certification.

UNIT 1 THE LAW ENFORCEMENT OFFICER PROFESSION
LESSON 3 The Criminal Justice System

◎ Lesson Goal

At the end of this lesson, you will understand the basic structures of the U.S. criminal justice system, the levels of criminal involvement, and how these affect your job as an officer.

Think About This

You are called to the scene of a theft. The person who called dispatch says her purse was stolen. Another person on the scene claims to have seen the crime take place. Additionally, the victim learns from her bank that her credit card was just used out of state for an online purchase. How do you determine the levels of criminal involvement of each individual in this situation?

STRUCTURE OF THE CRIMINAL JUSTICE SYSTEM

A law enforcement officer is one small piece of a large and complex structure known as the criminal justice system. Officers play an important role in this structure. Your ability to interact effectively with other parts of the system directly affects your job performance as an officer.

☑ LE113.1. Outline the basic structure of the U.S. criminal justice system

The system of **criminal justice** involves the maintenance and enforcement of criminal laws and includes the structures, functions, and decision-making processes of the agencies that deal with the management and control of crime and criminal offenders. The three main components of the criminal justice system are law enforcement, the court system, and corrections.

- **Law enforcement** enforces laws, maintains civil order, and protects the constitutional rights of everyone within the United States.
- The **court system** is responsible for the interpretation of laws. You will learn more about the court system in Chapter 3.
- **Corrections** enforces punishment and provides rehabilitation services as defined by the court system.

LAW ENFORCEMENT AGENCIES

The United States has four levels of law enforcement agencies: local or municipal, county, state, and federal. Each level is responsible for enforcing the laws within its jurisdiction or the geographical area in which it has authority. The following are some examples of the roles of agencies at each level.

☑ LE113.2. Describe the role of municipal, county, state, and federal law enforcement agencies

Local or municipal law enforcement agencies enforce the ordinances of the municipality as well as state laws within the jurisdiction of the agency. Examples include police departments and public safety departments.

County law enforcement agencies enforce county ordinances and state laws within the county (including unincorporated areas), oversee the county jail, and handle civil processing. Sheriffs' offices are county law enforcement agencies.

State law enforcement agencies enforce state laws within the state. Examples include the Florida Department of Law Enforcement and the Florida Highway Patrol.

Federal law enforcement agencies enforce federal laws across state lines and within the states. Examples include the Federal Bureau of Investigation and Immigration and Customs Enforcement.

CORRECTIONS

The corrections system in the U.S. has institutions at the local or municipal, county, state, and federal level. A general overview of the corrections system in the U.S. includes the following primary components.

☑ LE113.3.
Describe the primary components of the U.S. corrections system

- County jails—facilities where arrestees go through booking procedures and await trial, and convicted offenders serve a year or less detention.
- Juvenile assessment/detention centers—facilities that handle the processing and pretrial detention of juvenile arrestees. According to the Florida Statutes, a *juvenile* (sometimes referred to as a child or youth) means any person younger than 18. Officers should check their agency's policies and procedures for the proper detainment center for juvenile arrestees in their district.
- Prisons (federal and state)—correctional institutions that are maintained by the federal and state governments for confining convicted felons.
- Probation and parole—serve as alternatives to incarceration. Their purpose is to supervise the enforcement of specific restrictions on people who may have received a suspended sentence after conviction or who may be on parole.

Probation is a sentence placing a person under the supervision of a probation officer for a specified length of time instead of confinement. Probationers may have to serve their confinement sentence if they violate the terms of their probation.

Parole is the release of an inmate from a correctional institution before the conclusion of their court-imposed sentence. Under supervision, the person serves the remainder of the sentence in compliance with the specific terms of the release agreement. The person may have to return to the institution if they violate the release agreement.

LEVELS OF CRIMINAL INVOLVEMENT

Investigating officers must determine the identity of people involved in a criminal incident, which can include witnesses, victims, and suspected perpetrators of a crime. As a law enforcement officer, you must also determine what each person knows about the incident and whether a person participated in the crime, was a victim, or merely witnessed it. You

☑ LE113.4.
Distinguish between the people involved in a criminal incident

will be required to make initial determinations by questioning people, observing physical evidence at the scene, and reviewing documentation related to the incident.

Figure 1-1 illustrates how people identified in the reporting or commission of a crime may move from one designation to another as the criminal justice process proceeds. Note that not every role is represented and that one role does not necessarily lead to another.

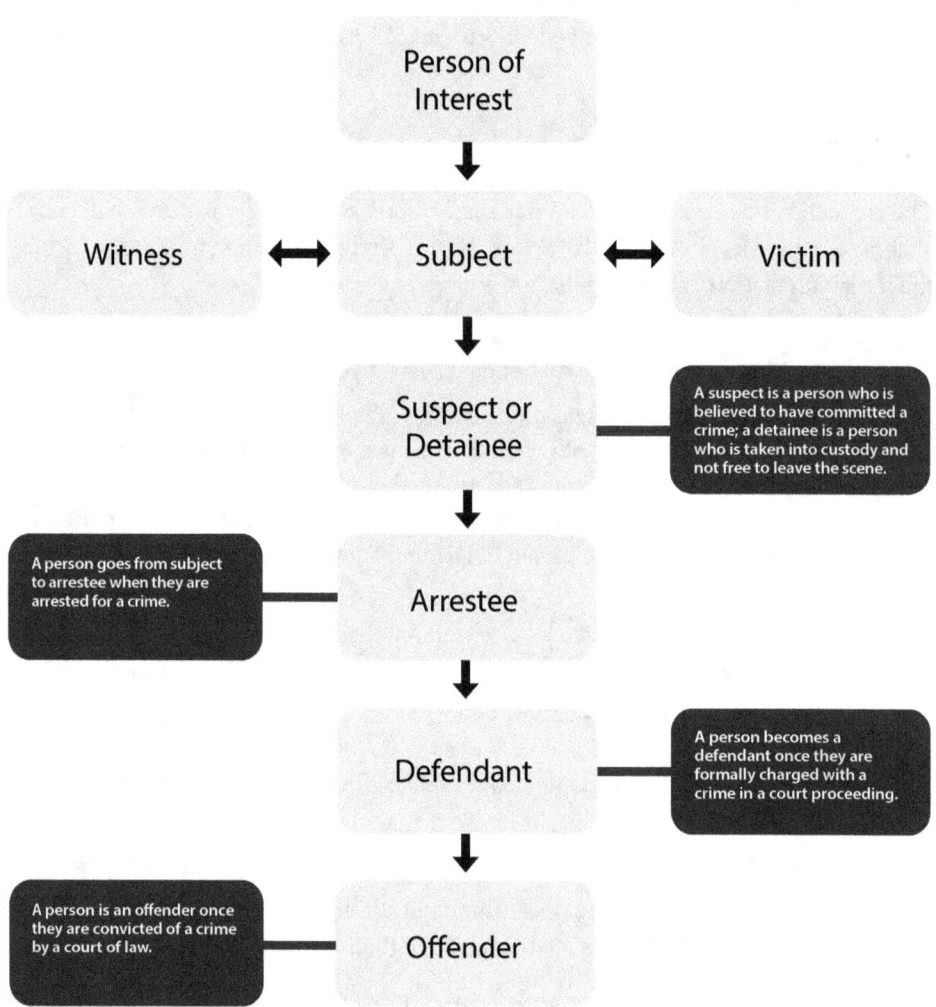

Figure 1-1 Levels of criminal involvement

You should become familiar with the following terms:

- ***complainant***—a person who reports a crime or alleges that a crime has been committed.
- ***witness***—any person who has information about some element of the crime or about evidence or documents related to the crime. A witness may have heard statements or observed events before, during, or after the crime and may have information about a piece of evidence associated with the crime or knowledge of some document related to the crime.

- *victim*—a person or entity that suffers an injury as a result of a crime. The injury may involve physical harm, loss of money, loss of property, or damage to property. Not all crimes have an individual victim. For example, the victim in the crime of unlawful possession of a controlled substance is the state of Florida.
- *confidential source*—a person who provides information in confidence about a crime, either from a sense of civic duty or in the expectation of some personal benefit or advantage, and whose identity is normally not disclosed unless required by law.
- *person of interest*—someone involved in a criminal investigation who has not been arrested or formally accused of a crime. It commonly refers to someone in whom the police are "interested," either because they are cooperating with an investigation or may have information that would help the investigation.
- *subject*—a known person accused or suspected of committing a crime. A subject may not have actually committed the crime.
- *suspect/detainee*—a person believed to have committed a crime. You may identify a suspect by:
    - directly observing that person commit the crime
    - indirectly through witness observations and statements
    - the suspect's own statements
    - learning of the person's identity based on evidence collected while investigating the crime
- *arrestee*—a person who is under arrest or who has been arrested.
- *defendant*—a person formally accused of committing a crime or a civil wrong in a court proceeding.
- *offender*—a person convicted of a crime in a court of law.

UNIT 1 THE LAW ENFORCEMENT OFFICER PROFESSION
LESSON 4 Chain of Command

Lesson Goal

At the end of this lesson, you will understand how the chain of command and the delegation of authority are important to the foundation of an effective organization.

Think About This

Officer Woods has lost a vital piece of evidence in a murder case. He knows he is required to report this through his chain of command. However, he consults his fellow officer instead of reporting to his supervising officer. What are some possible consequences for Officer Woods's violation of the chain of command?

CHAIN OF COMMAND

Most law enforcement agencies have a structure that is practical and hierarchical. Under this system, subordinates report to a single superior, and many agencies have an organizational chart that shows how the various jobs and positions are related.

☑ LE114.1. Describe the chain of command

Chain of command is the order of authority within an organization. It provides the links of authority and responsibility that join one level of an organization to another. Law enforcement agencies often assign ranks to the different structural levels of the organization. A typical rank structure in a law enforcement agency might be:

- sheriff/chief of police
- undersheriff or chief deputy/deputy chief of police
- colonel
- major
- captain
- lieutenant
- sergeant
- corporal
- deputy/officer/trooper

Your rank as an officer identifies where you are in the structural level of the organization. In most agencies, officers with ranks such as lieutenant, captain, and higher are regarded as command level.

Most organizations use the chain of command as a means of communicating and making decisions. A chief or sheriff cannot answer every question that subordinates might have on a given day, so most officers go to their immediate supervisor for help.

Following a chain of command enhances an agency's efficiency through coordinating communication channels and reducing confusion. There must be uniform channels for communication within the agency to manage the accomplishment of objectives. These channels must include both vertical and lateral communication.

☑ LE114.2. Describe the importance of following the proper chain of command

Vertical communication is a term for information from the agency head that flows down through the supervision levels to the lowest levels of the organization. The information that flows from the lowest levels to the highest is equally important.

☑ LE114.3. Differentiate between vertical and lateral communication

Lateral communication is communication across a level of the organization to employees on the same level within the chain of command.

All officers should operate within the chain of command and keep their immediate supervisor informed of their activities. Not following the chain of command can lead to the miscommunication of important information and data. Miscommunication can damage the relationship between you and your immediate supervisor and can result in confusion and a lack of coordination within the unit. In some situations, such as on patrol, your direct supervisor may not be available to answer an important question. This is when academy training comes into play, and you must make decisions to the best of your ability, knowledge, and training.

☑ LE114.4. Identify the consequences of not following the proper chain of command

Violating the chain of command may also result in insubordination. ***Insubordination*** can be a serious violation that is often the result of failing to follow orders. However, insubordination is usually determined on an agency basis and may differ depending on the situation.

DELEGATION OF AUTHORITY

Whether it is the chief of police, the sheriff, or the agency director, the consequences of everything that happens within the organization ultimately rest on one person. To effectively manage an organization, the person in command needs to assign decision-making authority to those under their command. When a person with authority grants decision-making authority to another person, it is called the ***delegation of authority***. On each level of the chain of command, there is a distribution of authority and responsibility. Knowing who has the authority to make decisions and who has the responsibility to follow through is the foundation of an effective organization.

☑ LE114.5. Explain what effective delegation of authority is

UNIT 1 THE LAW ENFORCEMENT OFFICER PROFESSION
LESSON 5 Procedural Justice

◎ Lesson Goal

At the end of this lesson, you will be able to practice procedural justice by using the LEED framework as well as understand the importance of police legitimacy for strengthening the bonds between you and the community you serve.

Think About This

You pull over a driver who is angry and confused about why he has been stopped by the police. What are some ways you can help stabilize the situation?

PROCEDURAL JUSTICE

Every single encounter you have with the public is a chance to shape how the public feels about law enforcement officers, so it is important to always practice procedural justice throughout your career.

☑ LE115.1. Explain why you should practice the concept of procedural justice and its four pillars throughout your law enforcement career

Procedural justice is an approach that focuses on carrying out justice in a fair and equitable manner. Research shows that when people believe they have been treated justly by law enforcement, they are more likely to comply and generally have a more positive view of law enforcement. Employing procedural justice in your duties as a law enforcement officer can make you more effective in your work.

Four main pillars compose the procedural justice approach:

1. Fairness and consistency of rule application—the perception of fairness is not just about the outcome; be consistent in your decision-making, and treat people with respect.
2. Voice and representation in the process—involve groups in the decisions that affect them and listen to their concerns.
3. Transparency and openness of the process—decisions are made without secrets and deception.
4. Impartiality and unbiased decision-making—decisions are based on relevance and data.

☑ LE115.2. Describe the four factors of the LEED framework

To practice procedural justice in your daily police work, it helps to remember the LEED framework:

- listen—give everyone you interact with a chance to tell you their side of the story.
- explain—always explain your actions.
- equity—make fair decisions.
- dignity—treat people with respect.

Practicing procedural justice minimizes tension and potential violence in law enforcement encounters with the public. For example, an officer who uses procedural justice when responding to a noise complaint explains exactly why they are there, gives the person who is accused of the violation a chance to explain the situation, is transparent about what will happen next, and treats the person with respect. The person might still receive a citation for the noise violation, but because they feel they were treated fairly, they are more likely to have a positive view of the interaction and less likely to commit the same violation in the future.

The three main roles discussed earlier in this chapter—supporter, stabilizer, and enforcer—all employ procedural justice. Even when you are acting as an enforcer and administering the law, always remember the four pillars of procedural justice. When arresting a suspect, allow them to speak if they want, explain your actions, be fair in your enforcement of the law, and treat them with dignity.

Figure 1-2
Four main pillars of procedural justice

A key component of procedural justice is the concept of police legitimacy. **Police legitimacy** happens when the community views law enforcement as fair, morally obligated to administer the law, and as a legitimate authority of power. A positive perception of law enforcement helps build and maintain the public's trust. The public's perception of law enforcement is incredibly important. Research shows that police legitimacy is more effective at stopping crime than traditional deterrence, such as fines or prison sentences. In addition to deterring crime, police legitimacy is also connected to building and maintaining the public's trust. Mutual respect between the public and law enforcement often results in a much safer situation for law enforcement officers and the communities they serve.

☑ LE115.3. Explain the importance of demonstrating police legitimacy by building and maintaining public trust

When the public does not have confidence in law enforcement, there may be negative consequences. For example, people who do not trust local law enforcement officers are usually less likely to report crimes. This can result in situations where the public believes they must be in charge of their own safety. These conditions can lead to more crime and people feeling unsafe in general. Strengthening the partnership between law enforcement and communities by using procedural justice can help reduce crime and keep your community more secure.

UNIT 2 OFFICER ETHICS AND CONDUCT
LESSON 1 Criminal Justice Ethical Concepts

> **◎ Lesson Goal**
>
> At the end of this lesson, you will understand the importance of ethical decision-making on and off duty and the ethical standards that you must practice as a law enforcement officer.

Think About This

You respond to a domestic disturbance, and you realize that the primary aggressor is a member of your command staff. What are your ethical considerations?

ETHICS

Ethics are the standards of conduct based on the principles of right and wrong defined by society. Ethics dictate how a person should behave, and laws and rules are derived from ethics.

☑ LE121.1. List examples of ethical decision-making while on or off duty

Your behavior as an officer must reflect ethical principles, as the role of law enforcement officer requires the ability to make ethical decisions. Ethical behavior in law enforcement includes:

- being honest in your work
- refusing to accept or offer gratuities
- preserving evidence
- giving true and impartial testimony
- obeying all laws and regulations
- protecting the civil rights of everyone
- respecting confidential and privileged communication
- speaking up if you see your fellow officers acting unethically

You have a duty to intervene if you see another officer(s) committing an offense, treating a community member with disrespect, or engaging in any behavior that would be deemed unethical.

Every action you take as a law enforcement officer, both on and off duty, should reflect ethical behavior; always keep in mind that your conduct will reflect on every other law enforcement officer. Your community will look to you to advocate for the highest ethical standards at every level and at all times.

INFLUENCES ON ETHICAL PROBLEM-SOLVING

During your career in law enforcement, you might be confronted by different situations that challenge your ethical decision-making and impact your approach to problem solving. These situations are not only limited to the workplace but can also arise from your personal life as well.

Your fellow officers can influence the way you respond to a problem by their attitudes, whether they are positive and upbeat or cynical and negative. The way you view your role and the roles of your peers will also have a large impact on your actions.

☑ LE121.2. Determine factors that have an influence on your ethical decision-making

Challenges in your personal life, including financial or legal troubles, can push you to consider using your position for personal gain. A law enforcement officer who abandons their ethical principles is no longer fulfilling their duty to serve the public. Be mindful of the fact that, while you have great influence as an officer, this influence is tied to a responsibility to the community you serve.

It is important that you look for positive role models early on in your career, both from inside your agency and in your personal life. Finding people in your life who model the type of ethical behavior you want to see in yourself can help ensure that you practice and uphold the high ethical standards required for an officer.

LAW ENFORCEMENT CODE OF ETHICS

The Law Enforcement Code of Ethics provides specific principles for law enforcement officers to follow. The Law Enforcement Oath of Honor gives officers a shorter version of these ethical values. The shorter version allows you to memorize the oath with ease and to recall it when confronted with an ethical dilemma or stressful situation. Always keep the Code of Ethics and the Oath of Honor at the center of your work. Doing so will help you focus on your responsibilities to the public.

Law Enforcement Code of Ethics

As a law enforcement officer, my fundamental duty is to serve the community; to safeguard lives and property; to protect the innocent against deception, the weak against oppression or intimidation, and the peaceful against violence or disorder; and to respect the constitutional rights of all to liberty, equality, and justice.

☑ LE121.3. Identify the approved ethical standards of conduct as provided in the Law Enforcement Code of Ethics

I will keep my private life unsullied as an example to all and will behave in a manner that does not bring discredit to me or to my agency. I will maintain courageous calm in the face of danger, scorn, or ridicule; develop self-restraint; and be constantly mindful of the welfare of others. Honest in thought and deed both in my personal and official life, I will be exemplary in obeying the law and the regulations of my department. Whatever I see or hear of a confidential nature or that is confided to me in my official capacity will be kept ever secret unless revelation is necessary in the performance of my duty.

I will never act officiously or permit personal feelings, prejudices, political beliefs, aspirations, animosities, or friendships to influence my decisions. With no compromise for crime and with relentless prosecution of criminals, I will enforce the law courteously and appropriately without fear or favor, malice or ill will, never employing unnecessary force or violence and never accepting gratuities.

I recognize the badge of my office as a symbol of public faith, and I accept it as a public trust to be held so long as I am true to the ethics of police service. I will never engage in acts of corruption or bribery, nor will I condone such acts by other police officers. I will cooperate with all legally authorized agencies and their representatives in the pursuit of justice.

I know that I alone am responsible for my own standard of professional performance and will take every reasonable opportunity to enhance and improve my level of knowledge and competence.

I will constantly strive to achieve these objectives and ideals, dedicating myself before God to my chosen profession…law enforcement.

Source: International Association of Chiefs of Police

Law Enforcement Oath of Honor

On my honor, I will never betray my integrity, my character, or the public trust.

I will treat all individuals with dignity and respect and ensure that my actions are dedicated to ensuring the safety of my community and the preservation of human life.

I will always have the courage to hold myself and others accountable for our actions.

I will always maintain the highest ethical standards and uphold the values of my community and the agency I serve.

Source: International Association of Chiefs of Police

UNIT 2 OFFICER ETHICS AND CONDUCT
LESSON 2 Unethical Behavior

Lesson Goal

At the end of this lesson, you will recognize unethical behavior that will damage your relationship with your community and your career as a law enforcement officer.

Think About This

You are eating at a fast-food restaurant with a fellow officer, and you are discussing the details of an arrest you just made. Your fellow officer finds the situation funny and begins to laugh. However, the sister of the woman you arrested is at the table next to you and has heard your conversation. Has an ethical violation occurred?

UNETHICAL BEHAVIOR

Society considers certain types of behavior unethical; laws make some of these behaviors illegal. There are several unethical behaviors that law enforcement officers should guard against.

For instance, officers should never engage in criminal offenses, such as bribery, perjury, and misuse of one's position or authority. **Bribery** occurs when you accept something for your benefit that influences your professional conduct or decision-making. **Perjury** is the offense of lying in court after taking an oath. Criminal violations differ depending on the situation in which a person commits perjury. Perjury is a felony in proceedings such as testifying in court or giving a deposition. Officers should also never reveal confidential information, engage in situations that present a conflict of interest, or accept inappropriate favors.

☑ LE122.1.
Recognize unethical behavior for a law enforcement officer

The Florida Statutes contain certain standards of conduct for officers and provide specific violations. Some of these violations include:

- perjury by false written declaration
- perjury when not in an official proceeding
- perjury in official proceedings
- perjury by contradictory statements
- false reports to law enforcement authorities
- false official statements
- bribery
- unlawful compensation or reward for official behavior
- refusal to execute criminal process
- misuse of confidential information
- witnesses accepting bribes

Misuse of Your Position

Never misuse the authority entrusted to you as a law enforcement officer. The Florida Statutes prohibit misuse of your position as a public employee:

> *No public officer, employee of an agency, or local government attorney shall corruptly use or attempt to use his or her official position or any property or resource which may be within his or her trust, or perform his or her official duties, to secure a special privilege, benefit, or exemption for himself, herself, or others.*

Examples of misusing your position may include having a family member's traffic ticket dismissed, using your badge to gain unauthorized entry to a concert, or wearing your uniform for the sole purpose of obtaining a discount at a local restaurant.

Confidential Information

You will spend a great deal of time collecting information through interviews with victims and witnesses. It is important to maintain privacy, trust, and loyalty when people volunteer information or act as sources of information.

☑ LE122.2. Explain inappropriate disclosure of confidential information

Do not gossip, discuss cases with anyone, or post about cases on social media. Do not share information with friends, relatives, or the public. This obligation applies to both off- and on-duty time. Examples of inappropriate sharing include divulging information from a criminal justice database, sharing crime scene photos, or disclosing information about victims, witnesses, or suspects. These actions may risk ongoing investigations and cause serious consequences for you and your agency. If you divulge confidential information for non-law enforcement purposes, you could face agency and CJSTC disciplinary action.

Conflict of Interest

In official law enforcement matters, you must not influence the actions of other people with whom you have significant personal, business, or employment relationships, as this creates a conflict of interest.

☑ LE122.3. Explain what conflict of interest means for a law enforcement officer

A **conflict of interest** is a situation, on or off duty, in which an officer is in a position to personally benefit from actions or decisions made in their official capacity. For example, you cannot arrest someone and then recommend your family friend who is an attorney to represent the arrestee.

Do not engage in any off-duty employment if the position compromises or would reasonably tend to compromise your ability to impartially perform your duties as a law enforcement officer. For example, you cannot be a private investigator and a certified law enforcement officer at the same time.

Accepting a gratuity may also present a conflict of interest. A **gratuity** is anything of value intended to benefit the giver more than the receiver. Do not take something given to you because of your position or authority. This is an ethical issue that law enforcement officers often face.

Whenever a situation involving gratuity arises, ask yourself the following:

- Does this person want something from me?
- Would I be offered this if I were not a law enforcement officer?
- What is expected in return?

For the public to maintain its faith in the integrity and impartiality of law enforcement officers and their departments, you must not engage in any situation that would present a conflict of interest.

Sexual Misconduct While on Duty

Every year, the CJSTC addresses numerous disciplinary cases of sexual misconduct while on duty. Penalties can range from probation to suspension to possible revocation of an officer's certification.

Sexual misconduct can include anything from asking a driver for a date when conducting a traffic stop to having sex on duty. There is always an inherent power imbalance between you and the public. For example, if you pull over a driver and ask them out on a date, they might feel that they have to say yes because you are a law enforcement officer. Remember that you are viewed as an authority figure and always serve as a representative of your agency as well as of the law enforcement profession.

☑ LE122.4. Describe sexual misconduct while on duty

Harassment in the Workplace

Everyone has a right to work in an environment free of harassment and hostile conditions. There are many different types of harassment, but all involve creating a **hostile work environment**, which is a workplace that is difficult or uncomfortable to work in because of a harasser's behavior. For example, if someone posts explicit photographs and posters in a break room, other employees might be less likely to use that communal space because they are uncomfortable with the photos.

In the work environment, harassment may occur in the form of **quid pro quo**, a Latin phrase that means "something for something." An example of quid pro quo harassment is when a supervisor demands sexual favors from an employee in return for allowing that employee to continue to work. The employee believes that any complaint will result in job loss.

Sexual harassment is unwelcome sexual advances, requests for sexual favors, and other verbal or physical conduct of a sexual nature. It is also a form of discrimination. Sexual harassment includes verbal and non-verbal behavior as well as physical actions. Verbal actions can include giving sexual compliments, pressuring someone for dates, or ridiculing someone with a sexual message. Non-verbal actions can include making facial gestures, displaying nude pictures, posting inappropriate messages on social media, or using suggestive body language. Physical actions may include touching and brushing against someone, hugging and patting, or horseplay.

☑ LE122.5. Describe behaviors that constitute sexual harassment that an officer should avoid

A workplace that allows sex-based discussions, humor, banter, or posters promotes a hostile work environment. For law enforcement employees, it is becoming increasingly difficult to define the workplace. Court cases have created a very wide definition of where people work, and as an officer, your workplace may be a police station, patrol car, or training academy. Therefore, make sure to be respectful everywhere you go and at all times.

RESPONSES TO HARASSMENT

Training and communication are key to understanding and preventing sexual harassment. Many agencies have trained staff members who handle sexual harassment complaints, procedures, and training.

☑ LE122.6. Identify appropriate responses to sexual harassment

Victims who experience harassment should report the behavior to a supervisor or member of management informally or formally, as agency policies dictate. If the conduct becomes criminal, the victim may make a report to the appropriate law enforcement agency. Remember, even if you are not a victim of harassment, if you observe someone being harassed, you should report that harassment. The victim may also file a complaint with the Equal Employment Opportunity Commission (EEOC) and consult with an attorney. The EEOC is the governmental agency that enforces compliance with the Civil Rights Act (Title VII).

To prevent liability, follow the law and your agency's policies. Avoid engaging in behavior that could be misinterpreted, and act professionally at all times. Address any sexual harassment as soon as it occurs to prevent escalation.

CONSEQUENCES OF SEXUAL HARASSMENT

☑ LE122.7. Describe the consequences of engaging in sexual harassment

The act of sexual harassment can be seen as a moral character violation. An officer who engages in sexual harassment may face severe consequences for their actions. The officer's agency may impose internal disciplinary action such as mandatory retraining, leave without pay, loss of rank, and termination. The CJSTC could revoke the officer's certification. If a lawsuit is filed, a court could impose monetary damage. In a criminal case such as stalking, assault, battery, or official misconduct, an officer could face imprisonment.

UNIT 2 OFFICER ETHICS AND CONDUCT
LESSON 3 Fair and Unbiased Policing

◎ Lesson Goal

At the end of this lesson, you will understand how biases affect interactions between people, including between law enforcement officers and the communities they serve. You will also learn how fair and unbiased policing can combat the harmful impacts of stereotyping, prejudice, and discrimination.

UNBIASED POLICING

Bias is the unfair treatment and attitude toward a group of people, and it is considered unethical behavior. Unbiased policing (also known as fair and impartial policing) is the equal treatment of any person you stop, question, search, detain, or arrest, regardless of the person's race, ethnicity, religion, gender presentation, sexual orientation, socioeconomic status, national origin, homeless status, mental or physical disability, age, or other self-defining characteristics. When you practice unbiased policing, you make decisions based on evidence and data rather than emotions and predetermined ideas of a person.

Bias can present itself in different ways. Someone with *explicit bias* is aware of their dislike of certain groups of people and might be openly hateful and biased in their actions. In contrast, *implicit bias* is a bias or prejudice that is present but not consciously held or recognized. It occurs when someone unconsciously makes judgments about others without being aware that they are making those judgments. Every person has implicit bias of some kind, including but not limited to, someone's education level, class level, or age. Our brains make these associations without our awareness. People develop implicit bias because of images in the media, a lack of exposure to diverse groups of people, and other societal factors.

☑ LE123.1. Compare explicit and implicit biases and how they impact a law enforcement officer

Because law enforcement officers must often make split-second decisions, it is critical for them to understand implicit bias. When you have to make quick decisions based on limited information, implicit bias can influence your actions without your awareness. Implicit bias cannot be eliminated overnight; being aware of it is only the first step in countering its consequences. Taking the time to slow down and think through your actions can also help.

Another part of confronting bias-based policing is acknowledging the complex history of policing in the United States. Being aware of this history can help you understand why some people might be afraid when they encounter a law enforcement officer. If you understand this and practice procedural justice, you can help strengthen the ties between you and the community you serve.

DISCRIMINATORY PRACTICES

Avoiding bias is just one step in fair and unbiased policing. You must also avoid stereotyping, prejudices, and discrimination.

Stereotyping is judging a group of people who are different from you based on your own or others' opinions or encounters. Both positive and negative stereotypes hurt because they categorize people unfairly. Additionally, judging a person based on stereotypes will cause you to miss valuable information and clues that could help save a life or solve a crime.

Law enforcement officers should also avoid prejudice and discrimination. *Prejudice* is an unjustified and baseless attitude toward a person because of their membership in a social group. These prejudices may grow from learned behavior and attitudes. *Discrimination* occurs when people choose to act on their prejudices. This type of behavior can break down the relationship between law enforcement and the communities they serve and can also lead to liability.

☑ LE123.2. Describe the relationship between stereotyping, prejudice, and discrimination

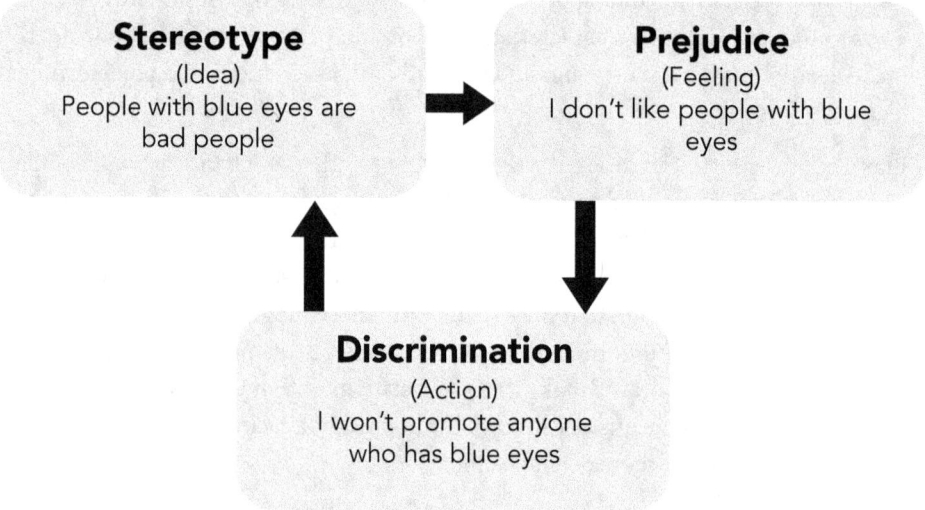

Figure 1-3
Discriminatory practices

Stereotypes, prejudices, and discrimination can cause you to misunderstand information or exclude vital information in an investigation. False assumptions may lead you to act on emotions rather than a planned response. Always avoid these unethical practices in your career as a law enforcement officer.

UNDERSTANDING DISCRIMINATORY OR BIASED-BASED POLICING

Officers should avoid any law enforcement action that targets a person based on a variety of group characteristics, including occupational status or the ability to speak English, as this constitutes discriminatory or bias-based policing.

Discriminatory or bias-based policing is the unequal treatment of any person, including stopping, questioning, searching, detaining, or arresting a person solely or primarily because of the person's race, ethnicity, religion, gender presentation, sexual orientation, socioeconomic status, national origin, homeless status, mental or physical disability, age, or other self-defining characteristics. Not only will this behavior negatively impact the relationship of the community with you and law enforcement in general, but it is also illegal and can bring criminal or civil penalties against you.

Some law enforcement agencies require officers to report demographic data, including race and gender, on some calls for service. This data assists agencies in investigating possible allegations of bias-based policing. Various laws and court rulings require this information to detect and eliminate unfair policing. It is your responsibility to treat everyone within the community equally.

☑ LE123.3. Describe what discriminatory policing is and how it can impact your career and relationship with the community you serve

UNIT 3 OFFICER WELL-BEING
LESSON 1 Adjusting to Shiftwork

> **◎ Lesson Goal**
>
> At the end of this lesson, you will understand methods used to adjust to shiftwork and what actions to avoid when adjusting to shiftwork.

Think About This

Two new officers have been reassigned to work the night shift. What can they do to ensure that they are well rested and alert during the whole shift?

As a law enforcement officer, you will work in shifts to ensure that the community you serve remains safe and protected. Often, you will be required to work rotating shifts that may include evenings, all-night shifts, weekends, and holidays. During these shifts, regardless of the time of day, you will need to be alert and ready to respond at a moment's notice. When not managed well, shiftwork may negatively affect your physical and mental health.

☑ LE131.1. Describe the challenges of shiftwork

Adjusting to shiftwork can be challenging because it can impact your time with family and friends, your sleep schedule, and your eating habits. At times, balancing your personal life and work may feel like a difficult task given the nature of shiftwork; however, know that there are ways to make the transition easier and less harmful to your physical and mental health. Some of these methods involve maintaining good communication, engaging in regular exercise, and developing good sleeping and eating habits.

☑ LE131.2. Explain methods of adjusting to shiftwork

Even with opposite sleeping schedules, it is still possible and important to maintain connections with the people who are close to you. You will need to communicate directly with them and let them know your schedule and the times when you will be asleep. If you live with others, a helpful suggestion would be to designate specific times when the household needs to be quiet to allow you to rest as well as times when you will be awake and able to interact. Post your schedule on the refrigerator or another place where others can see it.

☑ LE131.3. Discuss health risks associated with getting insufficient sleep

Establishing and maintaining healthy sleeping habits is important, even if you are working non-traditional hours. For example, there are health risks for people who get insufficient amounts of sleep. Chronic conditions like heart disease, high blood pressure, diabetes, obesity, and depression have been linked to sleep deficiency. In addition, people who are sleep deficient are more inclined to injuries and accidents. Sleep deficiency can also affect your focus, decision making ability, and reaction time similar to alcohol intoxication. Therefore, it is imperative that you consistently get 6–8 hours of good quality sleep.

If you are struggling to fall asleep because of your schedule, pay attention to light, sound, and temperature in your sleeping environment:

- light—when you go to sleep, make sure your room is as dark as possible. Blackout curtains can help with this as well as a sleep mask for your eyes. The blue light emitted from electronic devices can also affect your circadian rhythm, which is your body's natural way of telling you when to wake and when to sleep. Make sure to limit or eliminate your screen time prior to bed as it can create difficulties with falling asleep, which can then reduce the quality of your sleep.
- sound—noise can directly impact the quantity and quality of sleep you get. If possible, invest in tools that can help drown out noise that other members of your household might make during the day. For example, you may get quality sleep by owning noise-canceling earplugs or headphones or a white noise machine placed inside your room or on the outside of your door. Also, there are free apps available for you to download that provide white noise and other soothing sounds.
- temperature—lower temperatures have been shown to help people fall asleep quicker. If possible, try to cool your room as much as possible. Turn on a fan or lower your air conditioner. Temperatures between 60 °F and 65 °F have been shown to be ideal for falling asleep. Sleeping on cotton or bamboo sheets can also help you stay cool while sleeping.

☑ LE131.4. Describe helpful techniques for falling asleep

Adjusting to an irregular sleep schedule may tempt you to make decisions that will hinder your adjustment. So, it is important that you are using techniques that will help you to be successful in your career while also allowing you to maintain your overall health and well-being.

☑ LE131.5. Discuss actions to avoid when adjusting to an irregular sleep schedule due to shiftwork

When adjusting to an irregular sleep schedule due to shiftwork, avoid using sleeping pills or alcohol to help you sleep because both substances can become highly addictive and cause dependency. People who rely on sleeping pills or alcohol often need increasing amounts in order to achieve the same effect until, eventually, they are unable to fall asleep without the use of them.

Before bed, try to limit your intake of sugar, caffeine, and junk food. These types of foods and substances can interfere with your ability to sleep and can be harmful to your health. You should also avoid eating a heavy meal close to bedtime. Consuming a heavy meal so close to bedtime can affect the quality of your sleep. If you do decide to eat before bed, make sure it is a small, nutrient dense snack.

It is important to not deviate from your sleep schedule. Stay consistent, even on your days off. When you get home from work, create a routine, and try to go to sleep at the same time every day. Deviating from your sleep schedule can make it more difficult to adjust back. If you do have to transition to a new shift, try and do so gradually and avoid drastically changing the time you go to sleep.

UNIT 3 OFFICER WELL-BEING
LESSON 2 Officer Wellness

> ### ◎ Lesson Goal
>
> At the end of this lesson, you will be able to maintain your physical and mental health as well as your financial stability.

Throughout your law enforcement career, you will experience situations that could influence your physical and mental health as well as your financial stability. So, it is important that you recognize and understand that your health should rank high on your list of priorities. Remember, focusing on your overall well-being will allow you to better serve your community.

MAINTAINING PHYSICAL HEALTH

☑ LE132.1. Describe the best practices for establishing healthy eating habits

Although healthy eating habits are suggested for everyone, they are especially essential for law enforcement officers as aspects of the job can be physically taxing. In order to properly fulfill your duties, your body needs to be properly fueled. For example, try to eat a balanced diet that includes lean proteins, grains, vegetables, fruit, and dairy. Limit your daily intake of fat, sugar, and sodium in order to maintain a healthy weight and normal blood pressure.

Finding ways to eat a balanced diet can be very difficult for officers on busy schedules. You may be tempted to grab fast food during your shift due to time constraints; however, fast food can be high in fat and sodium content with minimal nutritional value. Eating out regularly also becomes very expensive and can easily lead to poor financial choices. Plan ahead by developing and prepping a week-long meal plan. Consider investing in good quality food storage, such as a thermos or portable insulated lunch container. This will allow you to bring nutritious meals from home, which will save you time and money. You may also benefit from eating healthy snacks like fruit and nuts throughout your shift. Starting these practices early on can help you maintain healthy eating habits.

Another way to focus on your overall well-being is to make sure you are properly hydrated during your shift. If you are thirsty, you are dehydrated and need fluids. Ensure you stay hydrated by carrying a bottle of water with you, and refill it as needed. Beverages that contain electrolytes can be beneficial after heavy workouts or intense physical activity. But keep in mind that these beverages may have high sugar contents.

In contrast, avoid drinking excessive amounts of caffeinated beverages like coffee and soda. If you develop a physical dependence on caffeine, you may feel symptoms of withdrawal when you eliminate it from your diet. Likewise, be aware of your alcohol consumption, frequency, and reactions.

If possible, find ways to relax that do not include alcohol, but if you do drink, carefully examine your intake and the effect it has on you. Excessive routine and binge drinking can have negative effects on your health and personal and professional life. Caffeine and alcohol can also cause sleep disturbances, so it is vital to limit your use of both.

It may seem difficult or even impossible to schedule time for exercise. However, routine exercise is very important for your overall health. Some benefits of routine exercise include:

- maintaining a healthy weight
- preventing weight gain
- combatting chronic conditions, such as high blood pressure, diabetes, and arthritis
- reducing anxiety and depression
- boosting energy
- promoting better sleep

☑ LE132.2. Discuss the benefits of getting routine exercise

You can exercise by finding a physical activity that you enjoy such as playing basketball or walking with friends and family. The Centers for Disease Control and Prevention (CDC) recommends engaging in a moderate-intensity activity 30 minutes a day for five days a week. If you cannot carve out scheduled time to exercise, incorporate more movement into your normal activities. For example, park further from your agency's building or take the stairs instead of the elevator.

Along with exercising your body through movement, you should also exercise your mind. Participate in activities that stimulate your mind, such as meditation, reading, or puzzles. These actions can enhance your overall well-being by temporarily removing you from the stressors of the day.

MAINTAINING MENTAL HEALTH

Mental and physical health overlap and are deeply intertwined. Just as it is important to take care of your body, it is equally important that you take care of your mind. Developing a work-life balance can help you maintain your mental health and keep up with your daily responsibilities. This means that you focus on law enforcement tasks when you are at work, and on non-work-related activities, such as spending time with family and friends, when you are at home. This balance is essential because it allows you to be present during the different areas of your life.

☑ LE132.3. Describe the best practices for maintaining mental health

While it is natural to connect with fellow officers at work, it is also necessary to keep your existing friendships outside of law enforcement and build new ones. Spend time with people who share common interests in hobbies, sports, or other activities. If you have a spiritual or religious affiliation, build support by joining activities related to your beliefs. This will help you stay connected to your community and remind you that you have an identity outside of your career.

In addition to building a community, it is essential for every officer to build their toolbox of mental health resources. Begin by finding out about the resources offered through your employer. Most agencies have an employee assistance program (EAP), which is a free and confidential program that provides consultation and treatment to employees to address and resolve personal and work-related challenges. Some agencies have peer support teams, chaplains, and culturally competent therapists. Culturally competent therapists are therapists who work with and understand the law enforcement career and are available to contact whenever you need them. The need might not arise for you, but you will have tools to help a fellow officer in need of additional support.

Finally, you should not let fear of judgement prevent you from seeking treatment. If you notice yourself feeling like your mental health is being challenged, make it a priority to seek out help. Think of it this way; if you were shot through the shoulder, you would not wait around to see if it will get better on its own. Instead, you would immediately seek out professional medical help. Just like physical health challenges, mental health challenges should also be taken seriously.

MAINTAINING FINANCIAL STABILITY

☑ LE132.4. Identify ways to maintain financial stability while employed as a law enforcement officer

Learning to make sound financial decisions is also part of caring for your overall well-being. Make sure you set yourself up for success by creating a financial plan that keeps your spending within your means. Create a budget that details your monthly expenses. This can help you easily track your spending and avoid impulse purchases. Consider the long-term effects that high-dollar purchases, such as expensive vehicles, have on your budget. One helpful suggestion is to save up for an expensive item and then, make the purchase in the future.

Spending beyond the means of your budget can also create additional stress when bills are due. Some officers work overtime or take second jobs to bridge the gap between their income and debt, which can reduce the time an officer spends with their family and friends. Working overtime and taking second jobs can also reduce the amount of time an officer has to relax from the challenges associated with the profession. Understand that steady employment does not guarantee a lavish lifestyle, and financial choices should be made with this in mind.

UNIT 3 OFFICER WELL-BEING
LESSON 3 Stress

⊚ Lesson Goal

At the end of this lesson, you will be able to recognize how the different types of stress impact your daily life and ways to manage stress more effectively.

Think About This

After a few months on the job, you notice that you are often tense, easily startled, and have difficulty sleeping and relaxing outside of work. What could be causing you to feel this way?

You will respond to high-stakes situations such as domestic disputes, child abuse cases, traffic accidents, and homicides. For victims, these situations may occur only once in a lifetime, but as a law enforcement officer, you may find yourself regularly in dangerous situations. It is vital that you be able to recognize and manage the stress that goes along with these difficult situations. **Stress** is the physical or emotional reaction to an event, situation, or threat (real or perceived). It can also be a physical or mental response to a demanding situation or change.

CATEGORIES OF STRESS

The level of stress you feel in each situation depends on your perspective and previous experiences as well as the type of threat. There are three general categories of stress:

- *routine stress*—happens on a daily basis and is a normal part of life. Some examples include the ordinary stresses of being a law enforcement officer, balancing home and work life, and taking care of day-to-day tasks for your household.
- *acute stress*—is often short-lived and occurs when you experience unexpected changes in your life, such as the end of a relationship, the death of a family member, or sudden unemployment.
- *traumatic stress*—occurs during major events like war, disasters, global pandemics, incidents of assault, or other events that cause you to feel that your personal safety, or the safety of others, is in danger. This type of stress can also result from incidents that may be less easy to identify, such as having chronic worries about your health and safety of others or hearing about how a fellow officer has been assaulted.

☑ LE133.1. Describe the three categories of stress

Remember, everyone has different perspectives and life experiences, and what may be stressful to you, may not be stressful to others. As a result, people may respond differently to certain situations.

RESPONSES TO STRESS

☑ LE133.2. List the three primary responses to stress

While stress can slow down your reaction time, cloud your judgment, or make you question your decisions, not all of its effects are bad. Stress can make you aware of potentially dangerous situations and prepare you to react. One of the body's defense mechanisms is the *fight-flight-freeze response*, which is the body's physiological response to a perceived or real threat. When this is triggered, your body may react in one of three ways:

- fight—the body prepares to face the danger head-on.
- flight—the body prepares to flee from a dangerous situation.
- freeze—the body fails to react.

Although the fight-flight-freeze response can be helpful in certain situations, experiencing this response every day may prime you to be stressed more often than not. It is important to strike a healthy balance between the right amount of stress to stay alert in case of danger while still being able to relax or unwind when the situation calls. You are encouraged to develop personal interventions to combat stress.

EFFECTS OF STRESS

☑ LE133.3. Describe some of the indicators of stress

While acute and routine stress may not initially appear to be as dangerous as traumatic stress, both can have negative effects on your life if not managed properly. Routine and acute stress responses include temporary increases in anxiety, tension, and irritability. Health-related stress responses include headaches, blood pressure changes, and loss of sleep. Job performance-related stress responses include inconsistent work habits and decreased productivity.

All categories of stress can also affect your personal relationships and damage your connections with loved ones. Long-term stress responses may include depression or suicidal thoughts. Failure to address stress may also result in chronic health problems, including disease, high blood pressure, and ulcers. Due to the nature of their duties, law enforcement officers are at greater risk for many of these conditions. Additionally, officers have a higher risk of suicide and substance abuse.

Monitor yourself as well as other officers for warning signs of stress. Some of the most common indicators are sudden behavioral changes, inconsistent work habits, accidents or injuries, frequent tiredness, sleeping and eating disorders, anxiety, alcohol and substance use, and complaints from other officers or members of the community. Reach out for help from a colleague, a licensed mental health professional, or your facility's EAP if you or a fellow officer is struggling with mental or emotional health.

☑ LE133.4. Identify signs that a fellow officer is coping poorly with stress

You will often work alongside other officers as a partner or on a team. For this reason, you may be one of the first people to notice that a fellow officer is having a difficult time coping with stress. Some signs that an officer may be having a difficult time coping with stress include:

- irritability
- attempts to isolate

- a change in behavior and how they interact with colleagues or the public
- hopelessness or emotional pain
- tardiness, absence, or other changes in job performance
- increased use of substances or other risky behavior, including high-risk sexual behaviors
- changes in physical appearance and hygiene, such as suddenly having an unkempt uniform or appearance, and excessive weight gain or loss

If you notice these signs in one of your colleagues, simply ask them how they are doing. You do not need to be a mental health professional to provide support. In fact, they may feel comfortable sharing with you because of your shared experiences in working in law enforcement.

☑ LE133.5. Discuss how to provide support to officers who are experiencing stress

Some suggestions to help you talk to an officer about their stress include the following:

- listen—often, people who are going through problems simply want a person to listen to them and give their full attention. Be patient and give the person time to tell you how they are feeling.
- reassure—let the person know that their feelings are normal and that they are not weak for expressing them.
- provide appropriate resources, such as a peer support team, a crisis text line, alcoholics anonymous, or your facility's EAP.
- follow-up—check in with the officer in a week and ask if they have used any of the resources provided. If not, ask them how you can help them reach out for assistance.

When you help your fellow officers, you are not trying to solve their problems. You are offering support and helping your colleague plan to help themselves. Listening, reassuring, providing resources, and following up will let them know that you are available to talk and that they are not alone.

IMPACTS OF TRAUMA

Along with other types of stress, traumatic stress comes with medical consequences. When you are frightened and nervous, your brain releases stress hormones that help you survive during life and death situations by allowing you to react quickly, such as in the fight-flight-freeze response. Even though stress plays an important role in keeping you safe during dangerous incidents, it can be harmful if experienced on a long-term basis. Repeated exposure to traumatic stress keeps the brain flooded with stress hormones even when you are not in a stressful situation. High levels of stress hormones have been linked to illness, anxiety, and increased risk of drug and alcohol use.

☑ LE133.6. Explain how trauma impacts the brain

While traumatic stress is a normal part of your job, feeling distressed by traumatic situations is not a failure on your part. It is your body's biological response to trauma. Understanding your body's biological responses will help you realize that when you are

impacted by traumatic stress. When you are feeling negatively impacted by stress, reach out to a peer or professional for help.

> LE133.7. Differentiate between post-traumatic stress and post-traumatic stress disorder

Post-traumatic stress is a natural reaction that involves physiological and psychological changes in response to a traumatic event. It is a normal reaction to a traumatic, stressful, or out of the ordinary situation. Post-traumatic stress usually occurs within 30 days of the traumatic event and generally resolves itself within days or weeks. However, if symptoms occur for more than a month, this could be signs of post-traumatic stress disorder. Unlike post-traumatic stress, post-traumatic stress disorder can only be diagnosed by a licensed clinician. Most officers will have post-traumatic stress at some point in their career; however, not all officers will experience post-traumatic stress disorder.

Due to the high levels of stress that law enforcement officers face, some go on to develop *post-traumatic stress disorder (PTSD)*, a pattern of biological stress responses that may develop after a single stressful event or a series of stressful events. Sometimes the sufferer is not the person threatened by the situation but someone who witnessed it.

PTSD SYMPTOMS

> LE133.8. Describe the symptoms of post-traumatic stress disorder that a law enforcement officer may experience

An officer with PTSD may display symptoms such as depression, anxiety, flashbacks, and recurring nightmares. The officer may become emotionally unresponsive or have an unpredictable outburst of anger due to intrusive thoughts of re-experiencing the event. Avoidance of reminders or anything associated with the event may be a coping mechanism to relieve stress.

Other symptoms of PTSD include the following:

- irritable or aggressive behavior
- reckless or self-destructive behavior
- problems with concentration
- difficulty falling or staying asleep or restless sleep
- hypervigilance

One of the symptoms of PTSD is hypervigilance, which is a sense of always being on guard that can make it difficult to disengage from stress. When someone is hypervigilant, they may have increased difficulty relaxing in situations that are not stressful, such as sitting in a restaurant with family or enjoying a day in the park with friends. This is different from vigilance, which is important for officers as it helps them identify and avoid dangerous situations as well as protect themselves and fellow officers from harm.

STRATEGIES FOR COPING WITH STRESS

Due to the challenges you will face, it is important to manage your stress effectively. You will be exposed to traumatic events more frequently and will need to develop healthy coping strategies in order to continue to protect your community.

In addition to maintaining your physical and mental health, establish and utilize your support system. Having a support system in place is another good way to cope with stress, and it will help with your mental health in the long run. A support system is a group of people who can offer you emotional and practical support. Your support system can be professional, personal, or a combination of the two, and it can be made up of one person or many people. An understanding support system can guide you through difficult times in your career.

Conversation can be a powerful tool when coping with stress; however, make sure that you choose someone trustworthy to share your concerns with. Sharing your feelings with a loved one, close friend, religious or spiritual advisor, counselor or doctor are a few options.

Along with talking with a trustworthy supporter, it is also vital that you build resilience. **Resilience** is the capacity to effectively cope with stress, trauma, and other serious problems. You can strengthen resilience by making your health a priority, seeking help from a licensed mental health professional, and connecting with people in your support group. You can also build resilience by practicing stress reduction activities, such as controlled breathing exercises, throughout your time on duty. Take time to disengage and fully unwind after your shift is over. Building your resilience will not happen overnight, and you do not have to do it on your own. Having resilience does not mean that you are unaffected by difficult situations; it means that you have healthy coping strategies and know when to reach out for help when you experience them.

☑ LE133.9. Discuss strategies for building resilience

UNIT 3 OFFICER WELL-BEING
LESSON 4 Substance Abuse Awareness and Suicide Prevention

> **Lesson Goal**
>
> At the end of this lesson, you will be able to recognize the impacts of substance abuse and understand the importance of suicide prevention in law enforcement.

Due to the high-stress environment associated with the law enforcement profession, some officers may develop poor coping strategies and turn to alcohol and drugs. These substances numb feelings that officers face from sustained exposure to traumatic events, which can affect both their mental and physical health. With this in mind, substance abuse is a growing concern in law enforcement because it not only places the officer at risk, but the community as well.

SUBSTANCE ABUSE AWARENESS

☑ LE134.1. Identify common substances being abused

In order to relieve some of the stress that comes from routinely facing dangerous situations, officers may turn to certain substances like alcohol and drugs. For example, officers may go drinking with their colleagues in order to feel accepted at their agency. If done frequently, alcohol use may develop into dependence, which may lead to substance abuse issues. Poor decisions like driving under the influence or being intoxicated on the job can end one's career and can be life-threatening to the officer and other members of the community.

While some officers may turn to alcohol to relax and cope, others may turn to drugs that have been prescribed, such as opioids or pain medications. Officers put themselves at risk daily while doing their jobs and sometimes, they may get injured. The genuine need for pain relief may lead to substance abuse issues. Other types of medications that officers may use are sedatives, such as anti-anxiety medications, muscle relaxers, and sleeping pills. These medications are very effective in creating a sense of calm for officers who are dealing with intense stress; however, officers may depend on them for everyday use.

☑ LE134.2. List the effects of substance abuse

Overtime, commonly used substances may negatively impact every aspect of a person's life. For example, long term use of alcohol and drugs can cause damage to major organs like the liver, kidneys, heart, and brain. The overuse of opioids and sedatives can lead to respiratory distress, coma, and even death. Substance abuse can worsen mental health issues such as depression and anxiety, while also impairing one's ability to make decisions. In addition, a person's usage of alcohol and drugs may damage their relationships and negatively affect their employment, since signs of abuse, such as frequent absenteeism and poor performance, can lead to job loss.

Since substance abuse affects a person's mind and body, they will most likely show some of the following signs and symptoms:

- slurred or slowed speech
- watery, bloodshot eyes
- impaired memory
- slower reaction times
- lack of coordination
- mood swings or personality changes
- sudden weight loss or gain
- deterioration of physical appearance

☑ LE134.3. List signs and symptoms of substance abuse

It is your responsibility to intervene if you notice signs that a fellow officer is on duty and appears to be under the influence of alcohol or drugs. If you suspect that a fellow officer is struggling with substance abuse, you can speak with them about utilizing agency resources, such as your facility's EAP or outside support groups. That officer may or may not follow your recommendations and, as a result, you may need to take additional steps by notifying a supervisor. Most agencies have a zero-tolerance drug and alcohol policy, so make sure to follow your agency's policy and procedures when involved in this situation.

☑ LE134.4. Describe how to respond to a fellow officer who appears to be struggling with substance abuse issues

Helping a fellow officer who is struggling with substance abuse can impact your emotions as well. Take time for self-reflection and self-care after this type of encounter. Self-reflection may involve thinking about your own behavior and habits and questioning what you can do to protect yourself from unhealthy choices. Self-care may include speaking with a fellow officer or counselor.

SUICIDE PREVENTION

Each day officers are often witnesses to tragedies, such as fatal car crashes, domestic violence, child abuse cases, and other life-threatening situations, that could impact their mental health. Suicide and suicidal ideation are also a growing concern in the law enforcement community.

Some officers you talk to may experience *suicidal ideation*, which is when a person has thoughts about ending their own life. Anyone can experience suicidal ideation, regardless of whether or not they are diagnosed with a mental illness. When someone experiences suicidal ideation, that does not necessarily mean they will die by suicide. However, it is important to take suicidal ideation seriously because it does increase the risk of suicide.

☑ LE134.5. Identify warning signs that a person may be planning suicide

Personal and professional challenges may become overwhelming and cause an officer to experience suicidal ideation. People who are planning suicide may show warning signs. Some of the signs you should look for include:

- expressing hopelessness and talking about wanting to die
- talking about being a burden to others

- feeling as though one's pain or stressors are inescapable
- sleeping too little or too much
- withdrawing or feeling isolated from family, friends, and loved ones
- displaying extreme mood swings
- increasing one's use of alcohol or drugs
- acting agitated or reckless
- saying goodbye to others and referencing the next life
- giving away important possessions

☑ LE134.6. Explain how to help officers who may experience suicidal ideation

If you suspect that an officer may be coping with suicidal ideation, you should ask them directly if they are having thoughts of harming themselves or taking their own life. A good question to ask would be "have you had any thoughts about killing yourself?"

Talking openly about someone's thoughts of suicide does not mean that you are pushing the person toward suicide. Instead, asking directly often makes people more likely to open up about those feelings, so they can receive help. If an officer shares that they are experiencing suicidal ideation, it may be helpful to respond in the following ways:

- Thank them for being honest with you.
- Let them know you are listening and that you support them in getting help.
- Offer to help them make an appointment with a mental health professional. You can do this either by calling someone with them or helping them make an appointment online.

If it would make it easier for the person, you may offer to go with them to their first appointment or be on the phone with them while they call to talk to a professional.

If an officer says that they do intend to kill themselves, stay with them and make sure they do not have access to weapons. If an officer does not want to get help or talk to someone, let them know that there are resources and that you are willing to help connect them at any time. Be familiar with your agency's policies and procedures and follow the guidelines when this situation arises.

If an officer says that they have a plan to end their life, ask if they have taken any steps to carry out the plan. If there is a plan, and steps to carry out the act have begun, then immediate intervention is needed. Follow your agency's policies and procedures to obtain immediate help for the officer in crisis. Some agencies may require you to report this information to a designated staff member. Remember that there is nothing wrong with reporting this information. You may save an officer's life. Follow up with the person after the crisis and offer continued support.

Helping a fellow officer who is experiencing thoughts of suicide can take a heavy toll on you. Be sure to recognize your own emotions and responses. Caring for yourself is vitally important. It may take some time to process through your own thoughts and feelings.

Take care of yourself and use coping strategies. Consider using some of the resources that your agency provides to come to terms with what you are feeling.

ASSISTANCE RESOURCES

Many agencies have resources available to their officers, and many of these are available through an EAP. The EAP at your agency can be a good first step to access several resources. EAPs are often designed to help employees address issues such as mental and physical health, family care-giving, and financial planning.

Many agencies also have peer-to-peer support assistance. People who participate in this program will often be fellow officers who have been trained to give support and listen to their colleagues. Peer-to-peer support can guide you to other resources available to assist you, but keep in mind that it is not a substitute for therapy with a licensed clinician. It is an additional option that allows you to share with someone who understands the profession.

☑ LE134.7. List available resources for managing mental health

There are also many outside resources available. A few options include:

- Alcoholics Anonymous
- Crisis Text Line
- Narcotics Anonymous
- 988 Suicide and Crisis Lifeline (formerly National Suicide Prevention Lifeline)
- Substance Abuse and Mental Health Services Administration (SAMHSA)
- The National Alliance on Mental Illness

Many organizations also help first responders and other public safety professionals. A few examples include:

- Badge of Life
- Blue HELP
- 1-800-COPLINE
- Center for Officer Safety and Wellness, International Association of Chiefs of Police
- Concerns of Police Survivors
- First Responder Support Network
- HEART (Healing Emergency and Response Team) 9/11
- Police Officers Providing Peer Assistance (POPPA)
- Safe Call Now
- The Vicarious Trauma Toolkit—Office for Victims of Crime

CAREER LONGEVITY

> LE134.8. Describe ways to develop personal resilience against trauma, compassion fatigue, and stigma for career longevity

Sustaining a career in law enforcement means being aware of the challenges you will face and knowing how to cope with them. Many people who work in careers that regularly place them in traumatic situations are at risk of developing secondary trauma and compassion fatigue. **Secondary trauma**, sometimes referred to as vicarious trauma, occurs when a person is exposed to the trauma of others and experiences physical or mental impacts. Experiencing secondary trauma may result in absences at work, inability to focus on tasks, and a shortened career. **Compassion fatigue** is the emotional exhaustion that comes from caring for others in emotional distress on a long-term basis. Symptoms of compassion fatigue include irritation, withdrawal from social situations, and feeling emotionally drained. Awareness of these possible complications is important because officers who neglect their mental health may not have the career longevity that they hope for. Additionally, officers who neglect their mental health could be putting their colleagues as well as the public at risk. Your fellow officers and the public you interact with need you to be dependable and calm even when situations are tense.

In the past, it was common to believe that people should deal with trauma and stress on their own. This was due to the stigma associated with mental health issues. **Stigma** is a set of negative and unfair beliefs that a society or group of people have about something. This can consist of officers making jokes or perpetuating stereotypes that can prevent people from getting professional help. Statements such as "just deal with it" or "you need to be tougher" will foster this stigma. Recognize that mental health is as important as physical health, and similarly, it sometimes requires the help of a professional.

Law enforcement officers may not seek help because they fear that this will negatively impact their careers. However, getting help from a licensed mental health professional is strictly confidential. There is only one exception and that is when the mental health professional has reason to believe that their patient is an immediate danger to themselves or others or if there is a case of child or elder abuse.

Building your personal resilience and taking care of yourself can help you cope with secondary trauma and compassion fatigue. Reaching out for help before you experience stress will help you with career longevity. It is recommended that, on top of your annual physical exam with your general medical practitioner, you also schedule an annual mental health checkup with a licensed therapist or psychiatrist. By doing so, you make it a habit to prioritize your mental health. You do not have to wait until you experience a crisis to seek help.

Chapter 2
Communication

UNIT 1 FUNDAMENTALS OF COMMUNICATION
  LESSON 1 Communication Basics / 45
  LESSON 2 Verbal and Non-verbal Communication / 48
  LESSON 3 Conflict Resolution and De-escalation / 51

UNIT 2 PROFESSIONAL COMMUNICATION
  LESSON 1 Knowing Your Community and Interacting With the Public / 54
  LESSON 2 Core Communication Competencies / 57

UNIT 1 FUNDAMENTALS OF COMMUNICATION
LESSON 1 Communication Basics

⊚ Lesson Goal

At the end of this lesson, you will be able to communicate effectively using empathy, courtesy, and professionalism while serving your community.

Think About This

While on patrol, a resident approaches you and says they are angry because of the increase of burglaries in their neighborhood. They begin to raise their voice and ask you why the police aren't doing more to protect their homes. How could you help de-escalate this situation?

COMMUNICATION METHODS

In this chapter, you will learn several communication skills that will make you safer and more effective in your work as a law enforcement officer. Officers who possess strong interpersonal skills can respond appropriately and potentially avoid triggering or escalating a crisis situation.

Communication involves the exchange of verbal and non-verbal messages. Communication methods include spoken or written language, gestures, facial expressions, and body movements. For communication to occur, the speaker must send their message in a way that the listener will understand. Then, the listener can show that they understand by responding.

☑ LE211.1. Define communication and the different methods to communicate

CHARACTERISTICS OF AN EFFECTIVE COMMUNICATOR

Law enforcement officers interact with people of many backgrounds, cultures, religious beliefs, and ethnicities. You should be able to adapt your communication style to fit the needs of the people you are interacting with and the situation at hand.

Communication barriers, unclear expression, or a failure to understand the other person's needs can all lead to miscommunication; when miscommunication occurs, it can create problems and potential safety issues for officers. Good communication skills can help prevent misunderstandings and the escalation of tensions, thereby keeping you and the community you serve safe. You can become a more effective communicator by practicing empathy, courtesy, and professionalism.

Empathy

Empathy is the ability to understand and care about the emotions of others. Think of it as a tactic you can use to help in the situations you will encounter as a law enforcement officer.

> **LE211.2.** Describe the role of empathy in effective communication

Empathy should not be confused with sympathy, which is feeling sad for someone. Instead, empathy allows you to connect with someone. When you are empathetic, you think about how that person must be feeling and how you would feel in that same situation.

Officers can use empathy in any setting to help keep situations safe. For example, you may respond to a call about a person loitering in front of a store. Use empathy to navigate the situation. Consider that this person might be fearful of the police and unsure of the situation. Think back to times when you were afraid or felt unsafe, and use these experiences to let this person know that you understand how afraid they might be.

Using empathy to put yourself in another person's shoes will also help you employ the four pillars of procedural justice. If you were in the same situation, you would want to be listened to, treated with respect and fairness, and know what was going on. These behaviors may seem basic, but in a stressful or volatile encounter, empathy can mean the difference between escalating into violence or keeping everyone safe and secure.

Courtesy

Courtesy is how you display professional conduct or show respect for others. The following tips may help you demonstrate courtesy as an officer:

- Be personal yet professional by introducing yourself by name and using the person's name to establish rapport.
- Treat every person you meet with dignity and respect.
- Avoid words, phrases, and sarcastic tones that may create barriers. An example is using the word "obviously" when the situation may not be obvious to someone else. Another expression to avoid is the phrase "you people," which establishes an instant separation between you and the people that you are addressing.
- When a person's request seems unrealistic, instead of focusing on what cannot be done, redirect the focus to what can be done.
- Explain what actions you are taking and why.

> **LE211.3.** Explain the importance of practicing courtesy throughout your career

Maintaining a professional, courteous demeanor will help you respond appropriately to situations and can make the public more likely to assist you.

> **LE211.4.** Describe how to demonstrate professionalism throughout your career

Professionalism

Professionalism is behavior that demonstrates good character and is marked by pride in yourself and your career. The characteristics of a professional include service, integrity, respect, quality, fairness, honesty, courage, compassion, moral and ethical leadership, trustworthiness, and common sense. Some examples of professionalism include:

- doing the right thing when no one is looking
- knowing your job and being competent

- dressing professionally
- maintaining a calm presence
- recognizing and admitting your mistakes
- being courteous
- practicing customer service
- maintaining your training and continuing education

Be mindful of your attitude and assume one that supports the professional behavior you should display every time you go to work. Your attitude shapes your expectations of what will happen in any given situation, and it affects how people perceive you. An officer with a professional and positive attitude is a valuable member of society and the law enforcement community.

Another way to maintain professional behavior is to practice the four pillars of procedural justice and the LEED framework—listen, explain, equity, dignity—in all your interactions. Remembering the LEED framework will give you guidelines to follow and make it easier to remain professional in a variety of situations.

PROJECTING A POSITIVE SELF-IMAGE

An officer's most valuable non-verbal tool is their command presence, and it is demonstrated in several ways. To have command presence, you must demonstrate confidence in your demeanor by maintaining a professional personal appearance, erect posture, alertness, and attention to your surroundings. Continued training, education, and experience are all things which will improve your self-confidence, credibility, and command presence.

Displaying a positive self-image extends to every role you play as a law enforcement officer and will vary depending on which role you are serving at the moment—the supporter, stabilizer, or enforcer. For instance, when acting as a supporter, maintain your command presence, but adjust it to fit the situation. Consider sitting down with a victim instead of standing over them when speaking to them. In this way, you are still in control of the situation and conveying ability but also making the victim more comfortable. Being aware of what role you need to take on will help you determine a suitable professional response for that situation.

☑ LE211.5. Explain the importance of having a positive self-image

Project a positive self-image in your physical appearance. It is the first non-verbal message you give upon arriving at a scene. Keep your uniform clean and pressed and your shoes shined. Maintain your personal hygiene. This demonstrates respect for your job and the people in the community you serve.

UNIT 1 FUNDAMENTALS OF COMMUNICATION
LESSON 2 Verbal and Non-verbal Communication

◎ Lesson Goal

At the end of this lesson, you will be able to interpret non-verbal and verbal communication while taking into consideration the context of the incident.

Think About This

You respond to a domestic disturbance at an apartment complex. When the tenant opens the door, he tells you that everything is fine, but he is sweating, breathing heavily, and has an expression of terror on his face. How can you read his non-verbal communication to help you assess the situation?

VERBAL AND NON-VERBAL CUES

The more you understand verbal and non-verbal cues, the greater your ability to communicate and choose responses appropriately. Constantly evaluating your verbal and non-verbal communication as well as the verbal and non-verbal communication of the people you are interacting with is important to your job and safety.

☑ LE212.1. Describe the elements of verbal and non-verbal communication

For example, you may observe that a person's **verbal communication** (what they say with words) during a traffic stop seems unemotional, but their non-verbal communication seems aggressive. **Non-verbal communication** is any message or signal sent from one person to another without the explicit use of language.

Some communication cues can include voice and tone, general appearance and dress, posture, body movement, facial expressions, touch, smell, personal space, and eye contact.

Voice and Tone

Verbal communication is not just what we say but how we say it. Pay attention to how you speak, and be mindful of your volume, tone, and inflection. Ask yourself and anyone else in the conversation these questions:

- What is the tone, volume, and pitch of the speaker?
- Does the speaker's tone of voice indicate sarcasm, confidence, compassion, anger, or another emotion?
- What words are being used, and how are they spoken?

General Appearance and Dress

Whether we recognize it or not, all of us make judgments based on a person's appearance. However, it is important to stay objective regarding a person's way of dressing.

Posture

How we carry ourselves can be an important non-verbal communication. Posture refers to the way we sit, walk, and stand and includes our bearing, subtle movements, and general presence. When evaluating someone's posture, consider the following:

- When you ask someone about their timeline on the date of a crime, does the person shift their weight or suddenly cross their arms?
- Does someone's non-verbal communication match what they are saying to you? Does the person's posture help validate or contradict what they say?

Body Movement

Body movement can offer vital non-verbal cues. We often use our bodies to communicate our attitude or our emotional state by facing or leaning toward a person or moving away from a person. Consider the following:

- When you interview someone, what is your body language saying? Do you lean forward to indicate interest?
- Does the person you are talking to exhibit physical indicators, including rocking back and forth, twitching their eyes, or shaking their legs? These behaviors could indicate that the person is nervous and is trying to self-soothe or could be indicators of fight or flight.

Facial Expressions

We are able to express various emotions through our facial expressions without saying a word. The good thing is that most facial expressions are universal. For example, the facial expressions for sorrow, joy, surprise, rage, disgust, and terror are the same across most cultures. When communicating with others, listen attentively and ask yourself:

- What facial expression is this person making, and does it provide additional information?
- Does the person's facial expression match the verbal message they are sending? A person may tell you that they are fine, but their facial expression may be one of rage.

Touch

Non-verbal behavior regarding touch also depends on the person. You may find yourself having to touch people to perform your duties. For example, when consoling a victim, you may give a reassuring pat on the shoulder to show empathy, or you may have to physically redirect someone to a particular location. Think about what messages you are giving to others when you touch them, and make sure to always respect someone's boundaries if they seem uncomfortable or don't want to be touched.

Smell

Sense of smell can sometimes be a barrier to communication. For example, some people may not share your expectations of personal hygiene, may have a medical condition, or may have dietary restrictions that cause them to smell differently. Avoid making judgments about the people with whom you interact.

Personal Space

Boundaries vary greatly from person to person. While it may be acceptable in some cultures to move into close proximity to communicate, it may not be in others. Be mindful that when you move within someone's personal space, you may make them uncomfortable and limit your ability to communicate with them.

Eye Contact

Your ability to establish, maintain, and understand eye contact will enhance your ability to communicate effectively. Factors such as cultural background, personality, nervous tension, emotional state, and medical conditions can influence someone's eye contact. Use your knowledge of eye contact to help determine someone's emotional state.

Two concepts that you should be aware of are mutual gaze and break of gaze. Mutual gaze is the common level of eye-to-eye contact that two people have when conversing. It usually starts when someone is trying to get someone else's attention. For example, as an officer interviewing a subject who appears hesitant to reveal information, you might establish mutual gaze by nodding your head and maintaining eye contact to encourage the subject to continue to talk.

A break of gaze usually occurs when a person unintentionally or intentionally drops their gaze from the person looking at them. This could be caused by:

- personality
- emotional state
- traumatic event
- cultural norms
- recalling information

If a person breaks their gaze, it may indicate any number of emotions or non-verbal messages. Do not be quick to assume that you understand their response if they are not making eye contact with you.

Effectively evaluating your verbal and non-verbal communication will prove useful when you have to conduct criminal investigations, interviews, traffic stops, and interrogations. As a general rule, evaluate verbal and non-verbal behaviors within the entire context of what is going on and take cultural factors into consideration. All communication is subject to misinterpretation because people may react differently in stressful situations.

UNIT 1 FUNDAMENTALS OF COMMUNICATION
LESSON 3 Conflict Resolution and De-escalation

◎ Lesson Goal

At the end of this lesson, you will understand the barriers to communication and how to use conflict resolution and de-escalation skills to resolve incidents with equity and dignity.

Think About This

You respond to a conflict between a homeowner and his plumber. The plumber is upset because he says the homeowner has not paid him for any of his services. The homeowner is cursing and claiming that the plumber did not do his job, so he refuses to pay. How could you help manage this conflict?

CHALLENGES TO EFFECTIVE COMMUNICATION

Anticipating potential conflict will help you prepare for any law enforcement duty. There are many verbal and non-verbal cues to be mindful of as situations unfold, but there are strategies for conflict management that can be tailored to your duties. Each situation is unique and should be approached with patience and empathy.

☑ LE213.1. Describe barriers to effective communication

There are some common verbal and non-verbal barriers that you should try to avoid when communicating such as:

- failing to explain your actions
- failing to listen to what the person has to say
- using dialect, slang, words that have multiple meanings, or different languages
- using curse words or slurs
- phrasing your message in a disrespectful way
- having prejudices or implicit biases that lead to false assumptions or stereotyping
- changing body language or tone abruptly
- using non-verbal communication that does not match your verbal communication
- using derogatory hand gestures or body movements

It is important to avoid barriers to effective communication, but you should be especially mindful of these barriers when:

- a person has physical or psychological disabilities or conditions, for example, speaking louder for someone who may be hard of hearing
- a person has a language difference or an accent
- environmental and situational distractions are present, such as background noise in a person's home like a crying child or a loud radio

> **LE213.2. Describe how to overcome communication barriers**

There are several ways to prevent common barriers to communication:

- Treat everyone with respect.
- Maintain appropriate eye contact so that you can read non-verbal cues.
- Keep sentences brief and to the point. Short sentences minimize distractions, especially in stressful, confusing, or noisy situations.
- Give clear, specific directions. For example, saying "stand next to the trunk of your car" is better than saying "move over to where I can see you."
- Use open-ended questions to promote communication without limiting the other person's responses to short or one-word answers. Avoid asking yes-or-no questions.
- Allow the person to give their side of the story.

Understand that there will be times when communication barriers will be beyond your control; however, using the communication strategies above may help reduce the frequency of these occurrences.

MANAGING CONFLICT

Officers frequently serve as mediators during a conflict, and conflict resolution is a part of either temporarily or permanently resolving a situation before it escalates. Properly managing conflict can increase the awareness and understanding of the people involved and help them accept a decision or outcome.

Common calls for service may often involve you mediating between juveniles and their parent(s) or caregiver(s). The following conflict resolution strategies may be used for both adults and juveniles by tailoring your approach to each individual situation:

- Separate the people involved, making sure they are in a safe location and they cannot communicate with one another.
- Render first aid, if needed.
- Gather information from all sides. Allow people to give their side of the story.
- When appropriate, explain what you are doing and what the people involved can do.
- Provide options and available resources.
- If possible, help mediate a compromise.
- Tell the people involved why you are or are not taking action.
- Act with dignity and leave people with their dignity intact.

Before you begin mediating, you will also need to determine if the conflict can be resolved or only managed. Know the resources available to manage the conflict and bring it to an appropriate conclusion. Establishing order by guiding the people involved in the dispute toward a peaceful end should be the main goal; however, keep in mind that not everyone may agree with the solution.

To manage conflicts effectively, you should employ active listening, understand human and cultural diversity, and practice self-control. You will learn about active listening later in this chapter. It is equally important to be well-informed of the law and your authority as well as how to appropriately apply both to a situation.

☑ LE213.3. Describe how to defuse a situation through conflict management

You should remain unbiased and calm when helping people with a dispute. Many situations have the potential to escalate to violence if not properly managed; some examples are domestic disputes, child custody exchanges, landlord-tenant disagreements, and civil disputes. If the situation escalates to violence, you must take steps to establish control, such as by calling additional personnel, re-deploying resources, issuing strong verbal commands, or using physical force or the threat of force. These actions are commonly referred to as de-escalation techniques and are designed to bring a volatile situation under control.

Remember that until you establish control, mediation and arbitration cannot take place; however, with the use of de-escalation techniques, you may regain or establish control of the situation so that you can manage or resolve the conflict.

Unfortunately, not all conflicts can be brought to a peaceful conclusion. Sometimes, you may need to take enforcement action, such as making an arrest. Know the limits of your skills, the law, and your authority and how to apply these to a situation appropriately.

UNIT 2 PROFESSIONAL COMMUNICATION
LESSON 1 Knowing Your Community and Interacting With the Public

⊚ Lesson Goal

At the end of this lesson, you will know how to interact fairly and professionally with your diverse community.

Think About This

You are interviewing witnesses at the scene of a traffic crash. One witness is with her grandmother who, upon seeing you, begins crying and steps behind her granddaughter in an effort to hide from you. Her granddaughter apologizes and explains that her grandmother is afraid of law enforcement officers. What might have happened to this woman to damage her trust in law enforcement?

COMMUNITY EXPECTATIONS

As an officer, it is important to become familiar with your community and its expectations. Community refers to the people and locations that make up the neighborhoods, institutions, and businesses in the area where you work.

☑ LE221.1.
Describe community expectations for law enforcement

Officers interact with and serve their communities every day, and how they behave can potentially harm or improve the relationship between the community and law enforcement. The community expects officers to behave in a courteous, efficient, and accessible manner, treating all people fairly with consideration and compassion.

☑ LE221.2.
Explain how professionalism helps you communicate effectively

When officers act professionally, they build trust and strengthen law enforcement's relationship with the community, and the community is more secure and protected from criminal elements. This is why displaying professional behavior when interacting with the community is as important as demonstrating proficiency with firearms or defensive tactics. On the other hand, behaving unprofessionally will have an adverse effect on how the community views law enforcement and can impact everyone's safety.

People sometimes form negative opinions of law enforcement based on how law enforcement has previously responded to calls for service in their communities. An officer's unprofessional reaction to a situation can destroy the goodwill that took years to build within a community. Surveys show that people will most likely complain about your behavior if you show disrespect or arrogance, humiliate people, or rush to judgment on situations before gathering all the facts. Communities also complain about officers who make assumptions and respond in inappropriate and biased manners.

Make sure to always demonstrate professionalism in your interactions. Demonstrating professionalism will help improve your communications with the general public and the community and make you more capable of carrying out your duties. Remember that you need the community's respect, support, and cooperation to provide effective law enforcement services.

COMMUNITY DEMOGRAPHICS

During the course of your duties as an officer, you will meet people from different countries and cultural groups, and you will communicate with people with various socioeconomic backgrounds, ages, physical abilities, religious beliefs, living situations, sexual orientations, political beliefs, and ideologies. People from these groups may feel fear or distrust or be uncomfortable when interacting with you. They may not understand how the criminal justice system works, or they may have had negative experiences with law enforcement in the past.

To improve your communication with diverse communities, learn the demographics and social characteristics of your community and demonstrate a sincere willingness to learn about those you serve. Learn about the belief systems of different cultures and make an effort to connect with community members. Recognize differences that may block your communication as well as similarities that may support your effectiveness. Ask yourself questions such as:

- Does my gender affect this situation?
- Is there a family or cultural hierarchy that I should be aware of?
- Is there a language barrier? If so, what can I do to communicate more effectively?

Recall the tips regarding non-verbal cues that were presented earlier in this chapter. Be aware of how eye contact, gestures, personal space, and facial expressions can affect your communication with diverse communities. Building rapport, respecting others, and taking the time to explain your actions can help you gain cooperation and lessen negative consequences. As the people you serve become used to how you police the community, they will begin to understand how local law enforcement agencies can partner with the community to prevent crime.

INTERCULTURAL COMMUNICATION

Culture is one of many factors that affect communication. Culture may be identified as the customary beliefs, social norms, and significant traits prevalent among a group of people or in a particular place. It is important to understand the concept of intercultural communication and how it can affect your job as an officer. Intercultural communication takes place when people from different cultures communicate. "Intercultural" can mean interethnic, interreligious, and interregional, as well as between genders.

☑ LE221.3. Describe cultural influences that can affect interpersonal communication

When intercultural communication is done poorly, it can result in miscommunication and division between you and your community. For example, some cultures prefer to establish rapport or an informal relationship before conducting business. If you attempt to question someone from a culture like this without establishing rapport first, the person might be less inclined to share information with you.

When you are *culturally responsive*, you are open to learning about new cultures, are respectful of cultural differences, and recognize the important role that culture plays in people's lives. You can improve your intercultural communication by being culturally responsive, and you can work on being culturally responsive by:

Learning about your community's:

- diverse populations
- faith organizations
- languages spoken
- cultural organizations
- small businesses

Demonstrating respect for the cultures of your community members:

- Culture is an important part of everyone's lives and identities. Showing respect for someone's culture can help make community members feel valued.
- Showing respect for other people's culture also leads to a better relationship between law enforcement and the communities they serve.

Being open to learning and fixing mistakes when they happen:

- If a community member corrects an error you have made regarding their culture, listen, accept responsibility, and do not be defensive.
- Recognize that making mistakes is part of the learning process. What is important is that you are willing to learn and grow.
- If you are not sure, ask. If you ask a question about someone's culture in a respectful manner, you open up a dialogue that can result in a relationship built on a foundation of respect.

Remembering that not everyone has the same experiences as you:

- Everyone sees the world in a different way because each person's experiences are unique.
- Take the time to talk to your community members and learn their perspectives.

You will need to dedicate time to build awareness and learn how to be culturally responsive. This will take some effort, but it will make you more effective as an officer.

UNIT 2 PROFESSIONAL COMMUNICATION
LESSON 2 Core Communication Competencies

◎ Lesson Goal

At the end of this lesson, you will understand the importance of self-talk and self-awareness in preparation for using the core communication competencies when serving your community.

Think About This

You are on your way to a call about possible child abuse. You realize this might be a difficult situation, and you need to keep your emotions in check. What are some ways you can prepare so that you remain professional while handling this incident?

PREPARING FOR AN INTERACTION

There are several techniques that can help you mentally prepare for the possible interactions you may have while on your way to a call or before a conversation. Some rely on self-talk and some employ self-awareness.

Self-talk is the practice of talking to yourself as you anticipate, encounter, or evaluate an event. Examples include recalling skills and information learned during training, applying agency policies and procedures, and visualizing a professional response. Visualizing the conversation can help you remain objective in a difficult situation by keeping your thoughts, verbal and non-verbal communications, and emotional responses in check while you assess a situation and complete tasks.

☑ LE222.1. Identify how self-talk and self-awareness can help with communication

While being aware of your own perceptions, assumptions, and limitations, you must also be aware that others have perceptions and assumptions of you. To communicate effectively, you must control your emotions and not allow them to dictate your words or actions. Remain open-minded, self-aware, and sincerely listen to the speaker without imposing cultural biases and values on the speaker. Focus on things you have in common to resist thinking about the other person in stereotypical or derogatory terms.

Be the calming presence, and do not allow your anger to escalate a situation. Hostility and rudeness have no place in an officer's relationship with the community. When on the receiving end of profanity or name calling, remind yourself that those individuals are attacking the profession and not you personally, so focus on their behavior rather than their language. If, for example, you have told a person to stop smoking in a public park, the person may become disgruntled and use profanity toward you. However, if they do as you have asked and put out their cigarette, that behavior matters more than what they are saying to you.

CORE COMPETENCIES

> LE222.2. Describe the core communication competencies and how to use them

Every officer should demonstrate the following 10 core communication competencies while performing their duties. These competencies will help you communicate and may also help you avoid volatile situations.

Introduction

The simple act of introducing yourself to a person and explaining the reason for your interaction may make a person feel more at ease.

Appropriate Questions

Asking the right questions can also make the communication process smoother. In Chapter 4, you will learn more about the best questions to ask depending on the situation.

Active Listening

Active listening skills are critical for law enforcement officers. Active listening involves:

- paraphrasing or restating the information the person provides based on your understanding of what they have said so that the person may want to continue to give you information. For example, "Okay, so far I understood you to say..."
- summarizing or repeating several of the major points to check understanding. For example, "Let me sum up what you said to make sure I understood everything correctly."
- clarifying or asking the person to explain or to repeat a part of the discussion that seemed unclear or that you did not hear. For example, "Would you mind repeating that last statement, please?"
- reflecting by stating the information in a way that allows the person speaking to know that you not only understand what they said but that you also recognize their feelings and emotions. When using reflection during a non-confrontational conversation, you should try to match the person's tone and body language to encourage the person to continue speaking. It does not mean that you agree with what they have said, but you have given them the courtesy of listening to them and have tried to understand how they feel.
- ensuring that you allow adequate time for the person to both comprehend what you have said and be able to respond to you. Show them that you have heard and understood their response.

Active listening involves focusing more on listening than talking. Listen so that you can gather important information, such as who, what, when, where, why, and how. Listening will help you communicate better when you need to speak.

Self-De-Escalation

If you find yourself becoming angry or emotional, take time to pause and reset your response. This process may include withdrawing from a conversation or having a fellow officer relieve you. As a law enforcement officer, you may meet people who react negatively to your authority. Remember that this is not an attack on you as a person but their reaction to law enforcement in general. Self-control will help you stay emotionally strong, even under considerable stress. Self-control includes your ability to detach from your personal feelings in a stressful situation or encounter.

You should understand what triggers your emotions and learn ways to manage them. If you cannot manage your emotional triggers, you may put your safety and health at risk.

Knowing and overcoming your weaknesses will help you gain self-control. When presented with a stressful situation:

- breathe smoothly, deeply, and evenly to maintain your composure
- be aware of things that irritate you
- exercise self-control over your reactions
- keep a professional attitude
- maintain an impartial outlook
- precisely execute your duties to help retain your self-control

When an officer loses self-control, the situation can quickly worsen and have a negative result. Your goal is to have a positive result.

Non-verbal Communication

Understanding the subtle differences between a person's spoken words and their non-verbal communication will improve your ability to communicate effectively. One of the things that makes communication so powerful is not only what is expressed but how it is expressed. Ways you can use non-verbal communication effectively include:

- indicating direction in a situation where it is too loud for verbal communication alone
- emphasizing commands, such as pointing in different directions to separate arguing parties
- complementing a verbal message, such as nodding to confirm the direction you have pointed a motorist to go
- confirming an action, such as nodding your head to indicate to the other person that you are listening
- substituting for the verbal message, for example, by extending your arm and holding your hand out to indicate that the person needs to stop

Environment and Audience Consideration

You must treat everyone with dignity and respect, so be mindful with whom, and where, you are speaking and remain empathetic and culturally sensitive. For example, if somebody does not speak your language, or is hearing impaired, be patient and attempt to provide that person with an interpreter.

Implicit Bias

Always take a moment to assess what implicit biases might influence a given situation.

Self-Awareness

Being aware of your own thoughts and behaviors can help you control yourself in a difficult situation. Recall that in Chapter 1 we discussed how self-awareness ties into your overall emotional intelligence. As you improve your emotional intelligence, you become aware of how you might react in a variety of situations. Having this awareness contributes to your overall safety because you will know how to prepare for the different situations you will encounter.

Procedural Justice

Procedural justice can be helpful in fostering relationships with your community members. Including procedural justice in your communications with the public means:

- explaining your actions
- giving the other person a chance to speak
- treating people with respect
- remaining transparent in your actions

Appropriate Conclusion

At the end of any interaction with a person, whether law enforcement action is taken or not, conclude by explaining what actions will or will not be taken and why. As explained earlier, treat every person with respect and leave them with their dignity intact.

Chapter 3
Legal

UNIT 1 INTRODUCTION TO LAW
- LESSON 1 Law Systems / 63
- LESSON 2 Constitutional Law / 66
- LESSON 3 Classification of Offenses / 69
- LESSON 4 Reading and Understanding Statutes / 71

UNIT 2 LEGAL CONCEPTS
- LESSON 1 Categories of Criminal Intent / 74
- LESSON 2 Standards of Legal Justification / 78
- LESSON 3 Search and Seizure / 85
- LESSON 4 Weapons and Firearms Possession / 94
- LESSON 5 Laws of Arrest / 96
- LESSON 6 Use of Force / 99

UNIT 3 LIABILITY
- LESSON 1 Types of Liability / 103
- LESSON 2 Protecting Officers Against Liability / 108

UNIT 4 COURT BASICS
- LESSON 1 The U.S. and Florida Court Systems / 111
- LESSON 2 Court Proceedings / 114
- LESSON 3 Court Orders / 118

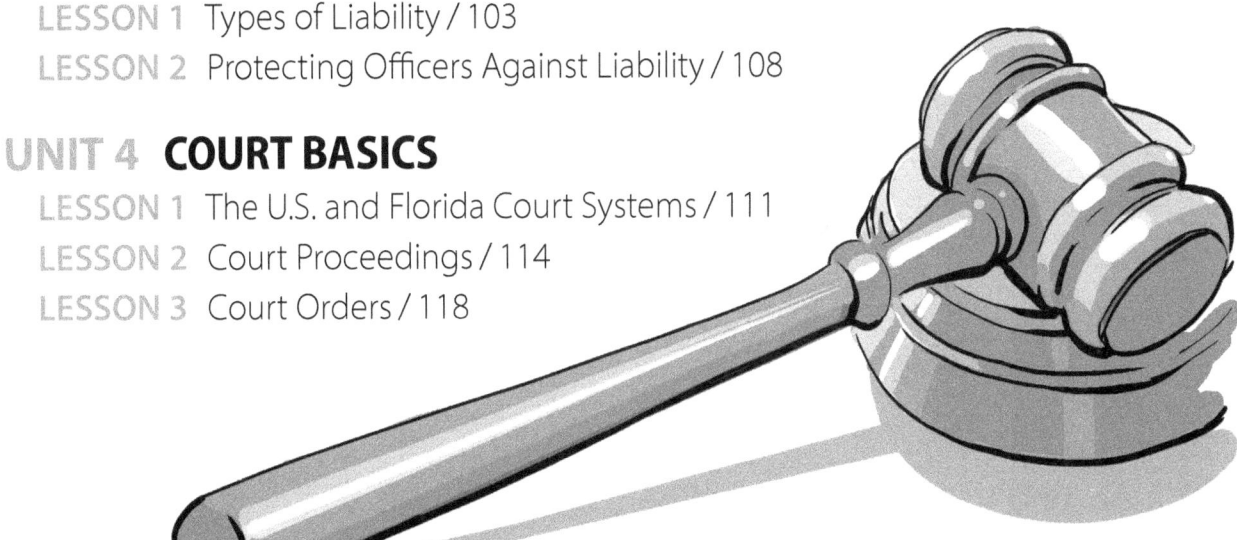

UNIT 1 INTRODUCTION TO LAW
LESSON 1 Law Systems

⊚ Lesson Goal

At the end of this lesson, you will understand types of laws and the importance of staying current with case law as well as your agency's policies and procedures when enforcing the law.

Your duties as a law enforcement officer include responding to calls, patrolling, determining violations of law, making arrests, knowing how and when to use force, and investigating crimes. You must have a basic understanding of federal, state, and local laws in order to act properly and effectively without infringing on individual rights. This chapter will provide a solid legal foundation to help you perform your duties.

SOURCES OF LAW

Laws protect our rights, freedoms, and lives and serve to maintain order, protect ownership of property, regulate certain businesses, and raise money for state and federal governments. There are several types of laws that govern the way we live in the United States, and one source of these laws is the U.S. Constitution.

The U.S. Constitution establishes the form of government in the United States, and it also outlines the representational government and its responsibilities within a three-branch structure. The legislative branch is responsible for creating laws, the executive branch (which you are part of as a law enforcement officer) is responsible for enforcing laws, and the judicial branch is responsible for interpreting the laws. Together, all three branches make up the federal government.

Constitutional law further defines the powers and limitations of each of the three branches. It also upholds standards set forth in the Constitution and the court decisions or interpretations of the Constitution handed down by the federal district courts and the United States Supreme Court.

☑ LE311.1. Explain the role of constitutional law

Florida has its own state constitution that generally parallels the U.S. Constitution. This means that the Florida Constitution affords Florida's residents the same level of rights or greater than they derive from the U.S. Constitution. The supremacy clause of the U.S. Constitution states that when laws conflict, federal law generally overrules state and local law. State law can be more restrictive than federal law, but it cannot undermine the federal standard.

Statutory law is written law enacted by Congress, state legislatures, or local governing authorities in response to a perceived need; it includes criminal, civil, administrative, and regulatory laws.

☑ LE311.2. Examine criminal law and its relation to ordinances and statutory law

Criminal law identifies behaviors deemed unacceptable by society; it also sets punishments for those behaviors.

Ordinances are laws enacted by a municipal (city) or county government. Local governments create ordinances that regulate matters of narrow application, such as curfews for minors, restrictions on the hours when alcohol may be sold, or parking regulations. Ordinances apply only within the jurisdiction of the governmental entity that enacted them. Some ordinance violations are criminal, while others are civil infractions. Ordinances cannot conflict with state, federal, or case law.

☑ LE311.3. Describe the role of civil law

Civil law is the legal action that a person takes to resolve a non-criminal private dispute with another person. The courts provide a forum for people to settle these disputes. Examples include child custody disputes, landlord-tenant disputes, and property boundary disputes. Your involvement with civil law situations generally does not permit law enforcement action beyond keeping the peace and referring to the appropriate court.

In civil lawsuits, the person filing the lawsuit must have a court-recognized cause of action. In law, a cause of action is a set of facts sufficient to justify a right to sue to obtain money, property, or the enforcement of a right against someone. In many situations, crime victims also have causes of action that allow them to sue the perpetrators of the crimes.

☑ LE311.4. Describe the role of administrative law

Administrative law is the body of law that establishes the operations and procedures of governmental agencies. It governs the internal operations of these agencies and ensures that they do not abuse their power. For example, division 11B, Florida Administrative Code (F.A.C.), governs the training and certification of law enforcement officers.

KEEPING CURRENT IN THE LAW

Case law is the body of law formed by the decisions of the court system, which is part of the judicial branch. These court-imposed decisions are based on the court's interpretation of constitutional provisions, and they clarify the meaning of a Florida statute or a Florida rule (F.A.C.) as applied to a specific set of facts.

☑ LE311.5. Recognize the importance of staying current with case law

Court decisions influence how you perform your duties. Once an appellate court creates a rule, known as a precedent, you are required to follow that rule unless a higher court changes the rule. An appellate court is responsible for hearing and reviewing appeals from cases that have already been heard in a lower court. Additionally, each circuit court ruling is binding for that jurisdiction. Because of this, there could be different case law in neighboring circuits. Know and follow the case law in your jurisdiction. The rules under which you operate will constantly change based upon revisions in statutes and the case law interpreting those statutes. You are responsible for keeping current with these changes.

There are a variety of sources that can help you stay current in statutory and case law, including agency bulletins, legislative updates, and official websites, such as the Florida Department of Law Enforcement, the Florida Office of the Attorney General, and the Florida Supreme Court. Avoid obtaining legal knowledge from unofficial sources, such as newspapers, television, radio, unreliable websites, and word of mouth. If you fail to stay up to date with changes to laws, you may risk exclusion of evidence at trial, case dismissal, administrative discipline, civil liability, or even criminal prosecution.

AGENCY POLICIES AND PROCEDURES

While the Constitution and the Florida Statutes direct your actions, law enforcement agencies establish policies and procedures to guide the daily activities of officers and to meet the specific needs of the agency. These policies and procedures will differ between agencies and can be more restrictive than state and federal laws.

Your agency will provide you with specific policies and procedures during your agency's training program, and it is important that you become familiar with them. This textbook does not cover agency-specific policies and procedures; however, there will be areas within this book that direct you to review your agency's policies and procedures for further clarification. Examples include policies on wearing body cameras, using conducted electrical weapons (CEWs), engaging in vehicle pursuits, maintaining uniform standards, and following arrest procedures.

☑ LE311.6. Explain the importance of staying current with your agency's policies and procedures

UNIT 1 INTRODUCTION TO LAW
LESSON 2 Constitutional Law

Lesson Goal

At the end of this lesson, you will understand the role of specific U.S. constitutional amendments while protecting the rights of the community you serve.

Think About This

While on patrol you give a woman a ticket for littering. After getting the ticket the woman curses at you and walks away. What amendment protects the woman's right to do this?

BASIC CONCEPTS OF THE U.S. CONSTITUTION

☑ LE312.1. Explain how the U.S. Constitution impacts your criminal justice role

As a law enforcement officer, your main objective is to protect the constitutional rights of everyone within the United States. The U.S. Constitution sets parameters within which the government operates and establishes laws. The Constitution also defines your authority to act. In any situation, you must be able to determine how to follow the law and abide by the limitations that the Constitution sets.

THE ARTICLES OF THE CONSTITUTION

The Articles of the Constitution form the Constitution's main body. Their purpose is to form a contract between the people of the United States and the legislative, executive, and judicial branches of the U.S. government. The Articles also spell out the responsibilities and authority of the three branches of government.

CONSTITUTIONAL AMENDMENTS OF SPECIAL NOTE

According to the Constitution, all people stand equal before the law and therefore share certain rights. Knowing a majority of these rights—such as the freedom of speech, protection against unreasonable searches and seizures, and prohibition of cruel and unusual punishment—will be important to your career as a law enforcement officer.

☑ LE312.2. Describe specific amendments that direct your actions as an officer

Many of the amendments in the Bill of Rights (the first 10 amendments to the U.S. Constitution) focus on the courts and the legislature, but the First, Second, Fourth, Fifth, Sixth, Eighth, and Fourteenth Amendments are of particular importance to law enforcement.

The First Amendment protects the freedom of speech, press, peaceful assembly, and religion. Situations you may encounter that may be protected by the First Amendment include protests, video recording of public activities, and the use of offensive language toward law enforcement.

The Second Amendment guarantees the right to bear arms. The Florida Statutes set forth the guidelines regarding firearms in the state of Florida. You will learn more about firearms later in this chapter.

The Fourth Amendment prohibits unreasonable search and seizure and may require a warrant signed by an independent magistrate (judge). Law enforcement activities affected by the Fourth Amendment include entry into homes, vehicles, luggage, purses, or other places where a person has a reasonable expectation of privacy, including their person. Stops and arrests, including the use of force, are considered seizures and must meet the reasonableness requirement of this amendment that provides certain exceptions to law enforcement.

The Fifth Amendment is best known for prohibiting compelled self-incrimination. It also requires grand jury indictment for capital crimes and prohibits double jeopardy and deprivation of life, liberty, or property without due process of law. **Due process** means that laws must be applied fairly and equally to all people, including a person accused of a crime. Furthermore, due process declares that the government shall not deprive anyone of their life, liberty, or property without cause.

There are two main types of due process:

- **Substantive due process** is the fair and consistent enforcement of the law. This means that people are treated fairly.
- **Procedural due process** refers to the procedures that must be followed to protect a person's rights during a criminal justice process. This means that everyone is entitled to every step in the criminal justice process.

The Sixth Amendment guarantees the right to a speedy and public trial, the right to a fair jury, the right to an attorney, the right to be informed of the nature of the charges, and the right to confront witnesses. Law enforcement activities affected by the Sixth Amendment relate to making contact with a suspect who is represented by counsel, and making sure reports and evidence are submitted in a timely manner.

The Eighth Amendment prohibits excessive bails, fines, and cruel and unusual punishment. An example of this is failing to provide necessary medical care to a person held in custody.

The Fourteenth Amendment expands the application of the Bill of Rights to state and local governments as well. This is done in the due process clause of the Fourteenth Amendment:

> No state shall make or enforce any law which shall abridge the privileges and immunities of citizens of the United States; nor shall any state deprive any person of life, liberty or property, without due process of law; nor deny any person within its jurisdiction of the equal protection of the laws.

The Constitution requires you to get the right result the right way. Failure to abide by these rules may result in the suppression of evidence and confessions, and civil or criminal liability toward you or your agency. Your community will count on you to uphold the Constitution and protect their rights.

Amendments of Special Note	
First Amendment	Protects the right to free speech, press, assembly, and religion
Second Amendment	Protects right to bear arms
Fourth Amendment	Protects from unreasonable search and seizure
Fifth Amendment	Protects against self-incrimination and guarantees due process
Sixth Amendment	Establishes a right to a speedy trial, impartial jury, and assistance of counsel
Eighth Amendment	Protects against cruel and unusual punishment and prohibits the use of excessive bail or fines
Fourteenth Amendment	Establishes due process and equal protection of the laws

UNIT 1 INTRODUCTION TO LAW
LESSON 3 Classification of Offenses

⊚ Lesson Goal

At the end of this lesson, you will understand the different classes of offenses and their penalties before making a lawful arrest.

Think About This

You have just arrested a man for taking a child at gunpoint while at the park. Based on his actions, what type of offense is this?

The term **offense** refers to a breach of law and is used to broadly describe criminal or non-criminal acts that are punishable under Florida law. Criminal offenses may be punishable by incarceration and classified as either misdemeanors or felonies. An offense for which the only penalty may be a fine, forfeiture, or other civil penalty is a **non-criminal violation**, also known as a civil infraction. A non-criminal violation does not constitute a crime and is not punishable by incarceration. An example of a non-criminal offense is a traffic violation, such as failure to yield the right-of-way.

☑ LE313.1. Explain the different types of offenses

ORDINANCE VIOLATIONS

Municipal and county ordinances can be criminal or non-criminal. A local criminal ordinance violation may carry up to 60 days in a county jail or a $500 fine, or by a fine and jail time. A non-criminal ordinance fine is not limited in amount; there are numerous municipal and county civil code violations that carry fines greater than $500.

MISDEMEANORS

A **misdemeanor** is any criminal offense that is punishable by a term of imprisonment in a county correctional facility of up to one year. Misdemeanors are classified by degrees based on the maximum penalty and fine associated with the offense.

☑ LE313.2. Differentiate between felony and misdemeanor offenses

- A second-degree misdemeanor carries a maximum penalty of 60 days in a county jail, a fine of up to $500, or both. An example of a second-degree misdemeanor is criminal mischief involving property damage totaling less than $200.
- A first-degree misdemeanor carries a maximum penalty of one year in a county jail, a fine of up to $1,000, or both. An example of a first-degree misdemeanor is criminal mischief involving property damage greater than $200 but less than $1,000.

FELONIES

A **felony** is any criminal offense committed where the maximum penalty is death or incarceration in a state correctional facility for more than one year. Felonies are classified based on the severity of the offense's maximum or minimum penalty. Each of the five felony classes are defined by the penalty and fine associated with it. Penalties and fines are set forth in the Florida Statutes:

- A third-degree felony carries a maximum penalty of 5 years in a state correctional facility, a fine of up to $5,000, or both. Aggravated assault is an example of a third-degree felony.
- A second-degree felony is punishable by a maximum of 15 years in a state correctional facility, a fine of up to $10,000, or both. Aggravated battery is an example of a second-degree felony.
- A first-degree felony carries a maximum penalty of 30 years in a state correctional facility, a fine of up to $10,000, or both. However, certain first-degree felonies specifically carry a maximum penalty of life incarceration in a state correctional facility. For example, kidnapping is a first-degree felony punishable by life incarceration.
- A life felony has varying penalties depending on the date and type of crime committed. The maximum penalty is life incarceration in a state correctional facility without the possibility of parole or probation, a fine of up to $15,000, or both.
- A capital felony is the highest class of felony. The penalty for offenses in this class is death or life incarceration in a state correctional facility without the possibility of parole. For example, first-degree murder is a capital felony for which the state may impose the death penalty. Note: the death penalty can be imposed for capital sexual battery on a child younger than 12 by a person 18 or older.

☑ LE313.3. Relate offenses to their associated penalties

	Classification	Degree or Application	Maximum Penalties and Fines
criminal offense	felony	capital felony	death or life incarceration without possibility of parole
		life felony	lifetime incarceration without possibility of parole, a $15,000 fine, or both
		felony—1st degree	30 years of incarceration, a $10,000 fine, or both. Some 1st degree felonies may receive a lifetime penalty depending on the crime
		felony—2nd degree	15 years of incarceration, a $10,000 fine, or both
		felony—3rd degree	5 years of incarceration, a $5,000 fine, or both
criminal offense	misdemeanor	misdemeanor—1st degree	incarceration for up to a year, a $1,000 fine, or both
		misdemeanor—2nd degree	incarceration for up to 60 days, a $500 fine, or both
local ordinance violation	civil or criminal	can be criminal in nature and require incarceration	incarceration for up to 60 days, civil penalty of up to $500, or both
non-criminal offense	infraction	includes non-criminal infractions or traffic violations	$500 fine, forfeiture or other civil penalty

UNIT 1 INTRODUCTION TO LAW
LESSON 4 Reading and Understanding Statutes

◎ Lesson Goal

At the end of this lesson, you will know how to find, understand, and reference the Florida Statutes when documenting a lawful arrest and identifying parties to a crime.

Think About This

While conducting a bank robbery, one robber wears a ski mask and wields a knife while his accomplice threatens customers with a gun stolen from a police officer. Which of these individuals will face enhanced penalties and why?

NAVIGATING THE FLORIDA STATUTES

The ability to read and understand the Florida Statutes is a critical function for law enforcement officers. The Florida Statutes can be found in many formats. Agencies may provide you with the necessary source materials. Always make sure that the source that you use is reliable and current.

☑ LE314.1. Explain how to find and read the Florida Statutes

Navigating through the Florida Statutes may be difficult without an understanding of how to read them; however, the more you familiarize yourself with them, the easier it will become to read the statutes. Digital versions of the statutes may offer a keyword search feature that you can use to narrow your search. Meanwhile, if you are searching a printed statute book, you can reference the index in the book.

READING THE FLORIDA STATUTES

The Florida Statutes are divided into chapters, sections, and subsections. Chapters are broad topics, and are broken down into sections, which are broken down into subsections.

In the example in Figure 3-1, the chapter is 812, Theft, Robbery, and Related Crimes, and the section is 812.014, Theft. The subsection is (1).

Generally, everything contained within subsection (1) outlines the actual crime itself. Subsections may be broken down into paragraphs, for example, (1)(a), (1)(b), which specify the elements or components of the crime. For some crimes, all elements of the offense must be met to establish that the crime occurred. However, in others, not all of the elements are required to establish the criminal act; in these instances, the end of the element is generally followed by the word "or." The later subsections commonly outline the penalties for the offense. For some offenses, the penalty is outlined in a separate section within the chapter.

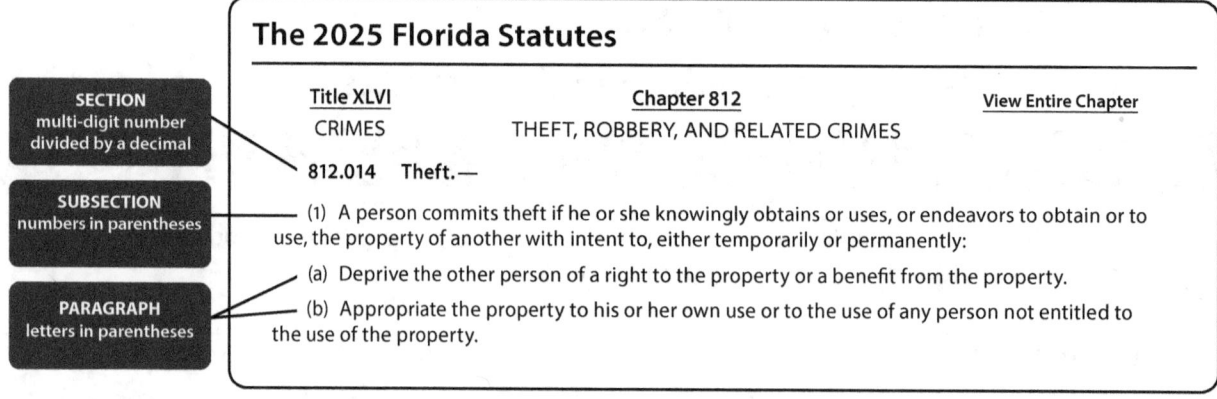

Figure 3-1
Statute organization

In some offenses, there are particular words that may have unclear meanings. Often, those words are defined at the beginning of the chapter, and sometimes they are defined at the beginning of a section. The last portion of a section provides a history of legislative changes relating to the statute.

ENHANCED PENALTIES

☑ LE314.2. Identify the conditions and criteria that result in enhanced penalties

An **enhanced penalty** is a sentence that is increased from one classification of offense to a more serious classification due to a prior conviction or the serious nature of the circumstances involved. Enhanced penalties are governed by federal and state laws, which vary from state to state. Examples of serious circumstances that may lead to an enhanced penalty include the following:

- committing violent offenses against law enforcement officers, correctional officers, state attorneys, assistant state attorneys, and judges
- wearing something (a mask or hood) to conceal identity while committing a felony or misdemeanor
- showing prejudice or discrimination while committing a crime (a hate crime)
- using a weapon while committing a crime
- unlawful taking, possessing, or using of a law enforcement officer's firearm during the commission of a crime
- committing a misdemeanor or felony that facilitated or furthered an act of terrorism

PARTIES TO A CRIME

Often more than one criminal defendant plays a role in committing a crime. When the participation and criminal conduct varies among the defendants, it is important to determine who is responsible for which crime, or aspect of a crime, and to what degree.

The Florida Statutes divide the parties to a crime into two categories: principal in the first degree and accessory after the fact.

A ***principal in the first degree*** is a person who commits any criminal offense, whether felony or misdemeanor, that aids, abets, counsels, hires, or persuades an offense to be committed or attempted. It includes a person that helps another person or other people to commit or attempt to commit a crime. A principal may be charged, convicted, and punished whether they were present when the crime is actually committed or attempted. For example, if a babysitter provides security codes to a friend for the purpose of that friend to commit a burglary and the burglary takes place without the babysitter being there, the babysitter is a principal in the first degree.

An ***accessory after the fact*** is a person who gives the principal any aid with the intent that the principal avoids or escapes detection, arrest, trial, or punishment. For example, if Janet shelters James in her garage for a night to help him avoid being caught by police after he had robbed a local convenience store, Janet is an accessory after the fact.

☑ LE314.3. Describe the two categories of parties to a crime

UNIT 2 LEGAL CONCEPTS
LESSON 1 Categories of Criminal Intent

◎ Lesson Goal

At the end of this lesson, you will understand the significance of intent and negligence when determining whether an act is criminal.

Think About This

During an altercation, Stephanie points a gun at her sister, Eliza, and shoots at her. Stephanie misses and accidentally shoots their nearby friend, Carol, instead. What category of criminal intent does this crime fall under?

DETERMINING A CRIMINAL OFFENSE

As a law enforcement officer, you will often have to determine whether a criminal offense was committed. Before a person can be charged with a criminal offense, you must answer two fundamental questions:

- Was a criminal act committed?
- Was there criminal intent?

☑ LE321.1. Describe the concept of criminal intent

Generally, to prove that a crime has been committed, it must be shown that a criminal statute or ordinance specifically prohibits the alleged act or omission and that the person committing the act or omission did so knowingly or intentionally. A criminal act must also have criminal intent. **Criminal intent** is the conscious decision someone makes to deliberately engage in an unlawful act, or to harm someone else. You may need to determine whether the elements of a criminal act are present and must have probable cause to believe that the person committed the crime. **Probable cause** is a fair probability or reasonable grounds to believe that someone committed a crime, based on the totality of circumstances. Proving criminal intent is fundamental to the criminal justice system because it is what separates an accident from a crime.

In most cases, a criminal offense requires a person to take some physical action or act toward committing the criminal offense. Mere thoughts do not constitute criminal liability. However, a person may also commit a criminal act by failing to act, that is, by omission. To base criminal liability on failure to act, you must first find that the person had a legal duty to act and not simply a moral duty.

To determine whether a statute specifically prohibits an alleged act or an omission to act, or to determine the necessary intent to commit the crime, determine what specific acts or facts must be present before a suspect can be charged with a crime.

CATEGORIES OF CRIMINAL INTENT

For a person to be guilty of a criminal offense, the offense must be defined so that the suspect engages in specific conduct or intentionally produces a specified result. Under criminal law principles, there are four basic classifications of intent: general intent, specific intent, transferred intent, and recklessness.

General intent is when a suspect intentionally commits an illegal act prohibited by law without considering the results of the illegal act. Examples of general intent are battery, assault, rape, kidnapping, false imprisonment, and involuntary manslaughter.

☑ LE321.2. Explain the legally recognized categories of criminal intent

Specific intent is the intent to commit a crime and the intent to deprive an owner of something permanently. Specific intent crimes refer to an individual's state of mind at the time the crime is committed accompanied by the physical act. These crimes usually are done intentionally, knowingly, purposely, or willfully. Examples of specific intent crimes are burglary, embezzlement, forgery, murder, robbery, and theft.

Transferred intent is when a crime is intended to harm one person and inadvertently causes another person to be hurt instead. The crime charged must bear some relationship to the actions of the defendant. Situations involving transferred intent are complex, and you should seek legal or supervisory advice before determining what crime, if any, to charge based upon a theory of transferred intent. Examples of transferred intent include a suspect striking a bystander unintentionally while attempting to commit a battery, or a person intending to shoot one victim missing their target and unintentionally striking a second victim.

Recklessness imposes criminal liability on defendants when they did not intend for a behavior to cause the resulting harm. Recklessness may result in civil or criminal charges. An example of recklessness is vehicular homicide.

NEGLIGENCE

Negligence is the failure to behave with the level of care that a reasonably prudent person would have exercised under the same circumstances. Negligence cases do not involve deliberate actions, but instead occur when an individual or entity is careless and fails to provide a duty owed to another person. Some examples of negligence can include:

☑ LE321.3. Describe the concept of negligence

- A person is looking at their phone instead of the road while driving a car and causes an accident.
- Someone unintentionally hurts someone else. For example, if John intentionally hits Bob during a fight, and then accidentally hits and injures Tom, John could be considered negligent.

The behavior usually consists of actions, but can also consist of omissions when there is some duty to act.

Elements of Negligence

> LE321.4. Describe the elements of negligence

To convict a defendant of a crime, the state must prove in criminal court that the individual committed all elements of a particular offense. In a civil (non-criminal) negligence action, the plaintiff must prove a different set of elements to find the defendant negligent.

The elements of negligence are—a duty to act with care, breach of the duty to act, causation or proximate cause, and damages. All four elements must be proved in a negligence action to recover damages. If any of the four elements is missing, the defendant cannot be found negligent.

A DUTY TO ACT WITH CARE

A duty is usually created by statute or contract. Duties may be general or specific. For instance, everyone who drives a vehicle in the state of Florida has a general duty to do so using reasonable care. An officer who is hired to direct traffic at an intersection has a specific duty to the people relying on that officer as they pass through the intersection.

BREACH OF THE DUTY TO ACT

The second element of negligence is a breach of duty. A breach is a failure of some kind. The term **breach of duty** means that the person unreasonably failed in the duty they were obligated to perform. A breach of duty is generally proved by evidence that the person violated a law or accepted practices, such as a departmental policy or rule. An officer may breach duty by not taking action when a reasonable officer should have taken action. For example, if an officer decides to wait for EMS instead of performing CPR on an injured person who is not breathing, and the person dies or suffers brain damage from lack of oxygen, the officer is liable for those consequences because the officer breached the duty of care.

CAUSATION OR PROXIMATE CAUSE

The third element of negligence is proximate cause, which means that the breach caused the harm. **Proximate cause** is the legal phrase for the link between the breach of duty and the harm caused (damages). In deciding proximate cause, the judge and jury will have to determine if the harmful event was a foreseeable outcome of the defendant's act or failure to act.

DAMAGES

> LE321.5. Explain two types of damages for negligence

The final element of negligence is damages. There are two main categories of damages: compensatory and punitive. **Compensatory damages** are monetary awards designed to compensate for the actual property damage, harm, or injury that the plaintiff suffers.

Compensatory damages may include general and special damages.

- General damages are those presumed to result from the defendant's actions. They include awards for pain and suffering, discomfort, humiliation, and emotional distress.
- Special damages are those actually caused by the injury. They are available to the plaintiff for lost earnings, medical expenses, destruction of personal property, and attorney's fees.

Sometimes when the jury believes the plaintiff's rights were violated but there is insufficient proof of measurable financial harm, nominal damages—damages in name only—are awarded.

Punitive damages are penalties intended to punish the defendant for their act and to warn others from doing the same act. They are awarded in addition to compensatory damages when the defendant acted with recklessness, malice, or deceit.

UNIT 2 LEGAL CONCEPTS
LESSON 2 Standards of Legal Justification

Lesson Goal

At the end of this lesson, you will understand the three standards of legal justification, their evolving levels, and the corresponding justifiable legal action.

Think About This

While on patrol at 2 a.m., you see someone sprinting across the street from an abandoned gas station. Do you have legal justification to stop, frisk, or arrest this person?

OFFICER'S JUSTIFICATION TO ACT

The U.S. Constitution guarantees a right of privacy to all individuals. This right, guaranteed by the Fourth Amendment, allows people to move about in public places free from police interference as long as they obey the law; however, if an officer has reasonable suspicion that someone has committed a crime, they can temporarily detain the person, frisk them during an investigative stop, or, where an officer has probable cause, arrest the person and search and seize property.

☑ LE322.1. Explain your legal justification to act

If you stop someone, you must be able to explain your actions in a legal context, and whenever possible, give the person a chance to ask you questions. This will help them understand what is happening. Law enforcement officers must develop a keen awareness of the legal justification at each point during an incident. Document your actions and be prepared to testify in court.

TYPES OF ENCOUNTERS

☑ LE322.2. Identify the three types of encounters

You will have many different encounters with members of the public. Three main types of law enforcement encounters include:

- consensual encounters
- investigative stops
- arrests

Every encounter is case and fact specific. What an officer does in one particular circumstance, given the specific facts, may be reasonable in that circumstance, but may not be reasonable for a different situation.

CONSENSUAL ENCOUNTERS

Many times, you will have encounters with the public that are nothing more than simple conversations. These encounters are not based on a violation of the law and are no different than when any members of the public talk to one another.

A *consensual encounter* occurs when an officer has voluntary contact with a person and a reasonable person would feel free to leave at any time. In addition, the person is free to refuse to answer any questions, decline to identify themselves, and ask that you leave them alone. A consensual encounter involves no coercion, no detention, and therefore is not a seizure under the Fourth Amendment. Examples of consensual encounters are asking a local baker how their business is doing or making polite conversation with a community member.

☑ LE322.3.
Describe consensual encounters

In determining whether an encounter was consensual, the court will look at all of the circumstances surrounding the encounter. To maintain the consensual nature of the interaction and not raise the level of encounter to an investigative stop, it is important to:

- allow the person to end the conversation at any time
- allow the person to leave at any time
- allow the person to have freedom of movement (for example, if you or your vehicle is blocking their path, the person is not or may not feel free to leave)
- not force the person to identify themselves
- not physically stop or restrain the person
- not frisk the person
- not give orders
- not make commands
- not use sirens or red or blue lights

A consensual encounter may be based on mere suspicion or no suspicion at all. Mere suspicion is sometimes described as a hunch or gut feeling based on law enforcement training and knowledge. The Constitution does not prohibit you from approaching pedestrians or motorists and engaging them in conversation. If you have mere suspicion, you can ask them if they are willing to answer questions, question them if they are willing to listen, or listen to what they have to say if they voluntarily approach to speak with you.

Mere suspicion does not grant any enforcement or legal authority, including detaining a person or conducting a search. Detaining a person or searching requires more than mere suspicion. Sometimes during a consensual encounter, an officer may develop reasonable suspicion or probable cause of a crime giving the officer the legal justification to temporarily detain or to arrest the person. The distinction between a consensual encounter and the next two types of encounters is that a consensual encounter is completely voluntary on the part of the person, and a reasonable person in the same circumstance would feel that they could leave at any time.

Mere suspicion or a need to investigate are not the only reasons for engaging in consensual encounters. Use consensual encounters to get to know your community members. By making conversation with the members of your community, you help strengthen the bonds between law enforcement and the public.

INVESTIGATIVE STOP

An officer can make an *investigative stop* only if the officer has reasonable suspicion that the person stopped was committing, is committing, or is about to commit a law violation.

An investigative stop, which is based on reasonable suspicion, is conducted for the limited purpose of investigating that reasonable suspicion. If further reasonable suspicion develops during the stop, then the encounter continues. However, once the purpose of the stop concludes with either no further development of a crime that created the reasonable suspicion, no other reasonable suspicion, or no cause to arrest, then the stop is over, and the suspect is free to leave.

REASONABLE SUSPICION

☑ LE322.4. Describe the concept of reasonable suspicion

Reasonable suspicion is the standard of justification needed to support an investigative stop. This means that you can articulate, or put into words, facts that support a suspicion that the person stopped may be involved in a law violation. The facts and circumstances must support the suspicion that a person committed a crime, is committing a crime, or is about to commit a crime.

Reasonable suspicion may be established through a number of sources such as personal observation, information from fellow officers, information from third parties such as informants, and BOLOs (be on the lookouts). A **BOLO** is a description of a vehicle or suspect, and any other information that would help identify the suspect.

Along with the time and location of the encounter and perceived smells or sounds, examples of personal observations could include:

- a person is running away or trying to evade someone
- a person is dressing or acting unusually
- a person is in a known high crime area

None of the listed observations alone justifies enough reasonable suspicion to make an investigative stop. Regarding high crimes areas, in *Illinois v. Wardlow* the U.S. Supreme Court ruled:

> An individual's presence in an area of expected criminal activity, standing alone, is not enough to support a reasonable, particularized suspicion that the person is committing a crime...But officers are not required to ignore the relevant characteristics of a location in determining whether the circumstances are sufficiently suspicious to warrant further investigation.

TERRY STOP AND FRISK

The *Terry* stop takes its name from an important 1968 U.S. Supreme Court case, *Terry v. Ohio*. In the original case, a law enforcement officer observed Terry and two associates repeatedly walking by and looking into a store window. The officer suspected that the men were examining the store to plan a crime. The officer confronted them, and when they did not respond appropriately, the officer grabbed the two of them and patted down their outside clothing. The officer discovered that the men had guns in their jackets. The two men were arrested and charged with illegally carrying concealed weapons. Terry argued that the search and seizure had violated his Fourth Amendment rights.

The Court disagreed and ruled that a law enforcement officer may frisk the exterior clothing of someone lawfully detained if the officer has reasonable suspicion to believe that the person is about to commit a crime, has committed a crime, or is committing a crime, and may be armed. A frisk, also known as a pat down, is not a full search. The scope of the frisk is limited to an external pat down of outer clothing and property being carried by the person.

☑ LE322.5. Explain the legal justification for a *Terry* stop and frisk

To reduce the possibility of a pat down violating the Fourth Amendment, you must be able to articulate reasons for believing the person has a weapon. You may not automatically pat down every person detained. The two elements required for a lawful pat down or frisk are that:

- The person is lawfully detained based on reasonable suspicion.
- The officer has reasonable suspicion to believe that the person possesses a dangerous weapon.

A frisk is not restricted to a person's body. Even the passenger compartment of a vehicle may be frisked, based on a reasonable belief that an occupant of the vehicle is armed and dangerous. The passenger compartment includes the area of a motor vehicle designed for the seating of the driver and other passengers of the vehicle. It does not include a locked glove compartment or the trunk. This might happen, for example, during a high-risk traffic stop of a vehicle that matches the description of an armed robbery suspect's vehicle. Further search will be justified only if the officer detects something readily apparent to be a weapon or immediately apparent to be contraband. Simply seeing a partially concealed firearm does not, standing alone, constitute reasonable suspicion or justify a frisk, since many people may lawfully possess a concealed firearm. If an illegal weapon or evidence of a crime is discovered during the detention, you may make an arrest if warranted.

An officer who conducts a valid stop and frisk as described previously, and in the process feels an item readily recognized as contraband, may seize that contraband. Known as the **plain touch/feel doctrine**, this rule allows the officer to seize the contraband even if it does not feel like a weapon. **Contraband** is anything that is illegal to produce, possess, or transport. The plain touch/feel doctrine does not permit any manipulation or groping of the object in an effort to identify it as contraband. The officer must be able to articulate that, based upon their training and experience, they immediately recognized the item as contraband. See *Minnesota v. Dickerson*.

The duration of a *Terry* stop is limited to the time reasonably necessary to accomplish the purpose of the detention. An investigative detention may become an arrest even if the officer does not initially intend to make an arrest. Questioning that prolongs the detention but is not justified by the purpose of the investigative stop is unreasonable under the Fourth Amendment. During the stop, the officer may not require the person to move from the location of the stop or its immediate vicinity. Doing so would turn the stop into an arrest.

You may lawfully use force during an investigative stop if you reasonably believe it protects your safety or the public's safety. You may use handcuffs if reasonably necessary, but you must be able to explain the reasons why force or restraints were necessary.

The Florida Legislature incorporated the *Terry* stop guidelines into the Florida Stop and Frisk Law, which requires probable cause before a weapons pat down is permitted. Case law, however, has held that in this context the term "probable cause" means reasonable suspicion.

PRETEXT STOPS

☑ LE322.6. Describe how an officer can legally conduct a pretext stop

If an officer has probable cause that a driver has committed a traffic infraction, or if the vehicle shows evidence of an equipment violation, such as a broken headlamp, the officer may stop the vehicle on that basis. Such stops are sometimes called **pretext stops**, because the officer stops the vehicle due to an equipment violation but really wants to investigate other, more serious criminal activity.

WHREN V. UNITED STATES

The case of *Whren v. United States* addressed pretext stops. Whren and a passenger were driving in an area known for high crime. Two officers patrolling the area noticed Whren's vehicle sitting at a stop sign for an unusually long time. Suddenly, and without using a turn signal, the vehicle sped off. The officers pulled over the vehicle based on the traffic infraction (failing to signal a turn) they witnessed. When the officers approached the vehicle, they saw that Whren was holding bags of cocaine, and they arrested both men.

Whren later argued that the search and seizure was illegal because when the officers pulled over his vehicle, they had no reasonable suspicion or probable cause to believe that he had illegal drugs in his possession. However, the Court ruled that the search and seizure was constitutional because the officers had probable cause to stop the vehicle for a traffic violation. The subjective reasoning of an officer for a stop is irrelevant so long as there is an objectively reasonable justification for the stop.

ARRESTS

Arrests are typically the most serious level of encounter and can involve lengthy searches or detentions. To make an arrest you may physically restrain an individual or use your authority to clearly indicate that the person is not free to leave. You must always have probable cause that a person has committed or is committing a crime in order to initiate an arrest.

PROBABLE CAUSE

The standard of justification required to make an arrest or conduct a search is probable cause. Because probable cause justifies greater invasions into a person's privacy, it is a stricter standard than reasonable suspicion.

As stated previously, probable cause is based on the totality of circumstances and is the fair probability or reasonable grounds to believe that a crime has been or is being committed.

☑ LE322.7. Describe the legal standard of probable cause

The U.S. Supreme Court stated:

> *In dealing with probable cause…we deal with probabilities…they are the factual and practical considerations of everyday life on which reasonable and prudent men, not legal technicians, act…Probable cause exists where "the facts and circumstances within [the arresting officers'] knowledge and of which they had reasonably trustworthy information [are] sufficient in themselves to warrant a man of reasonable caution in the belief that" an offense has been or is being committed.* Draper v. United States

> *[P]robable cause is a fluid concept—turning on the assessment of probabilities in particular factual contexts—not readily, or even usefully, reduced to a neat set of legal rules.* Illinois v. Gates

For example, seeing drug paraphernalia in open view in a car is probable cause to search the vehicle.

Developing Probable Cause

To establish probable cause, officers must be able to point to certain circumstances leading them to believe that a suspect committed a crime. The difference between reasonable suspicion and probable cause is the amount and quality of information the officer has concerning the commission of a crime by a particular suspect or that evidence of a crime is present in a place to be searched.

Illinois v. Gates also established the totality of circumstances standard of probable cause. This is the standard for all arrests and warrants. You must focus on all the circumstances of a particular case rather than one factor when determining probable cause for an arrest. Your knowledge, training, and experience will assist you with evaluating the totality of the circumstances.

Examples of Probable Cause

1. Officer Michaels arrives at Midtown Jewelry store moments after it was robbed and sees broken glass inside the store. A man claiming to be Sean, the owner, is on the scene. He holds what looks like keys to the store and is distressed. He tells Officer Michaels that a man, about 6'5" tall and weighing over 300 pounds, held up the store at gunpoint and escaped with rings and watches in a small brown paper bag. A few minutes later, less than a mile

away from the jewelry store, Officer Michaels pulls over a car for speeding. The driver matches the description of the robber, and on the seat next to him is a small brown paper bag and a couple of watches with the price tags attached. Though Officer Michaels did not see the robbery itself, the driver matches the unusual physical description of the robber and has property that looks like what Sean said was missing. Officer Michaels has probable cause to arrest the driver.

2. Officer Cole pulls over a car and its three occupants for speeding. The officer searches the car (with the driver's consent) and finds baggies of cocaine stashed behind an armrest in the backseat. All three occupants say they did not know the cocaine was in the car. Officer Cole has probable cause to arrest the car's occupants. In the absence of evidence demonstrating that the cocaine belonged to a specific occupant, Officer Cole could reasonably conclude that all of them knew about and possessed the cocaine.

Sources used to establish reasonable suspicion or probable cause must be those that the court recognizes as reliable.

☑ LE322.8. Describe legally recognized sources for developing reasonable suspicion or probable cause

Commonly recognized sources you will rely on include an informant, corroborated or verified anonymous tips, reliable and credible confidential information, lineups, and showups. Any information an officer legally obtains may be used to establish probable cause. Chapter 9 discusses commonly recognized sources further.

It is important to remember that each law enforcement encounter must have a type of suspicion to correlate with it:

- consensual encounters—no suspicion or mere suspicion
- investigative stops—reasonable suspicion
- arrests—probable cause

PROOF BEYOND A REASONABLE DOUBT

☑ LE322.9. Describe the legal standard of proof beyond a reasonable doubt

Before a person may be found guilty of a crime and sentenced, the prosecution must present evidence sufficient to prove guilt of each element of the crime beyond a reasonable doubt.

Proof beyond a reasonable doubt is the standard used to determine if a criminal defendant is guilty. This means that based on the facts of the case, there is no other reasonable explanation other than the defendant committed the crime. Although probable cause supporting a person's arrest may exist, without further evidence, the state may not be able to prove the case beyond a reasonable doubt. Therefore, the case may not be filed by the prosecutor.

UNIT 2 LEGAL CONCEPTS
LESSON 3 Search and Seizure

⊚ Lesson Goal

At the end of this lesson, you will understand the legal requirements for conducting a valid search or seizure, the role of probable cause, and contraband forfeiture.

Think About This

You pull over someone on a routine traffic stop and you see a bag of pills on the seat next to them. Do you have the right to seize the bag of pills?

FOURTH AMENDMENT GUARANTEES

The Fourth Amendment of the Constitution guarantees the protection of people from governmental intrusion into areas where they have a reasonable expectation of privacy. Some examples of reasonable expectation of privacy include a personal residence, a car, and a public restroom.

The Fourth Amendment prohibits searches and seizures unless they are conducted with probable cause and under reasonable circumstances. It states:

☑ LE323.1. Describe the protections of search and seizure in the Fourth Amendment

> *The right of the people to be secure in their persons, houses, papers, and effects, against unreasonable searches and seizures, shall not be violated, and no Warrants shall issue, but upon probable cause, supported by Oath or affirmation, and particularly describing the place to be searched, and the persons or things to be seized.*

A *search* occurs when an officer examines an area, person, or property for evidence in a place where a person has a reasonable expectation of privacy. A *seizure* occurs when an officer affects a person's right to have or control their property, usually by physically taking it. A seizure is also a physical arrest or detention.

SEARCH WARRANTS

The Fourth Amendment generally requires officers to obtain a search warrant before intruding into a place where an individual has a reasonable expectation of privacy. While there are numerous exceptions to the search warrant requirement, officers should always first obtain a search warrant when it is possible and practical.

A *search warrant* is a court order that authorizes law enforcement to conduct a search and seizure. The search warrant process is set up to protect people's rights by issuing a search warrant correctly. The search warrant must be issued to a person or agency with specific jurisdiction over the location of the search.

LE323.2. Describe the legal requirements to obtain a search warrant

To be valid, a search warrant must meet all of these legal requirements:

- It must be authorized and signed by a neutral magistrate or judge.
- It must be based on an affidavit that states sufficient facts to establish probable cause that evidence of a crime will be found in the place to be searched.
- The basis of the information in the affidavit must come from reliable sources.
- The affiant (the person who swears to the affidavit and signs it) may be anyone, but the person serving the warrant must have jurisdiction over the place chosen for the search.

Probable cause will be determined based on the totality of the circumstances. Courts also will consider how recent the information supporting the probable cause is and how likely it is that the evidence is still at the location to be searched.

The detailed description in the search warrant is a crucial element, designed to prevent an intrusion into the wrong location. The description must include directions to the place to be searched beginning from a known landmark, such as an intersection. The search warrant is valid only for the specific location it describes; it must also describe in detail the person or items to be seized. Officers must connect the seized items to criminal activity. For example, courts do not normally accept the general description "drugs" or "illegal controlled substances." They require law enforcement to name the specific drugs they expect to find.

EXCEPTIONS TO SEARCH WARRANT REQUIREMENTS

Under the Fourth Amendment, a search or seizure may be defined as the government intruding where a person has a reasonable expectation of privacy (REP). The three elements that compose a Fourth Amendment "search" are government, intrusion, and REP.

LE323.3. Explain the exceptions to the search warrant requirement

If any element is missing, it is not a search, and the Fourth Amendment is not involved. For example, if a person walks into his neighbor's garage, finds evidence of a crime, and calls the police, the evidence can be used, because the government was not involved in the search. If a suspect drops a bag containing controlled substances when an officer approaches him, the officer can seize the bag and use it as evidence, because the suspect abandoned his REP for the bag when he dropped it.

In both examples, one of the elements of a Fourth Amendment search is missing. If all three elements were present, however, the Fourth Amendment does apply. If the action by the officer is a search, and the officer does not have a search warrant, they must determine if one of the exceptions to the search warrant requirement applies. Some exceptions require probable cause, and some do not.

Probable Cause Required

The law presumes that a search without a warrant is invalid; however, there are a number of exceptions that require probable cause such as:

- plain view
- mobile conveyance
- exigent circumstances

PLAIN VIEW

Any contraband an officer can see can be seized without a warrant as long as three conditions are met:

- The officer is lawfully present in the place where they see the item.
- The item is in plain sight.
- The officer has probable cause to believe that the item is contraband or crime evidence.

First, the officer must lawfully be positioned where they can see the contraband. An officer responding to a domestic dispute who sees bags of cocaine sitting on the dining room table inside the residence can seize the cocaine, because the officer has answered a call for assistance. However, if the officer walks up to a house and looks in the window to see, they are not lawfully present in the place where the cocaine is seen, and the seized drugs would be excluded from evidence.

☑ LE323.4. Describe the three conditions that must be met to seize contraband in plain view without a warrant

Second, the seized item must be in plain sight or plain view. The officer may not move a blanket, for example, to see what is underneath. The use of a flashlight to light the area around the blanket is permitted, but any movement of the item will likely invalidate the search.

Third, the criminal nature of the seized item must be immediately apparent. An officer must know instantly that the item is contraband. In *Sawyer v. State*, a police officer saw a white pill on the console of a car and, thinking it was ecstasy, seized it. Testing proved the officer was correct. However, the court said that the pill's nature as an illegal drug was not immediately apparent upon first sight, so the evidence was not permitted.

MOBILE CONVEYANCE

Vehicles and other mobile conveyances must be licensed, registered, insured and are easily moved. Consequently, they have a reduced expectation of privacy and may be searched without a warrant.

☑ LE323.5. Explain when searching a mobile conveyance is legal without a warrant

A mobile conveyance search may be conducted without a warrant even if there may be time to obtain a warrant. Additionally, a mobile conveyance search does not have to occur at the same time as the stop. Probable cause is required for a mobile conveyance search.

This is sometimes called the **Carroll doctrine**, named for the case of *Carroll v. United States*. The scope of a search under the *Carroll* doctrine extends to the entire vehicle and to all containers where the evidence could reasonably be found.

United States v. Ross justifies probable cause in the search of a lawfully stopped vehicle, to include the search of every part of the vehicle and its contents. For example, a canine's positive alert on the exterior of a lawfully seized vehicle provides the probable cause justifying a complete search of the vehicle's interior, as well as any containers in it. In contrast, if an officer has probable cause to believe that a person prohibited has possession of a full-sized shotgun in their vehicle, they may not lawfully look inside the glove box or center console during the search.

Courts have held that it is not a search to use a certified police canine to detect odors of controlled substances by walking the canine around the exterior of the car, provided the sniff is completed before the end of the traffic stop. The length of the stop cannot be extended to wait for the arrival of the canine or for the sniff to be completed.

EXIGENT CIRCUMSTANCES

Exigent circumstances are certain emergencies, such as evidence destruction, an emergency scene, or a fresh pursuit that justifies a warrantless entry.

☑ LE323.6. Explain when the destruction of evidence permits a search without a warrant

Destruction of evidence is one of the exigent circumstances that permit search and seizure without a warrant. If you have probable cause to believe that contraband or evidence is in immediate danger of being destroyed, you do not need to obtain a search warrant before seizing the contraband or evidence. The law is clear, however, that the officer cannot create the exigent circumstance to justify a warrantless entry. *Hornblower v. State* justifies probable cause and search and seizure without a warrant, including entering a home when there is a detection of noise of scurrying activity and possible destruction of evidence. An officer may not knock loudly at a house when they have a hunch that drugs are being held there and announce, "Police officer," and then enter the house because he or she thinks the residents may be trying to destroy drugs inside. The officer must have probable cause to believe that the drugs are inside and are in immediate danger of destruction.

☑ LE323.7. Explain the fresh pursuit exception to the search warrant requirement

Fresh pursuit is the immediate and continuous pursuit by officers of a suspect who is fleeing to avoid arrest. A fresh pursuit is not restricted to a vehicle and applies to every mode of transport, including foot and bicycle. It permits a law enforcement officer to make an arrest of a fleeing suspect who crosses jurisdictional lines. This is an exception to the general rule that a Florida officer's arrest powers are limited to the jurisdiction of the agency that employs the officer. Fresh pursuit may be very brief and undramatic and not necessarily a high-speed pursuit.

The offense must have occurred within the pursuing officer's jurisdictional boundaries. If a criminal offense was committed for which a probable cause arrest may be made, the officer may leave their jurisdiction to arrest the suspect. The pursuit must be continuous and uninterrupted; however, the pursuing officer does not need to be in constant visual contact with the subject before making the arrest. The commission of the offense and the pursuit of the suspect must be closely related in time. When the arrest occurs in another jurisdiction, the arresting officer must notify the officer in charge of that jurisdiction and must take the suspect before a trial judge in the county where the arrest occurred.

Fresh pursuit also allows an officer to enter a residence or other private place while chasing a suspect. It generally requires these three conditions:

- probable cause that the suspect committed a serious crime
- immediate or continuous pursuit of the suspect
- probable cause that the suspect is in the premises that is being entered without a warrant

Any contraband or evidence in plain view found in the place entered in fresh pursuit will not be subject to suppression in court because of failure to obtain a search warrant. Officers must follow their agency policies regarding fresh pursuit, which may be more restrictive than state law.

The emergency scene exception involves a situation in which officers may make a warrantless entry to ensure their own safety or that of the public. For this exception to apply you must have an objectively reasonable basis to believe that someone is in immediate danger. For example, in the case of *Seibert v. State* officers were justified in entering a house, because they had an objectively reasonable basis to believe that a person was about to commit suicide. Once within the house, they discovered a murder victim while securing the person to prevent his suicide.

☑ LE323.8. Explain how an emergency scene relates to warrantless entry

There is no general crime scene or murder scene exception to the Fourth Amendment warrant requirement. Although officers responding to a homicide scene may conduct a protective sweep to make sure there are no more victims and that the assailant is gone, to search a crime scene further will require a warrant or a valid exception.

Probable Cause Not Required

Four additional search warrant exceptions require less than probable cause:

- consent searches
- inventory searches
- administrative searches
- search incident to arrest

CONSENT SEARCHES

Consent searches do not require probable cause, reasonable suspicion, or even mere suspicion. An officer may ask anyone for consent to search. If the consent is knowing and voluntary and the person giving consent has authority to do so, then the search is valid and any evidence obtained from it can be used in court. Officers do not need to advise people that they have a right to refuse. Many times, people who hide contraband will consent to an officer's request to search thinking that because they consented, the

☑ LE323.9. Explain the importance of consent when conducting a warrantless search

officer will assume they are not hiding anything and will not complete the search. The burden is on the prosecution to prove that consent was valid. Consent may be obtained verbally or in writing. It is the responsibility of the officer to document how the person gave consent. Your agency may have specific policies on how to document consent.

Voluntary means a reasonable person under the circumstances would feel that they could refuse the request for consent to search. So, for example, if an officer has possession of a driver's or passenger's identification while conducting a traffic stop, the court may not consider voluntary consent valid because the individual may not feel free to leave.

Under limited circumstances, consent to search may be implied. Examples of implied consent include, searches of airline passengers, searches of patrons attending sporting events, and searches of visitors to courthouses or other government buildings. Except for such limited situations, courts will not generally approve of warrantless searches based on implied consent.

Third-party consent to search may be valid if the third party has mutual access and control over the area to be searched. However, a search may not be done by consent of one co-tenant if another co-tenant is present and objects to the search. See *Georgia v. Randolph*. Unless they are the owner, a vehicle's passenger may not consent to the search of the driver's vehicle.

In cases involving juveniles, the consent of a parent or guardian will generally overrule objection by the child. A child may provide consent for a warrantless entry to a parent's home if the child shares the home with the parent and the parent is not physically present to grant or deny consent.

Consent may be withdrawn at any time during the search. While conducting the search, the person granting consent must be positioned in an area where they are able to communicate a withdrawal or revocation. Once withdrawn, officers must stop searching immediately. The scope of consent can be limited as well. For example, a driver may consent to the search of the vehicle's passenger compartment but not the trunk. Of course, if an officer develops probable cause to search at any time, the withdrawal of consent will be meaningless.

INVENTORY SEARCHES

When the driver of a vehicle is arrested, you must make sure the vehicle is properly secured. Next, it is important to conduct an inventory, which is a documentation of all valuable property in a vehicle and the description of the vehicle.

☑ LE323.10. Explain why a vehicle inventory does not require a search warrant

An inventory is not designed to search for evidence, but to protect the arrested person's property and to protect you and the agency from accusations of theft, loss, or damage to the vehicle. An inventory is permitted only if the vehicle is impounded. To *impound* means towing a vehicle at the direction of law enforcement. Follow your agency's policy to determine when and how the inventory must be conducted; for example, your agency's policy may recommend that the inventory must occur at about the same time as the impoundment of the vehicle. Any evidence or contraband found during an inventory may be used against a defendant in court.

ADMINISTRATIVE SEARCHES

Administrative searches generally do not require a warrant due to the setting or special conditions. Subjects of this type of search include students, public schools, people in government offices, government property (such as desks, lockers, and vehicles), people engaged in certain businesses or licensed activities, and people on probation or parole.

These types of searches generally do not require warrants because they are for regulatory purposes and usually are not conducted by a law enforcement officer. Because certain industries are heavily regulated, their expectations for privacy are reduced. Examples include searches of pawn shops, alcohol and tobacco establishments, and probationers. Agency policy will dictate the extent to which officers may be involved in assisting with such searches.

☑ LE323.11. Explain why an administrative search does not require a search warrant

SEARCH INCIDENT TO ARREST

When a person is lawfully arrested and taken into custody, they may be searched without a warrant. This is called a search incident to arrest and is reasonable under the Fourth Amendment. Incident here means an event that occurs in the process of conducting an arrest.

United States v. Robinson noted two historical rationales for the search incident to arrest exception: (1) the need to disarm the suspect to take them into custody and (2) the need to preserve evidence for later use at trial.

☑ LE323.12. Explain why searching someone under arrest does not require a search warrant

A search incident to arrest may be conducted only when two requirements have been met:

- First, there must have been a lawful custodial arrest. A search incident to arrest may not be conducted unless there is a confinement by an officer. An officer may not conduct a search incident to arrest when the officer issues a traffic citation or a notice to appear. There must be a physical, custodial arrest.
- Second, the search must be "substantially contemporaneous" or at the same time with the arrest. For example, a search done 10 minutes after an arrest will generally be valid, but one conducted an hour after the arrest will likely be invalid.

Chimel v. California defined the scope of a search incident to arrest as the arrestee's person and the areas "within the arrestee's reach" at the time of the arrest. However, *Thornton v. United States* clarifies that a search incident to arrest may also include the vehicle in which the arrested person was a passenger just before the arrest.

Under *New York v. Belton*, the scope of a vehicle search incident to arrest includes the entire passenger compartment and all containers located therein, open or closed. The trunk of a sedan is not considered part of the passenger compartment, but the rear area of a van or SUV is included in the search area. *Arizona v. Gant*, has further refined the scope of search incident to arrest situations involving vehicles. Officers may search the passenger compartment of a vehicle only when the arrestee is unsecured and the passenger compartment is within reaching distance of the arrestee or if it is "reasonable" to believe the vehicle contains evidence of the crime for which the subject was arrested. Officers should document the facts and circumstances on which they relied when making decisions regarding a search and be prepared to articulate those reasons at a deposition or hearing.

Abandoned Property and Open Fields

LE323.13. Explain how abandoned property and the open fields doctrine relate to a warrantless search

Searches of abandoned property and open fields are two search types that are often considered exceptions to the search warrant requirement. They are not technically searches, because the person does not have a reasonable expectation of privacy in the place to be searched. An example of abandoned property is the contents of a trash can that has been put out by the curb for pickup. The owner of the trash has abandoned any expectation of privacy in the trash, so officers may seize it and search through it without a warrant.

Open fields are those areas that are visible to people outside of the property and where the occupant has made no attempt at privacy. The Supreme Court has made a distinction between the **curtilage** (the enclosed space of ground and outbuildings immediately surrounding a structure) of someone's home and an open field. Whether particular property is an open field or curtilage depends upon the steps the occupant has taken to create an expectation of privacy and its common use. Fenced and posted fields are given a higher degree of constitutional protection than areas that do not have them.

THE SCOPE OF SEARCHES

An officer who conducts a probable cause search of a vehicle for a stolen gun and finds the gun in the glove box must stop searching unless there is probable cause to search for other specific items.

LE323.14. Describe the scope of searches legally permitted for a law enforcement officer

This is because the scope of constitutional searches that are permitted for officers is limited to the items being searched. The nature of the search should be based on the item the officer expects to find. For example, if an officer has probable cause to search a home for stolen refrigerators, searching drawers, clothing, and under the bed is unreasonable, because a refrigerator cannot fit in those places.

Whether conducting a search using a warrant or acting under a legally recognized exception, case law and statutes allow officers to search for these items:

- contraband
- dangerous weapons
- evidence
- suspects
- items used by the suspect to commit the crime
- objects obtained by the suspect as a result of committing the crime
- items defined by statute (chapter 933, F.S.—Search and Inspection Warrants)

FLORIDA CONTRABAND FORFEITURE ACT

The Florida Statutes give law enforcement agencies the authority to seize and forfeit certain property known as contraband articles.

Contraband articles include items that are illegal to possess, items used in the commission of a felony, and items purchased with the profits of felonious activity.

Forfeiture is a civil proceeding in which a law enforcement agency asks the court to transfer ownership of the property from the defendant to the law enforcement agency. The agency may then sell the property at auction, use the property for law enforcement purposes, or give the property to a public or non-profit organization. An example would be a law enforcement agency seizing the car of a drug dealer and after the forfeiture proceeding, the car could then be used for agency purposes.

Forfeiture deprives a person of interest of their property, so officers must have probable cause to seize the property. The Fourth Amendment guards against not only unreasonable searches but also unreasonable seizures. Officers must use great care in applying principles of constitutional search and seizure law before seizing property under the Florida Contraband Forfeiture Act. Illegal pretext stops, reliance upon drug-courier profiles, or racial or ethnic profiling must never be any part of the basis for a contraband seizure.

The purpose of the seizure and forfeiture of contraband is to further law enforcement's purposes of public safety, the safety of law enforcement officers, or the investigation and prosecution of criminal activity. Florida has established mandatory guidelines for seizure and forfeiture of contraband. Be familiar with these guidelines and your agency's forfeiture policies.

> ☑ LE323.15. Describe legal seizures under the Florida Contraband Forfeiture Act

UNIT 2 LEGAL CONCEPTS
LESSON 4 Weapons and Firearms Possession

Lesson Goal

At the end of this lesson, you will understand the laws regarding the ownership, possession, and use of weapons and firearms.

LAWFUL OWNERSHIP AND POSSESSION OF WEAPONS AND FIREARMS

Chapter 790 of the Florida Statutes addresses lawful ownership, possession, and use of firearms and weapons.

☑ LE324.1. Describe the lawful ownership and use of a weapon or firearm

In the state of Florida, a person younger than 21 may not purchase or transfer ownership of a firearm from a licensed importer, manufacturer, or dealer (s. 790.065(13), F.S.). As a result, a licensed importer, manufacturer, or dealer may not make or facilitate the sale or transfer of a firearm to a person younger than 21. These prohibitions do not apply to the purchase of a rifle or shotgun by a law enforcement officer, correctional officer, or a military service member. However, a person younger than 21 can still own or possess a firearm in accordance with chapter 790. For example, a person younger than 21 may own or possess a firearm that has been given to them as a gift or obtained by other lawful means. A person younger than 21 can also buy a firearm from a private party; however, it would be a criminal offense for a person to sell or otherwise provide a firearm to someone younger than 18 if it is sold or provided without consent from the minor's parent or guardian.

In addition to sales of firearms, the Florida Statutes address seizing firearms in situations where a person poses a danger to themselves or to others. Section 394.463, F.S., authorizes a law enforcement officer taking someone into custody for an involuntary examination under the Baker Act to seize and hold any firearm or ammunition the person possesses if the person poses a danger to themselves or to others and has made a credible threat of violence against another person. You will learn more about the Baker Act in Chapter 6.

LAWFUL USES OF WEAPONS AND FIREARMS

Following the decision in *McDaniels v. State*, an individual who is lawfully in possession of a firearm may openly carry that firearm in public unless another statute specifically prohibits it. Therefore, while a person under 21 may not purchase or carry concealed firearms under sections 790.065(13) and 790.06(2), F.S., open carry by individuals between the ages of 18 and 20 is not prohibited and cannot be treated as unlawful solely based on age.

However, there are still some restrictions in place in regards to carrying a weapon or firearm. For example, firearms are prohibited in specific areas, including schools (s. 790.115, F.S.) and county detention facilities (s. 951.22, F.S.). Statutes barring improper exhibition (s. 790.10, F.S.), possession by felons (s. 790.23, F.S.), and use of a firearm while under the influence (s. 790.151, F.S.) are also in effect. Finally, private property owners have the right to prohibit firearms on their premises under Florida's trespass laws. Officers must refer to their employing agency for the enforcement of weapons and firearms laws in their jurisdiction.

☑ LE324.2. Identify the circumstances where carrying a weapon or firearm is prohibited in Florida

LAW ENFORCEMENT OFFICERS SAFETY ACT

The Law Enforcement Officers Safety Act is a federal law that allows qualified and retired law enforcement officers to carry a concealed firearm in any jurisdiction in the United States, regardless of state or local laws.

To comply with the act, officers must carry two forms of documentation:

- photo identification issued by the agency for which they are currently employed or were separated from
- documentation which certifies that the officer has met, within the past 12 months, the active duty law enforcement standards for qualification for a firearm of the same type as the one they are carrying

RISK PROTECTION ORDERS

You may encounter situations that do not rise to the level of a criminal violation but have the potential for violence. In these situations, your agency may petition the court for a risk protection order.

A *risk protection order (RPO)* is a court order that temporarily restricts a person's access to firearms for up to one year in situations where they pose a significant danger to themselves or others by having a firearm or ammunition in their custody or control, or by purchasing, possessing, or receiving a firearm or any ammunition. The petition must:

☑ LE324.3. Explain the temporary restrictions permitted under risk protection orders

- have an affidavit made under oath stating the specific statements, actions, or facts that give rise to a reasonable fear of significant dangerous acts by the person
- identify the quantities, types, and locations of all firearms and ammunition that the person owns, possesses, and has in custody, or controls
- identify whether there is a known existing RPO governing the person

Situational awareness and maintaining officer safety will be important when given the responsibility of serving an RPO. When serving an RPO you will request the person to immediately surrender all firearms and ammunition they own and any license to carry a concealed weapon or firearm. Follow agency policies and procedures when initiating the petition for an RPO and when serving the order.

UNIT 2 LEGAL CONCEPTS
LESSON 5 Laws of Arrest

Lesson Goal

At the end of this lesson, you will understand the process of making an arrest with or without a warrant, issuing a notice to appear, and the role of a probable cause affidavit.

Think About This

An owner of a local clothing store has reported that one of their customers is currently shoplifting. When you arrive, you talk to the owner, and he points out the shoplifter who is now walking away from the store. Do you have the authority to arrest this person without a warrant and without having witnessed the crime yourself?

AUTHORITY TO ARREST

The Florida Statutes give law enforcement officers the authority to make arrests. An **arrest** is depriving a person of their liberty by legal authority. There are two types of arrests under Florida law: arrest with a warrant and arrest without a warrant.

☑ LE325.1. Describe the role of an arrest warrant after deciding to make an arrest

An **arrest warrant** is a court order authorizing and requiring law enforcement to take the individual named on the warrant into custody to answer for charges specified in the warrant. Obtaining an arrest warrant requires an affidavit containing probable cause.

The Florida Statutes authorize law enforcement officers to enter the residence of a wanted person to make an arrest, provided there is a reasonable belief the person named on the warrant is there. To enter a third party's residence to arrest a subject named in an arrest warrant, officers must obtain a search warrant or articulate the basis for an applicable search warrant exception. See *Steagald v. United States*.

WARRANTLESS ARRESTS

☑ LE325.2. List situations where officers can legally conduct a warrantless arrest

You may make a probable cause arrest without a warrant under the following circumstances:

1. The person has committed a felony or misdemeanor or violated a county or municipal ordinance in the presence of the officer.

2. The person committed a felony outside of the officer's presence, but the officer has probable cause to believe that the person committed it.

3. A warrant for arrest has been issued and is being held by another law enforcement officer or agency.

☑ LE325.3. List the statutory exceptions to the misdemeanor arrest requirement

4. The person has committed a misdemeanor that does not have to occur in your presence. These misdemeanor exceptions include:
    - carrying a firearm in violation of an injunction
    - battery

- retail theft
- traffic offenses related to crash investigation
- disorderly conduct on premises of establishment
- theft from a dining or lodging establishment
- trespass on school grounds
- possession of cannabis less than 20 grams
- stalking
- transit fare evasion
- criminal mischief
- trespass on certain properties
- acts of domestic violence
- a violation of injunction for protection
- sexual cyberharassment

NOTICE TO APPEAR

After an officer has developed probable cause, they may have the option to issue a notice to appear. A *notice to appear* is a written order that may be issued by a law enforcement officer in lieu of a physical arrest, requiring a person accused of violating the law to appear in court at a specified date and time.

It may be used only under limited circumstances for misdemeanor offenses, municipal or county ordinance violations, and criminal traffic violations. The officer advises the defendant of the charges and releases them at the scene if the defendant signs the notice and promises to appear in court.

☑ LE325.4. Explain when you may or may not issue a notice to appear

An officer may not issue a notice to appear in any of the following circumstances:

- The accused's identity cannot be verified.
- The accused refuses to sign the notice to appear.
- The officer has reason to believe that the continued liberty of the accused constitutes an unreasonable risk of bodily injury to the accused or others.
- The officer believes that domestic violence may have been involved.
- The accused has no ties with the jurisdiction reasonably sufficient to ensure their appearance, or there is substantial risk that the accused will refuse to respond to the notice.
- The officer has any suspicion that the accused may be wanted in any jurisdiction.
- The accused has previously failed to respond to a notice or a summons or has violated the conditions of any release program.

Make sure you follow your agency's polices when issuing a notice to appear.

PROBABLE CAUSE AFFIDAVIT

> LE325.5. Explain the role of the probable cause affidavit

A ***probable cause affidavit***, also called an arrest affidavit, is a sworn, written statement by a law enforcement officer establishing certain facts and circumstances to justify an arrest. This document is used by the judge to determine if there was sufficient probable cause to detain the individual. The assistant state attorney may also review the document to decide whether to file formal charges for the alleged crime. An officer should remember that the probable cause affidavit is an officer's statement of the facts made under oath and may be used by the defense attorney in preparing the defense.

UNIT 2 LEGAL CONCEPTS
LESSON 6 Use of Force

◎ Lesson Goal

At the end of this lesson, you will recognize the legal basis for using force by examining related court cases and statutes.

OBJECTIVE REASONABLENESS

An officer's use of physical force is restricted by case law, statutes, and agency policy. It is unlawful to go beyond the force that is necessary in any given situation.

Use of force can be defined as the effort an officer has to use in order to get an unwilling subject to comply to their lawful commands, and it can include the following:

- basic physical restraint
- less lethal force
- deadly force

☑ LE326.1. Explain use of force and the objective reasonableness standard

Section 776.06, F.S., defines **deadly force** as any force that is likely to cause death or great bodily harm. Any use of force by a law enforcement officer is serious and should be a last resort when de-escalation fails. You must be able to articulate the legal justifications for all of your actions when using any type of force.

The Fourth Amendment governs police contact with individuals by protecting people from unreasonable search and seizure by the government. When a law enforcement officer decides to detain, arrest, or use any level of force against a person, the officer's actions will be scrutinized through the reasonableness test of the Fourth Amendment. Objective reasonableness asks whether a reasonable officer would have used force in similar circumstances and whether the officer's actions were reasonable under the given circumstances.

As an officer, you can only use the force reasonably necessary under the circumstances to accomplish your lawful objectives. Always review your agency's policies and procedures on use of force.

Graham v. Connor

In *Graham v. Connor*, Graham asked a friend to drive him to a convenience store to purchase juice to manage the onset of a diabetic episode. Graham quickly entered, then exited the store after noticing a lengthy checkout line. Connor, a law enforcement officer watching nearby, suspected Graham of committing a robbery. Connor and other officers ignored Graham's attempts to explain his medical condition; he and

☑ LE326.2. Recognize case law for use of force measures

his friend were detained, and a struggle followed. After the officers were informed that nothing illegal had occurred at the store, Graham was transported home and released, having declined medical assistance. Graham was injured during the struggle and sued for officer use of excessive force.

The U.S. Supreme Court ruled that the use of force did not violate Graham's Fourth Amendment rights under these facts and circumstances. The Court held that the use of force by an officer is examined under the objective reasonableness standard of the Fourth Amendment. The use of force is to be judged from the perspective of a reasonable officer under the same circumstances without the benefit of hindsight. The Court clearly considered that officers are often required to make split-second, sometimes deadly, decisions in circumstances that are "tense, uncertain, and rapidly evolving." The Court concluded that the objective reasonableness test is not a precise or clear rule but requires a careful review of the facts and circumstances of each case, including the severity of the crime, whether the person posed an immediate threat to the safety of officers or others, and whether the person was actively resisting arrest or attempting to evade arrest by flight.

Tennessee v. Garner

The *Tennessee v. Garner* case involves restricting the use of deadly force on an individual fleeing from arrest. Garner, a 15-year-old juvenile, was running from officers after committing a burglary. Garner was shot and killed after disregarding commands to stop. The officers were acting under authority of a Tennessee statute that provided: "if, after notice of the intention to arrest the defendant, he either flee or forcibly resist, the officer may use all the necessary means to effect the arrest." Although Garner was fleeing arrest from the felony of burglary, he did not appear to the officers to be armed at the time or present any other immediate threat to the officers or public at the time he was fleeing. Garner's father sued and argued that his son's constitutional rights had been violated. The U.S. Supreme Court agreed and declared that use of deadly force to prevent the escape of all felony suspects, whatever the circumstances, is constitutionally unreasonable, and where the suspect poses no immediate threat to the officer and no threat to others, the harm resulting from failing to apprehend them does not justify the use of deadly force to do so.

The Court's test for the use of deadly force in making an apprehension considers the following justifications:

1. There is probable cause to believe the suspect committed a felony involving infliction or threat of serious bodily harm.
2. The use of deadly force is necessary to prevent escape.
3. The officer provides a warning, if feasible, and an opportunity to surrender.
4. There is probable cause that the suspect poses a threat of death or serious bodily harm to officers or others.

The use of force, including deadly force, is a seizure subject to the reasonableness requirement of the Fourth Amendment. All use of force actions by officers will be viewed under the scrutiny of the reasonableness requirement of the Fourth amendment and the courts will balance the nature and necessity of the intrusion on a person's Fourth Amendment rights against the importance of the government interest alleged to justify the intrusion.

FLORIDA STATUTES ON USE OF FORCE

The Florida Legislature incorporated the criteria set forth by the U.S. Supreme Court in *Tennessee v. Garner* regarding the use of deadly force in apprehending a fleeing felony suspect in s. 776.05, F.S.:

☑ LE326.3. Examine the Florida Statutes regarding an officer's use of force

> *A law enforcement officer, or any person whom the officer has summoned or directed to assist him or her, need not retreat or desist from efforts to make a lawful arrest because of resistance or threatened resistance to the arrest. The officer is justified in the use of any force:*
>
> *(1) Which he or she reasonably believes to be necessary to defend himself or herself or another from bodily harm while making the arrest;*
>
> *(2) When necessarily committed in retaking felons who have escaped; or*
>
> *(3) When necessarily committed in arresting felons fleeing from justice. However, this subsection shall not constitute a defense in any civil action for damages brought for the wrongful use of deadly force unless the use of deadly force was necessary to prevent the arrest from being defeated by such flight and, when feasible, some warning had been given, and:*
>
> *(a) The officer reasonably believes that the fleeing felon poses a threat of death or serious physical harm to the officer or others; or*
>
> *(b) The officer reasonably believes that the fleeing felon has committed a crime involving the infliction or threatened infliction of serious physical harm to another person.*

Other statutory provisions regarding the use of force that an officer should be aware of include:

> *776.051 Use or threatened use of force in resisting arrest or making an arrest or in the execution of a legal duty; prohibition. —*
>
> *(1) A person is not justified in the use or threatened use of force to resist an arrest by a law enforcement officer, or to resist a law enforcement officer who is engaged in the execution of a legal duty, if the law enforcement officer was acting in good faith and he or she is known, or reasonably appears, to be a law enforcement officer.*
>
> *(2) A law enforcement officer, or any person whom the officer has summoned or directed to assist him or her, is not justified in the use of force if the arrest or execution of a legal duty is unlawful and known by him or her to be unlawful.*

This provision is important in that officers must be aware that any use of force in addition to meeting the constitutional requirements set forth thus far must also be based on lawful arrest or the lawful execution of the officer's duties as described in subsection (2) of s. 776.051, F.S.

Section 776.06, F.S., defines deadly force as follows:

> (1) As applied to a law enforcement officer or correctional officer acting in the performance of his or her official duties, the term "deadly force" means force that is likely to cause death or great bodily harm and includes, but is not limited to:
>
> (a) The firing of a firearm in the direction of the person to be arrested, even though no intent exists to kill or inflict great bodily harm; and
>
> (b) The firing of a firearm at a vehicle in which the person to be arrested is riding.
>
> (2)(a) The term "deadly force" does not include the discharge of a firearm by a law enforcement officer or correctional officer during and within the scope of his or her official duties which is loaded with a less-lethal munition. As used in this subsection, the term "less-lethal munition" means a projectile that is designed to stun, temporarily incapacitate, or cause temporary discomfort to a person without penetrating the person's body.
>
> (b) A law enforcement officer or a correctional officer is not liable in any civil or criminal action arising out of the use of any less-lethal munition in good faith during and within the scope of his or her official duties.

Section 776.07, F.S., makes the following provision in reference to actual escape from custody by law enforcement or a correctional facility and should be distinguished from the legal requirements discussed earlier regarding a suspect fleeing from arrest:

> (1) A law enforcement officer or other person who has an arrested person in his or her custody is justified in the use of any force which he or she reasonably believes to be necessary to prevent the escape of the arrested person from custody.
>
> (2) A correctional officer or other law enforcement officer is justified in the use of force, including deadly force, which he or she reasonably believes to be necessary to prevent the escape from a penal institution of a person whom the officer reasonably believes to be lawfully detained in such institution under sentence for an offense or awaiting trial or commitment for an offense.

UNIT 3 LIABILITY

LESSON 1 Types of Liability

◎ Lesson Goal

At the end of this lesson, you will understand how liability will result from the consequences of not performing your duties or performing your duties incorrectly under the color of law.

Think About This

While teaching a safety course for high school students, an officer accidentally fires his gun and injures a student. How might the officer be found liable for this incident?

Liability issues may arise if you improperly perform a task or do not perform a task that you should have performed. If you do not fully understand and limit situations that give rise to liability, the potential for harm to both the agency you work for and yourself is great. You can suffer severe consequences including job loss, assessment of devastating monetary awards, or even a prison sentence if you are found liable.

Two types of liability are criminal and civil. They are not mutually exclusive; you can be prosecuted criminally and civilly for the same act. **Criminal liability** occurs if a person is found guilty of committing a crime and is sentenced to incarceration or other penalties. **Civil liability** is the responsibility for a wrongful act or an omission that injures a person or property and most often involves negligence. Penalties for civil liability are normally payment of money damages to the victim or the victim's heirs. Acquittal in a criminal case does not necessarily prevent civil liability.

☑ LE331.1. Differentiate between criminal and civil liability

Being found criminally or civilly liable for actions taken while performing law enforcement work can result in consequences that range from minor to catastrophic. It can cost an officer their freedom and result in financial ruin. For example, an individual can be tried for murder (criminal liability) and sued by the decedent's family for wrongful death (civil liability). In such cases, criminal charges are addressed first. Under state law, the officer's employing agency cannot pay the punitive damages; they must be paid by the individual officer. A civil judgment may result in a reprimand or brief suspension from work, but a criminal conviction can lead to loss of employment and decertification.

TORTS

A **tort** is a civil wrong in which the action or inaction of a person or entity violates the rights of another person or entity. Torts may be intentional, such as battery or false incarceration, or unintentional, such as negligence.

The difference is intent. For example, rarely does a person deliberately crash their vehicle into another person's vehicle; usually it is an accident. If the at-fault driver

☑ LE331.2. Explain the role of intent in intentional and unintentional torts was speeding or looking at a cell phone rather than the road, the driver could be sued for the unintentional tort of negligence. Battery is a deliberate act, so it is an intentional tort. Causing someone's death, called wrongful death in tort law, may result from a deliberate act such as shooting a gun into the air during a New Year's celebration. It may also result from an unintentional accident such as driving carelessly. Liability may result from either one.

NEGLIGENCE

You will recall from earlier that negligence may result in harm to another and involves a duty to care as well as a breach of duty.

☑ LE331.3. Describe examples of officer negligence

An example of officer negligence would be if an officer rear-ends the car in front of him because he was looking at the screen on his in-car computer. Since the officer breached his duty to act with reasonable care, he and his agency could be held liable for the damages caused by the crash.

Another example of negligence is an off-duty officer who leaves their loaded weapon on the kitchen counter in reach of their 10-year-old son. If the son takes the weapon to show a neighborhood friend and accidently fires the pistol, killing the friend, the officer could be held liable for the accidental death of the child because of the officer's negligence.

ACTS THAT LEAD TO CIVIL LIABILITY

The most common types of civil liability are related to arrests, searches, use of force, administration of first aid, and operation of vehicles. The same unlawful acts that result in civil liability may also subject the officer to criminal charges.

☑ LE331.4. Describe examples of officer actions that can lead to civil liability

An unlawful arrest occurs when an officer takes someone into custody without probable cause. Unlawful arrest is an intentional tort. If an officer makes an arrest without probable cause, they may be liable for false incarceration of the arrestee or for violating the arrestee's civil rights.

An unlawful search is a search or seizure performed without probable cause or reasonable suspicion. This sometimes happens inadvertently, for example, when a suspect is arrested on an outstanding warrant that is no longer valid. This can happen when the warrant has been served on the defendant but not cleared or removed from the computer system. This civil violation is based on an unlawful seizure of the person because the arrest was not supported by probable cause. This shows the importance of confirming the validity of a warrant before making an arrest.

An officer's excessive use of force against a suspect can lead to civil and criminal liability. An officer may use only the amount of force that is reasonable and necessary under the circumstances.

An officer who fails to provide appropriate first aid to someone who needs immediate medical assistance may face civil liability. The term **omission** means neglecting to perform what the law or duty requires. Officers may be liable not only for performing required actions improperly but also for failing to perform actions required of them.

Negligently driving a vehicle and causing damage to another vehicle or property will likely lead to civil liability. If an officer's negligent actions amount to recklessness, the officer may also be subject to criminal charges like vehicular homicide.

COLOR OF LAW

When an officer acts or purports to act in the performance of official duties under any law, ordinance, or regulation, they are acting under **color of law**. As a law enforcement officer, you do not have the right to commit acts that violate the law. Additionally, liability issues may arise if you improperly perform a task or do not perform a task that you should have performed.

☑ LE331.5. Explain the role of color of law as it relates to officer duties

Section 242 of title 18 of the United States Code (U.S.C.) prohibits anyone acting under color of law from intentionally depriving another person of a constitutional or other civil right.

> *Whoever, under color of any law, statute, ordinance, regulation, or custom, willfully subjects any person in any State, Territory, Commonwealth, Possession, or District to the deprivation of any rights, privileges, or immunities secured or protected by the Constitution or laws of the United States, or to different punishments, pains, or penalties, on account of such person being an alien, or by reason of his color, or race, than are prescribed for the punishment of citizens, shall be fined under this title or imprisoned not more than one year, or both; and if bodily injury results from the acts committed in violation of this section or if such acts include the use, attempted use, or threatened use of a dangerous weapon, explosives, or fire, shall be fined under this title or imprisoned not more than ten years, or both; and if death results from the acts committed in violation of this section or if such acts include kidnapping or an attempt to kidnap, aggravated sexual abuse, or an attempt to commit aggravated sexual abuse, or an attempt to kill, shall be fined under this title, or imprisoned for any term of years or for life, or both, or may be sentenced to death.*

When you violate the law, this will result in criminal liability. For example, if you commit an act that violates state or local law, the state attorney may bring charges against you. If you commit an act that violates federal law, the U.S. Attorney's Office may file criminal charges.

An officer's illegal act that causes injury or other serious consequences to a person may result in an FBI investigation to determine if the officer violated federal law. For example, a suspect's death due to law enforcement's use of force may result in a federal investigation, even when the local law enforcement agency or state attorney's office fully investigates the incident.

CIVIL VIOLATIONS OF FEDERAL CIVIL RIGHTS

A *civil rights violation* happens when an officer unlawfully interferes with the fundamental rights of another person, such as the rights to due process and equal protection under the law. Officers' use of force is often the basis for civil rights lawsuits. Law

☑ LE331.6. Describe civil violations of federal civil rights

enforcement officers who violate someone's civil rights may be subject to civil liability and even criminal prosecution.

In addition to criminal prosecution, an officer who violates an individual's civil rights may be subject to civil liability in federal court. The most common federal statutory basis used to sue law enforcement officers is 42 U.S.C. § 1983. The provisions of an action for civil rights violations are similar to the criminal provisions contained in 18 U.S.C. § 242. Before imposing liability, the court considers that both sections require proof that the officer acted under the authority of their agency and intentionally violated a clearly established constitutional or civil right of the victim. Officers who violate the civil rights of others may also be subject to discipline by the Criminal Justice Standards and Training Commission and their employing agency.

The double jeopardy clause in the Fifth Amendment to the U.S. Constitution prohibits anyone from being prosecuted twice for the same crime. However, the Fifth Amendment's double jeopardy bar does not prohibit criminal prosecution for civil rights violations even after acquittal of state criminal charges because the state and federal governments are two separate and distinct sovereigns. Each government operates its own criminal court system under its own set of laws. For example, an officer charged with aggravated battery for beating a suspect who resisted arrest may be acquitted of all state charges. After the acquittal, the federal government may indict the officer for criminal civil rights violations for the same incident. A state crime and a federal civil rights violation are different offenses even though they may arise from the same facts.

AGENCY LIABILITY

In a civil suit, the officer may not be the only defendant. Most suits also name the employing agency, its chief or sheriff, or other governmental officials because in most cases, the officer acted within the scope and course of authority. A plaintiff may sue the employing agency because it usually has more financial means than the individual officer. If the plaintiff proves at trial that the officer committed a tort or violated civil rights as part of the officer's duties, the employing agency is likely to be liable for damages through direct or vicarious liability.

☑ LE331.7. Differentiate between direct and vicarious liability

Direct liability arises in cases where the officer committed an intentional or a negligent tort in violation of the employing agency's orders or policies. An example is an officer's illegal use of force in arresting a suspect. The agency's liability is based on action it took or failed to take regarding the officer's alleged policy violation. Direct liability may result from the following:

- negligent hiring of a problem employee
- negligent assignment of duties to a person who is not able to perform them
- negligent retention of a problem employee
- negligent failure to adequately train an employee

Vicarious liability is when a person or entity is held responsible for the negligent actions of another person, even though the first person or entity was not directly responsible for the injury. In law enforcement, an officer's agency is often vicariously liable for damages caused by the officer's actions. Vicarious liability involves the indirect responsibility for officers' actions due to negligence in training, hiring, assignment, supervision, direction, and retention. For example, an agency may be held vicariously liable if an officer operates their patrol car in a negligent or inappropriate way that results in damages to property or personal injury to a member of the public.

UNIT 3 LIABILITY

LESSON 2 Protecting Officers Against Liability

◎ Lesson Goal

At the end of this lesson, you will have a basic knowledge of how officers and agencies are protected against liability, including sovereign immunity.

LIMITING LIABILITY AND OFFICER LEGAL DEFENSES

Law enforcement agencies adopt policies and procedures to help guide their sworn officers in performing their duties. There are federal and state laws that protect officers against civil and criminal liability and provide legal defenses, including sovereign immunity, acting within the scope of employment, qualified immunity, good faith, reasonable manner, justified acts, and emergency doctrine.

☑ LE332.1. Describe how to limit officer and agency liability

These policies are carefully developed to ensure officers comply with legal and ethical guidelines. Agency policies and procedures are developed and published for officers' benefit. By following such policies, you may avoid liability for acts taken while on duty.

Attending required and optional training also helps officers stay informed of current law and police practices. Awareness of changes in legal and practice guidelines helps officers avoid liability.

Sovereign Immunity

Sovereign immunity is derived from the common law idea that the king and his agents can do no wrong. The concept has been applied to state and local government agencies, including law enforcement. The sovereign immunity law under s. 768.28, F.S., is a limited waiver of this immunity.

☑ LE332.2. Describe the role of sovereign immunity in personal and civil liability

The sovereign immunity law provides one of the most important protections for government employees and law enforcement agencies. It includes a list of circumstances and requirements that must be met before the state, county, municipality, or a law enforcement entity or any of its employees can be sued in a state tort action. It also protects individual officers and government employees from personal liability and from being named as a defendant in a state civil lawsuit. This means that unless an officer or employee acts with willful or wanton disregard of someone's rights or property, the officer or employee must be dismissed from a state civil tort action.

Because the sovereign immunity law covers only state tort actions, it does not protect officers and employees named in federal civil rights actions. However, before a plaintiff can prevail in such a case, the plaintiff must show more than mere negligence on the part of the officer or employee.

Scope of Employment

Chapter 111, F.S., protects employees, including officers, charged with civil and criminal actions, if those actions occurred within the scope and course of the employees' employment.

Acting within the scope of employment refers to the range of reasonable and foreseeable activities that an employee does while carrying out the employer's business. If an employee acts outside the scope of employment, the employee may be held individually liable.

☑ LE332.3. Explain acting within the scope of your employment

To ensure that their actions are within the scope and course of their employment, officers should avoid willfully or wantonly infringing on others' rights. Chapter 111, F.S., contains the following two provisions:

- The employing agency may, but is not required to, reimburse legal costs for its employees who have been sued or charged with a crime.
- The employing agency may provide legal counsel for its employees who are sued in either state tort actions or federal non-criminal civil rights actions.

Note that an employing agency may opt not to defend an employee in a civil case, even if the action arose from within the scope of employment. However, if the employee prevails, the agency must reimburse court costs and reasonable attorney's fees. The employing agency may pay any final judgment, including damages, costs, and attorney's fees, arising from a complaint for damages or injury that resulted from any act or omission of the employee in a civil or civil rights lawsuit.

If the action is for an alleged civil rights violation or a similar federal statute, payments for the full amount of the judgment may be made by the employing agency unless the final judgment states that the employee intentionally caused harm.

PROTECTING OFFICERS FROM LIABILITY

Other ways in which officers may be protected from liability include qualified immunity, acting in good faith, acting in reasonable manner, committing acts justified under the law, and acting under the emergency doctrine.

☑ LE332.4. Describe ways an officer is protected from liability

Qualified Immunity

The defense of *qualified immunity* protects "government officials...from liability for civil damages insofar as their conduct does not violate clearly established statutory or constitutional rights of which a reasonable person would have known." See Harlow v. Fitzgerald. Qualified immunity protects public officials from being sued for damages, unless they violated a "clearly established" law of which a reasonable official in their position would have known. Qualified immunity also protects civil servants from the fear of litigation in performing the discretionary functions of law.

For example, a police officer decided to issue a notice to appear (NTA) rather than make a physical arrest for a battery that occurred during a bar fight. The person who was issued the NTA returns to the bar and physically attacks the bar owner. The officer would not be liable for not making the physical arrest because the act of issuing an NTA is discretionary.

Acts Done in Good Faith

To act in good faith, officers must be faithful to their duty and honestly intend to avoid taking undue advantage of others. Acts done in good faith are without malice, ill will, or the intent to unjustly harm anyone.

Acts Done in a Reasonable Manner

Officers must act in a reasonable manner when responding to any law enforcement situation. Reasonableness involves acting professionally within the law and agency policies and procedures. It can range from having a reasonable belief that a person has committed an offense and arresting the person for that crime, to determining what type of first aid to perform, to knowing what level of force is needed in a given situation. Reasonableness is judged objectively by asking if a reasonable officer in the same situation would have acted the same way.

Acts Justified Under the Law

Some seemingly forceful and offensive law enforcement actions can be justified under the law. This occurs in situations where case law or statutory law provides a defense for an officer's actions. For example, chapter 776, F.S., provides that an officer may use deadly force in self-defense or in defense of another from a threat of death or serious physical injury. Other Florida laws permit officers to commit what would otherwise be illegal acts such as:

- use of force in riots, s. 870.01, F.S.
- possession of controlled substances during a criminal investigation, chapter 893, F.S.

Emergency Doctrine

When an unforeseen emergency requires instinctive action, you are not required to use the same degree of care as when you have time to reflect. This is known as the *emergency doctrine*. However, you are still required to use due care. Reckless disregard of others does not qualify as an appropriate response.

UNIT 4 COURT BASICS
LESSON 1 The U.S. and Florida Court Systems

⊚ Lesson Goal

At the end of this lesson, you will be familiar with the structure of the Florida and federal court systems, including the roles of primary personnel.

Think About This

Two men kill a person and then transport the body outside of state lines to bury it. Which court will handle this case, and who is responsible for prosecution in the case?

The court system in the United States includes local, county, state, and federal courts. State judges in Florida are elected or appointed by the governor. Federal judges are appointed by the president. The federal courts are the highest courts in the United States and generally take precedence over the state courts.

The court system has the authority to try cases and to rule on legal matters within a particular area. This authority and the ability to rule within a specific territory or geographic area can be defined as jurisdiction. Courts can have general jurisdiction or limited jurisdiction. General jurisdiction allows a court to hear all kinds of cases within a geographic area. Limited jurisdiction is the power of a court to hear only certain types of cases. For example, family law courts can hear only family law cases, and small claims courts can hear only cases involving damages up to a certain monetary amount. State courts hear cases involving violations of state law. Federal courts hear only cases that are violations of federal laws, including constitutional violations.

STATE OF FLORIDA COURT SYSTEM

The state court system in Florida has four levels: county courts, circuit courts, district courts of appeal, and the Florida Supreme Court.

☑ LE341.1. Describe the structure of the Florida and federal court systems

County Courts

The 67 county courts have limited jurisdiction and manage the following legal issues:

- minor criminal offenses (misdemeanors), which provide a maximum sentence of one year or less in the county jail
- county and municipal ordinance violations, including traffic infractions (some counties use hearing officers)
- civil cases involving amounts of $50,000 or less
- the issuance of search and arrest warrants within the county

Circuit Courts

The 20 circuit courts manage the following legal issues:

- domestic relations cases, such as divorce, guardianship, and juvenile delinquency
- major criminal offenses (felonies), which can result in incarceration in a state correctional institution
- probate matters, such as the processing of wills and settling of the estates of deceased persons
- civil cases involving amounts of more than $50,000
- Baker Act and Marchman Act cases
- the issuance of search and arrest warrants within the circuit
- appeals from county court judgments

Florida District Courts of Appeal

The district courts of appeal are intermediate appellate courts of the Florida court system. They determine whether the law was applied correctly in the trial court. These courts consist of three judges and do not use a jury.

Florida Supreme Court

The Florida Supreme Court is the highest court in Florida. It consists of seven justices appointed by the governor. The supreme court hears cases regarding final orders imposing death sentences and appeals from lower state courts.

FEDERAL COURT SYSTEM

The federal court system has three main levels: district courts, courts of appeal, and the Supreme Court of the United States.

U.S. District Courts

Presided over by U.S. district judges, district courts are the federal trial courts assisted by magistrates. Magistrates, appointed by the district judges, are responsible for issuing warrants, making pretrial motions, and presiding over some civil cases, misdemeanor trials, petty cases, and preliminary hearings. The scope of the federal judiciary system includes all federal codes (criminal, civil, and administrative) in all 50 states, U.S. territories, and the District of Columbia.

Courts of Appeal

The courts of appeal hear challenges to district court decisions from courts located within its circuit, as well as appeals from decisions of federal administrative agencies.

Supreme Court of the United States

The U.S. Supreme Court is the highest court in the United States and the chief authority in the judicial branch. The Supreme Court hears appeals from the decisions of lower federal courts and state supreme courts, and it resolves issues of constitutional and federal law. However, constitutional amendments can overrule Supreme Court decisions.

The Supreme Court's most important responsibility is to decide cases that raise questions of constitutional interpretation. The Court decides if a law or government action violates the Constitution. This power, known as judicial review, enables the Court to invalidate both federal and state laws when they conflict with its interpretation of the Constitution.

PERSONNEL OF THE COURT

To function well, the court system requires many people to act in designated roles.

☑ LE341.2. Describe the roles of the primary personnel of the court system

The *judge* presides over the courtroom and decides questions of law.

The *prosecutor* represents the government's case. Each court has its own prosecutor. Each federal district has its own U.S. attorney and assistant U.S. attorneys. In the Florida state court system, the prosecuting office is the Office of the State Attorney. Each judicial circuit has its own state attorney and assistant state attorneys. The state attorney is responsible for filing formal charges in criminal cases.

The *defense attorney* represents the defendant's case. In Florida, defendants can be represented by an attorney they hired, a public defender who is appointed by the court, or, in certain circumstances, themselves.

Each county elects a *clerk of the court* who is responsible for maintaining the court's files and official records and issuing subpoenas. Deputy clerks are appointed to assist judges with court paperwork and proceedings.

The *court administrator* is responsible for the day-to-day administration of a court system. Their responsibilities can include arranging facilities and scheduling and facilitating the interaction of the court system with other components of the criminal justice system.

A *jury* is a group of citizens who determine questions of fact in a trial. Their responsibilities may differ depending on the particular case. A jury is not always required for a court to hear a case. In a non-jury or bench trial, the judge hears the case and renders a verdict.

A *bailiff* or a court deputy is, generally, a sworn law enforcement officer who is responsible for security in the courtroom.

The *court reporter* is responsible for making a record of the proceedings (not all court proceedings are recorded). Some proceedings may have voice or video recordings; others have written transcripts or merely notes from a court reporter.

UNIT 4 COURT BASICS
LESSON 2 Court Proceedings

Lesson Goal

At the end of this lesson, you will be able to describe the different types of court proceedings, including hearings, arraignments, depositions, meetings, and trials.

Think About This

You are the primary officer who responded to a call involving aggravated battery. The prosecutor has asked you to testify at the trial. What are some factors you must consider as the court process begins?

FIRST APPEARANCE HEARINGS

According to Florida law, the first appearance hearing must occur within 24 hours of the arrest. At the first appearance hearing, the judge appoints counsel if the defendant qualifies and desires it.

LE342.1. Describe the function of a first appearance hearing

The judge reviews the probable cause affidavit and other information to decide if there is probable cause that the defendant committed the alleged offense. The hearing allows the judge to ask questions about issues that may not be clear in the affidavit. Along with the judge, the state attorney (prosecutor) and public defender or their designated assistant will attend the proceeding.

All arrested persons go to a first appearance hearing, unless either of the following applies:

- A law enforcement officer issues a notice to appear in a designated court at a specified date and time, as an alternative to physical arrest.
- The arrested person bonds out from custody, or provides collateral, such as cash or property, to ensure they return to court for future hearings.

The rules in a first appearance hearing are more relaxed than those of a trial. Generally, hearing or trial protocols do not allow **hearsay** evidence (an out of court statement offered for the truth of the matter asserted) as admissible. However, hearsay is admissible in first appearance hearings. The first appearance hearing is adversarial. The defendant may also exercise the right to defend their position later in the court process, usually through pretrial motions to suppress evidence or dismiss the case.

LE342.2. Describe the role of an officer during a first appearance hearing

As an officer, you usually do not need to attend a first appearance hearing unless the prosecutor requests your appearance. Plan to attend the first appearance hearing if you need to clarify or supplement the affidavit or have information that was not included in the probable cause affidavit. You may provide any relevant oral testimony that you believe the judge needs to determine if probable cause exists. The law allows the judge to determine probable cause initially based on the probable cause affidavit.

ARRAIGNMENT

After the arrest, a hearing (arraignment) takes place where the charges are formally filed by the state attorney's office and read aloud to the defendant. This is when the defendant enters a formal response (generally a plea).

☑ LE342.3. Explain the functions of arraignments, pretrial releases, and bond hearings

PRETRIAL RELEASE

In a pretrial release, the defendant is released from jail pending the trial proceedings. The release generally begins with a bond. Conditions may be set for the defendant to abide by while awaiting trial. If the defendant violates these conditions, they may face new charges and the release revoked. A pretrial release may occur at the first appearance.

BOND HEARING

At a first appearance hearing, there may be discussion regarding bond and special conditions of pretrial release. Each circuit has its own bond schedule (pre-set amount for specific crimes). When a bond is not addressed in first appearance, a separate bond hearing may be held to determine if the defendant is eligible to bond out—and if so, the amount of the bond—based upon the defendant's criminal history, offense, and flight risk. The court may call upon you to provide insight into the defendant's flight risk and danger to the community. There can be further bond hearings, based on the judge's decision and the availability of resources for the defendant to bond out.

DEPOSITION

Before trial, you may receive a notice requiring you to give a deposition. A ***deposition*** is an official court proceeding in which the people involved, with the exception of the defendant, provide separate sworn testimonies regarding the facts of the case to one of the attorneys (defense or prosecutor) before the trial. It is the attorneys' chance to assess the case further and document your oral testimony before a trial or hearing.

An attorney from the state attorney's office will be present during the deposition; a judge will not be. At a deposition, the attorney asks questions about the case. A court reporter, or electronic recording device, will record all responses, transcribe them, and then print them for the case file and distribution to the involved people. In addition, you have the right to use your own recording device openly in the deposition. Later, during a criminal trial, the defense can discredit you if your testimony changes or you provide information that differs from the deposition statement. The defense attorney can also plan a defense against any testimony provided in your deposition that is harmful to the defendant.

As an officer, your deposition most often will be conducted with a defense attorney asking the questions. These questions should be reasonably relevant and important to the case. The Florida Statutes give law enforcement officers the legal right not to answer personal questions about their spouses, children, residential address, or phone numbers, or any

☑ LE342.4. Describe how to testify in a deposition

information not related to the case, unless directed by a judge. Do not answer questions that are "off the record." **Off the record** refers to information not recorded in an official document during a court proceeding. Always assume that anything you say could be used at a later time.

When the deposition ends, an attorney will ask if you wish to read the transcribed deposition or waive the review. It is not advisable to waive the review. Although you cannot demand changes, you can point out and notify the state and defense attorneys of errors or misstatements. Before the hearing or trial, review a copy of the deposition to refresh your memory before testifying.

SUPPRESSION HEARINGS

A *suppression hearing* occurs when the defense files a motion to suppress or to exclude certain testimony or evidence from a trial, alleging that your actions were improper and violated their client's rights. This hearing usually occurs before the trial but also may occur during the trial. The court will call on you to testify on your actions related to the stop, detention, arrest, search, seizure, statements, confessions, or evidence that the defense is trying to suppress.

PRETRIAL MEETING

In some circuits, a prosecutor will request a pretrial meeting with the victims, the witnesses, and the arresting officer. The purpose of the pretrial meeting is to give the prosecutor an opportunity to clarify facts of the case and deal with any inconsistencies.

TRIAL

The defendant selects a trial by judge or a trial by jury, unless the defendant is a juvenile. Juveniles are entitled to a trial by a judge, unless tried as an adult. The judge will read the statement of charges against the defendant. Each side is entitled to an opening statement. The prosecution presents the case by presenting the evidence which may include but is not limited to witness testimony and physical evidence. The defense may present a case that may be followed by possible rebuttal evidence by the prosecution, and then both sides finish with a closing statement. If it is a jury trial, the jury will receive instructions and decide the verdict. If there is no jury, the judge will decide the verdict. Your role in a trial is discussed in Chapter 9.

SENTENCING HEARING

Most often, a sentencing hearing occurs after a trial. A sentencing hearing can occur before a trial if the defendant pleads guilty or *nolo contendere*. If during a trial the defendant pleads guilty or *nolo contendere*, a sentencing hearing will occur that includes a review of the defendant's previous convictions. The state attorney's office may request that you attend a sentencing hearing.

At a sentencing hearing, both the defense and the prosecution have an opportunity to present evidence and testimony to recommend an appropriate sentence to the judge. The victim also has the right to make a victim impact statement. Your role is to provide the court with a complete picture of the defendant's actions, and the impact on the victim and society.

☑ LE342.9. Describe the function of a sentencing hearing

VIOLATION OF PROBATION HEARING

A *violation of probation (VOP)* happens when an offender does not abide by all conditions ordered by the court. A *violation of probation hearing* occurs when an officer accuses an offender of violating their probation or community control and the offender contests the violation. An offender, whose legal rights are not the same as those of a defendant, is not entitled to a jury trial. A judge conducts the hearing and makes the final decision whether the offender violated probation or community control. You may be asked to testify in a VOP hearing due to your involvement with the filing of the new charge that violated the person's probation, not that you were involved with the original charge.

☑ LE342.10. Describe the function of a violation of probation hearing

Similar to pretrial hearings, the rules are more relaxed in violation hearings than in trials. For example, hearsay evidence is admissible in violation hearings and can result in a finding by the judge of a violation if the direct evidence confirms the hearsay.

UNIT 4 COURT BASICS
LESSON 3 Court Orders

◎ Lesson Goal

At the end of this lesson, you will know the common court orders and how to serve civil processes and search warrants.

COURT ORDERS

☑ LE343.1. Describe the role of arrest warrants, capiases, or pickup orders when making an arrest

A court order is a legal document issued by a court or judge requiring a person to do or not do something.

Some of the court orders you will encounter most frequently are:

- A *subpoena*—a legal order for a person to appear before a court, imposing a penalty if a person does not comply
- A *capias*—a legal order for an arrest issued by the clerk of the court at the request of the state attorney's office (for example, a failure to appear in court)
- An *ex parte order*—a court order issued and signed by a judge that is initiated by one person in the absence of and without representation or notification of other parties
- A *pickup order*—a court order to take a juvenile into custody
- A *protection order*—a court-issued order that is meant to protect a person, business, company, establishment, or entity and the general public from harm or harassment
- A risk protection order (RPO)—a temporary *ex parte* order or a final order which revokes a person's constitutional right to possess firearms
- A *domestic violence protection order*—a court order issued by a judge to protect someone against domestic violence

ARREST BY COURT ORDER

When you receive a court order, review the document to determine the subject's personal information and the nature of the order. Use criminal justice databases and other law enforcement intelligence resources to confirm the person's identity and possible location.

The nature of the court order may provide information related to safety issues when making the arrest. For example, serving an arrest warrant for murder will be handled differently than an arrest warrant for retail theft.

You are required by s. 901.16, F.S., to tell the person the charge for the arrest, unless either of the following applies:

- The person flees or forcibly resists the arrest.
- Providing the information will endanger the successful completion of the arrest.

Once you have located the subject of the court order, place them under arrest and complete the necessary documentation. On all copies of the court order, you must sign, date, and document the time the court order was served.

SERVING CIVIL PROCESS

You may receive an assignment to serve a civil process, such as a witness subpoena, protective injunction, or eviction notice. Civil processes are issued by the court and are non-criminal in nature. Serving a civil process is a legal procedure in which a summons is delivered to a person to appear in court or at a legal proceeding. In this context, serving simply means official delivery of the court documents.

Civil processes are typically served by the sheriff or a special process server appointed by the sheriff. Except for witness subpoenas or eviction notices, civil processes can also be served by a municipal police officer or a private server by authority of the chief judge. The sheriff's office may have a civil process department, or officers may receive the assignment directly from their supervisor.

☑ LE343.2. Describe how to serve a civil process

Once you receive the assignment, review the information for the recipient's name and address and the nature of the civil process. Before serving the document, conduct a search in a criminal justice database to verify the address. Read the civil process beforehand so you know what information you need to tell the recipient. Understanding the nature of the civil process will allow you to determine whether a heightened awareness of officer safety is necessary.

Once you have located the recipient, provide a copy of the process to them. Be sure to tell the recipient what the civil process is for and any additional pertinent information.

Include a signature, date, and time on all copies of the civil process. Confirm delivery of the process by completing necessary service documentation, providing a copy of proof of service to the recipient, and returning service documentation to the clerk of the court or the sheriff's office. A failure to state the facts or to include the signature as required by the Florida Statutes invalidates the service.

ASSISTING IN THE EXECUTION OF SEARCH WARRANTS

Patrol officers may be required to assist in executing a search warrant. Search warrants vary in type and complexity. Executing a search warrant can be labor-intensive and may require the coordination of multiple officers and agencies, or it can be as simple as obtaining a DNA swab.

LE343.3. Describe how to legally execute a search warrant

When you are assigned to a search warrant team, you should respond to the designated briefing location and make contact with the operation officer in charge. During the briefing, you will get specific information about the operation, such as information on a suspect, the type, scope, and location of the search warrant, and safety concerns. Each officer will be given a specific task to complete, such as security perimeter, entry, search, crowd control, or transport. Be sure you understand your assignment and are properly equipped to complete the task.

While conducting the assignment, comply with the scope of the search warrant. Search warrants outline items to look for and also may identify specific locations or rooms to search. If you locate additional evidence or contraband, notify the operation officer in charge immediately. You may observe or encounter additional issues, such as crowd control, the presence of children, suspects fleeing the scene, aggressive animals, weapons, and booby traps.

Before leaving the scene, make sure that all equipment and evidence are accounted for and removed. A debriefing may be conducted following the execution of the search warrant to discuss the details of the operation. Points to discuss may include the overall outcome and the strengths and weaknesses of the operation.

Chapter 4
Interviewing and Report Writing

UNIT 1 BASICS OF INTERVIEWING
- LESSON 1 Taking Good Notes / 123
- LESSON 2 Preparing for the Interview / 127
- LESSON 3 Conducting the Interview / 131
- LESSON 4 *Miranda* and Laws of Interrogation / 138

UNIT 2 WRITING A REPORT
- LESSON 1 Reports / 142
- LESSON 2 Mechanics / 145
- LESSON 3 Elements and Principles of Effective Report Writing / 151
- LESSON 4 Reviewing a Report Before Submission / 158

UNIT 1 BASICS OF INTERVIEWING
LESSON 1 Taking Good Notes

◎ Lesson Goal

At the end of this lesson, you will understand the importance of taking good notes, what to include in your notes, and strategies for taking notes.

Think About This

You respond to a robbery of a local department store and interview multiple employees. When reviewing your notes later, you realize that you forgot to record some people's names and misspelled the department store's name. What issues will you have writing an accurate report?

WHY TAKE NOTES

Note-taking is the process of writing down information concerning an incident, event, activity, or statement. Accurate note-taking helps you remember facts, complete a report, and prepare for a deposition or trial. Good notes also provide documentation so that other officers who become involved in the incident can quickly learn the facts and important information about the case.

☑ LE411.1. Explain the purpose of note-taking when investigating an incident

WHAT TO RECORD IN NOTES

When responding to a call, you will need to gather preliminary information from a complainant, witness, victim, or other person of interest. Notes are the details you record about the event, interview, or persons involved. The information you gather in notes may aid in identifying evidence and in conducting future investigations.

Your notes should provide answers as to where, when, who, what, how, and why an incident occurred in order to write an accurate report.

☑ LE411.2. Identify the details of an incident and the basic questions that your notes should address

Where

"Where" documents the location of an incident, as well as the location of people and items involved. The "where" is a legal requirement that verifies the jurisdiction. This is generally one of the first pieces of information you will obtain. Note whether you were dispatched to a location or if the call was self-initiated, and document the incident location using as much detail as possible.

Example: "The incident occurred on State Road 33, about 3 miles east of Highway 99."

Describing "where" also includes documenting the location of evidence.

Example: "I saw the knife lying on the kitchen floor, under a chair."

When

"When" documents the date and time an incident occurred. The "when" of an incident is a legal requirement regarding the statute of limitation and the right to a speedy trial. If you cannot establish an exact date, determine a range of dates as closely as possible. For example, write "between Saturday, June 8, and Tuesday, June 11, 2026," instead of "unknown."

Record the time that you received the call from dispatch, arrived at the location, and completed the call for service. Capturing these specific dates and times is critical to the investigation and possible prosecution. The "when" should also include documenting key steps of your investigative process, such as obtaining consent, reading *Miranda* (which is discussed later in this chapter), locating a suspect, or the beginning and ending times of an interview.

Who

"Who" lists and describes everyone who may have information about what happened or who was involved in an incident. Describing "who" requires documenting more than a person's name. Capture the name, address, telephone number(s), age or date of birth, employment information, race, and sex of each person in your notes, and always request some form of photo identification such as a government-issued ID. Note any unique physical attributes, such as scars, body piercings, or tattoos, that might later help identify a person, and include information such as height, weight, type of clothing, hair color and length, and unique mannerisms or speech patterns.

You should also identify individuals as victims, witnesses, suspects, or other in your notes. Typically, officers note a person's status in the incident with a circled "v," "w," or "s" (abbreviated versions of victim, witness, or suspect). Document information seen, heard, and obtained from any person involved in an incident. In Chapter 5, you will learn about identifying information that can be verified through the criminal justice databases.

What

"What" describes information regarding the nature of an incident. As you describe the "what" element of an incident, consider questions such as "what happened (to what or whom)?"

For example, "the suspect struck the victim's windshield" describes what occurred to prompt a response from law enforcement.

Descriptive information might include specific details on the damage, theft, or loss of particular items. A detailed description of property should include the type, characteristics, serial number, model number, age, marks or inscriptions, and estimated value. Descriptions of vehicles should include the type, make, model, year, style, and exterior/interior color; license plate number; vehicle identification number (VIN); and any other identifying marks, such as scratches, dents, customizations, or decals.

When describing injuries to a person, always note the location, type, and extent of the injury and include a detailed description of what weapons or items were used in the incident.

How

"How" specifies how an incident occurred. This is often closely related to the "what" element. Include what object was used to commit the offense. The "how" should explain the action of an event as well as how different objects were used. For example, if a suspect hit the victim with a closed fist versus an open hand or used a weapon, such as a tire iron, those details should be written in your notes. Another example might be a suspect who used white spray paint to vandalize the side of a building with graffiti.

Describe in detail how an incident or activity was carried out. Through observation, you can often determine how an incident happened. Since your notes may be presented in court, it is crucial to document your actual observations and not merely your conclusions.

For example, in a burglary investigation, you may notice a doorjamb with fresh pry marks, indicating something was used to pry the door lock open. Instead of writing, "The door was pried open," you could write, "the doorjamb had fresh pry marks, indicating that the door was pried open."

Why

"Why" describes the reason for an incident and is sometimes called the motive, and it is possible that you will not discover the motive during the initial investigation. Each witness will give you information that is based on their own perspective of the event. Do not jump to conclusions based on the first or most vocal or talkative witness. Instead, gather and include in your notes information about possible motives and evidence of intent. Often, the motive forms part of the criminal intent for an offense.

Actions Taken

You will need to describe the actions that you have taken during the investigation. Remember to include the case number in your notes. You should document key elements of how you conducted your investigation and obtained information.

For example, you "lifted fingerprints from the scene," "located and arrested the suspect," "provided the victim with victims' rights brochures," and "documented the time *Miranda* warnings were given."

STRATEGIES FOR TAKING NOTES

Take notes throughout the process of collecting information. Sometimes, circumstances delay immediate note-taking, but the longer you wait to write down what you see or hear, the greater the chances are that you will forget some of the information. Notes taken in the field are intended to help refresh your memory as you complete reports; for this reason, you do not need to write everything word for word, but you should capture key points, facts, and details.

Timing

> LE411.3. Describe strategies for taking effective notes

While capturing information in a timely manner is important, taking notes while a complainant, witness, victim, or other person of interest is speaking may keep you from hearing some of the statements the person makes. As you recall from Chapter 2, a good technique is to listen closely and pause the conversation to ask for clarification and write down details. This method will allow you to hear and accurately record information. As you are taking notes, stay aware of your surroundings and officer safety.

Spelling

Correctly spell and accurately record all names, addresses, and other relevant information. Use the spelling on a person's legal identification if it is available. This will ensure that you have correctly documented their information. If the person does not have identification, ask them to spell or write out their name. You may be able to compare this information to criminal justice databases for accuracy, but be aware that not every individual will be listed in these databases. Sometimes, you may need to ask an interviewee about another person's name or contact information. If a person is not sure of the spelling of another person's information, write the word by sounding it out and try to find the correct spelling later. Inaccurate information may hinder or delay the investigative process.

Abbreviations

Using abbreviations can increase your note-taking speed, but you should adopt a consistent system for using abbreviations. When you abbreviate the first letters of the words "victim," "suspect," or "witness," circle them to avoid confusion. Abbreviations for race, ethnicity, and gender are usually uppercase and separated by a slash.

Examples include:

- W/H/F (White/Hispanic/female)
- B/M (Black/male)

REVIEWING YOUR NOTES

Reviewing your notes before leaving the scene is imperative. Make sure you have obtained all relevant information from involved parties, since you may not get another chance to speak with them. The accuracy of your report will depend on having good foundational notes.

Other note-taking strategies include using sketches and organizing notes with enough space to add new details during follow-up.

Your agency may have specific policies for retaining notes. Be familiar with your agency's policies before disposing of your notes.

UNIT 1 BASICS OF INTERVIEWING
LESSON 2 Preparing for the Interview

◎ Lesson Goal

At the end of this lesson, you will know how to thoroughly prepare for an interview, including the order of interviews and interviewee considerations.

Think About This

You arrive as backup for a noise complaint situation. The primary officer tells you to interview a group of young men who are standing in front of their residence. What are your next steps?

WHAT IS AN INTERVIEW?

Officers regularly gather information from victims, witnesses, and suspects during investigations. They interview victims and witnesses, sources, or complainants to find out what occurred, who was involved, and other important facts. This information is then used to develop probable cause against suspects.

An *interview* is a conversation with a person who has knowledge of an event or individual; it is not an arrest situation, and the person is free to leave. Many interviews result in obtaining *statements*, which are a person's permanent oral or written records that explain an incident. You will be required to take statements from witnesses, suspects, victims, or anyone who has information about a crime or incident. You will also administer an oath or affirmation when a person provides a statement. An *oath* is a solemn and formal promise to tell the truth regarding what one says or intends to do, often invoking God as a witness. An *affirmation* is a solemn and formal declaration in place of an oath, usually taken to avoid the religious implications of an oath. You will learn more about sworn statements later in this chapter.

☑ LE412.1. Describe the purpose of an interview

It is important to secure the scene before conducting interviews. Always remember that your safety is important. There is the possibility that an interviewee has a weapon.

PREPARATION TECHNIQUES

Recall from Chapter 2 that every interaction requires some sort of preparation. The pre-interview process involves planning who to interview and for what purpose. You will also determine where you will conduct the interview. If you plan to interview more than one person, you must also determine in which order to interview them. While you are planning, consider what information you need to get and how you will record the interview.

☑ LE412.2. Describe how to prepare for an interview

Planning includes knowing your agency's interview policies and procedures. These will dictate how you conduct your interview and will help you determine when you should administer an oath or affirmation. If your agency requires specific paperwork, be sure to have these forms prepared before conducting the interview. These may include an oath or affirmation form, or a written statement form.

When preparing for an interview, use criminal justice databases to check if the interviewee is a wanted person. You will learn more about the various criminal justice databases available to you and how to use them in Chapter 5. You should also gather and review any background information that is available on the interviewee.

Review any existing information that has been documented, such as initial reports, dispatch documents, crime scene notes, sketches, evidence, and supplemental reports.

INTERVIEWEE CONSIDERATIONS

☑ LE412.3.
Determine if any accommodations should be made to the interview process

An important part of planning the interview is determining an interviewee's ability to understand the nature of the interview. Take into consideration the interviewee's level of education, intellect, experience, culture, language, background, and whether they are an adult or a child. Remember to treat the interviewee with respect and dignity. This is a unique and stressful situation for the interviewee, and your demeanor and treatment of them will influence their view of law enforcement.

You may need to plan for accommodations for interviewees with unique circumstances. These may include the use of an interpreter, hearing assistance devices, or a sign language interpreter. Consider allowing the presence of caregivers and service animals. Make sure the interview location is accessible for interviewees who use mobility devices.

The environment should be appropriate for interviewees with developmental or medical conditions. Your agency will have a policy that you must follow when interviewing someone who has a developmental or medical condition, such as autism spectrum disorder. The Florida Statutes require that an interviewee on the autistic spectrum has the right to request that a mental health or other related professional be present at all interviews. In addition, the interviewee's parent or guardian has the right to make this request on behalf of the interviewee. If this request is made, you must make every effort to ensure that a mental health or other related professional is present.

ORDER OF INTERVIEWS

☑ LE412.4.
Determine the order of people to interview based on the incident

Part of planning for an interview is determining who to interview and in what order. An interviewee will fall into one or more of six categories: complainant, victim, witness, source, suspect, or other person who may have knowledge about the incident or people involved. Generally, you will interview the complainant or victim first, followed by witnesses. Typically, the suspect is the last person you interview.

Another way you can determine the order in which to conduct the interviews is by observing the attitudes of potential witnesses. You may want to interview witnesses who are more likely to cooperate first. If an interviewee is experiencing trauma from the incident, wait until they are stable before you conduct the interview. Empathize with the interviewee and make them feel as comfortable as possible.

PREPARING QUESTIONS

After you have identified the people involved in the incident, prepare your questions, and design open-ended questions to elicit as much information as possible about the incident. Open-ended questions encourage conversation and require the interviewee to think, reflect, and provide their opinions and feelings. These questions require more than "yes" or "no" answers, so the interviewee is more likely to answer open-ended questions with greater detail. Typically, these start an interview and help you establish rapport with the interviewee.

☑ LE412.5. Develop specific interview questions to establish elements of the crime

Examples of open-ended questions include:

- Who were you with? Who was involved? Who do you think did it?
- What happened? What did you see? What were the circumstances? What did they do?
- When did you realize something was happening? When, in terms of date and time, did the incident occur?
- Where did he throw the knife? Where did the incident occur?
- Why did you call for help? Why did the incident happen?
- How can I help you? How did the incident happen?

By contrast, closed-ended questions require a specific response, usually a "yes" or "no." Use these questions to get specific information. They can also be used as follow-up questions after open-ended questions to clarify details.

Examples of closed-ended questions include:

- What is your full name?
- Did you see the knife?
- Were you injured?

Avoid asking leading questions. Leading questions steer a person's responses to a specific conclusion. For example, saying, "Your husband hit you, didn't he?" assigns blame to a specific person. This technique prevents you from discovering details about an incident from the interviewee's perspective. The interviewee may interpret these questions as having a "correct" answer.

Instead, acquire information by asking questions that are objective and do not pre-judge the situation. For example, "How did you get injured? Who hurt you?"

TIMING AND LOCATION OF THE INTERVIEW

As the interviewer, you are responsible for creating an atmosphere that will encourage the interviewee to be honest and straightforward. Holding the interview in a place where the interviewee feels comfortable and safe—both physically and emotionally—improves the chances for an effective interview. An interviewee who feels comfortable may be more willing to cooperate.

☑ **LE412.6. Choose an appropriate and safe environment that is suitable for an interview**

Try to conduct interviews immediately or soon after an incident, and when possible, at the scene. This allows you to obtain the most accurate and helpful information. In some situations, you may have to conduct an interview at a later time, such as when the scene is too hectic, there are too many distractions, or when an interviewee has been injured. In such cases, it may be preferable to conduct the interview at your agency, station, or a medical facility.

If you are unable to speak with a witness at the scene, schedule a post-scene interview with them. The proper time to interview will depend on various factors including the physical condition and emotional state of the interviewee. It is best to conduct interviews in person.

The location of the interview is an important factor in successful interviewing. Whenever possible, interview each person in isolation. When you isolate the interviewee, it creates a sense of privacy. Doing so, along with treating them respectfully, will help you build rapport and gain the interviewee's trust. Whatever location you choose, it should be safe, out of the weather, free from distractions, and away from other witnesses, victims, and suspects.

UNIT 1 BASICS OF INTERVIEWING
LESSON 3 Conducting the Interview

Lesson Goal

At the end of this lesson, you will know how to properly conduct an interview, document information from an interview, and obtain sworn statements.

Think About This

While interviewing a witness, you notice that they are fidgeting and tapping their foot. What might their behavior indicate?

STAGES OF AN INTERVIEW

A planned interview has three stages: warm-up, primary, and closing. During the warm-up stage, you will establish rapport and build an understanding with the interviewee, so you must remain professional and impartial. Introduce yourself and make sure that the interviewee is physically and emotionally comfortable. Explain the purpose of the interview and why the information is important. Using procedural justice when interviewing someone can make them more likely to cooperate.

☑ LE413.1. Describe the three stages of an interview

During the primary stage, you will get information about the incident from the interviewee. Ask different types of questions, depending on the information you are seeking. Begin with a variety of open-ended questions to collect as much information as possible. If you want specific answers, need clarification, or want to help the interviewee refocus, ask closed-ended questions, such as "do you know where the suspect lives?" and "were you in the room when the fight started?"

During the closing stage, you will conclude the interview. Summarize and review all of the information that you collected for the report before the interviewee leaves. Ask any follow-up questions as needed. Verify their contact information in case additional questions come up later. Tell the interviewee that you appreciate their time and cooperation.

INTERVIEW LIMITATIONS

As you may recall from Chapter 1, there is often a power imbalance between law enforcement officers and the general public. You must be aware of the power that you hold when you are in uniform and how it can affect your interactions with people.

When you interview someone, document how the process is conducted and how the person consents to the interview. You have a lot of discretion when you conduct an interview, but there are some tactics that must be avoided:

☑ LE413.2. Identify inappropriate tactics to avoid when conducting an interview

- Do not make threats.
- Do not promise leniency.
- Do not create physical evidence for use during an interview.

Using these tactics during an interview may cause admissions, confessions, and evidence to be suppressed. It may also result in disciplinary action and civil liability for you and your agency.

BASIC INTERVIEW TECHNIQUES

> LE413.3. Describe basic interview strategies and evaluating outcomes

Three strategies to use during an interview include mirroring, minimal encouragers, and cognitive interviewing.

Mirroring is appropriately matching another person's speech patterns, gestures, body language, mannerisms, or posture. Position yourself so that your posture lets the interviewee know that you are actively listening to them. While you should be mindful of officer safety, turn your head and torso toward the interviewee and focus on them. Avoid indications that you are not paying full attention to the person, such as checking your watch or phone. Repeat what the interviewee says and rephrase their responses as questions and statements. Doing so will help clarify information or gather more details.

For example, if the interviewee says, "I was just standing there, and Jim came up and hit me as hard as he could. I hadn't done anything to him!"

You could respond with, "So, if I understand you correctly, you are saying that Jim hit you, and it was unprovoked?"

Minimal encouragers are brief statements that indicate that you heard what the interviewee said and want to hear more, and these can include non-verbal encouragers, such as nodding your head. Examples of verbal encouragers include "okay," "go on," "then what?" and "tell me more about that." Be patient and careful not to fill in gaps for an interviewee that might suggest a conclusion.

Cognitive interviewing tries to recreate the event, either physically or psychologically, to enhance memory recall. Cognitive interviewing helps develop a more accurate account of eyewitness events. It is effective with victims of crimes, and best applied in a private location. Start by asking the interviewee to think back to the original event, and then ask them to recall the physical surroundings (time of day, workspace, and so on) and describe how they felt at the time (for example, rushed or bored). Use questions related to the five senses to help prompt memories.

Be sensitive to language barriers and allow the interviewee enough time to answer questions. Keep in mind that you may have to repeat and explain questions.

You may encounter difficult interviewees. Strategies for handling these situations include keeping your composure, asking direct questions, and trying to reduce the interviewee's stress and anxiety. If an interviewee goes off topic, use closed-ended questions to get them back on task.

If the interviewee answered all of the questions pertaining to who, what, when, where, why, and how, you should have valuable results. If you did not receive answers to these questions, ask the interviewee follow-up questions. If you realize information is missing after the interview has concluded, plan a follow-up interview to obtain more information.

INTERVIEWING VICTIMS

A trauma-informed approach can be helpful with any victim, but it is highly recommended for victims of sexual offenses. This approach should be used in conjunction with a culturally sensitive response as described in Chapter 2.

All victims may experience some degree of trauma after a crime has been committed against them. A *trauma-informed approach* is a method of interviewing that acknowledges an interviewee's trauma; it includes maintaining a demeanor that is reassuring, empathetic, and non-judgmental. A traumatic event can distort the victim's perception of time and distance. Initially, the victim may not be able to answer certain questions accurately or in great detail.

☑ LE413.4. Describe how to interview a victim of sexual battery using a trauma-informed approach

Offer compassion and be patient with the victim. This may not be the first time that the victim has experienced trauma. Focus on the victim, talk to them directly, and ask them questions to establish rapport. Reassure the victim that you are there to help and to collect facts for an investigation.

INTERVIEWEE BEHAVIOR AND RESPONSE

Gathering information about an incident or a call to service is not just about recording the facts. You should also observe the behavior of the people you interview. As you learned in Chapter 2, people have unique verbal and non-verbal behaviors. The use of body language, personal space, and eye contact will vary from person to person, so do not stereotype or judge the interviewee's behavior based on your preconceptions. Be open-minded and relate to the interviewee as an individual.

At the outset of an interview ask biographical questions that will not produce stress or a deceptive response, such as the interviewee's name, date of birth, address, place of employment, and recent activities. Pay attention to verbal and non-verbal responses, including the interviewee's body language, tone of voice, and demeanor because it will help you establish how they usually behave and physiologically function. Remember that an interviewee may have had previous interactions with law enforcement that affect how they respond to you. Do not take this personally. Once you understand the interviewee's behavioral patterns, start asking questions about the incident.

☑ LE413.5. Describe how to respond to interviewee behaviors

Sometimes a person that self-identifies as a witness becomes a suspect. For this reason, be aware of behavior that might indicate that a person is not being truthful. Recognizing deception is a valuable skill, and you will develop this skill over time with practice and experience.

Observe the interviewee's physiological and behavioral changes as they respond to specific questions. For example, while asking an interviewee questions about their address and employment, they seem calm; however, when you begin asking them about the burglary that occurred the night before, they start tapping their foot, sweating, and repeating simple questions before answering them.

The interviewee's physiological and behavioral changes are possible indicators that they are hiding information or being deceptive. You will most likely see these changes when the interviewee responds to specific questions or statements. Certain body movements and facial expressions are indicators of deception. However, it is also possible that these reactions may be due to stress, nervousness, previous experiences, or medical conditions.

☑ LE413.6. Recognize common signs of deception by an interviewee

Some signs of nervousness, stress, and possible deception may include:

Physiological

- increased perspiration
- changes in skin color
- dry mouth
- observable increase in pulse rate
- observable change in breathing rate

Behavioral

- pausing or silence; speaking rapidly; changing tone of voice or volume of speech
- foot tapping; leg shaking
- finger tapping
- pacing; not sitting still
- refusing to look at the interviewer
- giving answers that appear rehearsed
- giving verbal responses that are inconsistent with non-verbal responses
- attempting to change the line of questioning
- being overly eager to help
- giving too much or too little clarification
- responding to questions with questions
- looking for an escape route
- asking for simple questions to be repeated

DEALING WITH CHALLENGING INTERVIEWS

☑ LE413.7. Identify ways to address mental health needs during and after an interview

Having a plan and strategy beforehand can help the interview go smoothly. However, you may encounter some challenging interviews that will cause you internal stress and discomfort no matter how much you have prepared. Conducting interviews for certain crimes may be especially difficult due to the circumstances surrounding the crime, the event, or because of personal experiences. As an officer, you must maintain professionalism and objectivity even when you hear disturbing or conflicting statements. This will require empathy and self-regulation. Reacting or giving in to your personal feelings in challenging interviews may create issues for you and your agency.

Remember to act professionally while conducting the interview but make sure to devote time to taking care of your mental health afterwards. You may also consider taking breaks during the interview process to refocus and gather your thoughts. Make sure to use the resources available to you through your agency and to use the strategies discussed in Chapter 1 for coping with stress. It is important to seek help for your long-term well-being and career longevity. In addition, remember to support your fellow officers if they experience a difficult time with an interview or express that they are struggling with something specific post interview.

OATHS AND SWORN STATEMENTS

When an interviewee makes a *sworn statement*, they provide written or oral facts under oath or with a penalty of perjury. Most jurisdictions require interviewees to make sworn statements. In these instances, you must administer an oath or affirmation.

When and how to administer an oath will depend on the circumstance and the policies of your agency and local state attorney's office. These policies can help you determine the preferred procedure, location, materials, equipment, and interpreters that you may need for the statement and oath. The Florida Statutes give you the authority to administer oaths while performing your official duties. However, it does not certify you as a notary. A person may object to taking an oath because of a religious or philosophical belief. In these cases, Florida law allows a person to make an affirmation instead of an oath.

☑ LE413.8. Describe how to legally administer an oath and obtain a sworn statement

Before administering an oath or affirmation, explain that it is perjury to give false information in a sworn statement. Instruct the interviewee to raise their right hand while you administer the oath or affirmation and ask the person, "Do you swear or affirm that the statement you are about to give is true and accurate to the best of your knowledge?" The law does not require a person to raise their right hand when giving an oath or affirmation. However, this well-known practice and gesture may impress upon the person the importance of telling the truth.

Written statements and audio or video recorded statements should be made under oath or affirmation. Put the interviewee at ease and remind them that the information they are providing will be used in the case. Be sure to preserve these statements in accordance with your agency's policies and procedures.

Written Statements

Use the information you have developed during your initial contacts to identify everyone who can provide a written statement. Be sure to follow your agency's policies regarding when and how to obtain written statements.

When you ask an interviewee to provide a written statement, explain the reason for the request, and be clear about what information should be included. If an interviewee writes a statement, ask them to write clearly and have them describe the incident to the best of their recollection. They should describe all property as well as every event, person,

☑ LE413.9. Describe how to obtain a written sworn statement

weapon, and vehicle involved in the incident. Read the statement and compare its content with your notes from the interview. If an interviewee says something important during an interview but leaves it out of the written statement, ask them to include the missing information. Clarify any information that you cannot read or do not understand.

An interviewee who is non-English speaking may write a statement in their preferred language. When this happens, one option is to have an officer who is fluent in that language review the statement. Always refer to your agency's policies regarding the use of translators.

If the interviewee does not read or write or has any other limitation, follow your agency's policies on how to prepare written statements. There are some guidelines that you may consider. You may ask questions or have the interviewee relay the information in their own words while you write the statement, but do not paraphrase or summarize the statements from an interviewee.

Under certain circumstances, it may be impossible to take a statement. Always document why a person did not provide a statement. For example, a person who is injured and requires immediate medical attention is often unable to give a statement at the scene.

If someone refuses to give a statement, indicate this information in your notes and written report. You cannot force someone to provide a statement; however, they can be subpoenaed and required to appear in court.

SIGNING STATEMENTS

☑ LE413.10. Describe how to obtain a signature on a written statement

When an interviewee submits a written statement, you must read it to verify that it is complete and legible before they sign the document. If you prepare the statement on the interviewee's behalf, read the statement back to the interviewee, make any necessary corrections, and ask the interviewee to sign and date the statement or make a thumb mark. Interviewees sign statements to prove the words are theirs. Also, a witnessing officer should sign the statement. At the end of the written statement, add the following phrase:

"Dictated by_____ and written by Officer_____."

In some situations, an interviewee may be injured, sick, or incapacitated and unable to sign the statement. In such cases, write the reason why the person was unable to sign the statement. If an interviewee refuses to sign their statement, note "refused to sign" at the bottom of the statement.

Electronic Statements

There are advantages and disadvantages to obtaining an electronic statement by recording an audio or video interview. An electronic recording can be beneficial because you can hear the entire interview, but one disadvantage is that some words or descriptions may not be clear, which can lead to misunderstanding the information. To prevent this, test the equipment before the interview to make sure that the recording device is working properly. As technology evolves, the use of in-car and body cameras have become prevalent in law enforcement. These devices are often used when responding to a call for service and will record initial interviews. Always be aware that audio and video recordings may be used in court, and in-car and body cameras are no exception.

Keep all interview recordings as evidence. Be familiar with your agency's and state attorney's office policies when using audio or video recordings during an interview.

☑ LE413.11. Describe how to obtain an electronic statement

When recording an interview, explain to the interviewee that you are recording and clearly state the following:

- your name
- the names of other people present
- your location
- the day and date of the interview
- the incident to be discussed
- the case number
- the type of incident

Record the administration of the oath or affirmation. Ask the interviewee to raise their right hand and indicate whether the interviewee has done so, and then administer the oath or affirmation.

If you have to suspend or pause the interview at any time, document the following information before resuming the recording:

- the reason for the suspension or pause
- that you are continuing the statement recording and include the date and time
- that you did not ask the interviewee any questions while the recording was suspended or paused

Pay attention to what the interviewee says during the statement. If you notice any discrepancies or if you need clarification, ask them to elaborate. At the end of the recording, state the following:

"This now concludes the statement of _____, regarding incident _____, case number _____. The time is now _____."

After completing an interview, document the information collected and include all evidentiary forms or log entries.

UNIT 1 BASICS OF INTERVIEWING
LESSON 4 *Miranda* and Laws of Interrogation

Lesson Goal

At the end of this lesson, you will understand how an interrogation is different from an interview. You will also understand when to conduct an interrogation versus an interview, when and how to give *Miranda* warnings, how to respond to an invocation of rights, and the standards for questioning juveniles.

Think About This

Your fellow officer is reading a suspect their Miranda *rights. However, the suspect does not speak English. How do you ensure that the suspect understands their* Miranda *rights?*

FUNDAMENTALS OF INTERROGATION

When suspects are identified through initial interviews, officers may detain and interrogate them. Conducting interrogations may depend on the officer's employing agency, so keep in mind that interrogations may be reserved for detectives at your agency.

☑ LE414.1. Identify the difference between an interrogation and an interview

An ***interrogation*** consists of questioning initiated by law enforcement that is directly or indirectly intended to elicit an incriminating response; it differs from an interview because the person being questioned has been detained and is no longer free to leave. In an interrogation, officers must follow certain legal rules to protect the detained suspect's rights and ensure that their statements are admissible in court.

MIRANDA DECISION

☑ LE414.2. Explain the importance of the *Miranda* decision for conducting a legal interrogation

In 1966, the U.S. Supreme Court decided the landmark case of *Miranda v. Arizona*. The decision in this case had a profound impact on law enforcement throughout the United States. Until the *Miranda* case, the law presumed that people knew their constitutional rights. The *Miranda* decision put the burden of explaining Fifth and Sixth Amendment rights on the law enforcement officer.

In *Miranda*, the Court decided that whenever a law enforcement officer questions a suspect in custody, the officer must advise the suspect of certain constitutional rights. These include the right to remain silent and the right to have an attorney present when being questioned by law enforcement. If you fail to follow the rules set forth in *Miranda*, any statement or admission obtained from the interrogation cannot be used in court.

There are four elements to the *Miranda* decision: custody, interrogation, understanding, and the free and voluntary waiving of rights. The *Miranda* requirements are necessary whenever a law enforcement officer conducts a custodial interrogation.

Custody

When a person is taken into *custody*, they have been deprived of freedom in a significant way. Generally, interviews at the scene—such as *Terry* stops, traffic stops, and roadside driving-under-the-influence tests—are not considered custody, because they are typically brief in nature. Handcuffing a person or otherwise restricting their movement so that they are not free to leave is considered custody. In deciding whether a person is in custody for the purpose of *Miranda*, courts ask two questions:

- What were the facts and circumstances surrounding the interrogation?
- Given those circumstances, would a reasonable person have felt they were not at liberty to end the interrogation and leave?

If, from all of the circumstances, it appears that the person is not free to end questioning and leave and a reasonable person in that person's place would believe that they are not free to leave, then the person is in custody, and *Miranda* warnings are required.

In *Ramirez v. State*, the court ruled that the determination of whether a reasonable person in the suspect's position would consider himself in custody for the purposes of *Miranda* requires consideration of the manner in which the police summoned the suspect for questioning; the purpose, place, and manner of custodial interrogation; the extent to which the suspect is confronted with evidence of his guilt; whether the suspect is informed that he is free to leave the place of questioning.

Note that when there are multiple officers present or emergency lights activated, it can create an environment in which a reasonable person might believe that they are not free to leave.

☑ LE414.3. Describe the concept of custody in relation to the *Miranda* decision

Interrogation

Many agencies in Florida refer to the process of interrogating or questioning a suspect as a "custodial interview"; however, Florida courts routinely use the term "interrogation." During an interrogation, officers may use direct or indirect questioning. See *Rhode Island v. Innis* and *Brewer v. Williams*.

Often, a suspect who is in custody will voluntarily give information even when not solicited through questioning. These are known as spontaneous statements and are admissible even if an officer does not advise the suspect of their *Miranda* rights. You may allow the suspect to continue talking, but you may not ask the suspect any questions without giving *Miranda* warnings. Basic questions posed to a suspect such as biographical data are not subject to *Miranda* rules.

☑ LE414.4. Explain the significant case law rulings on the *Miranda* decision

Understanding

You must ensure that the suspect understands their rights, taking into account their age, national origin, education, circumstances of the advising of rights, mental or physical disability, and whether or not they are under the influence of an intoxicating substance. Document any measures taken to address these issues for any future court proceedings.

☑ LE414.5. Explain the importance of a suspect understanding their rights

Waiver of Rights

Once you have advised the suspect of their *Miranda* rights, you are required to provide a waiver before questioning may begin. The waiver ensures that the suspect understands their rights and will speak with you. A written waiver is preferred but not essential, and it can be verbal or even implied. The waiver of rights must be freely and voluntarily given. You may not make any promises or coerce the individual to get a confession.

GIVING *MIRANDA* WARNINGS

☑ LE414.6. Describe when and how to administer a *Miranda* warning to a suspect

You are only required to provide a suspect with *Miranda* warnings when the elements of custody and interrogation are present. Once the *Miranda* warnings are required, you should read the rights one at a time from an agency-provided *Miranda* card or form. Not only will this guarantee that you do not forget or mix up any of the rights, but it can also enhance your courtroom testimony. Defense attorneys can do little with an officer who testifies that they always read *Miranda* rights from the card or form. It may also help you avoid liability for failure to follow policy.

Miranda Cards

Officers are usually issued a *Miranda* card to use when reading the *Miranda* rights to a subject.

Miranda Warning	Acknowledgment of Rights
1. You have the right to remain silent. 2. Anything you say can and will be used against you in court. 3. You have the right to call or obtain an attorney at this time and have one present now or at any time during questioning. 4. If you cannot afford an attorney and you want one before or at any time during questioning, one will be provided for you. 5. If you decide to answer questions now, you have the right to stop answering at any time during questioning.	*After the warning and in order to secure a waiver, the following questions should be asked and an affirmative reply secured to questions (1) and (3). If the individual has previously asked for an attorney, no valid waiver may be obtained, unless they initiated the conversation.* 1. Do you understand each of these rights I have explained to you? 2. Have you previously requested any law enforcement officer to allow you to speak to an attorney? 3. Having these rights in mind, do you wish to talk to us now?

Invocation of Rights

☑ LE414.7. Describe how to respond when a suspect invokes their *Miranda* rights

Remember that the *Miranda* warnings include several rights. If the suspect makes a clear and unmistakable request to invoke any of their rights under *Miranda*, all questioning must cease immediately.

If the suspect invokes only their right to remain silent, you may reinitiate the interrogation after "a significant lapse of time" as stated by the U.S. Supreme Court. On the other hand, if the suspect requests an attorney, you are not allowed to continue questioning unless the suspect's attorney is present or the suspect reinitiates communications. However, if a suspect reinitiates contact or conversation with you after having previously invoked their Fifth Amendment right, an entirely new *Miranda* rights advisement and waiver must be conducted and documented. Simply reminding the suspect of their previous *Miranda* advisement is insufficient as defined by *Quarles v. State*.

If in response to *Miranda* warnings an in-custody suspect invokes their right to counsel, you may reinitiate contact with the suspect if they experience a break in police custody of at least 14 days. Still, you should provide *Miranda* warnings to the suspect depending on the conditions of the interrogation (if in custody, etc.) as defined by *Maryland v. Shatzer*.

The Fifth Amendment right to counsel under *Miranda* is not crime specific. Once a suspect asks to have an attorney present during an interrogation regarding one charge, then the suspect cannot be questioned regarding any other charges without their attorney present.

JUVENILE INTERROGATIONS

The *Miranda* warning also applies to juveniles. A waiver of a juvenile's *Miranda* rights will be closely scrutinized by the court. See *B.M.B. v. State*, *Lee v. State*, and *State v. Roman*. Factors that the court will consider in determining if a juvenile understands their rights and the significance of waiving those rights include the juvenile's age, marital status, education, intellectual level, and experience in the criminal justice system. See *J.D.B. v. North Carolina*.

The standards for questioning a juvenile are the same as for adults. While there is no statutory requirement for a parent or guardian's consent before you may interrogate a child, the Florida Statutes require you to make a reasonable effort to contact parents or guardians when a juvenile is taken into custody. Document exactly what you say to a juvenile to indicate to them whether they are free to leave.

☑ LE414.8. Describe the standards for interrogating a juvenile

Juvenile interrogations may only last for a reasonable length of time. If a child is held for any length of time before the interrogation, note the length of the delay and any reasons for the delay. Also document the number of breaks and rest periods given to the child during the interrogation. Keep in mind that there is a limit to the number of times you can interview a child. Make sure you know both your agency and local court requirements.

UNIT 2 WRITING A REPORT
LESSON 1 Reports

Lesson Goal

At the end of this lesson, you will understand the importance of a well-written report, the potential uses and audience of a report, and what type of incidents require a report.

After you respond to an incident, you will prepare a written report. A **report** is a written document that gives information about an event, situation, occurrence, or incident. Your agency may refer to this type of report as an offense or offense-incident report.

☑ LE421.1. Explain the importance of submitting a well-written report

Writing reports is one of your critical job functions, so you should write clear, concise, and effective reports. A report reflects competence and professionalism not only in writing skills, but in all aspects of law enforcement work. A well-written report will:

- aid the state attorney's office in prosecutions
- reduce legal liability for you and your agency
- save your agency time and expense

You may have heard someone say, "If it isn't in the report, it didn't happen." This statement reinforces the point that it is your responsibility to include all important details in your reports. A poorly written report could result in a criminal going free or an innocent person going to jail. Write your report so that it can withstand the test of time because someone may need to refer to it years after the incident. For this reason, you are required to keep reports long after the case is closed. Statutes and agency policies dictate how long reports should be saved.

☑ LE421.2. List the common uses of law enforcement reports

Once submitted, your report becomes a public record and may be used in proceedings as an official representation of the facts surrounding the incident.

Reports are commonly used in:

- criminal and civil appeals
- criminal case filings
- criminal trials
- civil proceedings
- depositions
- drafts of probable cause affidavits
- internal affairs investigations
- pretrial proceedings
- probation and parole hearings
- research/examination of past events

- victim restitution hearings
- workers' compensation cases

Reports are also used for:

- continuing investigations
- coordinating law enforcement activities
- evaluating law enforcement officers' performance
- keeping other law enforcement officers informed
- planning future law enforcement services

READER CONSIDERATIONS

Before you write a report, consider the potential readers and the purpose of each report. The majority of people who will read your reports are not law enforcement officers. Readers will have varying life experiences, education levels, cultural backgrounds, and reasons for reading the report. To recognize the significance of writing a clear and complete report, consider that it may be read by any of the following people:

☑ LE421.3. List the potential readers of law enforcement reports

- other officers
- supervisors
- defense and prosecuting attorneys
- judges
- city, county, or state officials
- media reporters
- victims or their families
- suspects, defendants, or people convicted of crimes
- members of the public
- insurance companies

Each reader will develop an opinion about the writer based solely on the content or makeup of the report. For example, prosecuting attorneys will make crucial decisions about a case based on what they read in the report. On the other hand, defense attorneys will seek to exploit any weaknesses they see in the same report. Both will make assumptions about your competence.

In addition to considering the audience of the report, it is important to consider its tone. A report is a professional document and should be businesslike and objective. Report only the facts of the event and not your opinions. Use plain English.

INCIDENTS OR EVENTS REQUIRING REPORTS

You will not write every report the same way, so think about the situation and the circumstances before you begin writing. For example, a burglary report will require different information and may be in a different format than a report of found property.

> **LE421.4.** List common incidents that may require a report

Your agency may require you to submit a report for any of the following incidents:

- all crimes
- officer use of force
- suicides
- death
- missing or endangered persons
- runaway juveniles
- found property
- traffic crashes (under certain circumstances) as required by law
- miscellaneous non-criminal or suspicious incidents
- additional or supplemental information

A later lesson discusses another type of report, the probable cause affidavit, which was introduced in Chapter 3.

UNIT 2 WRITING A REPORT
LESSON 2 Mechanics

Lesson Goal

At the end of this lesson, you will be able to apply good vocabulary, appropriate parts of speech, and proper grammar when writing reports.

Think About This

Your supervising officer returns a recent report to you and says there are numerous grammatical errors. If no one had reviewed the report and it was later used in court, how might the report reflect on your abilities as an officer and your agency? Would it affect the outcome of the case?

It is easy to believe that the content is the most important part of a report. However, grammar, punctuation, and spelling are equally as important as the report's content. If the content reflects a good investigation but the report contains too many mechanical errors, the reader will be distracted from the message, and the reader may think you are incompetent and unprofessional. An effective report should be well-written and demonstrate a good command of language. It should be free of errors in sentence structure, grammar, and other writing mechanics.

GOOD VOCABULARY

Having a good and professional vocabulary is important when writing a report. When you encounter unfamiliar words and phrases, take the time to find their meanings and proper usage. When you expand your vocabulary, you increase your report writing skills and become more effective at precisely describing things that you are required to document.

☑ LE422.1. Describe strategies for using effective vocabulary

PROPER GRAMMAR

Proper grammar is defined by the guidelines and rules that govern a language's usage. It is important to be conscious of grammatical rules because, when you use correct grammar, your reader is more likely to understand your report.

You must recognize the parts of speech and use them properly to write a clear report. Refer to the parts of speech table for the basic elements that make up a sentence.

☑ LE422.2. Recognize the importance of using the correct parts of speech

PROPER SENTENCE STRUCTURE

A sentence is a group of words that contains a subject, a verb, and usually an object, and every sentence should express a complete thought. A singular subject should have a singular verb, and a plural subject should have a plural verb. In the incorrect

Part of Speech	Description	Examples
noun	people, places, things, actions, qualities, beliefs	The **officer** stopped the car. The **subject** fled from the **officers**.
pronoun	acts as a substitute for a noun	**They** stopped the car. **He** ran from **them**.
verb	expresses an action or state of being	The officer **ran** after the subject. The subject **was** fast.
adverb	describes, identifies, or quantifies a verb, adjective, or other adverb	The subject ran **quickly**. He became **extremely** exhausted.
adjective	describes a noun or a pronoun	The **heavyset** man was the subject. The **short** woman was also running.
preposition	links words and phrases and provides temporal, spatial, and logical relationships	The subject jumped **out of** the car, went **over** the retaining wall, and ran **into** the store.
conjunction	connects words with other words, clauses (parts of sentences) with other clauses	Officer Russ **and** I approached the car. I covered the car **while** he contacted the subject.

example, the verb *is* takes the singular form while the subject, Jim and Bob, is plural. The correct verb form for the plural subject is *are*.

✗ **Incorrect** Jim and Bob is brothers.

✓ **Correct** Jim and Bob are brothers.

☑ LE422.3. Describe how to use proper sentence structure when writing a report

Understanding the parts that make up a simple sentence will help you write clear sentences. The subject of a sentence tells you what or who performs an action. A verb states the subject's action, existence, or state of being. The object identifies the person or thing that is affected by or that receives the action of the verb. Not all sentences have objects, but many do.

John	hit	Monica.
subject	**verb**	**object**

A *sentence fragment* is a group of words that lacks a subject, verb, or object (when one is needed) or fails to express a complete thought. Notice how, in the incorrect examples, the sentence does not express a complete thought because either the subject or verb is missing.

- ✗ **Incorrect**   Witnessed a bank robbery in progress while on patrol. (missing subject)
- ✓ **Correct**   I witnessed a bank robbery in progress while on patrol.
- ✗ **Incorrect**   The gun on the floor next to the body. (missing verb)
- ✓ **Correct**   The gun was lying on the floor next to the body.

POINT OF VIEW, VOICE, AND TENSE

Point of View

Write reports in the first or third person depending on your agency's policies. Most reports are written in the first person.

First person is written from the author's perspective: "I saw," "I spoke," and "I arrived."

Third person is written from an outside perspective: "The witness saw," "The victim spoke," and "The officer arrived." Do not use personal pronouns such as "I," "me," or "my" in third person.

Active and Passive Voice

When writing your reports, use active voice, not passive voice. In active voice, the subject of the sentence comes before the verb and is clearly stated.

Example: "Ann struck John with a frying pan."

In this sentence, Ann is the subject and is placed at beginning of the sentence before the verb. John receives the action and is therefore the object. When you write in active voice, you tell the reader who or what is performing the action, what that action is, and what or who is receiving that action.

In passive voice, the object and the subject are reversed.

Example: "John was struck with a frying pan by Ann."

In this sentence, John is still the object because he still receives the action. However, the reader does not find out who struck him until the end of the sentence, so the reader has to backtrack in thought.

You can identify and correct passive voice by asking yourself whether a sentence starts with the subject performing the action. If it does not, rewrite the sentence so that the subject comes before the verb.

Tense

Most law enforcement reports are written in past tense because the events have already occurred. Make sure you use proper verb tenses. Writing in active voice does not mean that you must write in the present tense.

Example: "Ann struck John with a frying pan" uses active voice, past tense, and proper language. Make sure that the tense is consistent throughout the report.

When you use incorrect grammar and sentence structure, you damage your credibility. In addition, the report may appear inaccurate and unclear.

CORRECT SPELLING AND CAPITALIZATION

☑ LE422.4. Recognize the importance of using correct spelling and capitalization when writing a report

Spelling is an important part of writing a report, so make sure to spell words correctly. If you are using a computer to write your report, use the spellcheck feature. Remember, however, that spellcheck does not always know whether you used the correct word.

Example: "The thief took there money" might not be flagged by spellcheck, but it is still wrong.

Have another person proofread your report to make sure that you have used the correct words. If you are unsure of the spelling of a word, consider using a different word.

Examples: Instead of "penitentiary," you can use "prison." Instead of "contusion," you can use "bruise."

You can also use a dictionary to check your spelling when writing a report by hand. Whichever method you choose to check your spelling, use it consistently throughout the entire evaluation of the report.

Some agencies may recommend or require you to use all capital letters in a report. When you are not using all capital letters, follow these capitalization rules:

1. Capitalize the names of people, streets, cities, and states.

    "I spoke with the victim, Greg Alexander, at his house on 999 Monroe Street in Tallahassee, Florida."

2. Capitalize the names of organizations and buildings only when they are specific.

    "The neighborhood meeting will be held at the library." (non-specific)
    "The Oakbrook Neighborhood Association meeting will be held at the LeRoy Collins Leon County Public Library." (specific)

3. Capitalize holidays, days, and months.

    "Independence Day is on Saturday, July 4."

4. Capitalize geographic locations but not directional words.

    "She is from the South." (specific region or location)
    "I drove south on the road." (direction)

5. Capitalize the titles of professionals only when names are used.

> "I stopped the chief's daughter for speeding." (chief not named)
>
> "I stopped Chief Smith's daughter for speeding." (chief named)

6. Capitalize brand names.

> "Mr. Jones reported that someone stole his Smith & Wesson revolver."

PROPER PUNCTUATION

It's important to understand when to use punctuation such as commas, apostrophes, and quotation marks. Using improper punctuation can result in confusing or even misleading reports, so be sure to proofread your reports before submitting them.

☑ LE422.5. Recognize the importance of using correct punctuation when writing a report

Commas

The comma is one of the most misused punctuation marks. It is not always appropriate to insert a comma whenever you desire a pause. The following rules are specific to the use of commas:

1. Use a comma to separate two complete sentences joined by a coordinating conjunction. There are seven coordinating conjunctions: for, and, nor, but, or, yet, and so.

> I met with the victim, and she gave me a statement. (correct)
>
> I met with the victim, she gave me a statement. (incorrect)

If the two complete sentences are not joined by a coordinating conjunction, use a semicolon or period to separate them. Do not use a comma.

> I met with the victim, she gave me a statement. (incorrect)
>
> I met with the victim; she gave me a statement. (correct)
>
> I met with the victim. She gave me a statement. (correct)

2. Use a comma after an introductory clause. A clause is a group of words with a subject and verb that tells the reader what the sentence is about. Sometimes a clause can stand as an independent sentence, but when it needs more parts of speech to make sense, it is a dependent clause.

> When the alarm sounded, the burglar ran from the store. ("The burglar ran from the store" can stand alone as a sentence and is therefore an independent clause; "when the alarm sounded" is a dependent clause because it needs more parts of speech to make sense.)

3. Use a comma to separate items in a series of three or more items. A comma and a conjunction should appear before the last item.

> The victim said someone stole his digital camera, television, DVD player, radio, and computer.

4. Use a comma to separate non-essential phrases in a sentence. A phrase is a group of words that forms a grammatical unit, but it is not necessarily a complete sentence. A phrase is considered non-essential when you can omit it without changing the meaning of the sentence.

    The fingerprints, <u>which I found on the window</u>, belong to the victim.

5. Use a comma between two or more adjectives when they separately describe the same noun.

    Officers often work long, exhausting hours during an emergency.

6. Do not place a comma between two or more adjectives when the adjective before the noun changes what the noun is. One way you can test this is if you reverse the adjectives, and they do not make sense.

    He threw the <u>white toaster oven</u> at me. (You would not say, "He threw the toaster white oven at me.")

7. Use a comma to introduce a quote.

    The suspect yelled, "I'm going to burn his house down when I get out."

8. Use commas when writing dates and addresses. Remember to include a comma after the year, street name, and city.

    The robbery occurred on January 12, 2018, at 345 Monroe Street, Tallahassee, Florida.

Apostrophes and Quotation Marks

Other common punctuation to be aware of are apostrophes and quotation marks. The following are a few rules to keep in mind:

1. Use an apostrophe to show possession or to create a contraction. Possession means that a certain object or quality belongs to a person or thing.

    An <u>officer's</u> size and skill are factors to consider when deciding use of force.

2. A contraction is the result of combining two words. The only time you should use contractions in a report is when you document a direct quote.

    The suspect said, "I <u>don't</u> want any trouble."

3. Try to use a person's exact words in an incident report. If using a direct quote, place quotation marks around the person's words. Here is an example of a direct quote:

    Keith Roberts said, "<u>Go ahead and search.</u>"

4. Do not use quotation marks when paraphrasing or summarizing a person's statement.

    Keith Roberts gave me permission to search his car.

UNIT 2 WRITING A REPORT
LESSON 3 Elements and Principles of Effective Report Writing

Lesson Goal

At the end of this lesson, you will know the elements and principles of writing effective reports and probable cause affidavits.

Think About This

Officer Frey's report says, "I arrived at the smash and grab and had my fellow officer's six." How might this wording affect the use of this report in the future?

REVIEW NOTES

Review your notes and any statements before you write a report to make sure that you have all the facts. If you are missing certain facts, get them as soon as possible. For example, if a victim's date of birth is missing, contact the victim as soon as possible to get it.

Keep in mind that if you are wearing a body camera, the Florida Statutes allow you to request to review the recorded footage from the body camera before writing a report or providing a statement regarding any event pertaining to your duties.

> LE423.1. Describe how to review notes before writing a report

ORGANIZE INFORMATION

When you organize or group information, it is easier to efficiently write a report. You can organize information in one of the following two ways: by order of events or by category.

When you organize information by order of events, you organize chronologically, sorting the information by the date and time from the first event to the last. By organizing notes chronologically, you can easily write a narrative and explain what happened, when, and in what order.

When you organize information by category, you divide things into groups with things in each group sharing similar characteristics. Examples of categories include witnesses, victims, suspects, weapons used, and crime elements. This type of organization will help you because most report forms group information by type of information. Organizing notes this way before you write the report can minimize the risk of forgetting a piece of information. This practice is helpful for incidents that involve several witnesses or victims.

> LE423.2. Describe two methods for organizing information before writing a report

ELEMENTS OF AN EFFECTIVE REPORT

Report writing requires much more than filling in the blanks on a preprinted form. The largest and most important part of a report is the ***narrative***, a detailed account of an incident and events related to the incident. Normally, narratives are written in complete sentences and detail a sequence of events.

An effective report will not only have good content but also proper formatting. Format refers to the way that information is organized and presented in the report. Your report should present the material aspects of the case and the actions of the subjects, such as who they were with, who was involved, who they think did it, and who the victim is.

Factuality

☑ LE423.3. Recognize the importance of including only the facts in a report

A report must be factual. Include only the facts of the incident represented by the who, what, when, where, why, and how the action was taken. Do not include your personal opinions, judgments, hunches, or guesses in a report, and do not alter any information you obtained about an incident. If you do, it is considered falsifying the report, which is a criminal offense.

For example, consider this sentence: "The victim appears upset and fears for her safety."

A defense attorney might ask you why the victim was afraid. It is possible that you cannot remember and cannot accurately testify about what happened because you did not document the victim's statement or action that indicated why she feared for her safety. Therefore, try to get the victim to explain why she fears for her safety and include that in the report. In addition, different people might have different opinions of what it means to "appear upset."

Instead, it would be better to write, "Sandra's hands were shaking, and she was wiping tears from her face." This description will help the reader visualize Sandra's emotional state.

People could interpret the following statement in different ways: "Jim became uncooperative and belligerent." Instead, document Jim's specific actions and words without adding personal interpretations of his actions.

A better statement would be, "Jim stood in front of me in a fighting stance. When I attempted to handcuff him, he pulled his right arm away and yelled, 'I'm not going anywhere!'"

Include your observations of all witnesses, suspects, victims, and other officers involved in an incident. Report all sides of the story. For example, include an explanation given by each witness, even if the explanation contradicts information given by another witness, and do not alter or paraphrase their words. Do not include unnecessary or vague information, and do not include emotional, sarcastic, humorous, or opinionated content. Reports should only contain facts. Omit unnecessary words and irrelevant material. Remember that a well-written report shows that you are professional and competent, and it can be your greatest strength in court. If you write the report poorly, the defense may try to discredit it.

Clarity

☑ LE423.4. Describe how to write a report using clear and plain language

A report should be clear and allow only one interpretation of each sentence's meaning. Use plain and straightforward language to ensure that the report is clear. It is sometimes acceptable to omit the race or gender of a person from the narrative. For example, you can omit the race or gender when the information has already been documented in the victim, suspect, or witness description boxes on the appropriate agency form or log.

When you refer to a person for the first time, give their full name. In later references, make sure that you properly identify the individual; this is especially important when there are multiple people with the same or a similar name. Be consistent when you identify a person to prevent confusion.

Example: You would first reference the victim by writing "Jane Doe, victim;" afterwards, you may refer to her as "the victim."

If there are multiple victims, refer to them by their last names or their victim numbers in the report.

Example: "Jane Doe, Victim 1," and "Samuel Smith, Victim 2."

Follow your agency's policies for using abbreviations when you refer to victims, witnesses, or suspects in a report. If your agency's policies do not address these issues, comply with the requirements of the state attorney's office.

Conciseness, Completeness, and Accuracy

When you write a report, be concise and to the point. However, do not be so brief that the report is inaccurate, not detailed, or incomplete.

Examples:

"I observed the suspect fleeing the scene in a northerly direction away from me." (wordy)

"I saw Charles Baker running north on First Street." (concise)

To ensure accuracy, include all relevant facts and specific details from your notes and any statements in the report. Remember that you have obtained facts through interviews and investigations. Document all statements made by the victim, suspect, and witnesses. Document their exact words in quotation marks, the emotional state of the people involved according to what they say they feel or think, and indicate the approximate time of the incident in the report.

Proper Usage of Standard English

Standard English refers to the form of language used when speaking and writing wherever English is spoken and understood. Non-standard English is casual or regional, may involve slang, and sometimes does not follow recognized grammatical rules or spelling.

☑ LE423.5. Describe how to use Standard English when writing a report

Always prepare reports using Standard English and avoid using the following when preparing official reports:

- *jargon*—vocabulary used in a profession that has meaning only to the people who work in that particular field or profession. For example, "Signal Zero," "I got your Six," and "smash and grab" are terms that are familiar to law enforcement officers but not to civilians. Use only acronyms that people can recognize and spell them out the first time you mention them. An example would be Smith Memorial Hospital (SMH).

- *slang*—informal, non-standard words often used by regional or specific groups. Do not use slang in a report except when you are quoting someone. Examples include lol (laughing out loud), l8r (later), and ttyl (talk to you later).
- *textspeak*—comes from text messages and digital communications and consists of abbreviations, acronyms, or initials. It does not follow standard grammar, spelling, or punctuation rules. You may use textspeak as a convenient tool for taking notes; however, do not use textspeak in an official report. If you use texting language in a final report, you will appear unprofessional. In addition, you will give others the impression that the information you conveyed is not important. Always remember that the reports you prepare will become public record and may be used in court.

If a witness, victim, or suspect uses jargon, slang, racial slurs, or offensive language, report their exact words using quotation marks. These statements can be valuable to the investigation and point out a person's frame of mind.

You can use jargon, slang, and abbreviations when taking notes so long as you know their meanings, but do not include jargon, slang, textspeak, and abbreviations (except for abbreviations allowed by your agency) in your final report.

Legibility

☑ LE423.6. Explain the importance of using legible handwriting

If you handwrite a report, write clearly and legibly. In some cases, writing in all capital letters is a good solution to poor penmanship as long as doing so follows your agency's policies and procedures. Unless your agency specifies otherwise, use a black or dark blue ballpoint pen for clear legibility and the best photocopying quality possible. A perfectly written report is useless if no one can read it.

Timeliness

☑ LE423.7. Describe the timeline for completing and submitting a report

Complete your report as soon as possible after the incident. Doing so helps you avoid forgetting important details. When you immediately prepare a report, you may be able to recall important facts that you did not record in your notes.

After you complete a report, turn it in by the end of your shift unless your agency's policies state otherwise. If you submit the report late, you may hinder other operations, impact the investigation, and delay the preparation of a prosecution.

If you need to conduct further investigations, you may have to write a supplemental report.

Proper Identification of the Statute Violated and Elements of the Crime

When writing a report about a crime, be sure to properly identify the correct name of the crime and the statute that was violated, and outline the elements of the crime. If you do not provide this information, the entire report may be questioned. You will learn more about documenting the elements of crimes in Chapters 7 and 8.

Introduction, Body, and Conclusion

To present a clear narrative, a report should contain an introduction, a body, and a conclusion. The introduction of a report usually includes:

- the date and time of the incident
- the location of the incident
- the identity of the victim, suspect, or complainant
- your assignment and arrival time
- your name
- your initial actions

☑ LE423.8. Describe how to compose the three main parts of a report narrative

The body contains the narrative and a detailed chronological account of the incident. This section includes the investigative actions that you took, and it should address the elements of the crime. Often, the body of the report may contain one, two, or more paragraphs, depending on the complexity of the case and the number of people involved.

The conclusion explains how you resolved the situation. It also describes how you handled the information you obtained. It includes any citations you may have issued or any arrests you have made, and it documents the appropriate criminal charges.

Just because a report typically contains three sections does not mean you should limit the report to one paragraph per section.

The content of the narrative should answer the following four questions:

- Why were you there? For example:
  - Were you dispatched to a call at the location?
  - Were you flagged down while on patrol?
  - Did you see or think something occurred while on patrol?
- What did you observe? For example:
  - What did you see, hear, smell, or feel?
  - What were the crime scene conditions?
  - What did the people at the scene tell you?
  - Who else responded to the scene?
- What did you do? For example:
  - What investigative steps did you take?
  - What other actions did you perform (such as, CPR, response to resistance)?
  - Who did you interview?
  - Who did you notify about the situation?

- Did you collect any evidence?
- What did you do with any collected evidence?
• What were the outcomes? For example:
    - What crimes were committed?
    - Did you make any arrests?
    - What related documents were collected or disseminated?
    - Were any further actions or referrals required?

WRITING A PROBABLE CAUSE AFFIDAVIT

You will recall from Chapter 3 that a probable cause affidavit must be presented in court in order to justify an arrest. Depending on your agency's policies and procedures, you may be required to write probable cause affidavits.

> LE423.9. Explain how to write a probable cause affidavit

Use your agency's approved form for your jurisdiction, and record the suspect's personal identifying information in the affidavit. Before writing the affidavit narrative, review the following:

- evidence
- witness statements
- incident or supplemental reports

A probable cause affidavit must contain a description of the offense with sufficient facts to show the probable cause of each element of the charged offense. For example, to arrest someone for battery, you must show that the suspect intentionally touched or struck the victim against the victim's will. It should set out for the judge the facts and circumstances that justify the arrest. Some jurisdictions may require more information in the narrative, so follow your agency's policies and procedures.

Some of the facts in the affidavit may include the:

- date and time
- location
- city or county where the offense occurred
- offense charged and the correct Florida Statutes section number or county or municipal ordinance
- reason for the contact, seizure, or both
- any other information necessary to establish probable cause
- name of the victims (Florida law protects against the release of any identifying information of sexual battery victims)
- the accused's name, address, identifying information, and a description
- any statement made by the accused

- names and addresses of all parties present (including the names of supervisors)
- if and why a search occurred

The officer who made the arrest should review the narrative to make sure it is complete and accurate. Correct any grammatical or typographical errors before swearing to the truthfulness of the affidavit, and then sign it. Another officer, a notary, a deputy clerk, or a clerk of the court who administered the oath to the arresting officer must also sign as required by law. Attach any supplemental information to the probable cause affidavit. This information may include the names and addresses of essential witnesses, witnesses' statements, or a list of seized tangible evidence. Follow your agency's policies or rules on how to include, approve, and submit supplemental documents.

UNIT 2 WRITING A REPORT
LESSON 4 Reviewing a Report Before Submission

Lesson Goal

At the end of this lesson, you will be able to evaluate a report for factuality, clarity, correctness, and completeness.

You should always evaluate a report after you finish writing it. Take your time and carefully examine it. Make sure that you have included all of the relevant facts from your notes and any statements in an organized and accurate manner.

CONSIDERATIONS IN THE REVIEW PROCESS

Review the content in the report to see if you have included answers to the questions of who, what, when, where, why, and how, and any actions taken. Make sure to include details on the elements of the crime. Check to see if you have recorded all of the procedures that you followed, including notifications and victims' rights brochures if applicable.

☑ LE424.1. Explain how to evaluate a report for thoroughness and errors

To effectively evaluate a report for errors, review its content for the following:

- spelling—ensure that all words are spelled correctly.
- grammar—make sure that your verb tense is consistent and your sentence structures are correct. All sentences must be written using active voice.
- punctuation—check for the correct use and placement of punctuation, including commas, apostrophes, and quotation marks.
- capitalization—verify that the appropriate words are capitalized.
- vocabulary—select the appropriate words and use them correctly.
- typographical errors—assess for keystroke errors, especially for words that the spellcheck feature might miss.

Make sure the information is clear. The report narrative should flow properly, make sense, and contain complete sentences. Check to see if you need to add or delete any information. If audio or video recording is available, review it before finalizing the report to avoid any contradictions. When possible, have another officer read the report to catch any mistakes and verify that it makes sense before you submit it.

In addition to the resources in your textbook, there are online resources available to help you improve your grammar, punctuation, spelling, and vocabulary.

The following exercise will help you practice your proofreading skills. These skills are necessary for editing reports.

EXERCISE

Correct the following exercise using Standard English grammar rules, and make sure the narrative is free of jargon and slang:

> On 16 Feb 08 at 1220 hours this officer responded to 2615 Airport Av Apt 65, Ponte Vedra Beach, reference a disturbance. Upon arrival, this officer scoped out what sounded like a loud verbal dispute emanating from within the home. Subsequently, this officer made contact with the owner of the dwelling, Doris Wardley, to assure the safety of anyone inside the apt. The defendant advised that her TV was on and that what this officer heard was a movie on TV. The defendant appeared confrontational and hostile to this officer's presence. The defendant told this officer to get outta my face and attempted to shut the door with great force. this officer detected a strong odor that this officer recognized as marijuana coming from within the apt. this officer asked s1 if she had any illegal narcotics on her person. At stated time def provided a pack of rolling papers and a small baggie containing a green leafy substance from her right pant pocket. Such substance was tested using a dept issued kit. The examination results were presumptive positive for cannabis. Subj was placed under arrest and advised on her Mirandi Right. Def was transported to the slammer by this officer.

Chapter 5
Fundamentals of Patrol

UNIT 1 PATROL BASICS
- LESSON 1 Patrolling / 163
- LESSON 2 Officer Safety and Survival / 166
- LESSON 3 Electronic Communications / 170
- LESSON 4 Electronic Sources of Information / 174

UNIT 2 DUTIES ON PATROL
- LESSON 1 Initial Response / 178
- LESSON 2 Approaching and Contacting a Suspect / 182
- LESSON 3 Responding as Backup / 185
- LESSON 4 Behavioral Threat Assessment and Management / 186

UNIT 3 NON-CRIMINAL CALLS FOR SERVICE
- LESSON 1 Assisting Your Community / 189
- LESSON 2 Well-Being and Security Checks / 191
- LESSON 3 Death Notifications / 193
- LESSON 4 Animal Complaints / 195
- LESSON 5 Fire-Related Incidents / 196
- LESSON 6 Lost, Stolen, or Recovered Property / 198
- LESSON 7 Property Disputes / 200
- LESSON 8 Civil Disturbance / 202
- LESSON 9 Crowd Control / 204

UNIT 4 STRUCTURE AND AREA SEARCHES
- LESSON 1 Alarms and Searches / 206
- LESSON 2 Area Searches / 210

UNIT 5 ARREST PROCEDURES
- LESSON 1 Taking Custody of the Suspect / 214
- LESSON 2 Processing the Arrestee / 218

UNIT 1 PATROL BASICS
LESSON 1 Patrolling

Lesson Goal

At the end of this lesson, you will know how to create community partnerships and become familiar with your assigned patrol area.

Think About This

You are a new officer and have just been assigned to patrol a new community that you are not familiar with. What are some ways that you can get to know your community while on patrol? Why is this important?

Patrolling is the main activity that you will perform daily. This chapter provides an overview of the law enforcement techniques and tactics that you will use while on patrol. This includes the use of communications equipment, community-oriented policing, and officer safety and survival skills. It also explains how to respond to non-criminal calls, how to conduct structure and area searches, and provides resources that officers use while on patrol.

The primary purposes of patrolling are to maintain a public presence, enforce laws and ordinances, and deter crime. Patrolling an assigned area also includes building a relationship with your community by developing resident and community contacts and providing information to residents.

Reactive patrol is about responding to or dealing with a crime after it occurs. It requires responding immediately to an incident to increase the likelihood of catching a subject. This strategy exists in traditional policing where you are more likely to answer calls and take reports about recurring problems in your community.

☑ LE511.1. Differentiate between reactive and proactive patrol activities

Proactive patrol discourages criminal activity by having an officer regularly present in the area. To make your presence known, you must continuously travel through the patrol area and speak to people for short periods. You must talk to residents and interact with the public so that you can establish close ties with your community members, who you can turn to for information in the future.

COMMUNITY-ORIENTED POLICING

Community-oriented policing is a concept that encourages the community to work with law enforcement and address what causes crime and other issues affecting the community. The goal of community policing is to look at issues that are typical of certain neighborhoods and to work with the community to fight these problems.

Community-oriented policing has two main parts: community partnerships and problem solving. Community partnerships increase understanding and trust between law enforcement agencies and their communities. Community partners can include law enforcement representatives (elected, sworn, or civilian), government representatives

☑ LE511.2. Explain the concepts that contribute to community-oriented policing

(public housing and mental health agencies), and community representatives (local businesses, professional groups, and neighborhood leaders).

The second part of community-oriented policing is problem solving. Community partnerships allow law enforcement agencies to develop long-term, proactive programs and ways to address problems in the community. For example, you can make conversation with the owners of a local restaurant and the people who are dining there. Another way you can build community partnerships is by stopping to play basketball with youth that you see while out on patrol. Positive and professional relationships allow information sharing to learn about crime-related issues in the community. They also establish a bond and inform the community about the methods that law enforcement agencies use to perform their duties.

PREPARING TO PATROL

Duty Equipment Inspection

The equipment used while on patrol is vital to an officer's safety and effectiveness. Because you will rely on these tools, you must routinely make sure that each piece of equipment is working and is stored safely.

☑ LE511.3. Describe how to inspect duty equipment for functionality and safety

At the beginning of your shift, check all of the items on your duty belt to make sure all equipment is present and functional. You should have a working flashlight for every shift. Inspect patrol vehicles to make sure that all equipment is working, and make sure that the preventive maintenance on your vehicle is up to date. Regularly check the functionality of emergency equipment, such as fire extinguishers, biohazard gear, and first-aid kits. Never assume that others have maintained equipment.

If your agency permits or requires you to wear a body camera, you will be trained on its proper use, maintenance, and storage. You will also be trained on the types of law enforcement activities that you can or are required to record. Make sure you know these legal requirements as well as how long you must keep any data that your body camera records.

Roll Call

☑ LE511.4. Describe the purpose of a roll call

Roll call is a brief operational meeting that officers attend before starting a shift. It provides information about current issues to keep in mind while on patrol. Information shared at roll call comes from the oral instruction of supervisors and the records and reports of officers from previous shifts. Some agencies broadcast information using computer systems, radios, telephones, or other media. Record all roll call information that may affect your shift including BOLOs, addresses that require or request extra patrol, wanted and missing persons, stolen vehicles, stolen and lost vehicle license plates, suspicious incidents, officer safety bulletins, and safety concerns.

BECOMING FAMILIAR WITH THE PATROL AREA

One of the first things you will learn as a patrol officer is the layout of your assigned area, district, or jurisdiction. Your patrol area may remain the same or change daily depending upon factors related to staffing, the number of calls your agency receives, and individual assignments.

Before going on patrol, identify the boundaries of your assigned patrol area. Become familiar with your assigned area by learning about the major roads, landmarks, and community resources so that you can respond quickly. Always have a map with important landmarks and patrol areas highlighted.

☑ LE511.5. Explain how to become familiar with your assigned patrol area

Identify people in the area such as neighborhood watches, business owners, mail carriers, utility and sanitation workers, newspaper delivery people, or anyone who walks or drives through the neighborhood regularly. Be familiar with your community's resources such as shelters, social service agencies, or internal agency resources.

Throughout a shift, your patrol status will change. Inform dispatch about any changes to your availability and location while on duty. Know your patrol area so that you can recognize *suspicious activity*, which is any activity that is abnormal for a specific time of day in a particular area.

Knowledge of the law and community and good observational skills will help you determine whether any suspicious activity is a crime in progress. For example, while patrolling a neighborhood at 2 a.m., you may notice an interior vehicle light on. This could be an indicator of criminal activity such as a vehicle burglary.

Identify and remove dangers that can be a threat to public safety, such as removing the door of a discarded refrigerator or reporting a broken streetlight. This kind of proactive patrolling anticipates and removes potential hazards and protects your community.

PATROL METHODS

You can patrol in a variety of ways. Three of the most common types of patrol are done by motor vehicle, foot, and bicycle. Forms of specialized patrol include marine, mounted, air, all-terrain vehicle (ATV), motorcycle, and personal transporters.

The area you are patrolling dictates which patrol method to use. While using a vehicle allows you to cover larger areas, it can also isolate you from residents and divert your attention. Foot patrol has many advantages, such as allowing you to be visible to the public and accessible to your community. You will also be able to closely investigate community concerns and observe activity in specific areas.

☑ LE511.6. Compare the advantages and disadvantages of patrolling by vehicle and by foot

Patrolling on foot during the day or during the night has different advantages. During the day, you are highly visible to your community members and have greater access to the environment you are patrolling. This increased access can help you more efficiently observe minor details in your surroundings. At night, you can use darkness to conceal your approach to calls for service. Day or night, keep changing your patrol routine to keep others from predicting your patrol patterns. A combination of vehicle and foot patrol allows you to cover a large area and closely observe specific areas.

UNIT 1 PATROL BASICS
LESSON 2 Officer Safety and Survival

Lesson Goal

At the end of this lesson, you will be able to use your senses, training, and mental and physical fitness to preserve public and officer safety when serving your community.

Think About This

While on patrol, you approach a suspect as he pulls a gun out of his pocket. Which would be the best option for cover: a dumpster on your left or a wooden fence on your right?

Safety is an important aspect of your job as a law enforcement officer. To properly protect the public, you must also keep yourself safe. Officer safety should be assessed constantly. Stay alert at all times and maintain situational awareness. Improper training, poor planning, carelessness, and complacency can all contribute to officer fatalities and injuries. Other factors that impact your safety include the people you interact with, your view of the scene or people involved, your ability to communicate with dispatch, or whether or not a suspect is armed or can easily reach a makeshift weapon. The community partnership that you establish can help keep you safe. It is important to be aware of the entire situation as it evolves during a call for service, traffic stop, or any other encounter.

OBSERVATIONAL SKILLS

☑ LE512.1. Explain the role of observation while on duty

Observation is the act of recognizing an occurrence using your senses by noticing people, things, or circumstances. You can improve your observational skills through practice, such as memorizing descriptions of cars, people, and details at a scene. When observing others, take note of their appearance, height, weight, hair, clothing, approximate age, and other personal details. Focus on situations or behaviors that are important to law enforcement including what is usual or unusual activity within a certain area. Do not get distracted by a few elements, but observe the entire scene before making a judgment.

COVER AND CONCEALMENT

When you arrive at a scene, immediately identify cover and concealment areas that can be used to observe activity.

☑ LE512.2. Explain the difference between cover and concealment

Cover is anything that creates a bullet-resistant barrier between an officer and a threat, and it protects you from incoming gunfire. Examples of cover may include automobile engine blocks, brick walls, dirt embankments, concrete, steel, and thick wood. Keep your head and body protected by moving from cover to cover as you approach or advance on a shooter.

Concealment is an object or group of objects that creates a visual barrier between an officer and a threat but may not stop a projectile. These objects provide camouflage but will not stop incoming gunfire. Examples of concealment may include shrubs, fences, interior walls, and objects that keep you hidden from view and provide a position from which you can observe. It is preferable to use cover rather than concealment.

USING THE SENSES

Sight is often the starting point for observation. Be aware of various environmental and physical factors that can affect your vision. Visual defects like nearsightedness and farsightedness limit your vision if you do not wear corrective lenses. Lighting from objects, such as streetlights or fluorescent lamps, can distort color perception. Dimly lit objects tend to blend into the background and are hard to distinguish.

☑ LE512.3. Explain how to use your senses to identify safety concerns

Hearing that is affected by background noises, such as traffic, noises from residences, or environmental sounds, may prevent you from recognizing specific sounds that indicate a crime or incident is in progress.

Smell can help you identify dangerous or illegal substances. If you smell gasoline, petroleum products, natural gas, or gunpowder, you may determine that there is a potential threat; however, weather conditions or your health can affect your sense of smell. Odors in an outdoor environment can hide other smells, and substances with strong odors, like gasoline or ether, can inhibit your ability to smell. Some easily identifiable hazardous materials, such as chlorine gas or ammonia, are also harmful if inhaled. For example, fentanyl, in a fine-powdered form, can be fatal if inhaled and left untreated. Keep in mind that some hazardous substances are not easily recognized. Use caution when opening and closing containers (coolers, boxes, thermos-style containers) to identify contents. Do not smell the contents of a container, especially when dealing with any unknown substance.

Touch can help you identify items during a search or identify clues that can be used in an investigation. For example, touching tires or engines to check for heat will help determine if a vehicle was recently driven. When using your sense of touch, always wear gloves and appropriate personal protective equipment (PPE) to avoid touching something hazardous, such as biohazardous materials or fentanyl-laced drugs. Wearing gloves will also ensure that you do not disturb the crime scene.

While taste is an important sense, it should never be used to identify an unknown substance. Attempting to taste a substance to determine its origin will put you at risk for sickness or death if it is a drug or poison.

SAFETY AND SURVIVAL PROCEDURES

Under the stress of a survival situation, revert to your training. Survival readiness may include tactical preparedness, such as having a plan anytime you enter a building, firearm proficiency, physical fitness, situational awareness, and first-aid skills. Use mental conditioning or the will to survive, and practice tactical preparedness to respond quickly and safely to a situation. By studying, mentally rehearsing, and regularly practicing safety procedures, you can be prepared for difficult situations.

☑ LE512.4. Identify basic tactics to ensure officer safety and survival

The circumstances of a situation will dictate the tactics you use. Always be alert, and use your observational skills to identify potential dangers. Remember several basic safety tips when on duty:

- Practice **situational awareness**, which is the ability to pay attention to what is going on around you. It requires staying aware of your environment so that you remain alert and are able to respond appropriately. Do not become complacent. Visually assess your surroundings, the number of people at the scene, the position of their hands, and threats, such as weapons or items that could be used as weapons.

- Avoid **tunnel vision**, sometimes referred to as funnel vision, which is the narrowing of the field of view during a stressful event, such as a vehicle pursuit, foot chase, or armed confrontation. Tunnel vision can cause you to miss other possible danger signs. To avoid tunnel vision, scan your surroundings, practice controlled breathing and task-relevant self-talk.

- Always identify yourself as a law enforcement officer and give direct commands, such as "stop" or "don't move!" Speak in the appropriate tone of voice for the situation.

- If you believe a suspect is armed, call for backup units and use appropriate tactics to contact, control, and disarm the suspect. Disarm a suspect before leaving cover if possible. If you shoot a suspect, notify dispatch as soon as possible. Do not holster your weapon or rush to the injured suspect until you have deemed the suspect is no longer a threat or ensured that there are no other shooters or accomplices. Perform a self-check to make sure you are not injured, and communicate with responding backup. Stay behind cover and wait for backup officers before approaching the suspect. When appropriate, handcuff the suspect and provide first aid as needed.

- While in a patrol vehicle, you may face an attack from gunfire, firebombs, rocks, or other projectiles. If this happens, immediately get away from the area, roll up the windows, and turn off air conditioning to prevent chemicals from getting into the vehicle. Abandon your vehicle if it becomes disabled or if there is no other avenue of escape.

- If you are on foot and come under gunfire, seek immediate cover, call for assistance, and determine a safe approach for responding officers.

FACTORS THAT COMPROMISE OFFICER SAFETY

Officers have a variety of equipment, including firearms, intermediate weapons, ballistic vests, flashlights, electronic devices, and handcuffs. Vehicles may have spotlights, takedown lights, a public address (PA) system, emergency lights, and sirens.

☑ LE512.5. Describe the importance of maintaining equipment, level of training, and physical fitness

Check all equipment regularly, and keep it clean and in good working order at all times. Make sure all electronic devices are charged. If you do not use and maintain your equipment and it breaks down, you could be seriously injured or killed.

Train regularly and know how to use your equipment. If you do not keep yourself updated on training, you can cause serious injury or death to you or others. You might fire your weapon only once in the line of duty, and when that time comes, you must be fully prepared to use the firearm safely and effectively. Constant training will help you develop the mindset and attitude required to keep you and the public safe.

You need to be in good physical condition to handle the demands of dangerous situations. Being in poor shape puts you, other officers, and the public in danger. Getting enough sleep and having an exercise and wellness program is an important part of your fitness for duty.

Your ability to observe danger and signs of criminal activity is another important part of patrolling. If you are busy or distracted, you may miss potential danger signs and cause injury or death to yourself, other officers, or civilians.

☑ LE512.6. Recognize the importance of maintaining an appropriate mindset and situational awareness

When interacting with someone, pay attention to non-verbal cues. These cues involve a person's body language, such as where they place their hands and if they are leaning away from or toward you. Always be aware of a person's hand placement because you may be able to stop them from using a weapon if they have one.

Never assume that a call is routine. Each call is different, and you must be prepared to react properly to each situation. Responding to a call without the appropriate mindset or attitude may cause you to become complacent during a potentially life-threatening situation. The ability to remain alert and observe your surroundings is crucial. You are expected to confront dangerous situations, so rely on your training and experience, not emotional reactions, to perform your duties safely.

UNIT 1 PATROL BASICS
LESSON 3 Electronic Communications

Lesson Goal

At the end of this lesson, you will be able to practice professional use of mobile communication devices while on duty.

Think About This

Dispatch is routinely missing the first half of radio transmissions from Officer Rollins. What can she do to fix this situation?

☑ LE513.1. Identify the role of mobile communication devices while on duty

Law enforcement relies heavily on mobile communication devices such as radios, laptops, tablets, and smartphones. You may use mobile communication devices to access information regarding criminal records, driving history, and agency records, or you may use these devices to help complete a number of daily routine tasks such as checking in and out when on and off duty, viewing and receiving calls for service, receiving dispatch information to minimize radio traffic, and sending electronic reports to a supervisor.

Database access agreements and agency policies set rules on the dissemination of electronic information. All computer activity is recorded per the FBI's security policy and is subject to review under public records law. With this in mind, always be professional whenever you use any form of electronic communication. This includes texting, emailing, and communicating via the radio.

While mobile communication devices are useful, they can often distract and reduce your observation skills and safety. Minimize the use of these mobile devices while driving a patrol vehicle to avoid causing a crash.

USING THE RADIO

☑ LE513.2. Identify the importance of radio communication

The radio is the most common communication device that officers use. You will use the radio to send and receive vital information to and from dispatch or other officers, call for backup, or identify a suspect or wanted person. For your safety, it is essential to know how to use the radio.

Basic police radio communication depends on three types of equipment:

- dispatch console or base station
- vehicle-mounted radio
- portable or handheld radio

Most agency radio systems consist of multiple channels such as primary dispatch, talk around, and specialized. During critical incidents, dispatch can patch, or merge, radio channels so multiple agencies can communicate.

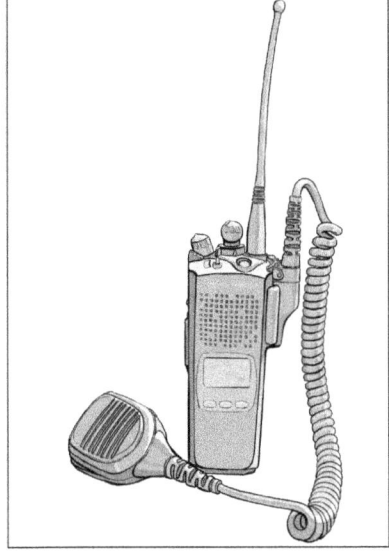
Figure 5-1 Handheld radio

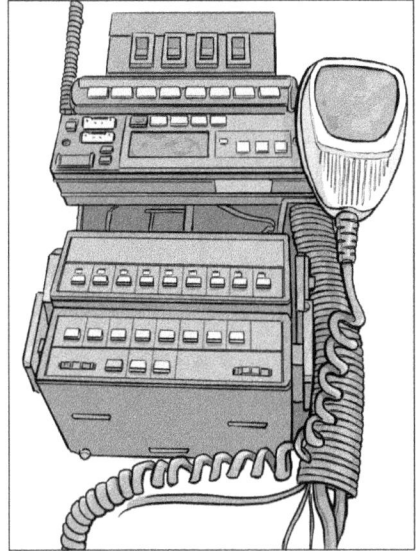
Figure 5-2 Vehicle radio

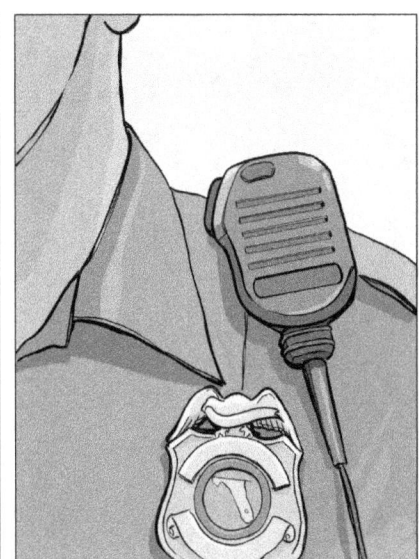
Figure 5-3 Shoulder microphone

Law enforcement uses many brands, models, and types of radios. However, radios generally have controls and indicators for power, volume, channel selection, and transmission.

☑ LE513.3. Describe the main components of radio equipment

COMMUNICATIONS PERSONNEL

Public safety telecommunicators (PSTs), also known as dispatchers, are the hub of contact for patrol officers. **Dispatchers** transmit calls, receive calls for assistance from officers, broadcast information about wanted and missing persons, check records, and perform many other tasks daily to assist patrol officers.

Dispatchers are generally non-sworn personnel who operate the radio and telecommunications systems. They typically work in a centralized area with access to telephones and other resources to assist you. Their duties include answering, receiving, transferring, and dispatching functions related to 911 calls. Dispatchers must do the following:

☑ LE513.4. Identify the duties of dispatch personnel

- dispatch law enforcement officers
- dispatch fire, rescue, and emergency medical services (EMS)
- dispatch other public safety services to the scene of an emergency
- provide real-time information from federal, state, and local crime databases

RADIO CONDUCT AND PROCEDURES

When using the radio, conduct all radio communication in a professional manner. Understand that you should have no expectation of privacy. Transmit sensitive information or criminal history details by radio only when there is an officer or public safety concern. Specialized units may use technology such as scrambled or encrypted channels to increase operational security.

LE513.5. Describe the professional use of law enforcement radio transmissions

Make sure you set your portable radio at the proper volume level. It should be loud enough for you to hear, but not so loud that it is disruptive. You may use an earpiece to prevent eavesdropping.

Transmit only information related to law enforcement business. Appropriate radio system use includes relaying the following information:

- law enforcement-related messages to other agencies
- driver license status and driver history
- calls for service
- criminal records checks
- hazardous material queries
- vehicle, boat, and aircraft registration queries
- road and weather conditions

Radio Protocol

Radio protocol describes the customs and regulations for constructing and transmitting radio messages. It also includes the proper use of codes and signals, which may be different among agencies and regions.

Some agencies use a phonetic-alphabet or uniform codes while others prefer plain talk, which is speaking in a clear, concise, professional manner without signals or codes. Radio codes and signals save airtime and express exact and definite meanings. They also keep radio communications consistent and professional. Use the appropriate codes when you are near a suspect to reduce the risks and dangers of exposing your actions.

LE513.6. Describe basic radio code systems

There are four basic radio codes:

- *Signals* communication is a system that uses the word "signal" before numbers; for example, "signal 0" often means an armed person.
- The *phonetic-alphabet* system uses the letters of the English alphabet to identify letters in voice communication; for example, "A" = Alpha, "B" = Bravo.
- The *numeric or 10-code* system uses the number "10" before other numbers that represent specific activities; for example, "10-15" often means prisoner in custody.
- The *alphanumeric code* system combines letters and numbers that may include officer call signs or vehicle license plate numbers; for example, "RVB632" may be spoken as "Romeo Victor Bravo Six Three Two."

Your agency might use codes that are different from these and will train you in their radio language. You are expected to become proficient in your agency's language when using a radio to communicate.

Before making a voice transmission, listen to make sure there is no other radio traffic. Press and hold the transmit button down for about one second before speaking, otherwise your first words will be lost. Use proper microphone techniques to send clear radio transmissions. Speak directly into the microphone with a clear, even tone of voice.

In stressful situations, your voice may fluctuate which can make the radio message difficult to understand. Keep your voice from fluctuating by controlling your breathing and using other stress management techniques. Be professional at all times.

Officers working high-priority calls may ask dispatch to designate a radio channel for emergency traffic only. Dispatch will then alert other officers to refrain from transmitting on that channel. Monitor transmissions from other units at all times in case other units need backup.

If your radio does not work, use another means of communicating. You may need to switch to another channel or call dispatch to report the failure.

INTERACTIONS WITH DISPATCH

Depending on your agency policies, you may have to notify dispatch whenever you go on or off duty. Checking in and out during your shift is important for your safety. Communicate with dispatch throughout your shift so that dispatch can send calls for service to you and monitor your status and safety.

Receiving and Answering Calls

Stay aware of all radio transmissions in case another officer is in trouble. When you receive a call from dispatch, respond with your assigned identification and current location. Record the information that dispatch provides, and do not leave anything to memory. This may include the type of complaint, incident location, and the suspect's description. Advise dispatch when you arrive at the scene of the call and if you need backup or any additional resources.

☑ LE513.7. Describe how to communicate with dispatch

Constructing the Message

Provide accurate information that is brief and concise. Plan your messages before transmitting them. Messages should provide essential information, such as officer identification, current location, the reason for the call, and information specific to the situation.

Officer-Initiated Transmission

While on patrol, you may see a situation that you need to investigate. Whenever you take self-initiated action during patrol, give dispatch the following information as applicable:

- your identification and location
- the type of situation (such as vehicle crash, fire, or disturbance)
- the type of assistance needed (such as backup, ambulance, or tow truck)
- a description of involved people or groups
- a description of the vehicle(s) (license information, color, make, and model)

UNIT 1 PATROL BASICS
LESSON 4 Electronic Sources of Information

Lesson Goal

At the end of this lesson, you will be able to use criminal justice information systems, including the Florida Crime Information Center (FCIC) and the National Crime Information Center (NCIC), while performing law enforcement duties.

Think About This

A new neighbor is moving into your subdivision, and you want to do a background check on him. What are the potential consequences of this action?

Querying is the process of gathering information by entering or running a search in a database for law enforcement purposes. It is sometimes called a vehicle check, records check, or wants and warrants check.

When you are on patrol and need information quickly, dispatch may conduct queries for you. You may also run the information yourself using a computer in your patrol vehicle. This lesson discusses some of the databases you will use and rely on in your daily work.

FLORIDA CRIME INFORMATION CENTER (FCIC) / NATIONAL CRIME INFORMATION CENTER (NCIC)

☑ LE514.1. Describe the type of information available through the FCIC and NCIC databases

The *Florida Crime Information Center (FCIC)* is a database housed at the Florida Department of Law Enforcement (FDLE) that provides statewide information on the following:

- people and property
- driver licenses and registrations
- wanted and missing persons
- stolen guns, vehicles, securities, and other property
- people's status files and computerized criminal histories
- concealed weapon licenses

FCIC is connected to the *National Crime Information Center (NCIC)*. NCIC is a national database maintained by the FBI, and it contains records of stolen, abandoned, and recovered property and wanted and missing person files. It also contains the National Sex Offender Registry as well as the files of people who are on supervised release, have active protection orders, are foreign fugitives or immigration violators, and are known or suspected terrorists or gang members. These records are from all 50 states, Canada, the U.S. Virgin Islands, the Commonwealth of Puerto Rico, and the District of Columbia.

FCIC INFORMATION SOURCES

FCIC contains the criminal histories of people who have been arrested in Florida. When a person is arrested, the booking agency first submits the person's arrest information and fingerprints to FDLE. FDLE then reviews the information and the fingerprints and creates a computerized criminal history (CCH) in FCIC. A state attorney's office, a clerk of court, and the Department of Corrections can add more charges, arrests, dispositions, and other information. CCH information is always changing. After using printed CCH information, destroy it by shredding or burning any copies.

To create a reliable record, agencies must enter information into FCIC accurately. That is why the information you record in arrest reports or on fingerprint cards must be correct, from the spelling of suspects' names to the laws they violated. You must provide the original report and any supplemental documents to enter the information into FCIC/NCIC. Follow your agency's policies and procedures when adding information to the system or when querying a database.

Only law enforcement agencies that are open 24 hours a day, seven days a week can enter data about stolen property and wanted and missing persons into FCIC. The entering agency is responsible for the accuracy, timeliness, and detail of the records entered as well as the removal of information when it is no longer needed.

FCIC/NCIC ACCESS AND RESTRICTIONS

FCIC/NCIC is a large system that contains sensitive information. For this reason, you must complete a Criminal Justice Information Services (CJIS) certification training course and pass a certification exam before you are allowed access to FCIC/NCIC. Users must also agree to a state and national fingerprint-based background check within 30 days of starting their job or of being assigned to an FCIC terminal. Computers with CJIS access must have physical security so that unauthorized persons do not have access to the system.

☑ LE514.2. Identify the certification requirements and restrictions for using the FCIC/NCIC system

All information contained in criminal justice databases is strictly for law enforcement use. The only exception is that you may give registration and lien information to towing companies.

Using the FCIC/NCIC system for purposes other than your law enforcement duties may result in disciplinary action, loss of your certification, and criminal charges. In addition, the agency that you work for may be held liable and could potentially lose access to the system.

FCIC/NCIC logs all user transactions; these can be electronically retrieved when requested. The logs are used for system compliance, criminal investigations, suspected system misuse, public records requests, and administrative purposes.

USING THE FCIC/NCIC SYSTEM

☑ LE514.3. Explain how to perform a database query of a person or property using the FCIC/NCIC system

You need to provide dispatch with as much of the following information as possible to perform an accurate FCIC/NCIC query:

- person query—provide the person's name, race, date of birth, and sex.
- stolen property query—provide basic information about the item.
- firearm—provide the serial number and the manufacturer.
- vehicle—provide the vehicle registration, the vehicle identification number (VIN), or the registration decal number.
  - vessel—provide the hull identification number (HIN), the vessel registration number, or the registration decal number. The FCIC/NCIC reply will describe the vehicle or vessel and include the owner's name and address.
  - other stolen property—provide information such as the item category and manufacturer and a description of the property, any distinct markings, its shape, or any other special identifiers.

When you query the FCIC/NCIC database, the results will show a list of possible matches if the data are the same or similar to the information submitted.

To make sure that the person or property is an exact match, you may need to provide additional information, such as the person's height, weight, scars, tattoos, birthmarks, Social Security number, and driver license number and the licensing state or authority; the vehicle's make, model, year, and bumper stickers; the firearm's model and caliber; and the property's engravings. An exact match in a database is called a **hit**. You, or your agency's designee, must confirm a hit to make sure that it matches the person or item before you arrest a wanted person or recover a missing person or stolen property. To confirm a hit, contact the agency that entered the information into the database to verify that the information is correct.

The purpose of the hit confirmation process is to make sure that the information in the system is active and matches the person or property of interest. The process also helps you avoid arresting someone by mistake when the warrant has expired or the information is incorrect. In addition, a hit confirmation provides more details on what action may be taken, such as arresting the suspect or confiscating the stolen property.

Even if the hit indicates that the entering agency does not require a wanted person's extradition, you should still contact the entering agency in case they desire a follow-up report. **Extradition** is the surrender of a fugitive to another state or nation that has jurisdiction.

CRIMINAL JUSTICE DATABASES

Sometimes, you may need to use other criminal justice databases when conducting a person or property check. Agencies may use additional criminal justice databases that are not listed here.

The Florida Department of Highway Safety and Motor Vehicles (FLHSMV) maintains an online search database known as the Driver and Vehicle Information Database (DAVID).

Authorized users have the ability to view the following:

- driver license applications, information, photographs, and signatures
- state-issued identification cards
- identification documents used by non-citizens
- driving and vehicle history for motorists
- insurance information
- records of vehicles or vessels registered in Florida

You can also request that a driver be reassessed for a driver license or a medical review through DAVID. For more information regarding driver reassessments or re-examinations, refer to Chapter 12. When you query DAVID about a vehicle or vessel registration, FLHSMV will also check the FCIC/NCIC database for stolen vehicles or vessels.

Members of the criminal justice community use the Criminal Justice Network (CJNet) to access many other valuable information databases. These include InSite (a statewide crime intelligence database), Florida's Integrated Criminal History System (FALCON), Child Abduction Response Team (CART), and the Florida Sexual Offender and Predator database. Your agency's policies and procedures explain which databases are available to you and how to access them.

Improper management of criminal databases and information is a misuse of your position. The Florida Statutes state that it is a felony to willfully, knowingly, and without authorization access or allow access to any criminal justice computer, computer system, or computer network. The computer networks in criminal justice that require authorized access include DAVID and FCIC/NCIC. An officer who accesses or allows access to any criminal justice computer, computer system, or computer network without authorization may be subject to prosecution.

☑ LE514.4. Identify the information available through criminal justice online sources

UNIT 2 DUTIES ON PATROL
LESSON 1 Initial Response

◎ Lesson Goal

At the end of this lesson, you will be able to safely respond to and approach a scene, gather initial information, and respond to a BOLO.

Think About This

You are dispatched to conduct a welfare check. You advise dispatch that you are en route, but you remain at lunch. An officer arrives first on scene to back you up and is attacked by a subject. What would have been a better initial response on your part?

RESPONDING TO A CALL

When receiving a call, evaluate the situation based on the information you receive from dispatch. Even though incidents vary, use the same basic steps when responding to calls for service. Once dispatch has notified you of an incident, respond and let them know you are on your way.

☑ LE521.1. Describe how to respond to a location using information from dispatch

Determine the safest response to the scene that will protect you, other officers, and the public. You may have access to electronic mapping systems to locate areas quickly. Keep these systems updated to have the most current maps, but also keep physical maps in your patrol vehicle. When selecting a route, identify the safest and quickest route to the location. The most direct route may not always be the quickest because of construction projects, street closings, or special events. Always consider traffic, time of day, school zones, and congested areas before deciding which route to take.

Collect as much information as possible about the call. Identify the type of incident, the location, the complainant's name, and their relationship to the location. Ask if this location has had other incidents. Use personal knowledge or information from dispatch to identify the risks in the area. Dispatch may also tell you if someone is injured.

While on your way, consider the safest arrival point and the possible threats at the incident. Threats may include weapons (firearms, knives, or explosives), things that can be used as weapons (broken glass, stones, sticks, baseball bats, or branches), and hazards (fire, downed electrical lines, or bad weather). These factors determine the number of officers that respond to a scene.

Plan how you will drive to the scene. You may not always want to use emergency lights and sirens. Depending on the nature of the call and agency policies, you may turn off the vehicle headlights at night to avoid detection when nearing a scene, such as when responding to a robbery in progress. You may need to reduce speed to avoid driving past the address and to avoid letting the suspects know you are there. Turn down the volume on your radio when you notify dispatch that you have arrived at the location.

ARRIVING AT THE SCENE OF A CALL

Once you have arrived, stop a short distance from the address. If other units are responding, you and other officers should coordinate the direction from which you all will arrive. You will have to determine the best place to park, so consider factors such as safe distance from the incident, the availability of cover and concealment, accessibility of the scene by other first responders and backup units, and evacuation routes.

Assess the area immediately surrounding the patrol car, and advise dispatch of any suspicious vehicles or people leaving the area. These descriptions may help when arresting suspects. Be aware of parked cars with motors running, and watch for hidden suspects who may attack you by surprise. An accomplice could be acting as a lookout or waiting in the area. If the call is a crime in progress, look for suspects leaving the scene.

Check for obvious clues, such as a vehicle parked in a lot that is normally empty at that time of day or the absence of a vehicle usually parked in a specific location. When exiting the patrol car, close the door gently and quietly. Be aware of items on you that make noise, such as loose change or keys. Follow these safety techniques before you exit your patrol vehicle and approach the scene:

- Secure the contents of your pockets and equipment on your duty belt.
- Turn your cell phone on silent mode.
- Scan the area for potential threats.
- Identify areas for cover and concealment.
- Avoid backlighting and silhouetting other officers.
- Maintain contact with dispatch throughout the incident.

OFFICER SAFETY WHEN APPROACHING A SCENE

Be sure to do the following as you approach a scene:

- Take and maintain the best tactical position, especially if you are waiting for backup.
- Approach suspicious vehicles on foot, and carefully check for occupants.
- Feel the hood of a vehicle for heat to determine if the vehicle was driven recently.
- Get close to buildings by moving behind parked cars, fences, trashcans, or shrubbery.

☑ LE521.2. Explain how to approach an incident scene safely

Walking in a low crouching position and taking an indirect route will help minimize the chances of detection. Constantly survey the building entrances and surrounding areas to ensure safety. When checking the exterior perimeter of a building, be careful when approaching corners, windows, and doors. Keep an eye out for animals, clotheslines, garbage cans, sprinkler heads, swimming pools, and other possible hazards.

When using a flashlight to examine the perimeter of a building, carry it in your support hand (your non-dominant hand). Hold it away from your body, so you do not make yourself a clear target. After shining the flashlight in an area, immediately move to a new position. Keep track of where other officers are, making sure not to shine the light on them. Since a flashlight temporarily impairs night vision, know where to aim the light before turning it on so that you do not blind other officers.

As soon as possible, determine the type of incident and if there is a need for backup. Determine if anyone has been injured and the extent of the injuries. Apply first aid and request medical assistance if needed. If you need to preserve the scene for investigation, use the available resources based on location.

GATHERING INFORMATION FROM COMPLAINANTS, VICTIMS, AND WITNESSES

At the scene of an incident, you must identify everyone involved. These include complainants, victims, witnesses, and suspects. As you gather information, remember to treat everyone involved with dignity and respect.

By assessing the scene and making these initial contacts, you can determine the type of complaint (civil, criminal, felony, or misdemeanor). Identify how much time has passed since the incident occurred, and if the suspect has left the scene and cannot be readily pursued, you can interview victims and witnesses for information that can help identify the suspect.

☑ LE521.3.
Describe techniques for interviewing complainants, witnesses, and victims

When interviewing a complainant, victim, or witness remember to do the following:

- Ask for identification and personal information, such as proper names, addresses, phone numbers, and other contact information.
- Be personal yet professional by introducing yourself by name and by using the person's name to establish rapport.
- Separate everyone and ask each complainant, victim, or witness to describe what happened. Then ask follow-up questions to clarify the incident. Ask them to describe the suspect and if they would be willing to identify the suspect later. These questions will help establish probable cause in the investigation.
- Take detailed notes of these accounts for documentation.

If they know the suspect, they may also have other information that can help find that person. Ask if they know any of the following information:

- the suspect's identity and description
- the suspect's location
- if the suspect can be violent or if the suspect has access to weapons
- the suspect's mode and direction of travel

These facts may help you find the suspect. If required, get written statements as these will help establish probable cause for an arrest.

BOLO

As you may recall from Chapter 3, a BOLO (be on the look out) gives a description of the subject, the subject's name, and any additional information that would help apprehend or locate them. Local, state, or national agencies issue BOLOs that may include descriptions of missing or wanted persons, stolen property, suspicious activity, or areas needing extra patrol attention.

BOLOs can contain a range of information, and they have no standard format or content. They may include printed information, photographs, verbal reports, electronic messages, or internet postings. A BOLO should include as much of the following information as possible:

- the subject's name and identifying information
- the location of the incident
- the reason for the BOLO
- the alleged violation or reason the subject is wanted
- the suspect's last known location and direction of travel
- a description or photograph of the person, vehicle, or property involved

☑ LE521.4. Describe valuable information a BOLO can provide when identifying a suspect

BOLOs are also issued for the following reasons:

- AMBER (America's Missing Broadcast Emergency Response) Alerts for missing and endangered children
- Silver Alerts for missing and endangered adults
- Blue Alerts for the capture of violent criminals who kill or seriously injure law enforcement officers
- Purple Alerts for missing disabled adults

You will learn more about alerts in Chapter 7.

Note the major points of each BOLO. Review information from current BOLOs to keep the information fresh while patrolling the assigned area.

Follow your agency policies when initiating a BOLO. If you arrive at the scene of an incident and are required to initiate an immediate BOLO, relay all significant information to dispatch. If you do not need to initiate a BOLO immediately, continue to gather and verify information to prepare a written BOLO. If you do not have enough information on a suspect, run a criminal justice database check for outstanding warrants, criminal history, and any additional information to include in the BOLO. Possible sources of photographs are prior arrest photos, driver license photos, security videos, and photos from family members.

☑ LE521.5. Explain how to initiate and cancel a BOLO

Cancel a BOLO when the subject of the alert is found, or the BOLO is deemed no longer necessary. You, a fellow officer, or dispatch should make sure that the cancellation goes through the appropriate messaging system.

UNIT 2 DUTIES ON PATROL
LESSON 2 Approaching and Contacting a Suspect

Lesson Goal

At the end of this lesson, you will understand the importance of safely approaching and interacting with a suspect using contact and cover officers.

Think About This

While approaching a female suspect, you observe that she is wearing tight clothing with no layers, and you see no obvious signs of a concealed weapon. You direct her to stop walking, but she turns and keeps going in another direction. You catch up to her to escort her to your vehicle, and she pulls out a large knife. What would have been a safer way to handle this situation?

APPROACHING A SUSPECT

☑ LE522.1. Describe how to safely approach a suspect

When developing a plan for contacting a suspect, decide if you should contact the suspect right away or wait for backup. Select an appropriate location and identify possible hazards. When approaching a suspect, consider their criminal history, behavior, and possible weapons. Always watch the person's hands and body language when talking with them. Watch for inconsistencies, such as if the suspect tells you that they came from one direction while pointing in another. Be aware of the presence of other people and possible escape routes for the suspect. Multiple suspects have the potential for adding extreme risk to your safety. Coordinating backup officers and establishing suspect control is critical to your safety.

☑ LE522.2. Explain the different roles of the contact and cover officer

Keeping safe when approaching a suspect is a coordinated effort between a contact officer and a backup or cover officer. Each officer fills a different role in the approach. Usually, the primary officer on the call is the **contact officer**. This officer is responsible for leading the approach and handling all communication with the suspect, including commands and interviews. This allows the suspect to be focused on one officer's voice instead of having multiple officers giving different directions at the same time.

The backup officer is the **cover officer** and is strictly responsible for officer safety concerns at the scene. The cover officer's responsibilities include observing the contact officer's interaction with the suspect and watching for hazards such as hostile crowds, traffic, or escape routes. Additional officers share cover responsibilities and assist the contact officer as requested.

INITIATING CONTACT AND ESTABLISHING COMMUNICATION WITH A SUSPECT

☑ LE522.3. Describe how to initiate contact with a suspect

When moving toward a suspect, do the following:

- Approach the suspect carefully.
- Keep your eyes on the suspect.

- Make sure that you keep a safe distance from the suspect.
- Stay alert to possible resistance or threats.
- Observe the suspect's position and body movements for indications of flight or assault.
- Continuously scan for weapons.

During contact, ask the suspect for information such as name, date of birth, address, Social Security number, and legal identification cards. Verify a suspect's identity via criminal justice databases, and check this information by comparing it with the information that the suspect has provided. If a criminal justice database, such as FCIC/NCIC, shows an outstanding warrant, you have the authority to detain the suspect pending confirmation and extradition. Once confirmed, arrest the suspect and transport them to the appropriate facility. If the issuing agency waives extradition, you must release the suspect. Follow your agency's policies and procedures regarding the documentation of your actions.

Continue to seek information by interviewing and observing the suspect. If you have a justifiable reason to believe that the suspect poses a threat or may flee, handcuff them upon initiating contact. If you believe the suspect is armed with a dangerous weapon, conduct a pat down search. If at any point the person is no longer considered a threat or deemed a suspect, remove the handcuffs.

☑ LE522.4. Explain what to do if a person resists arrest

Share all current information on the suspect with backup officers. If appropriate, establish rapport with the suspect to create a non-custodial atmosphere; doing so can help with other investigative efforts such as obtaining the suspect's consent for a search.

When initiating contact with a suspect, you may have to deal with uncooperative subjects. Common situations you will encounter while dealing with the public are resisting an officer with or without violence and giving false information when arrested or lawfully detained.

Resisting an officer without violence occurs when a person non-violently resists, obstructs, or opposes a law enforcement officer while they are performing their legal duties. For example, not obeying lawful verbal commands, refusing to be handcuffed, or refusing to provide identification would be considered resisting without violence. You should always request voluntary compliance when possible. If the person refuses to comply voluntarily, issue a verbal command. If the request and the command do not work, you have the authority to make the subject comply with the lawful order using techniques explained in Defensive Tactics. Even though the subject may be resisting, remember that you are obligated to maintain professionalism and treat the subject with respect.

Resisting an officer with violence occurs when a person knowingly resists or obstructs a law enforcement officer by committing or offering to commit a violent act toward a law enforcement officer while the officer is performing their legal duties. An example of resisting with violence is when a suspect violently fights with officers while being restrained and handcuffed. A person can still resist with violence while in handcuffs.

Never assume that the person is being compliant. Be ready to respond to violent resistance, and use techniques explained in Defensive Tactics to maintain your safety and gain control of the person.

People will sometimes provide false information, such as a fake name and date of birth, to disguise their real identity. Giving false identification occurs when a person who has been arrested or lawfully detained by a law enforcement officer gives a false name or otherwise falsely identifies themselves in any way to the officer. You may or may not pick up on the false information. Techniques to help identify people when you believe they are providing false information include the following:

- running a search of the person in DAVID
- asking for a Social Security number and comparing it to FCIC/NCIC
- asking for an address and comparing it to FCIC/NCIC or DAVID
- using a portable fingerprint scanner to establish identity

UNIT 2 DUTIES ON PATROL
LESSON 3 Responding as Backup

Lesson Goal

At the end of this lesson, you will be able to respond to a call as the backup officer while maintaining officer safety.

Think About This

You respond to a scene as the backup officer to transport an arrestee. Officer Smith arrested a woman for narcotics possession and has placed her in your patrol vehicle. At the request of the arrestee, you leave the window of your vehicle down. You leave your vehicle to assist Officer Smith with a search of the arrestee's vehicle, and when you return to your vehicle, you find that the arrestee is gone. What course of action should you have taken to prevent this situation from happening?

You will frequently be called to help other officers during calls for service, or you may decide on your own to provide backup based on the circumstances. Calls for backup may involve responding to non-life-threatening, high-risk, or life-threatening situations.

Non-life-threatening situations can range from assisting with administrative paperwork to providing additional equipment. High-risk situations may include assisting with serving a warrant, responding to a vehicle pursuit, or responding to a scene where the suspect is still present. Life-threatening situations may include dealing with an active shooter or a vehicle crash with serious injuries.

Backup officers can determine how to respond to a call based on several factors. These may include the nature of the call, the type of assistance needed, their familiarity with the area, or the demeanor of the requesting officer. Always stay in communication with the requesting officer, including visual and verbal contact. You can change your response according to the situation as more information is provided. For instance, a backup officer may respond in emergency mode to assist another officer engaged in a foot pursuit. If the primary officer advises dispatch that the suspect has been arrested and the situation is under control, the backup officer should downgrade their response.

LE523.1. Describe how to respond safely to the scene when providing officer backup

Upon arrival, survey the scene and maintain situational awareness. Backup officers should minimize flashlight use to keep others safe on the scene. Make visual or verbal contact with the primary officer to determine what type of assistance is needed. Always remain alert and avoid distractions such as using your cell phone. The role of the backup officer on a scene is to provide whatever assistance the primary officer needs.

UNIT 2 DUTIES ON PATROL
LESSON 4 Behavioral Threat Assessment and Management

Lesson Goal

At the end of this lesson, you will understand the role of behavioral threat assessment and management (BTAM) in identifying and preventing acts of targeted violence.

Think About This

You are notified of a local high school student's social-media post threatening to shoot up his school. After responding to the student's residence, you find that he has access to his father's firearm. The student claims the post was just a joke. What would your next steps be?

Despite a decrease in the overall violent crime rate over the past three decades, the United States has experienced a recent increase in the frequency and deadliness of targeted violence incidents, including mass targeted violence, such as active shooter incidents. **Targeted violence** refers to incidents of violence involving an identifiable person of concern (a perpetrator) who possesses the intent and capability to cause physical harm to an identifiable target (an intended victim). These incidents are goal-directed, premeditated, and predatory, and they may occur in or across many locations including homes, workplaces, schools, government offices, public events, hospitals, and places of worship.

☑ LE524.1. Describe the key findings regarding research on targeted violence

Practical research conducted by the U.S. Secret Service, FBI, and other government entities has revealed some key findings:

- Human behavior, particularly violent behavior, cannot be reliably predicted, but it may be prevented.
- No psychological or demographic profile exists for an active shooter or perpetrator of targeted violence, so profiling is not an effective tool for preventing targeted violence.
- Targeted violence is almost never impulsive or random. It is the result of organized thinking and behaviors, such as planning and preparation, which can be observed and reported.
- Mental health issues are rarely the main cause of targeted violence incidents.
- While communicated threats should never be ignored, persons of concern for targeted violence often do not communicate threats to a target or to law enforcement before they attack. Know that there is a difference between making a threat and posing a threat.

BEHAVIORAL THREAT ASSESSMENT AND MANAGEMENT PROCESS

Behavioral threat assessment and management (BTAM) is a proactive, investigative process used to identify, assess, and manage the risk of targeted violence posed by an identified or identifiable person. BTAM uses the law enforcement intelligence cycle to collect and analyze behavioral information about a person of concern. This includes observable, attack-related behaviors that indicate the perpetrator may be on a "pathway to violence." These behaviors may warn of future targeted violence against an identifiable target or the community in general.

The primary goal of BTAM is to prevent or mitigate acts of targeted violence, especially incidents of mass targeted violence, and its primary functions are to identify, assess, and manage people of concern within the local community.

☑ LE524.2. Describe the core functions of the behavioral threat assessment and management process

Identify

On patrol, you will respond to a variety of calls for service where you may see or hear something that leads you to identify a person of concern for future targeted violence. Collecting and reporting that information is critical to successfully preventing or mitigating targeted violence. Always follow your agency's policies and procedures for collecting and reporting this type of information. Information relevant to identifying persons of concern may include, but is not limited to, the following:

- a detailed description of the encounter that prompted concern
- your reasons for concern
- personally identifiable information for the person and any relevant witnesses

Assess

The core of BTAM is to assess a person's risk for future targeted violence against an identifiable target. Assessment involves collecting and analyzing behavioral information from all possible sources, including your own observations and knowledge. Trained BTAM professionals will primarily be responsible for this type of investigation. The quantity and quality of information reported directly impacts the accuracy of any assessment. Often, the best sources of information are relatives, friends, and close associates of the person of concern. You should consider the person of concern's current life circumstances, intimate relationships and close associations, financial status and resources, education and training, and mental and physical health. Information of critical importance includes, but is not limited to, the following:

- motive and intent communicated to third-parties
- ability and means to act, especially immediate access to firearms or other weapons
- access to the intended target
- the target's vulnerabilities

Manage

In BTAM, law enforcement agencies manage a person of concern using strategies based on the assessment to prevent or mitigate acts of targeted violence. You may be asked to assist BTAM investigators in managing a person of concern. A management strategy could include disrupting an immediate threat through arrest or protective custody, monitoring a person of concern's behaviors over time, enforcing legal process (for example, delivering a restraining order or a risk protection order), or referring the person to a mental or behavioral health care provider.

Remember that you may be the only member of law enforcement to observe critical information regarding a person of concern progressing along a "pathway to violence" before they attack. Reporting that information promptly and accurately is necessary to help prevent targeted violence.

UNIT 3 NON-CRIMINAL CALLS FOR SERVICE
LESSON 1 Assisting Your Community

◎ Lesson Goal

At the end of this lesson, you will be able to determine the appropriate resources to safely resolve non-criminal calls for service.

Think About This

You are the first to arrive on the scene of a vehicle crash with a fire. While you attempt to help the trapped driver out of the vehicle, you realize that backup has not arrived yet, and there are several bystanders on the scene. Should you ask them for assistance?

RESPONDING TO A NON-CRIMINAL CALL FOR SERVICE

While patrolling, you will respond to a variety of calls for service that are non-criminal in nature. A non-criminal call for service may range from a request to obtain specific information to a request to perform a security check on a building.

Every call for service requires you to respond in a professional manner and to adjust your command presence to fit the situation. The public's trust in you depends on whether your authority is seen as appropriate, proper, and just. If your authority is not seen as legitimate, the public may not cooperate. Remember that a seemingly simple incident can rapidly escalate into a criminal situation. Maintain your composure, display emotional intelligence, and proceed safely at all times.

When you arrive at the scene, find the complainant, and introduce yourself in a courteous manner. Listen to the person, and then determine what services the caller needs and whether you can assist or provide referrals. For example, you can serve a member of the public by providing information, pamphlets, or contacts (websites and telephone numbers) for the following agencies and services:

☑ LE531.1. Describe how to provide assistance during a non-criminal incident

- the Department of Veterans Affairs
- the Department of Children and Families
- local mental health services
- county clerks of court

Recall from Chapter 2 that, despite all of your best efforts, sometimes you may not be able to provide the expected level of service. In these situations, use your interpersonal skills to express your understanding of the situation and your empathy for the people involved, and explain why you cannot resolve the issue. For example, power outages or locked-out motorists do not require law enforcement intervention.

DIRECTING PEOPLE TO ASSIST

Most of the time, you will engage with a compliant person. However, there may be times when you need to call on bystanders to help. Typically, these are emergency situations such as rescuing a victim, providing first aid, or overcoming resistance from a suspect.

> LE531.2. Describe how to lawfully instruct the public to assist

Evaluate the scene to determine how much and what kind of help you need. Florida law authorizes officers to command assistance from the public in certain situations, such as apprehending or securing a person for breach of the peace or in the case of a rescue or escape of a person arrested upon civil process.

Determine the skill sets, physical limitations, and willingness of the public before commanding assistance. Be sure to give clear and specific instructions to people who are providing assistance. Under no circumstance should you instruct a member of the public to assist in a way that violates the law, exceeds their ability, or compromises their safety.

UNIT 3 NON-CRIMINAL CALLS FOR SERVICE
LESSON 2 Well-Being and Security Checks

Lesson Goal

At the end of this lesson, you will know how to safely check on the well-being of a person as well as the security of residences, buildings, or grounds.

Think About This

While on patrol, you drive by Mr. West's house. Typically, Mr. West is on his porch and waves at you, but on this day, you notice he is not outside. You decide to park your car, knock on the door, and check on him. As you approach, you hear cries for help. What do you do in this situation?

WELL-BEING CHECKS

You may notice a situation that requires a well-being check such as a bad odor coming from a residence or an abnormal presence of flies, which shows lack of activity. A person with medical issues may request law enforcement to routinely conduct well-being checks at their home. Dispatch may also receive a request from a resident's neighbor or relative to conduct a well-being check, and they should be able to research and confirm whether the subject of the well-being check has a call history at the location.

When you arrive at the location, notify dispatch if any vehicles are present, and conduct a brief search of the area for signs of unlawful entry or inactivity, such as an overflowing mailbox. Try to contact the person by knocking on the door or calling them on the phone. Look into the windows to determine the status of the person or identify indicators of distress. If appropriate, contact the property owner or management to obtain information about the person and about access to the location. Determine if the subject has been taken to a medical facility or has been arrested. Interview any neighbors to find out if they have information on the whereabouts of the person or if a neighbor has a key.

☑ LE532.1. Describe how to conduct a well-being check

If you cannot make contact with the person and no immediate signs of distress are present, contact dispatch or record your actions on your in-vehicle computer. Follow your agency's policies and procedures when notifying your chain of command.

In an emergency situation, follow your agency's policies and procedures when you have reasonable belief that a person is in immediate danger. In this situation, you may enter the property by force and search the premises. If you determine that you need immediate access to the person, you may need to call for backup or additional resources to assist with a forced entry. If necessary, provide first aid to the subject, contact dispatch to relay the person's status, or request additional emergency resources.

☑ LE532.2. Describe when you need to provide immediate assistance during a well-being check

When appropriate, contact the person who requested the well-being check to update them on the outcome and make any recommendations for future action. If you initiated the check, interview the person to determine who to contact for a follow-up.

SECURITY CHECKS

While patrolling an assigned area, you may conduct security checks of residences, buildings, or grounds. Residents may request security checks, or you or dispatch may initiate one. Notify dispatch when you arrive at the location, and park your vehicle at a distance from the building while observing the area.

☑ LE532.3. Describe how to conduct a security check

Use equipment, such as vehicle spotlights, flashlights, and radios, to help when you are conducting security checks. Look for suspicious indicators as you approach the scene. For example, be aware of open or unlocked doors, broken windows, damaged security equipment, or barking dogs. Other indicators of suspicious activity may be damaged plants or shrubs or items such as outdoor furniture or planters that are knocked over.

Run a vehicle check on any suspicious vehicles in the area. While walking the perimeter, check all entry points for signs of tampering. If you observe anything suspicious, get the property owner's contact information by locating any posted contact information, interviewing witnesses and neighbors, or asking dispatch to check for a property representative. Once you have contacted the owner or representative, ask them about circumstances at the property in relation to your observations. If there are indications of criminal activity, property damage, or loss, begin the appropriate investigative action. After you complete a security check, communicate the necessary information to dispatch.

UNIT 3 NON-CRIMINAL CALLS FOR SERVICE
LESSON 3 Death Notifications

Lesson Goal

At the end of this lesson, you will know how to deliver a death notification to the next of kin in a professional manner.

Think About This

You are responsible for notifying the next of kin after a fatal car crash, and the family cannot be reached in person. What do you do?

NOTIFYING THE NEXT OF KIN

You may be assigned to make a death notification when your agency conducts a death investigation or when it gets a request from another jurisdiction.

You can obtain the name, address, and telephone number of the deceased person's next of kin using criminal justice databases. If you use the DAVID emergency contact information (ECI), follow your agency's policies and procedures, and remember that ECI is for emergency purposes only and cannot be used as an investigative tool. After you have located the relatives, make a personal visit to the family, if possible.

Be sensitive to cultural and religious issues when handling this emotional situation. Before attempting to deliver a death notification, try to identify any language or cultural barriers. A victim advocate, an agency chaplain, or an interpreter may be helpful when you notify a relative or significant other of the death of a loved one. When responding in person, you may request a backup officer. Normally, this is a non-confrontational situation, but always practice officer safety.

☑ LE533.1. Describe how to deliver a death notification in a professional manner

If the next of kin lives in another state or town and is not accessible, contact the local law enforcement agency in that area, and request that one of their officers make the notification. Obtain that agency's telephone number by contacting dispatch, searching the internet, or performing queries within the FCIC/NCIC systems.

Although it is acceptable to notify the next of kin by telephone, this is the least preferred method. Do not make a telephone notification unless there is no other option. If you must notify the next of kin by telephone, call as soon as possible.

When you make contact with the next of kin, answer their questions concerning the deceased person's location and the circumstances surrounding the death. This will assist the family in dealing with the loss. If the investigation does not permit you to provide answers about the circumstances surrounding the death, explain this to the family. Follow your agency's policies regarding death notifications.

There are basic things you can do to display empathy when delivering a death notification. Be careful to avoid statements such as "I know how you feel" or "God never gives us more than we can handle."

The following are some recommendations when making a death notification:

- Be absolutely certain of the identity of the deceased.
- Make a clear statement that the death has occurred.
- Allow time for the venting of feelings.
- Obtain medical help if needed.
- Assist in notifying significant others.
- Make referrals for follow-up support services.
- Describe the procedure for identifying the deceased.

UNIT 3 NON-CRIMINAL CALLS FOR SERVICE
LESSON 4 Animal Complaints

Lesson Goal

At the end of this lesson, you will know how to safely respond to situations involving animal complaints.

Think About This

You get a call about a 3-foot alligator in a residential pool. What are some ways to handle this situation?

NUISANCE ANIMAL CALLS

You may respond to calls involving domestic, wild, and exotic animals. Domestic animals may include livestock or family pets, such as dogs and cats. Common calls involving wildlife include alligators, snakes, bears, raccoons, and birds. An ***exotic animal*** is any animal that is not native to Florida, such as pythons, parrots, and monitor lizards.

When arriving on scene, identify any immediate threat and injury that may require first aid, and call EMS as needed. Determine if the animal is running free, contained, injured, or aggressive. Once you establish the present state of the animal, you may attempt to capture the animal or contact animal control services or the Florida Fish and Wildlife Conservation Commission (FWC). Consider your level of experience and training before you attempt to capture or handle any animal yourself.

☑ LE534.1. Describe how to assist a person with an animal complaint

You may need to request additional resources, such as wildlife rehabilitators or nuisance animal trappers. If an animal threatens personal or public safety, or suffers a debilitating injury, use appropriate equipment and force.

UNIT 3 NON-CRIMINAL CALLS FOR SERVICE
LESSON 5 Fire-Related Incidents

Lesson Goal

At the end of this lesson, you will be able to identify the appropriate course of action when responding to a fire-related incident.

Think About This

While on patrol on the highway, you observe what appears to be smoke coming from a ditch on the side of the road. You stop to check it out and find a small grass fire from a discarded cigarette. What should your response be?

ROLE OF LAW ENFORCEMENT

If you arrive at the scene of an incident and see a fire, notify dispatch immediately and request assistance. Occupants in the surrounding area may need to evacuate. Contact a supervisor and follow your agency's procedures when considering evacuations.

☑ LE535.1. Describe your role during a fire-related incident

The primary responsibility of an officer after the arrival of fire department personnel is to assist the firefighters and the fire marshal in their investigation and to maintain crowd and traffic control.

RESPONDING TO A VEHICLE FIRE

When responding to a vehicle fire, ask dispatch for all relevant information regarding the incident. Dispatch may be able to provide the specific information on the fire, where it is, what is on fire, if anyone is trapped, and if fire rescue has been notified. You should notify dispatch when you arrive at the scene.

☑ LE535.2. Describe how to respond to a motor vehicle fire

When parking, consider the wind direction and speed, traffic conditions, and safe access for other responders. Use your vehicle to block traffic and to protect the area in which you and other officers will work.

Consider fire intensity, and if you determine that you cannot put out the fire yourself, request fire and rescue aid. Survey the scene for victims, hazards, and other threats to public safety. These may include hazardous materials, downed power lines, and any other materials that may present an immediate threat. Dispatch can assist in making contact with available emergency resources.

You may need to use other emergency equipment, such as cones or flares, to create a perimeter around the work area. Consider the proximity of the fire to oncoming traffic, property, victims, and witnesses when deciding on the size of the perimeter. You will learn more about setting up a perimeter in a later lesson. Move people, including the injured, away from the scene if possible.

Determine if the vehicle is occupied. If victims are present, begin rescue efforts to extract them. Move victims to a safe location, and provide first aid as needed. If victims are trapped beyond your rescue ability, make every reasonable effort to immediately extinguish the fire. Be aware of the capabilities and limitations of fire extinguishers. Foam fire extinguishers are best for paper or wood fires while CO_2 fire extinguishers are more suited for flammable liquids. Fire extinguishers may help gain access to trapped victims. Once the victims have been removed and if there is no immediate threat to life or property, secure the scene for the arrival of fire personnel. Highly flammable or combustible items in the vicinity must be evaluated and moved if practical.

Depending on the scope of the incident, you may be required to assist other responding resources. You may be asked to provide details of the incident, control traffic, maintain a perimeter, or possibly administer first aid. The fire may be the result of a traffic accident, and the scene will need to be preserved as much as possible for evidence.

FALSE ALARMS

A false alarm of a fire occurs when an alarm system is activated but no evidence of reasonable threat exists. The false alarm could be caused intentionally or due to a malfunction. If you are dispatched to a building for an alarm that has malfunctioned, this is not an offense. However, it becomes a criminal offense if someone has intentionally caused the alarm. When charging a suspect with false alarm of a fire, document that the suspect, without reasonable cause, circulated a false alarm of fire.

☑ LE535.3. Determine when an incident is a false alarm of a fire

UNIT 3 NON-CRIMINAL CALLS FOR SERVICE
LESSON 6 Lost, Stolen, or Recovered Property

Lesson Goal

At the end of this lesson, you will know how to respond to an incident involving lost, stolen, or recovered property.

Think About This

A person turns in a found backpack to the local police department where you work. As you are going through the contents of the backpack, you discover a laptop, a camera, and a phone. What do you do next?

While on patrol, you may need to handle lost, stolen, or recovered property. A person may call about a lost cell phone; a victim of a burglary may find their stolen property at a pawn shop; or a person may turn in prescription drugs or a valuable object to law enforcement. This lesson discusses general guidelines for responding to these types of incidents. However, follow your agency's policies and procedures when handling these types of situations.

LOST PROPERTY

☑ LE536.1. Identify the procedure for handling lost, stolen, or recovered property

Items that people commonly report as lost property include cell phones, driver licenses, license plates, credit cards, Social Security cards, any insurance-related claims, or any losses due to a natural disaster. Use a general information report to document these incidents. Get a description of the property and an estimate of its value. Precise descriptions of lost property are important for later identification and recovery. Note the unique distinguishing identifiers, such as scratches or unique parts, to help identify the property. On items with serial numbers or other unique identifying numbers, record the numbers in your report and enter it into FCIC/NCIC. Conduct an FCIC/NCIC database query and a local system search that will search for recovered property in local pawn shops. Keep in mind that lost property may turn into stolen property.

STOLEN PROPERTY

You may come across stolen property on routine patrol, during traffic stops or arrests, or from a concerned resident. Upon receiving stolen property, handle the property according to your agency's policies, which may include the following:

- conducting an FCIC/NCIC and local database search to verify the property as stolen
- requesting the entering agency to remove the item from the database after verifying it is stolen property
- attempting to identify the owner or the original case report to add a supplemental report

- photographing the item
- processing the item for physical evidence, including latent prints and touch DNA (discussed in Chapter 9)
- returning the item to the owner if there is no forensic value and documenting this action
- submitting the item as evidence if you cannot locate the owner or if there is forensic value
- forwarding any suspect or item identification to the appropriate department in your agency for a follow-up investigation

STOLEN PROPERTY IN THE CUSTODY OF PAWNBROKER

Stolen property is often sold to pawnbrokers. The Florida Statutes state:

> When an appropriate law enforcement official has probable cause to believe that property in the possession of a pawnbroker is misappropriated, the official may place a written hold order on the property. The written hold order shall impose a holding period not to exceed 90 days unless extended by court order. The appropriate law enforcement official may rescind, in writing, any hold order. An appropriate law enforcement official may place only one hold order on property.

RECOVERED PROPERTY

Recovered property may be abandoned, seized, or found. Inventory the items, complete a property/receipt form, and give the items to your agency's property clerk for storage or destruction. Take all of the necessary steps to identify the owner or determine if the items are evidence of a crime. If you have identified the owner and have deemed that the property is not evidence, attempt to return the property according to your agency's policies and procedures. If you determine the property is stolen, refer to the information under stolen property above. Property that is recovered is entered into FCIC/NCIC as recovered property.

Florida law allows an owner or operator of a theme park, entertainment complex, zoo, museum, aquarium, public food service establishment, or public lodging establishment to dispose of or donate any lost or abandoned property found on its site. However, the owner or operator must maintain a record of the property and hold the property for at least 30 days. If the property remains unclaimed after 30 days, the owner or operator may not sell the property, but must dispose of or donate the property to a charitable institution.

UNIT 3 NON-CRIMINAL CALLS FOR SERVICE
LESSON 7 Property Disputes

Lesson Goal

At the end of this lesson, you will know how to respond to disputes involving property boundaries, landlords and tenants, motor vehicle repairs, and repossessions.

Think About This

You respond to a residence where the homeowner complains about his neighbor's tree branches hanging over his side of the fence. The neighbor refuses to cut down the trees because she says it's not her problem. What action can you take in this situation?

PROPERTY BOUNDARY DISPUTES

Property disputes between neighbors are usually civil in nature. For example, a property owner plants trees in his backyard, but his neighbor says the trees are on his side of the property line. The property owners would need a recent survey to identify who owns the property where the trees were planted.

☑ LE537.1. Describe how to respond to property boundary disputes

This is considered a civil dispute and would need to be done outside of the criminal justice process. Advise the parties to seek the appropriate remedies in civil court.

LANDLORD AND TENANT DISPUTES

You will sometimes be called to disturbances that arise from landlord and tenant disputes. You need a general knowledge of what action, if any, you can take in these situations. The Florida Residential Landlord and Tenant Act governs most of the traditionally recognized rental arrangements for dwellings, such as apartments, town homes, duplexes, single-family housing units, and mobile home parks.

☑ LE537.2. Describe how to respond to a landlord-tenant dispute

In tenancy situations covered by the law, the only way a landlord can legally recover possession of the leased residence without the consent of the tenant is to file an eviction proceeding in the county court where the residence is located.

If the landlord is successful, a writ of possession will be issued by the court to the sheriff who is then authorized to evict the tenant and put the landlord in possession of the residence after a prescribed notice period. Be aware that, until legally evicted, a tenant has a right to enter the residence, and a landlord may not prevent entry by changing the locks.

You may physically evict a tenant only following a writ of possession. Any action without a writ that causes the removal of a tenant, whether physically removing the tenant's belongings from the residence or suggesting to the tenant that failure to leave may result in arrest, is likely to be considered a wrongful eviction.

The Residential Landlord Tenant Act does not apply in these three types of residential rental facilities: public lodging establishments, such as hotels and motels; medical, geriatric, educational, counseling, religious, or similar residency facilities; and recreational vehicle parks.

REPOSSESSION OF PROPERTY

When a person or company that is owed money (called a creditor), sells or leases property to a person who takes out a loan (called a borrower), the creditor may get a security interest or lien against the property in the form of a contract or security agreement. The contract allows the creditor to take the property as collateral if the borrower defaults or does not repay the loan. The creditor can enforce this stipulation by obtaining a **writ of replevin**, a court order that allows the creditor to take possession of the collateral after the borrower defaults.

Outside of a court order, Florida law allows one other option for repossession; a creditor may rely on **self-help repossession**, a process where the creditor takes possession of the collateral after default without a court order, only if the repossession can be done without a breach of peace. In this situation, your role as an officer is to keep the peace. You may not give legal advice to either the borrower or the creditor.

☑ LE537.3. Describe how to safely respond to repossession of property during a dispute

Creditors usually hire a recovery agent to repossess property. Types of property likely to be repossessed include motor vehicles, mobile homes, motorboats, aircrafts, personal watercrafts, all-terrain vehicles, farm equipment, and industrial equipment. Motor vehicles are the most common type of repossessed property.

When responding to a dispute or confrontation about the repossession of a vehicle, you may have to determine the following:

- if the vehicle has already been attached to the tow truck and is ready for transport or if the recovery agent is behind the steering wheel of the vehicle ready to drive away. In this case, the repossession is complete, and the recovery agent should be permitted to leave.
- if there is a breach of the peace. In this situation, the recovery agent cannot lawfully take the vehicle. You will learn more about breach of the peace in Chapter 8.

MOTOR VEHICLE REPAIR DISPUTES

You may sometimes be dispatched to disturbances at automobile repair shops regarding disputes over repair costs. The Florida Statutes permit a vehicle owner who refuses to pay the repair bill to take possession of the vehicle after posting a bond with the clerk of court. After a bond is posted for the amount of the repair invoice, including storage fees, the clerk will issue a certificate directing the repair shop to release the vehicle to the owner. If the vehicle owner refuses to pay the repair cost and removes the vehicle from the repair shop without posting a bond, then the vehicle owner should be investigated for theft.

☑ LE537.4. Describe the process for motor vehicle repair disputes

UNIT 3 NON-CRIMINAL CALLS FOR SERVICE
LESSON 8 Civil Disturbance

Lesson Goal

At the end of this lesson, you will know how to safely mediate a civil disturbance and maintain the peace during a civil standby.

Think About This

You respond to a call where someone asks to meet you for a child-custody exchange. What is your role in this situation?

☑ LE538.1. Describe how to mediate a civil disturbance

When responding to a call that is civil in nature, such as a landlord-tenant dispute or child custody issue, be aware that these incidents can become highly confrontational.

Evaluate the threat level with information relayed by dispatch, the location's call history, personal knowledge of the people involved, and your observations. Be vigilant, avoid complacency, and request backup based on the threat level of the situation.

Separate, identify, and interview all of the people involved to obtain information related to the incident. Through your assessment, interviews, and observations, verify whether a crime has been committed. You can also perform queries within the FCIC/NCIC systems to determine if any injunctions or warrants exist. An *injunction* is a court order that requires a person to do or refrain from doing specific acts, such as having no contact with a former spouse or a specific victim of domestic violence.

Once you have determined that the disturbance is civil in nature, provide information and resources that will help resolve the conflict. For example, you may assist people involved in a landlord-tenant dispute by referring them to civil court or mediation.

CIVIL STANDBY

There may be times where you are called to a *civil standby*, which is when an officer maintains the peace through officer presence while serving a court order or responding to a call for service. Civil standbys may be conducted in situations such as the execution of a writ of replevin, a child custody exchange, or a pretrial release order.

☑ LE538.2. Describe how to maintain order during a civil standby

Typically, a civil standby requires little action by the officer; your presence is enough to keep the incident calm. If your presence is not enough and the situation begins to escalate, you may separate both parties, recommend that one or both parties leave, or have them contact the clerk of the court or their attorneys. When necessary, separate and interview the parties to determine whether you need to take any enforcement action.

Remain impartial and use conflict management skills to prevent escalation of the situation. Refer to Chapter 2 for more information on conflict management skills.

Policies and procedures differ between agencies on whether a court order needs to be in place for an officer to conduct a civil standby, so it is important for you to be familiar with your own agency's policies and procedures.

UNIT 3 NON-CRIMINAL CALLS FOR SERVICE
LESSON 9 Crowd Control

Lesson Goal

At the end of this lesson, you will know how to safely control a crowd, demonstration, or riot using effective communication and observation skills.

Think About This

After a high school football game, a group of students gather outside the local gas station. Management reports that 15 to 20 students are cursing loudly and congregating outside in the parking lot. When you arrive, you estimate the crowd to be about 100 people. How do you handle this situation?

ASSESSING THE CROWD

You may be assigned to a special event detail, such as providing security for a sporting event, concert, fair, or political rally. You may also be asked to provide security for event facilities, attendees, and employees. Your agency will provide information regarding a command post for the event, level of enforcement, safety concerns, prohibited items, and other areas of concern. Always be aware of other officers' locations and maintain a high level of awareness for potential incidents that may require a response.

☑ LE539.1. Describe the role of law enforcement when responding to crowds

The First Amendment protects the right of peaceful assembly for the community. When the assembly of people is no longer peaceful, law enforcement is called upon to resolve the public disturbance. Instances where the Florida Statutes apply to assemblies, groups, or crowd control situations include the following:

- disorderly intoxication
- affrays and riots
- unlawful assemblies
- routs, melees, mobs
- breach of the peace and disorderly conduct

People may gather as long as they cause no disturbance and act within the scope of the law. Your duty is to determine if the demonstration or gathering is lawful based on state statutes and county and municipal ordinances. In Florida, permits may be required for planned events that anticipate a large crowd. You may have to respond to complaints about sudden crowds such as late-night bars closing or crowds leaving a venue.

IDENTIFYING THE PROBLEM

☑ LE539.2. Determine the threat level of a crowd, demonstration, or riot

Try to determine the threat level of the crowd, demonstration, or riot by observing the mood, location, direction of travel, and size of the crowd. Several things may affect the crowd's mood, such as the result of a sporting event or a controversial court ruling.

Identify if the crowd is organized and if anyone is leading or agitating the crowd. Some crowds may involve gang members, possibly displaying colors, symbols, and weapons. Monitor the situation from the best vantage point for collecting information, such as from a patrol car, a rooftop, or a video monitoring system. Relay information frequently to dispatch or any assisting agencies. Include critical information on crowd size and movement, observed weapons such as broken bottles, and any property damage. Report any level of escalation or de-escalation. Determine if the situation requires specialized assistance such as a supervisor's deployment of the riot squad, SWAT, canine, or mounted patrol; the fire department; or the public information office.

Any large gathering could be dangerous, so you must approach it carefully. If you decide to engage the participants of a crowd or demonstration, officer safety is your first consideration. Sheer numbers can be overwhelming for responding officers. Calling for assistance and waiting for backup are critical when engaging a crowd or demonstration. Although non-hostile crowds are more passive, never become complacent when dealing with large groups as things can quickly change. Safety is your main concern.

☑ LE539.3. Describe how to control a crowd, demonstration, or riot

It is sometimes difficult to remove or arrest members of a large group. The anonymity of a crowd may provoke the violent behavior of aggressive individuals. In large crowds, attacks can come from any direction, so always have an exit strategy and prevent crowds from cornering you or stopping you from leaving. A show of force or presence in numbers can be persuasive in calming a crowd.

Identifying why a group has assembled will help you better understand group goals and possible solutions for a peaceful dispersal. Look for signs and symbols on clothing or listen to what people say or chant to help you understand the gathering.

An important part of dispersing crowds and resolving group incidents is determining the leader or instigator. Identify this person by observing how the crowd interacts. Is there someone that the crowd rallies behind? Who does all the talking? Who seems to stand out most, talking the loudest and prompting activity? Answers to these questions may point to the group leader.

After backup has arrived, you may approach the leader or person responsible, separate them from the crowd, and interview them. Isolation allows you to speak to the leader without the influence of the group. Effective communication skills are essential in resolving conflicts involving many people. Speak in a professional manner, treating all parties with dignity and respect, to encourage cooperation. Tell the leader why officers are at the scene. The leader's willingness to cooperate is a major factor in subduing a threatening situation. Issuing a threat to arrest someone during initial contact may turn an otherwise peaceful event into a violent one. Request that the leader comply with laws and ordinances if the group has violated any.

Independent criminal violations may occur in a crowd, such as underage drinking or illegal narcotics usage. These violations must be addressed. For officer safety reasons, if intervention is feasible, use discretion when deciding on enforcement action. If you expect to make a physical arrest, observe the crowd's actions and determine if sufficient backup is present to ensure officer and public safety.

UNIT 4 STRUCTURE AND AREA SEARCHES
LESSON 1 Alarms and Searches

Lesson Goal

At the end of this lesson, you will know how to conduct a legal and tactically sound building search in response to an alarm or call for service.

Think About This

Officer Bentley responds to an alarm call for a vacant building and notices a front door is open. She enters the building to search for any suspects or criminal activity. Is this the right action? What else should she take into consideration?

RESPONDING TO SECURITY ALARMS

During patrol, you will respond to various alarms. Alarms can come from homes, retail stores, schools, government offices, or medical facilities, and may involve the following incidents:

- burglary
- robbery
- panic
- fire
- medical alert

There may also be cases when you respond to a false alarm. Your response and tactics will be determined by the type and location of the alarm. Factors to consider are life-threatening situations, danger to the public, or a significant loss of property. The alarm company may tell dispatch the cause of the alarm.

Some alarms are audible while others are silent, so adjust your response (lights and siren versus a stealth approach) to the type of alarm. Whatever the alarm type, remain aware of your surroundings and anticipate unknown risks. Some agency policies require at least two officers to respond to alarm calls. Other agencies make a second officer available under certain circumstances or at the request of the initial responding officer.

☑ **LE541.1.** Explain how to respond to an alarm call

Upon arrival, park your patrol vehicle at a safe distance from the building or residence. The location you choose depends on the situation (for example, parking up the road versus several doors down). Observe any vehicles present at the scene, and notify dispatch to run the license plate numbers. Do an overall assessment of the location, and notify dispatch of any evidence of forced entry, such as broken glass or open doors.

Try to identify the cause of the alarm. You can do this by observing the location and environment, interviewing people present, and getting information from dispatch.

This information may include a suspect description, false alarm notification, and the response from the property owner or a representative with key holder status. Several factors cause false alarms including weather conditions, animals, power outages, unintentional activation, or an open door.

If a crime has occurred and there are no suspects present, secure the scene. If a significant amount of time has elapsed and you have not located the suspects, begin an investigation.

If you determine that suspects are present, develop a tactical plan to apprehend them. Ask yourself the following questions:

- Do you need to establish a perimeter?
- Do the suspects know of the police presence?
- Do you need to conduct a building search?
- Do you need to call for additional resources like a canine or tactical team?

You may also respond to non-criminal or unknown alarms, such as fire or medical alarms. Your responsibility in these situations is to identify the issue and notify the proper agency to resolve the incident. Assist other agencies as needed. Usually, you will help with controlling the crowd, gathering witness statements, and providing additional community safety functions. You may also need to provide first aid until EMS arrives.

BUILDING SEARCH PRINCIPLES

At times, you will be required to conduct building searches, including calls for alarms, open doors, burglaries, and trespassing, and some of these incidents may turn into high-risk situations.

You must determine if a building search is legally allowed before conducting one. Recall the exigent circumstances that justify a warrantless entry from Chapter 3. If necessary, secure the exterior of the building with a perimeter. Direct people who are not involved to a safe location. If possible, obtain access to the property through the owner or a property agent.

☑ LE541.2. Explain the basic principles for conducting a building search for a suspect

Do not search buildings alone. Use additional resources, including other officers and a canine unit, if available. When you are working with a partner, establish a plan to search and secure the building.

Noise from jangling keys, loose change, cell phones, or radio volume can reveal your location during a search. Secure loose items and turn down the volume on phones and radios before you begin a search. When using a flashlight to search a building, remain aware of the presence of other officers and their locations, and do not shine your flashlight on other officers. Hand signals can be used to communicate, so work together and avoid becoming separated. Using these methods allows you to cover each other and reduces the risk of crossfire.

The greatest threat in a building search is the possibility of a suspect in hiding. Always remember that a suspect inside of the building can be armed and dangerous, so conduct a thorough and careful search because failure to do so can lead to fatal results. After the initial search, consider swapping search areas with your partner and conduct a secondary search of the premises to ensure that all areas were thoroughly searched.

BEFORE ENTERING A BUILDING

Determine how to enter a building based on how the doors and windows open. For example, before entering, note which direction the door opens by locating the hinges. Whatever the entry point, use the appropriate strategy to enter the building. Generally, you will enter buildings through a doorway.

Before entering a building, request an emergency radio channel through dispatch, and draw your firearm. In certain situations, you may knock and announce your presence to allow the people inside to exit or any suspects to surrender. For example, if you are doing a security check at a residence at 2 p.m. with an open door, you may want to announce your presence and purpose for entering. The situation may dictate your response, but be sure you have a plan before entering. Never enter too quickly. Stop, look, and listen.

Be cautious of anyone who may be hiding behind doors. When working in pairs, maintain visual contact, communicate, and be aware of each other's actions. Do not assume that your partner sees and hears everything you do. If either of you face a threat, give loud verbal commands. This will alert your partner to the situation and the threat.

ENTERING AND CLEARING A BUILDING

☑ LE541.3. Describe how to conduct a systematic building search for a suspect

Systematically search the structure, keeping track of cleared rooms or areas. As you move through a building, remain aware of **fatal funnels**, narrow spaces that restrict movement; these spaces are typically doorways, hallways, and windows. You should also be aware of **deep corners**, corners that cannot be visually cleared from the doorway and must be checked first upon entry. Be mindful of people hiding in shadows and dark areas. When you encounter these areas, make sure that the area is clear of threats and dangers before moving through them.

During the search, you will encounter a number of factors that will affect your tactics. These factors include stairways, locked doors, closets, attics, and various other barriers. Follow your agency's policies when dealing with special considerations during a search.

Before entering a room, visually clear as much of the room as possible. One technique for visually clearing a room is called "cutting the pie" or "edging." Stand to one side of the door and scan as many parts of the room as possible. When you enter a room, move deliberately.

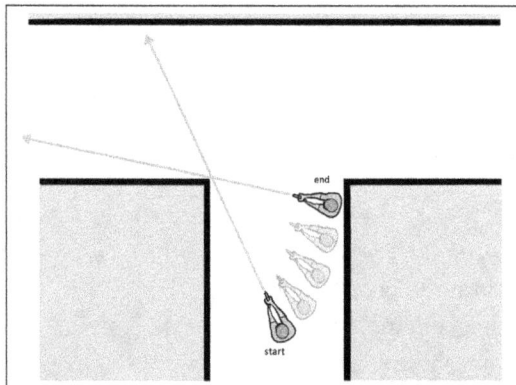

Figure 5-4
Cutting the pie

Two common methods for entering a room are the crisscross and buttonhook techniques. Whichever method you choose, be sure to coordinate with other officers.

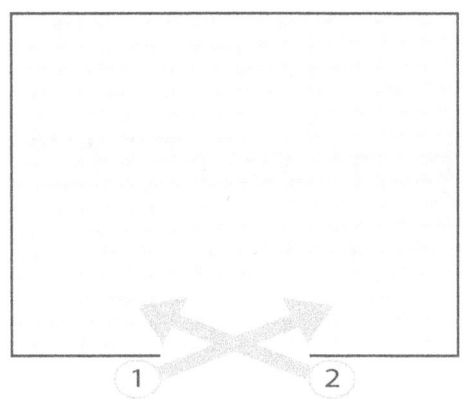 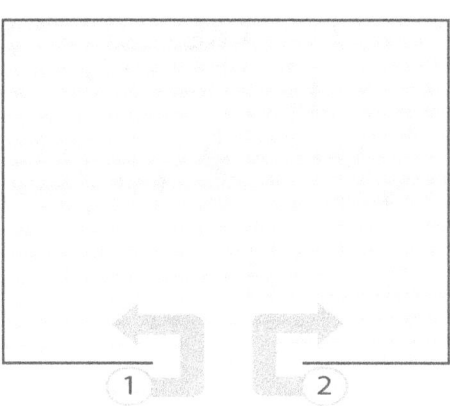

Figures 5-5 and 5-6
(left to right)
Crisscross technique
& Buttonhook
technique

In the crisscross technique, officers start on opposite sides of the doorway. They enter rapidly, one after the other, crossing to the opposite sides.

In the buttonhook (also called the wraparound) technique, an officer and a partner enter the room by hooking around the corner at the point of entry. They stand on opposite sides or on the same side of the door. They should wrap around the wall and into the room.

While searching, clear rooms of immediate threats, starting with the deep corners. It is important to stay together and search each room thoroughly before moving to the next. Communicate with your fellow officer your area of responsibility for each room while maintaining firearm safety. Keep in mind the scope of your search is limited to locating persons. After searching each room, consider closing the door or keeping the room under observation. Once you clear the building, return the building to the responsible person.

UNIT 4 STRUCTURE AND AREA SEARCHES
LESSON 2 Area Searches

⊚ Lesson Goal

At the end of this lesson, you will know how to maintain a perimeter when conducting a grounds search for a suspect and how to safely pursue a suspect on foot.

Think About This

During a consensual encounter, the person decides to flee. Do you have grounds to pursue them?

PERIMETERS

A *perimeter* is an area of containment surrounding the site of an incident. The size and scope of the perimeter depends upon the nature of the incident. It may include natural or artificial barriers.

Situations will occur where it will be necessary to create a perimeter. You can use a perimeter when securing a crime scene or during a search for suspects, a high-risk situation, a special event, or any incident where access to an area needs to be restricted to authorized individuals.

☑ LE542.1. Describe how to establish a perimeter

The situations calling for a perimeter can change constantly, but it is best to start with a large perimeter. As the situation changes, the perimeter can be adjusted to keep officers and the public safe. The primary officer or a supervisor will determine the need for a perimeter and necessary resources based on the knowledge of the surrounding geographical area.

While you may need to coordinate with several officers and resources to maintain an effective perimeter, a basic one can be set with minimal resources, usually by two officers. You can also create a perimeter using vehicle headlights, spotlights, barricades, and natural boundaries.

Use your resources in the way that best protects the safety of the public while limiting the movements of contained suspects. You may use other resources depending on the type of incident, the amount of time that has passed after the incident occurred, and the geographic configuration of the area. Resources may also include additional staff, a helicopter, or canines.

☑ LE542.2. Describe how to monitor a perimeter

If assigned to a post, ensure the integrity of the perimeter through constant observation and activities, and maintain contact with other officers to prevent people from entering or leaving a secured area. Report any notable information over the radio, such as if you observe any person matching the suspect's description. Take immediate action if someone attempts to enter or leave the perimeter.

Stay at your post until you are relieved or relocated, or the situation has been resolved. Perimeters can be effective even with limited resources by good planning and positioning.

GROUND SEARCHES FOR A SUSPECT

Often, suspects escape into an open area, the grounds surrounding a building, a neighborhood, or a business area. Officer safety is always the primary concern, so ask for backup and additional resources such as aviation or canine units as necessary.

The techniques for searching grounds are similar to building searches:

- Work with a partner because it is safer than working alone.
- Do not expose yourself as a target.
- Use available cover and concealment.
- Be aware of the noise you are making; move only as fast as you can to remain safe.
- Coordinate with other officers to avoid crossfire situations.
- Be aware of other noises, such as barking dogs or alarms, that may indicate a suspect's location or direction of travel.
- Be aware of areas that present a higher threat, such as low light or potential hiding areas.

☑ LE542.3. Describe how to search an open area for a suspect

Additional concerns that may complicate outdoor searches can include the following:

- uneven and varying terrain
- ambient lighting
- access to elevated hiding areas, such as trees or rooftops
- members of the public walking into the area
- weather

Exterior grounds searches are more difficult to contain than a building search. A number of factors that may affect your search tactics include fences, pools, vehicles, dead ends, and various barriers.

Encountering People During a Search

During a search, you may find people who have a legitimate reason to be in the search area. This includes employees, residents, or cleaning personnel. Consider any person in the search area a potential threat until you or another officer determine their status. Remember that this is a search for a suspect, not an evidence search, so you cannot search unreasonable places such as dresser drawers.

An encountered person may provide information regarding the incident. If you encounter an unverified subject, contact and detain them until you confirm their identity and status. Even if you locate a suspect, continue to search and clear the rest of the area,

☑ LE542.4. Recognize what to do if you encounter a person during a search and consider conducting a secondary search. If you find a suspect hiding, proceed with caution. This could determine your next course of action.

FLEEING SUSPECT ON FOOT

During a consensual encounter, if the person you are speaking to decides to flee, you do not have grounds to pursue. A person's flight is not enough to provide probable cause for an arrest, but it does contribute to a reasonable suspicion to detain the person for investigation. When you have reasonable suspicion to detain a suspect and the suspect flees, you have the legal authority to pursue.

☑ LE542.5. Describe how to safely pursue a suspect that flees on foot

During a foot pursuit, clearly communicate via the radio your location, your direction of travel, a description of the suspect, and possible charges. Continuously update dispatch with this information. Doing so will allow responding officers to provide support and establish a perimeter if needed.

Safety considerations during a foot pursuit include the following:

- the probability that the suspect is armed
- the seriousness of the offense committed
- the threat to officers and the public
- the location and potential for ambush
- the time of day and weather conditions
- the knowledge that the person is a known suspect who can be apprehended at a later time
- the number of officers versus the number of suspects at the scene
- the physical limitations and capabilities of the officer and suspects
- the availability of additional resources, such as canine, air support, or SWAT
- the ability to secure the patrol vehicle
- the suspect's and officer's familiarity with the area

Attempt to keep your eyes on the suspect. If you lose sight of the suspect, be aware of the possibility of an ambush. It is common for fleeing suspects to get rid of evidence or contraband while running. Immediately alert assisting officers via the radio to the location of discarded items.

A foot pursuit is an ever-changing, stressful event; you must constantly reassess officer and public safety during the pursuit. Be aware of the physiological effects of stress and fatigue during a foot pursuit. These effects include selective hearing, tunnel vision, and rapid breathing.

Deciding whether to pursue with a drawn firearm depends on the circumstances. Pursuing with a firearm in hand presents a number of significant safety hazards such as an accidental shooting. Certain conditions will present increased risks, such as corners, fences, wooded areas, swimming pools, and animals. When going around blind corners, slow down and tactically clear the corner. If you lose radio contact with dispatch, reevaluate the decision to pursue. You or your supervisor may decide to end a pursuit at any time or when the following occurs:

- the suspect's location is unknown
- you are unable to continue because of injury, fatigue, or unfamiliarity with the area
- you establish the suspect's identity, and they are no longer a threat

UNIT 5 ARREST PROCEDURES

LESSON 1 Taking Custody of the Suspect

◎ Lesson Goal

At the end of this lesson, you will know how to make a safe and lawful arrest and transport the arrestee to a secure facility.

Think About This

You are sent to the scene of a narcotics arrest to transport an arrestee for a narcotics detective. As you take custody of the arrestee, you begin to search the arrestee. The senior narcotics detective intervenes and tells you he has already searched them. What are the potential consequences if you do not search the arrestee?

MAKING A PHYSICAL CUSTODY ARREST

☑ LE551.1. Describe how to make a safe and lawful arrest

You will take certain steps when making a physical custody arrest. Inform suspects that they are under arrest and the reason for the arrest. Properly handcuff suspects, including double lock, before searching for weapons or contraband. Perform a custodial search using the proper techniques explained in Defensive Tactics. As you may recall from Chapter 4, *Miranda* requirements are necessary whenever you conduct an interrogation.

☑ LE551.2. Describe when and how to seize and secure personal property, evidence, and contraband

Separate the arrestee's personal property from evidence and contraband. Agency or detention facility policy will dictate what to do with personal property and contraband. You must seize any evidence and process it according to your agency's policies. You will learn more about processing evidence in Chapter 9. If you find any other evidence on or near the person, additional charges may apply.

☑ LE551.3. Describe how to explain the arrest process to family or involved people

At times, it may be necessary in an arrest situation to provide information to victims, witnesses, and possibly the arrestee's family members, all of whom may have a direct interest in the incident. Whenever reasonably possible, provide general information. Remember, this could be the only time that this person interacts with a law enforcement officer, and you want the interaction to be a positive one. Be empathetic while explaining the charges, the location to which the arrested person will be taken, the bail procedures, and the first appearance information.

State law and agency policies regulate what information can be released to the public. The investigative process does not necessarily stop once an arrest has been made. You may not release information about evidence, potential witnesses, or any other aspect of the crime because it may hinder the investigation or make you the subject of criminal prosecution.

People near the scene may be using personal mobile devices to record all aspects of the incident, including your behavior. This is not a criminal offense, and you cannot interfere unless the person recording the incident is actively obstructing the investigation.

There may be reporters present asking detailed questions at any scene. Most agencies have a designated public information officer (PIO) who is responsible for releasing information to the media. The PIO will be informed of the situation and prepare a response to media requests.

☑ LE551.4. Identify who is authorized to release information to the public about an arrest or ongoing investigation

ESCORTING THE ARRESTEE TO THE PATROL VEHICLE

You must maintain physical control of the arrestee during the entire escort. Use the escort techniques discussed in Defensive Tactics. This will ensure officer and arrestee safety and prevent the arrestee from falling or fleeing.

☑ LE551.5. Describe how to escort an arrestee to a patrol vehicle

Never assume that the arrestee has already been searched before placing them in a transport vehicle. Every time custody of the arrestee is transferred from one officer to another, conduct another search and secure all personal property, evidence, or contraband. Remember to treat the arrestee with dignity and respect at each point in their transport.

PREPARATION FOR TRANSPORT

When placing an arrestee in your vehicle, take the following actions:

- Make sure the window controls and door handles are disabled from the rear compartment to prevent opening from the inside. This may prevent an escape, injury to the arrestee or others, damage to property, or the destruction of evidence.
- Make sure the rear passenger compartment of your vehicle is clear of any drugs, weapons, or equipment.
- Thoroughly search the handcuffed arrestee and take immediate possession of all personal property, evidence, and contraband.
- Assist the arrestee into the transport vehicle. The arrestee will typically occupy the right rear passenger compartment of your vehicle.
- Secure the arrestee's seat belt.

☑ LE551.6. Explain how to safely restrain and secure a person and property for custodial transport

If required by your agency, notify dispatch of your destination with beginning and ending mileage. Some agency policies require special procedures, such as audiotaping or videotaping the transport. Following these guidelines will protect you and your agency from unfounded misconduct charges.

SPECIFIC TRANSPORT SITUATIONS

During transport there may be specific situations you will have to address.

☑ LE551.7. Explain how to safely transport an arrestee

- You cannot transport a juvenile in the same vehicle with an adult arrestee unless they are codefendants.
- Notify dispatch when you transport an arrestee needing medical attention to a medical facility or if you have requested EMS. When you need an ambulance to transport the arrestee, follow your agency's policies regarding your responsibility to accompany the arrestee.

- When transporting an arrestee with a disability or specific need, adjust transport procedures in a manner that doesn't compromise officer safety, for example, when transporting an arrestee with a service animal or a person with a motorized wheelchair.
- When transporting a pregnant arrestee, you may want to place restraints in the front of the arrestee.
- Consider weather conditions and temperature if you cannot transport the arrestee immediately after loading. Do not leave an arrestee in a hot car for an extended period of time. Make every effort to transport them in a timely manner.
- You may encounter additional obstacles, such as the arrestee's size, health, or medical condition. In these situations, you may need to request a larger transport vehicle or an ambulance, or adjust the arrestee's position.
- When arresting a person who appears to be under the influence or not in control of their physical functions, examine the person to determine if their actions may be caused by a medical condition. If you determine that their actions may be related to a medical condition, seek immediate medical attention.

While En Route

En route, you may encounter situations that cause interruptions. If this happens, find a safe place to pull over, notify dispatch of your location and mileage, notify your supervisor, and request backup.

These situations may include the following:

- The arrestee becomes combative or removes their restraints.
- The arrestee has a medical issue such as a seizure.
- The transport vehicle is involved in a crash or a malfunction.
- You encounter a life-threatening event.
- The arrestee escapes or attempts to escape.

Transporting an Incarcerated Pregnant Person

According to the Healthy Pregnancy for Incarcerated Women Act, you must not use restraints for an incarcerated pregnant person who is in labor, delivery, or postpartum recovery unless you determine that they present a substantial flight risk or another extraordinary medical or security circumstance makes restraints necessary. Since there are legal restrictions on the types and placements of restraint devices on pregnant prisoners, be sure to follow your agency's policies.

ARRIVAL AT THE DESTINATION

When you arrive at your destination, notify dispatch and report the ending vehicle mileage. Approach the appropriate drop-off point and obtain clearance to enter.

After arriving at the detention facility, secure your weapons in a locked location, such as the patrol vehicle's trunk, a weapons locker, or a lockbox at the drop-off point. Your agency and the detention facility will specify acceptable locked locations.

Gather all personal property taken from the arrestee, and safely remove the arrestee from the patrol vehicle. Maintain physical control of the arrestee during escort into the facility. Use verbal commands and physical direction. You are responsible for the arrestee until the facility staff receives them. Secured facilities can present certain hazards and dangers regarding officer safety, such as codefendants or other arrestees, so remain aware of your surroundings.

Provide appropriate documentation to the facility. After transporting an arrestee, thoroughly search the passenger compartment of the vehicle as soon as practically possible.

☑ LE551.8. Describe how to store your weapons safely before entering a secured facility

☑ LE551.9. Explain how to safely transfer an arrestee to a secured facility

UNIT 5 ARREST PROCEDURES
LESSON 2 Processing the Arrestee

Lesson Goal

At the end of this lesson, you will know how to safely transfer a juvenile or adult arrestee to a secure facility for processing.

Think About This

You respond to a burglary call involving a juvenile. What are some considerations when taking the juvenile into custody?

JUVENILE ARRESTS

You can take a juvenile to a secure booking area of a jail or an adult jail for temporary custody for no more than six hours, or for the purpose of fingerprinting and photographing them as long as the juvenile is out of the sight and hearing of adult arrestees.

☑ LE552.1. Describe your responsibilities when processing a juvenile in an adult detention facility

Most juveniles in adult jails or police lockups are waiting to be transported to an appropriate facility or are in pre- or post-court holding. Exceptions apply to a juvenile charged as an adult or when the court has emancipated or adjudicated the juvenile as an adult. Verify a juvenile's legal adult status through the Department of Juvenile Justice, court records, or criminal histories.

You are responsible for a juvenile who has a medical condition, a mental illness, or is experiencing the effects of substance abuse. You are also responsible until a parent, a guardian, or a representative of the Department of Children and Families assumes responsibility. Make thorough efforts to notify a juvenile's parents within a reasonable time after the arrest. You cannot release a juvenile on their own recognizance when custody is terminated. An adult relative, a qualified adult, or an organization must take custody of the child and acknowledge this by signing booking forms or charging documents. Your agency may have additional policies and procedures for processing a juvenile.

ENTERING THE DETENTION FACILITY

Many agencies use booking or intake officers (law enforcement or correctional officers) at the county jail. These facilities have their own policies and procedures, and you must know and follow them.

☑ LE552.2. List arrestee information to tell the booking officer

Tell the booking officer the following information:

- the charges against the arrestee
- any injuries the arrestee has
- if the arrestee is a juvenile

- if the arrestee was contaminated with pepper spray
- if a conducted electric weapon (such as a dart-firing stun gun) was used
- any threats made by the arrestee to oneself or others
- any known medical conditions

The transporting officer must give the booking officer any personal property previously removed from the arrestee. Do not give the booking officer any contraband or evidence collected from the arrestee. After this, transfer custody of the arrestee to the booking officer. The arresting officer must complete an arrest affidavit, and the affidavit must accompany the arrestee to the booking officer.

BOOKING

After the transfer, the booking officer processes the arrestee. This process includes fingerprinting, photographing, and inventorying personal property for safe keeping until the arrestee is released. Record the following personal information about the arrestee: name, race, sex, date of birth, Social Security number, criminal charges, and case number.

☑ LE552.3. Describe the role of the booking officer

Remember that FCIC/NCIC receives criminal history data from fingerprint cards, arrest, and correctional reports. Therefore, it is important to complete this information accurately. Booking photos provide a visual record of each arrestee. Many facilities can access existing photos from past arrests rather than taking new photographs. Learn your agency's procedures for taking fingerprints and for photographing arrestees. All crime evidence and seized contraband must be properly processed and packaged for safekeeping according to your agency's policies. Submit evidence using established procedures to maintain the chain of custody and reduce any legal challenges. Chain of custody will be discussed in greater detail in Chapter 9.

COMPLETING THE ARREST PROCESS

After you turn over the arrestee and the arrest affidavit to the booking officer, inform dispatch of the call's completion and its outcome.

☑ LE552.4. Assemble complete documents for arrestee processing

Document your arrests completely and accurately. Your documents should clearly convey investigative facts to assist in prosecution.

Chapter 6
Serving Your Community

UNIT 1 INTERACTING WITH YOUR COMMUNITY
- LESSON 1 Introduction to Responding to Your Community / 223
- LESSON 2 Serving the Elderly / 225
- LESSON 3 Serving Juveniles / 227
- LESSON 4 Serving Veterans / 229
- LESSON 5 Serving the Homeless / 232
- LESSON 6 Americans With Disabilities Act / 234
- LESSON 7 Serving People With Physical Impairments / 236
- LESSON 8 Serving People With Developmental Disabilities / 240
- LESSON 9 Serving People With Autism / 243
- LESSON 10 Serving People With Mental Illnesses / 245

UNIT 2 RESPONDING TO A PERSON IN CRISIS
- LESSON 1 Crisis Situations / 249
- LESSON 2 The Baker Act / 253
- LESSON 3 Suicide Risk / 256
- LESSON 4 Substance Abuse / 259
- LESSON 5 The Marchman Act / 262
- LESSON 6 Transportation and Documentation / 264

UNIT 3 IDENTIFYING AND RESPONDING TO HIGH-RISK GROUPS
- LESSON 1 Criminal Gangs / 266
- LESSON 2 Extremist Groups / 268

UNIT 1 INTERACTING WITH YOUR COMMUNITY
LESSON 1 Introduction to Responding to Your Community

Lesson Goal

At the end of this lesson, you will know how to respond to and interact with your community, including vulnerable adults.

Think About This

You receive a call from dispatch regarding a noise complaint due to a graduation party at a local residence. What are some techniques you could use when responding to this call?

A community's relationship with law enforcement can greatly affect how officers do their jobs. You can create opportunities for positive change by strengthening the trust between you and the community you serve; building trust begins with addressing residents' concerns and ensuring a safe community.

Responding to situations that have the potential to become volatile can cause reactions of inflexibility, aggression, fear, and anger. This can negatively affect the communication between you and your community and make conflict more likely. Additionally, taking things personally and reacting to perceived insults discourages effective policing. Good communication, critical thinking, and sound judgment are crucial for determining when you should use force and when you should try other methods to resolve conflict.

RESPONDING TO VULNERABLE ADULTS IN YOUR COMMUNITY

During your duties as a law enforcement officer, you will encounter vulnerable adults, such as the elderly, people with disabilities, and people with mental health disorders. A ***vulnerable adult*** is a person 18 or older whose ability to perform the activities of daily living or to provide for their own care or protection is impaired. Often this is due to a mental, emotional, sensory, long-term physical or developmental disability or dysfunction, brain damage, or the infirmities of aging.

Be sensitive and aware of people's differences and demonstrate respect for their limitations. Never dismiss or disregard a person because of their differences. Keep in mind the core communication competencies you learned in Chapter 2 and treat all people you encounter respectfully, accommodating any limitations they may have.

☑ LE611.1. Describe how to respond to incidents involving vulnerable adults

Techniques to use when responding to vulnerable adults include the following:

- Minimize distractions and disperse any crowds.
- Respect personal space and avoid physical contact.

- Remember to relax, breathe, and use calming body language.
- Allow the person's self-stimulating behaviors to continue if the situation allows unless there is immediate danger.
- Once the person has calmed, assist them as needed.

INTERACTING WITH YOUR COMMUNITY

☑ LE611.2. Describe how to interact with people in a courteous and polite manner

The way you interact with the people in your community can help keep encounters courteous and polite. When interacting with the public, maintain eye contact and speak directly to a person, even if an interpreter is present. In addition to the core communication competencies, other techniques you may use include the following:

- Speak clearly and in a respectful tone of voice.
- Use short, simple phrases while avoiding slang.
- Model the behavior you want to see.
- Maintain a calm and reassuring tone.
- Use encouragement throughout your encounter.

While communicating politely is essential, it is important to remember that any encounter with the public has the opportunity to become tense. The following techniques can help you maintain peace:

- Practice calming—defuse the intensity of the situation. Treat people with courtesy and speak politely to create a comfortable atmosphere for conversation. Practice active listening skills. Use a calm, low voice; keep intermittent eye contact; and maintain an appropriate reactionary gap.
- Assess the situation—be aware of behaviors, statements, and the possible role of substances.
- Consider the environment—be aware of the environment's effect as well as the current circumstances, including the presence of injuries or signs of substance abuse.

While using these techniques can prevent escalation, understand that they do not guarantee a peaceful resolution. In some cases, people will continue to escalate regardless of your efforts, but these techniques help you keep communication open and improve your ability to resolve the call.

Although many of your interactions with the public will be positive, as an officer, you will encounter people in some of the most difficult moments of their lives. Individual calls may not seem to noticeably affect you, but daily stress as a law enforcement officer may overlap with other personal stressors, such as financial or family issues. Cumulative stress is the buildup of routine and acute stress over time which can affect your mental and physical health. When managing your own stress becomes overwhelming, it may become difficult to maintain your composure and have positive interactions with the public. Taking care of your own mental and physical health and learning how to cope with stressors in a healthy way is vital for your career longevity.

UNIT 1 INTERACTING WITH YOUR COMMUNITY
LESSON 2 Serving the Elderly

Lesson Goal

At the end of this lesson, you will know how to identify and respond to the unique needs of people who are elderly in your community.

Think About This

You receive a call about an elderly person who cannot find their car in the mall parking lot and fears it may have been stolen. What considerations do you have while interacting with this person?

CHARACTERISTICS OF PEOPLE WHO ARE ELDERLY

Chances are high that you will frequently interact with older people in a variety of settings. Not all elderly people have the characteristics listed here, but they may struggle from physical or mental weakness to a degree that impacts their ability to care for or protect themselves.

According to chapter 825, F.S., an ***elderly person*** is:

> *a person 60 years of age or older who is suffering from the infirmities of aging as manifested by advanced age or organic brain damage, or other physical, mental, or emotional dysfunctioning, to the extent that the ability of the person to provide adequately for the person's own care or protection is impaired.*

☑ LE612.1. Identify some of the common characteristics of a person who is elderly

Common characteristics of an elderly person may include limited mobility, vision, or hearing, lack of strength, bone deterioration, or memory loss. They may live alone, with family members, in nursing homes, or be homeless.

You may encounter an elderly person who has wandered away from their home or living facility due to memory loss or declining health. In this situation, you may consider initiating a Silver Alert to aid in their rescue or recovery. You will learn about initiating a Silver Alert in Chapter 7.

Two common causes of memory loss in an elderly person include:

- dementia—an umbrella term used to describe an organic, progressive mental disorder characterized by loss of memory, an impairment of judgment and abstract thinking, and changes in personality.
- Alzheimer's disease—a progressive brain disorder that gradually destroys a person's memory and ability to learn, reason, make judgments, communicate, and carry out daily activities. As Alzheimer's progresses, a person may also experience changes in personality and behavior, such as anxiety, suspicion, or agitation as well as delusions or hallucinations.

INTERACTING WITH PEOPLE WHO ARE ELDERLY

> LE612.2. Identify ways to effectively interact with a person who is elderly

General guidelines for communicating with an elderly person are the same as with anyone else. You may use the following techniques:

- Make sure you understand the problem from their perspective.
- Explain what you can do to help them.
- Speak directly to them; establish and maintain eye contact as is appropriate based on cultural customs.
- Use a conversational tone and speak loudly only if necessary.
- Use caution when allowing caregivers to speak on behalf of an elderly person to eliminate any third-party agenda.
- Include them in all discussions concerning their welfare, and adjust your communication based on any disabilities or other limitations.
- Always treat them with dignity, respect, and patience.

If an elderly person becomes a victim of a crime, they may find it difficult to cope. Depending on the crime and the circumstances, the person may feel embarrassed and ashamed of being a victim. In addition to investigating the incident, you must address and calm their fear by showing empathy and compassion.

RESOURCES FOR PEOPLE WHO ARE ELDERLY

> LE612.3. Identify state and local resources that may assist people who are elderly

Knowing about the special needs of the elderly can help you ensure that older Floridians have the full protection of the law. The Department of Elder Affairs provides direct services to the elderly through its Division of Statewide Community-Based Services. Another important resource is the Florida Elder Helpline at (800) 96-ELDER. The helpline provides information to help older residents obtain specific local social services. The 211 helpline is another resource available to all persons, including the elderly, who are looking for resources or assistance in a variety of areas such as crisis counseling and disaster, housing, and food assistance.

UNIT 1 INTERACTING WITH YOUR COMMUNITY
LESSON 3 Serving Juveniles

Lesson Goal

At the end of this lesson, you will know how to identify and respond to the unique needs of juveniles in your community, including juvenile offenders.

Think About This

You receive a call about a teenager shoplifting at a local convenience store. When you speak with the teenager, she is uncooperative. What techniques would you use while interacting with the teenager?

CHARACTERISTICS OF JUVENILES

Young people generally reflect the values instilled in them by their families, schools, communities, and cultures. Ethnicity, socioeconomic status, expectations, and numerous other factors also affect a juvenile's characteristics and behaviors.

☑ LE613.1. Describe factors that can affect the decision-making abilities of juveniles

Some children are exposed to domestic violence either as victims or witnesses. They may hear one parent or caregiver threaten the other, observe a parent losing control, see one parent assault the other, or live with the aftermath of a violent assault. Many children are affected by hearing threats made to their caregiver regardless of whether the threats result in physical injury. These children are susceptible to post-traumatic stress disorder (PTSD) in addition to experiencing physical health issues and demonstrating behavior problems in adolescence, such as juvenile delinquency and alcohol or substance abuse.

Florida law defines a person younger than 18 years of age as a juvenile. While the age of legal maturity is 18, the brain is not fully developed until the age of 25. This is a possible explanation for the risky behavior or lack of impulse control that juveniles and young adults may exhibit.

JUVENILE OFFENDERS

Some juveniles may want to push the boundaries of the rules, both at home and in public, and they may show a high degree of irresponsibility, a lack of respect for authority, and unpredictable behavioral patterns, such as fighting, bullying, using weapons, and participating in gang-related violence. Without successful interventions, they may go on to become juvenile offenders. According to the U.S. Office of Juvenile Justice and Delinquency Prevention, juveniles who start offending when they are younger than 13 are more likely to become serious and violent offenders.

☑ LE613.2. Identify some of the common characteristics of juvenile offenders

Juvenile offenders may display manipulative and defiant behaviors when interacting with others, including law enforcement. The stability of a juvenile's home environment can determine to what degree that juvenile becomes involved in petty crimes. As an officer, you may have to respond to incidents where a crime was committed against a juvenile. Although physical assault is the primary crime committed against juveniles, bullying via social media is a growing issue.

INTERACTING WITH JUVENILES

You and other law enforcement officers can serve as role models and help steer potential juvenile offenders toward becoming law-abiding citizens.

☑ LE613.3. Identify how to effectively interact with juveniles

A high degree of self-control, patience, flexibility, and understanding is required to work effectively with juveniles. You must be able to adapt to whatever situation arises, whether dealing with the home environment, bullying, excessive school absenteeism, rebellion, or dangerous behavior. To build a positive relationship, provide information and support through empathy, comfort, and physical assistance, such as buying groceries for a juvenile who is trying to steal food.

When interacting with juveniles, you may need to interact with their families as well. Look for ways to provide guidance to juveniles and their families; this will help increase your support within the community and build relationships and networks that will benefit the overall law enforcement effort.

When dealing with juvenile offenders, you can take a variety of actions, depending on the seriousness of the problem and the evidence, if any, of misconduct. Your actions may involve issuing commands, informing the parents or guardians, conducting an investigation, arresting the juvenile, or releasing the juvenile. A juvenile younger than 7 years of age may not be arrested or charged unless the violation is a forcible felony or a third-degree felony of burglary or trespassing with burglary tools.

RUNAWAY CHILDREN

☑ LE613.4. Describe how to respond to a runaway child

Children who run away are at considerable risk of falling prey to horrible crimes. Always presume that the runaway child is in danger. You have no arrest authority for a child who is a runaway or an absentee from school; however, if you believe a child is a runaway, take the child into protective custody and contact the parent or legal guardian of the child. If you reasonably believe a child is an absentee, you can take the child into protective custody and deliver them back to the school system. If the parent or guardian is not available for a runaway child, contact the Department of Children and Families. Protective custody is not a criminal arrest.

UNIT 1 INTERACTING WITH YOUR COMMUNITY
LESSON 4 Serving Veterans

Lesson Goal

At the end of this lesson, you will know how to identify and respond to the unique needs of military veterans in your community.

Think About This

While on patrol, you pull over a driver for swerving between lanes. As you speak to the driver, he seems disoriented and irritated. You ask for his license and registration and notice a "Veteran" designation. What considerations do you have when interacting with the driver?

IDENTIFYING VETERANS IN LIFESTYLE TRANSITIONS

Veterans transitioning from active duty to civilian life possess unique experiences from military culture and combat. Cultivating a knowledge of military principles will prepare you to make a connection with veterans in your community. You may become a positive role model or potentially refer veterans to beneficial resources.

Visible signs of current or prior military experience may include the following:

- tattoos with military subject matter (e.g., a military branch logo)
- military ID provided alongside a driver license
- Florida driver license with "Veteran"; older licenses may have a "V"
- license plates and bumper stickers with military subject matter
- body language; a command presence
- military-style haircut
- blended clothing (e.g., such as a t-shirt with camouflage pants and a cap)

☑ LE614.1. Identify some of the characteristics of veterans or active-duty military personnel

As with all members in the community, veterans can be victims of crime or potential suspects or perpetrators of crime. If you suspect that a veteran has committed a crime, be aware that they might have a high level of weapons or defensive tactics training due to their prior or current military service, so maintain proper situational awareness. Be prepared to react quickly and appropriately if there is a threat to your safety.

INTERACTING WITH VETERANS

Because of their exposure to traumatic experiences, some veterans may have pronounced stressors caused by musculoskeletal injuries, neurological injuries, or psychological disorders. These disabilities may be significant but not necessarily immediately noticeable.

☑ LE614.2. Identify the physical and psychological stressors that some military veterans experience

Some veterans with psychological symptoms may know how to cover or hide their symptoms in society, especially if they were able to hide them while serving in the military. Those serving in the military may be hesitant to get the help that might improve their mental health.

☑ LE614.3. Identify some of the characteristics of a person with a traumatic brain injury (TBI)

Some veterans may have PTSD or a traumatic brain injury. A **traumatic brain injury (TBI)** is structural and often occurs as the result of sudden injury that causes damage to the brain, frequently resulting from combat. Some common signs and symptoms of TBI are loss of balance, slurred speech, disorientation, and irritability. As an officer, you need to be aware that symptoms of TBI may mimic behaviors of being under the influence of drugs or alcohol.

Law enforcement officers who are combat veterans suggest doing the following when responding to an incident involving a veteran:

- Gain their trust—gain trust to increase your odds of obtaining the person's cooperation and achieving your success.
- Do not corner the person—avoid cornering the person unless it is a dangerous situation where you must forcefully and directly engage with the person. If the situation quickly escalates, immediately request backup.

☑ LE614.4. Identify how to interact with a person who is a veteran

Cornering veterans, especially when they have a TBI or PTSD, is one of the biggest mistakes you can make. Combat veterans faced with this situation will usually choose to battle because that is their training. All veterans have undergone extensive defensive and offensive training and are familiar with a wide assortment of weapons. This can pose a very real threat to officer safety. A veteran with TBI or PTSD may have issues with substance abuse, mood changes, social judgment, and impulse control that can lead to unpredictable behavior.

If you are responding to an incident involving a veteran and cannot reach an understanding with them, consider asking for backup from another officer with a military background.

COPING BEHAVIORS EXHIBITED BY VETERANS

☑ LE614.5. Identify negative coping behaviors that a veteran may use

Veterans with PTSD may try to gain control over their environment by applying various coping behaviors that mask deeper issues. Some coping behaviors may do more harm than good. Common negative coping behaviors veterans use include:

- using substances—using drugs or alcohol to escape personal problems, to sleep, or to make symptoms go away. Substance abuse may lead to violence or bad decisions.
- avoiding situations, people, or things that are reminders of the trauma—avoidance behavior can lead to isolation and patterns of negative thoughts and feelings that prevent veterans from obtaining the needed social support.
- hypervigilance—being constantly on guard for danger, causing stress, fear, and exhaustion.

- feeling anger and resorting to violence—losing their temper easily and making careless choices.
- engaging in dangerous behavior—participating in dangerous or unsafe activities, such as beginning fights when upset, hurting oneself or others, or driving recklessly.
- working too much—working to avoid thinking about the trauma. Working can be another form of avoidance.

As an officer, recognizing negative coping behavior early in your interactions with veterans may help you avoid potentially dangerous situations and find better ways to serve them. Become familiar with the resources available for veterans in your community.

UNIT 1 INTERACTING WITH YOUR COMMUNITY
LESSON 5 Serving the Homeless

◎ Lesson Goal

At the end of this lesson, you will know how to respectfully interact with and provide support to people who are homeless in your community.

Think About This

You respond to a call from a local business owner who says that a woman has been sleeping in her car in his parking lot for the past two days. When you speak with the woman, she tells you that she is currently living in her car and has nowhere else to go. What should you do?

HOMELESSNESS

☑ LE615.1. Identify some of the characteristics of a person who is homeless

According to the Florida Statutes, **homeless** is defined as a person who does not have a fixed, regular, and adequate nighttime residence. One type of homelessness is "unsheltered," which refers to people who live in places not meant for human habitation—on the streets, in cars, in wooded areas, or in abandoned buildings. Others are "sheltered" but are still homeless because they are staying in homeless shelters or transitional housing until they find stable permanent housing of their own.

The experience of homelessness is traumatic, and daily survival is a challenge. People who are homeless are less likely to connect with community health care resources, engage fully in employment and education, or have stable relationships with friends and family. Homelessness worsens preexisting health problems, reduces the speed and likelihood of recovery, and exposes people to more health threats.

Many people who are homeless have committed what are considered "imprisonable offenses," such as thefts, burglaries, or other crimes of opportunity. In addition, without the security of a home, homeless people become vulnerable and easy targets for crime. They are often reluctant to report a crime because they lack the motivation to file a complaint or because they want to avoid contact with law enforcement.

RESPONDING TO PEOPLE WHO ARE HOMELESS

☑ LE615.2. Describe how to respond to a person who is homeless

Being homeless is not a crime, and it is rarely a choice. As an officer, you can provide information about services instead of making an arrest when interacting with people who are homeless. As with any interaction in the community, when a homeless person requests or needs assistance, treat them with dignity and respect, and be aware of the person's civil rights at all times.

Transporting a person who is homeless to an alternate location, such as a faith-based organization with related outreach or shelter services, may eliminate the original concern that required the attention of law enforcement. Many communities have programs and tent cities for people who are homeless to centralize services and offer safer locations for them. Become familiar with your local resources, including shelters and social programs provided through a crisis intervention team (CIT). Depending on your community, resources may be available to veterans, families, and youth who are homeless.

UNIT 1 INTERACTING WITH YOUR COMMUNITY
LESSON 6 Americans With Disabilities Act

© Lesson Goal

At the end of this lesson, you will know how to interact with and protect the rights of people who have a disability as defined by the Americans With Disabilities Act (ADA).

Think About This

While on patrol, you approach a vehicle and ask the driver to step out of the car. You see the driver reach behind the seat for her crutches. What considerations would you have during your interaction with this person?

The **Americans With Disabilities Act (ADA)** is a federal civil rights law that prohibits discrimination against people with disabilities in all areas of public life, such as jobs, schools, and transportation. As a law enforcement officer, you must understand the requirements of the ADA to effectively interact with people who have a disability.

☑ LE616.1. Identify the impairment criteria as defined by the Americans With Disabilities Act (ADA)

According to the ADA, a person with a disability is someone who has a physical or mental impairment that substantially limits a major life activity, has a record of impairment, or is regarded as having an impairment. A substantial limitation is a restriction of the way, condition, or amount of time in which a person can perform major life activities compared to non-impaired people.

Major life activities include caring for oneself, performing manual tasks, walking, seeing, hearing, speaking, breathing, learning, and working. Other major life activities include sitting, standing, and lifting, and mental and emotional processes such as thinking, concentrating, and interacting with others. Examples of impairments include back or spinal injuries, psychiatric or mental disabilities, neurological impairments, extremity impairments, heart impairments, drug addiction, diabetes, hearing impairments, vision impairments, and blood disorders. The most common disabilities that you will encounter are psychiatric or mental disabilities, neurological impairments, vision, hearing and speech impairments, and extremity impairments.

The ADA prohibits discrimination against a person with a disability in all services, programs, and activities provided to the public by state and local governments. Since a law enforcement agency is a public entity that provides state or local government services, it has an impact on your daily duties and responsibilities. The ADA does not prevent you from enforcing laws, but it does affect how you interact with people who have disabilities.

PROTECTING THE RIGHTS OF PEOPLE WITH DISABILITIES

Chapter 825, F.S., defines a ***disabled adult*** as:

> *a person 18 years of age or older who suffers from a condition of physical or mental incapacitation due to a developmental disability, organic brain damage, or mental illness, or who has one or more physical or mental limitations that restrict the person's ability to perform the normal activities of daily living.*

The disability substantially affects a person's life activities and may be present from birth or occur during a person's lifetime.

People with disabilities have the same rights as everyone else, and you must protect these rights. For example, some people with disabilities may not understand *Miranda* rights as they are usually explained. This is likely when people are in a stressful situation and have a disability that affects their ability to communicate. You should explain the *Miranda* rights so that the person can understand them. Keep in mind that the person's vocabulary and understanding of the concept of rights might be limited. Similarly, observations for intoxication, such as failure to walk a straight line, will be ineffective for people whose disabilities cause an unsteady gait.

☑ LE616.2. Describe how to ensure the rights of a person with a disability

When appropriate, make sure that someone who knows the person, such as a relative, friend, attorney, or agency staff member, is present when interviewing them. Record the interview, if possible. Document the disability in the interview or report and inform the state attorney's office of the disability as appropriate. If you arrest a person with a disability, inform correctional personnel of the disability.

INTERACTING WITH PEOPLE WITH DISABILITIES

It may not be immediately apparent that someone has a disability, but be aware that anyone can. Treat all people with respect; use a suitable tone of voice; and speak in an age-appropriate manner, even when you suspect a person may have a disability. Be attentive to how the person needs to communicate and interact, and make sure that your communication with them is as effective as communication with others.

☑ LE616.3. Describe how to interact with a person who has a disability

Some people with disabilities use a service animal, such as a dog trained to assist them with daily activities. Under the ADA, a service animal is defined as a dog that has been individually trained to do work or perform tasks for a person with a disability. The task(s) performed by the dog must be directly related to the person's disability. Examples of tasks include guiding a person who is blind, alerting a person who is deaf, alerting and protecting a person who is having a seizure, reminding a person with mental illness to take prescribed medications, or calming a person with PTSD during an anxiety attack.

A service animal for a person with a vision, hearing, or mobility impairment may or may not wear an identifying harness or vest. The person may have documentation showing that the animal is a service animal. However, no certification is required under the law. If it is apparent that the animal is a service animal, you may not question the animal's service. Under the ADA, in situations where it is not obvious if the animal is a service animal, you may ask only two specific questions: is the dog a service animal that is required because of a disability, and what work or task has the dog been trained to perform?

A person with a service animal is entitled to freely access public areas. If a person you arrest uses a service animal, you must arrange care for the animal. It is preferable to place the animal with a family member, a friend, or even a kennel rather than calling animal control. Follow agency policies and procedures when dealing with situations involving service animals.

UNIT 1 INTERACTING WITH YOUR COMMUNITY
LESSON 7 Serving People With Physical Impairments

◎ Lesson Goal

At the end of this lesson, you will know how to interact with and protect the rights of people with physical impairments.

Think About This

You respond to a dispute between two neighbors. The person reporting the issue is complaining that his neighbor keeps parking on his grass. You approach the neighbor and learn that she is hard of hearing. How would you handle this interaction?

MOBILITY IMPAIRMENT

A *physical or mobility impairment* is a functional limitation that affects one or more of a person's limbs. People with mobility impairments may have limited use of one or more of their extremities for walking, grasping, or lifting objects. They may need to use devices such as braces, canes, or wheelchairs to move around. Some people may have conditions such as arthritis or tendonitis that prohibit them from moving, sitting, or reaching. Even if a person does not have formal documentation of a disability, treat them with all the rights afforded to a person who has a disability according to the ADA.

☑ LE617.1. Describe how to interact with a person who has a mobility impairment

There are special considerations to keep in mind when communicating with a person who has a mobility impairment, such as maintaining good eye contact and asking if the person would like assistance before providing it. However, not all people who have a mobility impairment need assistance. Some activities may appear to be difficult, but the person may not need or want help. Do not be offended if the person declines your offer of assistance.

VISION IMPAIRMENT

Vision impairment is a loss or partial loss of sight that cannot be corrected by usual means, such as glasses. The types of vision impairments that you will encounter most often are blindness and partial sight. Blindness is a functional loss of vision. This definition applies both to people who cannot see at all (are unable to distinguish light from dark) and people who have some vision in one or both eyes. Partial sight is a visual impairment in which, after correction, objects still look dim or out of focus. People with partial sight may not see color well or at all or may lack peripheral vision, but they can still see and even read with magnifiers or other aids.

☑ LE617.2. Explain how to interact with a person who is blind or visually impaired

The following are tips for speaking to a person who is blind or visually impaired:

- Identify yourself and state any directions or instructions clearly and completely.
- State any information that is posted visually as well.

- Read out loud, and in full, any documents that the person needs to sign or, when available, provide a large-print version.

- Describe any procedures in advance so that the person will know what to expect. For example, before taking photos or fingerprints, explain to the person what you are going to do and what it involves.

- Provide special accommodations for them as victims, witnesses, and suspects. For example, when communicating with them, instead of pointing and saying, "Go over there," you might want to take them to where you are pointing.

- If the person is a victim of assault, reassure them that the assailant is no longer present.

HEARING IMPAIRMENT

A *hearing impairment* is any degree of hearing loss. The two classifications of hearing loss are hard of hearing and deafness.

A person who is hard of hearing may have hearing loss but not to the extent that they must rely primarily on visual communication, such as written notes or sign language. Hearing aids may not improve the person's ability to understand words but may increase their ability to hear sound.

Deafness is severe hearing loss to the extent that the person must rely primarily on visual tools, such as writing, sign language, and lip reading, to communicate.

Some people who are deaf or hard of hearing may have poor balance or slurred speech and may appear to be intoxicated. However, they are generally attentive to their surroundings as their eyes must see what their ears cannot hear. They may compensate for the loss of hearing with heightened visual awareness, and often indicate that they cannot hear by pointing to their ears or mouths, shaking their head "no," or making some other movement to indicate that they do not understand.

When interacting with a person who is deaf or hard of hearing, attempt to gain the person's attention first. A light touch on their arm should draw their attention and avoid a startled response. Once you have the person's attention, state the person's name before beginning a conversation. Face the person, maintain good eye contact, and speak clearly, slowly, and distinctly, using the appropriate volume without shouting.

☑ LE617.3. Explain how to interact with a person who is deaf or hard of hearing

Other things to keep in mind when communicating include the following:

- Avoid shouting or exaggerating your mouth movements. This will distort your speech, making it more difficult for them to understand you.

- Avoid using complex sentences and quickly changing topics as it can be confusing. If they do not understand a particular phrase or word, try to find a different way of saying the same thing rather than repeating the same message.

- Take turns speaking and pay attention to their expressions and body language. A puzzled look may indicate misunderstanding.
- Assess how much they understand by having them repeat back what they understood.
- Have them write down specific information such as time, place, phone numbers, and other relevant information.
- Be aware of environmental considerations. Try to minimize extraneous noises and avoid dimly lit rooms.
- If you have a conversation with a person who is deaf or hard of hearing and a third person, make sure that they understand everything you're saying to the third person.

For many people who are deaf or hard of hearing, sign language and other forms of non-verbal communication are their primary language. A qualified **sign language interpreter** is a person who can both receive and express information and interpret it effectively, accurately, and impartially through sign language. This definition recognizes that some types of communication require more sophisticated interpreting skills than other forms of communication. When communicating with a person who relies on sign language, speak directly to them and not to the interpreter.

If an interpreter is not available, you may need to ask the person to use pen and paper, saving the document as evidence relating to an incident. You can use aids, such as cell phone applications, a computer, a telecommunications device for the deaf or teletypewriter (TDD/TTY), or an assistive listening device (a sound amplifier with headphones) to help with communication. Also consider recording all exchanges with someone who is hearing impaired.

☑ LE617.4. Explain how to protect the rights of a person who is deaf or hard of hearing when making an arrest

Florida court cases involving defendants who are deaf or hard of hearing are sometimes dismissed because of events occurring before *Miranda* rights are explained. This emphasizes the importance of understanding the communication problems associated with hearing impairments. When advising a person who is deaf or hard of hearing of their *Miranda* rights, provide their rights in a manner understood by them, such as in writing or by using a sign language interpreter. If the person requests a sign language interpreter during a *Miranda* situation, you may not continue to question them until the interpreter appears. People who are deaf or hard of hearing cannot knowingly waive their rights unless the warning is given in a format they understand.

According to the ADA, a person who is deaf or hard of hearing has the right to choose what kind of communication help they need. The nature of the communication, the needs of the person requesting the assistance, and your agency's policies and procedures may determine whether the situation requires a qualified sign language interpreter or another communication aid, such as a TDD/TTY.

If the situation may be confrontational, do not rely on family members, friends, or children to provide sign language interpretation because you may receive biased information.

SPEECH IMPAIRMENT

A *speech impairment* is a physiological condition that causes a person to have difficulty in producing sound or understandable language. Speech impairment can result from hearing loss, a neurological disorder, a brain injury, or physical impairments such as a cleft lip or palate. Speech impairments have many forms, including voice and sound disorders, stuttering, slurring, lisping, and mumbling.

If you have trouble understanding someone's speech in a non-confrontational incident, ask if family members, friends, or neighbors can help. If no one is available, ask the person to repeat what was said or to use a pen and paper or electronic device. Do not use your personal cell phone for communication as it may be used as evidence. If using a pen and paper or electronic device to communicate, make the questions brief and clear, and save the paper as evidence or document the use of the electronic device.

☑ LE617.5. Explain how to interact with a person who has a speech impairment

UNIT 1 INTERACTING WITH YOUR COMMUNITY
LESSON 8 Serving People With Developmental Disabilities

Lesson Goal

At the end of this lesson, you will know how to interact with and protect the rights and dignity of people with developmental disabilities, including intellectual disabilities.

Think About This

You pull over a driver for failing to use his turn signal. When you approach the driver, he begins to repeat the same phrase over and over again and does not appear to understand you. What considerations do you have when interacting with this person?

DEVELOPMENTAL DISABILITIES

The Florida Statutes define a ***developmental disability*** as a disorder or syndrome that is attributable to intellectual disability, cerebral palsy, autism, spina bifida, Down syndrome, Phelan-McDermid syndrome, Prader-Willi syndrome; it is a disability that manifests before the age of 18, constitutes a substantial handicap, and continues indefinitely.

☑ LE618.1. Identify the characteristics of a person with a developmental disability

A developmental disability may affect a person's intellectual functioning and can make it harder for them to learn. The symptoms vary for each person depending on their condition. People with developmental disabilities may have substantial functional limitations in major life activities such as self-care, learning, mobility, the capacity to live independently, and the ability to be economically self-sufficient. As you perform your duties as an officer, keep in mind other possible characteristics of development disabilities such as limited vocabulary or possible speech impairment, difficulty understanding or answering your questions, or a short attention span.

INTERACTING WITH PEOPLE WITH DEVELOPMENTAL DISABILITIES

At some point in your career, you may respond to a call for service for breach of peace, a disturbance, or unusual or disorderly conduct that involves a person with a developmental disability. Be aware that there may be communication challenges, and try to contact a caregiver or family member who can help with communication.

☑ LE618.2. Describe how to interact with a person who has a developmental disability

The following are important tips for speaking to a person with a developmental disability:

- Allow extra time to exchange information.
- Speak directly to the person and not to their caregiver.
- Focus on their abilities rather than disabilities.
- Respect personal space as they may be sensitive to physical contact, lights, and sounds.

- Gather information to identify and eliminate any stimuli that are aggravating to them. Examples of aggravating stimuli can include an agitating caretaker, family member, object, noise, or animal.
- Interview people at the scene of the incident, and observe the actions of the person with a developmental disability.

If you are the responding officer, determine if any threats are present and if the person is a threat to themselves or to others by following officer safety protocols:

- Assess the scene to determine if medical assistance is needed.
- Apply first aid techniques or request EMS as appropriate.
- Request assistance from a CIT if appropriate.

Be aware of community resources that can assist, including mental health facilities, the Department of Children and Families, or crisis centers. Explain to the caregiver or family the resources available to successfully resolve the situation. Determine if the person with a developmental disability meets the criteria for the Baker Act or if they should be left with their legal guardian or caregiver. The Baker Act is discussed later in this chapter.

INTELLECTUAL DISABILITIES

Intellectual disabilities are types of developmental disabilities that are lifelong conditions characterized by slow intellectual development. A number of conditions, ranging from genetic conditions to illness and injury, can cause an intellectual disability. A psychological evaluation is required to diagnose an intellectual disability early in childhood. These disabilities cannot be cured, but using the appropriate modifications and accommodations can enhance a person's capabilities and independence. Depending on the person's level of disability, a person with an intellectual disability may be vulnerable to crimes of opportunity.

The majority of people with an intellectual disability function at a mild level of disability, which may not be easily identifiable. People functioning at this level can learn academic and prevocational skills with special training and can work within their community. People with a mild intellectual disability might not understand long-term consequences or be able to make appropriate choices, but they do sometimes realize when they have done something wrong.

☑ LE618.3. Identify the characteristics of a person with an intellectual disability

People with a moderate intellectual disability may recognize their own needs and wants but not immediately identify the needs and wants of others. People with a moderate intellectual disability can achieve a primary academic education and may be able to perform semiskilled work under direct supervision. They can be independent in familiar surroundings but may be easily frustrated with unfamiliar surroundings and circumstances. They may have trouble describing events in chronological order and may not understand cause and effect. While they may understand that they have done something wrong, they may not grasp the significance of their actions.

People with a severe intellectual disability have slow motor development and communication skills and are frequently under close and constant supervision, such as in a group home setting. They are usually encouraged to contribute to their own self-maintenance; however, they may not be fully capable of living independently.

People with a profound intellectual disability require constant care and supervision and may or may not have well-developed basic speech. Generally, you will not come into direct contact with them but will deal directly with the caregiver.

INTERACTING WITH PEOPLE WITH INTELLECTUAL DISABILITIES

LE618.4. Describe how to interact with a person who has an intellectual disability

You may respond to situations involving a person who has an intellectual disability. The following are tips for speaking to a person with an intellectual disability:

- Refrain from imposing a label upon their disability, and always defer to their preferred terminology.
- Treat them with dignity and respect.
- Use simple, short sentences to increase the likelihood that they will understand your message.
- Ask them to repeat what they have heard to show that they fully understand the message.
- Provide additional time to respond to questions.

When interacting with a person with an intellectual disability, a caregiver may provide reassurance, have a calming effect on the person, or may take extra precautions with the person's safety. The person with an intellectual disability may have a personalized piece of technology or some other form of identification that can assist you in contacting the caregiver.

People with intellectual disabilities may not be able to distinguish between abstract and concrete thought and might confess to crimes that they did not commit. They may be easily intimidated, eager to please, and generally agree with all authority figures. If there is a need for services, refer them to the Department of Children and Families; The ARC, which is a nationwide organization that provides resources for people with intellectual and developmental disabilities; or another local intake facility.

UNIT 1 INTERACTING WITH YOUR COMMUNITY
LESSON 9 Serving People With Autism

Lesson Goal

At the end of this lesson, you will know how to interact with people who are on the autism spectrum and how to ensure their safety while in custody.

Think About This

An office manager calls the police when two customers get into an argument at a local auto shop. As you speak to one of the customers, he avoids eye contact and repeatedly snaps his fingers. How would you handle this interaction?

AUTISM SPECTRUM DISORDER

Autism spectrum disorder (ASD) is a type of developmental disorder that is diagnosed in early childhood and continues throughout adulthood. It is characterized by language and social development delay and repetitive behaviors. Every person on the autism spectrum is unique and might have a variety of symptoms. Some people can live independently and show no external characteristics of the disorder while others require consistent support to function in daily life.

Autism can be difficult to recognize as it does not always have visual indicators. You will usually need to interact with a person to understand that they might be autistic. They may make limited eye contact, have difficulty responding to questions or directions, or repeat your words, which is also called echoing.

☑ LE619.1. Describe some of the characteristics of people who are on the autism spectrum

Autistic people may engage in coping skills known as ***self-stimulating behaviors***, also called stimming; engaging in these behaviors may allow an overstimulated person to calm down in a stressful environment or may provide an under-stimulated person with sensory stimulation. Examples include body rocking, hand flapping, skin picking, hair twirling, or finger flicking. Some people on the autism spectrum may also engage in self-injurious behaviors such as hand biting, self-rubbing, head banging, or scratching.

Autistic people are frequently the victims of crimes such as abuse, neglect, sexual battery, and robbery, and they are sometimes conspirators in crimes due to their trusting natures and their inability to understand social norms. You may receive calls for service because the community may see their behavior as abnormal, irrational, or predatory in nature. Understanding how to recognize and approach a person with autism can make a significant difference in the outcome.

INTERACTING WITH PEOPLE ON THE AUTISM SPECTRUM

☑ LE619.2. Describe how to interact with a person who is on the autism spectrum

The sooner you determine that you are interacting with a person on the autism spectrum, the sooner you can modify the way that you communicate to help you de-escalate an already tense interaction or avoid potentially escalating a situation. Often, an autistic person will have difficulty following verbal commands and interpreting body language.

The following are tips for interacting with an autistic person:

- Do not assume their mental capacity.
- Watch for unusual movements at stressful moments, and be patient if they become upset.
- Avoid using sarcasm and figurative language.
- Allow them extra time to answer your questions.
- Clarify what you are saying and check for understanding.
- Minimize distractions such as lights, sirens, loud crowds, and barking dogs.
- Use patience and do not take their behavior personally.

If you recognize self-injurious behavior, take the appropriate steps to ensure the person's safety. If you are preparing to interview an autistic person as a victim, suspect, or defendant, Florida law requires that certain requirements be met. See Chapter 4 for more detail.

ENSURING SAFETY WHILE IN CUSTODY

☑ LE619.3. Describe some safety concerns when taking someone with ASD into custody

There are added safety concerns to be aware of when taking a person with ASD into custody; these concerns include self-injurious behaviors and medical issues such as seizure disorders. The following techniques may help ensure safety while in custody:

- Evaluate the person for any injuries since indications of pain may not be apparent.
- Watch for signs of trouble breathing when restrained. Some autistic people may have poor muscle tone, so placing them in positions of restraint can pose a risk of suffocation.
- Alert the detention facility that you have a person with ASD in your custody so that they can take the appropriate steps to ensure that person's safety.

If there is a need for additional services, refer the person to the Department of Children and Families, the local mental health facility, the Center for Autism and Related Disorders (CARD), or the Autism Society of Florida.

UNIT 1 INTERACTING WITH YOUR COMMUNITY
LESSON 10 Serving People With Mental Illnesses

Lesson Goal

At the end of this lesson, you will have basic knowledge of common mental illnesses and how to respond to incidents involving people who might have a mental illness.

Think About This

You respond to a residence where a woman is concerned about her mother who is sweating, having difficulty breathing, and saying something bad is going to happen. After speaking to the daughter, you learn that her mother has anxiety. What are your considerations when speaking to the mother?

When responding to a call or disturbance involving a person who may have a mental illness, your concerns should be the same as in any other situation. Determine the nature of the environment, the setting or context of the situation, what has happened, and who is involved. People with mental illness have the same rights as anyone else.

UNDERSTANDING MENTAL ILLNESS

As defined by the Florida Statutes, ***mental illness*** is an impairment of the mental or emotional processes that exercise the conscious control of one's actions. Mental illness may hinder a person's ability to perceive or understand reality. A person with a mental illness may have a thought disorder, mood disorder, anxiety disorder, or personality disorder, and it is common for a person to have any combination of these disorders.

Mental illness is not directly related to intelligence and occurs in people of all intellectual abilities. It does not necessarily interfere with intellectual abilities, but it may require psychiatric evaluation and treatment.

☑ LE6110.1. Identify some of the characteristics of a person with a mental illness

Developmental disabilities are different from mental illness. Developmental disabilities deal with below average intellectual functioning and the ability to learn and process information whereas mental illness refers to disturbances in how people process their thoughts, emotions, and behaviors. Developmental disabilities occur before a person reaches adulthood while mental illness can occur at any time in a person's life.

As an officer, you are not a mental health professional, and you should not try to diagnose a person that you suspect might have a mental illness. Simply be aware of the situation, and follow your agency's policies accordingly.

Some medical conditions and the effects of certain substances that people take can mimic mental illness symptoms. People with mental illnesses who stop taking their medications or are overmedicated may also display symptoms. Medications help people with mental illnesses manage their symptoms in the same way that insulin helps a diabetic person manage their diabetes. When taken as prescribed, medications benefit people experiencing symptoms of mental illness. If a person stops taking their medication as prescribed, they may be at a greater risk of crisis or suicide.

Thought Disorders

☑ LE6110.2. Identify some of the characteristics of a person with a thought disorder

A thought disorder is a disturbance in a person's ability to create a logical sequence of ideas, which can appear as disordered speech or writing. You might be able to recognize thought disorders by observing their symptoms. Listen to what the person is saying and notice whether the person's thoughts seem disorganized and not logically connected.

You might also notice that the person reports hearing or seeing things that are not present or are not real. If so, this person is having a **hallucination**, a sensory experience in which a person can see, hear, smell, taste, or feel something that is not there. If a person is hearing voices, you may want to ask them "what are the voices saying?" rather than "what do you hear?" to discourage the person from thinking that you doubt they are hearing things.

While a hallucination involves a person's sensory experience, a **delusion** is a false belief that is firmly held despite obvious proof or evidence to the contrary; the delusion is this person's reality. For example, a delusional person could believe that they are someone famous or are being followed by the CIA. Symptoms of hallucinations and delusions are often present in people with thought disorders, such as schizophrenia.

Mood Disorders

☑ LE6110.3. Identify some of the characteristics of a person with a mood disorder

Mood disorders are emotional disturbances with long periods of excessive sadness, excessive joyousness, or both. The excessive sadness is different from the brief, situational depressive episodes that most people commonly experience with the loss of a loved one, job, or finances. A mood disorder is diagnosed when sadness (depression) or joyousness (mania) is overly intense, persistent, and significantly impairs the person's capacity to function. The person with a mood disorder may have multiple major depressive episodes and may be profoundly sad and suicidal, cry uncontrollably, or be unable to concentrate, eat, or sleep. During a manic episode, the person may be easily distracted or may have an exaggerated sense of self, powers, and abilities. Examples of mood disorders include major depressive disorder (MDD) and bipolar disorder (BD).

Anxiety Disorders

☑ LE6110.4. Identify some of the characteristics of a person with an anxiety disorder

An anxiety disorder is different from the occasional anxiety we all experience as the episodes of anxiety are more frequent, intense, and last longer. Anxiety becomes a disorder when it affects a person's daily ability to function. The disorder does not go away and can become worse over time; it can range in intensity from mild to debilitating, and triggers are often varied and not always conscious.

A person with an anxiety disorder may experience a panic attack with symptoms of a racing heartbeat, sweating, tension, and a feeling that something terrible is about to happen. The attack could be accompanied by chest pain or discomfort, trembling, choking, or a feeling that they are going to die. Anxiety disorders, such as obsessive compulsive disorder (OCD), may cause a person to have uncontrollable, reoccurring thoughts (obsessions) and behaviors (compulsions) that they feel the urge to repeat over and over.

Personality Disorders

A personality disorder is a deeply ingrained, non-psychotic, inflexible pattern of relating, perceiving, and behaving. Personality disorders involve a continuing pattern of inner experience and behavior that differs noticeably from the accepted behavior of a person's culture. It is serious enough to cause distress to the people around the affected person. Depending on the specific disorder, a person may display anxious, fearful, dramatic, emotional, or unpredictable behavior and impaired functioning (such as difficulties keeping a job or socializing). A person with a personality disorder may lie and exploit others for personal gain and pleasure, lack empathy, have no regard for right or wrong, or be unnecessary risk takers. Examples of personality disorders include antisocial personality disorder (ASPD) and narcissistic personality disorder (NPD).

☑ LE6110.5.
Identify some of the characteristics of a person with a personality disorder

RESPONDING TO PEOPLE WITH MENTAL ILLNESSES

Because some people with a mental illness can be unpredictable, keep everyone's safety in mind. Assessment of the situation and the person affected by mental illness must be ongoing throughout the contact.

If the initial contact is made through dispatch, get as much information as possible from the dispatcher. The more you know about the person, such as a diagnosed condition or medications they are taking, the better prepared you can be to make responsive decisions.

☑ LE6110.6.
Describe how to respond to a person with a mental illness

Speak to other people, such as family members or concerned residents, to seek information on the following:

- characteristics and specific behavior of the person
- relationship of the complainant to the person (if any)
- whether a crime is involved
- the availability of weapons to the person
- prior law enforcement contact
- the nature of any previous mental health conditions

Unless a crime of violence has been committed or a dangerous weapon is involved, respond to the incident with a person who is known or believed to have a mental illness in the same basic way you would anyone else. Only use emergency lights and sirens when urgent response is critical, and turn off these devices as soon as possible upon arrival. Emergency equipment can have a disturbing and negative impact on a person affected by mental illness, can potentially heighten the person's anxiety, and can hinder your efforts to calm the situation. Slow down your contact with the person and establish yourself as a helper rather than an enforcer.

INTERACTING WITH PEOPLE WITH MENTAL ILLNESSES

While you are not in a position to solve the problems of a person with a mental illness, the person you encounter may come into contact with law enforcement again in the future, and your actions may have a long-term impact on the person's perceptions toward law enforcement officers.

☑ LE6110.7. Identify how to interact with a person with a mental illness

When speaking with the person, exhibit a caring attitude without becoming authoritarian, overbearing, condescending, or intimidating. The following are tips for speaking with a person with a mental illness:

- Avoid basing your interaction on previous contacts with them.
- Speak at an appropriate level to their age and development, keeping in mind that mental illness has nothing to do with a person's intelligence.
- Be empathetic and engage in reflective listening.
- Ask if they are taking any medications, prescribed or illicit, and whether they are taking the appropriate dosage.
- Ask them what they are hearing or seeing only if they are experiencing auditory or visual hallucinations.
- Always maintain situational awareness and consider your safety.

UNIT 2 RESPONDING TO A PERSON IN CRISIS
LESSON 1 Crisis Situations

◎ Lesson Goal

At the end of this lesson, you will know how to recognize and respond to a person in crisis while remaining respectful and impartial.

Think About This

You respond to a call from a convenience store about a person in the parking lot who is pacing back and forth. He is sweating, has clenched fists, and appears to be very angry. The store clerk asked if he was OK, and he didn't respond. What could this person's behavior indicate?

Social service agencies are not qualified to enter extreme crisis situations, so law enforcement officers must respond to these incidents and are often the first on the scene. You may need to interact with community agencies to manage and resolve conflicts and make referrals to the appropriate agencies.

Crisis intervention is one of your most important roles as a law enforcement officer. A person in crisis might not have any help other than what you can provide, so it is your duty to recognize, respond, and intervene safely, professionally, and effectively. Each intervention is important to the person in crisis, their family, and the community.

☑ LE621.1. Describe your role during a crisis situation

You may encounter a crisis situation in various ways; it may come as a call for service from dispatch, an observation while on patrol, or an encounter during another call. Regardless of how you are introduced to the crisis, your goal is to ensure the safety of all people involved, assist the person or people in distress, restore or maintain peace, act on any law violations, and document the incident as appropriate.

It is important to remember that regularly interacting with people in a crisis situation may take a toll on your mental health since exposure to traumatic situations can be a risk factor in developing secondary trauma or compassion fatigue. Make sure to engage in healthy coping strategies that build your personal resilience; these strategies may include utilizing peer-to-peer support or other resources from your agency's EAP. Recognizing when you may be experiencing symptoms of compassion fatigue or secondary trauma ensures that you are able to perform your duties effectively during a crisis situation.

CHARACTERISTICS OF A CRISIS SITUATION

Crisis intervention is a potentially hazardous part of your duties as a law enforcement officer. The correct response to a crisis might require timely intervention, effective management of the incident, and referral to appropriate services.

If unmanaged, a conflict can quickly evolve into a crisis. A *crisis* is a time of intense difficulty, trouble, or danger especially when the affected person feels unprepared and pressured to take action or to make a decision. However, a crisis is also defined by the person's perception of and response to the event. If the person sees the event as significant and threatening, has used all of their coping strategies without success, and is unaware of or unable to pursue other alternatives, then a state of crisis exists.

☑ LE621.2. Identify the characteristics of a crisis situation

A crisis can add stress to a person's life or to an entire community. There are significant crises that people may experience at some point in time:

- death of a loved one
- a serious health issue
- financial loss
- job loss
- separation from family and friends
- natural disasters
- house fires
- vehicle accidents

Do not minimize or judge a person's reaction to a situation. You may not perceive the situation as a crisis; however, the person experiencing the crisis may see it as a traumatic event. For example, a traffic stop is a normal everyday occurrence for an officer, but it may be a crisis situation for the person who is stopped.

☑ LE621.3. Identify factors that influence how a person responds to a crisis

Economic, personal, and social dynamics, psychological elements, and physical considerations are all factors that may influence how a person responds to a crisis. If a crisis affects a person's self-image and community standing, it can significantly influence how they respond to the crisis. For example, a person who recently lost their job may have a more severe reaction to that occurrence if they have additional stressors in their life, such as little money held in savings, poor prospects of finding another job before the next mortgage payment is due, or their sense of self-worth is tied to their job. When these factors are present, the person might be more susceptible to crisis than a person who has a support network and the financial stability to go without income while searching for a new job.

BEHAVIORAL CHARACTERISTICS OF A PERSON IN CRISIS

☑ LE621.4. Describe common reactions of a person in crisis

The behavioral characteristics that a person in crisis may display include anger, cursing, making threats, and shouting. There may be additional physical signs such as the following:

- a flushed face
- heavy or rapid breathing
- clenching and unclenching of fists
- pacing
- pointing fingers
- tightening the lips
- clenching the teeth
- sweating
- an unreal calmness

The effect of the crisis and stress on a person may cause a diminished capacity for thinking and decision-making.

INTERACTING WITH A PERSON IN CRISIS

When interacting with a person in crisis, observe their behavior before taking any legal action, such as arrest, or before applying the Baker Act or the Marchman Act (discussed in greater detail later in this chapter). You may need to call for a crisis intervention team (CIT). Realize that not every instance requires legal action on your part; some crises can be resolved through effective communication. The following are tips for speaking with a person in crisis:

- Summarize their thoughts and feelings to help them feel validated.
- Use an empathetic, non-judgmental tone.
- Avoid minimizing their problems or giving advice.
- Avoid placing blame or criticizing their situation.
- Ask how you can help.

☑ LE621.5. Describe how to interact with a person in crisis

Understanding different phases of a crisis will help you when interacting with people in crisis. During the different phases the person may:

- realize they are unable to cope with the situation. Life may be out of control, emotions high, and reasoning ability low. Emotions can range from anger to rage or from fear to panic, all leading to confusion.
- struggle to resolve the situation using methods that have previously worked in a similar situation but do not in this instance. The person's failure to resolve the problem may lead to emotional blockage.
- be unable to solve the crisis and be overwhelmed by emotions. They may be unable to cope with the situation rationally, and the inability to cope combined with the loss of problem-solving skills may lead to diminished self-esteem. A downward cycle may begin thus interfering with their ability to cope.
- be open to suggestions and willing to try new options. They may begin to explain what the situation personally means and may begin to find answers.

CRISIS INTERVENTION AND REFERRAL

As an officer, you must decide if a person involved in a crisis can continue to safely care for themselves or if they must be removed from the situation for their safety. Refer to Chapter 7 for more information regarding crimes of abuse.

When dealing with a person in crisis, you must answer the following questions:

- Can the person care for themselves?
- Are they a threat to themselves or others?

☑ LE621.6. Determine the appropriate intervention for a person in crisis

You should be familiar with the different types of crisis intervention. Examples include the following:

- relocating the person to a safe environment
- taking the person into custody if they have committed a crime
- initiating an involuntary treatment referral via the Baker Act or Marchman Act
- making a referral for services
- arranging for or providing transportation as necessary

UNIT 2 RESPONDING TO A PERSON IN CRISIS
LESSON 2 The Baker Act

Lesson Goal

At the end of this lesson, you will know how to identify the criteria and action to take when interacting with a person who qualifies for services under the Baker Act.

Think About This

You respond to a call where a mother and daughter are present. The mother states that her daughter is threatening suicide. What actions would you take to prevent the risk of harm?

VOLUNTARY AND INVOLUNTARY PSYCHIATRIC EXAMINATION

You may respond to a call for service involving a person demonstrating that they are a danger to themselves or others. The Florida Mental Health Act of 1971, also referred to as the Florida Baker Act—or simply the **Baker Act**—provides people who have a mental illness, or who may harm or neglect themselves or others, with an emergency service and temporary detention for psychiatric evaluation and voluntary or involuntary short-term inpatient treatment.

☑ LE622.1. Describe the role of the Baker Act

A **voluntary examination** is the decision by a person to willingly seek a psychiatric evaluation for symptoms that may be due to mental illness. If a person is willing to seek treatment, ask them to submit to a voluntary examination. The person must be competent to make the decision and be at least 18 years old. If the person has been found to be incapacitated or incompetent to consent for admission or treatment, or if the person is younger than 18, ask the person's guardian for consent.

Do not rely on the Baker Act as a way to deal with difficult people; instead, use it for people who you have determined are a danger to themselves or to others. If you have determined the Baker Act is necessary, do not delay in implementing it; recognize that you are attempting to prevent self-harm, suicide, or another violent act.

The law requires that a person be extended the same rights whether under voluntary or involuntary status. All personal identifying information (name, date of birth, home or email address, phone number, and government-issued ID number) of a person who is voluntarily or involuntarily admitted for mental health treatment must be kept confidential and exempt from disclosure.

CRITERIA FOR THE BAKER ACT

☑ **LE622.2.** Identify the criteria to refer a person for a psychiatric evaluation under the Baker Act

The Florida Statutes state that a person may be taken to a receiving facility for involuntary examination under the Baker Act if there is reason to believe that the person has a mental illness and, because of their mental illness:

1. The person has refused voluntary examination after receiving a thorough explanation and disclosure of the purpose of the examination, or is unable to determine for themselves whether the examination is necessary; and

2. Without care or treatment, the person is likely to either:
   - cause serious bodily harm to themselves or others in the near future, as evidenced by recent behavior; or
   - suffer from neglect or refuse to care for themselves; such neglect or refusal poses a real and present threat of substantial harm to their well-being; and it is not apparent that such harm may be avoided through the help of willing, able, and responsible family members or friends or the provision of other services. (For example, an elderly person is not caring for themselves by bathing or eating.)

When a law enforcement agency receives notification that a person has communicated a specific threat to cause serious bodily injury or death to an identified person, appropriate action must be taken to prevent the risk of harm. This includes notifying the intended victim of the threat or initiating an RPO.

INITIATING A MENTAL HEALTH EVALUATION

☑ **LE622.3.** Describe your options for initiating a psychiatric evaluation under the Baker Act

The Baker Act provides several options for initiating a mental health evaluation and includes the following:

- the person volunteers to receive treatment
- the court is petitioned for an *ex parte* order (a court order issued and signed by a judge that is initiated by one person in the absence of and without representation or notification of other parties)
- the officer takes the person into custody, initiating an involuntary admission, and transports the person to the nearest receiving facility for a mental health evaluation
- a physician, clinical psychologist, psychiatric nurse, mental health counselor, marriage and family therapist, or clinical social worker executes a certificate stating that the person meets the criteria for examination under the Baker Act

IMPLEMENTING THE BAKER ACT

☑ **LE622.4.** Describe how to assess a person for a psychiatric evaluation referral

Determining if a person should be referred or taken into custody for a voluntary or involuntary psychiatric evaluation during a crisis depends on the specific situation. How the person interacts with you and with other people on the scene will help you decide if taking the person into custody is the appropriate course of action. Ask yourself the following questions:

- Has a crime occurred?
- If so, what was the nature of the offense, and what does the law say about it?
- Does the person have a residence or stable housing?
- Does the person have an established support system within the community?

Situations that involve the Baker Act have the potential to be volatile, and backup is highly recommended. Interview the person, the complainant, and any witnesses to gather information, and use this information to determine if you should take the person into custody under the Baker Act. When making contact with the person, use effective interpersonal skills to establish rapport. Assess the person's mental status by evaluating the following factors:

- the person's environment
- the behavior of and statements made by the person
- any self-inflicted injury of the person
- the complainant's or witness' statements

If needed, provide first aid and request EMS. After taking the person into custody, deliver them or have them delivered to a designated receiving facility. You must complete documentation, provide it to the receiving facility, and include it in your report.

UNIT 2 RESPONDING TO A PERSON IN CRISIS
LESSON 3 Suicide Risk

> **Lesson Goal**
>
> At the end of this lesson, you will know how to safely intervene in a potential suicide situation.

Think About This

You respond to a call and see a person standing on the ledge of a bridge. Upon initiating a conversation, you learn that he is unable to pay his bills and support his family. He says, "I just can't do this anymore." What considerations do you have as you interact with this person?

As an officer responding to a situation where a person is suicidal, you must remain aware of officer safety issues while also providing intervention. Be aware that an existing suicidal situation may be aggravated through the inappropriate handling of a distraught person. Suicide threat calls are life-threatening situations for everyone involved.

People with suicidal intentions have a diminished perceived value of life and may be more inclined to harm others. There are a variety of indicators and observations that you can use to assess a person's risk for suicide. A person with suicidal intentions may talk about committing suicide, attempt intentional self-injury, write suicide notes, or sketch death-related drawings.

INDICATORS OF SUICIDE RISK

☑ LE623.1. Identify characteristics of a person at risk for suicide

There are many factors that can lead someone to consider suicide. A person despairing over the loss of a loved one might contemplate suicide, or someone depressed by life stressors or who feels that their future is hopeless might consider suicide.

If a person talks about committing suicide, attempting self-injury, or formulating or has formulated a suicide plan, take them seriously. Not all people at risk for suicide show violence or anger; some can seem eerily calm. Most initial attempts do not result in death and are often a cry for help; however, always take an attempt seriously and use appropriate caution.

Behavioral changes that may indicate a person is contemplating suicide include giving away personal belongings, losing appetite, and engaging in self-destructive behaviors such as drinking, using drugs, or self-cutting. Other indicators include depression, obsessive talk about death, or intentional self-injury.

INTERACTING WITH A PERSON AT RISK FOR SUICIDE

☑ LE623.2. Describe how to interact with a person at risk for suicide

Communicating with a person at risk for suicide is a vital part of the intervention process. The following are tips that could help you intervene:

- Try to establish rapport and keep the person talking.
- Listen carefully to what they are saying and how they are saying it.

- Show support, empathy, and interest by talking directly to them without judgment.
- Convey patience, reassurance, and hope.
- Listen carefully to them so that you can learn how serious and immediate the suicide threat is and possibly what method the person plans to use.
- Observe their body language so that you may become aware of their motivation for suicide and willingness to accept intervention.
- Consider asking the person whether they are thinking of killing themselves and, if so, how they would do it.

INTERVENING WITH A PERSON AT RISK FOR SUICIDE

Before arriving at a scene with a person at risk for suicide, you should:

- request assistance, such as additional officers, EMS, or a CIT
- coordinate responsibilities and tactics with other responding officers and EMS
- request dispatch information about:
    - weapons at the scene
    - the person's intended method of suicide
    - the person's location and call history

Once on scene, immediately determine if the person has access to weapons. Be aware that the person could initiate a sudden attack on you or others. If there is no immediate threat to yourself or others, attempt to talk to the person. Clear the scene of bystanders and any weapons or potential weapons. Perform first aid and request EMS as necessary.

☑ LE623.3. Describe appropriate intervention and referral for a person at risk for suicide

Avoid intentionally exposing yourself to unnecessary danger to disarm a suicidal person. If attempts to speak to the person do not de-escalate the situation, use appropriate tactics, equipment, and verbal commands. You can use less lethal weapons, such as pepper spray, as the situation dictates.

These situations can be volatile, and you may have to resort to deadly force. Some people may attempt to end their lives by intentionally provoking officers to use deadly force. This is commonly referred to as *suicide by cop*.

Depending upon the circumstances of the scene, it might be necessary for you to remove the person from danger to a place of safety and remove any aggravating stimuli and onlookers. Do not leave the person alone.

A suicidal person needs evaluation from a medical or mental health service provider as soon as possible. If the person appears to meet the criteria for involuntary examination under the Baker Act, take them into custody and deliver them to the nearest facility. Notify the receiving facility of the possible suicide risk.

AVAILABLE RESOURCES

The National Suicide Prevention Lifeline (now known as the 988 Suicide and Crisis Lifeline) is a service available to anyone and may be contacted at any time by calling 988 or the previous phone number 1-800-273-TALK (8255). Other community resources, friends, religious leaders, and relatives may also be available to assist a person contemplating suicide.

UNIT 2 RESPONDING TO A PERSON IN CRISIS
LESSON 4 Substance Abuse

Lesson Goal

At the end of this lesson, you will know how to recognize illnesses that mimic substance abuse and the stages of substance abuse and treatment.

Think About This

While on patrol in the early morning, you pull over a vehicle for running a red light. When speaking to the driver, you notice his speech is slurred, and he appears confused. How would you handle this situation?

The nation's opioid epidemic is changing the way law enforcement does its job. Many law enforcement agencies are initiating programs aimed at treating people who abuse substances rather than putting them in jail. Officers play a critical role by targeting high-risk groups with prevention information and forming collaborations with public health agencies and drug treatment centers.

SUBSTANCE USE VERSUS SUBSTANCE ABUSE

Substance use is the intake of a substance that can lead to substance abuse. It can be a legal therapeutic prescription or an illegal recreational use of the substance. Substance use can include having a casual drink with friends, taking a prescribed drug according to label directions, or taking aspirin daily to prevent heart disease.

☑ LE624.1. Differentiate between substance use and substance abuse

Substance abuse (also referred to as substance misuse) is the inappropriate use of a substance that negatively affects the mind and body, adversely impacting a person's social or occupational life and psychological or physical health. Some examples of substance abuse include misusing prescribed medication, binge drinking, sniffing or inhaling glue, or using cocaine.

Substance abuse can quickly lead to substance dependence or addiction. Substance dependence is the physical and psychological loss of control due to a disruption of chemicals in the brain. Substance addiction is using a substance consistently in excess despite negative consequences.

Substance abuse can also lead to **overdose**, which is the accidental or intentional use of a dangerously large amount of a substance that can lead to death. Drug overdose is often underreported out of fear of arrest. Friends and relatives of someone who struggles with substance abuse can be protective or ashamed of the person or may not want to get involved. However, when a person is overdosing, friends or family may contact law enforcement in an attempt to save their life. Keep in mind that you cannot charge, prosecute, or penalize a person for possession of a controlled substance when someone acting in good faith seeks assistance for the person experiencing a drug-related overdose.

ILLNESSES THAT MIMIC SUBSTANCE ABUSE

☑ LE624.2. Identify symptoms of illnesses that can resemble substance abuse

Some illnesses and medical conditions have symptoms that mimic characteristics of substance abuse. Keep the following conditions in mind:

- Diabetic shock may cause a person to stagger and appear drunk; a diabetic coma may cause a person's breath to smell sweet, like a fruity alcoholic drink.
- An epileptic episode may cause a person to appear as if they are in a drunken stupor or confused state; during a severe episode, the person can become violent for brief periods of time.
- High blood pressure can sometimes cause people to become temporarily irrational.
- A head injury may cause people to be confused and aggressive.
- A stroke may cause a person to appear dizzy and confused, and they may vomit or lose consciousness.
- Parkinson's disease may cause a person to shake, slur their speech, or appear intoxicated.
- Cerebral palsy and Wernicke syndrome may cause a person to appear confused and have faulty muscular coordination or paralysis of the eye muscles.
- Degenerative diseases such as Alzheimer's and dementia may cause a person to stagger, act inappropriately, be forgetful, or wander aimlessly.

Some mental health issues can cause people to behave unpredictably and experience sensory hallucinations, such as sounds, physical sensations, or visions that can mimic the symptoms of substance abuse. Using illegal drugs, such as phencyclidine hydrochloride (commonly called PCP) and methamphetamine (commonly called meth), can cause mental illness symptoms such as hallucinations. Also, taking several prescriptions at one time can sometimes cause negative drug interactions that lead to symptoms imitating schizophrenia. An elderly person may take many prescribed medicines throughout the day and may accidentally abuse medications, potentially causing an overdose.

DRUG TREATMENT

☑ LE624.3. Describe stages of a drug treatment program

Some jurisdictions offer drug treatment court programs as a choice for people whose criminal charges are the result of substance abuse. Drug treatment court programs offer an opportunity for people who abuse substances to participate in an intensive, supervised program.

Detoxification is often the first step in a drug treatment program. It is the process of allowing the body to rid itself of a drug while managing the symptoms of withdrawal.

Withdrawal refers to the physical and mental symptoms that occur after chronic use of a drug is reduced or stopped. Symptoms vary depending on the drug but can include agitation, confusion, cramps, sweating, and convulsions. In extreme cases, withdrawal symptoms, if not managed appropriately, can lead to death.

AVAILABLE RESOURCES

You should become familiar with the local resources available to people struggling with substance abuse in your community. Many communities host self-help groups such as Alcoholics Anonymous, Narcotics Anonymous, or SMART Recovery.

UNIT 2 RESPONDING TO A PERSON IN CRISIS
LESSON 5 The Marchman Act

◎ Lesson Goal

At the end of this lesson, you will know how to identify the criteria for the Marchman Act and understand what action to take when interacting with a person who qualifies for services under the act.

Think About This

You respond to a call from a 60-year-old woman. She says that her 40-year-old son was fired from his job three months ago for attendance problems, and since that time, he has not been motivated to find a new job. He sometimes sleeps all day and night or stays awake for days at a time, and he often goes days without bathing. She is concerned there is a problem because of his behavior and that he is spending all his money on drugs. She wants to get him help but is not sure what to do. What are your possible interventions?

You may respond to a call for service involving a person who is significantly impaired by drugs or alcohol and potentially harmful to themselves or to others. In these circumstances, you may place the person in protective custody under the Marchman Act.

☑ LE625.1. Describe the role of the Marchman Act

The Hal S. Marchman Alcohol and Other Drug Services Act of 1993, commonly known as the **Marchman Act**, provides people in need of substance abuse services access to emergency services and temporary protected custody on either a voluntary or involuntary basis. In a voluntary admission, a person decides to enter a treatment facility for substance abuse and seeks services directly from the provider.

CRITERIA FOR THE MARCHMAN ACT

The Florida Statutes state the criteria for referring a person for involuntary admission into a facility under the Marchman Act.

☑ LE625.2. Identify the criteria to refer a person for substance abuse services under the Marchman Act

A person may be referred or taken to a receiving facility for involuntary admission for substance abuse if there is good faith reason to believe that the person is substance abuse impaired or has a co-occurring mental health disorder and, because of such impairment or disorder, the person:

1. Has lost the power of self-control because of substance abuse.
2. Is either:
    a. in need of substance abuse services, and their judgment has been so impaired that they are incapable of appreciating the need for services and of making a rational decision regarding the need for services; or
    b. likely to suffer from neglect or to refuse to take care of themselves; or the person has inflicted, has attempted or threatened to inflict, or, unless admitted, is likely to inflict physical harm on themselves, or another.

The Marchman Act also specifies other situations where you would take a person into protective custody or deliver them to a treatment facility. These situations may include:

- the person volunteers to receive treatment
- the court is petitioned for an *ex parte* order

A person's refusal to receive services does not mean that they lack judgment for the need of services.

The decision to arrest someone referred for voluntary or involuntary substance abuse or abuse services during an incident depends on the alleged crime and the person's state of being. As an officer, you will have to make your decisions on a case-by-case basis.

IMPLEMENTING THE MARCHMAN ACT

Situations involving the Marchman Act can be unpredictable, and backup is highly recommended. These calls may be initiated by the person, a family or household member, a member of the public, or by an officer who is at the scene with the person-at-risk. Interview the complainant or any witnesses who may be able to provide assistance in identifying the impaired person and the background and extent of their substance abuse.

When making contact with the person, use effective interpersonal skills in an attempt to establish a dialogue. Assess the person's physical condition through observation and their vital signs. If the impaired person is injured, incoherent, or non-responsive, request assistance from EMS. Information from the initial assessment can assist you in determining if the impaired person is an immediate threat to themselves or others.

☑ LE625.3. Describe how to assess a person for a substance abuse evaluation referral

After taking the impaired person into protective custody, deliver them to the appropriate or nearest designated receiving facility. Complete the Department of Children and Families form for the receiving facility and detail the circumstances under which the person was taken into custody in your report. According to Florida law, in the case of an adult, you are authorized to take the person to a detention facility within the jurisdiction.

UNIT 2 RESPONDING TO A PERSON IN CRISIS
LESSON 6 Transportation and Documentation

◎ Lesson Goal

At the end of this lesson, you will know how to transport a person in crisis as well as document the incident on the proper form.

Think About This

You receive a call from the wife of a person who just lost his brother in a car accident. She indicates that he and his brother were best friends, and her husband has said he wants to kill himself. Upon initiating a conversation with the husband, you learn that he has access to a firearm, and he says, "I want to end everything." You have determined to initiate a Baker Act. What procedures do you need to follow?

TRANSPORTING A PERSON IN CRISIS

☑ LE626.1. Explain how to transport a person in crisis to a medical or treatment facility

In addition to making a referral for services, you may have to transport a person suspected of having a mental illness or misusing substances to another location. Your agency will have a memorandum of understanding with receiving facilities that reflects a single set of protocols for the safe and secure transportation of the person and transfer of custody to a responsible person.

If a person is in need of psychiatric or substance abuse evaluation and treatment, you may arrange or provide for special transport to any of the following locations:

- a mental health facility
- a hospital
- a substance abuse treatment facility
- a jail facility
- a shelter or safe house

If the person is being assessed for the Baker Act or Marchman Act, follow your agency's policies and procedures regarding non-custodial transport and escort the person to the appropriate receiving facility.

DOCUMENTING A CRISIS SITUATION

☑ LE626.2. Document an incident involving the Baker or Marchman Act

Documenting the incident might include the following forms:

- Report of Law Enforcement Officer Initiating Involuntary Examination CF-MH 3052a
- Transportation to Receiving Facility CF-MH 3100
- agency-specific Marchman Act form(s)

Your agency reports should be as detailed as possible and include the person's and any victim's actions, reactions, physical condition, and appearance. Additional information should include witness statements, known medications, weapons involved, and the disposition of the incident. Documenting these incidents provides historical data and warns future responding officers of special hazards.

UNIT 3 IDENTIFYING AND RESPONDING TO HIGH-RISK GROUPS
LESSON 1 Criminal Gangs

> **Lesson Goal**
>
> At the end of this lesson, you will know how to recognize indicators of gang activity and the importance of documenting observable identifiers.

GANGS

☑ LE631.1. Describe common characteristics of criminal gangs

One of the most dangerous population groups that you may encounter is a criminal gang. The expansion of these groups and their violence and criminal activity have made them a national problem. The Florida Statutes define a **criminal gang** as the following:

> *a formal or informal ongoing organization, association, or group that has as one of its primary activities the commission of criminal or delinquent acts, and that consists of three or more persons who have a common name or common identifying signs, colors, or symbols including, but not limited to, terrorist organizations, transnational crime organizations, and hate groups.*

Criminal gang activity is any act committed with the intent to benefit or further the interest of a criminal gang. These activities may include theft, burglary, fraud, narcotics manufacturing and distribution, assault and battery, racketeering, witness intimidation, extortion, vandalism, arson, weapons and explosives, counterfeiting, and homicide. Typically, violent crime associated with gangs is attributed to hostility between rival gangs. As a result of this rival violence, members of the public are often caught in the middle and become victims.

WHY PEOPLE JOIN GANGS

☑ LE631.2. Identify reasons why some people join criminal gangs

Florida gangs are overwhelmingly comprised of young males between the ages of 13 and 23. Gang members may have experienced child abuse or neglect and can come from a disadvantaged socioeconomic background. Often, gang members are school dropouts, unemployed, and frequently in trouble with law enforcement. Individuals join gangs for a variety of reasons including the following:

- psychological needs—a sense of structure and discipline
- safety—a sense of security and protection
- social acceptance—a feeling of belonging
- self-esteem—a sense of confidence in oneself
- fame—a sense of power and prestige

Gangs may be organized for different reasons, such as race, ethnicity, territory, or tradition, and they often participate in similar types of criminal activity. Not all gangs have a formal organized structure, but they do generally serve the same purpose and participate in the same types of activities.

Gang members identify themselves and promote gang solidarity through the use of identifying symbols, such as graffiti and tagging, tattoos, hand signs, clothing and jewelry, colors, and music. These identifiers have special significance to each gang, and members go to great lengths to protect them from degradation by rival gangs. Become familiar with the types of gangs, gang identifiers, symbols, and activities in your community.

Most gangs require new members to prove their loyalty to the gang and to solidify their membership through an initiation process. Often these acts include committing criminal or sexual activity or being subjected to violence.

OFFICER SAFETY CONSIDERATIONS

Use extreme caution when dealing with gang members. Historically, gangs have very little respect for legal authority, and they typically do not honor the same rules and laws that govern society. Gang members have been known to use hand signs to silently communicate with other members to launch attacks against law enforcement. Some gang members may have paramilitary or law enforcement training, and others may be military veterans. As a result, they may have advanced knowledge of and training with combat and weapons tactics.

☑ LE631.3. Explain officer safety issues when interacting with criminal gangs

Gang members often use the home field advantage of their neighborhoods or turfs against law enforcement when officers respond to calls for service. Gang members tend to know their turfs better than law enforcement officers, and sometimes people within the neighborhood are sympathetic to gang members. As with any other group, build rapport and engage with members of the community. When dealing with gang members, do not make assumptions. Instead, observe and learn.

DOCUMENTATION

Documentation of gang activity is extremely important. Through documentation, a potential gang member can be statutorily labeled as a gang member. This documentation can then be used in prosecutions to enhance penalties. When you make contact with a gang member, or suspected gang member, you are encouraged to make notes to document their clothing, tattoos, and any other observable identifiers. Many members are proud of their gang affiliation and will pose for photographs while showing hand signs.

☑ LE631.4. Explain why it is important to document known or suspected criminal gang activity

Closely monitoring graffiti and tagging can help you and other officers keep track of gang conflicts and identify which gangs are present in an area. Documenting these activities can aid in developing a roster of gang members. If you find graffiti in your patrol area, photograph and report it according to your agency's policies and procedures, which may include painting over graffiti.

UNIT 3 IDENTIFYING AND RESPONDING TO HIGH-RISK GROUPS
LESSON 2 Extremist Groups

Lesson Goal

At the end of this lesson, you will know how to identify characteristics of extremist groups, their members, and associates.

Think About This

While on patrol, you observe a vehicle that appears to have a license plate from an area you do not recognize. Upon further inspection, you see the plate reads, "No driver license or insurance required/private mode of travel." You initiate a traffic stop, and upon contact with the driver, he says, "I am a free man traveling about the land, and I do not submit to your inquiry." How would you handle this situation?

CHARACTERISTICS OF EXTREMIST GROUPS

☑ LE632.1. Identify characteristics of extremist groups

There are certain organized groups, often known as extremist groups, which advocate violence and the illegal disruption of the lawful activities of others. Although much of their rhetoric is an expression of First Amendment rights, it can cross over to advocating violence. Be mindful that simply voicing antigovernment speech is not against the law, but seeking to advance that ideology through force or violence is illegal.

TERRORISM

☑ LE632.2. Identify characteristics of domestic terrorism

Terrorism is not isolated to foreign affairs. People who commit terrorist activities within the United States seek to intimidate the civilian population or influence the policy of government by intimidation or coercion. They may also seek to affect the conduct of a government by mass destruction, assassination, or kidnapping.

White supremacist groups are a common terrorism group within the United States. These groups share the ideology that the thoughts, beliefs, and actions of white people are superior to those of other races. These groups may commit violent criminal acts toward other groups of people who share different ethnicities or ideas.

SOVEREIGN CITIZENS

☑ LE632.3. Identify the ideology and characteristics of sovereign citizens

The ***sovereign citizen movement*** is a subculture of society that holds antigovernment beliefs and does not recognize federal, state, or local laws, regulations, or policies. Sovereign citizens participate as individuals or in groups without established leadership; they usually come together only in loosely affiliated groups to train, help each other with paperwork, or socialize and talk about their ideology. They sometimes refer to themselves as "constitutionalists" or "freemen," which indicates their decision to not recognize federal, state, or local laws, regulations, or policies.

Many sovereign citizens:

- attempt to establish their beliefs by filing legal documents to renounce their citizenship, return Social Security cards, and cancel birth certificates.
- believe in the Redemption Theory, which holds that the U.S. government went bankrupt when it replaced the gold standard with paper currency in 1933; this theory also contends that the U.S. government began using citizens as collateral in trade agreements with foreign governments and, therefore, doesn't act in the best interests of its citizens.
- believe in emancipating themselves from the U.S. government by refusing to either pay taxes, use a state driver license, or obey U.S. laws.
- may engage in criminal activities related to defrauding banks, credit institutions, and the U.S. government because they consider these organizations to be without merit.

Sovereign citizens are known for clogging the courts by filing hundreds of documents containing unintelligible language, a practice known as paper terrorism. The Florida Statutes prohibit people, including sovereign citizens, from filing false documents with the intent to defraud or harass others. If a sovereign citizen perceives they are provoked by a government official, the sovereign citizen may retaliate by filing nuisance property liens and frivolous lawsuits against the official, which would be legally binding until lawfully dismissed.

Although sovereign citizens tend to fight the government through nuisance legal tactics, they may also become extremely violent. Sovereign citizens can be especially dangerous to you during traffic stops. Be on guard for drivers who may try to distract you with confusing documents and animated arguments for sovereignty status; it may be an ambush.

INDICATORS OF SOVEREIGN CITIZENS

While these may also be useful to identify members of other extremist groups, the following are some indicators of potential sovereign citizens:

- antigovernment bumper stickers on vehicles
- homemade vehicle registration and license plates on vehicles
- use of personal seals, stamps, or thumb prints in red ink
- homemade ID from a non-recognizable territory
- spelling personal names in all capital letters or first and last name separated by a colon (e.g., JOHN DOE, jane: doe)
- signatures followed by: "under duress," "Sovereign Living Soul" (SLS), or the copyright symbol (©)
- excessive reference to the Bible, Constitution of the United States, U.S. Supreme Court decisions, or treaties with foreign governments

LE632.4. Identify how to recognize a sovereign citizen

Figure 6-1
Sovereign citizen license plate

Figure 6-2
Sovereign citizen license plate

☑ LE632.5. Identify the ideology and characteristics of militias

MILITIAS

Militias refuse to recognize the authority of municipal, state, and federal governments. Many of today's militias are connected by self-described patriot beliefs. Their most common beliefs are the following:

- The Second Amendment, the right to bear arms, is a cornerstone of the Constitution.
- Only well-armed people can enforce their own rights.
- Any form of gun regulation is a denial of their rights.
- The Sixteenth Amendment, allowing federal income tax, was authorized through fraud.

Militias view law enforcement officers as representatives of the government, which they feel is controlled by people who cannot be trusted to preserve law and order. Therefore, militia members train for preemptive attacks or ambushes by the government and are often arrested for weapons violations.

Chapter 7
Crimes Against Persons

UNIT 1 BASIC INVESTIGATIONS
- LESSON 1 The Investigative Sequence / 273
- LESSON 2 Victims' Rights and Brochures / 277

UNIT 2 CRIMES AGAINST PERSONS
- LESSON 1 Assault and Battery / 280
- LESSON 2 Domestic Violence / 284
- LESSON 3 Stalking Crimes / 289
- LESSON 4 Child Abuse / 291
- LESSON 5 Abuse, Neglect, and Exploitation of an Elderly Person or Disabled Adult / 295
- LESSON 6 Interference With Custody, Luring or Enticing of a Child, False Imprisonment, and Kidnapping / 299
- LESSON 7 Missing or Missing Endangered Persons / 302
- LESSON 8 Sexual Offenses / 306
- LESSON 9 Human Trafficking / 310
- LESSON 10 Respond to a Death / 312
- LESSON 11 Robbery / 316

UNIT 1 BASIC INVESTIGATIONS
LESSON 1 The Investigative Sequence

Lesson Goal

At the end of this lesson, you will know how to respond to any incident that has the potential for an arrest by following a basic investigative sequence that focuses on fairness in the process and the outcome.

Think About This

You are dispatched to an incident outside of a local bar involving two patrons engaged in a fist fight. Your field training officer (FTO) is busy writing a ticket across town, and you are faced with making the initial contact alone. What steps will you take?

One of the most important tasks assigned to a law enforcement officer is conducting an impartial investigation to bring a suspect to justice. Objective investigative work is one of the main ways officers earn the public's trust. The quality of an investigation undergoes great public scrutiny, so officers must conduct each investigation with attention to accuracy, detail, and professionalism. You establish a reputation in court and in public based upon the quality of your investigative work.

When you respond to a call for service, always preserve life first and then work to preserve the scene for investigation. Approach all incidents with compassion and a reassuring presence. You may need to assume your role as a stabilizer or an enforcer based on the circumstances of the incident. Understand your basic responsibilities and any agency limitations when responding to crimes against persons.

Follow basic investigative steps and use a systematic approach to each investigation. Although each investigative situation is unique, this lesson outlines the basic sequence of events you will follow when you respond to a call involving a potential crime. Refer to the basic investigation sequence (Figure 7-1) throughout this chapter and the next. Follow the basic steps outlined in Chapter 5 for driving and responding to a scene.

SCENE SAFETY

When you approach the scene of a building, do not stand directly in front of the door to avoid a fatal funnel situation. Immediately identify yourself and state the purpose of your visit. Move to and maintain a position of advantage, such as somewhere you cannot be attacked from behind. Stay out of doorways, and visually assess the scene, taking note of the number of people present. Observe their hands, body language, and facial expressions. Scan the room for hazards, such as possible weapons, dangerous pets, or possible hiding places.

☑ LE711.1. Describe how to approach the scene entrance safely

Some incident scenes can be chaotic. There could be injured victims, witnesses yelling, and possible suspects on the scene with weapons. Ask witnesses or victims if there is anyone present who may have a weapon. Deal with any immediate threats first.

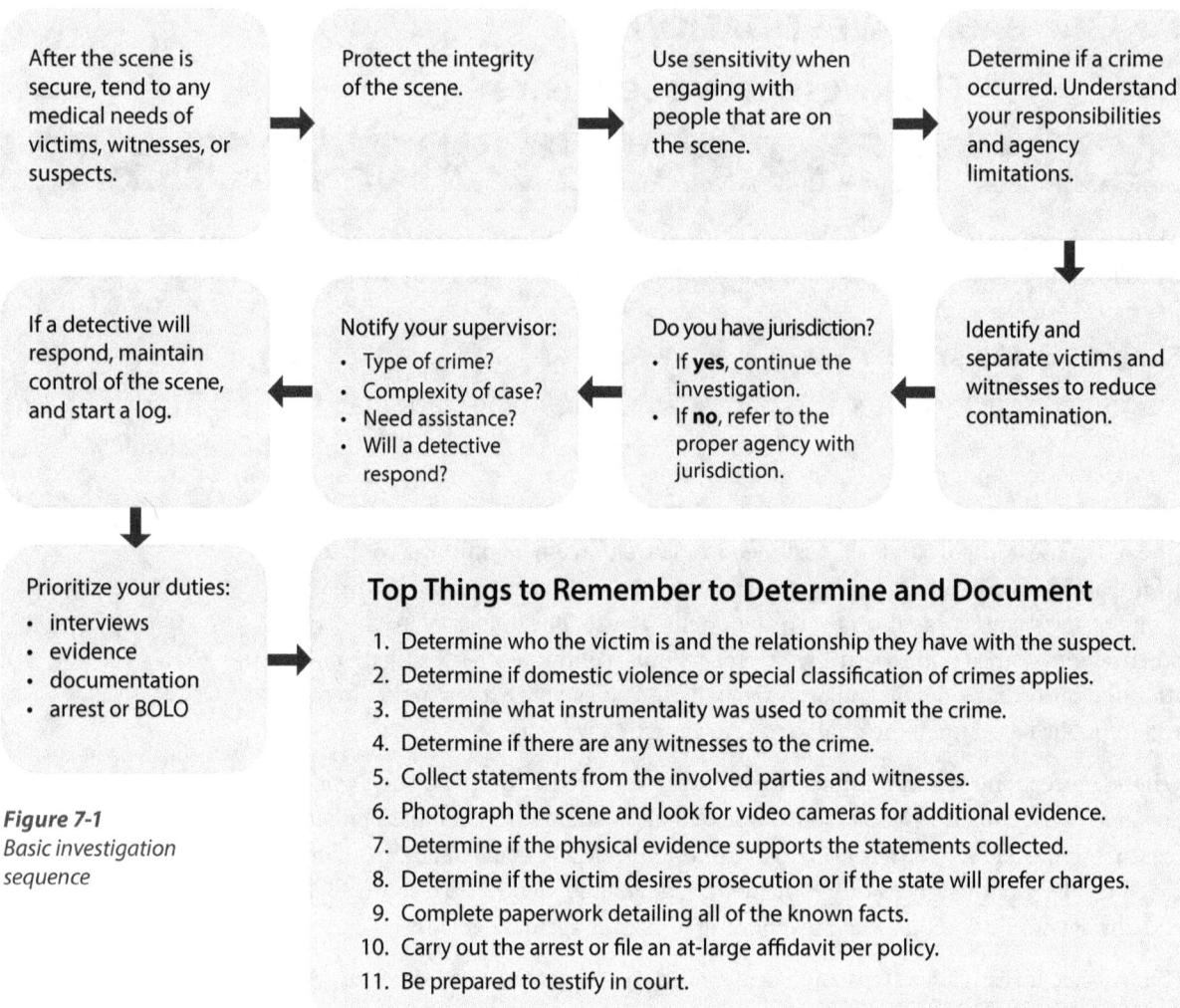

Figure 7-1
Basic investigation sequence

☑ **LE711.2.** Describe how to stabilize the incident scene before providing first aid

Your initial response to a call, and how you approach a scene, can influence the level of cooperation you receive from the victim, witnesses, and anyone on the scene. Use communication techniques to calm the situation and maintain control. Keep in mind that no two incidents are alike, and each may require a distinct response. Loud sounds can increase tension and make it difficult to communicate. Turn down noise sources, such as music systems and televisions, and ask bystanders to step away.

Once the scene is relatively calm, determine if anyone is sick, injured, or under the influence of drugs or alcohol. They may appear incoherent or may exhibit abnormal behavior and not respond. Use first-aid skills to tend to any medical needs. You may need additional assistance from EMS.

☑ **LE711.3.** Describe how to engage with people on the scene

Encourage the people involved to sit down, but only after you have determined that there are no weapons in the area. Sitting reduces a person's mobility and their access to weapons, exits, or other people. Reduce scene contamination by controlling who enters the area and establishing a crime scene. Keep watching for any changes and request backup, if needed. Talk to the people involved with sensitivity and respect. Do not allow yourself to get caught up in the tensions of the scene. Remain neutral, maintain officer safety, and use verbal de-escalation techniques to defuse the situation.

COURSE OF ACTION

There may be a lot of people present when you arrive at a scene, and those directly involved may not be immediately obvious. Identify who is involved through observation and answers to the following questions:

- Who is the victim?
- Are there any impartial witnesses to the crime?
- Does the victim have a relationship with the suspect?

☑ LE711.4. Determine if a crime actually occurred

Assess any involved person's physical, intellectual, and emotional well-being, and how likely they are to be violent. Understanding the role of each person involved in an incident provides a foundation for identifying the victim of a crime. Keep in mind the concept of personal space. People prone to violence or who have experienced abuse may require more personal space.

As you continue through the investigative process consider:

- Did you collect statements from the victim and witnesses?
- What are the instrumentalities of the crime? **Instrumentalities of the crime** are the items used by the defendant to commit a crime.
- Does the physical evidence support the statements collected?
- Did you photograph the scene and look for additional evidence?

Use walls or a doorway to separate and break eye contact between the involved people. This will help them focus their attention on you and can also reduce the potential for verbal insults and physical threats. Your behavior can affect the situation, either defusing or escalating it. Be professional at all times, and display empathy and compassion toward the victims. Make eye contact when talking to people on the scene while maintaining an awareness of your surroundings.

Understand your responsibilities for making an arrest, whether you have jurisdiction, and whether to refer to your state attorney's office. Notify your supervisor if you are making an arrest or if you need more resources, such as crime scene technicians, detectives, or medical assistance. Contact dispatch to initiate a BOLO if the suspect is not on the scene. If a detective is able to respond, provide them with any information gathered and assist them as needed or directed. Continue to maintain the scene and start a log, which you will learn how to do in Chapter 9.

☑ LE711.5. Determine your course of action

Make the arrest if needed, file the affidavit, make a referral to the state attorney's office, and document the incident following your agency's policies and procedures.

The following are additional questions to ask:

- Does domestic violence or special classification of crimes apply?
- Does the victim want to prosecute, or will the state press charges?
- Did you complete paperwork detailing all of the known facts?

Provide the victim with a case number and the primary officer's name, and explain the follow-up procedures. Your agency may require the victim to agree to prosecute the suspect before you can take any action. Provide the victim with the appropriate brochures, and document this in your report.

The remainder of this chapter and the following two chapters discuss crime specific procedures in greater detail. If you are acting as backup, the general role of the backup officer discussed in Chapter 5 applies in an incident that results in an arrest. Additional duties may also be assigned.

Once you fulfill your obligations as the responding officer, allow yourself some time to reflect on the emotional impact of the situation. The nature of certain crimes can leave some people feeling distressed in the immediate aftermath and possibly long after the fact. Remember, everyone may find different situations upsetting based on their personal experiences or life circumstances. For example, if someone has a close relationship with an elderly relative, they may find cases of elder abuse particularly upsetting while others do not. Consider that you or other officers may be negatively affected by certain situations, even if it is not always obvious right away. Sometimes other officers, or even you yourself, may be able to operate normally during a tough call, but later begin to experience emotional difficulties. It is important to not only recognize when your emotions are affecting your work, but also use appropriate coping strategies, as discussed in Chapter 1, and check in with your peers.

UNIT 1 BASIC INVESTIGATIONS
LESSON 2 Victims' Rights and Brochures

◎ Lesson Goal

At the end of this lesson, you will be able to inform victims of their rights and provide them with the appropriate victims' rights brochures or cards.

VICTIMS' RIGHTS

One of your responsibilities as an officer is to interact with victims and witnesses of crimes. In some cases, being a victim is a person's first experience with the criminal or juvenile justice systems. When someone is a victim of a crime, they have certain rights.

Marsy's Law requires that officers provide all victims and their families the following information. Victims have the right to:

- due process and to be treated fairly and respectfully
- freedom from intimidation, harassment, and abuse
- accurate and timely notice of all of the case's public proceedings, including pleas, trials, and sentencings
- reasonable protection from the accused and any person acting on behalf of the accused within the judicial process
- prevent the disclosure of information or records that could be used to locate or harass the victim or their family
- consult with the prosecuting attorney concerning any plea agreements, when setting bail, participation in pretrial diversion programs, defendant release, restitution, sentencing, or any other disposition of the case
- be informed of all post-conviction processes and procedures, and participate in such processes and procedures
- return of property no longer needed as evidence
- full and timely restitution
- proceedings free from unreasonable delay
- be informed of these rights and may seek the help of an attorney

☑ LE712.1. Explain the rights and services available to victims, witnesses, and their families

The following brochures explain these rights and the services available to victims. You can find them in a variety of languages on the FDLE website. Your agency should provide specific versions of the information in the form of brochures or cards that include local contact information for victims. Because the Florida Statutes mandate distributing this information, document in your report that you gave them to the victim.

BROCHURES

☑ LE712.2. Describe the information in the *Victims' Rights Brochure*

You must give crime victims a *Victims' Rights Brochure* or an information card at the crime scene or during the investigation. The brochure provides the following information:

- the availability of crime victim compensation
- crisis intervention services, bereavement counseling, social service support referrals, community-based victim treatment programs
- the role of the victim in the criminal or juvenile justice process
- the stages of the criminal or juvenile justice process
- the right of the victim to be informed, present, and heard during criminal or juvenile justice proceedings, or, if the victim is incarcerated, the right to submit written statements

☑ LE712.3. Describe the domestic violence information in the *Notice of Legal Rights and Remedies* brochure

Victims of domestic violence must also receive a *Notice of Legal Rights and Remedies for Victims of Domestic Violence, Dating Violence, Repeat Violence, Sexual Violence, Stalking* brochure at the earliest opportunity. The brochure discusses:

- definitions of domestic violence, sexual violence, dating violence, repeat violence, and stalking
- what Florida's domestic violence law means and how it can help victims
- what to do if the abuser violates an injunction
- the victim information that is exempt from public inspection
- who the victim should contact for more information

☑ LE712.4. Describe the sexual battery information in the *Sexual Battery—Your Rights and Services* brochure

Victims of sexual battery must also receive a *Sexual Battery—Your Rights and Services* brochure, published by the Florida Council Against Sexual Violence. The brochure provides the following information:

- a definition of sexual battery
- the rights of victims and the compensation, resources, and services available to them
- possible compensation for medical care
- what evidence may be collected

☑ LE712.5. Decide which brochure to provide a victim, witness, or family member

DISTRIBUTION OF BROCHURES

	all crime victims and witnesses	victims and witnesses of domestic violence	victims and witnesses of sexual battery	victims and witnesses of domestic violence that involve sexual battery
Victims' Rights Brochure	✓	✓	✓	✓
Marsy's Law card or brochure	✓	✓	✓	✓
Notice of Legal Rights and Remedies		✓		✓
Sexual Battery—Your Rights and Services			✓	✓

LEGALLY REQUIRED TRANSPORT

You may also be legally required to transport victims and witnesses of certain crimes, such as domestic violence, sexual battery, or child abuse.

Follow your agency's policies and procedures for transporting juveniles, members of the opposite sex, witnesses, and victims. When you finish transporting a person, conduct a vehicle check after they have exited the vehicle.

UNIT 2 CRIMES AGAINST PERSONS
LESSON 1 Assault and Battery

Lesson Goal

At the end of this lesson, you will know how to respond to an incident involving assault and battery and determine when to make an arrest and whether an assault or battery charge merits reclassification.

Think About This

You respond to an incident at a bar. When you arrive at the scene, the bartender tells you that one of their customers walked into the bar with friends and spotted her boyfriend cheating on her with someone else. The customer ran over to the two of them and began yelling obscenities. How are you going to approach this incident and determine if the customer is committing a crime?

Some of the most common calls for service involve disputes and fighting. Your role in these types of incidents is to de-escalate the situation to prevent a serious crime with possible injuries.

ASSAULT

☑ LE721.1. Determine if an incident is assault or aggravated assault

Chapter 784, F.S., outlines the elements of both assault and battery. An assault involves verbal or non-verbal threats. For example, if someone walks up to you within striking distance and suddenly raises their fist in a manner that puts you in fear of being harmed, even if they do not say a word, they commit assault. A person who commits assault commits a misdemeanor of the second degree.

For *assault*, document that the suspect:

- intentionally and unlawfully threatened, by either word or act, to do violence to a victim
- at the time, appeared to have the ability to carry out the threat
- created in the mind of the victim a well-founded fear that violence was about to take place

For *aggravated assault*, document that the suspect committed all the elements of assault and in addition, made the assault with a deadly weapon without intent to kill, or with an intent to commit a felony. A weapon is a deadly weapon if someone uses or threatens to use it in a way likely to cause death or great bodily harm. Even if a person points a gun at the victim with no intention of firing it, this is aggravated assault if the victim fears the person will shoot them. A person who commits aggravated assault commits a felony of the third degree.

BATTERY

For *battery*, document that the suspect did either of the following:

- actually and intentionally touched or struck the victim against their will
- intentionally caused bodily harm to the victim

☑ LE721.2. Determine if an incident is battery or aggravated battery

Aggravated battery includes the element of intent or knowing that you will cause great bodily harm. If the victim is pregnant at the time of the battery, whether the suspect knew or should have known they were pregnant, this upgrades a battery charge to aggravated battery.

For *aggravated battery*, document that the suspect committed battery, and either of the following:

- intentionally or knowingly caused great bodily harm, permanent disability, permanent disfigurement to the victim
- used a deadly weapon

FELONY BATTERY

For a *felony battery*, document that the suspect actually and intentionally touched or struck a victim against their will and caused significant injury, great bodily harm, permanent disability, or permanent disfigurement to the victim. When a suspect has one prior conviction for battery, aggravated battery, or felony battery and commits any second or subsequent battery, the charge is reclassified from a misdemeanor battery charge to a felony battery charge. Felony battery does not involve a conscious intent to cause great bodily harm; however, it does include the intent to touch or strike a victim against their will.

☑ LE721.3. Determine if an incident is felony battery

Domestic battery by strangulation is a felony battery that is battery against a family or household member or someone with whom the victim is in a dating relationship. The abuser knowingly and intentionally impedes the victim's breathing or circulation against their will by applying pressure to the throat or neck or by blocking the victim's nose or mouth.

RESPOND TO ASSAULT OR BATTERY

Follow the basic investigative sequence outlined in the first lesson of this chapter. Your initial focus will be officer safety and de-escalating the tensions between the people involved in the incident. Determine if a crime actually occurred based on the elements of assault and battery and if the suspect used something to commit the crime, such as hands, fists, feet, or an object or weapon.

☑ LE721.4. Describe how to respond to assault or battery

Occasionally there are situations that may not rise to the level of a criminal violation but have the potential for violence. In these instances, your agency may consider obtaining a risk protection order (RPO) on the person who poses the threat for violence.

RECLASSIFICATION

Under specific circumstances, or when certain elements are present while committing an assault or battery, the crime is reclassified to a more serious class of offense and carries a stronger sentence than the original crime.

☑ LE721.5. Determine when an assault or battery charge merits reclassification or a change in the degree of the offense

Reclassification can occur when the victim is 65 or older or is one of the following:

- an employee of a public or private school
- a sports official
- an emergency medical care provider—ambulance driver, emergency medical technician, paramedic, registered nurse, or physician
- a firefighter or police explorer
- a public transit employee
- a criminal justice officer—law enforcement officer, correctional officer, correctional probation officer, federal law enforcement officer, or fish and wildlife law enforcement officer
- a traffic accident investigation officer, traffic infraction enforcement officer, or parking enforcement specialist
- a security officer employed by the board of trustees of a community college

Refer to chapter 784, F.S., for a full list of cases when reclassification can occur. To reclassify the crime properly, establish that the victim was performing job duties at the time of the assault or battery and the suspect knew or should have known the victim was one of the workers listed in chapter 784, F.S., at the time of the assault or battery.

You may respond to an incident at a jail or correctional facility. Assault or battery of a correctional facility employee requires five more elements to reclassify the crime:

- The suspect was in custody in a correctional facility.
- The suspect intentionally touched, struck, or attempted to touch or strike the victim against their will by throwing, tossing, or expelling blood, saliva, chewed food, semen, urine, or feces at the victim.
- The suspect intended to harass, annoy, threaten, or alarm the victim.
- The victim was a correctional facility employee.
- The suspect knew the victim or had reason to know the victim was a facility employee.

WARRANTLESS ARREST

Chapter 901, F.S., allows you to make an arrest for assault without a warrant in either of the following situations:

- The assault occurs in your presence.
- The assault occurs during a domestic violence situation.
- The assault occurs upon a law enforcement officer, a firefighter, an emergency medical care provider, a public transit employee, or another officer.

This statutory chapter also allows officers to make a warrantless arrest for battery if there is probable cause to believe that a misdemeanor has been committed and that the person accused is the perpetrator of the crime. Probable cause may consist of physical evidence or sworn statements.

☑ LE721.6. Describe when you can make a warrantless arrest for assault or battery

UNIT 2 CRIMES AGAINST PERSONS
LESSON 2 Domestic Violence

Lesson Goal

At the end of this lesson, you will know how to respond to an incident involving domestic violence and determine the appropriate course of action and charges, if necessary.

Think About This

Timothy is 15 and yells at his mother when he gets angry. One time, Timothy argues with his mother and shoves her into a wall. In fear, she runs into her bedroom, locks the door, and calls the police. Is this domestic violence? How will you respond to this incident?

DOMESTIC VIOLENCE CRITERIA

LE722.1. Determine when an incident meets the criteria for domestic violence

Chapter 741, F.S., defines **domestic violence** as any assault, aggravated assault, battery, aggravated battery, sexual assault, sexual battery, stalking, aggravated stalking, kidnapping, false imprisonment, or any criminal offense resulting in physical injury or death of one family or household member by another family or household member.

Family or household member means spouses, former spouses, people related by blood or marriage, people who live together as if a family, or who have lived together in the past as if a family, and people who are parents with a child in common. With the exception of people who have a child in common, the family or household members must currently live or, in the past, lived together in the same single dwelling unit.

In Florida, when you arrest a person during a domestic violence incident, the actual criminal charge will not be for domestic violence. Instead, the charge may be assault, aggravated assault, battery, or aggravated battery. The relationship between the perpetrator and the victim determines if the incident is domestic violence.

The most dangerous time of a domestic violence call is when you approach, as the abuser may know that you are coming. When you arrive immediately consider:

- Are there weapons?
- Have there been previous calls to this location?
- Is the incident in progress?
- Is the abuser on the scene?

If, after thorough investigation, evidence indicates there is probable cause that an offense occurred, and the involved persons are family or household members, arrest the abuser. Arrest is the preferred response only for the primary aggressor, not for a person who acts in a reasonable manner to protect themselves or a family member from violence.

DETERMINE THE ABUSER

With your backup officer, obtain each person's statements separately. Try to determine the abuser early on. Consider the following factors to help identify the abuser and make an arrest:

- Compare physical evidence to statements.
- Compare injuries to statements. Does the injury fit the story of the person who claims self-defense? Typical defensive wounds include bruising or cuts on outer forearms, back, backs of legs, palms, or inside fingers or fingertips.
- Compare statements from the victim, witness, and suspect.
- Consider evidence or patterns of assault and coercion; include physical, sexual, and psychological abuse.
- Assess the verbal and non-verbal communication of the involved persons.
- Consider the emotional state, use of physical stature for intimidation, and fearfulness of involved persons.
- Consider past incidents of violence.
- Consider violent physical acts, such as damaged property or injured animals.
- Determine if the suspect has destroyed any security or surveillance devices.
- Look for broken or damaged doors, window locks, or cell phones.
- Look for red flags of economic abuse or dependency, such as whether the abuser took the only credit card, checkbook, cell phone, or set of car keys.

☑ LE722.2. Determine the abuser in a domestic violence incident

DATING VIOLENCE

Dating violence is violence between people who have or have had a continuing and significant relationship of a romantic or intimate nature.

The criteria for dating violence is based on:

- a dating relationship within the past six months
- the character of the relationship, including the expectation of affection or sexual involvement
- the frequency and type of interaction occurring over time and on a continuous basis

☑ LE722.3. Determine when an incident meets the criteria for dating violence

The decision to investigate, arrest, and charge does not require the victim's consent. You are not liable in any civil action for an arrest based on probable cause, enforcement of a court order, or service of process in good faith arising from an alleged incident of dating violence.

RESPOND TO A DOMESTIC VIOLENCE INCIDENT

Follow the basic investigative sequence outlined in the first lesson of this chapter. Your initial focus will be officer safety and de-escalating the tensions between the people

☑ LE722.4. Describe how to respond to a domestic violence incident

involved in the incident. An incident that involved domestic violence will require additional documentation and reporting.

Getting details of the incident from the victim and suspect can be difficult because of the intensity of the situation. If either or both refuse to provide adequate information, turn to witnesses, including children, who were present during the incident. If there are no witnesses, you may need to rely on observable evidence at the scene, such as physical injuries or broken furniture.

☑ LE722.5. Describe how to document evidence in a domestic violence incident

Physical evidence is incredibly important in a domestic violence investigation. Photograph and document evidence carefully, or document the lack of evidence. It may be necessary for you to return in 24 to 48 hours to document or collect more evidence or information, including photographs of physical injury and property damage. Physical evidence can help solve a case involving an uncooperative victim or witnesses. You will learn about evidence collection in Chapter 9.

If you decide to arrest the abuser, tell the victim and the suspect why and where you are transporting the suspect. An adult suspect arrested for an act of domestic violence must remain in custody until brought before the court for a bail determination.

Like dating violence, the decision to investigate, arrest, and charge does not require the victim's consent. You are not liable in any civil action for an arrest based on probable cause, enforcement of a court order, or service of process in good faith arising from an alleged incident of domestic violence. A backup officer may need to transport the victim and any children to a domestic violence center.

When probable cause for arrest does not exist, you and the backup officer will explain the options available to each party separately, such as:

- getting counseling
- acting on information provided in the *Notice of Legal Rights and Remedies* brochure
- getting help from local social service agencies
- arranging for transportation to a domestic violence center or safe location

It is unlawful to disclose the location of the domestic violence center you transported a victim to.

NO CONTACT ORDER

☑ LE722.6. Describe the role of a no contact order

A no contact order prohibits any oral or written communication with the victim (or person named in the order); physical or violent contact with the victim; or presence within 500 feet of the victim's residence, vehicle, or workplace, or a specific place that the victim (or person named in the order) visits regularly. A no contact order is typically part of the pretrial release conditions imposed on someone arrested for committing a crime against another person, which would typically include incidents of domestic violence. Chapter

901 F.S., allows you to make a warrantless arrest for a violation of a no contact order if the original arrest was for an act of domestic violence.

INJUNCTIONS

Although an injunction is a civil action, its violation has criminal consequences. Law enforcement honors injunctions from other states or countries and can advise a victim to ask the local clerk of the court to reissue the injunction in Florida if the victim is now residing here.

Be sure to let victims know that they can go to the courthouse and file for an injunction. The victim must complete an affidavit, explaining why they need the protection. All forms are free of charge from the clerk of court. A judge reviews the affidavit and grants or denies the request.

☑ LE722.7. Describe the role of an injunction in a domestic violence incident

An injunction often involves custody of the victim and respondent's children. The violation of a custody arrangement outlined in an injunction will generally remain a civil matter unless the respondent violates one of the conditions given in chapter 741, F.S. If you determine the circumstances of the custody dispute are civil in nature, maintain the status quo and document the incident on the appropriate report. Chapter 901, F.S., allows you to make a warrantless arrest for a criminal act that is in violation of an injunction for protection.

Victims of domestic or dating violence often hesitate to obtain an injunction for fear that the abuser may retaliate. An option for the officer may be to petition the court for a risk protection order, following agency policies and procedures.

CHILD TO PARENT DOMESTIC VIOLENCE

Child domestic battery occurs when a child commits an act of violence against a parent, sibling, or other family member living in the home.

When you interview a child and family members, determine if the violent behavior is an isolated event. After gathering essential information, refer the family to appropriate interventions, refer the child to another family member's home or a respite diversion program to "cool off," or make an arrest based on the ongoing risk level of harm to others.

☑ LE722.8. Describe how to respond to child to parent domestic violence

The circumstances surrounding each child domestic battery incident are unique and require an individualized response. Refer families to the Florida Network of Youth and Family Services for local and statewide resources for emergency shelter services and individual and family counseling.

DOCUMENTATION

Florida law requires you to document any allegation of domestic violence with a written report. If you do not make an arrest and do not clearly write the reason why in your report, you and your agency may assume liability should the persons involved re-engage in violence and injury occurs.

☑ LE722.9. Describe how to document a domestic violence incident

Florida law also requires you to send a domestic violence report to your nearest local, certified domestic violence center within 24 hours of receiving notification of the reporting of the incident.

☑ LE722.10. Describe the purpose of a lethality assessment when responding to a domestic violence incident

Along with submitting a report, you are legally required to make a good faith attempt to perform a lethality assessment of the victim if the domestic violence call involves an intimate partnership. A ***lethality assessment*** is a tool that first responders use during a domestic violence call to predict the likelihood that a homicide will occur between intimate partners. The Office of Violence Against Women defines intimate partners as people who are married, living together, dating, or sharing a child. However, the term can also apply to people that have previously been married, have lived together before, or have dated in the past.

Before administering the lethality assessment, determine who the victim and the abuser (or aggressor) are, and ask the victim if they are either current or former intimate partners. When giving the lethality assessment, you will ask the victim a set of 12 questions and based on the victim's responses you may be required to advise the victim they are in a potentially lethal situation. You must document the results of the lethality assessment in your report, including the absence of a lethality assessment if the victim was unable or unwilling to provide enough information.

> **📌 Note**
>
> Remember, you are responsible for referring all victims of a domestic violence incident to the nearest certified domestic violence center and offering them resources and services, even if they are not in a potentially lethal situation.

UNIT 2 CRIMES AGAINST PERSONS
LESSON 3 Stalking Crimes

Lesson Goal

At the end of this lesson, you will know how to respond to incidents involving stalking and cyberstalking and determine the appropriate course of action and charges, if necessary.

Think About This

Michael began following his ex-wife, Cheri, soon after their divorce. He leaves notes on her car, parks his truck in front of her house, and repeatedly phones her at work and at home. She tells him to leave her alone but does not report it to law enforcement at first. Michael increases the frequency and intensity of this behavior, so Cheri decides to contact law enforcement as this behavior has occurred every day for over two months. How will you respond to this incident?

STALKING

Stalking involves unwanted and repeated attention, contact, or harassment by the suspect toward the victim. It can easily escalate as the suspect progresses to possessive and controlling behavior. Stalking is not limited to people who have an existing relationship. Sometimes the suspect is a stranger to the victim. It can occur as a cluster of incidents in a brief period of time or repeated over a long period of time.

Chapter 784, F.S., outlines the elements of stalking. Stalking occurs when the suspect willfully, maliciously, and repeatedly follows, harasses, or cyberstalks the victim. ***Maliciously*** means wrongfully, intentionally, without legal justification or excuse, and with the knowledge that injury or damage will or may be caused to another person or their property. Stalking may not come to the attention of law enforcement until the situation has progressed to another crime, such as sexual battery, aggravated assault, or murder.

☑ LE723.1.
Determine if an incident is stalking

AGGRAVATED STALKING

Aggravated stalking occurs when the suspect willfully, maliciously, and repeatedly follows, harasses, or cyberstalks the victim, and makes a credible threat to the victim. A ***credible threat*** is a verbal or non-verbal threat, or a combination of the two, that places someone in reasonable fear for their safety or the safety of their family and friends.

☑ LE723.2.
Determine if an incident is aggravated stalking

CYBERSTALKING

The Florida Statutes provide two definitions of cyberstalking. ***Cyberstalk*** means (1) to engage in a course of conduct to communicate, or to cause to be communicated, directly or indirectly, of words, images, or language by or through use of electronic mail or electronic communication, directed at, or pertaining to a specific person, or (2)

☑ LE723.3.
Determine if an incident is cyberstalking

to access the online accounts or internet-connected home electronic systems of another person without that person's permission, causing substantial emotional distress to that person and serving no legitimate purpose in both cases.

Some juveniles may have a false perception that they are anonymous on the internet and use social media to abuse others. They may use it to respond to or carry on a disagreement that can escalate to bullying and cyberstalking. Other forms of cyberstalking include cyberintimidation and sexual cyberharassment.

RESPOND TO A STALKING INCIDENT

☑ LE723.4. Describe how to respond to stalking

Interview the victim to gain the facts surrounding the stalking, such as frequency, method, and any electronic device information. Ask the victim to provide screenshots of text messages or social media pages, and physical copies of notes.

Determine if the information meets the elements of stalking, aggravated stalking, or cyberstalking, and if you have jurisdiction based on where the stalking occurred. To avoid destroying any information, do not touch any electronic devices, such as a cell phone, laptop, or desktop computer. Notify your supervisor based on the complexity of the case, if there are weapons involved, or if you need additional assistance, such as a specialized detective or a victim's advocate. A backup officer may transport the victim and any children to a domestic violence center.

UNIT 2 CRIMES AGAINST PERSONS
LESSON 4 Child Abuse

Lesson Goal

At the end of this lesson, you will know how to respond to an incident involving child abuse, neglect, and abandonment while considering the role of the child protective investigator.

Think About This

Tracy is a 14-year-old middle-schooler, and she is arguing with her father at the dinner table. Her father calls her defiant, and she argues that she is merely sarcastic. As they continue to argue, her father tells her to stand up; he grabs her by the arm and slaps her. Tracy does not notice any marks on herself, but her teacher notices marks on the back of her arm and calls the Florida Abuse Hotline. How will you respond to this incident? What are some of the first tasks you need to do?

CHILD ABUSE

In Florida, a parent has the right to discipline their child in a reasonable manner. Corporal punishment by a parent or legal custodian for disciplinary purposes does not constitute abuse when it does not result in substantial harm to a child. If a reasonable parent or adult would not engage in a damaging act toward a child for any valid reason, especially when the primary purpose is to cause the child unjustifiable pain or injury, the act is deemed malicious and is child abuse. Chapter 827, F.S., outlines the elements of child abuse.

For **child abuse**, document that the suspect knowingly or willfully abused a child younger than 18 by:

- intentionally inflicting physical or mental injury,
- committing an intentional act that could reasonably be expected to result in physical or mental injury, or
- actively encouraging another person to commit an act that results in or could reasonably have been expected to result in physical or mental injury to a child.

☑ LE724.1. Determine if an incident is child abuse or aggravated child abuse

Chapter 39, F.S., defines **physical injury** as death, permanent or temporary disfigurement, or impairment of any bodily part. Different types of harm can include:

- sprain, dislocation, or cartilage damage,
- bone or skull fracture, brain or spinal cord damage, or traumatic brain injury,
- injury to any internal organ,
- asphyxiation, suffocation, or drowning, or
- burns or scalding, cuts, lacerations, punctures, or bites.

Mental injury from child abuse is an injury to the intellectual or psychological health of a child. Expert testimony from a mental health professional determines if a child victim cannot function within the normal range of behavior because of child abuse.

For *aggravated child abuse* of a child younger than 18, document that the suspect:

- committed aggravated battery upon a child,
- willfully tortured a child,
- maliciously punished a child,
- willfully and unlawfully caged a child, or
- knowingly or willfully committed child abuse, causing great bodily harm, permanent disability, or permanent disfigurement.

CHILD NEGLECT

Child neglect occurs when a caregiver fails to provide food, nutrition, clothing, shelter, medicine, and medical services essential for the well-being of a child, regardless of the age. Child neglect is more than a failure to use ordinary care; it is gross and deliberate negligence, committed with disregard for the safety of a child.

☑ LE724.2. Determine if an incident is child neglect

For child neglect, document that the suspect was a caregiver for the child and willfully failed to provide the care, supervision, and services necessary to maintain physical or mental health, or failed to make a reasonable effort to protect a child from abuse, neglect, or exploitation by another person.

In the context of child neglect, a *caregiver* means a parent, adult household member, or other person who is responsible for a child's welfare or who might have legal custody of a child. *Legal custody* means:

- a legal status created by a court: the court appoints an entity, whether an agency or an individual (for example, DCF, or a member of a child's extended family), to be a custodian or guardian,
- the right to have physical custody of a child and the right and duty to protect, nurture, guide, and discipline a child, or
- the right to provide a child with food, shelter, education, and ordinary medical, dental, psychiatric, and psychological care.

CHILD ABANDONMENT VERSUS SURRENDERING AN INFANT

☑ LE724.3. Explain the difference between child abandonment and surrendering an infant

Chapter 39, F.S., defines *abandonment* as a situation involving a parent, legal custodian, or caregiver who, while being able, makes no significant contribution to a child's care and maintenance or has failed to establish or maintain a substantial and positive relationship with a child, or both. A parent does not commit child abuse, neglect, or abandonment if the parent surrenders an infant approximately 30 days old or younger at a hospital, emergency room, EMS station, or fire station. When the parent leaves an infant at one of these designated places and expresses an intent to leave the infant and not return, they are not exposing a child to unreasonable risk of harm.

Chapter 383, F.S., further outlines the treatment of surrendered infants and their parents. The Florida Statutes define an *infant* as a child a licensed physician would reasonably believe to be about 30 days old or younger. Unless there is actual or suspected child abuse or neglect, a parent has the right to remain anonymous when surrendering an infant. You may not pursue or follow a parent who surrenders an infant under s. 383.50, F.S.

ABUSIVE HEAD TRAUMA

In a child, a traumatic brain injury is an injury to the head and brain of an infant or child younger than 6 years of age, usually as the result of violent shaking or blunt impact. This type of head trauma is a sign of child abuse. In First Aid, you will learn how to recognize and provide emergency care to an infant or child younger than 6 years of age with head trauma and brain injury.

☑ LE724.4. Describe an incident of abusive head trauma

Once the infant or child is in the care of EMS, your role shifts to conducting the initial investigation for child abuse. The role of the parent or caregiver in abusive head trauma is considerable and may be difficult to understand if they seem pleasant and forthcoming with information. Most parents or caregivers do not intend to kill or injure a child, just punish, or get them to stop crying; however, these caregivers are still responsible for their actions.

CONTRIBUTING TO THE DELINQUENCY OR DEPENDENCY OF A CHILD

For contributing to the delinquency or dependency of a child younger than 18, document that the suspect committed an act that:

- caused, tended to cause, encouraged, or contributed to a child becoming a delinquent or dependent child or a child in need of services, or
- by act, threat, command, or persuasion, induced or endeavored to induce a child to commit or perform an act, follow a course of conduct, or live in a manner that causes or tends to cause the child to remain a delinquent or dependent child or a child in need of services.

☑ LE724.5. Determine if an incident is contributing to the delinquency or dependency of a child

A person 21 years of age or older who impregnates a child under 16 years of age contributes to the delinquency of the child, even if the victim agreed to the act.

RESPOND TO CHILD ABUSE, NEGLECT, OR ABANDONMENT

Responding to an incident involving child abuse can be emotionally difficult. When you arrive at the scene, you must determine if there are any injuries and if anyone needs immediate medical treatment. Look for signs of physical abuse, such as bruises, welts, burns, fractures, and cuts.

☑ LE724.6. Describe how to respond to child abuse, neglect, or abandonment

Sometimes you meet with or escort a child protective investigator (CPI) from DCF to the scene. Due to the hostile nature of domestic calls, you will provide security for the unarmed CPI while they conduct an assessment to determine if a child is in immediate danger. The Florida Statutes authorize a CPI to remove children from a parent or caregiver's custody and control without a custody order. If this occurs, make sure that the child's removal happens with as little trauma as possible.

☑ LE724.7. Separate the victim of child abuse or neglect from the suspected abuser

Physically separate a child from the alleged abuser to prevent additional harm to the child and to prevent them from seeing or hearing each other. Pay attention to how a child interacts with any adults or siblings and if their demeanor suggests fear when they are in the room.

Conduct a thorough interview of all persons on the scene, at a reasonable location of your choice, out of earshot of the child, and considering officer safety. Interview the parents or caregivers and obtain a statement regarding the allegations of child abuse or neglect. This is a preliminary interview to lock in a statement, dismiss any retaliatory accusations, or establish a suspect's identity. Often an investigator or a very experienced patrol officer conducts a child interview.

Determine whether a crime has occurred and if abuse or neglect of a child occurred. If it did occur, find out who is responsible. Decide what actions are necessary to protect the victims, which may include removing a child from the environment. If the child's life or health is in such danger that they must be removed from their surroundings, or if you reasonably believe a child has been abandoned, abused, or neglected, contact your supervisor and the Florida Abuse Hotline at 800-962-2873. Follow the basic investigation process outlined at the beginning of this chapter. Document the incident regardless of whether a crime has occurred.

Using procedural justice can help reduce tensions and limit the trauma experienced by all parties. Maintain a professional, impartial, and proactive response. Explain your actions and provide the children with a chance to speak and ask questions. Keep in mind that both the child and the adults involved in the incident are experiencing trauma. Treating all involved with dignity and respect can de-escalate and calm the situation.

REPORTING REQUIREMENTS

☑ LE724.8. Describe how to document child abuse, neglect, and abandonment

The Florida Statutes require all individuals to report any suspicion or knowledge of child abuse, neglect, or abandonment by calling the Florida Abuse Hotline. The identity of the person reporting the abuse is confidential information. Include this identifying information in your report, but do not disclose it to anyone involved in the incident. Most reporters can remain anonymous; however, statutes require people in certain professions, including law enforcement, physicians, and teachers, to provide their names to the hotline when reporting.

Do not place the CPI's personal identifying information (date of birth, home address, etc.) in your report as employees of DCF have the same confidentiality protections as law enforcement.

UNIT 2 CRIMES AGAINST PERSONS
LESSON 5 Abuse, Neglect, and Exploitation of an Elderly Person or Disabled Adult

Lesson Goal

At the end of this lesson, you will know how to respond to an incident involving abuse, neglect, or exploitation of an elderly person or disabled adult while considering the role of the adult protective investigator (API).

Think About This

Dispatch sends you to the home of Martha, who is 75 and blind. She called dispatch because her dog is not coming when called, but she can hear the dog whining somewhere in the house. Martha tells you that she lives with her son, and he was angry at her because she wouldn't give him money. She thinks that he kicked her dog before leaving the house. You find the dog and carry the dog to Martha, who asks you to call a cab for her. While you are calling for a cab, Martha discovers that credit cards are missing from her wallet. How will you respond?

ABUSE OF AN ELDERLY PERSON OR DISABLED ADULT

Abuse of an elderly person or disabled adult occurs when the suspect knowingly or willfully subjects an elderly person or disabled adult to behavior that could reasonably be expected to result in the physical or psychological harm or death of the elderly person or disabled adult. Document that the suspect:

- intentionally inflicted physical or psychological injury,
- committed an intentional act that could reasonably be expected to result in physical or psychological injury,
- actively encouraged another person to commit an act that resulted in or could reasonably have been expected to result in physical or psychological injury, or
- intentionally and without lawful authority isolated or restricted access to family members for any length of time that could reasonably be expected to result in physical or psychological injury or to conceal criminal activity.

☑ LE725.1. Determine if an incident is abuse or aggravated abuse of an elderly person or disabled adult

Aggravated abuse of an elderly person or disabled adult occurs when the suspect:

- commits aggravated battery upon an elderly person or disabled adult,
- willfully tortures, maliciously punishes, or willfully and unlawfully cages the victim, or
- knowingly or willfully abuses the victim and causes great bodily harm, permanent disability, or permanent disfigurement.

NEGLECT OF AN ELDERLY PERSON OR DISABLED ADULT

Neglect of an elderly person or disabled adult occurs when the suspect willfully fails to provide the care, supervision, and services necessary to maintain the physical or mental health of an elderly person or disabled adult or fails to make a reasonable

☑ LE725.2. Determine if an incident is neglect of an elderly person or disabled adult

effort to protect the victim from abuse, neglect, or exploitation by another person. The abuse may be repeated conduct or a single incident that can result in a serious physical or psychological injury, or a substantial risk of death.

The suspect must be the caregiver for the victim. A caregiver here means a person who has been entrusted with or has assumed responsibility for the care of an elderly person or disabled adult and their property. A caregiver includes, but is not limited to, relatives, court-appointed or voluntary guardians, adult household members, neighbors, health care providers, and employees and volunteers of facilities (a facility means any location that provides day or residential care for people who are elderly or disabled). Your observations might determine whether a caregiver is providing adequate food, nutrition, clothing, shelter, supervision, medicine, and medical services that would be essential to the well-being of the elderly person or disabled adult.

EXPLOITATION OF AN ELDERLY PERSON OR DISABLED ADULT

Adults who are elderly or disabled can be more dependent on others because of limitations and unique needs. This dependence, along with physical or mental vulnerability, places them at an increased risk of being financially exploited by friends, family, and other trusted individuals. Given the nature of the relationship between the victim and the suspect, victims may have difficulty identifying a crime has occurred and are often reluctant to report crimes committed against them. Look beyond the surface of a situation to understand the dynamics that may be occurring.

The elderly person or disabled adult may have a fiduciary, or someone who is legally responsible for managing their health and well-being or makes decisions regarding their property and finances. The fiduciary may call themselves a guardian, trustee, or an agent under durable power of attorney. Do not assume that an exploitation situation is a civil matter. When you determine the incident shows signs of the crime of abuse, neglect, or exploitation, consider the ongoing abuse, neglect, or exploitation a criminal matter and not just a family matter. Contact your supervisor for guidance.

☑ LE725.3. Determine if an incident is exploitation of an elderly person or disabled adult

Exploitation of an elderly person or disabled adult occurs when the suspect:

- knowingly obtains or uses, attempts to obtain or use, or conspires with another to obtain or use an elderly person's or disabled adult's funds, assets, or property with the intent to temporarily or permanently deprive the victim of the use, benefit, or possession of the funds, assets, or property, or to benefit someone other than the victim; or

- abuses a special relationship between them and the elderly person or disabled adult that results in an unauthorized seizure or other qualifying social, financial, or physical hardship or neglect suffered by the elderly person or disabled adult.

The elements of exploitation may appear similar to fraud or theft but should be charged as exploitation because of the victim's vulnerability and the suspect's relationship with them. Exploitation frequently occurs with abuse or neglect of an elderly person or disabled adult, which is something to be alert for when responding to these types of calls.

INITIAL RESPONSE TO ELDERLY OR DISABLED ADULT INCIDENTS

You may encounter suspected abuse, neglect, or exploitation when responding to a well-being check or domestic violence incident. Determine if there are any injuries to the victim or other household members, and decide whether anyone needs medical treatment. Look for signs of physical abuse, such as bruises, welts, burns, fractures, lacerations, and abrasions. Remember, signs of abuse, neglect, or exploitation may not be obvious. If the victim is in immediate danger and an API is not present, contact your supervisor.

☑ LE725.4. Determine if the elderly person or disabled adult is in immediate danger of abuse, neglect, or exploitation

Some questions to consider are:

- Does it appear that someone is taking care of the person?
- Do you smell urine or feces on the person or in the room?
- Do you smell rotting food?
- Can you find enough food in the kitchen and refrigerator?
- Is the person receiving regular medical care?

ADULT PROTECTIVE INVESTIGATOR

Sometimes you will meet with or escort an API to the scene. Should the API have reason to believe a situation presents a risk of death or serious injury and is unable to obtain consent for access to a premise, they can conduct an emergency forcible entry without a court order.

You will keep the API safe and secure while they conduct a social services investigation. Your job will be to conduct a criminal investigation to determine if a crime has occurred. Always document the incident even if you do not find evidence of a crime.

☑ LE725.5. Differentiate the officer's role from the adult protective investigator's role

The API will decide whether to remove the victim from the home, and when and where to place the person in protective custody. The law authorizes an API to conduct an emergency removal without a court order, along with specified medical personnel or law enforcement, for a victim who lacks capacity to consent when there is a risk of death or serious physical injury. If this occurs, help the API lawfully conduct their duties and ensure the safety of everyone involved.

GATHER INFORMATION

Take extra time to be sensitive to the person's needs; observe carefully, speak clearly, and have patience. Victims may be embarrassed, afraid, angry, or confused. Physically separate the victim from the suspect. Determine if the victim's disability or vulnerability affects their ability to communicate or their capacity or memory. Document their emotional and mental response, including the inability to recall details or provide an accurate account. If the victim tells you that they consented to the alleged criminal activ-

☑ LE725.6. Describe how to interview the people involved when conducting an initial investigation of abuse, neglect, or exploitation of an elderly person or disabled adult

ity, this should not end your investigation as they may lack the capacity or be unduly influenced into providing consent. Interview the primary caregiver to get a statement about the allegations.

COURSE OF ACTION

☑ LE725.7. Describe how to respond to abuse, neglect, and exploitation of an elderly person or disabled adult

After the initial interviews and assessment of the scene, work with the API to determine the best course of action to ensure the victim's safety. Tell the victim, their guardian, or someone acting on behalf of the victim that they may consider filing an injunction for protection against exploitation of a vulnerable adult or a domestic violence injunction as discussed in a previous lesson. If the victim is elderly and needs legal assistance, refer them to the Florida Senior Legal Helpline at 888-895-7873, or if disabled, refer them to Disability Rights Florida at 800-342-0823.

Chapter 415, F.S., authorizes you to provide transport, or arrange for transport, of an elderly person or disabled adult to the appropriate facility.

REPORTING REQUIREMENTS

Like child abuse, the Florida Statutes require everyone to report any suspicion or knowledge of the abuse, neglect, or exploitation of vulnerable adults, disabled adults, and elderly persons by calling the Florida Abuse Hotline.

☑ LE725.8. Describe how to document abuse, neglect, and exploitation of an elderly person or disabled adult

Always protect the identity of the reporting person during this type of investigation. If the initial report came from the Florida Abuse Hotline, the API may not reveal the reporting person to you because of confidentiality laws. Most reporters can remain anonymous; however, statutes require people in certain professions, including law enforcement and physicians, to provide their names when reporting.

UNIT 2 CRIMES AGAINST PERSONS
LESSON 6 Interference With Custody, Luring or Enticing of a Child, False Imprisonment, and Kidnapping

Lesson Goal

At the end of this lesson, you will know how to respond to an incident involving a child custody dispute, interference with custody, luring or enticing of a child, false imprisonment, and kidnapping while using multiagency resources as appropriate.

Think About This

While on patrol, you observe a woman who is parked alongside another car with her children in the back seat. A man gets out of the other car, and the two began to argue. After a lengthy argument, the woman gets back into her car and drives away with the children in the back. The man sees you across the parking lot, walks over to your patrol car, and reports to you that his ex-wife just interfered with a custody agreement. How should you respond?

INTERFERENCE WITH CUSTODY

Chapter 787, F.S., outlines the elements of interference with custody, luring or enticing of a child, false imprisonment, and kidnapping. To establish probable cause for **interference with custody**, document that the suspect knowingly or recklessly took or enticed, or aided, abetted, hired, or otherwise procured someone else to take or entice, a minor or incompetent person from the custody of the parent, guardian, public agency, or any other lawful custodian, or is the parent, whether natural or adoptive, stepparent, legal guardian, or relative who has custody and who took a minor or incompetent person with malicious intent to deprive the other person of their right to custody. The parent or guardian must have knowledge of the court order regarding custody or receive notice of the pending proceeding to meet the elements of interference with custody.

☑ LE726.1. Determine if an incident is interference with custody

The law does not apply to a parent fleeing with a child and who is the victim of domestic violence or believes that they are about to become a victim of domestic violence or believes that their action was necessary to preserve the child from danger. It is unlawful for any person, in violation of a court order, to lead, take, entice, or remove a minor beyond the limits of the state or to conceal the location of a minor with personal knowledge of the order.

Follow your agency's policies and procedures regarding interference with custody incidents. Document these incidents even when you do not make an arrest. If a child is later reported missing, there will be records of interference with custody incidents that may be able to provide investigative information.

You may encounter a child custody situation in which parents have separate, conflicting court orders issued from different states. The Florida order will not necessarily be the proper and enforceable one. Recall that you may not enforce a court order issued

☑ LE726.2. Describe how to respond to conflicting child custody orders from different states

by another state or jurisdiction unless the court domesticates—or follows a process to recognize and adopt—an out-of-state or county court order through a petition process. These cases involve application of the Uniform Child Custody Jurisdiction and Enforcement Act and can be legally complex. Do not attempt to determine which order is enforceable; instead, contact your supervisor to determine how to proceed.

LURING OR ENTICING A CHILD

The difference between interference with custody and luring or enticing a child is that interference with custody does not involve the intention to commit other crimes while luring or enticing requires the suspect to have the unlawful intention to commit other crimes, such as sexual battery.

☑ LE726.3. Determine if an incident is luring or enticing a child

For *luring or enticing a child*, document that the suspect:

- is 18 years of age or older
- intentionally lured or enticed, or attempted to lure or entice, a child under the age of 14 into or out of a structure, dwelling, or conveyance for other than a lawful purpose

FALSE IMPRISONMENT

☑ LE726.4. Determine if an incident is false imprisonment

False imprisonment is often associated with domestic violence. For *false imprisonment*, document that the suspect forcibly, by threat or secretly confining, abducted, imprisoned, or restrained the victim against their will without lawful authority.

Confining a child younger than 13 years of age against their will and without the consent of their parent or legal guardian is also false imprisonment.

KIDNAPPING

The difference between false imprisonment and kidnapping is that kidnapping includes the intent to commit other felonies. False imprisonment does not require an intention to commit any crime other than the confinement, abduction, restraint, or imprisonment. Kidnapping can also involve moving the victim.

☑ LE726.5. Determine if an incident is kidnapping

For *kidnapping*, document that the suspect forcibly, secretly, or by threat, confined, abducted, imprisoned, or restrained the victim against their will without lawful authority and acted with intent to do at least one of the following:

- hold the victim for ransom or reward or as a shield or hostage
- commit or help with the commission of a felony
- inflict bodily harm upon or terrorize the victim or another person
- interfere with the performance of any government or political function

For an incident to be kidnapping, the confinement, abduction, or imprisonment must not be slight, inconsequential, or merely incidental to the other crime committed (see below). Kidnapping is often associated with armed robbery and sexual battery crimes.

Kidnapping is both a state and federal violation. Kidnapping a child younger than 13 years of age is a life felony when committed with any of the following crimes:

- aggravated child abuse
- sexual battery
- lewd or lascivious battery, molestation, conduct, or exhibition
- child prostitution
- exploitation of a child
- human trafficking

INITIAL RESPONSE

If you determine an incident is interference with custody, luring or enticing of a child, false imprisonment, or kidnapping without a significant threat to the victim's well-being, follow state and agency guidelines. Notify your supervisor and command staff immediately. Contact dispatch and issue a BOLO. If the approximate location of the suspect or victim is known, request assistance and specialty support, such as:

- canine, air, and additional specialized support units
- the fire department, FBI, and FDLE
- an AMBER Alert, if applicable
- a child abduction response team (CART)

LE726.6. Describe how to respond to interference with custody, luring or enticing of a child, false imprisonment, or kidnapping

Be aware of potential evidence and investigative leads when working these types of crimes. You can lose leads if evidence is not appropriately gathered and preserved early on in the investigative process.

UNIT 2 CRIMES AGAINST PERSONS
LESSON 7 Missing or Missing Endangered Persons

◎ Lesson Goal

At the end of this lesson, you will know how to respond to an incident involving a missing or missing endangered person and when to begin the process for activating an AMBER Alert, Silver Alert, Purple Alert, or Blue Alert.

Think About This

You respond to a call involving a mother, who frantically tells you that her 6-year-old daughter never came home from school. She tells you that she called the school and was told that her daughter got on the bus, but the babysitter confirmed that her daughter never arrived at the house. The mother provides you a physical description of her daughter and what she was last seen wearing and carrying with her. How will you respond to this call?

DEFINITIONS

A *missing child* is a person younger than 18 whose temporary or permanent residence is in Florida, whose location has not been determined, and who is reported missing to a law enforcement agency.

A *missing adult* is a person 18 or older whose temporary or permanent residence is in Florida, whose location has not been determined, and who is reported missing to a law enforcement agency.

An *endangered person* is any one of the following:

- a missing child younger than 18 years of age
- a missing adult younger than 26 years of age
- a missing adult older than 26 years of age and believed to be in danger or the victim of criminal activity
- a missing adult 18 years of age or older who meets the criteria for a Silver Alert or a Purple Alert
- depending on agency policies, a person with diminished, developmental, or intellectual capacity, regardless of age

MISSING CHILD ALERT

☑ LE727.1. Describe a Missing Child Alert

In order to issue a Missing Child Alert, the following four criteria must be met:

1. The child must be younger than 18.
2. The law enforcement agency's preliminary investigation must conclude that the child is in danger of serious bodily injury or death.

3. Descriptive information or a photograph of the child must be available.
4. The agency of jurisdiction must approve the issuance of the Missing Child Alert.

AMBER ALERT

A Missing Child Alert may evolve into an AMBER Alert. FDLE, along with state, local, and private partners, operates the statewide Florida AMBER Alert with the purpose of publicly broadcasting critical information about an abducted child as quickly as possible via radio, television, road signs, text messages and alerts, and the internet.

☑ LE727.2. Describe an AMBER Alert

An AMBER Alert must meet five criteria:

1. The child must be younger than 18 years of age.
2. There must be a clear indication of abduction.
3. The local law enforcement agency of jurisdiction must recommend the activation.
4. A detailed description of the child, the abductor, or the vehicle to broadcast to the public (use a photo when available) must be available.
5. The law enforcement agency's investigation must conclude that the child's life is in imminent danger of serious bodily injury or death.

Follow your agency's policies and procedures for initiating an AMBER Alert.

SILVER ALERT

The statewide Silver Alert aids local law enforcement in the rescue or recovery of a missing adult who suffers from dementia, Alzheimer's disease, or other mental disability. Under the plan, the local investigating agency activates the Silver Alert and notifies the media, issues neighborhood telephone alerts, and uses other technologies to communicate with people who live in the community.

☑ LE727.3. Describe a Silver Alert

If the missing adult uses a vehicle during the incident, law enforcement can activate the statewide dynamic messaging system and other advisory methods through the Missing Endangered Persons Information Clearinghouse (MEPIC), which coordinates with the Florida Department of Transportation (FDOT) and the Florida Highway Patrol (FHP) to broadcast vehicle information about the missing person to motorists and the public.

To qualify for a Florida Silver Alert, the subject must be 60 years of age or older, or a person aged 18 to 59 who lacks the capacity to consent, and the person must have an irreversible deterioration of intellectual faculties that has been verified by law enforcement.

The incident must also meet the criteria for FDLE, FDOT, or FHP to activate dynamic message signs:

1. Local law enforcement has already activated a local or regional alert by contacting a media outlet in their own and surrounding jurisdictions.
2. Local law enforcement's investigation must conclude that the disappearance poses a credible threat to the person's welfare and safety.

3. There must be a description of the vehicle and a license plate number to display.
4. Local law enforcement must verify the vehicle and license plate information.
5. A local law enforcement agency must have entered the missing person into FCIC and issued a statewide BOLO to other law enforcement and 911 centers.

The Florida Department of Elder Affairs is another resource for local law enforcement to aid in the rescue or recovery of cognitively impaired missing persons. It can provide an email alert notification through the Aging Services Network; this includes area agencies on aging, community-care lead agencies, providers, and volunteers.

PURPLE ALERT

The statewide Purple Alert aids local law enforcement in the rescue or recovery of a missing adult who has one or more of the following:

- a mental or cognitive disability that is not Alzheimer's disease or a dementia-related disorder
- an intellectual or developmental disability
- a brain injury
- another physical, mental, or emotional disability that is not related to substance abuse

Local law enforcement may broadcast an alert if the missing adult's disappearance indicates a credible threat of immediate danger or serious bodily harm to themselves, and they cannot be returned to safety without law enforcement intervention. The missing adult must not meet the criteria for activation of a Silver Alert.

Law enforcement must notify the media in the jurisdiction where the missing adult is believed to or may be located and may broadcast the alert on lottery terminals. Your agency may also open a case with MEPIC and, if a vehicle is involved, coordinate with FDOT and FLHSMV to activate dynamic messaging signs.

BLUE ALERT

☑ LE727.4. Describe the role of the Blue Alert

The Florida Blue Alert uses technologies employed by the AMBER Alert to notify the public of critical information when a law enforcement officer has suffered serious bodily injury, is killed, or is missing while in the line of duty, and the suspect poses a serious threat to the public. In some of these cases, more information is available for broadcast, such as a detailed description of the suspect's vehicle, other means of escape, or the license plate of the suspect's vehicle.

Under the Blue Alert Plan, FDLE, FLHSMV, FHP, and FDOT immediately broadcast important information about the suspect when this information could prevent further harm or help apprehend the suspect. Law enforcement issues a Blue Alert to the public through the Emergency Alert System broadcasts on television, radio, and dynamic message signs located along highways.

RESPOND TO A MISSING PERSON INCIDENT

As soon as you determine that the person is missing, contact your supervisor. MEPIC provides specific guidelines for conducting a missing persons investigation. The initial search should include buildings and areas where someone last saw the missing person. Make sure the person is not inside the residence, especially when searching for children, who may hide in closets and small crawl spaces. Evaluate the contents and appearance of the missing person's room, home, car, and other personal spaces to learn if items are missing. Hairbrushes, drinking glasses, toys, and other items are sources of fingerprints, DNA, and scent. Look for diaries, computers, cell phones, game systems, and other electronic devices that may contain evidence and useful information.

☑ LE727.5. Describe how to assist with the investigation of a missing or missing endangered person

If the missing person is not in the building, conduct a neighborhood canvass. Consider how far the missing person could travel based on their physical condition and where they were seen last. Secure the area where someone last saw the person, and control entry and exit points if the situation seems to be a criminal abduction or if you suspect foul play.

Children with ASD, especially those who are severely affected, might wander or escape from a safe environment and seek bodies of water in nature (streams, ponds, lakes) or swimming pools. If a child with ASD is reported missing, law enforcement agencies must immediately notify all on-duty officers, local media outlets, and law enforcement in neighboring counties.

Should you find the missing person alive, make sure they receive necessary medical attention and contact the assigned investigator.

ADDITIONAL RESOURCES

The National Center for Missing and Exploited Children (NCMEC) works with law enforcement, families, and professionals on issues related to missing and sexually exploited children. NCMEC has a missing children hotline that serves as the national clearinghouse for information related to these issues.

☑ LE727.6. Describe additional resources for missing persons incidents

A Child Is Missing, Inc., offers free assistance to law enforcement to help recover missing people, including children, teens, and the elderly. After providing this organization with the missing person's information, a recorded message will be developed and sent to homes and businesses within the requested radius. Your agency may use this assistance during an AMBER or Silver Alert to supplement strategies for locating a missing person.

A child abduction response team (CART) is a multi-agency team that assists law enforcement to provide an organized and planned response to an abducted, missing, or endangered child. Rapid response is critical to the safe rescue of a child. Call one of FDLE's regional operation centers to obtain CART assistance.

UNIT 2 CRIMES AGAINST PERSONS
LESSON 8 Sexual Offenses

Lesson Goal

At the end of this lesson, you will know how to respond to incidents involving a sexual offense against a child, an adult, or an elderly person or disabled adult using a trauma-informed response.

SEXUAL BATTERY

Sexual battery is one of the most underreported crimes because the victim may be embarrassed or may actually have a continuing relationship with the suspect. A victim may also feel that the suspect will take revenge if the crime is reported, or they may feel like law enforcement cannot apprehend the suspect. Sexual battery victims might also fear further victimization or fear that they will not be believed during the investigation and in subsequent courtroom proceedings.

☑ LE728.1. Determine if an incident is sexual battery, including the victim's ability to provide consent

Sexual battery is non-consensual oral, anal, or female genital penetration by, or union with, the sexual organ of another or the anal or female genital penetration of another by any other object; however, it does not include an act done for a medical purpose. Consent does not include coerced submission and does not mean that the victim failed to offer physical resistance. The law also recognizes certain categories of people who are incapable of giving consent; these categories include the following incapacities:

- *mentally defective*—a person who has a mental disease or disorder that renders them temporarily or permanently incapable of judging their conduct
- *mentally incapacitated*—a person temporarily incapable of judging or controlling their own conduct due to the influence of a narcotic, anesthetic, or intoxicating substance administered without their consent or due to any other act committed upon them without their consent
- *physically helpless*—a person who is unconscious, asleep, or for any other reason physically unable to communicate unwillingness to an act
- *physically incapacitated*—a person who is bodily impaired or handicapped and substantially limited in their ability to resist or flee

☑ LE728.2. Determine if an incident is sexual battery of a child

The crime of sexual battery of a child is a felony with varying criminal degrees depending on the following factors:

- age and mental and physical capacity of the victim
- type of force used
- threat or use of a deadly weapon
- type of injuries received
- relationship of the child to the suspect

INITIAL RESPONSE TO SEXUAL BATTERY

Sexual battery victims experience a significant amount of trauma, so it is important to follow a trauma-informed approach when responding to a sexual assault. Listen and make observations to put the victim at ease and pave the way for an investigator.

☑ LE728.3. Describe how to respond to a victim of sexual battery

The Sexual Battery Victims' Access to Services Act provides victims of sexual battery access to medical intervention, advocacy, crisis-intervention, and recovery services. Chapter 794, F.S., requires you to provide or arrange for transportation of victims of sexual battery to an appropriate medical facility or a rape crisis center.

The victim's body and clothes contain valuable evidence. Gaining that evidence is a priority for the investigation. Discourage the victim from using the restroom, showering, washing their hands or face, or discarding any clothing or feminine hygiene products. Inform the victim why it is important to collect and maintain evidence, even if they are uncertain if they want to participate in the prosecution process at the time of the initial investigation.

Follow your agency's policies and procedures when arranging for a sexual battery exam and collecting a victim's clothing. Only medical personnel can perform medical intervention, in the form of an exam, using a sexual offense evidence kit or rape kit.

Once you arrange for medical intervention, contact a victim advocate following your agency's policies and procedures. Coordinate with the advocate to attend to the victim's emotional needs and to encourage the victim to cooperate with the process. The advocate should be able to accompany the victim to a medical facility or rape crisis center.

☑ LE728.4. Describe how to collaborate with a victim advocate when responding to a sexual battery

REPORTING REQUIREMENTS

Documenting sexual battery includes a forensic report, a medical report, and a criminal report. Agencies must submit a sexual offense evidence kit or other DNA evidence for forensic testing to the statewide criminal analysis laboratory system within 30 days of receiving it.

☑ LE728.5. Describe how to document sexual battery

Qualified medical personnel should provide the victim's medical report to law enforcement when complete, and it must be included in your final report. It is your responsibility to write the initial criminal report, and your initial and final reports must include a chronological description of what occurred as well as any actions you took to help the victim and gather evidence. Document the victim's appearance, condition (for example, bruises, scratches, and defensive wounds), and emotional state.

RESPOND TO LEWD AND LASCIVIOUS OFFENSES

Lewd and lascivious conduct is any sexual act considered to be highly offensive and contrary to common standards of behavior. The Florida Statutes provide the following definitions related to these offenses.

☑ LE728.6. Describe how to respond to a lewd and lascivious offense

- **Sexual activity**—the oral, anal, or female genital penetration by, or union with, the sexual organ of another or the anal or female genital penetration of another by any other object; however, sexual activity does not include an act done for bona fide medical purposes.
- **Consent**—actively agreeing to do something or giving permission for something to happen; it is intelligent, knowing, and voluntary consent, and does not include submission by coercion. Consent does not mean the failure by the alleged victim to offer physical resistance to the offender.
- **Coercion**—the use of exploitation, bribes, threats of force, or intimidation to gain cooperation or compliance.

Lewd and lascivious offenses may include battery, molestation, conduct, or exhibition. The level and classification of the offense varies depending on the age of the victim. Another consideration is whether the victim is a vulnerable adult.

RESPOND TO UNLAWFUL SEXUAL ACTIVITY WITH CERTAIN MINORS INCIDENT

☑ LE728.7. Describe how to respond to unlawful sexual activity with certain minors

Chapter 794, F.S., addresses sex offenses involving a person 24 years of age or older who engages in sexual activity with a minor aged 16 or 17. Notify your supervisor regarding the type of crime and complexity of the case, and request additional assistance and a victim advocate.

SEXUAL OFFENSES INVOLVING CHILDREN

☑ LE728.8. Identify sexual offenses involving children

The Department of Justice classifies child pornography as a form of child exploitation that can be prosecuted on the federal level. The Florida Statutes define *child pornography* as any image depicting a minor engaging in sexual conduct or any image that has been created, altered, adapted, or modified by electronic, mechanical, or other means, to portray an identifiable minor engaged in sexual conduct. It includes children posing in a lewd and lascivious manner or performing a sexual act. It is illegal to produce, possess, or distribute child pornography.

If you respond to a call involving child pornography on a computer or an electronic device, under no circumstance should you touch the device or attempt to find more images on it. Recovery of electronic data involves complex and highly specialized expertise, and you may inadvertently eliminate or spoil evidence by trying to do it yourself.

Many predators and pedophiles use chatting and email to coordinate traveling to meet child victims. They may also use computers to solicit sexual performances by children. A sexual performance can include a play, motion picture, photograph, dance, or any other visual representation exhibited before an audience.

Be aware that many sexual offenders and predators on probation or parole cannot have any pornography in their possession and may be court ordered not to have a computer at all. Do not allow the suspect, if present, to touch the computer or any electronic device. Contact your supervisor and ask for help.

SEXUAL OFFENSES COMMITTED BY JUVENILES

Juvenile sexual abuse is any sexual behavior a minor engages in that occurs without the consent of the other person, without the other person's being in a position of equality with the minor, or because of coercion. Juvenile sexual offender behavior ranges from non-contact sexual behavior to varying degrees of direct sexual contact.

Non-contact behavior can include making obscene phone calls, exhibitionism, voyeurism, and the showing or taking of lewd photographs. If you determine that an image was possessed by a minor or sent from a minor to other minors, this is sexting. *Sexting* occurs as a crime when a minor uses a computer or other electronic device, such as a cell phone, to transmit or distribute a nude photograph or video to another minor. Sexting is a crime even if both minors consent to the act.

Except as required by agency policies and procedures and restrictions on juvenile interviewing, your investigation will not be different from investigating an adult. If you have reasonable cause to suspect that a child is the victim of a known or suspected juvenile sexual offender, contact the Florida Abuse Hotline. Follow your agency's policies and procedures for the best approach to responding to these types of sexual offense incidents.

☑ LE728.9. Differentiate between investigating an incident involving a juvenile sex offender and an adult sex offender

UNIT 2 CRIMES AGAINST PERSONS
LESSON 9 Human Trafficking

Lesson Goal

At the end of this lesson, you will know how to respond to an incident involving human trafficking by recognizing labor and sex trafficking, child victims, and the importance of taking a victim-centered approach.

Think About This

You pull over a car for an expired license plate. The driver and the female passenger appear nervous, and they provide inconsistent stories. The driver tells you that he was driving the woman home, but when you question the woman, she tells you that she recently met the driver, and he suggested she sell her body for sex. He drives her places to have sex with people, and she charges them for sex and receives a portion of the proceeds. The driver consents to a search of his car, and you find a cell phone containing a nude picture of the woman, which she says she sent to the man by mistake. How should you respond to this incident?

HUMAN TRAFFICKING LAWS

Human trafficking is a form of modern-day slavery that involves holding people, including minors, in forced service for commercial sex trade or otherwise legitimate labor. It involves long-term, ongoing captivity, exploitation, and control of victims.

☑ LE729.1. Determine if an incident is human trafficking

Chapter 787, F.S., defines **human trafficking** as transporting, soliciting, recruiting, harboring, providing, enticing, maintaining, purchasing, patronizing, procuring, or obtaining another person for the purpose of exploitation of that person. Two threshold questions will help determine if a person is a victim of human trafficking:

1. Did the suspect recruit, transport, or hold the victim in the service of another for labor or commercial sex acts?
2. Did the suspect get or keep the victim's service through force, threats, psychological manipulation, or confiscation of legal documents?

Victims of human trafficking are subjected to force, fraud, or coercion for the purpose of sexual exploitation or forced labor. Force here means physical violence that may include beatings, sexual battery, shootings, or physical confinement. Fraud includes false or deceptive offers of employment, marriage, or a better life. Coercion includes:

- using or threatening to use physical force against any person (typically family members of the trafficking victim)
- restraining, isolating, or confining or threatening to restrain, isolate, or confine any person without lawful authority and against their will
- using lending or other credit methods as debt bondage
- destroying, concealing, removing, confiscating, withholding, or possessing immigration or identification documents

- causing or threatening to cause financial harm to any person, including high extension of credit, loan sharking, or fraudulent employment contracts
- enticing or luring any person by fraud or deceit
- giving a person a controlled substance so that they can be exploited
- using threats of deportation or other federal or state legal proceedings against the victim

Neither federal nor state human trafficking laws require an element of force, fraud, or coercion to determine sex trafficking of children younger than 18 years of age or an adult believed by the person to be a child younger than 18. Additionally, it is a capital felony if a child less than 12 years of age or a person who is mentally defective or mentally incapacitated is trafficked for the purpose of sexual exploitation.

RECOGNIZE HUMAN TRAFFICKING

As a patrol officer, you may encounter human trafficking masked as another crime or incident, such as drug possession, sexual assault, prostitution, or shoplifting. While one factor alone is not enough to indicate trafficking, it may be enough to suggest further investigation. You are in a key position to identify potential victims during traffic stops or on routine calls for service, such as domestic violence, child abuse, and incidents of truant or runaway children.

Living and working conditions for human trafficking victims can be unusual. Victims may live on or near work premises, reside in overcrowded living spaces, be restricted or have controlled communications, or be forced by traffickers to move frequently. Victims often lack individual transportation. They do not have identification (a birth certificate, visa, or passport) because traffickers take these documents as a form of control. Often a third party, or one person, will insist on interpreting for an entire group or an individual.

☑ LE729.2. Recognize the indicators of labor trafficking and sex trafficking

RESPOND TO A HUMAN TRAFFICKING INCIDENT

As a new officer, you are most likely going to report suspected human trafficking incidents to a special unit for further investigation; however, as the initial law enforcement contact, you can help establish rapport with the victim and gather preliminary information.

It is critical that you recognize that the person is a victim of a crime, not a suspect, and that the success of any investigation relies on the victim's cooperation. Their testimony will be crucial to prove the existence of force, fraud, or coercion, unless they are a minor.

☑ LE729.3. Describe how to respond to human trafficking using a victim-centered approach

Ask basic identifying information. If the people present are not willing to provide this, move to more involved questions to determine relationships between the parties. Based on the answers to these questions and if you suspect that something is wrong, encourage the potential victim to trust you enough to disclose information needed to detain the potential trafficker. Try to convey a sense of safety, bringing the victim away from the location where you encountered them. Victims may be reluctant to speak to a law enforcement officer, so follow the approach for trauma-informed interviewing.

UNIT 2 CRIMES AGAINST PERSONS
LESSON 10 Respond to a Death

◎ Lesson Goal

At the end of this lesson, you will know how to respond to an incident involving a death by understanding the manner and cause of death, the role of the medical examiner, and the variety of emotions on the scene.

Think About This

You are dispatched to the death of a 78-year-old man. Upon arrival, the family tells you that the man never woke up this morning; when they went into his bedroom to check on him, he was stiff and cold to the touch. The family says that he has had minor heart problems in the past but that he has not been to a doctor in several years. They already contacted his doctor, but he refused to sign the death certificate. There appears to be nothing suspicious or out of place at the scene. How do you respond to this incident?

All law enforcement officers will respond to the scene of a death at some point in their careers. When you are the primary responding officer, always consider officer safety first, provide first aid as necessary, and then preserve the scene for further investigation.

MANNER AND CAUSE OF DEATH

The cause of death may not be immediately apparent as some injuries may not cause a great deal of external blood loss. The *cause of death* is the specific injury or disease that leads to death.

☑ LE7210.1. Identify indicators of the manner and cause of death

While observing the body, look for obvious or abnormal signs of trauma, such as the presence of blood, cuts, gashes, or bruising. Look for an obvious fatal injury, such as a bullet hole in the head or chest. Notify your supervisor or investigator of any signs of trauma, obvious fatal injury, or abnormality to the body. A body that is cold to the touch may indicate that the person is dead and will not respond to resuscitation. The eyelids may remain open if they were open at the time of death.

The *manner of death* is the determination of how the injury or disease leads to death. The five manners of death are: natural, accident, suicide, homicide, and undetermined.

Homicide is the unlawful act of one human taking the life of another. Chapter 782, F.S., has subsections that identify types of homicide, including murder, justifiable homicide, vehicular homicide, manslaughter, and DUI manslaughter.

After death, a body goes through a process of changes that include:

- *rigor mortis*—the stiffening of body muscles after death
- *lividity*—the color changes from the settling of blood due to gravity, often black and blue
- *algor mortis*—the postmortem cooling of the body

Evidence of changes is most valuable if assessed as soon after death as possible because these indicators change over time. Body physique, individual variation, and environmental conditions can cause postmortem changes. You may use rigor mortis and lividity to help determine the position of the body at death, and it may indicate whether someone moved the body after death.

NOTIFY THE MEDICAL EXAMINER

When any person dies in Florida by criminal violence, accident, suicide, suddenly (when the person has a history of good health), or through any suspicious or unusual circumstance, the Florida Statutes require law enforcement to notify the Medical Examiner (ME) as soon as reasonably possible. As authorized by the ME, coordinate the release and transport of the body to the local morgue, a mortuary, or a crematorium. Do not disturb the body until authorized by the ME.

☑ LE7210.2. Describe the role of the Medical Examiner's Office

The officer and the ME cannot determine the cause and manner of death independently. The ME, in conjunction with law enforcement's investigation, makes the final determination on the cause and manner of death only after completing their investigation, which can take weeks.

If the death is by apparent natural causes or was expected, such as a patient in hospice care or with a terminal disease who was seeking treatment, notify the deceased person's physician of the death. You may find prescription bottles at the scene; examine the bottles for the doctor's name. With this information, contact the doctor for notification of the death. The physician may sign the death certificate. If you cannot locate the physician or the physician refuses to sign the death certificate, contact the ME's office.

☑ LE7210.3. Determine when to notify the deceased person's physician

IDENTIFY THE DECEASED

There are several ways that you can identify a deceased person. The final identification must be 100% positive before contacting next of kin or releasing information to the family. It is vital not to release a name without having physical evidence to confirm it. Premature release of a name later found to be incorrect can be devastating to family members of both the misidentified and the actual deceased individual.

Identifying a deceased person can be as simple as obtaining the driver license information (DAVID, fingerprint scanner) and comparing the photo to the body. There may be people on the scene who know the person and will tell you the deceased's name, but do not base your identification solely on this. Documents on the scene, identification found on or near the body, prescription bottles, and other items that identify a person, while helpful, may not always be those of the deceased. Depending on the condition of the body, one or more of these may not be possible, yet they may be helpful in identifying the deceased positively.

☑ LE7210.4. Describe how to verify the identity of a deceased person

INITIAL RESPONSE TO A DEATH

The tone you establish at the beginning of the preliminary investigation will have a direct impact on the cooperation of the people at the scene and the information they are willing to offer during interviews. You may be responsible for an investigation in its entirety or for a preliminary one with another investigator or the ME providing follow-up.

☑ **LE7210.5.**
Describe how to initiate crime scene procedures at a scene with a death

It is essential that you secure and protect the integrity of the scene. Do not move or touch anything. If there is a witness or suspect on the scene who needs medical attention, provide appropriate first aid.

Always approach the area as a crime scene and consider it a homicide until the information you gather consistently indicates otherwise. Determine the scope and size of the crime scene to avoid destroying or contaminating possible evidence. Remember to apply universal precautions and use PPE. If the scene is in a public location, place a visual barrier (such as crime scene tape) between the scene and the public without cross contaminating any evidence. Scan the area surrounding the body for potential hazards or evidence by performing a 360° visual sweep of the perimeter.

INTERVIEW

☑ **LE7210.6.**
Describe how to interview witnesses at the scene of a death

Identify, separate, and begin to interview witnesses and take statements. Interview the person who last saw the dead person alive and the person who found the body. Be sure to ask about anything that the witness may have observed or heard, and ask about the exact position the deceased individual was found in because the position of the body is crucial to the investigation. If they have been moved, this can cause confusion and difficulty in obtaining information that the ME will need in order to determine what caused or contributed to the death.

Consider asking:

- How did you find the body?
- Did you move the body?
- Do you know this person?
- What was happening with them immediately before their death?
- What was happening with them in the days or weeks before their death?
- Did they have a healthy lifestyle?
- Did they consume drugs or alcohol?
- Did they have any known medical conditions?
- Who was with them before their death?

INITIAL INVESTIGATION

☑ **LE7210.7.**
Describe how to conduct an initial investigation of a death

Determine if you have jurisdiction in this incident. If you do not, refer the incident to the proper agency and hold the scene until additional assistance arrives. If you do have jurisdiction, notify your supervisor and provide information related to the incident, including information from the witnesses. If a detective will respond, maintain the scene and start a log.

If a detective is not responding and you are tasked with conducting the entire investigation, begin to preserve any evidence that you locate. Failure to collect, document, or gather evidence makes it difficult to go back and undo the damage done to the integrity of the investigation. You will learn more about processing a crime scene and evidence in Chapter 9.

EMOTIONAL RESPONSE TO A DEATH

Death scenes can be chaotic and tragic and crowded with emotional family members and witnesses. Families have the right to receive a thorough investigation, so they can understand the true medical cause of the death.

Prepare for the family's responses, keeping in mind that they may be in shock, distraught, and most likely confused. You may need to repeat information several times. Try to understand the family's level of grief and empathize with what they are experiencing. People respond to death in many ways. Do not jump to any conclusions about the way a family reacts based on how you would respond if you were in this situation. Remain professionally distant but display respect to family members and loved ones to minimize their trauma.

☑ LE7210.8.
Describe the different responses people can have to a death

RESPONSE TO AN INFANT DEATH

The Centers for Disease Control and Prevention (CDC) defines an infant as a baby younger than a year old. Infants can die from a number of causes, such as abuse, neglect, infection, disease, accident, or intentional harm. Sometimes it is difficult to determine how an infant died.

Sudden unexpected infant death (SUID) is a diagnosis given only after an investigation rules out all other possible causes of death. This includes a comprehensive examination of the death scene, an autopsy, and a review of the infant's medical history. A complete death scene investigation is often the only way to determine the cause of death. Commonly reported types of SUID include:

☑ LE7210.9.
Describe the causes of sudden unexpected infant death (SUID)

- sudden infant death syndrome (SIDS)
- accidental suffocation and strangulation in bed
- other deaths from unknown causes

View the infant's body and check for a pulse, respiration, and reflexes as appropriate. In most cases the infant's skin is altered (blotchy, blue, or gray), which may give the appearance of bruising. There may be frothy, blood-tinged mucus draining from the infant's mouth or nostrils.

Respond to this incident the same as you would other death investigations, as if a homicide, until determined otherwise. A thorough written documentation of the incident that includes your response is the final step in the preliminary investigation of any death.

☑ LE7210.10.
Describe how to respond to an infant death

UNIT 2 CRIMES AGAINST PERSONS
LESSON 11 Robbery

⊚ Lesson Goal

At the end of this lesson, you will know how to respond to an incident involving a robbery and follow up with a canvass of the surrounding area.

Think About This

A cashier is working the midnight shift at a convenience store when someone enters the store and tells the cashier to open the register or they'll be shot. The cashier can't see any weapon on the suspect but doesn't want to assume that they don't have a gun, so they open the register. Terrified that the suspect might shoot anyway, the cashier gives them the contents of the register. What crime has been committed?

ROBBERY

☑ LE7211.1.
Determine if an incident is robbery

Chapter 812, F.S., outlines the elements of robbery. **Robbery** occurs when the suspect:

- takes money or other property from the victim,
- intends to permanently or temporarily deprive the victim of their money or other property and takes it for their own or someone else's use, and
- uses force, violence, assault, or places the victim in fear during the incident.

If the suspect committed the robbery while armed, or becomes armed during the robbery, this will change the degree of the offense to armed robbery.

ROBBERY BY SUDDEN SNATCHING

☑ LE7211.2.
Determine if an incident is robbery by sudden snatching

In robbery by sudden snatching, the property must be on the victim's person, not just next to them, and the victim does not necessarily have to resist while the crime is being committed. Document that the suspect:

- took money or property of some value, from the victim's person
- intended to permanently or temporarily deprive the victim of their property and took it for their own or someone else's use
- in the course of the taking, the victim was or became aware of the taking

In contrast to robbery, there is no requirement that the suspect used force, violence, or threats. Chapter 8 discusses the differences between robbery and theft in greater detail.

HOME-INVASION ROBBERY

☑ LE7211.3.
Determine if an incident is a home-invasion robbery

While often confused with burglary, which involves breaking into a home with or without the victim(s) present, a home-invasion robbery occurs when a suspect enters a victim's home while the victim is present and aware that the crime is occurring. For *home-invasion robbery*, document that the suspect:

- entered the dwelling of the victim and intended to commit robbery
- while inside the dwelling, committed robbery
- used force, violence, assault, or placed the victim in fear during the robbery

If the suspect is armed while committing this crime, the penalty is enhanced.

CARJACKING

The elements of carjacking are similar to robbery, except that the suspect took a motor vehicle. For *carjacking*, document that the suspect:

- took the motor vehicle from the victim
- intended to permanently or temporarily deprive the victim of their motor vehicle and took it for their own or someone else's use
- used force, violence, assault, or placed the victim in fear during the incident

☑ LE7211.4.
Determine if an incident is carjacking

If the suspect is armed during the carjacking, this enhances the penalty.

INITIAL RESPONSE TO ROBBERY

Your initial response to a robbery will vary depending upon information obtained from dispatch, which should indicate whether the robbery is in progress, or delayed (over with, completed) and the suspect has fled the scene.

You may respond to a call other than a robbery where, upon arrival, you find a robbery has occurred or is occurring. Approach a robbery in progress according to your agency's policies and procedures. After the scene is secure, tend to any medical needs of victims, witnesses, or suspects. Protect the integrity of the scene, and contact dispatch to initiate a BOLO if the suspect fled.

☑ LE7211.5.
Describe how to respond to a robbery

If the robbery has already occurred, secure the scene with crime scene tape to prevent contamination and to allow for processing evidence. Determine where the suspect entered the scene, where they walked around, and where they exited. Determine if there is video surveillance in the areas the suspect entered or exited, and request information regarding access to the digital information.

Engage persons on the scene with respect while explaining your actions along the way. When asking questions, keep in mind that some victims may be experiencing trauma from the event. Ask if they can provide a complete description of the suspect and include how the suspect concealed, displayed, or used any weapons. Finally, if possible, ask if they can provide a complete itemized list of the property that was taken along with serial numbers, if applicable. Discuss the answers to all of these initial questions with the follow-up investigator, if necessary.

After verifying that a robbery occurred, notify your supervisor to determine the level of assistance needed from additional resources, including crime scene or assigned investigators. It is common for an investigator to request that the responding officer exclude certain details in the preliminary report for verifying confessions or leads as the investigation progresses. If a detective will respond, maintain the scene. Should you respond to a bank robbery, notify the FBI, and work the scene following your agency's policies and procedures.

In most incidents involving robbery, additional backup officers will be dispatched. Backup officers may conduct a neighborhood canvass to assist with locating witnesses or suspects.

CANVASS

A *canvass* is an inquiry of all possible sources of information surrounding the incident or crime scene, and it happens most often when the suspect leaves the scene. At times, you may conduct a canvass for another officer or investigator, so if you obtain vital information, relay it immediately to the lead officer or investigator. When in doubt about the information, contact the lead officer or investigator and convey the new information directly.

☑ LE7211.6. Describe how to conduct a canvass of the area surrounding a crime scene

The best time to conduct a canvass is immediately after the crime or as soon as possible after it has occurred. It may require additional officers depending on the size of the area or the type of incident being investigated. Canvassing an area near the incident or crime scene may reveal additional witnesses, victims, suspects, or evidence.

Walk the perimeter of the crime scene to identify places where people may have been able to see or hear what happened. Identify houses or businesses with a clear view of the scene or that are within hearing distance. Make inquiries at each location beginning with those closest to the scene.

Developing relationships with members of your community may allow you to do your job more effectively. When contacting residents, be professional and courteous to build rapport and encourage cooperation. Explain that you are investigating an incident that occurred at a particular time and in a particular place, and be careful not to reveal the details of the investigation, such as the names of victims and potential suspects, the seriousness of the crime, or how the crime was committed. Ask whether the person or any other member of the household or business remembers seeing or hearing anything around the time of the crime. Always exercise caution during the canvass because you may actually knock on the suspect's door.

Be sure to document contact information and responses to questions from anyone you interview during the canvass. Include specific details about what they heard or witnessed no matter what information they provide, even if they report knowing nothing. Be sure to document any residences that are vacant or where there is no response.

Chapter 8
Crimes Involving Property and Society

UNIT 1 **PROPERTY CRIMES**
- LESSON 1 Theft / 321
- LESSON 2 Criminal Mischief, Trespassing, and Burglary / 325
- LESSON 3 White-Collar Crimes / 330
- LESSON 4 Crimes Against Animals / 334

UNIT 2 **CRIMES AGAINST SOCIETY**
- LESSON 1 Loitering or Prowling, Disorderly Behavior / 338
- LESSON 2 Illicit Drugs and Vice Crimes / 342

UNIT 1 PROPERTY CRIMES
LESSON 1 Theft

◎ Lesson Goal

At the end of this lesson, you will know how to respond to an incident involving petit or grand theft and incidents involving a stolen vehicle or property.

Think About This

Lynda was sitting on a bench at the bus stop. She placed her purse on the seat next to her and got distracted by some loud teenagers across the street. Eric walked behind the bench she was sitting on and lifted her purse off the bench and ran away. What crime did Eric commit?

People commit crimes involving property to interfere with or obtain money, property, or some other benefit from a victim. The primary result is to deprive someone of the use or enjoyment of their property. The secondary result can involve physical or mental harm to the victim.

THEFT

Chapter 812, F.S., outlines the elements of theft. *Theft* occurs when a person:

- knowingly obtains or uses, or tries to obtain or to use, the property of another
- commits such actions with the intent to, either temporarily or permanently, deprive the other person of their right to the property or any benefit from it
- takes the property for their own use or to the use of any person not entitled to it

☑ LE811.1. Determine if an incident is theft

Robbery is different from theft or burglary. Robbery is a crime against a person because it involves some sort of taking directly from another individual. By contrast, theft (and burglary) are property crimes, and lack this direct person-to-person element. Be careful not to confuse the two.

Property can be anything of value and includes real property, tangible or intangible, personal property, and services. Services are anything of value that results from someone's physical or mental labor or skill, or from the use, possession, or presence of property. This includes:

- repairs or improvements to property
- professional services
- private, public, or government communication, transportation, power, water, or sanitation services
- lodging accommodations
- admissions to places of exhibition or entertainment

Even though the victim of a theft may not be present at the time of the incident, they can provide information helpful to the investigation, such as a description of the stolen property, including unique characteristics or serial numbers. The victim can also tell you the value of the item and the last time and place they saw it. They may know who discovered that the item was missing and if there were any witnesses to the theft.

If the value of property stolen during a theft is $100 or more, but less than $750, the offense is a first-degree misdemeanor of *petit theft*; if the person who commits petit theft has two or more convictions for any theft, the crime becomes a third-degree felony. Theft of property valued at less than $100, or if the value of the property cannot be established, is a second-degree misdemeanor.

Grand theft involves the theft of an item with a value of $750 or more, the theft of an item specified by statute regardless of its value, or the theft of an item with a value of $40 or more from a dwelling or from the unenclosed area of land surrounding a dwelling. Grand theft can be a felony of first, second, or third degree.

Theft also includes identity theft and fraud, not just theft of property, funds, or assets. Florida law reclassifies theft to a higher degree if the victim is a person 65 or older.

☑ LE811.2. Determine if an incident involves obtaining food or lodging with the intent to defraud

Chapter 509, F.S., outlines the elements of the theft of obtaining food, lodging, or other accommodations with the intent to defraud. This occurs when a person orders and eats a meal in a restaurant or occupies a room in a public lodging establishment, and then refuses to pay. When a business operator and an officer follow the terms of this statute, the court cannot hold either criminally or civilly liable for false arrest, false imprisonment, or unlawful detention.

RESPOND TO A THEFT

☑ LE811.3. Describe how to respond to a theft

Contact the complainant, store manager, or loss prevention officer (LPO), upon arrival. Obtain a verbal statement to determine if a crime has been committed. Ask if there is any video of the incident and if the suspect is still on the scene. Identify any other witnesses and review surveillance videos. If the suspect is on the scene, and you determine that a crime has been committed, obtain a suspect statement before making the arrest. Remember to follow the principles of procedural justice when interacting with the suspect. Try to obtain official witness statements. Photograph the items before returning any stolen property. Obtain a receipt or itemized list of items stolen to document their value.

Notify your supervisor if you are making an arrest or if you need more resources, such as a crime scene unit or EMS. Call for backup if the suspect becomes belligerent or violent, or if there are multiple suspects related to theft rings. If a detective responds, brief them on the incident. Contact dispatch to initiate a BOLO if the suspect flees the scene.

A backup officer may assist with recovering and photographing evidence and obtaining an itemized list of stolen property.

RETAIL THEFT

A business can also be a victim of theft through shoplifting, embezzlement, skimming from cash registers or petty cash, smash-and-grab attacks, hijacking of delivery trucks or their cargo, quick-change artists, or theft of agriculture, services, or construction site materials. You can arrest someone for retail theft without a warrant even when the offense is not committed in your presence. **Retail theft** involves someone working alone or conspiring with others to:

- take or carry away merchandise, property, money, or negotiable financial or legal documents
- alter or remove a label or price tag
- transfer merchandise from one container to another
- remove a shopping cart, with the intention of depriving the merchant of the items or their full retail value

It is a felony to possess, use, or attempt to use any anti-shoplifting or inventory control device counter measure to defeat the security scanner.

The operator of the facility or a law enforcement officer with probable cause can take the suspect into custody in a reasonable manner and for a reasonable amount of time for recovering the value of the property, or for prosecution.

☑ LE811.4. Determine if an incident is retail theft

RESPOND TO A MOTOR VEHICLE THEFT

Ask the victim to describe the vehicle, to show you where they parked the car, and if they have their car key. Determine if a family member may have a key or may have taken the vehicle. Look for broken glass where the car was parked or for drag marks that indicate a vehicle may have been towed. Call dispatch to find out if the vehicle was towed for repossession. If the vehicle was parked outside a business and not listed in a tow log, ask to view the exterior surveillance videos.

If you conclude that the vehicle was stolen, determine its proper ownership, and query DAVID to obtain vehicle information. Activate any tracking devices that the vehicle may have. Contact dispatch to initiate a BOLO. Give dispatch the license plate number, a description of the vehicle, including any dents or special identifiers, and the VIN to enter into FCIC/NCIC.

Sometimes during a domestic dispute involving separated or divorced people, one of them may take a vehicle. Exercise caution in cases where the complainant and suspect both claim ownership of the vehicle. A person may borrow a friend's vehicle and not return it to the owner. These may be civil matters. Follow your agency's policies and procedures for dealing with these types of situations.

☑ LE811.5. Describe how to respond to a motor vehicle theft

RESPOND TO A RECOVERY OF A STOLEN VEHICLE

☑ LE811.6. Describe how to respond to an incident involving recovering a stolen vehicle

There are times when you investigate a suspicious vehicle. Stolen vehicles may have broken side and vent windows, a poorly attached license plate, or scratched door locks. There may be a punched-out hole below the door lock, a punched-out ignition, or a damaged steering column. If you recover a stolen vehicle, notify dispatch so that they can report the recovery to FCIC/NCIC, as well as to the vehicle owner. If you suspect that a vehicle is stolen, verify the vehicle by the VIN, license plate number, engine number, hidden number or component part numbers, or other identifying characteristics. The VIN plate on most domestic and foreign cars is on the driver's side dashboard, seen through the windshield, or on the driver's side doorjamb.

RESPOND TO A STOLEN PROPERTY INCIDENT

☑ LE811.7. Describe how to respond to a stolen property incident

When responding to dealing or trafficking in stolen property, document that the suspect trafficked in or tried to traffic in property that the suspect knew or should have known was stolen. If the sale price for property is substantially below the fair market value, the property may be stolen. Dealing in stolen property is a first- or second-degree felony.

If a victim locates their stolen property in a pawnshop, put a hold on the item or seize it as evidence. Get information on the suspect from store personnel. People dealing in stolen property sometimes do so under false names. Pawnshops require a thumbprint on the transaction sheet, which you can collect as evidence. Obtain the store video surveillance, if available. Often a detective will conduct a follow-up investigation on these types of crimes.

DEALING IN STOLEN PROPERTY

☑ LE811.8. Determine if an incident involves dealing in stolen property

Metals, electronics, jewelry, and firearms are commonly trafficked stolen items. When a person sells, transfers, distributes, or otherwise disposes of stolen property knowing or having reason to know that the property is in fact stolen, this person commits the crime of dealing in stolen property.

If you have probable cause to believe that a suspect stole an item, and the suspect resists reasonable efforts to recover the property, charge the suspect with resisting in addition to theft.

UNIT 1 PROPERTY CRIMES
LESSON 2 Criminal Mischief, Trespassing, and Burglary

Lesson Goal

At the end of this lesson, you will know how to respond to an incident involving criminal mischief, trespassing, or burglary, and how the Florida Statutes can enhance the penalties.

Think About This

A neighbor is watching a home while the owners are away on vacation. Dispatch sends you to the house after the neighbor reported that graffiti appeared on the garage door overnight. While interviewing the neighbors, you learn that a group was seen outside the home the night before. What crime has been committed?

CRIMINAL MISCHIEF

Criminal mischief is the willful and malicious damage of property belonging to another person. As outlined in chapter 806, F.S., it can include injury or damage to property, such as graffiti or other acts of vandalism.

☑ LE812.1. Determine if an incident is criminal mischief

For criminal mischief, document that:

- the suspect injured or damaged by any means real or personal property
- the property belonged to the complainant
- the injury or damage was willful and malicious

Photograph the damage for your report. Conduct a neighborhood canvass to gather information about the suspects. Based on your agency's policies and whether there is a suspect, conduct a follow-up investigation. Provide the victim with the appropriate victim brochures and document this in your report.

The Florida Statutes enhance the penalties for criminal mischief based upon several factors, including the value of the property.

☑ LE812.2. Describe statutory enhancements associated with criminal mischief

- Criminal mischief is a second-degree misdemeanor if the property damage is $200 or less.
- It is a first-degree misdemeanor if the damage is greater than $200 but less than $1,000.
- The crime is a third-degree felony if the value of property damaged totals $1,000 or more.
- If the suspect has one or more prior convictions for criminal mischief, a subsequent offense is a third-degree felony, regardless of the amount of damage.
- Any person who willfully and maliciously defaces, injuries, or damages by any means any place of worship or any religious article contained therein is guilty of a third-degree felony if the damage is over $200.

TRESPASSING

☑ LE812.3. Determine if an incident is trespassing

Trespassing, as outlined in chapter 810, F.S., occurs when a person:

- willfully enters or remains in any structure or conveyance, without being authorized, licensed, or invited
- willfully enters or remains in a structure or conveyance after the owner tells them to leave or when a trespassing notice is posted
- having been authorized, licensed, or invited, a person is warned by the owner or lessee of the premises, or by a person authorized by the owner or lessee, to depart and the person refused to do so

In trespassing, a person authorized means an owner or lessee, or their agent, or any law enforcement officer whose agency has received written authorization from the owner, lessee, or their agent, to communicate an order to depart the property in the case of a threat to public safety or welfare.

☑ LE812.4. Describe additional types of trespassing based on the location and intent

Based on the location or intent, a person can be guilty of trespassing in several ways. These trespassing offenses are misdemeanors when the following applies:

- a notice against entering or remaining is communicated or posted and a person disregards it
- someone enters and remains on a property and intends to commit another offense
- someone stays on the premises after law enforcement gave them a warning
- a transient person living in a residential property refuses to leave after law enforcement directed them to, even if the officer has a sworn affidavit from the property's owner
- someone is not authorized, licensed, or invited to enter or stay on a school campus
- a student who is suspended or expelled enters or stays on a school campus or any other campus the school owns
- someone is on a school campus without legitimate business to be there

These trespassing offenses are felonies:

- trespassing on a designated, posted commercial horticulture property
- trespassing on a designated, posted agriculture site for testing and research
- trespassing on a designated, posted agricultural chemical manufacturing facility
- trespassing on school property while in possession of a firearm or weapon
- trespassing on a designated, posted domestic violence shelter
- launching a projectile (using a firearm, bow, or crossbow) across someone else's land with the intent of taking or killing an animal
- entering and remaining on a designated, posted construction site
- trespassing on a legally posted operational area of an airport with the intent to injure a person, damage property, or impede operations

RESPOND TO TRESPASSING

Interview the complainant, property owner, person authorized to act on behalf of the owner, witnesses, and the suspect. Determine if there is posting on the property that clearly designates no trespassing on private property; photograph this if needed. Determine if there are any valid trespassing agreements in place that allow you to arrest a suspect for trespassing.

Make sure that you have jurisdiction, as property can expand into other private or public property; for example, someone could be walking on the beach and be accused of trespassing on private property.

☑ LE812.5. Describe how to respond to trespassing

BURGLARY

Burglary is the unlawful entry into any structure with the intent to commit a crime inside. Chapter 810, F.S., outlines the elements of burglary and classifies burglaries according to the type of location entered, such as a dwelling, structure, or conveyance. Penalties are more severe for a dwelling than a structure or conveyance. For burglary, document that the suspect:

- entered a dwelling, structure, or conveyance owned by or in the possession of the complainant
- at the time of entering the dwelling, structure, or conveyance, had the intent to commit a crime in that dwelling, structure, or conveyance
- was not licensed or invited to enter the dwelling, structure, or conveyance, and the premises were not open to the public at the time of the entering

☑ LE812.6. Determine if an incident is burglary

Trespassing involves being somewhere you do not own without the owner's permission. Burglary also involves being somewhere you do not own without the owner's permission, but with the intention to commit another crime, such as theft. Recall that robbery involves taking property from someone by force or fear. People will often tell you that they have been robbed when they were not at home; however, they have been burglarized.

☑ LE812.7. Differentiate between trespassing, burglary, and criminal mischief

Generally, any damage caused as the result of an unlawful entry, such as kicking in a door or breaking a window, is not criminal mischief, as that is a lesser offense. However, when the suspect clearly and intentionally vandalizes the home during a burglary, an additional charge of criminal mischief can apply.

The Florida Statutes enhance the penalties for burglary when:

- the suspect commits assault or battery upon any person during a burglary
- the suspect is or becomes armed within the property
- the suspect uses a vehicle to cause damage to the property
- the suspect causes more than $1,000 of damage to the property
- the dwelling, structure, or conveyance was occupied at the time of the burglary

☑ LE812.8. Describe statutory enhancements associated with burglary

☑ LE812.9.
Determine if an incident involves possession of burglary tools

Burglary tools may include screwdrivers, pliers and wrenches, pry bars, or spark plugs but can also be anything used to gain entry during a burglary, such as a rock or concrete block. Burglars may use several methods of entry, such as entering through unlocked doors and windows or using a hidden key, removing hinge pins, breaking glass, or kicking in the door.

Other techniques include prying a door or window frame, slipping, pulling, or picking the lock, or using a bump key—a key in which the suspect has cut the pin positions to the lowest level so that striking it at just the right moment will "bump" open the lock. Burglars may also use a garage door opener or electronic decoder for keyless entries.

For possession of burglary tools, document that the suspect:

- intended to commit burglary or trespass
- had in their possession a tool, machine, or implement they intended to use in committing burglary or trespass

RESPOND TO BURGLARY

☑ LE812.10.
Describe how to respond to a burglary

Burglary is one of the crimes that you will investigate most frequently. When you arrive at the scene of a burglary, determine if the burglary is in progress or delayed (occurred in the past). If the burglary is in progress, notify your supervisor, call for backup, set a perimeter, and request additional resources.

If the burglary is not in progress, obtain a statement from the victim. Call for backup if indicated in your agency's policies and procedures. Conduct a walk-through with the victim. Tell the victim how important it is to preserve any evidence and secure the crime scene. Should video footage of the incident provide a description of a suspect, and the burglary occurred within the past several hours, immediately contact dispatch to initiate a BOLO.

Agency policies will dictate if you will process the crime scene or additional resources will conduct the follow-up investigation. If a detective will respond, maintain the scene and start a crime scene log, which you will learn about in Chapter 9.

Establish the time frame for the incident, ask the victim when they left the building and when they returned. Determine the entry and exit points the burglar used, and note any disturbed areas and possible evidence for processing. Obtain detailed information from the victim, such as the description and value of any items taken. Remember to obtain serial numbers, owner-applied numbers, or special identifiers. Refer to the basic investigation flow chart for investigating this crime and consider conducting a neighborhood canvass.

Backup officers may secure the scene, conduct an area canvass, and assist in processing the scene for evidence.

PROTECTING ARCHAEOLOGICAL SITES

Chapter 267, F.S., outlines the elements of prohibited practices on archaeological sites. You may respond to a call concerning a violation of an archaeological site and will need to assess the scene. If you believe a crime was committed, secure and protect the scene, notify a supervisor, and inform local, state, or federal park rangers of the incident and any recovered evidence. It is a misdemeanor to walk on an archaeological site and remove an object; it is a felony to dig into the site to retrieve an object.

☑ LE812.11. Describe how to respond to a violation of an archaeological site

UNIT 1 PROPERTY CRIMES
LESSON 3 White-Collar Crimes

> **◎ Lesson Goal**
>
> At the end of this lesson, you will know how to respond to a variety of financial crimes such as fraud, telephone scams, phishing, and identity theft.

Think About This

You respond to a call from dispatch involving an older man who claims he was robbed. When you arrive on the scene, Tom is standing in the doorway with his bank statement in his hand. He is extremely upset and claims that all of his money is gone. He tells you that someone has been using his debit card to make purchases in Nevada, he has never been to Nevada, and now he doesn't have any money. What actions should you take?

The expression white-collar crime refers to a range of frauds committed by individuals, business professionals, and government officials. These crimes do not involve a threat of physical force or violence but rather dishonesty, cover-up, or abuse of trust.

FRAUD

☑ LE813.1. Describe the different types of fraud

Fraud is the intentional falsification of the truth to induce another person or other entity to part with something of value or to surrender their legal right to it. Current forms of fraud can include credit card fraud, bank fraud, cashing a fraudulent check, and identity theft. Officers will most often respond to a delayed credit card fraud and file an incident report. Occasionally, you may respond to an in-progress incident of a fraudulent check, fraudulent use of a credit or gift card, or someone using counterfeit funds.

IN-PROGRESS FRAUD

Forgery and Uttering

☑ LE813.2. Differentiate between forgery and uttering

There are two aspects of forgery: forgery and uttering a false instrument. *Forgery* is falsely making, altering, forging, or counterfeiting a public record, certificate, legal document, bill of exchange, or promissory note, with intent to injure or defraud someone. *Uttering* is knowingly exhibiting or publishing a document or attempting to cash a check by claiming the check and the endorsement are real. Uttering a false, forged, or altered record, deed, or other instrument with the intent to injure or defraud someone is a third-degree felony under Florida law.

The most common types of forgery an officer may encounter are forged signatures or endorsements on a check, use of a fictitious name, and forgery by altering the signature. Chapter 831, F.S., outlines the elements of uttering forged bills, checks, drafts, or notes.

Fraudulent Check

The primary complainant for in-progress fraudulent checks is the financial institution. The victim is the person from whom the funds were drawn. Before or right after arriving, ask the complainant if the subject is on the scene and get a subject and vehicle description, as they may pass you when exiting the bank or business. If the suspect is present, call for backup if necessary.

☑ LE813.3. Describe how to respond to a fraudulent check incident

If the suspect is not on the scene, collect the altered financial or legal document that was uttered and process it as evidence. Photograph the front and back of the document for your incident report. Interview any witnesses, such as the teller, clerk, or manager, and obtain a statement. Ask for a copy of the surveillance video, immediately view it, if possible, to identify a suspect, and contact dispatch to initiate a BOLO. Determine if a crime has been committed and follow your agency's policies and procedures regarding requesting additional resources, such as a detective. Ask the complainant or victim if they want to prosecute the suspect when identified and document this in your incident report.

You may take the initial complaint for these types of incidents; however, an economic crime investigator typically investigates fraud.

CREDIT CARD FRAUD

Chapter 817, F.S., outlines the elements of fraudulent credit card use. Credit card fraud is the unlawful use of a credit card to obtain property, goods, or services. This includes unlawful or unauthorized use of information to obtain credit by using any false, fictitious, revoked, or expired credit card, credit card number, or other credit device, or using any credit card without the owner's authority.

☑ LE813.4. Determine if an incident is credit card fraud

Suspects will fraudulently obtain and use debit or credit cards through falsified applications, burglary, theft, or robbery. A thief can also solicit a credit card number by calling unaware victims or by retrieving information on hotel room key cards.

Skimming is the act of extracting a customer's credit card information by using a skimming device. The skimmer attaches to a point of sale device and stores the customer's information as the payment is processed. More sophisticated skimmers can be wireless.

It is a felony if a suspect fraudulently uses a victim's credit card within a six-month period, two times or more, or charges $100 or more on the victim's card.

The primary complainant for most credit card offenses is the account holder. The primary victim of the theft is the issuing financial institution. Other victims may include the merchant where the credit card was fraudulently used and the person whose name was forged on the card.

Ask the complainant if they are still in possession of the card and document this in your report. Obtain the card number and expiration date on the card. Determine if a crime actually occurred. Explain to the victim that although the purchases may have been made out of state, you will file an incident report, which will provide a case number for

☑ LE813.5. Describe how to respond to credit card fraud

them to submit to their financial institution. You may take the initial complaint for these types of incidents; however, an economic crime investigator typically investigates fraud.

Ask the victim if they want to prosecute the suspect when identified and document this in your incident report. Encourage the complainant to contact their financial institution and place a hold on any more transactions to the account, and to contact a credit bureau to notify them of the fraud. Your agency may have educational material for these victims regarding how to prevent becoming a victim in the future.

TELEPHONE SCAMS

☑ LE813.6. Determine if an incident involves a telephone scam

Some phone or email solicitors misrepresent a bank, government agency, or relative and threaten to arrest the victim should they refuse to pay a fictitious debt or provide money to bail someone they know out of jail.

When responding to an incident involving any form of digital communication, such as phone calls, emails, or text messages, be aware that the true location and identity of the user can easily be hidden. By using modern internet-based applications, a phone number can quickly and easily be created to represent a specific area regardless of where the user is actually located. Voice over Internet Protocol (VoIP) services are one example of a modern communication method, which allows someone to create a phone number and use it anywhere in the world where they can connect to the internet.

PHISHING

☑ LE813.7. Determine if an incident involves phishing

Phishing uses fake digital communication that mirrors a legitimate business to obtain personal and financial information from unsuspecting victims. Suspects use this information to steal identities, bank accounts, or credit availability.

When examining any internet-based communication, consider that a suspect can hide their true identity by using an internet connection publicly offered by a coffee shop or a victim's unsecured (not password protected) network. In that case, the internet protocol (IP) address the suspect used will belong to an unrelated, innocent party.

Because of the unique considerations and details associated with investigating digital communications, consult with the appropriate division within your agency before taking any action based solely on a digital communication.

IDENTITY THEFT

☑ LE813.8. Describe the information used in identity theft

Identity theft is the unlawful possession or use of a person's identifying information to commit acts of fraud, such as apply for credit or loans, acquire services, establish or take over accounts, and commit crimes.

☑ LE813.9. Describe how to respond to identity theft

You may take the initial complaint for this type of incident; however, a detective typically investigates identity theft. Determine if you have jurisdiction based on whether the victim is a resident of your jurisdiction or if the fraudulent activity occurred in your jurisdiction.

Ask the victim if they have any idea how their identity may have been compromised. If the crime occurred outside of your jurisdiction, file an incident report to provide a case number for documentation purposes and to allow for a subsequent investigation.

Ask the victim if they want to prosecute the suspect if identified and document this in your incident report. Encourage the victim to contact their financial institutions and at least one of the major credit bureaus to notify them of the identity theft. Provide any educational material that your agency might have regarding how to prevent further victimization. Your agency may have a Florida identity theft victim kit to provide to the victim.

UNIT 1 PROPERTY CRIMES
LESSON 4 Crimes Against Animals

© Lesson Goal

At the end of this lesson, you will know how to recognize and respond to incidents involving crimes against animals.

Think About This

You respond to a call from dispatch involving a dog that is reported to be malnourished and tied up with a short leash in a backyard. When you arrive at the home, a neighbor reports that the homeowners moved out a week ago and that they have not seen anyone provide food or water for the dog since the homeowners left. How should you respond to this incident?

Many people consider their animals to be companions, but legally animals are personal property. Despite this classification, animals are still recognized as living beings that experience fear and pain, so there are certain legal standards of animal welfare that protect them from experiencing undue or prolonged suffering. It is important to investigate crimes against animals not only to protect animals, but also to protect people, since there are direct links between animal abuse and other crimes. For example, if someone is abusing or neglecting animals, they may also be abusing or neglecting other members in the household or engaging in other illegal activities. Sometimes, you may initiate an arrest on the grounds of animal cruelty when victims of other crimes, such as battery, are unwilling to press charges. By recognizing and responding to crimes against animals, further abuse of both people and animals may be prevented.

RECOGNIZE CRIMES AGAINST ANIMALS

☑ LE814.1. Define animal cruelty and the statutes related to it

Most crimes against animals are prosecuted based on chapter 828, F.S., which covers laws regarding animal welfare. In Florida, animal cruelty is a first-degree misdemeanor offense. A person commits animal cruelty by doing any of the following:

- unnecessarily overloading, overdriving, or tormenting an animal
- depriving an animal of necessary food or shelter
- unnecessarily mutilating or killing any animal, or causing the same to be done
- carrying in or on any vehicle, or otherwise, any animal in a cruel or inhumane manner

Aggravated animal cruelty occurs when a person intentionally commits an act to any animal or when a person who owns or has custody or control of any animal fails to act, which results in the cruel death, or excessive or repeated infliction of unnecessary pain or suffering. Aggravated animal cruelty is a third-degree felony offense.

Animal confinement or abandonment is a first-degree misdemeanor offense. A person commits animal confinement or abandonment by doing any of the following:

- confining any animal in any place and failing to supply the animal with a sufficient quantity of good and wholesome food and water
- keeping any animals in any enclosure without wholesome exercise and change of air
- abandoning any animal in a street, road, or public place without providing for the care, sustenance, protection, and shelter of such animal

Keep in mind that more than one statute from chapter 828, F.S., may apply depending on the nature of the suspected crime. For example, a person charged with animal fighting may also be charged with animal confinement if the animals are kept in cages without access to fresh air, food, or water.

Animal fighting is a crime against animals that is a separate offense from animal cruelty and animal confinement or abandonment. Chapter 828, F.S., defines animal fighting as fighting between roosters or other birds or between dogs, bears, or other animals. This statute also defines **baiting** as attacking with violence, provoking, or harassing an animal with one or more other animals to train it for fighting or to cause an animal to engage in fights with or among other animals. In addition, baiting means the use of live animals in the training of racing greyhounds.

☑ LE814.2. Define animal fighting and the statutes related to it

According to the Florida Statutes, it is a third-degree felony to participate in animal fighting by, but not limited to, staging, promoting, betting on, or attending animal fights. Animal fighting is an intentional and organized crime often associated with other illegal activities such as buying and selling narcotics, trafficking humans and animals, purchasing illegal firearms, gambling, and engaging in other criminal gang activities.

While there is a wide range of crimes against animals, you may encounter a few types more frequently than others. Some of the types of crimes against animals you may come across during your patrol route include the following:

☑ LE814.3. Identify common types of crimes against animals

- animal neglect—the animal lacks sufficient food, water, shelter, or medical care.
- animal hoarding— a form of neglect that occurs when an owner or caretaker collects so many animals that they are unable to provide minimum standards of care.
- intentional acts of animal cruelty—the animal is purposefully harmed in a way that causes unnecessary pain and suffering.
- animal abandonment— the animal is left alone by their owner or caretaker in a public area or residence without providing the proper care, food, water, protection, or shelter.
- animal sexual abuse—any sexual act between an animal and a person for the purpose of sexual gratification, abuse, or financial gain.

It is important for patrol officers to be aware of the signs of these crimes, so they can be properly identified and investigated.

LE814.4. List signs of crimes against animals

Often crimes against animals may be discovered during other calls for service. For example, evidence of a crime against an animal may be found during your response to a call regarding a noise disturbance or a domestic violence incident. If there are signs that there is an animal in a home or on a property, you should make inquiries about the animal's condition. Signs of crimes against animals can include the following:

- extremely thin animals
- dirty or matted fur
- patches of fur missing
- a collar that is too tight or heavy, or is embedded in the animal's skin
- lack of needed medical attention
- injuries or scarring
- lack of adequate shelter, food, or water
- living conditions that include excess feces, garbage, or broken glass
- inappropriate size cage for the animal to stand up and turn around
- weakness, limping, or the inability to walk properly

LE814.5. Discuss incidents of animals in a parked motor vehicle

Another example of a common call for service that may involve crimes against animals includes responses to incidents of animals left in a parked motor vehicle. Leaving an animal inside a parked motor vehicle is not necessarily a crime; however, it becomes illegal when the conditions inside the car endanger the animal. In Florida, dangerous conditions are generally from high temperatures. Signs of animal distress in a parked motor vehicle may include the following:

- excessive panting or drooling
- a tongue that has visibly turned dark purple (if the animal is a dog)
- frantic behavior from the animal, such as pawing at the window or trying to stick its nose out
- loss of bowel control
- sluggish and unresponsive behavior

If exigent circumstances are present, and the animal is in imminent danger of harm, follow your agency's policy on removing the animal from the vehicle. Immediately after removing the animal, measure and document the temperature both inside and outside the vehicle as well as the conditions outside. Measuring and documenting the temperature provides additional evidence, which in turn can help bring about charges for the owner of the animal.

You may be called to a scene where a person is upset because another person, acting in good faith, has damaged their vehicle to rescue an animal inside. Chapter 768, F.S., provides immunity from civil liability for rescuing a vulnerable person or domestic animal from a motor vehicle if certain conditions are met, such as if the motor vehicle is locked, or there is no reasonable method for exiting, and there is a good faith and reasonable belief that entry is necessary because the vulnerable person or domestic animal is in imminent danger of harm. However, the person must still notify law enforcement or call 911 before or immediately after entering the vehicle.

RESPOND TO CRIMES AGAINST ANIMALS

You will follow the same basic investigation process when responding to crimes against animals, just as you would for any other crime. Much like how child protective investigators are involved in cases of child abuse, you will need to involve additional resources when responding to cases of crimes against animals. These additional resources may include animal control services, veterinarians, or law enforcement investigators.

When you arrive to the scene, you are responsible for determining if a crime occurred based on the evidence found, securing the scene, locating the animals' owner, collecting information from witnesses, and preserving evidence. You must also assess the severity of the crime by considering the state of the animal, particularly if there are any visible injuries, as well as the animal's living conditions. Communicate with your chain of command in cases of exigent circumstances or if there is a need for additional resources such as a veterinarian, or animal control services for the housing and transport of the animal for medical treatment.

☑ LE814.6. Describe how to respond to crimes against animals

Photograph the animal, the surrounding area, and conditions you found the animal in, and include this information in your report. An animal will never come to court as evidence, so documentation such as photos, videos, statements, and reports must be able to clearly show what happened. Document the incident even if you determine a crime has not occurred. This documentation is important if there are future calls to the residence regarding crimes against animals or other crimes against persons such as child abuse or domestic violence.

UNIT 2 CRIMES AGAINST SOCIETY
LESSON 1 Loitering or Prowling, Disorderly Behavior

⊚ Lesson Goal

At the end of this lesson, you will know how to respond to an incident involving loitering, prowling, breach of the peace, disorderly conduct, or disorderly intoxication as well as understand how to coordinate with other officers when responding to an open house party.

Think About This

You respond to a call from a grocery store manager who is claiming that a man is loitering in front of their store and drinking. When you arrive, you see that the man is sitting on the ground in front of the store and drinking a beer. He says he just needs a few minutes to collect himself, and then he will walk home. What should you do?

LOITERING OR PROWLING

☑ LE821.1. Determine if an incident involves loitering or prowling

Standing or waiting around idly or without apparent purpose is not a criminal act. However, to linger or hang around in an area without any apparent purpose for being there in a place, at a time, or in a manner not usual for law-abiding people, and under circumstances that raise alarm or immediate concern for the safety of people or property in the vicinity is **loitering or prowling**.

Some things to consider in determining whether to be alarmed or concerned are if the person:

- flees when a law enforcement officer appears
- refuses to identify themselves
- attempts to conceal themselves or any object
- will not explain why they are there and what they are doing

> 📌 **Note**
>
> The fact that a person is out at odd hours, without showing any other suspicious activity, does not necessarily justify an investigative stop.

☑ LE821.2. Describe how to respond to loitering or prowling

Initiate a consensual encounter to dispel any concerns you may have. Explain exactly why you want to talk with them, give them a chance to explain why they are there, be transparent about what could happen next, and always treat them with respect. A loitering and prowling charge will require articulating in your report and in court the totality of the circumstances to support an arrest.

Call for backup before making that initial contact. Take a few minutes to observe the person. Be respectful and give them an opportunity to identify themselves and explain their presence and conduct. Remember that the person is free to leave at any point during a consensual encounter. Should the encounter move from a consensual encounter to an interview, based on reasonable suspicion, you may need to issue a *Miranda* warning to conduct further questioning.

Unless there is probable cause of some other offense, if the person voluntarily explains their presence and conduct, and the explanation eases your alarm, release them without charge. If you fail to release them, the court may dismiss the case and you may face civil liability for a false arrest. The court will not convict the person if it appears that the explanation given by them was true and, if you believed it, would have eased your alarm or concern.

These types of incidents pose significant officer safety issues that require a backup officer. Backup officers may stand by for officer safety, check for warrants on the subject, and check the building exterior for broken windows or unlocked doors.

BREACH OF THE PEACE AND DISORDERLY CONDUCT

Breach of the peace or disorderly conduct is not a catchall statute; however, it does include brawling, fighting, or an affray. An affray occurs when someone consents to fight with another person to terrorize other people in a public place. Urinating in public is also disorderly conduct, not an exposure of sexual organs. To meet the conditions of breach of the peace or disorderly conduct according to chapter 877, F.S., the person's actions must endanger the safety of another person or property and occur in a public place or on public transportation, causing a public disturbance. In this context, a **public place** means somewhere the public has a right to be and to go, such as a grocery store or hospital.

☑ LE821.3. Determine if an incident is breach of the peace or disorderly conduct

For the offense of **breach of the peace or disorderly conduct**, document whether the suspect's action:

- corrupts public morals
- outrages public sense of decency
- affects the peace and quiet of people who may witness it
- causes a brawl or a fight

A person who simply curses at others or officers may not be arrested for disorderly conduct unless other factors are present that would threaten the safety of the officer or others. Unless a person's words actually incite a reaction from onlookers that might create a danger to others, such as shouting "fire" in a crowded theater, freedom of speech protects the person from arrest. When you are on duty, you cannot be a victim of breach of the peace.

DISORDERLY INTOXICATION

Intoxication is more than merely being under the influence of an alcoholic beverage. Intoxication means that after consuming substances, a person loses normal control of their body, mental faculties, or both. According to chapter 856, F.S., for **disorderly intoxication**,

☑ LE821.4. Determine if an incident involves disorderly intoxication document that the suspect was intoxicated and endangered the safety of another person or property, or was intoxicated or drank alcohol in a public place or public transportation, and caused a public disturbance.

The difference between disorderly conduct and disorderly intoxication is the element of intoxication. Taken alone, the person's admission that they consumed substances is not enough to prove beyond a reasonable doubt that they were under the influence; however, consider this admission along with other evidence.

RESPOND TO BREACH OF THE PEACE, DISORDERLY CONDUCT, OR DISORDERLY INTOXICATION

☑ LE821.5. Describe how to respond to breach of the peace, disorderly conduct, or disorderly intoxication

This is an opportunity for you to use verbal de-escalation techniques to calm the involved persons. Separate the suspect from any witnesses. Call for backup, or additional backup, as these incidents can pose significant officer safety issues. Backup officers may assist with crowd control.

Interview any witnesses to the incident and collect statements. Document evidence of intoxication by identifying specific indicators, such as slurred speech, bloodshot eyes, or staggered gait. Determine if a crime actually occurred, or if you should consider using the Marchman Act.

RESPOND TO AN OPEN HOUSE PARTY

☑ LE821.6. Determine if an incident involves an open house party

Chapter 856, F.S., outlines the elements of allowing an open house party. An **open house party** is a social gathering at a residence that is legal unless minors at the party consume alcohol or drugs. This term does not apply to using alcoholic beverages or other substances at legally protected religious observances or activities. For the offense of an open house party, the Florida Statutes require that the suspect:

- is 18 or older
- had control over the residence at the time of the party
- allowed an open house party at the residence
- allowed a minor to possess or consume alcohol or drugs at the residence during the party
- knew that the minor possessed or consumed alcohol or drugs at the residence during the party

The law expects adults to take reasonable steps to protect and prevent minors from engaging in these activities. Chapter 562, F.S., outlines the elements of the crime of selling or giving alcoholic beverages to a person younger than 21.

☑ LE821.7. Describe how to respond to an open house party

Most agencies will send multiple officers to an incident involving an open house party, as teenagers may scatter and drive under the influence. Call for additional backup if needed. Check with dispatch to determine if the residence has had prior similar calls. Question the partygoers to determine if they are underage and drinking or using drugs.

Document evidence of intoxication or drug use by identifying specific indicators, such as slurred speech, bloodshot eyes or dilated pupils, or staggered gait. Find the teenager that lives there, ask for their parent or caregiver's contact information, and contact them.

Interview the parents or caregivers to determine if a crime has been committed, and make an arrest if necessary. Ask if they had knowledge of the party and the presence of alcohol or drugs, and ask if they knew who purchased these. If the parents are home while the open house party was going on or knew of the party and the presence of alcohol or drugs, the offense may be contributing to the delinquency of a minor in addition to an open house party violation.

Based on the circumstances and your agency policies and procedures, stand by while the parents or caregivers pick up the underage partygoers under the influence.

UNIT 2 CRIMES AGAINST SOCIETY
LESSON 2 Illicit Drugs and Vice Crimes

Lesson Goal

At the end of this lesson, you will know how to respond to an incident involving possession of a controlled substance, drug paraphernalia, or drug trafficking as well as how to recognize vice crimes and the characteristics of organized crime.

Think About This

You respond to a call from a store where a pharmacy tech is reporting a woman who is requesting her second refill of narcotic pain medications in the same week. The pharmacy tech believes the woman has a stolen prescription pad and is misusing narcotics. How do you handle this situation?

ILLICIT DRUGS

☑ LE822.1. Determine if an incident involves illegal possession of a controlled substance

There are many sources of illicit drugs in the United States. Drugs are smuggled, diverted, and intercepted from legitimate and illegal sources. You may encounter drug manufacturing in clandestine laboratories or cultivation grow houses through information from a concerned resident or while responding to a call from dispatch. Common methods used to transport drugs include both private and public transportation and shipments via commercial delivery companies, as well as the U.S. Postal Service. Suspects may conceal drugs in items such as children's toys or other commodities.

Illicit Use of Prescription Drugs

Prescription drugs are not necessarily illicit; however, misuse of prescription drugs is common in Florida. People may engage in "doctor shopping" or steal prescription pads to illegally obtain pharmaceuticals to meet their needs. Recent changes in the prescription drug monitoring program have contributed to a rise in opioid abuse.

It is illegal to drive under the influence of medical marijuana just as it would be with any other prescription medication that impairs your ability to drive.

☑ LE822.2. Describe how the Florida Comprehensive Drug Abuse Prevention and Control Act schedules legal and illegal drugs

The Florida Comprehensive Drug Abuse Prevention and Control Act, or chapter 893, F.S., places all controlled substances regulated under existing federal law into one of five schedules based on medicinal value, harmfulness, and the potential for misuse and addiction. Historically, controlled substances' names and formulas change intermittently.

The Drug Enforcement Administration (DEA) website contains information about the schedules of controlled substances, facts about commonly misused substances, color photos, methods of use, behavioral characteristics, signs, symptoms, and duration of effects.

For possession of a controlled substance, document that the suspect:

- knew that the illicit, controlled substance was present
- exercised control or ownership over the illicit, controlled substance
- knew the substance was an illicit, controlled substance

☑ LE822.3. Describe how to establish probable cause for illegal possession of a controlled substance

Florida law provides the following definitions to clarify the meaning of possession:

- *Possession* means to have personal charge of or exercise the right of ownership, management, or control over the thing possessed. Possession may be actual, constructive, or joint.
- *Actual possession* means the controlled substance is in the hands of or on the suspect, or in a container in the hands of or on the suspect, or so close as to be within ready reach and is under the control of the suspect. Mere proximity to a controlled substance is not sufficient to establish possession over the substance when it is not in a place that the suspect has control.
- *Constructive possession* means the controlled substance is in a place over which the suspect has control, or in which the suspect has concealed it.
- *Joint possession* means two or more suspects may jointly possess an article, exercising control over it. In that case, each of those suspects is in possession of that article.

If a suspect has sole possession of a controlled substance, infer or assume the suspect had knowledge of its presence. If a suspect does not have exclusive possession of a controlled substance, do not infer or assume the suspect had knowledge of its presence. Be aware that a person's presence in a room or building where there are drugs or other contraband does not necessarily mean the person has committed a crime.

DRUG TRAFFICKING

Chapter 893, F.S., outlines the quantities or weight of specific illicit, controlled substances that increase a possession charge to a drug trafficking charge:

☑ LE822.4. Determine if an incident involves drug trafficking

- cannabis, excess of 25 pounds, excess of 300 plants
- cocaine, excess of 28 grams
- hydrocodone, excess of 28 grams
- methamphetamine (meth), excess of 14 grams
- MDMA (ecstasy), excess of 10 grams
- oxycodone, excess of 7 grams
- LSD (acid), excess of 1 gram

Trafficking in illicit drugs is a felony. Florida law requires a minimum mandatory prison sentence for drug trafficking.

DRUG PARAPHERNALIA

> LE822.5. Identify a variety of drug paraphernalia

Drug paraphernalia is all equipment, products, and materials of any kind that are used or intended to:

- plant, propagate, cultivate, grow, harvest,
- manufacture, compound, convert, produce, process, prepare,
- test, analyze,
- pack, repack, store, or
- contain, conceal, transport, inject, ingest, inhale, or otherwise introduce a controlled substance into the human body.

Pipes, rolling paper, straws, or spoons are not drug paraphernalia until you can prove that they are being used or intended to be used to deliver an illicit drug. Possession of drug paraphernalia is a misdemeanor. Document that the suspect possesses any item that is used, intended to be used, or designed to be used as drug paraphernalia.

RESPOND TO POSSESSION OF A CONTROLLED SUBSTANCE

> LE822.6. Describe how to respond to illegal possession of a controlled substance

When responding to an incident involving possession of a controlled substance and the suspect is incapacitated, seek medical attention. Begin your initial investigation and consider:

- calling for backup, as these types of incidents pose officer safety issues, can have a crime scene that needs to be searched, and can contain quantities of evidence
- interviewing the suspect
- getting consent to search from the suspect or establish probable cause for a search
- searching the suspect for contraband
- requesting a narcotics canine unit
- conducting a presumptive test
- following basic crime scene processes for the recovery of any evidence
- photographing the illicit substance as you found it in the exact location you found it
- if a crime occurred, making an arrest after establishing probable cause

As part of establishing probable cause and before making an arrest for possession of illicit drugs, conduct a presumptive field test of the substance using a kit provided by your agency. A presumptive test can establish that the sample is an illicit substance. Be careful and always use PPE when collecting and handling evidence in narcotics cases. Notify your supervisor if you make an arrest.

VICE CRIMES

Vice crimes include offenses, such as alcohol and tobacco violations, gambling, and prostitution. Alcohol and tobacco violations are the vice crimes that most frequently involve people younger than 21. Chapters 562 and 569, F.S., state that any adult that provides someone younger than 21 with alcohol or tobacco commits a misdemeanor. Possession of alcohol by someone younger than 21 is also a misdemeanor; however, possession of tobacco by someone younger than 21 is a non-criminal violation.

☑ LE822.7.
Determine if an incident involves a vice crime

You may also respond to calls involving unlicensed establishments selling alcohol, moonshine operations, or establishments selling alcohol after hours. Vice investigations involve undercover work and develop information through intelligence, including confidential informants and surveillance operations.

Chapter 849, F.S., outlines the elements of gambling. Gambling offenses that you may encounter include bolita (a popular numbers game, especially in south Florida), dog or cock fighting, high-stakes card games, off-track betting, youth athletic events, or craps games on the street. For gambling, document that the suspect played or engaged in a game of chance (including cards, keno, roulette, faro, dice, domino, or other games of chance) at any place, by any device, for money or other thing of value.

☑ LE822.8.
Determine if an incident is gambling

RESPOND TO PROSTITUTION

Chapter 796, F.S., outlines the elements of prostitution. Prostitution is often associated with adult entertainment venues, massage parlors, escort services, and certain internet dating services. Street prostitutes tend to be located in particular geographical areas and truck stops. Prostitutes may be victims of human trafficking, especially if they are younger than 18. If the person is younger than 18, the law requires that you take them into custody and contact DCF.

☑ LE822.9.
Determine if an incident is prostitution

Consider surveilling the area. Approach the person and conduct a field interview. While maintaining officer safety, treat the person with respect and dignity. Should you encounter a person with a sex buyer, separate and interview them separately to establish any relationship. Ask dispatch to run an FCIC/NCIC check to confirm their identities and determine if they have any outstanding warrants. At the end of your preliminary investigation, determine if a crime actually occurred. Complete your paperwork detailing all the known facts.

ORGANIZED CRIME

An organized crime operation has these basic characteristics:

- It has a specific structure, usually hierarchical or paramilitary.
- It has both criminal businesses and legitimate, for-profit or not-for-profit businesses.
- It provides a product or service in a particular market and rarely shares areas of crime or territory with other organized crime groups.
- The loss of one source of income will not necessarily eliminate its profit.

☑ LE822.10.
Describe the basic characteristics of organized crime

The higher-level personnel of the organization are relatively insulated from liability. The business structure is designed to protect them from infiltration by law enforcement and regulatory agencies. Members of the organization that you will encounter will be street level criminals. Members will attempt to intimidate or coerce witnesses and members of law enforcement and the judicial system. Organized crime promotes public corruption, street crime, and gang activity and can have a significant negative impact on the economy.

Organized crime is often associated with gambling, loan sharking, narcotics, prostitution, human trafficking, extortion, pornography, white-collar crime, fencing, public corruption, numbers games, auto theft, drive-by shootings, adult entertainment, and money laundering. Some of the methods law enforcement uses to combat organized crime are asset forfeiture, concentration on vice offenses, intelligence gathering, interagency cooperation, and prosecution under the Racketeer Influenced and Corrupt Organization (RICO) Act.

Chapter 9
Crime Scene Follow-Up Investigations

UNIT 1 THE CRIME SCENE
  LESSON 1 Evidence Rules and Concepts / 349
  LESSON 2 Secure and Protect the Crime Scene / 352
  LESSON 3 Manage Victims, Witnesses, and Suspects / 355
  LESSON 4 Document the Crime Scene / 358
  LESSON 5 Evidence-Handling Procedures / 361

UNIT 2 FOLLOW-UP INVESTIGATION
  LESSON 1 Review Initial Information and Pursue Leads / 371
  LESSON 2 Gather Information on an Unknown Suspect / 374
  LESSON 3 Gather Information on a Known Suspect / 376
  LESSON 4 Showup, Photographic Array, and Photo Lineup / 378

UNIT 3 PREPARING FOR COURT
  LESSON 1 Testimony / 382

UNIT 1 THE CRIME SCENE
LESSON 1 Evidence Rules and Concepts

Lesson Goal

At the end of this lesson, you will know how to apply the rules and concepts of evidence to a crime scene and follow-up investigation to support a successful prosecution.

Think About This

Dispatch sends you to an in-progress burglary. When you arrive, the investigator asks you to collect evidence. What type of evidence might you look for?

A *crime scene* is the site or sites where a crime has occurred, including an area or areas that contain evidence from the crime committed. A crime scene can be a location, a person, a place, or an object associated with criminal behaviors. Fingerprints, photographs, physical evidence, and eyewitness testimony that you collect at a crime scene may prove that the suspect committed the crime.

Making sure that evidence is collected in a correct and timely way helps officers understand what happened at the crime scene. The rules and concepts of evidence guide officers toward completing the investigation successfully.

FUNCTION OF EVIDENCE

The Florida Evidence Code, found in chapter 90 of the Florida Statutes, provides the basic concepts and rules of evidence that may be used in a criminal or civil proceeding. *Evidence* is anything that tends to prove or disprove the existence of a fact. There is a legal distinction between evidence and proof. Evidence is information that is allowed in court while proof is the effect produced by that information.

Evidence has three basic functions when offered in court:

- to prove or disprove a crime
- to support or undermine other evidence
- to help determine an appropriate sentence

☑ LE911.1. Describe the role of evidence in court

TYPES OF EVIDENCE

There are two broad types of evidence: direct and indirect (or circumstantial). *Direct evidence* proves a fact without an inference or presumption, which, if true in itself, conclusively establishes that fact. For example, direct evidence that someone was speeding would be the admission by the driver that they were speeding, speed measurement device results, and testimony from eyewitnesses who saw the driver speeding.

☑ LE911.2. Differentiate between direct and indirect evidence

Indirect or circumstantial evidence requires an inference or presumption to establish a fact rather than personal knowledge or observation. An example of indirect or circumstantial evidence is eyewitness testimony that the defendant entered the victim's home around the time of the crime. It requires the judge or jury to infer or assume from the evidence that the defendant committed the crime.

Direct and indirect evidence presented in court can be testimonial, physical, or documentary.

☑ LE911.3. Differentiate between testimonial, physical, and documentary evidence

Testimonial evidence is a witness statement that tends to prove or disprove facts about the case. It includes the testimonies of law enforcement officers, experts, and other witnesses. Testimonial evidence is generally less reliable than physical evidence because people perceive events differently, do not remember accurately, or lie completely.

Physical or real evidence refers to actual objects offered to prove or disprove facts about a case. This evidence plays a direct part in the crime in question. Examples include items such as trace evidence, biological and touch DNA evidence, impression evidence, firearms evidence, electronic evidence, chemical, or toxicological evidence, and questioned documents evidence. When you correctly identify, protect, collect, preserve, transport, and analyze physical evidence, it is less likely to deliver false results. A later lesson in this chapter discusses how to process physical evidence. Physical or real evidence is crucial for the prosecutor because it gives the jury something to touch and take back to the jury room while they conduct deliberations.

Physical evidence can either be fruits of a crime, instrumentalities of a crime, or contraband. *Fruits of a crime* are the objects obtained by the defendant because of committing the crime. An example is money stolen by a bank robber. Instrumentalities are the items used by the defendant to commit the crime. The crowbar used by a burglar to gain entry into the building is an instrumentality of the crime. Contraband is any property that is illegal for a person to possess based on statute, ordinance, or rule. For example, child pornography found on a computer is both contraband and evidence.

Documentary evidence is anything written or printed that is offered to prove or disprove facts pertaining to the case. It includes bank records, medical records, or a certified copy of a driving history.

ADMISSIBILITY OF EVIDENCE

Admissibility of evidence refers to the legal requirements that must be met before a jury can see or hear about the evidence; the evidence must be deemed relevant and real so that the court may receive it.

☑ LE911.4. Recognize the importance of ensuring that crime scene evidence is admissible

Admissibility of evidence protects the defendant's constitutional rights, guards the jurors from being misled or confused, and can expedite a trial.

The admissibility of evidence also depends upon several factors.

- The officer must obtain the evidence legally and preserve it properly.
- The evidence must be relevant to the case.
- The evidence cannot be unfairly prejudicial, confusing, or based on hearsay.

The fruit of the poisonous tree doctrine holds that the court may exclude evidence from trial if the officer obtained it illegally. For example, if an illegal interrogation leads to the discovery of a murder weapon, the court may exclude both the information obtained from the interrogation and the weapon. The good-faith exception doctrine holds that if you execute a search warrant that you believe is valid, but a court later determines that the warrant has a legal error, the court may still admit any seized evidence.

PRIVILEGED COMMUNICATION

The Florida Evidence Code recognizes that the need to protect communications within certain relationships is more important than the admissibility of evidence obtained from those communications. Some examples of privileged communications include communication between a sexual assault counselor and a sexual assault victim, and communication between a domestic violence advocate and a domestic violence victim. These types of interactions between two parties are private, protected, and confidential, and their disclosure cannot be forced.

☑ LE911.5. Describe the role of privileged communications

UNIT 1 THE CRIME SCENE
LESSON 2 Secure and Protect the Crime Scene

◎ Lesson Goal

At the end of this lesson, you will know how to secure, protect, and manage a crime scene independently or as part of a team to support the successful prosecution of a crime.

Think About This

You are driving to an incident that quickly becomes a robbery crime scene. There are several persons involved, most of them are spectators, and you already know that one of them is injured. What actions will you take before and after you arrive?

The purpose of an investigation is to determine what happened during an incident, identify and locate the suspect, and develop enough evidence to establish probable cause to make an arrest. The preliminary investigation focuses on establishing whether a criminal act has been committed and, if so, what type, when, and where it was committed. The initial or preliminary incident report should clearly document the initial investigative steps taken at the scene.

You may be the first responding officer to a crime scene. Your first priority is to secure, protect, and preserve the scene to avoid contaminating any evidence. Protecting and securing the scene begins when you arrive and ends when you release the scene to an investigator or from law enforcement custody.

Your second priority must be to search for, identify, document, collect, and maintain the physical evidence. The successful prosecution of a case will depend on the actions of the first responding officer and the state of the physical evidence at the time it is collected. Often, officers think that the arrest is the end of their participation in a criminal case; however, they remain an integral part of the prosecution process until the case is resolved.

RESPOND TO A CRIME SCENE

When dispatch sends you to a potential crime scene, the operator will identify the nature and location of the alleged crime, as well as the complainant's name and relationship to the scene location. Dispatch may also inform you if someone is injured.

☑ LE912.1. Describe crime scene information that you need from dispatch

While driving to the scene, consider key questions that will help you assess the situation adequately:

- What is the location?
- Are any weapons involved?
- Has the complainant indicated the suspect's location?
- How many individuals are involved?

- How many officers are necessary to safely contain or control the situation?
- Do you need additional services?
- Do you need special equipment?
- Are any special concerns or dangers associated with the call?

SECURE A CRIME SCENE

After finding the incident's location, identify officer safety concerns, any victim or witness injuries, and the need for backup. Secure the potential crime scene(s). Before conducting your investigation, make sure the crime occurred within your jurisdiction. Look for sources of information about, and evidence of, the crime when securing the scene.

The size of the crime scene depends on the type of crime, the type of evidence, and the location of the evidence; for example, a burglary may involve an entire apartment complex or just one apartment. Use personal observations and statements from victims and witnesses to assist in determining the extent of the scene. Crime scene perimeters should be larger rather than smaller. It is easier to reduce the size of a perimeter than to enlarge it. A larger crime scene also helps keep crowds away from evidence.

Attempt to locate and identify the point of the suspect's entry to and exit from the crime scene by visually inspecting the scene. Evidence of entry or exit might include broken glass or pry marks around doorways. Identify the pieces of evidence farthest from the center of the crime scene. Establish boundaries for the crime scene and guard against unnecessary entrance by blocking off the area with crime scene tape. A supervisor or investigator assigned to the case may later decide to adjust the original boundaries or perimeter of the scene, based on the size and the type of crime scene.

☑ LE912.2.
Determine if a crime scene is life threatening or threatening to officer safety

☑ LE912.3.
Determine the probable extent, size, and scope of a crime scene

☑ LE912.4.
Determine a single access point for authorized personnel

PROTECT A CRIME SCENE

Once you establish the crime scene perimeter, do not allow any unauthorized removal or alteration of any evidence. Curious, unauthorized people can damage, contaminate, or destroy evidence at a scene. Do not allow them to enter the secured crime scene area. Officer safety is also at risk when unauthorized people enter a scene.

Protect the scene until you or someone with your agency can photograph and document it. Different crime scenes may require different methods of protecting the evidence. Recognizing threats to the evidence will help determine the appropriate method of protection. For example, in the case of an outdoor crime scene involving degradable, easily destroyed, biological, or trace evidence, protect the evidence from weather elements such as rain, hail, lightning, or wind. The same evidence located inside a temperature-controlled house would not require the same level of protection. Once you determine the nature of the scene and the type of crime you are investigating, you can decide how best to protect it.

☑ LE912.5.
Determine how to position authorized personnel, crime scene tape, and natural barriers

Instruct people to move behind the crime scene tape, advising that refusal may result in arrest. You have the authority to arrest any person who, after receiving a warning, crosses an area marked by crime scene tape.

☑ **LE912.6.** Determine your legal authority to secure and protect a crime scene

Before you enter the scene to process evidence, determine if the location is public or private property. Public property is for the use and enjoyment of the public and is open to the public. Private property belongs to an individual and is not open to the public. A person occupying private property has an expectation of privacy that no one can violate without a search warrant or a valid exception to the warrant requirement. An officer has permission to enter private property based on exigent circumstances to conduct a sweep for potential suspects, to provide first aid, or if there is an indication that evidence will be lost, destroyed or removed prior to obtaining a search warrant or consent to search.

☑ **LE912.7.** Describe how to create a crime scene log

The primary officer or investigator will designate a point of entry and exit and will assign an officer to maintain a crime scene log at that location. The ***crime scene log*** is a document that details the name, rank, and agency of each person entering or leaving the scene; the date and time of the person's entry or exit; and the reason the person was at the scene. If the investigator designates more than one point of entry or exit, they will assign an officer to each location and notify all officers to use the access point(s). The officer posted at the access point must document these details in the crime scene log. The log provides proof of crime scene security and validates the evidence collected at a crime scene. Officers not assigned to the crime scene do not have access just because they are law enforcement officers.

If the evidence becomes contaminated or altered in any way, document the incident in your report. Include information about the original condition of the evidence and the events leading to its damage or destruction.

☑ **LE912.8.** Describe how to relinquish a crime scene to authorized personnel

Upon arrival, the supervisor or investigator will usually coordinate duties such as evidence collection, securing the scene perimeter, and other assignments. They will also assign shifts for officers, taking weather and staffing limitations into consideration. The size and type of crime scene search will determine the number and type of personnel or resources needed for processing the scene. Agency policies, procedures, jurisdiction, and available resources will also factor into how to proceed. Larger agencies have specialized crime scene units that can process the scene and collect evidence. Other agencies require responding officers to process scenes. In some cases, agencies may call for outside assistance, such as FDLE's crime scene personnel. Ultimately, the responding officer's supervisor will decide whether to request crime scene or investigative assistance and determine crime scene jurisdiction for crime scene service.

UNIT 1 THE CRIME SCENE
LESSON 3 Manage Victims, Witnesses, and Suspects

⊚ Lesson Goal

At the end of this lesson, you will know how to manage victims, witnesses, and suspects at a crime scene and gather and share information with a supervisor or investigator.

Think About This

Dispatch sends you to help another officer with an incident involving a disturbance. When you arrive, there is one person sitting on the curb with an icepack on their face and several others standing around them. One person is yelling, and the first responding officer is trying to calm them down. What are some of the first tasks you need to perform?

IDENTIFY PEOPLE ON THE SCENE

Crimes scenes are rarely the orderly, calm, and perfectly secured areas that are portrayed on television or in the movies. In reality, crime scenes can be emotionally charged and chaotic because of the persons involved. There may be victims, witnesses, and sometimes suspects present. As discussed in Chapter 1, you will need to constantly shift between the three officer roles of supporter, stabilizer, and enforcer.

At the scene of an incident, identify all the people involved, including complainants, victims, witnesses, and suspects. A person can belong to more than one of these categories. For example, the victim may also be the complainant, or a person first identified as a witness may become a suspect as the investigation progresses.

☑ LE913.1. Identify who to question at a crime scene

When establishing which people may have information, ask those present where they were and how they were involved in the incident. Determine their degrees of involvement and roles in the incident. You may not have the time or the resources to question all of the people at the scene, so determine who has the most information and knowledge of the incident. Ask the victim or the complainant who was present during the crime or event to name any potential witnesses of the incident. In addition, ask witnesses if anyone else was involved and, if so, what their roles were. This will help verify individual statements.

In your notes, document the names, dates of birth, genders, races, addresses, and telephone numbers of all people involved. Ask vital witnesses to stay at the scene for interviewing. Witnesses may try to leave or remain in the background when you attempt to ask them questions. People who do not want to be involved may say little or nothing so that they can leave the scene quickly.

SEPARATE INVOLVED PEOPLE

☑ LE913.2. Explain the process for separating victims, witnesses, and suspects

In a criminal investigation, you must keep victims, complainants, and witnesses separated. Tell them not to talk to each other or discuss the incident with anyone until after you complete their interview. This keeps them from coordinating their accounts of what happened. Place people in separate locations, near the crime scene area, but in a place that poses no risk of contaminating evidence. Ideally, they should be far enough apart so that they cannot hear or see each other. If separate rooms are not available, isolate people within one large room by placing them on opposite sides of the room with their backs to each other. Make sure that there is enough distance between them so that they cannot have physical contact. Another possible controlled area is inside of a patrol car. However, due to space limitations, place only one person in each car. If necessary, another officer can stay with each person to ensure control and safety.

Separating involved people will help each one focus on what they saw or heard and maintain the integrity of their statements. Multiple witnesses who have experienced the same event never recall the same details. A witness overhearing another person describe the same event may be tempted, even unconsciously, to repeat the other witness's version of the crime. Working together, they may come up with accounts that differ from the facts.

Some of the people involved may try to intimidate others into giving false information. Make sure that, while victims or witnesses are giving statements, no one can intimidate them visually or verbally. If a suspect or another witness attempts to influence witnesses' statement, you may need to remove them from the scene.

An interviewee may want to help the suspect by diverting evidence of involvement away from them. People involved may also try to pass evidence, such as a weapon or contraband, to each other to hide it.

Separating family members during a crisis might make a difficult situation worse. Use your best judgment and react with empathy when assessing whether separating family members is necessary. In a child abuse incident, for example, separation of certain family members may not be appropriate.

If an interviewee is suffering from physical or mental trauma, make a note to interview this person later when they have recovered. For safety reasons, always maintain visual contact with victims, witnesses, complainants, and suspects.

INJURED PEOPLE

☑ LE913.3. Describe how to gather information related to victim injuries

When injured people are at the scene, responding officers may have to provide first aid. If you are providing emergency first aid and the victim does not have life-threatening injuries, consider asking the victim direct, fundamental questions about how they sustained the injury, such as the following:

- Who hit you?
- What did the suspect use to hit you?

- Where were you hit?
- Where were you standing when you were hit?
- When were you hit?
- How were you hit?
- Why were you hit?

Look at the victim's injuries and record detailed observations in your notes, keeping in mind that you will use them to create reports and refresh your memory when testifying. Florida law allows officers to review footage from their body-worn camera which will assist in this process. Note whether the information the victim provides appears to be consistent with the injuries and evidence at the scene. Checking for consistency requires noting specific information regarding the location, size, and type of injury. Tell the victim to notify law enforcement if bruising intensifies so that the injuries can be photographed as documentation as bruises tend to change color with time. Record the names of medical personnel who provide services to the victim because the court may call any of them as a witness.

SHARE INFORMATION WITH A SUPERVISOR

Share the following information with your supervisor or the investigator:

- when the incident occurred
- how it occurred
- where it occurred
- all evidence gathered or specific items that are still the focus of a search
- descriptions of all property involved in the incident (obtained from complainants, victims, or witnesses who can identify the property)
- the names and descriptions of victims, witnesses, and possible suspects
- a description of the suspect's vehicle, if applicable and if known
- any special concerns on the scene such as biohazards, a hostile crowd, at-large suspects, and severe injuries
- how the scene is being handled and protected
- the scene's boundaries and protection measures
- a plan for the continued investigation of the incident and the search for evidence
- the identity of the public information officer who is communicating with the media (When dealing with the media or designating an assigned authorized spokesperson on the scene, refer to your agency's policies and procedures.)

☑ LE913.4. List the information to provide to the chain of command

UNIT 1 THE CRIME SCENE
LESSON 4 Document the Crime Scene

Lesson Goal

At the end of this lesson, you will know how to photograph and sketch the crime scene and associated evidence, including evidence on a person, while ensuring privacy and dignity.

Think About This

You respond to an incident that results in a dead homeowner. You and a fellow officer have secured the crime scene and interviewed the witnesses. What steps should you take to document the crime scene before you begin to collect the evidence?

PHOTOGRAPH THE CRIME SCENE

☑ LE914.1. Determine when to photograph a crime scene

Photographing the scene is the first event that should take place when documenting a crime scene. Photographing allows people who were not present at the original scene, including the court and the jury, to gather information and "visualize" how the crime scene looked on the day you responded. Photos or sketches also help victims and witnesses refresh their memory as time goes by.

Broadly, crime scene photography moves from general to specific; take overall, midrange, and then close-up photographs. Begin at the perimeter of the crime scene and take a series of shots by framing an all-inclusive or four-corner view of the scene. The midrange view shots show the relationship between the evidence items within the scene.

☑ LE914.2. Describe the appropriate photographic equipment to document a crime scene

Close-up shots show the details of a specific item of evidence and must include a **scale or identifier**, which is an object that is used to establish the size and original position(s) of evidence and draw attention to relevant objects at a crime scene; examples include rulers, cards with rulers on them, a *Miranda* card, or a dollar bill. For example, if your crime scene is a room, the overall would be photographs of the room from all four corners. The midrange would be photographs of the sofa, and the close-up would be the blood on the sofa. For the photographs of the blood on the sofa, you would use a ruler to identify the size of the area. Look at all photographs after taking the pictures to make sure that they are in focus.

☑ LE914.3. Describe how to photograph a crime scene

Use proper lighting so that the photographs are neither too dark nor too light to see detail. Proper lighting also avoids glare and flashback from a mirror or glass. Standard camera flashes will project only 9–12 feet. Consider flood lighting with a flashlight, or using your vehicle spotlight or headlights if the overall picture requires you to photograph the scene from more than 9–12 feet away.

Photographic framing is composing the photograph so that it depicts what you are trying to document. For example, in overall or midrange photography, overlap the photos to show the relationships of items in the crime scene. All objects photographed must be important or relevant to the scene. Avoid including bystanders, other officers, your equipment, or pets in crime scene photographs.

You can use a flashlight for enhanced lighting. Use oblique lighting, better known as side lighting, when photographing shoe/tire impressions or tool marks. This lighting technique uses the flashlight at a low angle to show details by creating shadows on the surface of the impressions. Keep extra batteries for both the camera and the flashlight.

Use your agency issued digital camera with a flash, and do not use a personal cell phone camera. Avoid using an agency-issued cell phone camera; the court may subpoena the information on your phone. Follow your agency's policies and procedures regarding the use of a body camera to photograph a crime scene.

Photographing perishable, transitory, or fragile evidence ensures its documentation and preservation. Examples of perishable evidence can include blood, footprints, and tire impressions, or trace evidence, such as hair or fibers. Transitory evidence is evidence that can blow or wash away. Fragile evidence can include a bullet hole in glass held in place by a thin window tint. Based on the circumstances at the scene, you need to photograph these types of evidence first.

☑ LE914.4. Describe how to photograph specific types of evidence in the crime scene

When photographing specific items, such as blood drops, weapons, or tire marks, place a scale or identifier in the photograph with the evidence to establish the original positions and draw attention to relevant objects or evidence. The scale or identifier should be as close as possible to the item you are photographing to avoid creating optical illusions that misrepresents the actual size of the item (items looking larger or smaller based on placement of the scale or identifier). Most agencies provide rulers or cards with rulers on them. Other examples of scales or identifiers are *Miranda* cards, dollar bills, or coins.

☑ LE914.5. Explain where to place a scale or identifier

PHOTOGRAPH PEOPLE

A person can be a crime scene or part of a crime scene. Visible evidence that can be present on the victim or witness includes bruises, lacerations, broken bones, gunshot wounds, blood, and trace or transfer evidence. A suspect does not have the right to refuse photographing injuries, such as scratches from the victim or blood evidence.

Apply the same photographic perspectives—overall, midrange, and close-up—when documenting injuries and evidence on people. Use a scale or identifier to document the extent of the injury. Photographs of individuals should be taken in an area that affords privacy for the person being photographed. Be sure that the individual approves the officer taking the photographs and the officer who is acting as the witness in the space. If you need to take photographs of an injury to any external genital organs, provide the victim options regarding which officer will observe and which officer will photograph the injuries.

☑ LE914.6. Describe how to photograph evidence on a person

SKETCH THE CRIME SCENE

A crime scene sketch supplements your field notes and photographs and helps with report writing. Sketches aid in the reconstruction, explanation, and permanent recording of an incident. They can show positions of objects in relation to one another that are not easily visible in photographs.

☑ LE914.7. Determine when to sketch a crime scene

If you are going to sketch the crime scene, do this after photographing the scene and before you begin any detailed work. Use sketches to document where you recovered evidence in the scene. You may use the sketches during interviews with witnesses, victims, and suspects to correlate testimony. If you use these sketches during an interview, include them in the report, as they are admissible in court.

DOCUMENT PHOTOGRAPHS AND SKETCHES

☑ LE914.8. Describe how to document the photographs or sketches of a crime scene and evidence on a person

Before you begin to photograph or sketch a crime scene or a person, write the following information on a piece of paper or whiteboard and take a photograph; you may also type the following information into the electronic device that you will use to sketch or take the photograph:

- case number
- location
- date and time
- officer's name

Indicate in your report that you photographed or sketched the crime scene or person. You will need to be able to testify that the photographs or sketch are true and accurate representations of the crime scene or person as they appeared when you sketched or took the pictures.

UNIT 1 THE CRIME SCENE
LESSON 5 Evidence-Handling Procedures

Lesson Goal

At the end of this lesson, you will know how to search for and recognize several types of evidence; collect, package, and preserve evidence; and initiate a chain of custody.

Think About This

Dispatch sends you to a residence after receiving a call from someone who stated that their partner attacked them. You arrive at the apartment complex and find someone with cuts and bruises on their face and arms and wearing torn clothing. Your fellow officer notices drug paraphernalia on the dining room table next to a bag of white powder. The victim tells you that the drugs belong to their partner and that they keep guns in the apartment. How are you going to proceed with processing the evidence?

Cautionary Note: Always use the appropriate standard precautions and apply PPE when searching and handling evidence. Keep in mind that exposure to certain substances can be harmful or fatal.

SEARCH FOR EVIDENCE

The type of crime committed determines the types of evidence to search for at a scene. For example, at a burglary scene, search for evidence of illegal entry, such as pry marks on a doorframe or broken windows. When searching, use a systematic approach or pattern. The type of crime scene will help dictate the pattern. Study the whole scene first and keep in mind that the relationships of the items' positions may be important.

Use one or more of the following search patterns:

- *grid*—often used indoors, this is a variation of the strip/line search pattern. Searchers overlap a series of lanes in a cross pattern, making the search more methodical and thorough.
- *spiral*—usually used outdoors by one person. The searcher begins at a certain point and walks in increasingly larger circles to the outermost boundary of the search area.
- *strip/line*—usually used outdoors by several people. Divide the search area into lanes. Have one or more people search each lane by moving in both directions, examining all areas.
- *zone/quadrant*—used for vehicle searches, both indoors and outdoors, or a large area. Divide the area into four different sections and search each area using one of the patterns above.

☑ LE915.1. Describe how to conduct a building or grounds search for evidence

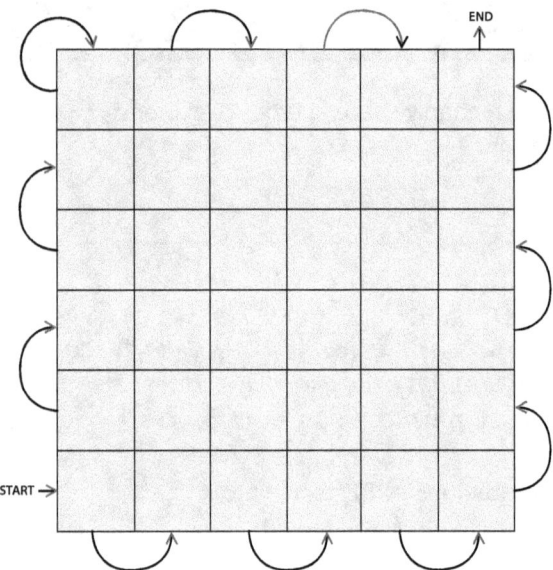

Figure 9-1 Grid search pattern

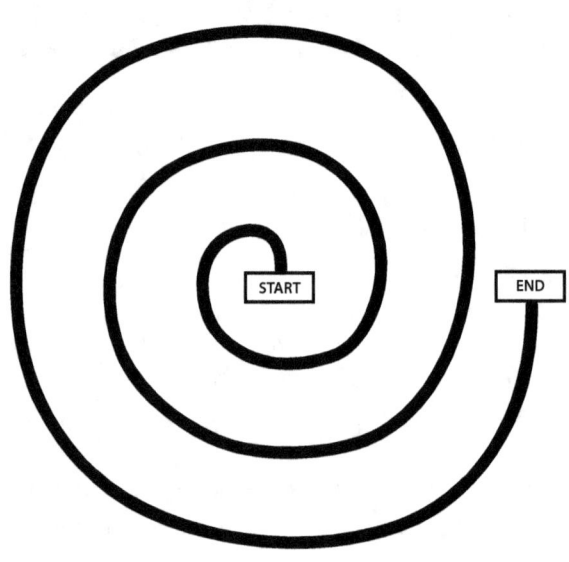

Figure 9-2 Spiral search pattern

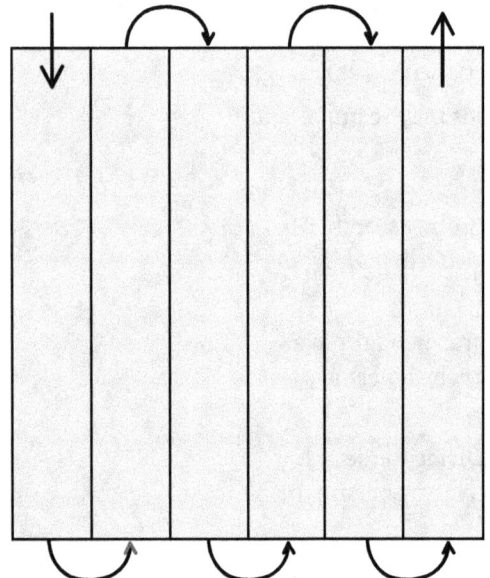

Figure 9-3 Strip/line search pattern

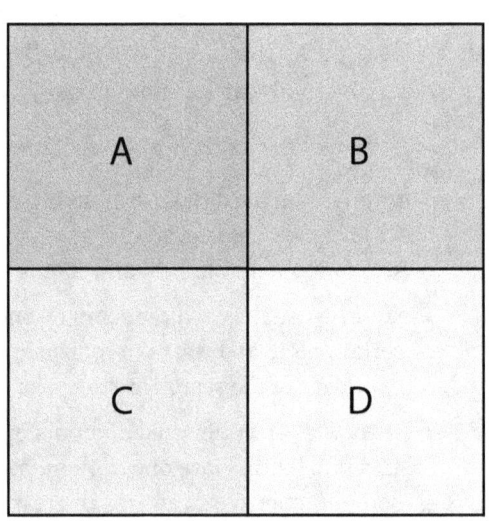

Figure 9-4 Zone/quadrant search pattern

TYPES OF PHYSICAL EVIDENCE

At any crime scene, the victim, witness, and suspect usually leave or take away some sort of evidence. A few examples of evidence that you may find and collect are fingerprints, shoe impressions, blood, fibers, hair, tool marks, paint scratches, broken glass, body fluids, controlled substances, electronics equipment and computers, firearms, broken or damaged materials, tire track impressions, documents, and bones.

☑ LE915.2.
Identify the types of evidence found at a crime scene

trace evidence	hair, fibers, clothing, paint chips, transfer evidence, glass, wood, soil, dirt
biological evidence	blood, semen, saliva, bones, teeth, body tissues, hair, touch DNA
impression evidence	fingerprints, tire, shoe, footprints, bite marks, tool marks
firearms evidence	weapons, projectiles, gunshot residue, cartridge cases, tool marks, database information
electronic evidence	cell phones, thumb drives, laptops, notebooks, tablets, computers, smart home and security devices, external hard drives, digital cameras, CDs, DVDs, VHS tapes, answering machines, digital recording devices
chemistry or toxicological evidence	blood alcohol levels, drugs, poisons
questioned documents evidence	checks, bank statements, address books, wire transfers, credit cards, phone bills, photographs or cameras, photocopies

Try to identify the possible sources of evidence. You should create a triangle of evidence (see Figure 9-5) that connects both the suspect and the victim to the scene. Talking with the victim and witnesses can help determine what evidence belongs to whom. For example, if a substance appears to be blood, determine whether the victim or the suspect might be injured. Some evidence will be unidentifiable, but the crime scene unit or laboratory can assist in identifying, comparing, and interpreting such evidence. Some surfaces may have contaminants that require expert processing.

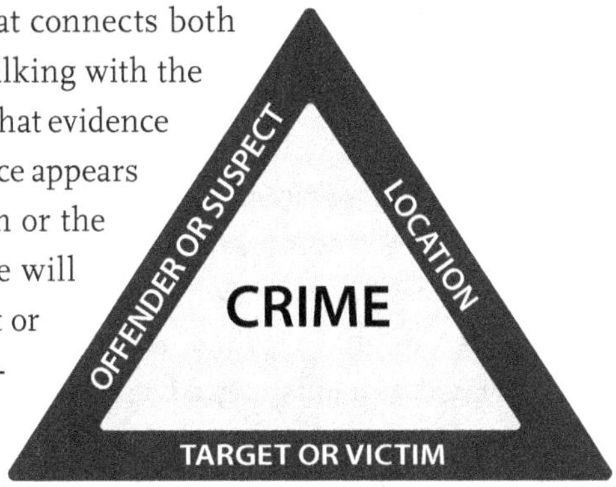

Figure 9-5
Triangle of evidence

Never handle evidence with your bare hands. Practice standard precautions and apply PPE whenever you handle or collect evidence. PPE will protect the evidence from contamination and you from exposure to dangerous substances. Depending on the type of evidence you are collecting, you may need booties, facemasks, goggles, aprons, and other

☑ LE915.3.
Determine the type of PPE to apply before collecting evidence

protective clothing or gear. Change gloves between collecting each piece of evidence needing DNA analysis.

Change PPE as often as necessary. Do not become a source of cross-contamination. If you touch the victim, witness, or suspect and then touch the crime scene wearing the same gloves, touch DNA may cross-contaminate the scene.

☑ LE915.4. Describe the appropriate packaging materials for evidence

There are special considerations for handling specific types of evidence. Proper tools, equipment, containers, and packaging help prevent contamination and degradation of evidence. For example, wet evidence, such as items soaked with body fluids or living plant material, must be air-dried, packaged in breathable containers, such as paper bags, or both. If packaged improperly, wet items will deteriorate to a point where they have no value as evidence. Place each piece of evidence collected for DNA analysis in its own, separate container. Your agency's policies and procedures will identify specific evidence-handling procedures.

TRACE EVIDENCE

☑ LE915.5. Identify the types of trace evidence

Trace evidence is small quantities of material transferred from a victim or suspect to each other or to a crime scene. Trace evidence can include human hair, animal hair, textile fibers and fabric, rope, feathers, soil, glass, and building materials. Microanalysis is the process of analyzing trace evidence with a microscope to determine a possible source or origin.

Sometimes fibers transfer between the clothes of the victim and the suspect. Fibers can come from clothing, carpet, rope, vehicle carpeting, upholstery, or other common articles. Fiber analysis can reveal the manufacturer and other information about the source item. The relationship that fiber evidence has to the victim, the suspect, or the crime scene is crucial in many cases. Broken windows, torn screens, or other sharp edges may snag fibers during a suspect's entry into or exit from a building. When the inside of a vehicle is part of a crime scene, examine the seat belts, airbag, steering wheel, and other places for fibers. Holding a flashlight to create sidelight and using a magnifying glass may help you spot fiber evidence.

Comparing and matching fragments from a broken piece of glass can indicate a relationship between the victim, the suspect, and the crime scene. The crime laboratory can analyze the glass pieces and compare characteristics, such as color, density, thickness, and type of glass (tempered window, non-tempered, headlight, and bottle), to match and identify their origin. In addition, if a suspect or victim is near a piece of glass when it breaks, glass fragments may contaminate the person's body, shoes, and clothing. The direction of force or the order in which glass is broken can determine on which side of the glass the suspect stood, thus establishing the suspect's entry or exit path.

Paint transfer can provide useful evidence in solving crimes such as a hit-and-run crash. Samples may show that paint at the scene and on the suspect's vehicle came from a common source. Tools used to gain illegal entry into buildings and safes can leave paint residue. Sometimes, soil from a crime scene attaches to a suspect or victim's clothing, shoes, tires, or other objects, and the person transports it to another location.

BIOLOGICAL EVIDENCE

Biological evidence left at crime scenes may contain DNA. Consider all objects at a crime scene as possible sources of DNA evidence. The most common biological specimens include blood, semen, or saliva. Crime laboratory experts can identify these body fluids and, if needed, conduct DNA analysis. Sexual assault cases may require an examination of semen evidence. Pieces of evidence that may contain saliva and require examination include cigarette butts, drinking straws, soda and beer cans, masks, bottles, and bite marks.

☑ LE915.6. Identify the types of biological evidence

The crime laboratory can test for the presence of blood and if it is of human origin. Blood type and DNA identification are also possible with a blood sample. Blood evidence may include blood pooled on the floor, a wet or dried stain on upholstery or carpet, or a sample collected from the victim or the suspect after the incident. Experts can analyze the direction of blood spatter to determine the type of weapon, the direction of the attack, and the relative size of the attacker. Advancements in DNA analysis allow for the detection of identifiable evidence in objects that made contact with a victim or suspect for a short time.

In some cases, teeth can serve as identification and evidence. If you discover human skeletal remains, contact your supervisor. Because of the nature of the evidence, a medical examiner or a trained forensic specialist should see the bones at the site as discovered.

Certain types of biological evidence require a specific technique or expertise to collect. Follow your agency's policies and procedures when dealing with these types of evidence.

IMPRESSION EVIDENCE

Working edges of tools leave distinct marks on surfaces. Never try to fit a suspect's tool into a mark. You may need to collect the entire damaged surface and submit it to the lab to compare with the suspect's tool. Comparing the fracture sites of two or more parts of a broken, torn, or cut object and determining whether they were once whole can provide strong evidence in court. Do not attempt to reconstruct the items or process fingerprints from the pieces before submitting them. If it is not possible to submit the entire damaged surface as evidence, follow your agency's policies and procedures for proper processing.

Footprints, shoe impressions, and tire impressions at the scene can link a suspect to a crime when they match an object in the suspect's possession. You can find these types of impressions in mud, soil, or another pliable material. Shoe or tire prints can remain on wood, tile, paper, or paint, or in dust, blood, or grease. Crime scene technicians can cast certain impressions, such as shoe or tire impressions. Photograph these items as well to preserve them as evidence.

☑ LE915.7. Identify the types of impression evidence

Teeth can provide dental evidence in the form of bite mark impressions that can lead to the identity of the suspect. Photograph bite marks as soon as possible with a scale or identifier. There is a high likelihood of saliva being present in bite marks as well.

FINGERPRINTS

Consider all objects at a crime scene as possible sources of fingerprints. A foreign substance, like wet paint, blood, grease, ink, or dirt, transfers and makes readily visible *patent prints*, which form from the friction ridges or corrugated lines on fingers. A *plastic print* is a molded or embedded fingerprint that you can easily see, created by touching an impressionable surface, such as fresh paint, wax, bar of soap, or mud. Follow your agency's policies and procedures regarding photographing visible prints and determining the best method to collect and preserve this evidence.

Latent prints are among the most valuable and common types of physical evidence at a crime scene. Although generally invisible to the naked eye, *latent prints* result from body residues left behind when the friction ridges of the hands or feet make contact with a surface. By examining the submitted evidence, the crime lab may be able to determine the presence of latent prints and determine if they are identifiable.

☑ LE915.8. Identify possible locations of latent fingerprints

When looking over a crime scene for places to locate latent fingerprints, consider how the suspect may have approached the scene, what they may have touched, how they moved inside the scene, and how they left the scene. By tracing this, you may be able to find locations to process latent prints.

Consider the types of surfaces that may be involved. To have the possibility of latent prints, you must have a surface that is conducive to having latent prints on it, for example, a rough concrete surface versus a smooth glass surface.

Capturing latent prints can help identify the suspect(s) in the crime you are currently investigating. Once latent prints enter the print database, the database may be able to solve unsolved past crimes and crime analysts may be able to identify suspect(s) in other crimes.

☑ LE915.9. Describe how to protect the latent fingerprint location

Make sure to preserve the latent prints you find. If you think an environmental issue, such as rain, may damage a latent print, collect the print before it becomes damaged or protect the item from the environmental factor. You may have to cover, move the item (after documentation), or even collect it as evidence for later processing by the crime lab. Before moving the item and to prevent destruction of the latent print, photograph the print with a scale or identifier in a RAW+JPEG setting on a point and shoot camera. This setting allows the raw image to remain unaltered. You cannot alter a raw image using imaging altering software.

If the object the prints are on makes it difficult to collect the prints or photographing them is beyond your skill level, collect the surface object for the crime lab to process or, if possible, have a crime scene technician respond to the scene.

☑ LE915.10. Identify the equipment for collecting latent prints

Most agencies provide officers with a basic latent fingerprint kit that includes gloves, black and light gray powder, a brush, lifting tape, and fingerprint cards. If your agency authorizes you to lift prints, have an adequate supply of materials on hand and get training in how to use them. Lifting latent prints is a basic skill of law enforcement. The ability to lift a latent print directly relates to your attention to detail. Lifting a print is often a "one shot" opportunity and should be treated as such. Take care to avoid smudging or smearing existing latent prints when handling and packaging evidence.

Follow these guidelines when dusting for and lifting latent prints:

☑ LE915.11. Describe how to collect latent prints

1. Wear gloves to avoid contaminating the area with your own fingerprints and DNA. Be careful not to wipe possible prints off the surface.
2. Hold a flashlight at an angle, and look for obvious signs of a latent print.
3. Take your brush and lightly dab into the powder once you find a target area.
4. Tap and twirl the excess powder off the brush in the jar of powder. Use it sparingly, because it tends to get on everything. It is better to use too little than too much.
5. Lightly brush from side to side, or swirl the brush, on the target area. If the powder adhered to the print is too thick, brush off the excess powder with a clean brush and adjust the amount of powder.
6. When you find a print, apply the lifting tape in the following manner:
    a. Place a suitable fingerprint card on a flat surface nearby so that it is ready for the print you lift.
    b. Turn under the end of the lifting tape to form a tab.
    c. Extend the lifting tape to a distance long enough to cover the print.
    d. Place the rolled end of the lifting tape just above the latent print, but keep it off the print.
    e. Make sure that you do not trap foreign matter or air bubbles under the lifting tape.
    f. Smooth from the tabbed end of the lifting tape back toward the rolled end or vice versa. Use your finger, pen, or another object to smooth out the lifting tape and release any trapped air. It is the same basic process as putting a decal on a window. With time and practice, you will develop your own technique for applying the lifting tape.
7. Slowly lift the lifting tape containing the developed prints from the same end that you started rolling the lifting tape over the print. Be careful not to touch the tape to another surface, such as your gloves.
8. Carefully place the lifting tape on the fingerprint card in the same way that you placed the lifting tape over the print. Place the print in the designated place on the correct side of the card.
9. On the back of the fingerprint print card, record the date, case number, the location within the crime scene where you retrieved the fingerprint, and any other information your agency's policies and procedures require. Be careful not to damage the print.
10. Follow your agency's policies and procedures to submit latent print cards as evidence.

LE915.12.
Describe the role of elimination prints

Elimination prints allow fingerprint analysts to distinguish between prints belonging to victims, witnesses, or possible suspects. To make this distinction, take fingerprints from anyone who may have been at the crime scene to eliminate their prints from the pool of suspects.

FIREARMS EVIDENCE

When recovering a firearm or ammunition at a crime scene, follow agency policies and procedures for handling such evidence and apply PPE to avoid contaminating the firearm or ammunition with your fingerprints and DNA. This may be properly securing the firearm and making it safe or leaving it in place for further investigation.

LE915.13.
Describe how to safely examine a firearm as evidence

If you are responsible for collecting a firearm as evidence, be sure to do the following:

- Always properly secure the weapon.
- Remove the magazine.
- Clear all ammunition from the chamber or cylinder.
- Carefully examine the weapon to identify the manufacturer, country of origin, serial number, model number, and caliber.
- Document this information in your field notes as you will need this information for your database check and final report.

LE915.14.
Describe the role of FCIC/NCIC when determining the status of a firearm

Place the weapon in a firearm or evidence box; put the magazine and the ammunition in a separate container. Use the serial number to conduct an FCIC/NCIC database check on the firearm. This will tell you if the firearm is lost, stolen, or found. Under no circumstances should you insert any object into the barrel of the firearm, as it may damage the rifling in the barrel of the firearm. Rifling is the grooves inside the barrel of a firearm that provide unique characteristics of that specific firearm.

If an object contains an embedded bullet, do not attempt to remove it. A laboratory can examine firearms for fired bullets, cartridge cases, and shotgun shells to determine if the suspect's weapon fired them. Analysts can also identify tool marks, after-market modifications, and serial number restoration as well as examine bullets recovered from a crime scene.

ELECTRONIC EVIDENCE

LE915.15.
Identify the types of electronic evidence

Electronic devices are commonly found at crime scenes and can often store vital evidence. Types of devices can include cell phones, tablets, laptops, and desktops. Media storage can include thumb drives, external drives, removable disks, tapes, digital cameras, and other data storage equipment. Do not manipulate or attempt to operate any part of the equipment to avoid possible damage to it. Computer evidence recovery is a complex task that requires highly specialized training. Follow your agency's policies and procedures for computer evidence recovery. Consider placing a mobile electronic device in "airplane mode" to keep the owner from accessing it remotely or in an antistatic Faraday bag that will prevent any communication with the seized device.

When you find a cell phone at a crime scene, you may not access the information contained in the cell phone unless you have consent from the owner or a search warrant. The U.S. Supreme Court, in *Riley v. California*, ruled that it is unconstitutional to search a cell phone without a search warrant unless there are officer safety concerns or exigent circumstances. This should not stop you from asking for consent to search a cell phone.

Keep in mind that technology is constantly changing. Stay current with your agency's policies and procedures regarding collection, processing, and storing of electronic evidence.

CHEMICAL OR TOXICOLOGICAL EVIDENCE

The crime laboratory's chemistry section analyzes substances to determine the presence or absence of any controlled substance listed under chapter 893, F.S. Analysts prepare reports of their findings and often testify in court on the results of their analyses. In certain criminal investigations where you believe the suspect or victim is using alcohol or drugs, you may submit an FDLE public records request and obtain an analysis from the toxicology section of a crime laboratory. These cases usually result from investigations of DUI, sexual assault, and death.

You should be able to identify a variety of controlled substances and drug paraphernalia by sight or odor. In some cases, you will use a field test kit to test a substance before collecting and packaging it as evidence. When collecting drug paraphernalia, package sharp objects, such as needles or syringes, in puncture-proof packages clearly labeled with the words "WARNING: SHARPS." PPE is essential when encountering any chemical or biological substances.

☑ LE915.16. Identify the types of chemical or toxicological evidence

A particularly hazardous substance you may encounter is fentanyl or carfentanil (a more potent version of fentanyl), which you can absorb through mucous membranes in the mouth, nose, or eyes. You may find these in powder form, mixed with heroin or cocaine, as pills, capsules, eye drops, or blotter paper, or disguised as other drugs such as hydrocodone or oxycodone. When you encounter any substance that you suspect to be fentanyl or carfentanil, follow your agency's policies and procedures for field-testing, collecting, packaging, and transporting. Use PPE such as gloves, long sleeves, a surgical or dust mask, and eye protection. Conduct field-testing in an open environment with no wind. You should have another officer nearby, preferably one with naloxone, which is the antidote for opioid overdose, to assist you if exposed to the substance. When packaging, mark the package as "suspected fentanyl." Use caution when transporting, and place it in the trunk of your vehicle. If you encounter large amounts of powder, evacuate the area immediately and call a hazmat team. When exposed to even a small amount, follow your agency's policies and procedures for decontamination. Signs of exposure include:

- disorientation
- difficulty speaking or walking
- slowed pulse
- nausea
- slow, shallow breathing
- respiratory arrest

You may notice signs of exposure within minutes, hours, or days. Immediately notify other officers on the scene, your supervisor, dispatch, or emergency medical assistance. Follow the protocols described in the First Aid chapter when responding to fentanyl exposure, and refer to your agency's policies and procedures for administering naloxone.

QUESTIONED DOCUMENT EVIDENCE

☑ LE915.17.
Identify the types of questioned document evidence

A document is anything containing a mark to convey a message. Questioned documents need examination to verify that they could be evidence. Questioned documents may also contain latent fingerprints and DNA. Carefully handle all documents found in a crime scene to preserve their conditions. Document analysts use a variety of scientific methods to examine documents for alterations, erasures, handwriting analysis, indentations, ink comparisons, and machine impressions. Analysis may answer questions about the document's authorship and authenticity.

When you find money at a crime scene, follow your agency's policies and procedures for handling it as evidence, and always be careful to avoid any appearance of impropriety. Should you believe money found at the scene is counterfeit, document it, and collect the money as evidence. Your agency will have a process for contacting and sending the money to the Secret Service. FCIC/NCIC maintains a database of counterfeit currency with information, such as:

- suspects under investigation
- any information that may lead to the apprehension of the counterfeiters
- the denomination, serial number, and location the suspect passed or transacted the money

CHAIN OF CUSTODY

When you recover evidence of any kind, begin a *chain of custody* to document everyone who handled the evidence as well as when, why, and what changes, if any, were made to it. A chain of custody document proves that the evidence submitted in court is the same evidence collected at the crime scene.

☑ LE915.18.
Describe how to initiate chain of custody

Follow your agency's policies and procedures for documenting chain of custody to help eliminate ethical and legal concerns about handling and preserving evidence. A property receipt, written or electronic, typically records the chain of custody. Florida law states that it is a felony to alter, destroy, conceal, or remove any record, document, or other item with the purpose of impairing its truth or availability in a criminal trial or investigation. The chain of custody for any item of evidentiary value will potentially encounter challenges in future court proceedings. For this reason, it is critical that the information on the chain of custody form is accurate and completed by every person who handled the evidence.

UNIT 2 FOLLOW-UP INVESTIGATION

LESSON 1 Review Initial Information and Pursue Leads

Lesson Goal

At the end of this lesson, you will know how to initiate a follow-up investigation through incident report analysis, by following leads, and by working with field contacts and confidential sources of information.

Think About This

After returning to the station from an animal cruelty call, your supervisor states that you need to conduct the follow-up investigation on the call. What steps will you take, and what resources will you need to complete this process?

INITIATE A FOLLOW-UP INVESTIGATION

A follow-up investigation is a continuation of the initial investigation to determine if a crime occurred; however, it can also complete the investigation by identifying a suspect. Agency policies and procedures determine to what extent you will pursue a follow-up investigation. In some agencies, this responsibility lies with the investigations section. In other agencies, responsibility for follow-up investigations may fall to the primary officer dispatched to the call. Regardless of who completes the follow-up investigation, the tools and skills required to complete the investigation are the same.

When initiating a follow-up investigation, review the preliminary report to identify the investigative leads to pursue. A follow-up investigation can include contacting witnesses, victims, and potential suspects; reviewing evidence; locating additional evidence; and writing a capias request, probable cause affidavit, or arrest warrant. The prosecutor may need more information to make a filing decision and may request a follow-up investigation.

☑ LE921.1. Describe how to initiate a follow-up investigation

ANALYZE INCIDENT REPORTS

To begin a follow-up investigation, locate and review the records of the initial or preliminary investigation, and establish a case file as required by your agency. Compare the list of victims, witnesses, and suspects with the case information to ensure its accuracy; review listed evidence; and determine if there is evidence that has not yet been located or analyzed. Identify any witnesses who were not available for an interview at the time of the incident or crime.

Identify collected evidence that needs further processing or examination. If there is a potential suspect, identify evidence that may connect the suspect to the victim and the crime scene. Conduct a criminal history check to determine whether the suspect has fingerprints on file for comparison to any latent fingerprints found at the crime scene.

FOLLOW LEADS

☑ LE921.2. Explain how to identify leads

A lead provides more information on a case that requires further investigation. Leads create avenues for follow-up and can come from many sources, such as anonymous tips, confidential sources, social media, forensic analysis, surveillance footage, and victim and witness statements.

☑ LE921.3. Explain how to determine the value and validity of leads

Evaluate and document all leads to determine their value and prioritize them for follow-up based on content. Leads such as latent fingerprint identification and DNA that identify a suspect can be high-priority leads. Anonymous tips with little detail can be low-priority leads; however, they may still produce valuable information.

Determine whether officers conducted a canvass of the area near the crime scene. If a canvass occurred, identify any residences or businesses where law enforcement was unable to contact potential witnesses. You may need to conduct a secondary canvass of the area surrounding the incident or crime scene to make contact with people at homes or businesses where there was no response during the initial canvass. Consider re-canvassing the same homes or businesses for any additional information.

Interviewing medical personnel and analyzing victim injuries can also provide information related to a crime. Remember to follow HIPAA regulations.

FIELD CONTACTS AND CONFIDENTIAL SOURCES OF INFORMATION

Field contacts are common sources of information that are developed through community policing and can assist you in completing an investigation. A ***field contact*** is any person you have contact with while on patrol—such as a concerned resident or an anonymous complainant—who does not necessarily generate an incident report.

☑ LE921.4. Recognize the importance of building relationships for sources of information

Field contacts are often key to solving a case. Follow the guidelines outlined in community policing when maintaining relationships with members of the community and establishing a network of sources of information.

Field contact information can be helpful; however, evaluate this information carefully. Consider who the contact is and what their relationship to the victim or suspect may be. Even though a person with an agenda may not always be a good source of accurate information, they may provide names or other leads worth following.

Verify a field contact's information using known case facts or information from public records or following other leads. For example, if a field contact provides a suspect's vehicle description and location, you can use this information to check if it matches the information from the facts of the case. If it does, follow that lead. If information from the field contact is substantial, document the information in your field notes, as required by chapter 119, F.S. Information from a field contact may be exempt from use if it relates to an active investigation or intelligence. Forward the information to the appropriate department within your agency as this information may be valuable to another ongoing investigation.

There is a difference between a field contact and a confidential source. As discussed in Chapter 1, confidential sources are people who furnish police with information about crimes, primarily for personal benefit or advantage and rarely out of a sense of civic duty. Both provide information; however, a confidential source may or may not receive compensation for information. Never promise a field contact or a confidential source any type of reward, favor, or reduced sentence.

☑ LE921.5. Differentiate between the roles of field contacts and confidential sources

There is also a difference between a confidential source and a documented confidential informant. A documented confidential informant is a type of confidential source that an officer recruits and manages based on their agency's guidelines. Your agency will provide special training for officers who work with confidential informants, which includes preserving the safety of the confidential informant, law enforcement officers, the suspect, and the public.

UNIT 2 FOLLOW-UP INVESTIGATION
LESSON 2 Gather Information on an Unknown Suspect

Lesson Goal

At the end of this lesson, you will know how to gather information on an unknown suspect through crime patterns and a suspect's modus operandi.

Developing an unknown suspect takes a team approach, often with the help of an outside agency or an analyst.

MODUS OPERANDI

In criminal investigations, **modus operandi (MO)**, a Latin phrase meaning "mode of operating," refers to a distinct pattern of criminal behavior or procedure that is used to identify someone. People are creatures of habit. If something works one time, they tend to think it should work the next time.

☑ LE922.1. Describe how to find an unknown suspect based on modus operandi

This pattern often shows up in criminal activity. The same person or group may have committed similar crimes that follow a pattern or the same or similar MO. These similarities are important information. A person's modus operandi may include repeatedly using the same method of entry when committing burglaries, stealing similar types of items, choosing victims who share similar characteristics, such as age, gender, and ethnicity, or committing their crimes with similar locations, days, and times.

CRIME PATTERNS

☑ LE922.2. Identify criminal suspects based on crime patterns

Develop potential suspects by locating reports of crimes similar to the crime you are investigating. Review reports for similarities such as type of crime scene, time, and day of occurrences, methods and points of entry and exit, and evidence found at the scenes. Review reports in which suspects were arrested and look at similarities in MO.

If you find two or more crimes that appear to have been committed by the same suspect, an MO can help you narrow the field of suspects. It can also help you determine the suspect's motivation, skill, experience, transportation, age, and size. For example, a burglary suspect, who commonly enters through small bathroom windows more than 5 feet high with no evidence of using a ladder, is likely tall and thin or very agile. A suspect who steals property that is large and heavy, such as a large screen television, will likely have a medium- to large-sized vehicle.

When comparing the MO, consider the following questions:

- Was the crime well-planned or committed impulsively?
- If there was entry into a building or vehicle, was it forcible, or was a key or lockpick used?

- Did the suspect use other tools? If so, what kind of tools?
- If theft was involved, what was stolen, and how much did the suspect take?
- What damage was done, and why? Did the suspect vandalize items that they could not take? Did the suspect do careless damage to things that got in the way in order to access a door or fence?
- If this was a crime against a person, what weapon, if any, did the suspect use? What verbal commands did the suspect give? What was the physical description of the suspect?
- What was the motivation for the crime? Was it profit, revenge, fun, opportunity, hate?
- Did the suspect use any other resources in the crime?
- Were any unexplained items left at the scene?

Consider searching the Department of Correction's list of released inmates or the supervision status of former inmates. It may provide web-based information on all incarcerated and supervised offenders. Use this database to compare release dates of certain types of offenders with currently developing crime trends.

UNIT 2 FOLLOW-UP INVESTIGATION
LESSON 3 Gather Information on a Known Suspect

Lesson Goal

At the end of this lesson, you will know how to gather information from additional sources when searching for a known suspect or wanted person.

GATHERING INFORMATION

Having a known suspect might appear easier than having an unknown suspect; however, this is just the beginning of the follow-up investigation. Officers must find the suspect and then connect the suspect to the crime and the crime scene for a successful prosecution.

LE923.1. Describe sources of information for a known suspect

When you have a possible known suspect, learn as much as you can about the suspect. A check of public records, criminal history, law enforcement reports, interview reports, driving records, and traffic citations can provide valuable information about your suspect. Public records can provide you with current and prior addresses. Knowing where a suspect has resided can help you locate the suspect, recover stolen property, and identify other crimes with the suspect's MO and any criminal associates. Incident reports and traffic citations can provide you with information about the suspect's whereabouts at the times of reported crimes. Criminal history and law enforcement reports can provide you with information regarding MO.

When gathering information, there are two main types of records—private and public. Private records of privately-owned businesses or organizations, including privately owned utilities, are not open to the public or law enforcement and require court orders to access them.

Public records of government entities and publicly owned utilities are records that, with few exceptions, you may access on demand. Public records from federal, state, county, and city databases can provide additional information regarding the suspect's address, employment information, and other essential facts. Agency policies and procedures dictate which databases are available to you and how you can access them. Social media can provide considerable information regarding a suspect.

Records pertaining to juvenile arrests and incidents with law enforcement are restricted from the public by Florida law. The Florida Statutes do not restrict law enforcement's access to juvenile information through criminal justice agencies; however, there may be limits on how you may use that information. School resource officers are a good source of information regarding juvenile offenders.

SEARCHING FOR A KNOWN SUSPECT OR WANTED PERSON

Review information from the initial incident report, and victim and witness statements, to get a physical description of the suspect. Should the initial report lack adequate information, re-interview the victim and any witnesses, and follow any leads of known associates or family members.

After obtaining the suspect's full name and demographics, conduct criminal justice database searches on DAVID and FCIC/NCIC to compile an accurate physical description of the suspect, address, or vehicle. This combined information can provide a likely location of the wanted person, including their residence, place of employment, or public or private locations that they regularly visit. Remember that you may need a warrant.

☑ LE923.2. Explain how to determine the location of a suspect or wanted person

Maintain constant contact with dispatch when physically searching for a wanted person, and update your location and status to maintain a high level of officer safety. This information is critical when searching for an armed suspect. If you are unable to arrest the wanted person, initiate a BOLO for the suspect, and pass any suspect information to the next shift and the appropriate department within your agency.

☑ LE923.3. Describe how to maintain contact with dispatch when searching for a suspect or wanted person

Depending on agency resources, the threat level of the suspect, and the location of the suspect, you may need additional officers to make an arrest. Take immediate action when arresting a wanted person who is suspected of committing a violent crime and who presents an immediate danger to the public. Agency resources that can assist in searching for a wanted person may include canine, aerial support, SWAT, or a fugitive taskforce.

☑ LE923.4. Identify additional resources when arresting a suspect or wanted person

UNIT 2 FOLLOW-UP INVESTIGATION
LESSON 4 Showup, Photographic Array, and Photo Lineup

ⓞ Lesson Goal

At the end of this lesson, you will be able to conduct a showup and a live or photo lineup that is legally defensible in court.

Think About This

You respond to a bank robbery in progress. When you arrive, the clerk tells you that the robber has already left the bank and fled down the street. What actions can you take to identify the suspect?

SHOWUP

A *showup* is the presentation of a possible suspect to a witness for identification, and it occurs at the same time or soon after the incident occurred and near the incident or crime scene.

☑ LE924.1. Explain when it is appropriate to use a showup

Use a showup in an immediate situation, such as battery or robbery by sudden snatching, as it can result in an immediate arrest. Typically, the officer who identifies the potential suspect will detain the suspect. Do not move the potential suspect to bring them to the victim or witness. The primary responding or backup officer will take the victims and witnesses separately to that officer's location to identify the potential suspect; for example, in separate patrol vehicles. To avoid the potential suspect from being able to see the victim or witness, use vehicles with a dark window tint.

Before conducting a showup, do the following:

- Interview all victims or witnesses separately to obtain a description of the suspect.
- Determine if the victim or witness has personal knowledge of the crime (the victim or witness saw the suspect clearly enough to identify the suspect's features).
- Determine if the victim or witness has the ability to accurately discuss the matter, directly or through an interpreter, and clearly understands their duty to tell the truth.
- Determine if the victim or witness demonstrates competence, attentiveness, a sound state of mind, and a lack of prejudice.
- Determine if a suspect matching the victim's or witness's description has been located near the incident.
- If there are multiple victims or witnesses, determine if circumstances will allow the prompt display of a single suspect to each victim or witness.

Showups are suggestive by nature. You can minimize this by using proper procedure.

To conduct a legally defensible showup, you must do the following:

- Coordinate the showup as quickly as possible, without compromising the investigation, to limit the legal impact of the suspect's detention.
- Caution the victim or witness that the person they will be looking at may or may not be the suspect. Avoid providing any verbal or non-verbal feedback to the victim or witness during the identification process.
- Take the victim or witness to the location of the suspect, not the suspect to the victim or witness.
- Ask the victim or witness if they recognize the suspect; do so in a way that avoids influencing the identification.
- Make sure that there is adequate lighting for the victim or witness to have a clear view of the potential suspect.
- Visually conceal the victim or witness from the suspect.
- Consider recording the showup with your body camera or other recording device.
- Document all statements of identification and non-identification. Document any comment made by the victim or witness during the entire process, word for word. Document any non-verbal communication or action that the victim or witness makes. If a victim or witness cannot identify the suspect, document why.

☑ LE924.2. Describe how to conduct a legally defensible showup

LINEUPS

When a showup is not a consideration or is unsuccessful in identifying a suspect, a lineup should become a part of your follow-up investigation. A lineup can be a live lineup or a photo lineup. Florida law provides requirements that all law enforcement officers must follow when conducting a lineup, whether a live lineup or a photo lineup.

☑ LE924.3. Differentiate the procedures for a live lineup and a photo lineup

Live Lineup

A *live lineup* is a procedure that displays a group of people to a victim or eyewitness, so they can identify the perpetrator of a crime and eliminate any suspects. An *eyewitness* is a person who can identify another person by sight as someone involved in a criminal proceeding. Live lineups are resource-intensive as the agency must schedule additional people who look similar to the suspect to appear with the suspect in the lineup.

Photo Lineup

A photo lineup is an alternative to a live lineup. A *photo lineup* is a procedure that displays a photo array to a victim or eyewitness, so they can identify the perpetrator of a crime and eliminate any suspects.

Photo Array

A *photo array* is a selection of photographs compiled to show to a victim or eyewitness, in a non-suggestive manner, in order to identify a suspect. When used in a photo lineup, a photo array is an efficient tool; it is usually easier to compile an adequate number

☑ LE924.4. Describe the function and development of a photo array

of photographs of people who look similar to the suspect than to assemble a group of people who resemble the suspect. A photo array should have a minimum of six photographs, which includes a minimum of five filler photographs with only one photograph of the suspect. Filler photographs are photographs of people other than the suspect that complete the array. Each photograph should be of a different person with physical characteristics similar to those of the suspect, all formatted alike.

ADMINISTRATORS

☑ LE924.5. Recognize the roles of the independent administrator and lineup administrator

A lineup administrator is the person who conducts the lineup. Ideally, the lineup administrator should be independent of the investigation. An independent administrator is a person who is not participating in the investigation of the criminal offense and is unaware of which person in the lineup is the suspect. The independent administrator should conduct the lineup and provide instructions to the victim or witness.

When an independent administrator is not available, you will assume the role of the lineup administrator, and you must use one of these accepted procedures for conducting a photo lineup:

- an automated computer program that can automatically administer the photo lineup directly and prevents the lineup administrator from seeing the lineup until after the procedure is complete
- randomly numbered, shuffled folders containing photographs that are presented to the eyewitness in such a way that the lineup administrator cannot see which photos correspond to specific folders until after the procedure is complete

The intent is that the structure of the lineup achieves neutral administration and prevents the lineup administrator from knowing which photograph is being presented to the victim or witness. Regardless of what method you use, do not allow the lineup administrator to see or track which photograph the victim or eyewitness is viewing until after the procedure is completed.

PHOTO ARRAY PRESENTATIONS

Number all photographs and filler photographs used in the array before presenting the array to the victim or eyewitness. The photo lineup can occur simultaneously or sequentially.

☑ LE924.6. Differentiate between simultaneous and sequential presentations

Simultaneous presentation occurs when the independent administrator presents a group of photographs to the victim or eyewitness all at once and at the same time. When the independent administrator is presenting the photo array simultaneously, they will instruct the victim or eyewitness to mark which photograph is the suspect and have the victim or eyewitness sign and date the array.

Sequential presentation occurs when an independent administrator presents individual photographs to the victim or eyewitness one at a time.

Agency policies and procedures will specifically indicate whether simultaneous, sequential, or both methods of conducting the photo array are authorized. Consult your agency's legal adviser or the state attorney's office that is handling investigations for help selecting the authorized method.

You will obtain a sworn statement from the victim or eyewitness regarding the lineup results.

ACKNOWLEDGEMENT

No matter the method used, the independent administrator will read standardized instructions to the victim or eyewitness to ensure consistent administration of the photo lineup.

The victim or eyewitness must acknowledge receiving the instructions before reviewing the photo array. If they refuse to sign the acknowledgment, document the refusal and sign the acknowledgment yourself.

☑ LE924.7. Describe how to instruct the eyewitness to sign the acknowledgment

The Florida Statutes mandate using these instructions; however, your agency's policies and procedures may add additional instructions.

Eyewitness Instructions

1. The perpetrator might or might not be in the lineup.
2. The lineup administrator does not know the suspect's identity *(except that this instruction need not be given when a specified and approved alternative method of neutral administration is used).*
3. You should not feel compelled to make an identification.
4. It is as important to exclude innocent persons as it is to identify the perpetrator.
5. The investigation will continue with or without your identification.

Carefully document or record, word for word, any comment that the victim or eyewitness makes during the entire lineup process. Note any non-verbal communication or action of the victim or eyewitness in the investigative file. If the victim or eyewitness makes an identification, document the precise photograph they select. If the victim or eyewitness is unable to identify a suspect, document why. Preserve the entire photo array as evidence. Document the process and the forms used in the lineup in the investigative file.

☑ LE924.8. Explain how to document a lineup

UNIT 3 PREPARING FOR COURT
LESSON 1 Testimony

Lesson Goal

At the end of this lesson, you will know how to prepare for and give courtroom testimony as well as respond appropriately to cross-examination tactics.

Think About This

You are scheduled to testify in court on a case that happened over six months ago. How will you prepare?

PREPARING FOR A PRETRIAL MEETING

Testifying in court can be a stressful experience. When it is your turn to speak, everyone in the courtroom is looking at you and listening to what you have to say. The defense attorney or judge may challenge your answers and cross-examine you, presenting a situation where you may become flustered and make mistakes. Begin to prepare for this event now and make sure that you participate in the mock trial that accompanies this lesson.

☑ LE931.1. Describe how to prepare for a pretrial meeting

Before a pretrial meeting, thoroughly review all the available case documentation. Discuss the case with the appropriate agency personnel, such as your supervisor, watch commander, or crime scene and evidence personnel. Be prepared to discuss the questions of who, what, when, where, why, and how related to the facts of the case, all evidence, and any other information relevant to your involvement in the case.

The prosecutor will ask you to provide details on the case, so you must know or have access to everything about the case. Be familiar with all of the issues that could affect a successful prosecution. For example, the prosecutor may discuss the admissibility of evidence and may ask you to bring evidence to the trial, and they will ask about any evidence that was obtained. Identify whether evidence supports or does not support the facts presented in the probable cause affidavit, and never enhance facts or manufacture evidence to fill in for any missing elements of the crime. Remain truthful, honest, and accurate when discussing the case with the prosecutor.

Try to identify potential weaknesses in the case. Help the prosecutor effectively deal with known problems by pointing out any conflicting statements or problems in the documentation of evidence and the errors you or another officer may have made. You have a continuing obligation to keep the prosecutor informed of any developments in the case.

You must know the case well enough to identify any special issues or situations that may require special arrangements, such as an interpreter, an appropriate supervisor for a child witness, and necessary accommodations for people with disabilities.

PREPARE FOR TESTIMONY

To prepare for a court proceeding, such as a deposition, hearing, or trial, review the reports that you created as well as the complete case file, including all other reports, photos, videos, evidence, and the chain of custody.

☑ LE931.2. Explain how to prepare for testimony

Discuss the case with the state attorney's office to identify and understand areas of weakness relevant to testimony and to clarify any concerns that the state attorney may have. Identify witness information and give it to the state attorney's office, and be prepared to answer questions on all relevant facts and to testify from memory. You will refer to reports only for specific details and only after requesting permission to refer to them. The court can use case documentation to identify correct and credible answers. Assume that the defense attorney knows everything you know. With full preparation, you can meet your legal and ethical obligations to give the important facts when the state attorney or defense attorney begins the line of questioning.

Checking in with the prosecutor and following their instructions gives you and the prosecutor time to address last-minute concerns. Recognize that a prosecutor usually has a large docket of cases and goes from one case to another every day, so the prosecutor may ask you to go over relevant details and major facts one more time. Never take a case lightly.

- Always prepare for testimony the same way.
- Review all case documentation.
- Discuss the case with the prosecutor.
- Follow the guidelines for giving an effective testimony.

PROVIDE TESTIMONY

Giving testimony may take place in an attorney's office, in the judge's chambers, or on the witness stand. In the courtroom or the judge's chambers, the involved parties will usually refer to the attorneys as "counsel."

Professional Demeanor

If you are to appear at a trial or hearing before or after a shift, look professional and dress in uniform unless your agency has differing policies. Remove objects, such as keys and loose change, from your pockets, and turn off radios and cell phones as these may cause distractions. How you prepare and present yourself can affect the success of your testimony. Always use good posture, be attentive, and place your hands on your knees or the arms of the chair and never over your mouth. Convey confidence, not arrogance or evasion, and avoid fidgeting or showing other signs of nervousness.

Rule of Sequestration

Sometimes a judge invokes the *rule of sequestration*, which forbids anyone who will testify from discussing any aspect of a case with anyone but the involved attorneys.

You are not permitted inside the courtroom or within hearing distance of the courtroom when other witnesses are giving testimony. Florida law states that you must follow the judge's orders completely when they invoke or impose the rule. Violating the rule of sequestration may mean the judge will penalize or punish the witness. The judge may instruct the jury to disregard the testimony of the witness or strike it from the record. The judge could even declare a mistrial. Whether or not the judge invokes the rule, you must never communicate with a juror or known potential juror, except as directed by the court. If you observe a possible violation, report it immediately to the courtroom bailiff or the judge.

Before testifying, you will take an oath or make an affirmation that your testimony is the truth. Typically, the clerk of the court, a court reporter, the judge, or another designated court personnel will ask you to raise your right hand and then ask, "Do you swear or affirm to tell the truth and nothing but the truth?" In a firm way, answer, "I do." Do this while standing or sitting up straight, and looking at and listening attentively to the person administering the oath. You are now required to testify truthfully.

Answer Questions

☑ LE931.3. Explain how to testify

Look directly at the attorney or judge and listen carefully to the questions they ask. When an attorney or judge asks questions, pause before answering to collect your thoughts. Make sure that you understand the questions and that you answer them accurately, clearly, and completely. Pausing also gives the prosecutor time to object if the question is objectionable. If necessary, you can state that you do not understand a question or you can ask the judge or attorney to clarify or repeat the question.

Never volunteer additional information; only answer the question that is asked. However, you can respond to closed-ended questions with more than a yes or no answer if the answer requires a more detailed explanation, but never answer a question with a guess. It is acceptable to say, "I don't know," when necessary. The judge may permit you to explain why you do not know. Resist the urge to fill silence with extra testimony.

Things to Avoid

Avoid suggestions to enhance your testimony or to strengthen a case as you could be committing perjury. Do not alter your answer to match someone else's, even if it means giving testimony that contradicts that of another officer. Because a court reporter is documenting what people in the courtroom are saying, the court can use earlier testimony to rebuke you later in the court process. Testifying truthfully keeps your testimony consistent, makes it credible, and keeps you out of trouble.

The appearance of prejudice destroys credibility. Avoid showing biases and prejudices, and always use plain, professional language—not slang or police jargon. For example, do not state that you are "burning my CI"; instead, state that you are "revealing the identity of my confidential informant." Avoid derogatory statements, sarcasm, witty comments, or ridicule as these are all unprofessional.

Avoid speaking in a monotone. Use of military time is appropriate, but be prepared to convert times to a.m. or p.m. Be courteous and use proper titles such as "your Honor," "ma'am," and "sir." Face the judge while responding to the judge's questions, and face the jury when responding to the prosecutor or the defense attorney.

Never address or refer to the defense attorney as a public defender. Doing so can cause a mistrial as it may make the jury aware that the defendant cannot afford other representation.

If you or a close relative is the victim of a crime, you may feel a need to ensure the "proper" prosecution of all defendants. However, you must not let personal experiences and beliefs affect your ability to be fair and objective. This principle also applies to cultural, ethnic, and gender issues. Avoid displaying extraordinary interest in the case. Display interest of a professional nature and not a personal one.

All answers to relevant questions are for the record as the court will record testimony. Your job is to provide an accurate and complete testimony of the available facts, not to steer the case.

OBJECTIONABLE QUESTIONS

Just as with a deposition, attorneys may occasionally ask improper questions. Maintain the same demeanor for the defense attorney and the prosecutor; do not change your attitude when responding to the opposing counsel's questions. Challenging your credibility is the opposing counsel's job and is usually not personal.

Once someone makes an objection, the judge will either sustain or overrule it. If you hear an objection, stop speaking until the judge rules. If the judge sustains the objection, you should not answer the question, and if the judge overrules the objection, you must answer the question.

☑ LE931.4. Describe how to respond to objectionable questions

There are several types of objectionable questions. One type calls for someone to make a conclusion. Answering this type of question requires you to make a decision on an issue, which is the job of the jury or judge. For example: "Based on your knowledge of the facts of this incident, would you say that Mr. and Mrs. Smith have a violent relationship?" Irrelevant questions may prompt you to give answers that have no direct bearing on the facts. For example: "Officer, are you married?" Some questions go beyond the proper scope of questioning, having nothing to do with the case. For example: "Do you arrest more men than women?" Remember that you can always pause to give the state attorney time to object when the question is objectionable.

CROSS-EXAMINATION TACTICS

Attorneys may use a variety of tactics during a criminal trial to discredit, misrepresent, or confuse you. Be aware of this, and go into court with basic techniques to overcome those tactics.

LE931.5. Describe how to respond to cross-examination tactics

A defense attorney may try to give the impression that you are inept, unreliable, or lacking in confidence.

> **Question:** "You mean to tell this court and jury that you have made only one prior arrest? Is it true you had been a sworn officer for only three months when you arrested Mr. Smith?"

> **Technique:** Convey professionalism, knowledge, and confidence and give firm, decisive answers. If necessary, the state attorney will ask appropriate follow-up questions.

A defense attorney may be confrontational or badger you to make you angry. The defense attorney hopes to affect logic and calmness and reveal your temperament.

> **Question:** "I have asked this question three different times in three different ways. What do you not understand?"

> **Technique:** Pause, stay calm, remember the defense attorney's motive, and speak deliberately.

A defense attorney may fire questions at you rapidly, giving you no time to think about or answer the questions properly. The attorney hopes to confuse you into giving inconsistent answers.

> **Question:** "Did you actually see Mr. Smith hit his wife? How do you know what really happened? Where was Mrs. Smith in relation to Mr. Smith when you first arrived?"

> **Technique:** Ask the attorney to repeat the questions one at a time and take time to consider each question one at a time. Speak deliberately and remain calm.

To get as much information as possible and to lull you into a false sense of security, a defense attorney may try to build rapport to create answers that favor the defense. The defense attorney may also try to lead you to say that you are an expert when that is not the case.

> **Question:** "I didn't realize you knew so much about domestic violence. Do you consider yourself an expert on the subject? You should!"

> **Technique:** Stay alert and control your ego. Focus on the facts of the case, and do not let the attorney's statements become confusing or distracting.

By mispronouncing your name, forgetting your title, or verbally demoting you, a defense attorney implies that you are of little significance. The attorney wants you to lose concentration and focus on the error, not the question.

> **Question:** "Sergeant Harrington? You said Mr. Jones was caught breaking into the back door with a tire tool. Is that correct? Oh, I'm sorry. You're a Captain. Whatever. Just answer the question."

> **Technique:** The first time that the defense attorney uses your wrong name, title, or rank, politely correct them. If the attorney persists, ignore their behavior and focus on the question.

A defense attorney may draw a conclusion, make an assumption, or suggest a response and then ask you if that is your answer. The attorney wants to confuse or mislead you.

> **Question:** "Your entire testimony here today actually points to Mrs. Smith as the aggressor, correct?"

> **Technique:** Correct inaccuracies, and avoid letting the attorney use them to draw incorrect conclusions. By concentrating carefully on the facts and answering the question accurately without expressing opinions, you will not let the defense attorney succeed in baiting you.

To prevent the judge or jury from considering pertinent facts and details, a defense attorney may demand a "yes" or "no" answer to a question that needs explanation.

> **Question:** "Did you see the gun in the defendant's hand or not? Yes or no?"

> **Technique:** Qualify your answer by saying that you cannot answer, "yes" or "no," then give the facts and details such as saying, "I cannot tell you yes or no. All I can tell you is that I saw a small shiny object in the defendant's left hand."

A defense attorney may reverse or rephrase your words, intending to convince the jury that you lack confidence in your own statement.

> **Question:** "Where did you see them in relation to the car?"

> **Officer:** "They stood toward the front."

> **Question:** "So they were standing at the front bumper?"

Officer: "They stood between the tire and front door."

Question: "But you just told us they were near the front of the car, right?"

Technique: Pay attention to what the attorney asks. Pause and avoid agreeing to misstatements. Always listen intently whenever the attorney repeats an answer, remember what they said, and correct any error they make in restating the answer.

A defense attorney may repeat and rephrase questions, hoping you will give inconsistent answers.

Question: "Was the defendant riding a green or red bicycle?"

Officer: "It was blue."

Question: "Was she riding in the dark?"

Officer: "Yes."

Question: "Could it have been green, blue-green, or black?"

Officer: "I already answered."

Technique: Pay attention to what the attorney asks. Provide the correct answer, avoid displaying frustration, and restate the correct answer.

Chapter 10
Traffic Incidents

UNIT 1 TRAFFIC BASICS
- LESSON 1 Traffic Law and Legal Terms / 391
- LESSON 2 The Florida Driver License, Registration, and Insurance / 394
- LESSON 3 The Uniform Traffic Citation / 401

UNIT 2 RESOLVING TRAFFIC INCIDENTS
- LESSON 1 Parking Violations / 405
- LESSON 2 Abandoned, Disabled, or Unattended Vehicles / 406
- LESSON 3 Search and Inventory of an Impounded Vehicle / 408
- LESSON 4 Directing Traffic / 410

UNIT 1 TRAFFIC BASICS
LESSON 1 Traffic Law and Legal Terms

Lesson Goal

At the end of this lesson, you will know basic traffic definitions and legal terms as well as identify common traffic violations.

The primary goal of traffic enforcement is to encourage drivers to comply with all traffic laws and to drive safely. Traffic enforcement includes all aspects of law enforcement related to vehicles, roadways, and pedestrians. This includes directing traffic, issuing citations, and handling unattended, abandoned, or disabled vehicles. This chapter will provide you with the necessary information about traffic laws and procedures and will lay the foundations for you to practice excellent traffic enforcement.

TRAFFIC ENFORCEMENT

Traffic enforcement will likely make up a large portion of your interaction with the public, and it involves more than writing citations for speeding or equipment violations. It covers all aspects of law enforcement related to vehicles, roadways, and pedestrians, including traffic stops. Because driving is such a primary means of transportation, it constitutes a major aspect of public safety and serves as a key point of contact between law enforcement and the public.

Through effective traffic enforcement and engagement with drivers, you can prevent or solve crimes and identify situations such as:

- car theft and carjacking
- people with outstanding warrants and escaped prisoners
- drivers with suspended licenses
- abused, kidnapped, and runaway children
- illegal weapons
- drug use or trafficking
- minors in possession of alcohol
- impaired drivers under the influence of alcohol or chemical or controlled substances
- criminals fleeing crime scenes
- uninsured motorists
- human trafficking
- terrorist activity

☑ LE1011.1. List the benefits of traffic enforcement

TRAFFIC LEGAL TERMS

To enforce traffic laws, you need to know some legal terms as they are defined in the Florida Statutes.

A *driver* is a person who is in physical control of a vehicle or is controlling or steering a vehicle in tow.

A *pedestrian* is a person on foot on a road, berm, shoulder, or sidewalk.

A *vehicle* is every device in, upon, or by which any person or property is or may be transported or drawn upon a highway, except personal delivery devices, mobile carriers, and devices used exclusively upon stationary rails or tracks. Examples of vehicles that you can pull over are a bicycle, an electric scooter, or a riding lawn mower.

A *motor vehicle* is:

- an automobile, motorcycle, truck, trailer, semitrailer, truck tractor and semitrailer combination, or any other vehicle operated on the roads, used to transport persons or property, and propelled by power other than muscular power
- a recreational vehicle designed as temporary living quarters for recreational, camping, or travel use, that is self-motorized or mounted on or pulled by another motor vehicle
- not a traction engine, road roller, personal delivery device, special mobile equipment, vehicle that runs only on a track, bicycle, swamp buggy, moped, or motorized scooter

An *autonomous vehicle* is equipped with technology that senses the environment and allows the vehicle to move on the road without a person actively controlling or monitoring, such as a driverless, self-driving, or robotic car.

A *roadway* (road) is a portion of a highway used for vehicular travel that does not include the berm, shoulder, or sidewalk.

A *street or highway* has several legal definitions:

- the entire width between the boundary lines of a public space for vehicular traffic
- the entire width between the boundary lines of privately owned space for vehicular traffic by the owner or those given permission by the owner; or any limited access road owned or controlled by a special district when a county or municipality exercises traffic control jurisdiction
- an area not open to public vehicular traffic, such as a runway, taxiway, ramp, clear zone, or parking lot within the boundaries of an airport owned by the state, county, municipality, or political subdivision
- a space used for vehicular traffic on a controlled access basis in a mobile home park recreation district and open to the public

A *laned highway* is a road divided into two or more clearly marked lanes for vehicular traffic.

A *limited access facility* is a road adjacent to private property to which the property owners have no right or easement to; however, the owners may have access to the light, air, or view over the property. Examples can include a road with signage prohibiting or limiting access for trucks, buses, or commercial vehicles.

A *private road or driveway* is a privately owned space that owners and people who have permission from the owners use for vehicular traffic.

A *state road* is a highway the Department of Transportation designates as a state-maintained road.

An *intersection* has two legal definitions:

- the area within the connection of the lateral curbs or boundary lines of two or more roadways of two highways joined at approximately right angles or any other angle that may connect the two roads
- where a highway includes two roadways 30 feet or more apart, every crossing of each roadway of the divided highway by an intersecting highway is a separate intersection

A *crosswalk* is an area of a road within an intersection, distinctly marked on the surface to indicate a pedestrian crossing. The marks connect the lateral lines of the sidewalks on opposite sides of the highway from the curbs or, in the absence of curbs, from the edges of the road.

A *sidewalk* is the area that pedestrians use between the curb, or lateral line of a roadway and the adjacent property lines.

A *bicycle path* is any road or path open to bicycle travel. An open space or a barrier separates a bicycle path from motorized vehicular traffic and is often located either within the highway right-of-way or within an independent right-of-way.

Traffic Statutes

Some traffic violations may result in criminal charges; others are civil infractions and non-criminal in nature, including moving and non-moving violations. Some infractions may require a mandatory court appearance. Many of the civil traffic infractions in chapters 316, 320, and 322, F.S., are punishable by fines, court costs, driving school, or community service hours. A driver with a civil traffic infraction does not face incarceration; they have no right to a trial by jury or court-appointed lawyer. The driver may elect a hearing before a judge or hearing officer. Refer to chapter 318, F.S., for ways to deal with a traffic infraction, including appeals, fees, and limitations.

☑ LE1011.2. Describe common non-criminal and criminal traffic violations

Chapter 316, F.S., provides regulations regarding bicyclist and pedestrian activities you should watch for to maintain roadway safety. For example, bicyclists should use lights at night and pedestrians should cross a roadway at a marked crosswalk.

UNIT 1 TRAFFIC BASICS
LESSON 2 The Florida Driver License, Registration, and Insurance

◎ Lesson Goal

At the end of this lesson, you will know the different formats of driver and vehicle licensing, proof of insurance requirements, and common licensing violations in Florida.

Think About This

You stop a vehicle at 11 p.m., and the driver hands their license to you. You see that the driver is 16. What do you do?

THE FLORIDA DRIVER LICENSE

The ***Florida driver license*** is issued to Florida residents who have passed the Florida Department of Highway Safety and Motor Vehicles (FLHSMV) tests, allowing them to legally drive in Florida. FLHSMV is the agency responsible for issuing driver licenses, motor vehicle titles, license plates, and vessel registrations. FLHSMV also issues Florida identification cards. A Florida ID card is not a driver license but a form of identification. Because it resembles a driver license, be careful not to confuse it for one. An individual cannot have both a valid driver license and a valid Florida ID card or more than one driver license.

☑ LE1012.1.
Describe what a driver in Florida must do when you request their driver license

All drivers in Florida must have a valid driver license from Florida, another state, or an entity approved by the state of Florida or the U.S. government. Drivers must show their driver license when asked by a law enforcement officer.

If you stop a vehicle and the driver is unable to produce a valid driver license, request another form of photo or military ID, or conduct a database query. If the driver is licensed but does not have the license with them, determine whether to issue a citation for failure to carry and exhibit the license upon demand and collect a fingerprint where it is required on the citation. A person may not legally operate a motor vehicle if they do not have a valid driver license.

☑ LE1012.2.
Describe how to verify that a driver is licensed to operate a motor vehicle

Florida law does not allow anyone to drive with a suspended, revoked, canceled, or disqualified license. The charge for doing this is a moving violation if the driver does not know their license is no longer valid. It is a misdemeanor if the driver knows that their license is suspended. It is a felony if a person habitually drives with a suspended license. A driver license also cannot be faded, altered, mutilated, or defaced. If you confiscate the driver's license due to suspension, mutilation, revocation, or altered data, dispose of it according to your agency policies and procedures.

Foreign visitors are not required to obtain an international driving permit. However, they must be in the country legally and carry a valid driver license from their country of origin while operating a motor vehicle.

LICENSE FORMAT

There are different formats of driver licenses that depend on the date the license was issued. You need to know the basic features of all formats, as you will encounter all in routine patrol and traffic enforcement.

Florida has three types of driver license:

- commercial
- non-commercial
- learner's

☑ LE1012.3.
Describe the types, classes, and formats of valid Florida driver licenses

The Florida driver license also has four classes: A, B, C, and E. The classes indicate what type of vehicle a driver can operate legally, and the gross vehicle weight rating (GVWR) of vehicle they are allowed to drive.

Licenses issued to drivers 21 and older have a horizontal format. Licenses issued to drivers younger than 21 have a vertical format. The color header of a license identifies the license type and class.

- Blue: Commercial Driver License (CDL)—Classes A, B, and C
- Green: Driver License—Class E
- Orange: Learner's License—Class E

A FLHSMV-issued identification card has a red header.

Florida's driver licenses have several security features that can only be seen under a black light.

Post-2017 Format

The currently issued Florida driver license has three headshots on the front, one of which is transparent. It also has a light blue Florida seal. On the back is another headshot and an image of the state of Florida that rests against ocean waves.

For qualified drivers, a red safe driver label appears near the front center of the card, above the issue date. A tactile feature appears on the bottom right side of the card, with designations located above the smaller headshot. For the front of the learner's license, a tactile feature appears on the bottom left side, with designations located on the bottom right of the card. The reverse side displays 1D and 2D barcodes.

Pre-2017 Format

Florida driver licenses issued before 2017 have a very different format. Card types and license classes are identified by the following color headers:

- Yellow: Learner's License—Class E
- Green: Driver License—Classes D and E
- Blue: Commercial Driver License (CDL)—Classes A, B, and C

An officer will need to closely inspect older formats to obtain required information, including the expiration date. Florida identification cards issued before 2017 have a pink/red header.

ENDORSEMENTS, RESTRICTIONS, AND DESIGNATIONS

☑ LE1012.4. Describe the endorsements, restrictions, and designations of Florida driver licenses

An *endorsement* is a special authorization printed on a Florida driver license permitting a driver to operate certain types of vehicles or transport certain types of property or number of passengers. Some examples of endorsements include operation of motorcycles, school buses, or combination vehicles with double or triple trailers.

A *restriction*, printed on a Florida driver license, may limit a driver from operating certain types of motor vehicles or require that they meet certain conditions when driving any motor vehicle. For example, someone who needs corrective lenses may be restricted from driving without them. Other restrictions may require a person who is hard of hearing to wear hearing aids when driving or require a driver without full use of their legs to have hand controls for the brake and accelerator.

A Florida driver license may also include *designations*, which inform you of a person's health condition or public safety status. For example, a license for a person with diabetes may display "insulin dependent" in red print. Designations are called informational alerts before 2017.

Endorsements, Restrictions, and Designations Beginning in 2017

Beginning in 2017, motorcycle-also and motorcycle-only endorsements are designated by an "A" or "O" in the endorsement field on the front of the card and by "A-MTRCL Also" or "O-MTRCL Only" on the back of the card. Motorcycle endorsements are not spelled out on the front of the license.

More information is available in the Driver and Vehicle Information Database (DAVID) for drivers who are deaf or hard of hearing, so that officers have the ability to see this information while running the driver's license. Chapter 6 discusses ways of interacting with people who are deaf or hard of hearing.

The following designations are required by law for individuals registered in the Florida Sexual Offender and Predator System. These appear on the front of the license in the bottom right corner:

- "Sexual Predator" for sexual predators
- "943.0435, F.S." for sexual offenders

Lifetime designations appear on the back of the license under the headshot and are represented by various symbols.

Endorsement, Restriction, or Designation	Symbol
Deaf/Hard of Hearing	🦻
Developmentally Disabled	**D**
FWC Lifetime Boater	⚓
FWC Lifetime Freshwater	🐟
FWC Lifetime Hunting	🦌
FWC Lifetime Saltwater	🐠
FWC Lifetime Sportsman's	🔫
Insulin Dependent	INSULIN DEP
Organ Donor	♥DONOR
Veteran	*V*ETERAN

Two designations can appear on the bottom right of a Florida driver license or ID card:

- D—upon request by a person who has a developmental disability, or by the parent or guardian of a child or ward who has a developmental disability, FLHSMV will issue a driver license or an identification card with a D.
- V—any honorably discharged U.S. military veteran may have a veteran designation placed on their driver license or ID card.

Pre-2017 Endorsements, Restrictions, and Designations

Before 2017, required endorsements and restrictions appear on the front of a driver license. Explanations of the endorsements and restrictions are on the back. For drivers authorized to operate a motorcycle, "Motorcycle Also" or "Motorcycle Only" appear on the front under the expiration date.

A sexual predator alert is indicated as "s. 775.21 F.S.," or a sexual offender alert as "s. 943.0435 F.S.," in the right corner in black.

CLASSES OF FLORIDA DRIVER LICENSES

☑ LE1012.5. Differentiate between the various classes of Florida driver licenses

Beginning in 2017, the license class type is located at the top right of the license, either near or below the Department of Homeland Security Real ID-compliant gold star emblem. Real ID-compliance means that Florida meets the federally established security standards for state-issued driver licenses and ID cards.

Licenses issued before the 2017 changes display the license class type on the front and back.

- CLASS A—required for drivers of trucks or truck combinations with a gross vehicle weight rating (GVWR) of 26,001 pounds or more, provided the towed vehicle is more than 10,000 pounds.

- CLASS B—required for drivers of straight trucks (all axles attached to a single frame) with a GVWR of 26,001 pounds or more.

- CLASS C—required for drivers of vehicles transporting placard-able amounts of hazardous materials, or for drivers of vehicles designed to transport more than 15 people (including the driver) with a GVWR of less than 26,001 pounds. You will learn more about hazardous materials and placards in Chapter 14.

- CLASS E—required for drivers of any non-commercial motor vehicle with a GVWR of less than 26,001 pounds. This includes passenger cars, 15-passenger (including the driver) vans, trucks or recreational vehicles, and two- or three-wheel motor vehicles 50 cc (cubic centimeters) or less, such as mopeds or small scooters. Farmers and drivers of authorized emergency vehicles are exempt from obtaining a commercial driver license, but they must obtain a Class E license.

- CLASS E Learner—required for drivers with a learner's license and limited to driving motor vehicles weighing less than 8,000 pounds. In addition, the driver must be accompanied by a person 21 or older who holds a valid driver license and who occupies the closest seat to the right of the driver. The learner may initially drive only during daylight hours. Three months after receiving the learner's license, they may drive until 10 p.m. A driver with a learner's license may not operate a motorcycle without a motorcycle endorsement. For more information on the Class E learner's license, visit the FLHSMV website.

There are six exemptions to the requirement to hold a commercial driver license.

Commercial Driver License (CDL) Exemptions

- Drivers of authorized emergency vehicles that are equipped with extraordinary audible warning devices (lights and sirens) that display red or blue lights and are on call to respond to emergencies
- Military personnel driving military vehicles
- Farmers transporting farm supplies or farm machinery, or transporting agricultural products to or from the first place of storage or processing or directly to or from market, within 150 miles of their farm
- Drivers of recreational vehicles used for recreational purposes
- Drivers who operate straight trucks (single units) that are exclusively transporting their own tangible personal property which is not for sale
- An employee of a publicly owned transit system who is limited to moving vehicles for maintenance or parking purposes exclusively within the restricted-access confines of a transit system's property

VEHICLE LICENSE PLATES

FLHSMV issues standard and specialized license plates. While the majority of specialized plates are "vanity" plates displaying the owner's nickname or commemorating a college, sports team, or cause, some have specific uses and restrictions. For example, some plates are limited to commercial or government vehicles. Others are based on the owner's status, such as a state legislator. There are also specialized plates that must have additional prefix characters or descriptions not preprinted on the plate. Some examples include various Florida universities, breast cancer awareness, antique vehicle, and Purple Heart plates.

☑ LE1012.6. Describe the format and components of valid Florida vehicle license plates and vehicle registrations

VEHICLE REGISTRATION

Any vehicle in the state of Florida must have a valid registration to operate on Florida roads. Vehicles with out-of-state registrations are required by law to be registered within 10 days of the owner either becoming employed, placing children in public school, or establishing residency. People who live in another state and commute to work in Florida are exempt from this licensure and tag requirement. However, their license and tag registration must be current in their state of residency.

Vehicles with expired registrations may not be operated legally on the roadways of Florida. Registrations are renewed semiannually, annually, or biannually. Registrations expire at midnight on the registered owner's birthday, with the exception of vehicles weighing more than 5,000 pounds gross vehicle weight (GVW). Any vehicle over 5,000 pounds GVW expires on December 31.

Validation Decal and Registration Card

A vehicle registration comes with a validation decal and registration card. The validation decal will have its own identification number, along with the month and year when the registration will expire. This will be displayed on the top right corner of the registered vehicle's license plate. The registration card contains important data unique to the registered vehicle and its owner. Appearing on the card are the decal number with the expiration date, and important vehicle information such as the plate number, vehicle description, and vehicle identification number (VIN) with the owner's name and address. Information from the license plate and vehicle registration must match.

PROOF OF INSURANCE

☑ LE1012.7.
Describe how to verify a driver's proof of insurance

Every owner of a motor vehicle in the state of Florida must register the vehicle and must maintain property damage liability insurance. When a driver fails to show valid and current proof of insurance in paper or electronic form, it is a non-moving violation. If a driver presents you with an electronic form, only view the document and nothing else on the device. FLHSMV may suspend a license or put a seize tag order on a registration for an owner who does not maintain liability insurance. The only way to verify the current validity of the insurance information is for the operator to provide a current hard copy or digital copy of their insurance card.

COMMON DRIVER AND VEHICLE LICENSING VIOLATIONS

☑ LE1012.8.
Describe common driver and vehicle licensing violations

While on patrol, you will encounter several types of driver and vehicle licensing violations. The most common violations will involve the improper or unlawful use of vehicle registrations or driver licenses. The following table lists examples of statutes commonly violated and the associated licensing violations.

Examples of Statutes Commonly Violated

Statute	Description	Violation
s. 320.0605, F.S.	Certificate of registration; possession required	Failure to display registration
s. 320.07, F.S.	Expiration of registration	Operating a motor vehicle/using a mobile home with an expired registration
s. 320.131, F.S.	Temporary tags	Unlawful use of temporary tag
s. 322.03, F.S.	Drivers must be licensed; penalties	No driver license
s. 322.15, F.S.	License to be carried and exhibited on demand; fingerprint to be imprinted upon a citation	Driver license not carried/exhibited on demand
s. 322.16, F.S.	License restrictions	Violation of restriction
s. 322.32, F.S.	Unlawful use of license	Possession/display/permitting use of suspended/revoked/canceled/disqualified driver license
s. 322.34, F.S.	Driving while license suspended, revoked, canceled, or disqualified	Operating vehicle while driver license suspended/revoked/canceled/disqualified

UNIT 1 TRAFFIC BASICS
LESSON 3 The Uniform Traffic Citation

Ⓞ Lesson Goal

At the end of this lesson, you will know when and how to issue an electronic or paper uniform traffic citation (UTC).

The *uniform traffic citation (UTC)* is for traffic offenses described in chapters 316, 318, 320, and 322, F.S. The UTC form is the only report that you need to complete for a traffic offense, unless it is a crash scene; then a traffic crash report is also required. Traffic crash reports are discussed in Chapter 12, Traffic Crash Investigations. The UTC is used if the officer believes that the violation was due to the aggressive careless driving by the operator or for failure to stop at a traffic signal. Use the UTC for certain non-traffic felonies and misdemeanors that can result in suspension or revocation of the person's driver license. You must issue a citation to anyone accused of any offense that requires revocation of a driver license, according to s. 316.650, F.S.

Many agencies use the electronic version of this form; other agencies use the paper book format. Complete both forms the same way.

ELECTRONIC UTC

When you complete an electronic citation, electronically submit the citation to the clerk of the court's office. You may have to print a copy of the citation for your agency before electronically submitting it. Give the driver a copy of the UTC. The driver may request that you send them a copy of the UTC via email or they may request a printed copy. Follow your agency policies and procedures regarding electronic citations.

☑ LE1013.1.
Describe how to issue an electronic uniform traffic citation (UTC)

PAPER UTC

If using the paper format, your agency will assign UTC books with a preprinted number. It is your responsibility to account for each UTC in this book. If a UTC is lost or destroyed before you give it to the driver, document the circumstances of the loss or destruction in the UTC book. It is official misconduct to dispose of a UTC in a manner other than as required by s. 316.650, F.S. FLHSMV tracks all UTC numbers to ensure integrity in issuing citations. Each law enforcement agency must keep records of and account for all citations supplied to them.

☑ LE1013.2.
Describe your responsibility to account for assigned UTC books

There is a receipt on the front of the UTC book that you must sign to acknowledge that you received the book. Your agency may have additional procedures for assigning citation books and may use these receipts to assist with internal control and record-keeping. Once you sign a receipt for a UTC book, inspect the book to make sure that the citations are in correct numeric sequence and that the book contains 25 three-part citations. Inspect the sequential numbers assigned to the book to make sure that the numbers on the book are the same as the numbers on the citations contained in the book and listed on your receipt.

FLHSMV maintains an inventory of each UTC book distributed to a specific agency. Agencies cannot transfer UTC books to other agencies. If you leave employment with an agency, turn your UTC books over to your immediate supervisor. FLHSMV periodically conducts audits of UTC books.

Completing a Paper UTC

☑ LE1013.3.
Describe how to issue a paper UTC

The instructions for completing the uniform traffic citation are in the *Uniform Traffic Citation Procedures Manual* available on the Florida Highway Safety and Motor Vehicles website. Review the description and procedures sections of the manual, and:

1. Make sure that the hard divider separates the set (three copies of the citation) from the other sets in the book.
2. Use a pen with a hard tip, such as a black ballpoint pen, when printing to make sure that the information is legible on all three copies.
3. Clearly fill in each data field or "X" the appropriate box based on the requested information at the top of each category.
4. Complete all applicable sections and leave blank any that are not applicable.

Sometimes FLHSMV returns a UTC to the issuing agency for correction or clarification. Common errors include:

- illegible handwriting
- failure to list a statute and subsection number that correspond to the violation
- failure to either check or write in a violation
- incorrect entry of the driver's date of birth

Distributing a Paper UTC

☑ LE1013.4.
Describe the three parts of a paper UTC

The paper UTC form HSMV 75901 contains three copies: one for the court, the driver, and for the officer's records.

PART ONE (WHITE)—COMPLAINT—RETAINED BY COURT

This part serves as a sufficient complaint for both civil and criminal cases. Judges and clerks use the reverse side of part one to document court actions. Submit a citation to the clerk of the court within five days after you issue the citation to a driver.

PART TWO (YELLOW)—SUMMONS—DRIVER'S COPY

The driver receives part two. The reverse side notifies people who are charged with traffic infractions that do not require a court appearance of their options when answering the offense charged.

PART THREE (PINK)—OFFICER'S COPY

Either you or your agency keeps part three to maintain accountability and a record of the court's action. You may want to keep a copy for your field notes in case you have to testify in court.

EXPLAINING AND ISSUING THE WARNING OR CITATION

It is important that you understand Florida traffic laws well enough to explain the offense to someone unfamiliar with them because it is your responsibility to make sure that the driver understands the violation. State the specifics of the violation slowly and clearly, making sure that the driver understands the verbal warning, the written warning, or the citation. Point to the section on the citation where you checked the violation and wrote specific information about the incident.

☑ LE1013.5. Describe how to explain the traffic violation and the driver's options for responding to a UTC

Explain to the driver their options for responding to the citation, as indicated in detail on the back of the driver's (yellow) copy, part two.

- Moving violations may include paying a civil penalty or requesting a hearing in traffic court. Some moving violations require a court appearance, and others allow attendance and completion of a driver improvement course, if eligible.
- Non-moving violations include paying a civil penalty or choosing a hearing in traffic court.
- Criminal violations require a court appearance on a scheduled date.

If charged with operating a motor vehicle that is in an unsafe condition or is not properly equipped, a driver may choose to provide certified proof of correction of the condition or equipment problem.

If charged with failure to display a valid driver license, registration, or proof of insurance, or with a vehicle safety violation, the driver may choose to enter a plea of *nolo contendere* (no contest).

The driver must then provide proof of compliance to the clerk of court within 30 days and pay a fine and court costs if charged with any of the following:

- safety of vehicle; inspection (s. 316.610, F.S.)
- failure to display a valid driver license (s. 322.15, F.S.)
- failure to possess a valid registration (s. 320.0605, F.S.)
- failure to maintain proof of insurance (s. 316.646, F.S.)

SIGNING THE UTC

Most citations no longer require the driver's signature, but if the driver has committed a violation that requires a hearing, ask the driver to sign the UTC, and explain that signing is not an admission of guilt.

☑ LE1013.6. Describe obtaining the driver's signature on a UTC

These violations are serious in nature and include the following:

- any infraction that results in a crash that causes the death of another person (s. 316.027, F.S.)
- any violation that results in a crash that causes serious bodily injury of another person (s. 316.1933, F.S.)
- any violation of passing a school bus, on the side of the bus where children enter or exit, while the bus is displaying a stop signal (s. 316.172, F.S.)
- any violation of dropping loads from vehicles (s. 316.520, F.S.)
- any violation of exceeding the speed limit by 30 mph or more (s. 316.183, s. 316.187, or s. 316.189, F.S.)
- any violation of driving with a suspended license (s. 322.34, F.S.)
- any violation of leaving the scene of an accident (s. 316.061, F.S.)

If the violation is criminal and you are issuing an electronic citation to the driver, print a copy and instruct the driver to sign it before submitting it to FLHSMV. Add any relevant notes to the electronic ticket that can be referred to should the driver later contest the citation in court. When you issue the citation, certify by signature that you delivered the citation to the driver cited. The signature may be electronic, electronic facsimile, or written. Check the block that certifies that the driver received a copy of the violation. This certification is evidence that you served the driver with the citation.

Refusal to accept and sign a UTC requiring a court appearance is a criminal violation under s. 318.14, F.S., that may result in arrest. If a driver refuses to sign the citation, use effective communication and de-escalation skills to gain compliance. Stress that signing the UTC is not an admission of guilt or a waiver of rights. Explain that refusal to accept and sign the citation might result in arrest. If the driver still refuses to sign, place them under arrest, and issue them another UTC for refusal to sign a citation.

UNIT 2 RESOLVING TRAFFIC INCIDENTS
LESSON 1 Parking Violations

◎ Lesson Goal

At the end of this lesson, you will know the different types of citations to use when enforcing parking violations.

Think About This

You find a vehicle parked in a disabled parking spot with nothing to designate that the driver has the proper paperwork to park there. However, as you are writing a ticket, the driver approaches you to tell you that they have a disability, but they forgot their placard. What do you do?

While on patrol, you may be assigned to enforce various parking violations, such as parking illegally in a handicapped parking space, blocking a fire lane, or blocking a sidewalk. Enforce parking laws and ordinances by issuing a UTC for a violation of the Florida Statutes and a county or municipal citation for a violation of local ordinances.

If your agency uses a municipal or county parking citation to enforce the Florida Statutes on stopping, standing, or parking, complete and attach the citation to the vehicle in violation. The statute also requires you to attach the citation in a safe, conspicuous place (usually under the windshield wiper).

Anyone who parks in a designated disabled parking space must have the proper permit. A permit may be displayed by either a placard or on a specialty license plate. Drivers who do not have permits and park in a designated disabled person's parking space commit a non-moving traffic violation.

The Florida disabled permit will have the Florida driver license or ID card number of the authorized user. Anyone who unlawfully uses a disabled person's parking permit commits a criminal violation.

☑ LE1021.1. Differentiate between a UTC, municipal parking citation, and county ordinance citation when enforcing motor vehicle parking laws

UNIT 2 RESOLVING TRAFFIC INCIDENTS
LESSON 2 Abandoned, Disabled, or Unattended Vehicles

◎ Lesson Goal

At the end of this lesson, you will know how to respond to an abandoned, disabled, or unattended vehicle.

ABANDONED VEHICLES

☑ LE1022.1.
Describe how to safely approach an abandoned vehicle

An *abandoned vehicle* has no driver, or the person responsible for the vehicle is unknown. These vehicles may be disabled, illegally parked, or a potential crime scene. Abandoned vehicles should be investigated to determine if a crime has occurred, such as a vehicle theft or burglary. Look for evidence of forced entry or of another crime. For example, a broken window may indicate a stolen vehicle.

When responding to an abandoned vehicle complaint, your first concern is to identify public safety hazards, which may range from roadway obstruction to a mobile meth lab. Use caution when approaching an abandoned vehicle.

Survey the scene for anything that may compromise officer safety or indicate a crime has occurred. Be aware of your surroundings, and approach from the rear. After it is safe to do so, you may need to have the vehicle moved due to dangerous conditions.

☑ LE1022.2.
Describe sources of vehicle owner information

Once you resolve all perceived safety concerns, attempt to locate the owner. The most common sources of vehicle and owner information are the license plate number and the vehicle identification number (VIN). You may also obtain information about the vehicle or owner from the complainant, people in the area, or available computer databases.

If you make contact with the owner, determine the status of the vehicle. Based on the information you receive, first secure the vehicle by making sure that it is locked. Next, you may have the owner remove the vehicle, arrange for it to be towed and impounded, or, if it is not a hazard, leave it in place. When the vehicle is in violation of a local or state law, issue a citation and take action according to your agency policies.

DISABLED AND UNATTENDED VEHICLE TOWING PROCEDURES

A *disabled vehicle* is not drivable. An example is a vehicle on the side of the highway with a flat tire. An *unattended vehicle* is a vehicle that the driver has left, the engine is still running, the key is still in the ignition, and the brake is not set. An example of an unattended vehicle is a vehicle parked illegally and the driver of the vehicle has stepped away to make a delivery.

If the vehicle is disabled and the owner or driver is present, they may request that a specific tow company respond. In this case, the owner or driver will make the removal arrangements. However, if the owner or driver is not present, use FCIC/NCIC to determine if the vehicle is reported as stolen. Conduct an inventory of the vehicle for towing purposes in accordance with your agency policy.

☑ LE1022.3. Describe how to respond to disabled or unattended vehicles

UNIT 2 RESOLVING TRAFFIC INCIDENTS
LESSON 3 Search and Inventory of an Impounded Vehicle

Lesson Goal

At the end of this lesson, you will know how to search the exterior and interior of a vehicle, conduct an inventory, and process contraband found in an impounded vehicle.

Think About This

You arrest a subject for a DUI and tow the vehicle. Three days later, the owner of the vehicle claims that a smartphone is missing from their car. Why is it so important to complete a thorough inventory of a vehicle?

VEHICLES INVOLVED IN A CRIME

In *New York v. Belton*, the scope of a vehicle search incident to an arrest includes the entire passenger compartment and all containers located inside the vehicle whether open or closed. The trunk of a sedan is not considered part of the passenger compartment, but the rear area of a van or SUV is included in the search area. In *Arizona v. Gant*, the scope of the search incident to an arrest has been further defined. Officers may search the passenger compartment of a vehicle only when the arrestee is unsecured and the passenger compartment is within reaching distance of the arrestee or if it is "reasonable" to believe the vehicle contains evidence of the crime for which the subject was arrested.

If a vehicle is evidence and needs to be held under the control of the investigating agency, a wrecker service should transport the vehicle to a designated secured location. Treat the vehicle as a crime scene until it is processed by the proper personnel. Follow your agency policies regarding securing vehicles as evidence. A secured storage facility will be used to maintain the chain of custody and to make sure that evidence is free from tampering.

Vehicles that are seized under the Florida Contraband Forfeiture Act will be thoroughly inventoried and taken to a secured location.

EXTERIOR/INTERIOR VEHICLE SEARCH

☑ LE1023.1. Describe how to search vehicle compartments and cargo areas

A vehicle search is conducted only when authorized under the Florida Statutes, for example, when probable cause exists or consent is given. Use personal protective equipment, such as goggles and gloves, when necessary.

When searching a vehicle, use a logical search process that allows you to be consistent and thorough. Make sure that all compartments are checked. Be aware of hidden compartments that can be used to conceal weapons and contraband. Suspicious buttons or switches may indicate hidden compartments. Avoid unnecessary damage to the vehicle. The authority to search a vehicle's trunk is determined by the purpose of the search. Your agency policies and procedures determine how you conduct a search on a locked vehicle.

INVENTORY

Impounding is the legal process of placing a vehicle in a lot or tow yard. A vehicle is impounded when towed at the direction of law enforcement. Follow your agency policies to determine if a vehicle should be impounded.

If a vehicle is to be impounded because it is disabled, abandoned, or unattended, or because it was involved in a traffic crash, the Florida Statutes require you to conduct an inventory of the vehicle and document all its contents. Failure to conduct the inventory constitutes a misdemeanor if the owner is not present.

When taking a vehicle inventory, document the vehicle's overall condition, mileage if available, damage, all contents, and equipment. An inventory is conducted to protect you and the agency from false claims of lost, stolen, or damaged property. An inventory of a vehicle is a recognized exception to the Fourth Amendment search warrant requirement. You do not need probable cause to inventory a vehicle, because the purpose of an inventory is to document items in or on a vehicle, not to search for evidence of a crime. Courts have upheld the legality of an inventory when the agency has an established written policy regarding inventories that the agency's employees follow.

☑ LE1023.2.
Describe how to conduct a motor vehicle inventory

If you observe contraband, such as controlled substances, weapons, or burglary tools, seizure of the item falls under the "plain view doctrine." If you seize contraband, consult your agency policies regarding the documentation and recovery of evidence inside the vehicle.

☑ LE1023.3.
Describe how to process contraband found in an impounded vehicle

After a decision is made to impound a vehicle, remove the vehicle from the scene. Agencies will provide inventory forms to document all items of value for reporting purposes.

An inventory should not be used in place of a lawful search. However, evidence located during an inventory can be used to further a criminal investigation. When conducting an inventory or a search of a vehicle, complete the appropriate form and attach it to the related report.

UNIT 2 RESOLVING TRAFFIC INCIDENTS
LESSON 4 Directing Traffic

Lesson Goal

At the end of this lesson, you will know how to safely direct vehicle and pedestrian traffic.

Think About This

A storm takes down multiple tree limbs and power lines in your town. You are called to a section of road that has a downed power line, and a school nearby is about to let out for the day. What are your first priorities? What is your course of action?

DIRECTING VEHICLE TRAFFIC

You may be called to direct traffic for many reasons, including road obstructions, traffic crashes, special events, utility repairs, or inoperable traffic signals.

Scene Survey and Roadway Obstruction

☑ LE1024.1. Describe how to respond to the scene of an obstructed roadway

When approaching the scene, assess for scene safety, such as downed power lines, hazardous materials, and active threats. Determine the cause of any road obstruction, which may include a traffic crash, debris, disabled vehicles, downed power lines, and pedestrian traffic. Park the patrol vehicle in a safe location and according to agency policy. Activate the vehicle's emergency lights to urge motorists to use caution and slow down.

☑ LE1024.2. Describe how to clear an obstructed roadway

Depending on the amount of traffic and traffic patterns, you may need to request additional help. If safe and possible, remove any obstruction. You may request assistance from bystanders while removing the obstruction.

If any road damage is severe enough to pose a danger to vehicle traffic, direct traffic around the damage and request assistance from the appropriate department to respond and provide barricades or road signs. If the scene is a traffic crash or crime scene, follow the guidelines you will learn in Chapter 12 Traffic Crash Investigations.

Traffic Safety

☑ LE1024.3. Identify appropriate safety and traffic warning equipment

Whether it is day or night, wear a reflective safety vest to be more visible to motorists. The type of safety hazard will help you decide on the appropriate safety and traffic warning equipment. Depending on the situation, you may use whistles, flashlights, traffic control devices, direction wands, reflective vests and gloves, and a traffic control box.

Directing Traffic

☑ LE1024.4. Describe how to determine alternative routes to redirect vehicle traffic

Each situation and location presents challenges for directing vehicle traffic flow. Identify what options are available for rerouting traffic based on the specific situation, your knowledge of the area, and environmental factors. Determine whether traffic can be safely routed through or around the immediate area. If the traffic must be routed away from the area, first identify alternate routes, such as alleyways, side streets, or parking lots. When choosing an alternate route, consider factors such as school zones, time of day, local business hours, and any community events. The selected route must also be able to sustain the level of traffic flow.

When directing traffic, determine the best place to stand, as well as the appropriate equipment to use for motorists to see you. The center of an intersection provides the greatest visibility, but it may also be the most hazardous. If you are not at an intersection, find the safest possible location from which to direct traffic. Avoid standing between two vehicles or directly in front of or behind a vehicle. Always allow yourself a path of escape. If additional emergency vehicles are responding, stop traffic and create access for these emergency vehicles.

☑ LE1024.5.
Describe how to direct vehicle traffic

If handling traffic flow from more than one direction, try to give equal time to each direction of traffic; however, heavier lanes of traffic should be allowed to flow for longer periods. If directing traffic in an intersection, follow typical traffic signal patterns to reduce confusion and improve traffic flow.

Get the drivers' attention when directing traffic by being seen, heard, and making clear hand movements. At night or during bad weather, drivers may have difficulty seeing or hearing you. Use the orange flashlight cone to enhance signals given with a flashlight. Flashlight signals mirror those of hand signals.

Signaling

To stop traffic:

- Point at the driver being directed to stop and make eye contact.
- Raise one or both hands with your palm toward the driver until they stop.
- Use an audible signal to alert drivers.

To start and maintain traffic flow:

- Point at the driver being directed to start, and make eye contact.
- Rotate your hand with palm up, bending at the elbow, and bring it toward you.
- Coordinate traffic direction with other officers when applicable.

To turn traffic flow:

- Direct turns only when they can be accomplished safely.
- Direct turns by pointing at the driver until eye contact is made, then point in the direction of the turn.

Audible signals:

- Whistles can be used along with hand signals.
- One long blast signals motorists to stop.

- Two short blasts signal motorists to proceed.
- Multiple short blasts may be used to gain the attention of drivers not responding to your signals.

Normal vehicle traffic patterns can resume once you confirm that the obstruction is removed or the road issue is resolved. Stop all lanes of traffic, remove and deactivate all traffic warning equipment, and signal drivers to continue normal traffic patterns.

DIRECTING PEDESTRIAN TRAFFIC

☑ LE1024.6. Describe how to direct pedestrian traffic

You may be called to direct pedestrian traffic for coordinated events or unplanned incidents, such as parades, sporting events, festivals, natural disasters, critical incidents, or disabled traffic signals. Regardless of the nature of the event or incident, wear a reflective safety vest and carry appropriate equipment as required by your agency. This may include a whistle or wand.

Planned Events

Coordinated events are typically planned in advance with established pedestrian routes. You may attend a pre-event briefing to obtain your duty location, responsibilities, and assigned time.

While directing pedestrian traffic from the duty location, maintain situational awareness to ensure the safety of all pedestrians and motorists. Some pedestrians may be guided by a service animal or white cane, indicating their partial or total blindness. Signals used to direct vehicle traffic can also be used to direct pedestrian traffic. When directing pedestrian traffic, make sure that all vehicle traffic has stopped before allowing pedestrian traffic to flow, that pedestrian walkways are not blocked, and that you are positioned between pedestrians and vehicles while remaining visible at all times.

Unplanned Events

Unexpected or unplanned circumstances can arise at any time and require a plan to safely reroute pedestrians out of the area. Inform the event coordinator of any adjustments to the established pedestrian traffic route. When setting up the plan, consider the following:

- traffic volume and speed
- number of pedestrians present
- duration of the traffic congestion
- availability of any traffic control devices
- geographic area
- nature of the event
- most efficient and safest route
- staging of traffic control equipment
- need for more resources
- any environmental hazards

During an unplanned event, people may become emotionally charged or panicked; therefore, engage in empathetic listening and apply procedural justice when interacting with the public. Be sure to use a command presence and provide clear instructions to maintain and establish order at the scene.

Chapter 11
Traffic Stops

UNIT 1 UNKNOWN-RISK TRAFFIC STOPS
- LESSON 1 Communication With Drivers / 415
- LESSON 2 Initiating the Stop / 417
- LESSON 3 Conducting the Stop / 421

UNIT 2 HIGH-RISK TRAFFIC STOPS
- LESSON 1 Initiating the Stop / 429
- LESSON 2 Conducting the Stop / 432

UNIT 1 UNKNOWN-RISK TRAFFIC STOPS
LESSON 1 Communication With Drivers

Lesson Goal

At the end of this lesson, you will know how to professionally interact with people during a traffic stop.

Think About This

You stop a vehicle, and when you begin to communicate with the driver, you realize that they do not speak English. How do you handle this situation?

The goal of every traffic stop is to promote driver education and safer roadways. During traffic stops, you may issue a uniform traffic citation or warning, you may make an arrest, or you may find that someone needs help.

DECREASING TENSION AND INCREASING COOPERATION

Exercise procedural justice and remain professional at all times. Traffic stops can be tense, and how you interact with those in the vehicle could shape the way they view law enforcement.

When stopped, a driver may react with embarrassment, anger, fear, or excuses, and tensions may rise. You can minimize negative and potentially unsafe results by conducting yourself professionally and following your training. Using the following guidelines can help you practice procedural justice and reduce tension in a traffic stop:

- Greet the driver and passengers politely, introduce yourself and your agency, and tell them why you stopped them.
- Give the driver the chance to speak.
- Request their driver license, registration, and proof of insurance.
- Explain why you made the stop. Describe the violation in terms of what you saw the vehicle, not the driver, do.
- Allow the driver to talk or vent; remain polite and focused, conveying to the driver that you are listening to them.
- Keep a pleasant expression, a calm tone of voice, and a non-confrontational interview stance while maintaining officer safety.
- Establish a command presence by using words that convey professionalism and respect.
- Respond politely to any argument from the driver; simply explain your observations and the violation, if any. Whether or not you issue a warning or citation, listening respectfully will help many people calm down and accept the situation.

☑ LE1111.1. Describe how to interact with people involved in a traffic stop to encourage cooperation

- Emphasize the importance of the enforcement action by explaining the seriousness of the violation, such as the risk of a crash or other circumstance. Do not lecture the person on what they did wrong.
- Keep the detention time as short as possible.
- End the interaction by saying "thank you for your cooperation," or "drive safely."
- Courteously provide the person with your rank, name, and badge or ID number upon request.
- Maintain your awareness of officer safety throughout the stop.
- Refer the driver to the appropriate person within your department if you are unable to answer all the driver's questions.

When dealing with a difficult or disrespectful driver, you may be tempted to respond with anger. If the encounter gets heated, it is important to respond with professionalism and a level head.

Use a reasonable tone of voice and give the driver the option either to comply with your request or be detained further for their non-compliance. A rational and reasonable approach will often defuse a situation that could otherwise escalate with an angry response from you. The person you stop could be stressed, tired, sick, or afraid. Use empathy to place yourself in their position. Do not take anything personally that a driver says to you.

BRIDGING COMMUNICATION AND LANGUAGE BARRIERS

Language barriers can hinder communication. For example, some drivers may speak a language other than English. Determine the driver's ability to understand you throughout the traffic stop. They may be fearful based on previous encounters with law enforcement, confused as to why they were stopped, or concerned about what they should do during the stop.

☑ LE1111.2. Describe how to bridge communication and language barriers

Request an interpreter through dispatch. If an interpreter is not available, try to communicate as best as you can by using gestures. Follow your agency's policies on the use of translation mobile phone applications or when using a passenger as an interpreter for the driver. Your agency may have a translation service available. Drivers with hearing impairments may also require assistance, though some can read lips. Writing notes back and forth may be a good method in such a situation.

Encourage communication by employing procedural justice strategies.

- Treat people with respect.
- Listen to what they have to say.
- Make fair decisions.
- Explain your actions.

When communicating with people during a traffic stop, your professional behavior should be a positive reflection of your agency and is a vital part of fostering positive relationships with members of your community.

UNIT 1 UNKNOWN-RISK TRAFFIC STOPS
LESSON 2 Initiating the Stop

Lesson Goal

At the end of this lesson, you will know when and how to initiate a safe and professional unknown-risk traffic stop.

Think About This

While patrolling at night, you notice a car with a broken taillight and initiate a traffic stop. The road you are on is a secluded state highway. The driver continues for miles before finally stopping in a gas station parking lot. What are some possible reasons why the driver didn't immediately pull over?

Traffic stops are among the most frequent activities that officers perform. A **traffic stop** is the lawful and temporary detention of a pedestrian or driver of a vehicle for the purpose of traffic enforcement.

Although officers conduct traffic stops regularly, you should not become complacent when conducting one. There is a potential risk of harm each time you make a stop. Many officers are injured or killed during traffic stops. Traffic stops require that you apply officer safety skills and situational awareness at all times.

DECIDING TO MAKE A TRAFFIC STOP

You may decide to make a traffic stop while driving, or when your vehicle is stopped or parked. Choose a safe parking place where you can monitor vehicle movement and watch for traffic violations. For example, when watching drivers at a traffic light intersection, park your patrol vehicle where it does not obstruct traffic flow but can enter the road quickly and safely to make a stop. Safe places include areas with a wide shoulder, available parking areas, and areas with an unobstructed view of oncoming traffic when entering the road.

A traffic stop begins the moment you observe a violation that merits a stop. Some of the reasons to stop a vehicle include BOLOs, reasonable suspicion, or probable cause. All traffic stops begin as an **unknown-risk traffic stop** because the potential risk of the situation is unknown to you at the time of the stop. You may stop a vehicle if the driver commits a traffic infraction or to assist a motorist whose vehicle is having mechanical trouble. You may have reasonable suspicion that a driver has committed, or is about to commit, a crime. Other justifications for a traffic stop can be to investigate suspicious behavior or to investigate a vehicle or occupant matching a BOLO description. During the stop, keep in mind that all vehicle occupants are innocent until proven guilty.

☑ LE1112.1. Describe circumstances that justify making a lawful traffic stop

Once you see a lawful reason for a stop, decide whether it is necessary, prudent, and safe to stop the vehicle. If immediately stopping the driver may endanger you or other motorists, do not make the stop. Unsafe conditions for a stop include heavy traffic, construction, or roadway conditions that do not allow room to pull over. For example, a bridge is not a safe place for a traffic stop.

If you are driving to an emergency call or an in-progress crime, or are transporting a prisoner, stopping a driver for a traffic violation is generally not practical. However, a reckless driver who is immediately endangering the lives of others may justify a stop, even if stopping means abandoning an earlier call. Your agency's policies will dictate what takes priority in these situations.

STEPS FOR INITIATING AN UNKNOWN-RISK TRAFFIC STOP

There are 10 steps for completing an unknown-risk traffic stop. The first four steps involve initiating the stop. Some steps may happen at the same time.

Step 1: Follow the vehicle through traffic until it is safe to make the traffic stop.

Step 2: Notify dispatch of the traffic stop.

Step 3: Select a safe location to stop.

Step 4: Activate emergency equipment to communicate the stop to the driver.

Step 1: Follow the Vehicle Through Traffic Until It is Safe to Make the Traffic Stop

☑ LE1112.2. Describe how to follow the driver until it is safe to make a traffic stop

Use defensive driving techniques to catch up with the vehicle, follow at a safe distance, and signal all lane changes. A well-executed traffic stop should have a minimal effect on traffic flow. Consider calling for backup, based on your agency's policies and procedures. You may have to follow the driver's vehicle for an extended period before you can initiate a safe stop or before requested backup arrives.

Continuously observe the vehicle from the time of the violation until you complete the stop. Note the vehicle's description, including its type, make, model, year, color, plate number and state of issue, and any vehicle descriptors, such as condition, bumper stickers or decals, dents, or a truck toolbox. Observe the driver and any passengers for unique identifiers such as glasses, hat, hair, or beard.

Step 2: Notify Dispatch of the Traffic Stop

☑ LE1112.3. List the information to provide to dispatch during an unknown-risk traffic stop

Your safety depends on how much information you can gather before making a traffic stop. Relay the following general information to dispatch:

- your radio identification number
- your location, such as the street, cross street, house number, or mile marker
- your general direction of travel: north, south, east, or west
- a description of the driver's vehicle, including color, make, approximate year

- the license plate number and state of issue
- the number of occupants and descriptions if possible
- the need for backup or other assistance as required

Location information is crucial on interstates and divided highways. If the situation escalates and you become injured or cannot use the radio, dispatch can pinpoint your location. If the final stop location changes, update dispatch immediately.

Provide enough information so that dispatch can perform a database check before you approach the vehicle or before the stop, as it might reveal important information about the operator or vehicle.

Step 3: Select a Safe Location to Stop

Select a safe location to initiate the stop. Plan to conduct the stop in an area that gives the driver a place to stop safely, preferably in a well-lit location with a low traffic volume.

☑ LE1112.4. Describe how to select a safe location for an unknown-risk traffic stop

Be ready to adjust and react quickly to any developments once the driver stops their vehicle. Any suspicious activity by the driver or passengers can increase the level of risk. Request backup based on your evaluation of the situation and agency policies and procedures.

Consider traffic flow when planning the traffic stop. **Traffic flow** is the general speed and direction of vehicle or pedestrian movement. Weather conditions, school zones, construction zones, and neighborhood activities all affect traffic flow and can slow drivers and cause congestion. In addition to traffic flow, certain road and traffic conditions increase the potential for danger for both the officer and the driver. These include merge areas, intersections, and acceleration lanes. If you have an assigned patrol zone, become familiar with normal traffic flow, speed limits and the locations where the limits change, and changes to traffic flow and conditions at different times of day.

Except in emergencies, choose a location where the driver can maneuver out of the flow of traffic. The location should be a place where both you and the driver can avoid the danger of passing vehicles. Passing traffic is not the only risk, as stopping a vehicle in a populated area may create a volatile and dangerous scene. Other drivers may slow down to see what is happening, which can cause a traffic jam or hazard. Be aware of your situation and safety at all times.

Check the width of the road and the shoulder to make sure that both you and the driver are far enough off the road so that other vehicles can pass. This reduces the potential for crashes, especially in a congested area where other drivers may not be able to change lanes to give you extra room.

Try to pull off onto a level spot or a slight downgrade. Stopping on an upgrade may cause a large vehicle to roll into the patrol vehicle. Do not make a stop on a blind curve, on or close to a ramp, close to a crest of a hill, or where road conditions could cause other vehicles to hit the patrol vehicle.

Take special precaution when conducting stops in areas where children are present, such as school zones or parking lots.

Step 4: Activate Emergency Equipment to Communicate the Stop to the Driver

Signal the driver to pull over using your lights and siren. Once you signal the driver, you have limited control over where the driver will stop.

Your interaction with the driver may begin before you signal the driver to stop. The driver may indicate that they know you are asking them to stop. They may look into the rearview mirror and make eye contact with you, signal a lane change to pull over, or suddenly reduce speed. Once the driver acknowledges that you have directed them to stop:

- Follow the vehicle as the driver changes lanes.
- Follow the vehicle at a safe distance.
- Direct the driver to a safer location if you are uncomfortable with the initial location.

☑ LE1112.5. Describe when to activate the patrol vehicle's emergency equipment

Begin communicating the stop by pulling your patrol vehicle directly behind the driver's vehicle. You are required to turn on your emergency notification equipment once you are in a safe location to make the stop. Emergency notification equipment includes emergency lights, siren, headlights, the PA system, and a horn. It may not be necessary to use all the emergency notification equipment to communicate during the stop. Follow your agency's policies.

Use flashing emergency lights when conducting traffic stops. Emergency lighting systems differ among agencies, and each driver reacts differently to them. Some might panic and stop in the left lane, skid to a stop, or swerve. Others ignore the lights. If this happens, tap the siren for one or two seconds. The patrol vehicle's high beams, spotlight, and takedown lights (white lights facing forward on the light bar) will help to conceal you from the driver's view. Leave the emergency lights on at all times to warn oncoming traffic during the stop.

If the stop occurs at night, spotlights can provide additional lighting. Consider turning on the patrol vehicle's high beams, unless they interfere with oncoming traffic or restrict your vision by reflecting off the driver's rear bumper or other object. To illuminate the interior of the driver's vehicle, activate the takedown lights if your patrol vehicle is equipped with them. This also prevents the driver from seeing into the patrol vehicle.

Stay far enough behind the vehicle so that you can react to any situation. Use safety precautions, such as avoiding traffic lanes, watching for pedestrians, and protecting the driver. If you need to move to a safer location, give clear, firm verbal directions using the PA system. You might say, "Driver, proceed into the parking lot ahead to the right," or "Driver, pull your vehicle farther to the right." If the driver flees instead of stopping as instructed, you should follow your agency's protocol regarding vehicle pursuit.

UNIT 1 UNKNOWN-RISK TRAFFIC STOPS
LESSON 3 Conducting the Stop

Lesson Goal

At the end of this lesson, you will know how to conduct a safe and professional unknown-risk traffic stop.

STEPS FOR CONDUCTING AN UNKNOWN-RISK TRAFFIC STOP

The last six steps involve conducting the stop. Some of the steps may happen at the same time.

Step 5: Park the patrol vehicle.

Step 6: Conduct a visual assessment of the vehicle and occupants.

Step 7: Exit the patrol vehicle.

Step 8: Determine the safest approach technique.

Step 9: Interact with the driver and passengers.

Step 10: Choose a course of action.

Step 5: Park the Patrol Vehicle

Because of roadway conditions, traffic, and other environmental factors, each traffic stop is unique. After stopping the driver in a safe location, park your patrol vehicle a safe distance behind the driver's vehicle, about 1½–2-car lengths behind the vehicle.

If the driver stops on the right side of the road, position your patrol vehicle in the *offset-angle position*. Align the center of your vehicle's hood with the taillight of the driver's vehicle and point your vehicle's nose outward into the flow of traffic. This vehicle position creates a safety corridor for you to walk when approaching the stopped vehicle. Turn your wheels away from traffic. Angling the vehicle may also provide cover if the driver shoots a weapon.

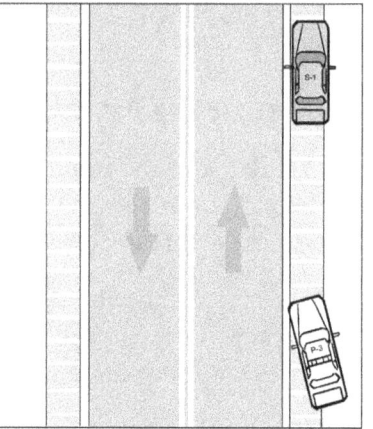

☑ LE1113.1. Determine how to park the patrol vehicle safely after the driver stops

Figure 11-1 Offset-angle positioning

If needed, use the PA system to direct the driver to move their vehicle further to the right to improve safety and reduce the obstruction of traffic.

Due to environmental conditions or roadway obstacles, you may have to conduct a traffic stop on the left side of the road.

In emergencies or less than optimal conditions, you may have to conduct a traffic stop on the roadway. Move your vehicle to the far outside of the driving lane and place it in an offset-angle position.

POSITION THE BACKUP PATROL VEHICLE

☑ LE1113.2. Describe how the backup officer should park their patrol vehicle in relation to the primary officer's car to prevent a crossfire situation

The backup officer should park their patrol vehicle at a safe distance behind the primary officer's vehicle. Depending on the conditions of the traffic stop, the backup officer may offset their vehicle to the left or the right of the primary officer's vehicle.

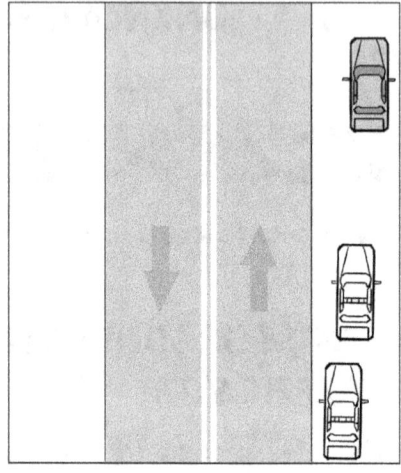

Figure 11-2 Offset positioning

The backup officer should not use the front emergency lighting, to avoid blinding or silhouetting the primary officer, and should use only rear emergency lights. The backup officer should approach the driver's vehicle along the passenger's side of the primary officer's vehicle.

Step 6: Conduct a Visual Assessment of the Driver's Vehicle and Occupants

☑ LE1113.3. Describe how to visually assess the vehicle, driver, and passengers for officer safety

Assess the vehicle for signs of danger before you exit your patrol vehicle. Visually assess the vehicle from the safety of your vehicle. If the occupants try to exit their vehicle, your discretion and agency's policies will determine whether you order them back into the vehicle.

Look for signs of criminal activity. If the vehicle's rear end appears to be significantly lower than the front, the vehicle could be carrying stolen merchandise, drugs, tools, a person, or a corpse.

Step 7: Exit the Patrol Vehicle

☑ LE1113.4. Describe how to safely exit the patrol vehicle

After checking for oncoming traffic in the rearview and side-view mirrors, exit your vehicle quickly. A silent exit from the patrol vehicle may give you time to approach the driver's vehicle and assess the situation before the driver reacts.

Quietly secure your vehicle door so it will not blow open and strike a passing vehicle. Adjust your portable radio volume to low. Continuously observe the driver's vehicle and all its occupants. Be prepared to transition to a high-risk vehicle stop based on your threat assessment.

If a situation seems dangerous, request backup and wait for its arrival before taking any further action. If you receive information about, or become aware of, a threat, consider returning to your patrol vehicle and transitioning to procedures for a high-risk traffic stop. High-risk traffic stops are explained later in this chapter.

Step 8: Determine and Apply Appropriate Approach Techniques

When you exit the patrol vehicle, use available cover. To prevent injury, avoid walking between your patrol vehicle and the subject's vehicle. The driver could reverse their vehicle or another vehicle could accidently strike your vehicle, pinning you between the two vehicles. Stay out of the flow of traffic.

☑ LE1113.5. Describe how to safely approach the vehicle

Be aware of brake lights or reverse lights. At night, avoid crossing in front of the headlights, which would reveal your position. If you need to approach the passenger's side of the driver's vehicle, walk behind your vehicle. Consider keeping your flashlight off while on approach until you make contact with the driver and passengers.

Look at the license plate for clues that the plate may not belong to the driver's vehicle:

- the way the plate is attached, suggesting the license plate is from another vehicle
- the age of the license plate attachment relative to the age of the plate (for example, shiny, new bolts on a dirty plate)
- an expired registration sticker or tampered-with decal, suggesting it was removed from another plate
- paint or dark film on the license plate
- the presence of dead insects on the plate, suggesting it was the front plate of another vehicle

Check the trunk for signs of damage, such as pry marks or a hole in the trunk where the lock should be. These are common signs of a stolen vehicle. Push down on the trunk as you approach the vehicle. Doing so will lock in anyone hiding inside the trunk. However, be aware that modern technology allows someone to open the trunk from the inside of the vehicle or the inside of the trunk.

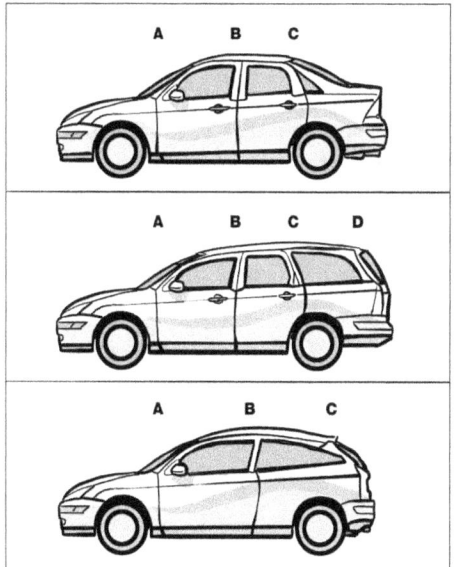

Touch the trunk lid during every traffic stop, even if the trunk lid appears closed. This transfers your fingerprints to the vehicle, which will serve as evidence of your contact with the vehicle if the traffic stop deteriorates into a crime scene, the driver flees, or you go missing.

APPROACH THE VEHICLE—DRIVER SIDE OPTION

Approach the driver's vehicle cautiously, constantly assessing the situation. Do not fix your full attention on any one part of the scene, but rather scan the entire vehicle and its occupants for suspicious movements. Examine the interior of the vehicle while looking through the rear window into the rear seat. Try to determine the number of passengers, the position of the rear seat, and the presence of any potential weapons or contraband.

Figure 11-3
Vehicle pillars

Stay close to the driver's vehicle. Depending on conditions and location, a flashlight may be needed during daytime. If a flashlight is used, keep it in your support hand.

When approaching the vehicle, if you see a passenger in the backseat, stop at the back edge of the rear window, also known as the C-pillar. Remain behind the C-pillar for cover. Instruct the driver to roll down all the windows on the driver's side of the vehicle so that you can easily observe the passengers in the backseat. If there are no passengers in the backseat, stop at the back edge of the driver's window, also known as the B-pillar. Remain behind the driver's B-pillar for cover. This gives you a position of tactical advantage while maintaining a safe distance when talking with the driver.

APPROACH THE VEHICLE—PASSENGER SIDE OPTION

The occupants of the vehicle will expect you to approach on the driver's side. Approaching on the passenger's side of the vehicle may give you extra time to listen and observe if the driver is concealing something on their right side, for example, a weapon, an alcoholic beverage, drugs, or drug paraphernalia.

Observe if there is a popped or damaged ignition, which may indicate a stolen vehicle. A *popped or damaged ignition* refers to popped open plastic housing around the steering column's base and exposed ignition wires pulled forward to start the car without a key.

At this point during the traffic stop, call for backup if the situation suggests a potential threat.

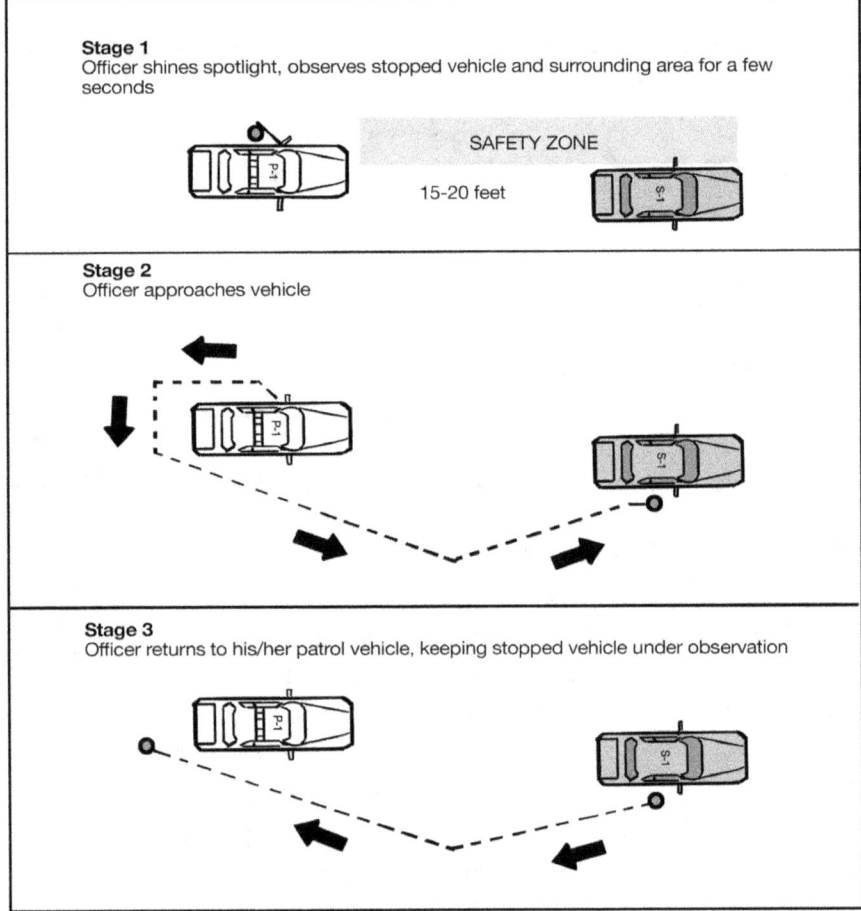

Figure 11-4
Passenger side approach

CALL THE DRIVER BACK TO THE OFFICER'S PATROL VEHICLE—"NO-APPROACH" OPTION

If you do not feel safe approaching the vehicle, you may use the *no-approach tactic*, which calls the driver to the patrol vehicle. Consider using the no-approach tactic if the driver's windows are tinted dark, if there are multiple occupants, or if you cannot see what is going on inside the driver's vehicle.

If you decide to call the driver back to the patrol vehicle, assume a tactical position behind one of your patrol vehicle pillars, the driver's or passenger's side door, or the rear of the patrol vehicle. Do not remain seated in your car. If the driver is looking at you directly or through a side or rearview mirror, you can motion the driver to come back to the patrol vehicle, or use the PA system to direct the driver to walk toward the patrol vehicle. As the driver approaches, be observant, especially of the driver's hands, for any signs of aggression or the presence of a weapon.

☑ LE1113.6. Describe how to conduct the "no-approach tactic"

Step 9: Interact With the Driver

INITIAL INTERACTION

There are three main objectives during the initial interaction with the driver:

1. When interacting with the driver, begin by identifying yourself as a law enforcement officer, especially if you are not in uniform. As discussed in Chapter 2, display a courteous but commanding presence, and you are less likely to encounter resistance. Make sure your expression, tone of voice, body position, gestures, and words are professional, respectful, and polite even while you are being assertive.

2. Explain the reason for the stop. Describe what you observed the vehicle, not the driver, doing, and request the required documentation. For example, an explanation for the stop might include the observation that the vehicle's taillights are not working. Allow the driver to offer an explanation, such as vehicle malfunction. If the driver states they have a medical condition that explains the violation, contact dispatch to request medical assistance for the driver and arrange for a relative or responsible person to remove the vehicle or have it towed.

3. Ask the driver to provide their driver license, registration, and insurance information. You may ask the driver where they keep the documents. This will help you predict where the driver's hands will move. If the driver reaches to open the glove compartment or other inside compartment, request that they do it slowly. Pay close attention to both of the driver's hands. The driver could use the reaching hand as a distraction while going for a weapon or object with the other hand. Expect the driver to retrieve this information from a wallet, glove compartment, or center console. Never accept a wallet from the driver. Instead, ask the driver to remove the license from the wallet. This prevents the driver from later making accusations of theft.

Observe the driver's and passenger's behavior for signs of a threat, such as:

- moving excessively and nervously
- watching you intently, beyond normal curiosity
- moving toward the floorboard or backseat
- making excessive motion, beyond natural curiosity
- sitting in a rigid, wooden posture

☑ LE1113.7.
Describe how to interact with a driver while maintaining officer safety

Use observation skills, safe positioning, and safe distancing when interviewing the driver or passengers. If the situation becomes dangerous or unstable, increase the distance between you and the stopped vehicle. Be aware that the driver or passengers may have lethal opioid drugs, such as fentanyl, in the vehicle. Follow your agency's policies and procedures regarding administering an emergency opioid antagonist if you encounter these types of opioids, as they may pose a life-threatening situation.

DRIVER AND VEHICLE INFORMATION

☑ LE1113.8.
Describe how to verify the driver's identity and vehicle ownership

Verify that the information on the driver's license is current. Compare information on the vehicle registration to the VIN, make, model, and year of the vehicle. If the driver does not have identification, ask for their Social Security number. Confirm that the insurance information is current and applicable to the driver's vehicle. A driver can provide proof of insurance in either a uniform paper or electronic format, as approved by FLHSMV.

While the Florida driver license has the designation for sex as either F for female or M for male, several states have a third sex or gender option, usually designated by the letter X. If you encounter a driver with an X on their license, or an individual whose appearance does not match the sex on their license, follow your agency's policies and procedures on how to enter the data into the system. As you talk with the person, treat them with the same respect you would show to anyone else; for example, if you are not sure how to address the person, ask what their preference is.

LEGAL CARRY OF A WEAPON

☑ LE1113.9.
Describe how to respond if you suspect that there is a firearm in the vehicle

The driver or a passenger may state that they have a weapon on their person or in the vehicle despite not being required to do so. Regardless, if you have reasonable suspicion that there is a firearm in the vehicle, ask for its location. If you determine that a firearm is readily accessible to anyone in the vehicle, follow your agency's policies and procedures on how to proceed with the traffic stop. For more information regarding the lawful ownership and possessions of weapons and firearms, refer to Chapter 3.

PASSENGER INFORMATION

☑ LE1113.10.
Describe how to obtain passenger information

The driver is the only occupant in the vehicle required to provide documentation. However, should you suspect other occupants of a violation or crime, request their documents that provide accurate personal information such as:

- driver license or state-issued identification card (with picture)
- school picture identification

- military ID
- permanent resident card (green card)

After obtaining the driver's and passengers' documentation, complete the criminal justice database checks or request dispatch to complete them. Remember to keep an eye on the vehicle and its occupants while you run the database checks. The information from DAVID and FCIC/NCIC can be useful during traffic stops. Recall from Chapter 5 that these databases provide information on people with outstanding arrest warrants nationally, driver licenses, and vehicle registrations. If your query returns a hit, and you confirm the identifying information with the entering agency, take the appropriate action, which may include making an arrest or impounding the vehicle.

Step 10: Choose a Course of Action

You may decide to take no action, issue a verbal warning, issue a written warning, issue a citation, or make an arrest. The law, your agency's policies and procedures, and the circumstances of the violation affect your enforcement options. Some agencies do not permit officers to issue written or verbal warnings. Handle civil traffic infractions for a juvenile in the same way as for adults.

☑ LE1113.11. Explain the actions you may take for a traffic violation

Weigh the seriousness of the offense and the road, weather, and traffic conditions when deciding a course of action. You may request that the driver and any passengers stay in the driver's vehicle or ask them to move to a designated area away from the vehicle but within your sight. This can make attacking you from behind more difficult as you choose or implement your course of action.

Complete the traffic stop by returning the driver's documents with a copy of the warning or citation and any relevant public information pamphlets that your agency may provide. Professional behavior can make this interaction easier if you clearly explain options for handling the citation. Do not argue about the merits of the citation with the driver.

Traffic stops are documented in many ways, such as through dispatch, computer, written warning, UTC, in-car video system, or body camera. If the driver expresses a desire to make a complaint against you, politely explain the process for doing so and notify your supervisor according to your agency's policies and procedures. Allow an upset driver time to calm down before the driver leaves. When the driver is ready, make sure they are able to re-enter traffic safely. Return to your vehicle and clear the traffic stop with dispatch.

ARRESTS DURING TRAFFIC STOPS

During a traffic stop, you may develop probable cause to justify an arrest of a driver or a passenger for an offense that came to your attention during your investigation. Whether you make a physical arrest or take some other action will depend on the nature of the offense, the severity of the circumstances, and your agency's policies and procedures.

☑ LE1113.12. Determine when to make a lawful arrest for an unrelated offense during a traffic stop

Before making an arrest, you should call for backup. When the backup officer arrives, work together on the best strategy to conduct the arrest. Keep in mind that during an arrest, there is always potential for resistance or violence. Remember to maintain a professional standard of conduct at all times.

DISPOSITION OF THE VEHICLE AND PASSENGERS

If you arrest a driver during the course of a traffic stop, you will have to decide what to do with the vehicle and any passengers.

> LE1113.13. Describe how to remove passengers and the vehicle from the scene after arresting the driver

Treat the passengers with dignity and respect. Witnessing a friend or family member being placed under arrest will cause some individuals to react or become emotional. Depending on the offense, you may search the vehicle, impound it, or retain it for evidence. If you impound it, follow agency policies and procedures to inventory the contents of the vehicle and remove and secure any driver or passenger possessions. You may arrange for a third party to remove the driver's vehicle or leave it at the scene with the owner's consent. If the vehicle is stolen, follow agency policies and procedures. If the vehicle must be impounded, contact a wrecker to take the vehicle to the impound lot.

UNIT 2 HIGH-RISK TRAFFIC STOPS
LESSON 1 Initiating the Stop

Lesson Goal

At the end of this lesson, you will know when and how to initiate a safe and professional high-risk traffic stop.

Think About This

What are some of the factors that would lead an officer to conduct a high-risk traffic stop?

A *high-risk traffic stop* happens when you reasonably believe that the vehicle was stolen or used in the commission of a felony, or that the occupant(s) of the vehicle:

- has committed, or is committing a forcible felony or a crime of violence
- may be armed and dangerous
- may have an active violent felony warrant
- poses a higher risk to yourself or the public

Unknown-risk traffic stops become high risk when any of the above criteria are present. A high-risk traffic stop requires you to think and act quickly, and to rely on your training and agency policies.

Listening, observing, coordinating with other officers, and maintaining constant communication are especially critical during high-risk traffic stops.

STEPS FOR INITIATING A HIGH-RISK TRAFFIC STOP

There are 10 steps for completing a high-risk traffic stop. The first four steps occur when the primary officer initiates the stop. Some of the steps may happen at the same time.

☑ LE1121.1. List the steps to safely initiate a high-risk traffic stop

Step 1: Identify a vehicle or a suspect.

Step 2: Identify the location of the stop.

Step 3: Coordinate with other officers.

Step 4: Initiate the stop.

Step 1: Identify a Vehicle or a Suspect

You might receive information about a BOLO during roll call or over your vehicle computer while on patrol. If you identify a vehicle or suspect who matches the details from the BOLO, notify dispatch that you may have located the vehicle or suspect.

☑ LE1121.2. Identify vehicle and suspect information to provide to dispatch before making a high-risk traffic stop

Request a secure channel, and provide dispatch your location and travel direction, and the suspect's vehicle's location and description including:

- vehicle make, model, and year (when identifiable)
- vehicle color
- plate number and state of issuance
- any visible damage to the vehicle
- special markings, such as neon lights, bumper stickers, writing on windows, decals
- aftermarket modifications, such as truck boxes, spinning rims, tow hitches, winches
- officer safety issues, such as tinted windows, gun rack, grill guard, raised chassis
- number and a description of the occupants

If dispatch confirms the driver and vehicle information you provided, you have reasonable suspicion to initiate the stop. Follow the suspect's vehicle and maintain constant visual contact with the vehicle. Know your agency's policies and procedures for safe vehicle speeds when following a suspect in a vehicle. Do not turn on the emergency equipment. If backup is unavailable from your agency, ask dispatch to request assistance from another agency.

Do not conduct a high-risk traffic stop alone unless the driver's behavior forces action. Conduct the stop alone only if the driver's actions or vehicle movement places you, the driver, or the public at immediate risk.

WAITING FOR BACKUP

☑ LE1121.3. Describe how to request and wait for backup

It is recommended that you request and, if possible, wait for backup before acting in a high-risk traffic stop situation. Maintain contact with dispatch and responding units at all times. As circumstances change, update dispatch and backup on the movement and route of the suspect's vehicle, activity of the occupants in the vehicle, and any observations of weapons or contraband. Regular updates to dispatch can prevent confusion and can direct backup officers to the correct location. Communication is an important task for you in any traffic stop. Periodically ask dispatch to provide the location and estimated time of arrival (ETA) for the backup units. An accurate ETA may help you plan for the safest stopping location.

Step 2: Identify the Location of the Stop

☑ LE1121.4. Identify an appropriate location to conduct a high-risk traffic stop

Determine a safe location to stop when backup officers arrive. Attempt to locate a place that is well lit, has light or no traffic, few or no pedestrians, and provides plenty of room for all vehicles.

An ideal, safe stopping location should have an unobstructed view between the suspect's vehicle and the patrol units, and to avoid public harm, be:

- visible to approaching traffic and all involved officers
- in a place that vehicular and pedestrian traffic can be stopped or redirected to a safe location
- away from heavy pedestrian and vehicle traffic
- large enough to accommodate two or more backup units
- on a wide and straight roadway
- in an open or rural area rather than a business area

Step 3: Coordinate With Other Officers

Usually, the initiating officer serves as the primary officer. There are exceptions to this rule. For example, a canine unit may relinquish the role of primary officer to a patrol officer.

If possible, attempt to stop all vehicular and pedestrian traffic. When backup officers arrive, the primary officer chooses a safe stopping location. Using the radio, the primary officer directs the responding patrol units to positions of backup or control of the driver and passengers. Backup officers should know what is expected of their positions to work safely and effectively as a team.

When there is enough backup to initiate the high-risk stop, the primary officer provides dispatch the location of the stop, and information regarding the driver's and the passenger's actions and behavior.

Step 4: Initiate the Stop

All officers must turn on their patrol vehicle's emergency lights to direct the driver to stop, and are to keep them on throughout the entire stop. This includes takedown lights, high beams, and spotlights. The lights may help protect officers from potential attack by the suspect. Using blinding light for safety can be effective during day or night.

The primary officer may use a siren if the driver does not respond to the emergency lights and may use the PA system to give directions to the driver to pull over. If the driver flees and does not stop as directed, you should follow your agency's protocol regarding vehicle pursuit.

UNIT 2 HIGH-RISK TRAFFIC STOPS
LESSON 2 Conducting the Stop

◎ Lesson Goal

At the end of this lesson, you will know how to conduct a safe and professional high-risk traffic stop using verbal commands.

The last six procedural steps for the primary officer to take when involved in a high-risk traffic stop are as follows. Some of these may happen at the same time.

STEPS FOR CONDUCTING A HIGH-RISK TRAFFIC STOP

Step 5: Position the patrol vehicles.

Step 6: Decide officer assignments.

Step 7: Issue commands.

Step 8: Secure the suspects.

Step 9: Clear and search the vehicle.

Step 10: Conclude the stop.

Step 5: Position the Patrol Vehicles

POSITIONING THE PRIMARY PATROL VEHICLE

☑ LE1122.1. Describe how to safely position the primary and backup patrol vehicles

Once the vehicle stops, the primary officer positions their patrol vehicle so that the driver's door of the suspect's vehicle is immediately visible. Officers should stop at a safe distance behind the suspect's vehicle, 15–20 feet, as more distance provides more protection. Officers should also keep their patrol vehicle engines running in case they need to react to changes in the situation. If your siren is activated, turn it off.

Agency policies and the physical situation (terrain, type of intersection, whether it is a highway or street, officer safety) help officers determine how far to offset the primary patrol vehicle. Generally, the primary patrol vehicle should offset toward the driver's side of the suspect's vehicle.

Lastly, make sure you leave room for a takedown area. A ***takedown area*** is a tactical area of advantage for the officer to handcuff and search the driver or passengers. The takedown area is always in front of a fan, wedge, or other patrol vehicle formation. The back of the patrol vehicle formation is preserved as the "safe zone." The safe zone is always behind the patrol vehicle formation and the place where secured suspects are thoroughly searched before being placed in a patrol vehicle.

POSITIONING THE BACKUP PATROL VEHICLES

The positioning of the backup vehicles will also be dictated by the location and terrain of the stop. A high-risk traffic stop usually involves many backup units. Position the first backup patrol vehicle to the right of the primary patrol vehicle and facing the suspect's vehicle. Position all backup vehicles at least two door widths apart so that all vehicle doors can open completely, facing the suspect's vehicle.

Focus the backup vehicle's takedown lights, high beams, and spotlight on the suspect's vehicle. Position a third vehicle (or fourth) to one side or to the other of the fan formation. If you choose to position a patrol vehicle at the rear of the primary patrol vehicle, turn off the forward-facing emergency lights.

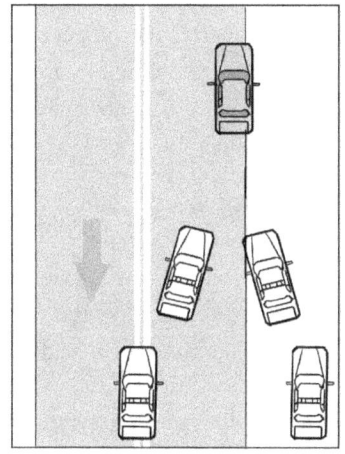

Figure 11-5
The wedge formation

TAKING COVER USING THE PATROL VEHICLE

Exit your vehicle and use available cover for safety after the suspect's vehicle has stopped and all patrol vehicles are positioned. Your patrol vehicle is usually the most effective and readily available cover; this includes the door frame and the rear of the vehicle. However, there may be instances where other environmental cover will offer better protection.

☑ LE1122.2.
Describe how to use a patrol vehicle as cover

Once all officers are in position, they should draw their firearm, and based on the environment, orient the muzzle in the appropriate ready position that does not obstruct the officer's vision with their finger off the trigger and indexed on the frame. Visually locate all other responding officers, and be mindful of other officers in your crossfire. The situation will dictate your position.

PURSUIT CONSIDERATIONS

If the driver pulls away after you initiate the stop, make a second attempt to pull over the vehicle. If the driver does not stop, the primary officer must decide whether the situation is legal, feasible, necessary, and meets their agency's criteria for pursuit. If a supervisor advises against pursuing or advises canceling the pursuit at any time, all officers must comply.

☑ LE1122.3. Identify when to conduct a vehicle pursuit that is legal, feasible, and necessary

If the vehicle stops and any suspects flee the vehicle, initiate a BOLO, set up a perimeter, and continue with the high-risk stop. Relay the details of the fleeing suspects to other responding officers. If the suspect vehicle begins to flee from the stop and then crashes, initiate a BOLO, set up a perimeter, and follow the high-risk traffic stop procedures.

Step 6: Decide Officer Assignments

TAKING COMMAND OF THE HIGH-RISK TRAFFIC STOP

Hold a brief discussion to determine the roles of the responding officers. While the primary officer assumes command of the high-risk traffic stop, the situation dictates who verbally controls the movements and actions of the driver and passengers. Only one officer should give instructions.

> LE1122.4. Differentiate between the roles of the primary and backup officers

Most of the time the primary officer verbally controls all occupants from the driver's side one at a time. Use loud, concise, clear commands. The contact officer should approach the suspect after the suspect is placed in a position of tactical disadvantage. The contact officer is responsible for handcuffing the suspect and searching the suspect before securing them in a patrol vehicle. The cover officer provides defensive protection for the contact officer during the arrest.

All officers must maintain situational awareness throughout the incident. There can be many officers moving within the traffic stop location. There will be noise, lights, and a heightened sense of anxiety. Keep yourself and your team safe during the incident by paying attention to what is happening around you. Practice deep breathing, remain focused, take your time, and recall your training.

Step 7: Issue Commands

VERBAL COMMANDS

You may use the PA system to identify yourself as a law enforcement officer. Maintain cover when giving voice commands. Instruct all occupants to put up their hands to where they are clearly visible.

If the driver does not immediately respond to your command, repeat the command. If they are still unresponsive, reassess and follow your agency's policies for the situation at hand. If an occupant absolutely refuses to exit the vehicle, treat them as a barricaded suspect and consult your agency's policies.

> LE1122.5. List the possible verbal commands to give to the driver

The following is an example of the verbal commands the primary officer can issue to control the occupants of the vehicle:

1. "Roll down all the windows."
2. "Raise your hands again where I can see them." (If the vehicle's windows are heavily tinted and the occupants are not easy to see, instruct the occupants to put their hands outside the windows so they remain visible.)
3. "Turn off your engine." (Note that because of newer car technology, there may not be a key in the ignition.)
4. "Remove and place your keys or key fob outside on the roof of your vehicle."
5. "Open your door from the outside with that same hand."
6. "Put your hand back above your head."
7. "Exit the vehicle on the driver's side. Do not close the driver's door. Keep it open."
8. "Keep your hands visible and put them above your head while facing away from me."

Once the driver has exited the vehicle, the primary officer can continue issuing the following commands:

1. "Step away from the vehicle."
2. "Extend your arms above your head."
3. "Lift the back of your shirt by the collar."
4. "Slowly turn in a complete circle."
    a. Look for any weapons or obvious bulges from possible weapons as the driver turns in a circle with their shirt lifted.
    b. If you observe a weapon, advise the driver that if they move toward their weapon, you will use appropriate force. Refer to the techniques you learned in Defensive Tactics.
5. "Stop, turn, and face away from me."
6. "Place your hands back in the air."
7. "Slowly step backward toward the sound of my voice."
8. If the vehicle has four doors, instruct the driver to:
    a. "Stop at the back door." (of a four-door vehicle)
    b. "Open the back door."
    c. "Continue backing up until I tell you to stop."

The contact officer will take over and issue commands to the driver directing them to the takedown area to be secured and searched. Where you handcuff the driver and passengers may vary. Some agencies handcuff all suspects near the front tires of the backup vehicle, leaving the back of the primary vehicle as a "safe zone." Other agencies take all suspects to the back of the backup vehicle to search and secure.

Step 8: Secure the Suspects

DETAINING THE DRIVER

Once the driver is in the takedown area, the contact officer tells the driver to kneel, lie prone, or assume another position of disadvantage. Holster your firearm, approach the driver, and handcuff them. Conduct a cursory pat down and secure any weapons.

☑ LE1122.6. Describe how to detain the driver appropriately

Walk the handcuffed driver behind the cover of the backup vehicle. Thoroughly search the driver. Follow up with a conversation about any remaining passengers and weapons. Place the handcuffed driver into a patrol vehicle. Once you secure the driver in the vehicle, move to a position of cover and draw your firearm, orient the muzzle in a safe position, based on the environment, that does not obstruct your vision with your finger off the trigger and indexed on the frame.

REMOVING PASSENGERS FROM THE SUSPECT'S VEHICLE

☑ LE1122.7. Describe how to remove the passengers from the suspect's vehicle

Do not remove any passengers from the vehicle until you secure the driver in the patrol vehicle. However, if the driver is uncooperative and refuses to exit their vehicle, remove the passengers from the vehicle. Only one suspect should be taken out of the vehicle at a time. Never take another suspect out of the vehicle until the previous suspect is secured in the back of a patrol vehicle and all officers are in or returned to position.

Follow the same procedures as used for the driver to individually remove, secure, and search each passenger. Instruct the last passenger exiting the vehicle to leave the door open, make sure all passengers are secured and, when possible, separate all suspects.

The *plus one rule* assumes that if you find one of something there is another. When you believe that you have removed all passengers from the suspect's vehicle, command any hidden passengers to make themselves known.

Step 9: Clear and Search the Vehicle

If there is no response to the command, more than one officer should cautiously approach the suspect's vehicle with their weapons pointed at it. The officer with the best vantage point should give commands to any discovered passenger. Only one officer should issue commands to prevent confusion. If a discovered passenger refuses to come out, consider retreating back to the patrol vehicle.

☑ LE1122.8.
Describe how to search the suspect's vehicle for hidden passengers

The officers who perform the systematic visual search of the vehicle will check the vehicle's interior for hidden passengers. After the interior is clear, retrieve the keys or remote to open the trunk. Move cautiously to the trunk area when attempting to clear it. One officer unlocks the trunk while another officer holds it down to prevent it from suddenly opening. After the trunk is unlocked, officers should assume a safe position, pointing their firearms at the trunk and making sure they are not in a crossfire position. An officer should lift the trunk lid and clear it. The vehicle may be a crime scene. Follow your agency's policies for searching the vehicle.

Step 10: Conclude the Stop

☑ LE1122.9.
Describe how to conclude a high-risk traffic stop

After the scene is secure and all is safe, the primary officer notifies dispatch to discontinue emergency radio traffic. Follow proper arrest procedures if you are arresting the driver or any passengers. If the occupants of the vehicle are not the suspects, explain the reason for the stop (for example, their vehicle matched the description of a vehicle used in a robbery), and release them.

Circumstances and your agency's policies and procedures will dictate the disposition and documentation of the high-risk traffic stop, such as seizing, impounding, or releasing the vehicle.

Document the incident, including:

- all information gathered from the time of roll call to locating the suspect
- confirmation of the warrant
- contact with and possible arrest of the suspect
- any seized evidence

Chapter 12
Traffic Crash Investigations

LESSON 1   Introduction to Traffic Crash Management / 439
LESSON 2   Assess a Traffic Crash Scene / 441
LESSON 3   Secure a Traffic Crash Scene / 444
LESSON 4   Injuries at a Traffic Crash Scene / 447
LESSON 5   Gather Traffic Crash Information / 449
LESSON 6   Gather Traffic Crash Evidence / 452
LESSON 7   Driver Information Exchange / 459
LESSON 8   Issue a Traffic Citation / 460
LESSON 9   Clear the Traffic Crash Scene / 462
LESSON 10   Complete a Traffic Crash Report / 463
LESSON 11   Manage Unique Traffic Crashes / 468

LESSON 1 Introduction to Traffic Crash Management

Lesson Goal

At the end of this lesson, you will know the basic steps of traffic crash management and how to safely approach a traffic crash scene.

Law enforcement officers conduct traffic crash investigations using a systematic approach, similar to the approach they use when responding to a robbery, battery, or homicide. This approach includes responding to, assessing, and protecting the scene; gathering and evaluating information and evidence; returning the scene to the normal condition; taking appropriate enforcement action; and documenting the crash.

TRAFFIC CRASH LAWS

A *traffic crash* is a collision involving one or more vehicles in motion causing property damage, personal injury, serious bodily injury, or death. A traffic crash is often the result of an unintentional non-criminal act. When someone crashes a vehicle to cause damage or injury intentionally, the incident is not a crash but a crime, such as aggravated battery or murder. The majority of traffic crashes do not involve criminal activity; however, treat each traffic crash as a potential crime scene until you determine the crash did not result from a criminal act.

Understanding Florida traffic laws will help you make these determinations as well as manage a crash scene within the law. You will also need to be able to defend these decisions in court by associating the corresponding Florida law to the facts of the incident. Chapter 316, F.S., State Uniform Traffic Control is the statutory chapter that governs traffic crash investigations in Florida.

LE1201.1. Describe the role of Florida law in investigating a traffic crash

10 STEPS TO MANAGING A CRASH SCENE AND INVESTIGATION

You must react quickly to a traffic crash incident and immediately begin to manage the scene. Although you may find yourself performing several steps at one time and some steps may occur in a different order, these 10 basic steps should occur during a traffic crash investigation.

Step 1: Approach the traffic crash scene safely.

Step 2: Assess the scene of the crash.

Step 3: Secure a safe environment at the crash scene.

Step 4: Provide first aid to injured people, if necessary.

Step 5: Gather traffic crash information.

LE1201.2. List the 10 steps for managing a crash investigation

Step 6: Investigate to determine how and why the crash occurred.

Step 7: Complete driver exchange of information.

Step 8: Take enforcement action.

Step 9: Return the scene to normal as quickly as possible, if appropriate.

Step 10: Document the crash.

Step 1: Approach the Traffic Crash Scene Safely

☑ LE1201.3. Describe how to approach a traffic crash scene

After getting a call from dispatch for a traffic crash, drive immediately and safely to the scene. Safety is a critical component when responding to the scene of a crash. Follow sound driving principles, and use lights and sirens while following your agency's policies and procedures as well as statutory requirements.

Get as much information as possible from dispatch regarding the traffic crash location, such as street names, addresses, or mile marker numbers, as well as vehicle descriptions, roadblocks, and other relevant information. The information you gather from dispatch will enable you to have a plan for managing the crash scene once you arrive. Make parking decisions quickly based on the nature of the traffic scene.

LESSON 2 Assess a Traffic Crash Scene

Lesson Goal

At the end of this lesson, you will know how to assess a traffic crash scene and its jurisdiction, how to respond if there is a fire or hazardous materials, and when to request additional resources.

Step 2: Assess the Scene of the Crash

Your initial response will include a quick assessment to decide if you need to request additional assistance. As you approach, analyze the scene from a distance to identify the extent of the traffic crash, the number of involved vehicles, and the risk for fire or hazardous materials. If there appears to be a need for additional resources, have them dispatched. You can always cancel them if you determine at a later point they are no longer necessary.

LOCATE ALL INVOLVED VEHICLES OR PEOPLE

Locating all involved vehicles, people, and damaged property will identify the parameters of the total traffic crash scene. Determine vehicle paths by examining evidence left on the road and surrounding property, such as skid marks, and damaged road signs, landscaping, or buildings. Thoroughly, yet quickly, scan the entire scene. Keep in mind that there may be vehicles or people involved in the traffic crash that have left the scene or are not immediately visible during your initial assessment. For example, vehicles or people projected over embankments or shrubs, or into gullies or waterways may not be immediately visible.

☑ LE1202.1. Describe how to locate all vehicles and people involved in a traffic crash

MANAGE ANY FIRES

Look for dangers and hazards at the crash scene such as the potential for fire, or downed power lines or wires. This can be difficult to identify immediately, as crash damage can block recognition of a fire, and poor weather and darkness can conceal downed power lines.

A small fire may be minor enough to immediately manage with the fire extinguisher in your vehicle. If necessary, request assistance from the fire department. In the event of a vehicle fire, decide how to evacuate everyone on the scene to a safe location. When selecting a safe location, consider the amount of traffic, the weather and wind direction, and the buildings in the area affected by the crash. Be aware of the location of crash debris, such as small pieces of metal and glass, which can pose additional threats to both vehicles and pedestrians.

☑ LE1202.2. Describe how to manage fire hazards at the scene

Use verbal commands and gestures to direct everyone at the scene away from the fire and toward the designated safe location. If the scene is large in scope and contains many people, use your vehicle's public address (PA) system to direct them away from the scene.

IDENTIFY HAZARDOUS MATERIALS

Dispatch might send you to a traffic crash scene involving a vehicle carrying hazardous material, which can pose a significant danger. A **hazardous material (hazmat)** is any substance or material that, when released, may cause harm, serious injury, or death to humans or animals, or harm the environment. Chemical, biological, radiological, nuclear, and explosive (CBRNE) threats include both industrial and weaponized chemical hazards. Industrial chemical hazards occur when hazardous materials are released due to accidents. Some examples include accidents involving tankers or semitrailers, railroad cars, gasoline stations, and manufacturing plants.

☑ LE1202.3. Describe how to respond to a traffic crash scene involving hazardous materials

Before approaching the scene, look for hazardous conditions, such as fluids on the ground, clouds of gas or smoke, or people lying injured on the road. Use binoculars to determine if the vehicle's contents are hazardous by locating a placard on the back or side of the vehicle.

The **Emergency Response Guidebook (ERG)** identifies hazardous materials, outlines basic actions for first responders, recommends areas of protective action, and gives responders an initial safety plan. Refer to the *ERG* to verify the contents of the vehicle and the recommended minimum evacuation distances in all directions. It is available in print, online, or as a mobile app.

The *ERG* is composed of color-coded sections. The white section includes the introduction, instructions, guidance, and placards. The yellow and blue sections identify material, while the orange section lists response guidelines related to potential hazards, public safety, and emergency response. Finally, the green section contains information on evacuation details for certain materials.

The U.S. Department of Transportation (DOT) has established the United Nations/North American (UN/NA) four-digit numbering system to identify hazardous materials. You may be able to identify a material using the *ERG* by finding any one of the following:

- the four-digit number on the placard or orange panel on the container
- the name of the material on the shipping papers or packaging
- the number of the material on the shipping papers or packaging

If you suspect the presence of hazardous materials, direct people on the scene to evacuate toward an upwind location. Enter the crash scene using extreme caution. Chapter 14 contains more information about hazmat incidents and using the *ERG*.

MANAGE ADDITIONAL RESOURCES

☑ LE1202.4. Recognize the need for additional resources at a traffic crash

Traffic crash scenes may require special arrangements for:

- directing traffic, establishing and maintaining roadblocks
- obtaining medical assistance
- completing searches
- taking photographs, measuring tire marks, processing evidence

- making an arrest
- towing oversized, hazardous, or commercial vehicle traffic
- completing paperwork

Additional resources may include:

- the traffic homicide investigative unit of your agency, the county sheriff's office, or the Florida Highway Patrol (FHP)
- the fire department or hazmat team
- DOT
- FHP Commercial Vehicle Enforcement
- local or state traffic engineering
- crime scene investigators

Contact dispatch to arrange for additional resources and relay any unusual details, hazards, dangers, or medical issues relevant to the scene. A backup unit will generally follow the instructions of the primary unit and help with whatever the primary unit needs.

DETERMINE JURISDICTION

The ***first harmful event***, or the first event during a traffic crash that caused injury or property damage, will determine the jurisdiction, time, place, and type of crash. The first harmful event determines the time, place, and type of crash. Evidence of the first harmful event may be crash debris, fixed property damage, broken glass, gouge marks, or scrape marks.

☑ LE1202.5. Determine the jurisdiction of the traffic crash

Should the first harmful event occur outside of your jurisdiction, stay at the crash scene to protect the public and the scene until the proper agency arrives. You might be able to assist with the investigation or provide help with traffic control, depending on your agency's policies. Some agencies may have policies governing how to investigate a crash with multijurisdictional boundaries.

When you are unable to determine the jurisdiction of the traffic crash scene, remain on the scene. Contact FHP, as they have statewide jurisdiction, or refer to your agency's policies and procedures. If the crash scene involves a traffic homicide or serious bodily injury, call dispatch and wait for a traffic homicide investigator.

If a crash is suspected to be the result of a criminal act involving homicide or serious bodily injury, do not move the vehicles or any items within the scene until after the traffic homicide investigator assesses the scene and documents the evidence, or until otherwise directed.

LESSON 3 Secure a Traffic Crash Scene

⊚ Lesson Goal

At the end of this lesson, you will know how to safely secure a traffic crash scene considering vehicle position, reflective clothing, warning devices, traffic diversion, and property and evidence protection.

Step 3: Secure a Safe Environment at the Crash Scene

Traffic crash scenes draw drivers' attention away from the road and can lead to staring or distracted driving. This slows traffic flow and can become a hazard since drivers tend to focus more on the crash and less on driving around the scene. Many secondary crashes happen because of distracted drivers. Nighttime crash scenes compound this hazard because visibility is limited. People who struggle with driving at night find it difficult to adjust from the bright lights around a crash scene. Emergency vehicle lights, heavy traffic, or movement on and off the road can reduce visibility. Traffic conditions, weather conditions, buildings, signs, and terrain can also influence a driver's ability to see the road and any vehicles on it.

Following your immediate assessment, securing the scene will require quick thinking and swift action. Decide where to park your patrol vehicle, what reflective clothing to wear, and which warning devices to use to divert traffic and protect the scene.

POSITION YOUR VEHICLE

☑ LE1203.1.
Describe how to position your vehicle at a crash scene

The primary tool for controlling traffic is your vehicle, as it warns motorists of the crash scene. Position your vehicle to protect the scene, prevent additional crashes, and redirect the flow of traffic. Park your vehicle in a safe location visible to oncoming traffic, away from hazards, and to avoid damaging any evidence.

Turn on your patrol vehicle's emergency lights as a caution or alert. Adjust the headlights to low beam so you do not blind drivers approaching from the opposite direction. Keep your emergency lights on throughout the traffic crash management process.

PERSONAL SAFETY

☑ LE1203.2.
Recognize the importance of wearing reflective clothing

It is extremely important, while directing traffic or investigating a crash scene, that you remain visible to oncoming traffic. Wear a reflective vest over your uniform; however, be sure you still have access to your gun belt. A flashlight with a wand attachment and reflective gloves will increase your visibility. Work facing oncoming traffic whenever possible. This will enable you to see hazardous situations that might develop.

RELOCATING CRASH VEHICLES TO A SAFE LOCATION

☑ LE1203.3.
Describe when to relocate crash vehicles

If circumstances allow, move vehicles out of the roadway to prevent accidents, encourage traffic flow, and create room for emergency vehicles to access the crash site.

There are exceptions to this rule:

- a traffic crash with injuries or fatalities
- the vehicles are too disabled to move
- the crash scene is a crime scene that will need processing

Before allowing drivers to relocate their vehicles, get their driver licenses and direct them where to move the vehicles, or to where you want to continue processing the incident. Follow your agency's policies and procedures for relocating the vehicle of a traumatized or incapacitated driver. You may need to mark the final rest points of all four tires with chalk or whatever your agency uses.

POSITION WARNING DEVICES

Your agency may use outside resources, such as the public works department, to provide additional warning devices. Warning devices for alerting and directing motorists include:

- barricades
- flares or fuses
- message boards
- signs
- traffic cones, reflective triangles

Based on multiple crash scene factors, decide what type of warning devices to use, how many will be required, and how to position them to prevent further damage or injury. Consider the following factors:

☑ LE1203.4. Describe how to position warning devices

- the extent of the scene or the size of the area that needs protection—determine the distance between the first harmful event and the final resting place of vehicles and debris. The final resting place, or *final rest*, is the point when all movement resulting from the crash comes to a halt.
- the number of traffic lanes—consider how quickly drivers can react to the traffic disturbance and change lanes.
- the normal speed of travel on the road—place the warning devices farther away from the scene the faster the traffic is moving. If you requested backup, position one of the officers at the first warning device.
- environmental conditions—consider how warning devices appear to oncoming traffic in rain or fog.

Flares or fuses can serve as effective warning devices at night, are visible during the day, and are easily stored in the trunk of your patrol vehicle. Before placing flares, make sure there are no flammable items, liquids, chemicals, or hazardous materials within the crash scene. If there is the chance of a hazmat situation, use the *ERG* to determine a safe distance away from the scene to place a flare or fuse. Be aware of drought conditions and keep flares or fuses away from dry grass on the side of the road, or any other combustible material that could cause a wildfire.

DIVERT TRAFFIC

☑ LE1203.5.
Describe how to divert traffic around a crash scene

Figure 12-1 is an example of a traffic crash scene involving two disabled vehicles on a two-lane road. The officer parked the patrol vehicle in the road to block oncoming traffic from the crash scene and placed flares or cones in front of, alongside of, and behind the involved vehicles. Generally, law enforcement agencies in Florida use this type of placement method, as it draws the attention of drivers to the cones or flares, and directs them to drive around the scene.

An alternative placement method involves parking the patrol vehicle near the scene with the emergency lights activated on the road. This serves not only as a physical barrier to protect the scene, but as a warning device for rerouting other road users when flares and cones are not available.

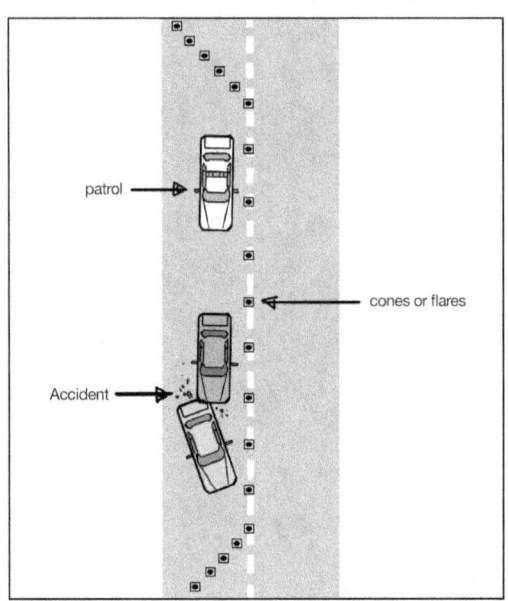

Figure 12-1
Traffic cones or flares

If there is no safe way to protect the scene from traffic using barricades, flares or fuses, signs, or traffic cones, then create a roadblock. The roadblock can prevent injury or damage to motorists and protect the crash scene. When setting up a roadblock, try to avoid redirecting traffic through residential areas, schools, and playgrounds. Immediately inform dispatch of the roadblock and redirection of traffic. Your agency will relay the information to the appropriate resources and other affected jurisdictions. Be sure to inform dispatch how long you think it will take to clear the scene and reopen the road. It is your responsibility to direct traffic around the crash scene until the road is completely clear.

PROTECT PERSONAL PROPERTY AND EVIDENCE

☑ LE1203.6.
Recognize the importance of protecting personal property at a crash scene

In addition to protecting the traffic crash scene for officer, traffic, and scene safety, you must protect personal property. If a traffic crash exposes driver or passenger property, such as phones, purses, wallets, or anything that was in their vehicles, take a moment to return them to the motorist or secure them in a vehicle. Should any of the involved vehicles require a tow, document on the tow receipt any personal property remaining in a crash vehicle.

A traffic crash scene can become a crime scene, so it is important to use the crime scene processing techniques covered in Chapter 9. If a crash is suspected to be the result of a criminal act involving homicide or serious bodily injury, do not touch or move anything except those who are injured. If you cannot move them, then move only those things surrounding them that could be hazardous or life threatening.

Vehicles used in the commission of a crime and involved in a traffic crash that results in death or serious bodily injury must be preserved for further investigation. Do not move these vehicles until after an investigator assesses the scene and documents the evidence, or until otherwise directed. If the crash includes serious bodily injury or a homicide, request a traffic homicide investigator to process the scene.

LESSON 4 Injuries at a Traffic Crash Scene

Lesson Goal

At the end of this lesson, you will know the main types of traffic crash injuries and ensure that EMS arrives on the scene.

Think About This

You are responding to a traffic crash and notice the driver appears to need medical attention. EMS has not arrived yet. What is your course of action?

Step 4: Provide First Aid to Injured People

TRAFFIC CRASH INJURIES

A traffic crash may involve people with injuries ranging from non-visible to severe or fatal trauma. Your first-aid training should prepare you for responding to trauma-related issues associated with a traffic crash.

Traffic crash injuries are classified into six legal categories that you will use in your incident report:

☑ LE1204.1. Describe the main types of traffic crash injuries

1. none—no injury.
2. *possible injury*—any injury reported or claimed that is not a fatal injury, suspected serious injury, or suspected minor injury. Examples include momentary loss of consciousness, claim of injury, limping, or complaint of pain or nausea. A possible injury is reported by the individual or is indicated by their behavior, but no wound or injury is readily evident.
3. *non-incapacitating injury*—a non-disabling injury, such as a laceration, scrape, or bruise.
4. *incapacitating injury*—a serious bodily injury that is non-fatal, resulting in one or more of the following:
   - severe laceration resulting in exposure of underlying tissues/muscles/organs or significant loss of blood
   - broken or distorted extremity (arm or leg)
   - crush injuries
   - suspected skull, chest, or abdominal injury other than bruises or minor lacerations
   - significant burns (second- and third-degree burns over 10% or more of the body)
   - unconsciousness when taken from the crash scene
   - paralysis

5. *fatal injury*—an injury resulting in an individual's death within a 30-day period after the traffic crash accident.
6. *non-traffic fatal injury*—a fatality that is unrelated to the traffic crash accident, such as a heart attack, natural causes, suicide, or homicide.

The Florida Statutes further define a **serious bodily injury** as an injury to a person, including the driver, which consists of a physical condition that creates a substantial risk of death, serious personal disfigurement, or protracted loss or impairment of the function of a bodily member or organ.

EMS AT A TRAFFIC CRASH SCENE

During the initial call reporting the traffic crash, dispatch will ask the caller if there are any injured people on the scene. If there are, dispatch will send emergency medical services (EMS) to the scene.

☑ LE1204.2. Describe how to manage injured people at a crash scene

If you arrive first, locate all of the people involved in the crash. If the scene involves injured people, determine the extent of the injuries. Remember your first-aid training and determine if you can move them immediately to a safe location and provide first aid until EMS arrives. If you cannot move them, try to remove any hazards surrounding them, and provide first aid in place.

If EMS is not present when you arrive, you are responsible for making sure EMS is on the way to the scene by contacting dispatch.

LESSON 5 Gather Traffic Crash Information

Lesson Goal

At the end of this lesson, you will know how to gather information from people at a traffic crash scene.

Think About This

You begin interviewing one of the drivers from the scene of a crash. At first, it seems like the driver was alone in the vehicle, but then he mentions that his kids were there at the time of the crash. You ask him where his kids are now and he says their mother picked them up after the crash so they could go home right away. What should you have done first to get this information earlier?

Step 5: Gather Traffic Crash Information

After you secure the traffic crash scene, aid the injured, and protect any evidence or personal property, you should begin gathering information related to the traffic crash from people on the scene. It is common for those involved in a crash to be emotionally upset, regardless of the severity of the crash. Your role is to remain calm and empathetic to the crash victims while managing the scene and investigating the crash. Remember to practice the three roles of a law enforcement officer—supporter, stabilizer, and enforcer—that you learned in Chapter 1.

OBTAIN DRIVER'S INFORMATION

After determining which driver(s) and vehicle(s) were involved in the crash, ask them to provide their driver licenses, vehicle registrations, and proof of insurance. Injuries or other special circumstances may prevent the driver from providing this information immediately. However, according to the Florida Statutes, a driver involved in a crash resulting in injury or death, or damage to another vehicle or property, if able, must provide this specific information to you at the scene. You must document this information in your traffic crash report and verify it in DAVID, FCIC/NCIC, and other appropriate databases.

☑ LE1205.1. Identify the information to collect at a crash scene

Ask the driver if there were any passengers in the vehicle, whether or not you see passengers present at the scene. This ensures that you know, rather than assume, how many people were in the vehicle at the time of the crash.

INTERVIEW PEOPLE ON THE SCENE

Before interviewing people at the crash scene, you must make the distinction between the drivers involved, those who witnessed the crash, those who may have heard, but not seen, the crash, and those who are providing information based on the final location of the vehicles. Keep in mind that witnesses are not legally obligated to give any information or provide a statement about a traffic crash.

Sometimes, witness accounts are all a traffic crash investigator can rely on when determining how the crash occurred. Passenger statements are voluntary, and the information they provide is important. However, if a driver involved in a traffic crash is unable to give a report or a statement about the crash, Florida law requires passengers to make a statement on behalf of the driver.

Separate drivers from witnesses to prevent them from influencing each other's statements or recollections. Do not allow drivers to discuss what happened with anyone on the scene, including other drivers and witnesses. Witnesses may occasionally be hard to separate, especially if the crash scene involves injured family members. Locate safe places for the drivers, passengers, non-motorists, and witnesses to stand or sit while you are interviewing others. A safe location may be:

- away from oncoming traffic
- protected from environmental conditions
- out of the path of emergency vehicles at the scene

☑ LE1205.2. Recognize the importance of interviewing and obtaining statements at the crash scene

When deciding the order of interviews, be mindful of independent witnesses who choose to be on the scene because of their good intention to help. They usually provide more accurate and reliable information about the traffic crash. Be courteous and do not detain them at the scene any longer than is necessary to collect their statements and information.

To help witnesses recall specific events and details of the crash, try to interview them close to where they were at the time of the crash. Some witnesses may have had a better vantage point of the crash than others. Even if there are no passengers immediately identifiable, you need to make sure that you are not missing a passenger for any reason. When interviewing a passenger, determine the passenger's relationship to the driver to identify any potential biases in their statements.

Verify the drivers' and each witness' ability to understand your request for a statement about the traffic crash. It is best to ask open-ended questions, as described in Chapter 4, when conducting interviews. Ask questions that will clarify what happened and resolve any discrepancies between witnesses' statements. Ask questions such as, "Can you give me information about the crash?" and "Can you tell me how this person was hurt?"

During each interview, record the interviewee's contact information, such as their name, current street address, and phone number, for your report and in case you need to follow up on the interview later. If EMS needs to transport an injured person to a hospital, get that person's contact information and conduct a follow-up interview.

First responders, such as EMS or fire department personnel, may also have valuable information concerning the post-crash events. For example, people involved in the crash may have made spontaneous statements about the crash in their presence. Document in your report any indications of impairment caused by injury, dementia, intellectual disability, intoxication, medication, or any other cause that may affect the drivers' or witnesses' comprehension or memory.

Some traffic crash situations such as DUIs, hit-and-runs, or serious bodily injury investigations may require you to take written or recorded statements. These can be useful when investigating a traffic crash, such as confirming other witnesses' testimonies at the scene or for prosecuting drivers in court. Written or recorded statements also help collect more accurate information by prompting involved people to record their information immediately after the crash. Having witnesses write statements about what they saw and heard will help you obtain valuable information. Witnesses who write their own statements will free you up to perform other on-scene tasks.

People manage their emotions differently, so remember to practice empathy when gathering information from anyone that is involved in or is a witness to the crash.

LESSON 6 Gather Traffic Crash Evidence

Lesson Goal

At the end of this lesson, you will know how to determine why and how a traffic crash occurred by gathering evidence at the scene.

Step 6: Investigate to Determine How and Why a Traffic Crash Occurred

PHASES OF A TRAFFIC CRASH

The three phases of a traffic crash are pre-collision, at-collision, and post-collision. Knowledge of each phase will help you determine how and why the crash occurred, and how the vehicle reached its final resting place after the crash.

☑ LE1206.1. Describe the three phases of a traffic crash

Phase 1—the pre-collision phase begins when the driver becomes aware of a danger or hazard.

- The point of perception occurs when the driver becomes aware of a danger or hazard.
- *Reaction time* is the length of time between the point of perception and the beginning of the evasive action.
- *Evasive action* is any action the driver takes to alter the speed or direction of a vehicle or to avoid danger or hazard, such as applying the brakes, turning the steering wheel, or moving the vehicle out of the way.
- The point of no escape is the point in time when the crash is inevitable, regardless of the evasive action taken.

Phase 2—the at-collision phase begins with the time of the initial impact or contact.

- Encroachment occurs when vehicles, property, or people begin to enter the same space at the same time and make contact, and where the first injury or damage may occur. The driver may still be able to take evasive action to reduce the severity of the crash.
- Maximum engagement is the point at which the vehicles, property, or people crush together to the greatest extent.

Phase 3—the post-collision phase (disengagement) begins when the vehicles, property, or people separate, either naturally or from post-crash intervention by a person.

- A second impact can occur in chain reaction collisions or when one vehicle glances off another into the path of a third vehicle or object.

VEHICLE DYNAMICS DURING A TRAFFIC CRASH

Basic physics states that an object in motion continues to remain in motion until acted upon by an external force. Vehicle dynamics refers to vehicle movement during and after a collision. It can help you determine how and why the crash occurred and the area of collision. The *area of collision (AOC)* is the location of the first harmful event, or the first damage-producing event in the traffic crash. The AOC indicates the area where the collision occurred, assists you in determining the direction a vehicle was traveling, and the probable location of the debris field. The point of impact is the place where a moving vehicle or object struck another vehicle, another object, or the road.

☑ LE1206.2. Describe the vehicle dynamics in a traffic crash

Struck or moved objects in the path of the vehicle may alter the vehicle dynamics and help determine the AOC by showing the path a vehicle followed either before or after the crash. Look for objects or items at the scene moved from their original location and inconsistent with the original direction of the vehicles or with the direction of force. Examining these objects, the vehicle dynamics, the AOC and point of impact, may help explain damage done to all the vehicles and whether there may have been other factors involved in the crash.

The following examples will illustrate vehicle dynamics in a traffic crash. The actual result will depend on the size, weight, and speed of the vehicle.

- Example 1—a vehicle is traveling north, striking a second vehicle traveling east. Expect the two vehicles to travel into the northeast quadrant.
- Example 2—a vehicle is traveling south, striking a second vehicle traveling west. Expect the two vehicles to travel into the southwest quadrant.
- Example 3—a vehicle is traveling south, striking a second vehicle traveling east. Expect the two vehicles to travel into the southeast quadrant.
- Example 4—a vehicle is traveling north, striking a second vehicle traveling west. Expect the two vehicles to travel into the northwest quadrant.

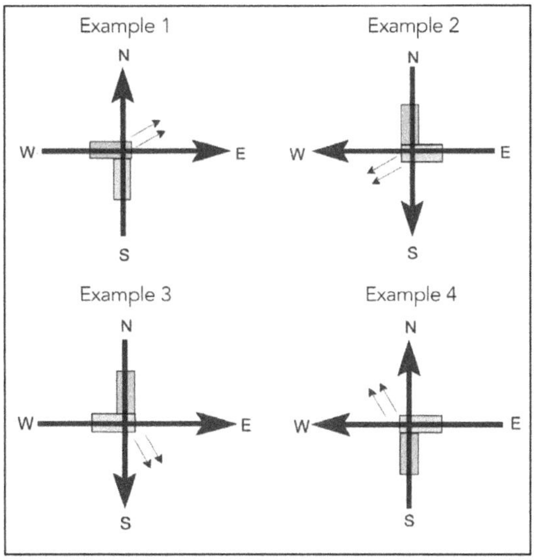

TRAFFIC CRASH EVIDENCE

Interpreting traffic crash evidence correctly can also help determine how and why the crash occurred. The involved vehicles may have pre-existing damage from past crashes. The road may also have pre-existing damage, such as skid marks and debris from other incidents.

Figure 12-2 Vehicle dynamics in a crash

VEHICLE EVIDENCE

Pre-existing damage is any damage existing on a vehicle before the crash. It is usually identifiable as damage that does not fit the pattern of the crash and appears rusted, dirty, or weathered.

☑ LE1206.3. Identify vehicle evidence found at a crash scene

Contact damage is any damage that did not exist on a vehicle before the crash. Contact damage results from the direct pressure of any object in a collision or rollover and appears as:

- scrape marks or striations (parallel scrapes or scratches) on the body of the vehicle
- material rub-off, such as paint from the other vehicle (called paint transfer), rubber, or tree bark
- fiber transfer, such as from a person's clothing
- hair or blood
- punctures to or imprints on a bumper, guardrail, or other fixed object

Contact damage should tell you the part of the vehicle hit first by examining the direction of the damage on the vehicle and tracing the damage backwards to the first appearance of damage. Contact damage should be consistent with other physical evidence, statements from people involved, and independent witnesses.

Induced damage is any damage that did not exist before the crash, but, unlike contact damage, is not visually evident at the crash scene. Induced damage often occurs as bending, breaking, crumpling, twisting, distortion, or buckling of vehicle metal.

ROAD EVIDENCE

☑ LE1206.4. Identify road evidence at a crash scene

A *gouge* is a cut into the surface of the road where some part of the vehicle removed the road surface material. For example, a bolt on the underside of a vehicle cuts into the pavement, leaving a trench or gouge in the road at the AOC. A gouge may indicate an AOC.

A scrape is a broad area of a hard surface covered with many scratches, striations, or streak marks made without great pressure by a sliding metal part. Scrapes occur between the AOC and the point of the vehicle's final rest.

Runoff is a pool or trail of fluids escaping from a vehicle because of impact. Quite often, hard impacts will make radiators, hoses, and brake lines burst. When this occurs, the liquid will run out of the vehicle onto the road. Often, these liquids will leave a trail from the AOC to the final resting place. While not pinpointing the exact location of the AOC, runoffs can provide evidence of the general location.

Debris is loose material spread across the road due to the crash. Debris can be dirt, liquids, vehicle parts, and other materials from the involved vehicles. Identifying where debris begins on the road may help indicate the AOC. Locating vehicle parts such as bumpers, headlights, and tail light lenses can also indicate the AOC and the direction a vehicle was traveling. Vehicle parts continue to move in the direction of the force of the impact until stopped by an object or the road surface.

The forces involved in collisions cause the debris from the vehicle to fall loose and in the direction of the force. Matching the damage on the vehicles to the debris found at the scene may serve as additional evidence in determining the AOC. For example, if a vehicle's rear reflectors are red and there are yellow reflector pieces lying on the ground, you can conclude this debris did not come from this crash. Recently broken glass has sharp, well-defined edges; by contrast, glass that has been on the road for some time will have rounded edges.

TIRE MARKS

A *surface mark* is any mark created by a vehicle's tire at a crash scene. Each type of surface mark on the road at the scene can provide specific information.

Tires can create several different types of marks, depending on:

- the road surface
- what the brakes are doing
- how the vehicle is accelerating or decelerating
- what the steering wheel is doing during the traffic crash

☑ LE1206.5. Describe the types of tire marks left on the road at a crash scene

Your task is to determine which mark came from which vehicle, and from which tire of the vehicle.

A skid mark is the black mark left by a tire sliding while it is unable to rotate. Skid marks tend to be straight, although they can show some curvature due to asymmetrical braking (not all brake pads lock simultaneously) or the crown of the road. These factors can make the vehicle depart from a straight-ahead path. The tire grooves are generally visible and easy to see in a skid mark. Front tire skid marks tend to be darker than rear tire marks, as weight shifts toward the front of the vehicle when braking. The outside edges of the tire mark may be darker than the inside area. Rear tire skid marks tend to be even in appearance with no dark outside edges.

When a vehicle brakes hard, tire rotation will stop before skid marks begin. The tires leave a light discoloration, or shadow mark, which is often difficult to see on the road. This discoloration, or incipient skid or impending skid mark, is the type of skid mark left by an anti-lock braking system (ABS). The incipient skid is the place you will begin to measure the skid mark. It is temporary and may be visible for only 15 to 20 minutes after the crash.

Anti-lock braking system (ABS) scuff marks are the patterns left by a vehicle with anti-lock brakes when a driver brakes hard. A scuff mark is a tire mark from a wheel that is both rotating and slipping on the road surface. The ABS prevents the wheels from locking by rapidly applying and releasing the brake while allowing the driver to remain in control of the steering. Vehicles equipped with ABS may leave faint, intermittent, visible skid marks. These marks do not resemble solid skid marks and may disappear 15 to 20 minutes after the incident.

Intermittent skid marks are a series of heavy skid marks with long gaps of more than 15 feet between them, caused by a driver who rapidly applies and releases the brakes, to stop the vehicle. Skid marks made by a bouncing vehicle that just struck a pothole or bump in the road are not continuous. However, the length of the skid mark and the length of the space between them are uniform, consistent, and less than 3 feet to 4 feet apart.

Skip skid marks are a series of skid marks, usually short in length with irregular intervals between them. This pattern appears on the road when a vehicle has a sudden load shift from braking hard, causing the vehicle to bounce. Skip skid marks are typically from trailer vehicles. However, a vehicle skidding on a bumpy road can also make this type of mark.

Offset skid marks are skid marks that indicate a sudden change in the direction of a tire due to collision forces. They are the direct result of the movement of the vehicle by the force of collision and occur at the moment of impact. The only item of evidence pinpointing the exact AOC on the road is offset skid marks.

A squeegee mark is a strip of dry pavement remaining after a vehicle skids on a wet road. The locked tire acts similarly to a window squeegee by removing water from the skid path. Due to the way these marks are made, they disappear quickly and are temporary evidence.

A **furrow mark** is a type of trench dug by locked tires moving across a soft surface such as gravel, sand, grass, or dirt. The furrow is shallow at the beginning of the skid and deepens with a piling of the surface material in front of the tire at the place where the vehicle finally rests.

A scuff or yaw mark occurs when a vehicle loses tire traction from entering a curve too fast or from oversteering. The tires continue rotating but slide sideways at the same time, leaving marks that remain on the road. Scuff or yaw marks are always curved and will show a sideways striping or striation from the side motion of the tires. Scuff or yaw marks may be evidence of the driver beginning to lose control of the vehicle.

Acceleration scuff marks result from rapid acceleration from a stop, causing the tires to produce gradually fading dark tire marks.

A tire print is a mark left by a tire rolling over a soft material such as sand or dirt, or rolling through a liquid on a hard surface, such as oil, which leaves an identifiable pattern matching the tread of the tire.

PHOTOGRAPH THE TRAFFIC CRASH SCENE

The best way to preserve the location of evidence found at the traffic crash scene is with a combination of photographs, measurements, and sketches. Photographs serve as a true and accurate depiction of the crash scene. You can use photographs later to recall facts and discover information that you may have overlooked at the scene. Photographs also serve as evidence to prosecute traffic violators and document the extent of damage.

Photographs of a traffic crash scene:

- record the scene's physical condition
- supplement other documentation
- aid in drawing conclusions about the crash
- can assist a traffic homicide investigator in reconstructing the crash

Photograph the crash scene immediately after the emergency is under control, but before someone can disturb the evidence or alter the scene. Record the date, time, and person taking the photographs. Photograph all relevant evidence and damage from several angles. For the involved vehicles, photograph all the corners, sides, approach paths, and the AOC. Your agency policies and the severity of injuries determine how you will photograph evidence in a crash investigation.

☑ LE1206.6. Describe what to photograph at a crash scene

MEASURE THE TRAFFIC CRASH SCENE

After photographing the traffic crash scene, take measurements to document distances, locations, and the length of tire marks and roadway evidence. Use crash scene measurements to precisely locate significant objects in the crash, to document the events of the crash accurately, and to later ensure accurate testimony in court. When taking measurements at the crash scene, be aware of safety issues for people on the scene.

Instruments to measure evidence include, but are not limited to:

- rolling measuring wheels
- fiberglass and steel measuring tapes of various lengths
- laser measuring devices

☑ LE1206.7. Describe how to measure the location of evidence at a crash scene

Measure the temporary evidence first:

- the AOC
- scuff marks
- squeegee marks
- tire marks
- skid marks
- tire prints
- gouges and scratches
- debris of any type
- vehicle parts
- liquids or runoff
- any item damaged or struck as a result of the crash
- the final resting positions of vehicles and bodies

Measure more permanent evidence as soon as practical:

- road dimensions
- sight distances
- grade or slope
- locations of traffic-control devices
- distances between landmarks

MEASURE SKID MARKS

If a crash is suspected to be the result of a criminal act involving homicide or serious bodily injury, after photographing the crash scene and taking measurements of other evidence, a traffic homicide investigator uses mathematical formulas to calculate the possible speed a vehicle was traveling when the skid occurred.

☑ LE1206.8.
Describe how to measure skid marks

The procedures for measuring skid marks include determining how many wheels were skidding and matching each skid mark to a specific wheel. Investigators use the following abbreviations to identify which tire made a specific mark on the road:

LF—left front	RF—right front
LR—left rear	RR—right rear

To measure skid marks, locate the beginning, the end, and all gaps made by each wheel and mark using an agency-approved method. Photograph the skid marks again after making your marks. In the case of an offset skid mark, measure the skid in two parts, recording the two lengths separately.

1. Record and label the distance from the beginning of the skid to the beginning of the offset.
2. Record and label the distance from the beginning of the offset to the end of the skid.
3. Measure each surface mark separately when the marks cross multiple surfaces, such as the road, sidewalk, landscaping, or lawn.

Common mistakes that affect accurate measurements include:

- identifying the wrong type of surface where the skid marks were made
- incorrectly identifying the beginning of a skid mark
- including gaps when measuring the skid

FIELD SKETCH THE TRAFFIC CRASH SCENE

Record the locations and lengths of all skid marks and other evidence at the crash scene in a field sketch. A *field sketch* is a rough drawing of the scene. The sketch uses simple symbols to indicate the details of the crash.

☑ LE1206.9.
Describe how to draw a field sketch of a crash scene

Use whatever symbols you choose, but use them consistently. This sketch will help document information concerning the crash and help recreate the crash scene diagram later. The amount of detail on the sketch will depend on the seriousness of the crash, the amount of evidence, or the information collected. The sketch should include only significant factual and observable items. When drawing a field sketch, clearly indicate all relevant evidence and measurements in the sketch. The field sketch should be consistent with any photographs taken and may be used as evidence in court along with the final sketch. The field sketch may also be used to complete the crash diagram later.

LESSON 7 Driver Information Exchange

ⓘ Lesson Goal

At the end of this lesson, you will know how to facilitate a driver information exchange and complete the appropriate form at a traffic crash scene.

Step 7: Complete Driver Exchange of Information

You, or the drivers, must complete a driver exchange of information form at all traffic crashes. Explain to the drivers involved in the crash that state law requires them to complete the form and then exchange the completed forms with each other. Exchanging driver information is important, not only because the law requires it, but because it also provides insurance companies with the necessary information to process claims for damage.

☑ LE1207.1. Recognize the role of the driver information exchange at a crash scene

If the officer completes the crash report, the exchange of information is still included as part of the report and the officer is responsible for providing the drivers with this information. The officer is also responsible for submitting the report within 10 days if it meets the criteria outlined in chapter 316, F.S. If the officer is not present, Florida law requires drivers to exchange information and report that information to FLHSMV within 10 days of the traffic crash incident.

Whether you determine the traffic crash incident does or does not require a written report, use form HSMV 90011S:

☑ LE1207.2. Describe how to complete the Driver Report of Traffic Crash (Self Report) or Driver Exchange of Information form (HSMV 90011S)

- Driver Report of Traffic Crash (Self Report)
- Driver Exchange of Information form

Show the drivers what fields to complete and where to sign, as each agency may have a different version of the form. The driver of each vehicle must provide the following information:

- name
- current street address
- driver license or learner's permit number
- registration number of the vehicle they are driving
- insurance information

Instruct them to print legibly using a black ballpoint pen. Each driver should sign and date their completed form before exchanging the form with the other driver involved in the traffic crash. If you do not use the HSMV 90011S for driver exchange of information, provide each driver or non-motorist with the other party's driver and vehicle information.

You may come across a driver who cannot adequately read or complete the form due to language or physical limitations. Practice empathy and patience. Provide reasonable accommodation by gathering the required information, completing the form for the driver, and instructing the driver to sign and date it. This helps to make sure that the information provided is valid and accurate. Drivers can also complete the form online on the Florida Highway Safety and Motor Vehicles website.

LESSON 8 Issue a Traffic Citation

Lesson Goal

At the end of this lesson, you will know how to identify traffic violations and issue citations based on evidence found at the scene.

Step 8: Take Enforcement Action

All of the evidence found on the crash scene, when viewed as a whole, should provide an accurate location of the AOC and point to how and why the crash occurred.

LE1208.1. Determine whether to issue a citation based on evidence at the scene

Compare your observations of the vehicle and road evidence, and statements from drivers, passengers, and witnesses, for consistency and validation of the events. Include any contributing factors, such as the conditions of the road, lighting, and weather. Contributing factors also include distracted driving, such as looking at a cell phone, eating, or grooming. Once you determine how and why a crash occurred, identify any violations, and issue citations.

TRAFFIC VIOLATIONS

LE1208.2. Describe the main types of violations associated with a traffic crash

The following are three types of traffic violations usually associated with traffic crash situations:

1. *contributing traffic violation*—this violation is a direct cause or contribution to the traffic crash itself, such as a vehicle running a red light and striking another vehicle. These types of violations include, but are not limited to:
   - driving too fast for the conditions
   - violating the right-of-way
   - driving left of center
   - making an improper U-turn
   - making an improper pass
   - having defective equipment
   - violating a traffic control device
   - running a red light
   - running a stop sign
   - driving carelessly
   - texting while driving

2. *non-contributing traffic violation*—this violation has no direct bearing on the cause of the traffic crash; you discover it during the investigation. Examples include an expired license plate, driver license violations, lack of insurance, or seat belt violations.

3. ***non-traffic violation**—*this violation is a criminal offense discovered during the traffic crash investigation. An example would be a quantity of cocaine discovered while taking inventory of one of the wrecked vehicles, or an outstanding warrant on a driver.

Surprisingly, vehicle defects cause few traffic crashes. In most crashes, at least one driver commits one or more contributing traffic violations. Most are the result of driver error. In a two-vehicle crash, both drivers may have committed violations. In addition to uncovering the primary violation, you are responsible for detecting other violations drivers may have committed and taking the appropriate law enforcement action.

TRAFFIC CITATIONS

For each traffic violation, issue a UTC, identify the specific violations, and note the relevant statute. Indicate on the citation any information related to court location and scheduling. Anyone you cite for a violation that requires a mandatory hearing must sign and accept that the citation indicates a promise to appear. For example, a crash that causes death or serious bodily injury will require a mandatory hearing.

For all other infractions that do not require a hearing, certify that you issued a UTC to the person cited when their signature is not required, as *prima facie* evidence (sufficient evidence to establish a fact or raise a presumption unless someone disproves or rebuts).

☑ LE1208.3. Describe when to certify a citation

LESSON 9 Clear the Traffic Crash Scene

Lesson Goal

At the end of this lesson, you will know how to safely clear a traffic crash scene of vehicles and debris.

Step 9: Return the Scene to Normal as Quickly as Possible, if Appropriate

Officers have an additional responsibility at a traffic crash scene, which includes returning the scene to the same condition it was before the crash, if possible. This can be as simple as removing hazards and debris from the road.

☑ LE1209.1. Describe how to remove vehicles and debris from a crash scene

Florida law requires drivers of operable crash vehicles to move their vehicles off the road. If a vehicle is immovable, request a tow truck to remove both the vehicle and any associated debris from the road.

If part of the crash assistance involves a hazardous materials incident, follow your agency's policies or call in the hazmat team. If hazardous materials are not involved, the scene may need a cleanup team to remove debris. Always follow your agency's policies.

☑ LE1209.2. Describe how to terminate a crash scene

Before leaving the scene, scan the area and make sure you have retrieved and stored all equipment (for example, tape measure, blanket, flashlight, cones, barricades, and identifying markers) in your vehicle. Finally, verify that the road is safe for normal traffic flow before removing any traffic redirection equipment. Contact the appropriate agency to repair or replace any traffic control signs or devices.

Make sure that you have taken all necessary law enforcement actions, such as:

- verified that all forms have been completed and copies distributed to the appropriate people
- issued all appropriate citations
- returned all personal documents (for example, driver license, vehicle registration, and proof of insurance) to their owners

If a safety risk still remains on the scene or you make an arrest, stay at the scene until the danger no longer exists or until you make other arrangements for scene safety.

LESSON 10 Complete a Traffic Crash Report

Lesson Goal

At the end of this lesson, you will know how to correctly complete the appropriate traffic crash report forms to document the traffic crash.

Think About This

You are dispatched to a two-vehicle crash and, upon arrival, one vehicle has to be towed. What type of report has to be completed?

Step 10: Document the Crash

FLORIDA TRAFFIC CRASH REPORT FORMS

FLHSMV creates and publishes the Florida Traffic Crash Report forms and the *Uniform Traffic Crash Report Manual*. These forms and the instruction manual are available from the FLHSMV website.

FLHSMV is the official records custodian for completed crash reports and is responsible for all applicable records retention requirements. It publishes two basic forms related to traffic crashes:

- HSMV 90011S—functions as a Driver Report of Traffic Crash (Self-Report) or a Driver Exchange of Information
- HSMV 90010S—Florida Traffic Crash Report, which functions as a Long Form, a Short Form, or an Update Form

HSMV 90010S—LONG FORM

You have a duty to investigate and submit a long form for traffic crashes that meet any of the following criteria:

- The crash resulted in the death of, the personal injury to, or any indication of complaints of pain or discomfort by, any of the people involved in the crash.
- A driver left the scene that involved damage to attended vehicles or property.
- A driver drove while under the influence.
- A vehicle was rendered inoperable to a degree that required a wrecker to remove it from the crash scene.
- A commercial motor vehicle was involved.

Your agency may have additional criteria that will require you to submit a long form for a traffic crash.

☑ LE12010.1. Determine when to complete a Florida Traffic Crash Report HSMV 90010S—Long Form

Before completing the form, assemble all the information related to the crash:

- validated identification information of the involved drivers
- verified vehicle registration
- verified license plate number
- verified VIN
- verified proof of insurance
- information gathered from drivers, passengers, non-motorists, and witnesses
- evidence collected, including any measurements, and your field sketch
- road and environmental conditions
- EMS run or call number and department
- DOT/Motor Carrier (MC) number for commercial motor vehicles

☑ LE12010.2.
Describe how to complete the Florida Traffic Crash Report HSMV 90010S—Long Form

The long form includes several sections that you will need to complete as thoroughly and accurately as possible using the crash manual.

- Event section—crash report fields or characteristics section.
- Vehicle section—vehicle information, characteristics, events, and consequences of the motor vehicle involved in the traffic crash.
- Person section—person data elements, characteristics, actions, and consequences to the people involved in the crash.
- Narrative section—a description of all key events in the crash, including the pre-collision, at-collision, and post-collision phases. The investigating agency report number and the eight-digit HSMV crash report number must be identical to all other report pages. Provide a narrative of events. The narrative needs to match the diagram on the Diagram page.
- Diagram section—illustration of the traffic crash scene with all key events in the crash, including the pre-collision, at-collision, and post-collision phases. The diagram needs to match the narrative.

DRIVER RE-EXAMINATION OR MEDICAL REVIEW

☑ LE12010.3.
Describe how to request a re-examination or medical review of a driver involved in a crash

You may question the driving ability of a driver who caused or contributed to the cause of a traffic crash. If you believe that a driver has a physical or mental impairment, indicate that on the Person page of the long form by checking "Recommend Driver Re-exam." You have three ways to explain why you recommend the driver for re-examination:

- Explain the request in a separate standalone paragraph on the Narrative section of the Florida Traffic Crash Report HSMV 90010S—Long Form.
- Attach a completed Medical Reporting Form, HSMV Form 72190, to the Florida Traffic Crash Report HSMV 90010S—Long Form.
- Request a "Report Driver for Medical Review" in DAVID. This is the preferred method for requesting a re-examination or medical review of a driver in addition to requesting on the Long Form.

To finalize the report form, check the "Long Form" box in the upper-left corner. Complete the entire form following the guidelines in the manual. Number the pages beginning with "page 1 of ___." Submit the form to FLHSMV within 10 days of completing the investigation. Keep a copy with your agency and provide a copy to each driver.

DIAGRAM SECTION

Use the Diagram section to illustrate how the traffic crash occurred. The diagram is the finished product showing what occurred during the crash. It should be able to stand alone and match the description in the Narrative section.

Carefully prepare a drawing of your field sketch and notes using diagraming software or a traffic crash template. The template or software will help make diagramming easier and more accurate. If drawing by hand, the template is the primary tool for completing a professional-looking crash diagram. Both the software and the template provide a number of scales of measure, angles, curves, straight edges, cutouts, and symbols to help you diagram the scene. The most common symbols are cars, trucks, trailers, motorcycles, pedestrians, signs, traffic signals and lights, buildings, camera directions, and directional arrows.

☑ LE12010.4. Describe how to complete the diagram page of the Florida Traffic Crash Report HSMV 90010S—Long Form

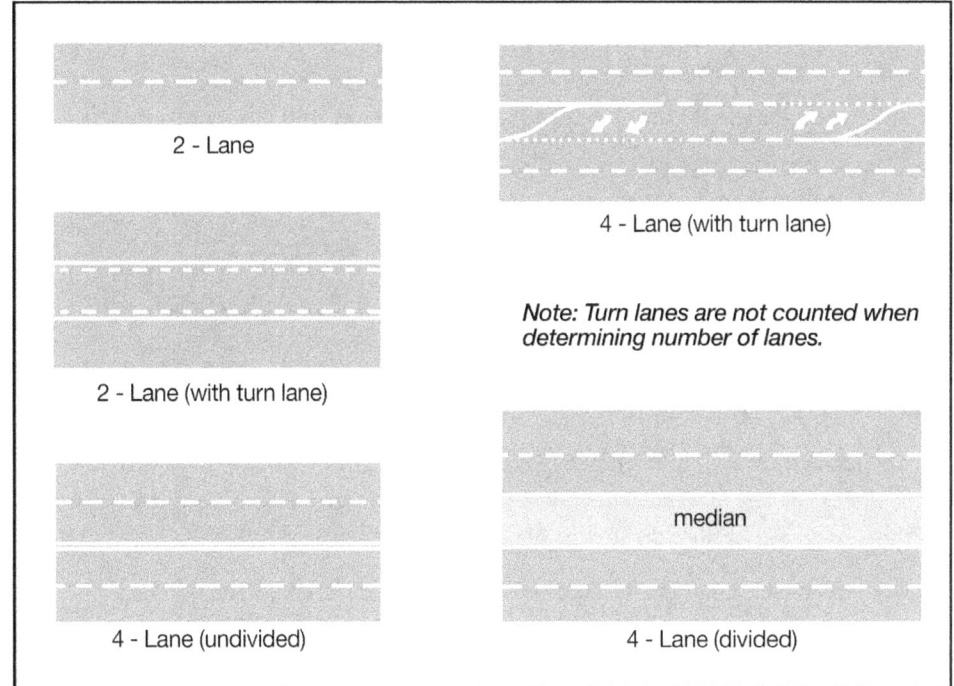

Figure 12-3
Counting number of lanes

Diagram the crash scene using the bird's-eye view, that is, depicting a scene as if looking down from an altitude or distance, just as when sketching a crime scene. Include only relevant items so the diagram will not be cluttered and will be easy to read and understand. Position the center of the diagram template on the page to correspond with the approximate center of the AOC. Draw the road, including all lanes, turn lanes, bike lanes, and the median. Label the road names. Insert the vehicles, pedestrians, and any other information from your field sketch.

Each vehicle should have a directional arrow on it to indicate the front of the vehicle and the direction of travel. Label each vehicle with a number in a circle that corresponds to the assigned vehicle number in your report. Show the directional movement of the vehicles before the crash, by drawing solid directional arrows behind the vehicles to indicate where they were coming from as they approached the AOC. To draw the vehicle movement after impact to the place of final rest, use dashes for the directional arrow.

If using the template and if the crash scene has debris or there is extensive damage to the vehicles or to property, freehand draw the vehicle damage, debris, or other details. Use the suggested symbols for freehand drawings provided with the template.

The final diagram should be professionally prepared with all appropriate entries, measurements, a legend of symbols, and a "not to scale" notation. At a minimum, document the following information in the diagram:

- location of traffic crash (road names)
- road markings and width of each lane
- north directional arrow placed upward or to the right when looking at the page
- any physical evidence on the road (such as skid marks, ruts, holes, standing water, vehicle debris)
- each vehicle's position pre-collision, at-collision, and post-collision
- where the vehicle was located at final rest on your arrival at the scene, even if the vehicle was moved
- measurements of skid mark length and road dimensions

If any people were ejected from the car or if any pedestrians were hurt, mark where they came to final rest, including the distance they traveled.

HSMV 90010S—SHORT FORM

☑ LE12010.5. Describe how to complete the Florida Traffic Crash Report HSMV 90010S—Short Form

Use the short form to report other types of traffic crashes that do not require the long form. Check the box marked "Short Form" in the upper-left corner. Complete the report with the exception of the narrative or diagram:

- Event section—crash report fields or characteristics section
- Vehicle section—vehicle information, characteristics, events, and consequences of the motor vehicle involved in the traffic crash
- Person section—person data elements, characteristics, actions, and consequences to the people involved in the crash

Remember to provide your signature in the Narrative section even though you are not completing the Narrative section. Number the pages beginning with "page 1 of ___." Submit the form to FLHSMV within 10 days of completing the investigation. Keep a copy with your agency and provide a copy to each driver.

HSMV 90010S—UPDATE FORM

You must update all open traffic crash investigations every 30 days until you close the investigation. Use the update form to update information previously recorded on the original traffic crash report using the long or short form.

Check the box marked "Update Form" in the upper-left corner. Complete only the appropriate updates, upgrades, or continuing information. Indicate in the Narrative section the updates you made to the report. Examples of new or updated information may include blood-alcohol content (BAC) results, insurance information, any injury status change, hit-and-run follow-up information, or corrections to the original report.

☑ LE12010.6. Describe how to complete the Florida Traffic Crash Report HSMV 90010S—Update Form

Continue the page numbering from the initial report. For example, if the initial report is six pages long, the update form begins with page seven. Keep a copy of the update form with your agency and provide a copy to each driver.

COMMON ERRORS

Traffic crash report forms are fairly easy to complete; however, officers sometimes make errors, or fail to provide adequate or correct information regarding:

☑ LE12010.7. List common errors in completing the Florida Traffic Crash Report forms

- intersection type or junction type
- vehicle-towed indicator
- first harmful event
- motor vehicle in transport
- Florida driver license check
- posted speed limit
- ejection
- airbag deployment
- time that the scene was cleared
- time on scene and time dispatch
- matching code identifier and code description
- number for each identifier
- appropriate box for type of form
- current addresses; using the address on the driver license as current instead of asking the driver(s) for a current address
- crash date when there is a difference between the crash date and date of report
- military time as opposed to the 12-hour clock system
- HSMV crash report number in the proper box or Narrative/Diagram page
- location of the crash
- number of road lanes (only travel lanes are counted; turn lanes do not apply)
- required endorsement for the vehicle operated by the drivers
- test results for blood-alcohol content (BAC). If you do not know the test results for BAC when you complete the report, enter "pending."
- update of BAC testing information when results become known
- update of the agency case number after the system goes down and then becomes operational

LESSON 11 Manage Unique Traffic Crashes

◎ Lesson Goal

At the end of this lesson, you will be able to manage traffic crashes that shift from a civil to a criminal investigation and crashes with unique circumstances.

Not all traffic crash situations are alike. Some crash scenes may involve unattended vehicles, property damage, or a single moving vehicle or may occur in a gated or private community. Other crash scenes can be the result of a criminal activity, such as a hit-and-run or a DUI driver, or may be part of a different criminal act. Traffic crashes that result in serious bodily injuries or a fatality will challenge your skills and may demand additional law enforcement actions.

SHIFTING FROM CIVIL TO CRIMINAL TRAFFIC CRASH INVESTIGATION

Initially, you will conduct most crash investigations as a civil investigation. A driver has a statutory duty to make a report and provide information to the officer making the crash report. This information will become part of your civil investigation.

At some point in the civil investigation, you may find evidence that could shift it to a criminal investigation. You must separate the civil crash investigation from the criminal crash investigation by specifically telling the driver that the civil crash investigation is complete, and a criminal crash investigation is beginning.

✦ Note

You cannot include any information that the driver has provided during the civil investigation in the criminal investigation.

You cannot use a driver's statement from the civil portion of the investigation admitting they drove one of the vehicles, except if there is other evidence that places the driver behind the wheel while committing the crime. Be sure to follow procedural justice when using observations made during the civil investigation. For example, noting odors, balance issues, and slurred speech would be used to support the reasonable suspicion of impairment that led to the criminal investigation.

The same statutory duty that requires drivers to provide information during a civil investigation of a traffic crash also prohibits that information from becoming self-incriminating if the civil investigation becomes a criminal investigation. The driver has a legal *crash privilege* which allows them to provide information during a civil investigation of a traffic crash that prohibits that information from becoming self-incriminating if the civil investigation becomes a criminal investigation. You cannot use any driver statements given during the civil investigation portion as evidence in a criminal trial.

When you tell the driver that your investigation is changing from a civil to a criminal one, their crash privilege ends. This is known as "changing hats." If the driver is no longer free to leave because you are detaining them, you must read them their *Miranda* rights. Questions you asked during the civil investigation that support criminal charges, you must ask again, allowing you to use the new answers as evidence in the criminal investigation. The changing hats rule applies not only to DUI offenses but to any crime revealed during a traffic crash investigation, such as illegal drug possession.

☑ LE12011.1.
Describe how to shift from a non-criminal to a criminal crash investigation

HIT-AND-RUN VEHICLE CRASH

If one of the vehicles involved in a crash leaves the scene, consider this a hit-and-run; based on the elements, this may be a misdemeanor or a felony.

If there are witnesses, ask them to describe the fleeing vehicle, the driver, or both. Contact dispatch to initiate a BOLO, if necessary.

☑ LE12011.2.
Describe how to locate the driver of a hit-and-run incident

The following are useful tools when following up on a hit-and-run investigation:

- written statements from all witnesses and the victim
- a description of vehicle damage or unique identifiers
- the direction the vehicle fled in the BOLO
- the time that passed between when the hit-and-run driver fled the scene and the officer arrived on the scene
- license plate information provided by victims or witnesses
- video if the incident occurred at a video-equipped intersection
- debris from the hit-and-run vehicle to help determine the vehicle make and model

When checking for video footage of an incident, carefully scan the immediate area to see if there is closed-circuit television (CCTV) or video surveillance on area buildings or businesses. Witnesses may also have a video of the event on their phones; you may be able to procure that video from them according to your agency's policies.

If the vehicle has remained on the scene and the driver has fled, carefully look for clues of the driver's presence such as left-behind wallets, purses, purchase receipts, and DNA from airbag deployment. Crash privilege does not apply to hit-and-run suspects. They are not protected under this rule. As a result, you will read *Miranda* rights to the suspect before you start an interview.

TRAFFIC CRASH INVOLVING UNATTENDED VEHICLE OR PROPERTY

Dispatch may send you to the scene of a crash that involves an unattended or parked vehicle damaged during a traffic crash. You should identify the owner of the vehicle and notify them of the damage. Give the license plate number to dispatch, which should

☑ LE12011.3.
Describe how to notify the owner of an unattended vehicle or property damaged from a crash

be able to provide the owner's contact information. A traffic crash can also damage roadside property, such as a billboard, fence, or mailbox. Notify the owner of the damaged property by attempting to contact them directly. If the owner is not readily obvious, a witness or neighbor may be able to provide the owner's name and contact information. If attempts to locate the property owner fail, leave your contact or driver exchange information on the damaged property, on the door, or send a registered letter to the owner. Dispatch should be able to search property tax or utility records for owner information.

SINGLE-VEHICLE CRASH

☑ LE1201.4.
Explain how to identify the driver of a single-vehicle crash

Sometimes, when you arrive at the scene of a single-vehicle crash, the driver is outside of the vehicle. Often there is a wheel witness who can establish what happened and identify that the person standing at the scene is the same person who got out from behind the wheel of the vehicle after the crash.

When no witness is present, you may have sufficient evidence to prove that the person behind the wheel during the crash is the person outside the vehicle. You may also see evidence inside the vehicle, such as interior damage or skin and blood on deployed airbags that is consistent with that person's injuries.

Searching the vehicle interior is legal under the *Carroll* doctrine, which gives you permission to search any part of a crash vehicle if probable cause indicates that the vehicle contains evidence of a crime. After providing dispatch with vehicle information, if the driver is not the owner of the vehicle, contact the owner to determine who was driving it. Once you identify the driver, interview them to compare any driver injuries with evidence found in the vehicle, such as bruising from a deployed airbag or a seat belt. If you cannot locate the driver of a crashed vehicle involved in a felony, consider using a canine team to track the driver's scent from the seat of the vehicle to a potential suspect.

TRAFFIC CRASH INVOLVING A FATALITY OR SERIOUS BODILY INJURY

☑ LE1201.5.
Explain how to manage a traffic crash involving a fatality or serious bodily injury

If a traffic crash results in life-threatening injuries or death, protect the scene as you would a crime scene. Do not move any vehicles or objects within the scene. Do not disturb anything inside the vehicle. Maintain scene integrity by immediately securing the area and following the protocols for a crime scene, as described in Chapter 9. Notify your supervisor and request a traffic homicide investigator as dictated by your agency's policies and procedures.

Sometimes, when the traffic crash involves a death, the crash itself may not be the cause. These situations can be difficult to determine during the initial investigation. However, investigate all crashes involving deaths in the same manner until you discover that an intentional act or a significant medical event caused the traffic crash. An example of an intentional act could be suicide or vehicular homicide. If a significant medical event preceded or contributed to the crash, investigate the scene as a traffic crash until the medical examiner provides a cause of death that is unrelated to the crash.

DRIVER IMPAIRMENT AS THE CAUSE OF THE CRASH

Be alert to evidence and indicators of driver impairment from drugs, alcohol, drowsiness, or health problems. If the crash investigation reveals that the driver may be under the influence of drugs or alcohol, advise the driver that you are ending the civil investigation and beginning a DUI criminal investigation.

☑ LE12011.6. Explain how to manage an impaired driver at a crash scene

Chapter 13
DUI Traffic Stops

UNIT 1 DUI BASICS
- LESSON 1 Effects on Society and Deterrence / 475
- LESSON 2 Alcohol and Drug Impairment / 476
- LESSON 3 Legal Issues / 479
- LESSON 4 DUI Field Notes / 483

UNIT 2 CONDUCTING THE DUI INVESTIGATION
- LESSON 1 DUI Detection Process / 485
- LESSON 2 Phase One—Vehicle in Motion / 486
- LESSON 3 Phase Two—Personal Contact / 489
- LESSON 4 Phase Three—Pre-arrest Screening / 491

UNIT 3 STANDARDIZED FIELD SOBRIETY TESTS
- LESSON 1 Horizontal Gaze Nystagmus / 492
- LESSON 2 Walk and Turn / 496
- LESSON 3 One Leg Stand / 499

UNIT 4 CONCLUDING THE DUI INVESTIGATION
- LESSON 1 Law Enforcement Action / 501
- LESSON 2 DUI Report Writing / 505

UNIT 1 DUI BASICS
LESSON 1 Effects on Society and Deterrence

◎ Lesson Goal

At the end of this lesson, you will know the effects of DUI on society and strategies to deter impaired driving.

Drivers who are under the influence of drugs or alcohol pose a hazard to themselves and others. This chapter provides information on how a law enforcement officer detects impaired driving, administers field sobriety tests, makes arrests when appropriate, and records the evidence of a DUI offense.

EFFECTS ON SOCIETY

Impaired driving is a major cause of traffic fatalities in the United States. Drivers show impairment for many reasons. These include alcohol, drugs, medical conditions, and mental or physical disabilities.

Everyone bears the cost of impaired driving. Property damage, financial burden, injury, and death are all parts of the cost. Impaired drivers are more likely to take excessive risks, have slow reaction times, and are less likely to wear seatbelts. An important part of providing public safety is keeping roadways safe by detecting, investigating, and removing impaired drivers.

☑ LE1311.1. Discuss how impaired driving affects public safety

DETERRENCE

Driving under the influence (DUI) is both a societal and a law enforcement problem. The public and law enforcement must work together to accomplish the goal of reducing the number of impaired drivers through education and deterrence. Education is an essential part of preventing impaired driving. Law enforcement not only enforces the DUI laws but also takes the time to educate the community through schools, civic groups, and special events.

☑ LE1311.2. Describe law enforcement and community strategies to prevent impaired driving

Deterrence is another major part of the solution. Successful DUI deterrence includes increased enforcement activity and identifying the cues and clues of impairment. Legal penalties for a DUI conviction include fines, incarceration, and a suspension of driver license.

One of the primary tools you'll use during a DUI investigation are the SFSTs. *Standardized field sobriety tests (SFSTs)* are three accurate and reliable tests used to determine alcohol or drug impairment.

UNIT 1 DUI BASICS
LESSON 2 Alcohol and Drug Impairment

ⓞ Lesson Goal

At the end of this lesson, you will understand the effects that alcohol and drugs have on the human body when driving a motor vehicle.

ALCOHOL AND THE HUMAN BODY

Alcohol is a central nervous system depressant. It is among the most commonly used substances in the United States. Alcohol may cause the impairment or loss of fine motor skills, hand-eye coordination, and judgment. Often, an alcohol-impaired person does not recognize their level of impairment.

☑ LE1312.1. Describe how the body processes alcohol

The human body processes alcohol through the following physiological processes:

- *absorption*—the process by which alcohol enters the bloodstream
- *distribution*—the process by which the bloodstream carries alcohol to the body's tissues and organs
- *metabolism*—the process by which the body breaks down alcohol for elimination
- *elimination*—the process by which the body expels alcohol through exhaled breath, sweat, tears, saliva, and urine

Any amount of alcohol can affect a person's ability to drive. The degree to which alcohol affects a person depends on how much alcohol they consume, the length of time over which they consume it, the individual physiology and physical size of the person, and whether the person has eaten any food.

☑ LE1312.2. List common behaviors of a driver impaired by alcohol

Common mental and physical effects of alcohol may include the following:

- slowed reactions and perception-reaction time (PRT)
- poor judgment
- risk taking
- poor coordination

DRUG CATEGORIES

Some drug-impaired drivers look and act very much like alcohol-impaired drivers, while others look and act very differently. Drug-impaired drivers are dangerous to themselves and to everyone else on the road.

☑ LE1312.3. List the seven categories of controlled and chemical substances that impair driving

To convict a person of driving under the influence of drugs, the drug must be a controlled substance as defined in chapter 893, F.S., or a chemical substance as indicated in s.

877.111, F.S. Drugs that impair drivers fall into seven major categories based on the observable signs and symptoms the drugs produce.

1. CNS (central nervous system) depressants—alcohol, antidepressants, barbiturates
2. CNS stimulants—amphetamines, cocaine
3. hallucinogens—ecstasy, LSD, and psilocybin
4. dissociative anesthetics—PCP and ketamine
5. narcotic analgesics—heroin, morphine, and opium
6. inhalants—aerosols and paint thinner
7. cannabis—marijuana and medical marijuana

Polydrug Use

You may encounter drivers who are impaired by **polydrug use**, which is using drugs from two or more drug categories at the same time.

Examples of polydrug use include:

- drinking alcohol while smoking marijuana or taking pain medication
- sprinkling PCP on marijuana joints
- combining heroin with cocaine

These combinations often increase impairment. Impairment can also occur when a person combines alcohol with prescription medication.

> ☑ LE1312.4. List examples of polydrug use

MEDICAL MARIJUANA

Section 381.986, F.S., permits the medical use of marijuana by qualified patients with specific medical conditions. A qualified patient, or the qualified patient's caregiver, must be in immediate possession of a Medical Marijuana Use Registry (MMUR) identification card when in possession of marijuana or a marijuana delivery device. During a traffic stop, they must provide the card to you upon request. The card does not exempt the person from criminal offense or prosecution related to impairment resulting from the medical use of marijuana. Possession of the card does not relieve a person from any requirement under law to submit to a breath, blood, urine, or other test to detect the presence of a controlled or chemical substance.

> ☑ LE1312.5. Describe the statutory requirements for a medical marijuana patient driving in Florida

MEDICATION EFFECTS

Some driver behaviors and physical reactions may indicate that the impaired driver is under the influence of medication. The driver may have prescription bottles or leftover pills with them in the vehicle. The driver may tell you they are taking medications, or their driver license may show that they are required to wear a medical alert bracelet.

> ☑ LE1312.6. Discuss how to determine if a driver is under the influence of medication

A driver may be lawfully in possession of prescription medication. However, if the effects of the prescribed medication impair the person's ability to drive, treat the driver the same way you would treat someone who is impaired by illegal drugs or alcohol.

MEDICAL CONDITIONS THAT MIMIC IMPAIRMENT

☑ LE1312.7. Determine if a medical condition impairs a person's ability to drive

Certain medical conditions may look like drug- or alcohol-induced impairment. To determine if a medical problem might cause a driver's impairment, check whether the driver has a medical alert card, bracelet, or if it is indicated on their driver license. Some medical conditions that may produce abnormal behavior include epilepsy, diabetes, head injury, or cognitive problems (dementia or Alzheimer's).

High or low blood-sugar levels may cause a person with diabetes to drive erratically. Their breath could smell like alcohol, or they could seem disoriented or impaired.

If you suspect a medical condition is causing impairment, call EMS. If you do not think the driver is having medical issues and there are signs of drug or alcohol impairment, continue with the DUI investigation.

UNIT 1 DUI BASICS
LESSON 3 Legal Issues

Lesson Goal

At the end of this lesson, you will know the legal limits and elements for a DUI arrest.

Think About This

You stop a vehicle. The driver is younger than 21, and you notice signs of impairment. You can smell the odor of an alcoholic beverage. What do you do?

LEGAL TERMS

To successfully enforce DUI traffic law, you should be familiar with Florida's DUI laws, stay up to date on case law, and know relevant terms. According to Florida Statutes, a person is **driving under the influence (DUI)** if they are driving or in actual physical control of a vehicle while impaired by alcohol or certain chemical or controlled substances to the extent that the person's normal faculties are impaired. **Normal faculties** include a person's ability to see, hear, walk, talk, judge distances, drive an automobile, make judgments, act in emergencies, and normally perform the mental and physical acts of daily life. Recall that drivers who are deaf or hard of hearing, or have a developmental disability, may have a designator on the front and back of their driver license. Use your training and sound judgment to make the distinction between a disabled driver and a person who is driving under the influence.

A person is in **actual physical control** of a vehicle if the person is physically in or on the vehicle and has the capability to operate the vehicle, regardless of whether the person is actually operating the vehicle at the time. Someone can be arrested and prosecuted for a DUI even if they were not actually driving. For example, a person who is asleep or passed out in the front seat of a vehicle, with the key in their possession, is in actual physical control of the vehicle and is subject to arrest.

You can arrest a person for DUI on any road on public or private property within the state of Florida. You can also arrest a person for DUI even if the person is driving a vehicle other than a motor vehicle, such as a bicycle, golf cart, or ATV.

ARREST AND EVIDENCE GATHERING

Section 316.193, F.S., states that a person commits the offense of DUI if the person is driving or in actual physical control of a vehicle, and the following applies:

   a. The person is under the influence of alcoholic beverages, any chemical substance set forth in s. 877.111, F.S., or any substance controlled under chapter 893, when affected to the extent that the person's normal faculties are impaired;

☑ LE1313.1.
Describe the elements required for arrest and conviction for DUI in Florida

b. The person has a blood-alcohol level of 0.08 or more grams of alcohol per 100 milliliters of blood; or

c. The person has a breath-alcohol level of 0.08 or more grams of alcohol per 210 liters of breath.

The Florida Statutes establish a legal presumption based on the driver's blood- or breath-alcohol level. If the driver's alcohol concentration was 0.08 or higher, a jury is to presume that the driver was under the influence of alcohol to the extent that their normal faculties were impaired.

Section 316.1934, F.S., states that evidence of a blood- or breath-alcohol level greater than 0.05 but less than 0.08 does not necessarily mean that the driver was under the influence of alcohol to the extent that their normal faculties were impaired. A jury cannot make any presumption based on this evidence. However, a jury may consider the alcohol concentration with other competent evidence, such as the driver's driving pattern, the officer's personal contact with the driver, and the SFSTs, to determine whether the driver was under the influence of alcohol to the extent that their normal faculties were impaired.

Sometimes a DUI investigation results from a crash investigation rather than a traffic stop. A crash investigation must be completed before you begin your DUI investigation. Recall from Chapter 12 that you need to change hats and formally transition to a DUI criminal investigation by making a verbal statement to the driver. Questions you asked during the crash investigation that support criminal charges, you must ask again after you have read the driver their *Miranda* rights. This allows you to use the new answers as evidence in the criminal investigation.

Miranda Warning During DUI

☑ LE1313.2. Determine when to issue a *Miranda* warning during a DUI traffic stop

You are not required to give a *Miranda* warning during a traffic stop when you temporarily detain a motorist to ask a few brief questions and issue a citation. This comes from the decision made in *Berkemer v. McCarty*, in which the U.S. Supreme Court ruled the following:

- A *Miranda* warning applies to interrogations involving minor traffic offenses.
- Routine questioning of a driver during a traffic stop is not an interrogation.

Miranda warnings are not required before you administer the SFSTs; however, when determining whether to advise of a *Miranda* warning during a DUI investigation, follow your agency's policies and procedures.

Implied Consent

Under s. 316.1932, F.S., **implied consent** refers to the fact that any person who accepts the privilege of driving a motor vehicle in Florida has consented to submit to testing for drug or alcohol impairment. This only refers to chemical testing as outlined in the Florida Statutes and not the SFSTs.

☑ LE1313.3. Describe the role of implied consent during a DUI traffic stop

This means that if an officer lawfully arrests a driver for driving or being in actual physical control of a motor vehicle while under the influence, the driver must submit to a breath, urine, or blood test to determine the alcohol content or the presence of a chemical or controlled substance in their breath, urine, or blood. Note that implied consent applies specifically to motorized vehicles. If a motor vehicle is not involved, the driver is not subject to implied consent.

Even if implied consent applies, you should still explain your actions to the driver. When a driver refuses to submit to a breath, urine, or blood test, the law enforcement officer, corrections officer, or certified breath test operator must read or provide the implied consent warning.

The Florida Statutes require law enforcement officers to explain to the driver that there are penalties associated with the refusal to submit to a lawful physical or chemical testing. If the driver refuses to submit to a lawful breath, urine, or blood test after a DUI arrest, their driving privilege will be suspended for a period of one year for the first refusal, or for a period of 18 months if their driving privilege has previously been suspended or they have previously been fined for refusing to submit to a lawful breath, urine, or blood test.

Additionally, law enforcement officers are required to explain that if the driver refuses to submit to a lawful test, they commit one of the following:

- a misdemeanor of the second degree for the first refusal to submit to a lawful breath or urine test after a DUI arrest; or
- a misdemeanor of the first degree if they refuse to submit to a lawful breath or urine test after a DUI arrest and their driving privilege has previously been suspended or they have previously been fined for refusing to submit to a lawful breath, urine, or blood test after a DUI arrest.

After you read the implied consent warning to the driver, ask the driver again if they will submit to the test. The refusal to submit to lawful tests upon the request of a law enforcement officer is admissible into evidence in any criminal proceeding.

Refusal Affidavit

If a driver refuses to submit to a breath, urine, or blood test after the implied consent warning, complete a refusal affidavit along with a DUI citation. Sign and forward the refusal affidavit to the FLHSMV as part of the DUI arrest report. You must read the implied consent warning for each test you request that is refused.

☑ LE1313.4.
Describe how to issue a citation for a DUI offense of refusal

Conduct an FCIC/NCIC, DAVID, or criminal history database search to see if a driver has had a previous citation for refusal. Issue the DUI citation and the uniform traffic citation (UTC) for the second refusal to submit to testing.

COMMERCIAL MOTOR VEHICLE DUI

A person who has any alcohol in their body may not drive or be in actual physical control of a commercial motor vehicle (CMV) in the state of Florida. Follow your agency's policies and procedures for CMV-related enforcement.

☑ LE1313.5.
Determine if a driver of a commercial motor vehicle is impaired

If you arrest a driver for DUI while operating or in actual physical control of a motor vehicle or a CMV, the driver may lose their commercial driver license (CDL) for one year, subject to an administrative hearing. This penalty applies if the driver refuses to submit to a breath, urine, or blood test to determine alcohol concentration or if the driver is driving a CMV with an alcohol concentration of 0.04 or higher, even if the decision to arrest is not made. Other conditions and penalties may apply, depending on the circumstances. If you suspect a DUI violation, conduct a DUI investigation.

DRIVERS YOUNGER THAN 21 (0.02 VIOLATION)

☑ LE1313.6. Determine if a driver younger than 21 is impaired

It is unlawful for a person younger than 21 years of age, who has a blood-alcohol level or breath-alcohol level of 0.02 or higher, to drive or be in actual physical control of a motor vehicle. Section 322.2616, F.S., outlines instructions for conducting a traffic stop involving a driver younger than 21.

1. Conduct a DUI investigation. If the subject is not arrested for DUI, proceed with the 0.02 investigation, based on the odor of alcohol on their breath.

2. Request the driver to submit to a breath test, using an approved testing device. A violation of this section is not a traffic infraction or a criminal offense, and being detained on this violation does not constitute an arrest. The driver is subject to administrative action by FLHSMV, which may suspend driving privileges by issuing a notice of suspension to the driver at the time of the offense.

3. If the driver refuses to submit to a breath test, read the implied consent for a 0.02 violation. If they still refuse, issue a notice of license suspension for the 0.02 violation.

4. Follow your agency's policies and procedures to deal with the vehicle and driver.

UNIT 1 DUI BASICS
LESSON 4 DUI Field Notes

⦿ Lesson Goal

At the end of this lesson, you will know how to take clear and descriptive field notes to support a DUI report.

NOTE-TAKING GUIDELINES

You will need to recognize, gather, and document facts and circumstances that establish reasonable suspicion to stop and investigate a driver suspected of impaired driving.

Your notes will document your observations of impairment at the time the incident occurred and will provide the information necessary to establish the evidence and elements of the DUI offense. The court may subpoena your field notes as evidence. Your field notes help you to complete the DUI report forms and support successful prosecution of the driver.

☑ LE1314.1. Recognize the importance of taking clear and descriptive field notes in a DUI investigation

Taking notes is one of the most important tasks in a DUI investigation. The evidence you observe, and document is largely sensory (sight, smell, hearing) in nature and is extremely short-lived. As such, it is important to take notes throughout the entire DUI detection process.

Develop your own shorthand or structured note-taking system to improve the effectiveness of handwritten field notes. Use clear and descriptive language that creates mental pictures of the facts, circumstances, and events. Below is an example of how you can write your notes to explain the specific information you will later need to put in your report. Refer to Chapter 4 for more information on taking notes.

Unclear Language	Descriptive Language
Driver appeared drunk	Driver's eyes bloodshot; gaze fixed; hands shaking
Smelled alcohol	Odor of alcoholic beverage on driver's breath
Vehicle stopped in unusual manner or location	Vehicle struck or climbed curb; stopped on sidewalk
Vehicle crossed the centerline	Vehicle completely crossed the centerline into the opposing traffic lane

LE1314.2. Describe the information to include in DUI field notes

Whenever possible, complete DUI field notes before you leave the site of the arrest. You will use these notes to refresh your memory, write the arrest report, and testify in court. During the DUI investigation, accurately note the following:

- descriptions of the vehicle in motion, including observations of the vehicle and the vehicle stop
- descriptions of the vehicle, the location, weather, terrain, and the date and time the incident occurred
- personal contact with the driver, including observations of the driver's manner of speech (also admissions), attitude, and clothing; note any physical evidence collected
- the results of the investigation
- any other evidence specific to the incident

UNIT 2 CONDUCTING THE DUI INVESTIGATION
LESSON 1 DUI Detection Process

Lesson Goal

At the end of this lesson, you will know the three phases of the DUI detection process to determine sufficient probable cause for arrest.

Before you determine whether or not to arrest a driver for a DUI offense, you must identify and gather evidence using the DUI detection process. The **DUI detection process** requires you to identify and gather evidence to determine whether or not a subject should be arrested for a DUI violation; it begins when you first suspect that a driver may be impaired and ends when you determine there is or is not sufficient probable cause to arrest the person for a DUI offense. A DUI investigation involves three phases of detection:

- Phase one: vehicle in motion—observing the way the driver operates and stops the vehicle
- Phase two: personal contact—observing and speaking with the driver face to face
- Phase three: pre-arrest screening—administering the SFSTs to the driver to determine if there is probable cause to arrest for DUI

LE1321.1. Describe how the DUI detection process can provide probable cause for arrest

The DUI detection process does not always include all three phases. Sometimes the officer does not have the opportunity to observe the driver operating the vehicle. Examples can include:

- a scene where the driver is passed out behind the wheel of a vehicle that is not in motion
- a traffic crash scene
- a request for motorist assistance

Sometimes you may be unable to conduct the SFSTs on the driver. This can include situations where the driver is physically unable to perform the SFSTs, the driver is transported to the hospital, or the driver refuses to submit to the SFSTs.

At the conclusion of each phase of the DUI detection process, you will need to decide whether to continue to the next phase.

Officers who are successful in the DUI detection process:

- know what to look, listen, and smell for
- apply their knowledge and skills whenever they come into contact with someone who may be under the influence of drugs or alcohol
- have the skills to ask the right kinds of questions
- properly administer the SFSTs
- properly document all phases of the DUI detection process

UNIT 2 CONDUCTING THE DUI INVESTIGATION
LESSON 2 Phase One—Vehicle in Motion

◎ Lesson Goal

At the end of this lesson, you will know whether to stop a vehicle based on the information gathered in phase one of the DUI detection process.

Think About This

You stop a vehicle for a traffic violation. You recognize that the driver may be impaired and ask them to step out of the vehicle to conduct the SFSTs. The driver exits the vehicle and does not successfully complete the SFSTs as demonstrated and instructed, and does not exhibit the cues or clues required. What factors would you consider when making your arrest decision?

Phase one begins when you observe the vehicle in motion. You may notice a vehicle because of a traffic violation, an equipment violation, or an expired registration. You may notice unusual driving actions, such as weaving within a lane or moving at slower than normal speed.

☑ LE1322.1. Describe the role of reasonable suspicion for conducting a DUI traffic stop

You have three choices: stop the vehicle for further investigation, continue to observe the vehicle, or take no action. Based on your observations, decide if there is reasonable suspicion to instruct the driver to stop. Ask yourself these questions:

- What is the vehicle doing?
- Do I have a reason to stop the vehicle?

If you decide to stop the vehicle, continue to observe the driver's actions as they respond to your signal to stop. Take note of any additional cues of a possible DUI violation. A *cue* is a reminder, prompt, or a signal to do something, such as taking law enforcement action or observing the vehicle more closely.

DUI CUES

While on patrol, you might see many signs of an impaired driver. These can be anything from a traffic statute violation to a driving observation—there can be multiple indicators of driving impairment. You must carefully observe driving patterns and violations.

☑ LE1322.2. List driver impairment cues for a vehicle in motion

Anything unusual may indicate that there is impairment, a vehicle problem, or a medical emergency. The following are some of the visual cues that may indicate an impaired driver.

Lane position

- weaving
- weaving across lane lines (lane departure)
- drifting

- straddling a lane line
- swerving
- almost striking an object or vehicle
- turning with a wide radius

Speed and braking problems

- stopping problems (too far, too short, or too jerky)
- accelerating or decelerating unnecessarily
- varying speed
- driving 10 mph or more under the speed limit

Vigilance problems

- driving without headlights at night
- failing to signal or signaling that is inconsistent with the action
- driving in opposing lanes or the wrong way on a one-way road
- responding slowly to traffic signals
- failing to respond or responding slowly to an officer's signals
- stopping in the lane for no apparent reason

Judgment problems

- following too closely (tailgating)
- conducting an improper or unsafe lane change
- making an illegal or improper turn
- driving off the roadway
- stopping inappropriately in response to the officer
- appearing to be impaired

DUI Motorcyclist Visual Cues

Driving impairment cues for motorcyclists include:

- drifting during a turn or curve
- trouble dismounting
- trouble balancing at a stop
- problems turning (unsteadiness, sudden corrections, late braking, improper lean angle)
- weaving
- moving erratically while going straight
- operating without lights at night
- driving recklessly (for example, driving on one wheel or at high speeds)

☑ LE1322.3. List impairment cues for a motorcyclist

- following too closely
- running a stop light or sign
- evading the officer
- going the wrong way

VEHICLE STOP

☑ LE1322.4. List driver impairment cues when stopping the vehicle

After directing the driver to stop the vehicle, the impaired driver may show additional evidence of DUI, such as:

- attempting to flee
- not responding
- responding slowly
- swerving abruptly
- stopping suddenly
- striking the curb or another object

☑ LE1322.5. Describe the concept of divided attention

Some of these cues occur because the stop places additional demands on the driver's ability to divide their attention among various tasks. **Divided attention** is the ability to concentrate on two or more tasks at the same time. While under the influence of alcohol or drugs, a driver's ability to divide attention is impaired. An impaired driver may have difficulty steering, controlling the accelerator, signaling, or making driving and stopping decisions (such as whether to stop, turn, speed up, or slow down).

Once the driver stops the vehicle, do not ask them to move their vehicle to a safer location. Telling an impaired driver to move their vehicle could create an unsafe situation for everyone.

UNIT 2 CONDUCTING THE DUI INVESTIGATION
LESSON 3 Phase Two—Personal Contact

◎ Lesson Goal

At the end of this lesson, you will know whether to administer the SFSTs to a driver based on information gathered in phase two of the DUI detection process.

Sometimes, phase one may not be possible, so you may move on to phase two. This phase has two major evidence-gathering tasks and one major decision.

- Task one—observe and talk with the driver in the vehicle.
- Task two—observe the driver exiting the vehicle.

Based on these observations, you have to make a major decision. Administer the SFSTs, continue dialoguing with the driver while looking for additional evidence, or finish the contact if you do not observe any impairment.

TASK ONE—OBSERVE AND TALK WITH THE DRIVER

The first task of phase two—observe and talk with the driver—begins as soon as both the driver's vehicle and the patrol vehicle have come to complete stops. It continues through your approach to the vehicle and involves all conversation between you and the driver. In some cases, your initial face-to-face contact with the driver may give you the first indications that the driver is impaired. For example, you stop a vehicle for an equipment violation and notice signs of impairment only as you talk with the driver. Whether or not the driver is impaired, treat the driver and all occupants with fairness, dignity, and respect as you search for clues.

☑ LE1323.1. Describe how to gather evidence during an impaired driver traffic stop

Use your senses when observing the driver to provide clues of alcohol or drug impairment. What do you see or smell? During a DUI investigation, a *clue* is a piece of evidence that suggests impairment. Clues are also the behaviors observed during the performance of the SFSTs. Some observable signs of impairment include:

☑ LE1323.2. List observable clues of driver impairment

- bloodshot eyes
- soiled clothing (urine, feces, vomit)
- alcohol containers, drugs, or drug paraphernalia
- odor of alcoholic beverages or marijuana smoke
- cover-up odors like breath spray or tobacco smoke
- fumbling with driver license or paperwork or with motor vehicle controls

Talking with the driver does not replace the SFSTs but can still be useful for obtaining evidence of impairment to establish reasonable suspicion. Use techniques that apply the concept of divided attention, which will require the driver to concentrate on two or more things at the same time.

☑ LE1323.3. Describe how to conduct a divided attention test for driver impairment

For example, while the driver is seated in their vehicle, ask for two things in one request. Ask the driver to produce both their driver license and the vehicle registration. If the driver forgets to produce both documents, produces documents other than the ones requested, or passes over their license, registration, or both while searching through wallet or purse, this may indicate impairment.

☑ LE1323.4. List verbal clues of driver impairment

An impaired driver may:

- respond slowly
- ask you to repeat questions
- repeat your questions or comments
- provide incorrect information
- change answers
- slur their speech
- admit to drinking
- provide inconsistent responses
- use abusive language

Once reasonable suspicion is evident, ask the driver to exit the vehicle. If there is not reasonable suspicion, let them go.

TASK TWO—OBSERVE THE DRIVER EXITING THE VEHICLE

☑ LE1323.5. List the impairment clues of a driver who is exiting the vehicle

Instruct the driver to exit the vehicle, and keep officer and driver safety in mind at all times. Safety considerations take precedence over all other considerations.

As the driver exits, observe their behaviors. Look for clues, that the driver:

- cannot follow instructions
- cannot open the door
- leaves the vehicle in gear
- climbs out of the vehicle
- sways or staggers while walking
- leans against the vehicle or another object
- places their hands on the vehicle for balance

At this point in the DUI detection process, the officer will make the decision on whether or not to proceed to phase three.

UNIT 2 CONDUCTING THE DUI INVESTIGATION
LESSON 4 Phase Three—Pre-arrest Screening

Lesson Goal

At the end of this lesson, you will know why the SFSTs are used to determine a driver's level of impairment.

Phase three of the DUI investigation is the pre-arrest screening process, which involves administering the SFSTs. For many years, law enforcement officers have used standardized field sobriety tests to determine whether a driver is too impaired to operate a vehicle. Officers now use the SFSTs to assess a driver's level of impairment, develop probable cause for arrest, and produce test results as evidence in court.

The SFSTs consist of the Horizontal Gaze Nystagmus test and two psychophysical tests: Walk and Turn and One Leg Stand. **Horizontal gaze nystagmus (HGN)** is an involuntary jerking that occurs as the eyes move toward the side. A **psychophysical test** is a divided attention test that measures a person's ability to perform mental and physical tasks at the same time.

The reliability of the SFSTs applies only when the officer:

- administers the exercises in the prescribed, standardized manner
- uses the standardized clues to assess the driver
- employs the standardized criteria to assess the level of impairment of the driver

☑ LE1324.1. Describe how to maintain the reliability and validity of the SFSTs

If you change any of the SFST elements, you may compromise the reliability of the tests. The SFSTs are components in determining whether probable cause exists to arrest the driver for DUI.

The National Highway Traffic Safety Administration (NHTSA) published studies that validate the SFSTs for use across the country. According to the research, officers made correct arrest decisions 91% of the time based on the three SFSTs. These studies supported arrest decisions at, above, or below a 0.08 blood concentration level.

SELECT A SAFE LOCATION

Before conducting the SFSTs, select a safe location, away from vehicle or pedestrian traffic and on a level surface that has ample lighting. At night, use lights to illuminate the location, and, if possible, minimize distracting lights.

☑ LE1324.2. Describe a safe location to conduct the SFSTs

UNIT 3 STANDARDIZED FIELD SOBRIETY TESTS
LESSON 1 Horizontal Gaze Nystagmus

⊚ Lesson Goal

At the end of this lesson, you will know how to administer, interpret, and document a nystagmus test.

NYSTAGMUS

The first SFST in the pre-arrest screening process is the Horizontal Gaze Nystagmus (HGN) test. **Nystagmus** is an involuntary jerking of the eyes. Many types of nystagmus can occur naturally, environmentally, or from medical conditions. When a person is impaired by drugs or alcohol, nystagmus may be observed. The person experiencing nystagmus usually does not know it is occurring. **Resting nystagmus** is the involuntary jerking of the eyes as the person looks straight ahead. This condition, though not frequently seen, usually indicates a pathological disorder or high doses of a dissociative anesthetic drug, such as PCP.

You should make note of any abnormalities observed or reported by the driver, then proceed with the Horizontal Gaze Nystagmus (HGN) test. The higher the degree of impairment, the sooner you will observe the nystagmus.

HGN TESTING

☑ LE1331.1.
Describe how to administer an HGN test

When you administer the HGN test, keep your weapon side away from the driver for safety. Give the following instructions:

1. "I am going to check your eyes. Do you wear glasses or contacts?" (If they are wearing glasses ask them to remove their glasses.)
2. "Stand with your feet together—heels and toes—and your hands down at your side." (The subject may also be seated.)
3. "Keep your head still and follow this object with your eyes only."
4. "Do not move your head."
5. "Do you understand the instructions?"

While administering the HGN test, have the driver follow the motion of a small object with their eyes only. Position the object about 12–15 inches from the driver's nose and slightly above their eye level. The object may be the tip of a pen or penlight, an eraser on a pencil, or a fingertip, whichever contrasts with the background. Begin with the driver's left eye, then the right, and examine each eye twice.

☑ LE1331.2.
Determine the driver's resting nystagmus

1. Check for resting nystagmus and equal pupil size. (Note unequal pupil size and if present, question the subject about it.)

2. Check for equal tracking. Equal tracking is the ability of the eyes to track together as they follow an object. Check that the driver's eyes can track together by moving an object smoothly across the driver's entire field of vision two times. If the eyes do not track together, it could indicate a possible medical condition, injury, or visual impairment. Ask the driver if they have a medical condition or injury that hinders one or both eyes from tracking together as this could possibly affect nystagmus observed. Check to ensure that the driver's pupils are equal in size. If you observe unequal pupil size, it could indicate a possible medical disorder or injury.

3. Check for *lack of smooth pursuit*. Lack of smooth pursuit occurs when the eye of an impaired driver jerks or bounces as the eye follows a smoothly moving stimulus. In contrast, the eye of an unimpaired driver will follow smoothly like a marble rolling across a smooth pane of glass. Check the driver's left eye by moving the stimulus to the right. Move the stimulus smoothly at a speed that requires approximately two seconds to bring the driver's eye as far to the side as it can go. While moving the stimulus, look at the driver's eye and determine whether it is able to pursue smoothly. Next, move the stimulus all the way to the left, back across the driver's face, checking if the right eye pursues smoothly. Movement of the stimulus takes approximately two seconds out and two seconds back for each eye. Then repeat the procedure.

☑ LE1331.3. Describe how to observe lack of smooth pursuit

4. Check for *distinct and sustained nystagmus at maximum deviation*. The distinct and sustained nystagmus at maximum deviation clue occurs when the gaze of the eye has moved as far as it can go toward the shoulder, and no white is visible at the outside of the eye. You can observe the eye jerk when it is held at maximum deviation for a minimum of four seconds. Have the driver hold the eye at that position for a minimum of four seconds while you observe the eye for distinct and sustained nystagmus. Move the stimulus all the way across the driver's face to check the left eye, holding that position for a minimum of four seconds. Then repeat the procedure. Some people exhibit slight jerking of the eye at maximum deviation even when unimpaired, but the jerking will not be evident or sustained for more than a few seconds. When impaired by alcohol, the jerking will be more pronounced, sustained for more than four seconds, and easily observable.

☑ LE1331.4. Describe how to observe distinct and sustained nystagmus at maximum deviation

5. Check for the *onset of nystagmus prior to 45°*, which is the point when the eye is first seen jerking prior to 45°. Onset of nystagmus prior to 45° is also a clue that a driver has an alcohol concentration above 0.08. Conduct two passes starting at 0° beginning with the subject's left eye. Move slowly until you see nystagmus. If you observe nystagmus, hold the position and confirm that nystagmus is distinct and sustained. If you do not see nystagmus, continue until 45°. Return to 0° and repeat with the right eye. The movement from 0° to 45° should take a minimum of four seconds. This estimate of a 45° angle is a critical factor in checking for onset of nystagmus before 45°. If the point at which you first see the eye jerking begins before 45°, it is possible that the driver has an alcohol concentration above 0.08 or has taken drugs.

☑ LE1331.5. Describe how to observe the onset of nystagmus prior to 45°

Figure 13-1
Onset of nystagmus prior to 45°

☑ LE1331.6.
Describe how to administer the VGN check

6. Check for vertical gaze nystagmus. **Vertical gaze nystagmus (VGN)** is the involuntary jerking of the eyes as they move upward and are held at maximum deviation for a minimum of four seconds. Hold the stimulus slightly above eye level 12–15 inches from the driver's nose. Be aware of your position in relation to the driver at all times. Raise the object until the driver's eyes are elevated as far as possible. Hold for about four seconds. Watch closely for evidence of the eyes jerking up and down. Repeat for two passes. There is no known drug that will cause VGN without causing at least four clues of HGN. If VGN is present and HGN is not, it could be a medical condition.

7. VGN was not included in the SFSTs in the original research; however, it is a reliable indicator of a high dose of alcohol for that individual and can also be caused by certain drugs.

The maximum number of clues that may appear in one eye is three. The maximum number of total clues observed is six.

1. Lack of smooth pursuit (left eye)
2. Lack of smooth pursuit (right eye)
3. Distinct and sustained nystagmus at maximum deviation (left eye)
4. Distinct and sustained nystagmus at maximum deviation (right eye)
5. Onset of nystagmus before 45° (left eye)
6. Onset of nystagmus before 45° (right eye)

The indications of impairment build upon each other. For example, if you do not have lack of smooth pursuit then you will not have distinct and sustained nystagmus at maximum deviation. Based on the research, if you observe four or more clues, it is likely that the driver's alcohol concentration is above 0.08. Using this criterion, you should be able to classify about 88% of drivers accurately.

☑ LE1331.7. Discuss how to interpret the HGN test

In your notes, record any facts, circumstances, conditions, or observations that may be relevant to the test, for example, if you observe the odor of an alcoholic beverage on the driver's breath at the time of the test. You may observe other clues during the HGN test, such as: inability to keep the head still, noticeable swaying, or self-incriminating statements. Examples of conditions that may interfere with a driver's performance of the HGN test include wind or dust irritating the eyes, or visual or other distractions.

☑ LE1331.8. Describe how to document nystagmus results

UNIT 3 STANDARDIZED FIELD SOBRIETY TESTS
LESSON 2 Walk and Turn

◎ Lesson Goal

At the end of this lesson, you will know how to administer, interpret, and document a Walk and Turn test.

Think About This

You are administering the SFSTs, and the driver tells you they cannot do the Walk and Turn and One Leg Stand because they have bad knees. You administer the HGN, and they exhibit the clues for impairment. Do you make the arrest?

WALK AND TURN TEST

☑ LE1332.1.
Describe the optimal conditions for conducting the Walk and Turn test

Conduct the Walk and Turn (WAT) test on a stable, level, and non-slippery surface, if possible. Make sure there is enough room for the driver to complete nine heel-to-toe steps. Certain drivers, such as those with back, leg, or inner ear problems, may have difficulty performing this test. Give them an opportunity to remove their shoes if they feel their shoes would prevent them from doing this test.

The Walk and Turn test consists of two stages: the instructions stage and walking stage.

Instructions Stage

In the instructions stage, you tell the driver how to position themselves before walking and have them demonstrate the position.

☑ LE1332.2.
Describe how to provide instructions for the Walk and Turn test

Give instructions and demonstrate from a safe position from the driver. Do not turn your back to the subject.

1. "Place your left foot on the line." (real or imaginary)
2. "Place your right foot on the line ahead of your left foot with the heel of your right foot against the toe of your left foot."
3. "Place your arms down at your sides."
4. "Maintain this position until I have completed the instructions. Do not start to walk until told to do so."
5. "Do you understand the instructions so far?" Make sure the driver indicates that they understand.

The instructions stage divides the driver's attention between a balancing task (standing with toes facing forward while maintaining the heel-to-toe position) and an information-processing task (listening to and remembering instructions).

Look for the following clues:

- The driver cannot keep balance during instructions.
    - Record this clue if the driver does not maintain the heel-to-toe position throughout the instructions. The feet must actually break apart.
    - Do not record this clue if the driver sways or uses the arms to balance but maintains the heel-to-toe position.
- The driver starts walking too soon: The driver begins to walk before you tell them to.

During the instructions stage, record the number of times each clue appears.

☑ LE1332.3. Interpret the driver's behavior during the instructions stage of the Walk and Turn test

Walking Stage

In the walking stage you tell the driver how to walk to complete the test and have them walk.

Give instructions and demonstrate from a safe position from the driver:

1. "When I tell you to start, take nine heel-to-toe steps on the line, turn, and take nine heel-to-toe steps back." (Demonstrate a minimum of three heel-to-toe steps.)
2. "When you turn, keep your front foot on the line, and turn by taking a series of small steps with the other foot, like this."
3. "While you are walking, keep your arms at your sides, watch your feet at all times, and count your steps out loud."
4. "When I tell you to begin, take nine heel-to-toe steps down the line. On the ninth step, keep your forward/front foot on the line, and take a series of small steps to turn around. Return nine heel to-toe steps back down the line." (Demonstrate.)
5. "While walking, watch your feet at all times, keep your arms at your side, and count your steps out loud. Once you begin, do not stop until the exercise is completed."
6. "Do you have any physical injuries or limitations that would keep you from completing this test?" (If the answer is yes, move on to the next test and record their answer in your notes.)
7. "Do you understand the instructions?" Make sure the driver indicates that they understand.
8. "Begin and count your first step from the heel-to-toe position as 'One.'"

☑ LE1332.4. Describe how to provide instructions for the walking stage of the Walk and Turn test

At the end of the test, examine each clue and only record each clue once. The maximum number of clues observed for any driver is eight; however, you can observe each clue multiple times.

LE1332.5.
Interpret the driver's behavior during the walking stage of the Walk and Turn test

Look for the following clues:

- Stopping while walking.
- Failing to walk heel to toe—the driver leaves a space of more than ½ inch between the heel and toe on any step.
- Stepping off the line—the driver places one foot entirely off the line.
- Using arms for balance—the driver raises one or both arms more than six inches from the sides to maintain balance.
- Turning incorrectly:
    - The driver removes the front foot from the line while turning.
    - The driver has not followed directions as demonstrated, spins or pivots around, or loses balance while turning.
- Taking the incorrect number of steps—the driver takes anything other than nine steps in either direction.

LE1332.6.
Describe how to document Walk and Turn clues

Record any facts, circumstances, conditions, or observations that may be relevant to this test in your notes. Based on the research, if you observe two or more clues, it is likely that the driver's alcohol concentration is above 0.08. Using this criterion, you should be able to classify about 79% of drivers accurately.

Other clues may be observed during the Walk and Turn test, such as not counting out loud, counting an incorrect number of steps, turning in the wrong direction, or uttering incriminating statements during the test. Conditions that may interfere with the driver's performance of the Walk and Turn test can include wind and other weather conditions, the driver's age or weight, or the driver's footwear. If the driver is unable to safely complete the test, you may stop the test early. Document the reason the test was stopped.

UNIT 3 STANDARDIZED FIELD SOBRIETY TESTS
LESSON 3 One Leg Stand

Lesson Goal

At the end of this lesson, you will know how to administer, interpret, and document a One Leg Stand test.

ONE LEG STAND TEST

Conduct the One Leg Stand test on a stable, level, and non-slippery surface, if possible. Certain drivers, such as those with back, leg, or inner ear problems, may have difficulty performing this test. Give them an opportunity to remove their shoes if they feel their shoes would prevent them from doing this test.

☑ LE1333.1. Describe the optimal conditions for conducting a One Leg Stand test

The One Leg Stand test consists of two stages: the instructions stage and the balance and counting stage.

Instructions Stage

In the instructions stage you tell the driver how to position themselves and have them demonstrate the position.

Give instructions and demonstrate from a safe position from the driver:

1. "Stand with your feet together and your arms at your side."
2. "Maintain this position until told otherwise."

☑ LE1333.2. Describe how to provide instructions for the One Leg Stand test

The instructions stage divides the driver's attention between a balancing task (maintaining a stance) and an information-processing task (listening to and remembering instructions).

Balance and Counting Stage

In the balance and counting stage you tell the driver how to complete the test and then have the driver perform it.

Give instructions and demonstrate from a safe position away from the driver:

1. "When I tell you to do so, raise one leg, either one, about 6 inches off the ground, foot pointed out, parallel to the ground, both legs straight, and look at the elevated foot."
2. "Count aloud in the following manner: 1001, 1002, 1003, 1004, and so on until I tell you to stop."
3. "Do you understand the instructions?" (Make sure the driver gives you verbal confirmation that they understand)
4. "Begin the test."

☑ LE1333.3. Describe how to provide instructions for the balance and counting stage of the One Leg Stand test

Time the One Leg Stand for 30 seconds with a time-measuring device. Note which leg the driver lifts.

The balance and counting stage divides the driver's attention between balancing (standing on one foot) and counting aloud. At the end of the test, examine each clue and only record each clue once. The maximum number of clues observed for any driver is four; however, you can observe each clue multiple times.

☑ **LE1333.4.** Interpret the balance and counting stage of the One Leg Stand test

Look for these clues:

- Swaying while balancing—the driver sways in any direction while balancing.
- Using arms to balance—the driver raises their arms 6 or more inches from the side of the body to maintain balance.
- Hopping—the driver hops to maintain balance.
- Putting the foot down:
  - The driver puts their foot down one or more times.
  - The driver puts their foot down during the 30-second count (record the count number when it happens).

☑ **LE1333.5.** Describe how to document the One Leg Stand test clues

In your field notes, record any facts, circumstances, conditions, or observations that may be relevant to this test. Based on the research, if you observe two or more clues, it is likely that the driver's alcohol concentration is above 0.08. Using this criterion, you should be able to classify about 83% of drivers accurately. Other clues may be observed during the One Leg Stand test, such as incorrect counting or bending of the knees.

Conditions that may interfere with the driver's performance of the One Leg Stand test can include wind or weather conditions, the driver's age or weight, or the driver's footwear. If the driver is unable to safely complete the test, you may stop the test early. Document the reason the test was stopped.

UNIT 4 CONCLUDING THE DUI INVESTIGATION
LESSON 1 Law Enforcement Action

Lesson Goal

At the end of this lesson, you will know whether to arrest an impaired driver and continue the investigation with a breath, urine, or blood test.

PROCEDURES FOR DUI CRASHES

When conducting a DUI crash investigation, identify a *wheel witness*, someone who can place the driver in actual physical control of the vehicle at the time of the crash and who can provide a statement of observations of the crash and driver. If there is no wheel witness, collect other evidence that places the driver in actual physical control of the vehicle.

☑ LE1341.1. Describe how to conduct a DUI crash investigation

Any statements the driver makes during the crash investigation will not be admissible in any criminal proceedings. Once the crash investigation is complete, evidence is collected, and witness statements and information are exchanged between involved drivers.

Tell the driver the following:

- The crash investigation is complete, and you are now beginning a DUI investigation.
- You are issuing the *Miranda* warnings and will ask if they understand their rights.
- You will be conducting the SFSTs to determine if they were able to drive a vehicle safely.

Any signs of impairment collected during the crash investigation can be used when deciding if you have reasonable suspicion to conduct a DUI investigation and probable cause for a DUI arrest. If the driver is arrested for a misdemeanor DUI, follow the same procedures for the collection of breath, urine or blood as if it were a DUI traffic stop. If the driver is arrested for DUI involving serious bodily injury or death, ask for a voluntary blood test or obtain a warrant. Follow your agency's policies and procedures.

DECISION TO ARREST

Based on the totality of the DUI investigation, you will need to make the decision whether to arrest the driver for DUI. The decision to arrest the driver should follow the evidence collected during the DUI detection process.

If probable cause does not exist, do not arrest. Whether or not you make the arrest, you need to remain respectful and treat the driver with dignity throughout the process. Follow your agency's policies and procedures regarding the decision to arrest.

☑ LE1341.2. Determine if probable cause exists to arrest a driver for DUI

During a traffic crash investigation, you may arrest the driver on a DUI charge if there was enough physical evidence that the driver was impaired at the time of the crash. Physical evidence should be based on your observations, the results of the SFSTs as well as the pending results of a breath, urine, or blood test. Become familiar with the guidelines of your local state attorney's office and your agency's policies and procedures before making an arrest during a traffic crash incident. Many DUI offenses are misdemeanor crimes; however, there are times when the offense is a felony, such as in the event of serious bodily injury, death, or multiple prior convictions.

POST-ARREST EVIDENCE

After the arrest you will attempt to collect breath, urine, or blood tests. If the driver refuses to take the tests, fill out the refusal affidavit, as explained earlier.

Breath Test

Section 316.1932, F.S., outlines the criteria for conducting a breath test for alcohol impairment. A certified breath test operator (BTO) is required to administer the breath test on an arrested driver following agency's policies and procedures. The BTO should administer the breath test as close as possible to the time that the stop was initiated.

☑ LE1341.3. Describe how to observe an impaired driver before conducting a breath test

You may not use a portable breath test (PBT) device to determine probable cause for a DUI arrest. After a DUI arrest, a certified BTO or a designee assigned by the BTO monitors the driver face to face. The observation must be for a continuous 20 minutes. Document in your field notes when the observation period begins.

Before the 20 minutes begin, make sure that the driver does not have any foreign objects in their mouth, such as tobacco, fingers, hair, rubber bands, razor blades, or paper clips. Instruct the driver to remove any such object(s). Examples of things that do not affect the breath test are braces, dentures, crowns, fillings, or tongue piercings.

During the 20 minutes, make sure that the driver is not eating or drinking anything (alcohol, mouthwash, gum, candy, breath mints). If the driver vomits, instruct them to rinse their mouth with water. If any of the above occurs, start another 20-minute observation period. Document the occurrence and record the time you end and restart the observation period.

If the results of the breath test indicate an alcohol concentration of 0.08 or higher, complete a DUI citation. Write the breath test results on the citation.

If the results of the breath test indicate an alcohol concentration below 0.08, complete a UTC for the charge of DUI based on the probable cause for the arrest.

If the driver refuses to submit to the breath test, complete a DUI citation, and mark the box for "Refusal."

To request a breath sample, the subject must be under physical arrest.

Urine Test

Section 316.1932, F.S., outlines the criteria for conducting a urine test. If a breath test result is below a 0.08 and you have probable cause to believe the person is impaired by substances other than alcohol, request a urine test. The urine test should determine if the drugs in the person's system cause physical impairment.

☑ LE1341.4.
Determine when to ask an impaired driver for a urine test

The driver must take the urine test at a detention facility or any other facility, mobile or otherwise, that is equipped to administer urine tests, according to your agency's policies and procedures. Write "urine results pending" in the comments section on the UTC.

If the driver refuses to submit to the urine test, complete a DUI citation, and mark the box for "Refusal."

To request a urine sample, the subject must be under physical arrest.

Blood Test

Section 316.1932, F.S., outlines the criteria for conducting a blood test. The test can be administered if either of the following applies:

☑ LE1341.5.
Determine when to obtain a blood test from an impaired driver

- You have reasonable suspicion to believe the person was under the influence of alcohol or a chemical or controlled substance while driving, or in actual physical control of a motor vehicle.
- You were unable to conduct a breath test because it was impractical or impossible. For example, if the driver has an injury on their mouth that prevents them from blowing while taking the breath test. Document the reason you could not administer the breath test.

If possible, request the driver of the vehicle to submit to a voluntary blood draw or obtain a warrant. A person does not have to be under arrest for you to request a blood draw under implied consent. However, all blood draws (in the absence of voluntary consent) will require a warrant.

Officers can request that a lawfully arrested person, suspected of impaired driving and who appears at a medical facility, submit to a blood draw.

All blood draws must occur at a medical facility or in an ambulance for treatment. Only authorized personnel can perform the draw. You are responsible for ensuring that the blood collection follows established procedures by verifying that:

☑ LE1341.6.
Describe how to verify the procedures of a blood draw

- The blood kit is not expired.
- The blood is collected in the appropriate vial.
- The kit is identified with the driver's name, the date, and the time the blood was collected as well as the initials of the person who drew the blood.

Complete all paperwork contained in the blood kit or agency specific paperwork.

Using a Drug Recognition Expert

☑ LE1341.7. Describe the role of a drug recognition expert (DRE)

A certified *drug recognition expert (DRE)* is someone specially trained to investigate incidents involving drug-impaired drivers. They may be called to testify in court, in significant detail, and provide expert opinions regarding drug impairment. Contact a local DRE, once an arrest has been made, to assist in the investigation of a suspected drug-impaired driver if it is part of your agency's policies.

UNIT 4 CONCLUDING THE DUI INVESTIGATION
LESSON 2 DUI Report Writing

Lesson Goal

At the end of this lesson, you will know how to complete a DUI report that will support testimony in court.

DUI CITATION

The DUI citation is very similar to the UTC; however, the DUI citation is for a DUI with an alcohol concentration of 0.08 or higher, or when the driver refuses a breath, urine, or blood test after their arrest. Complete the DUI citation the same way as a UTC.

The DUI citation is a charging document and is required to authorize FLHSMV to suspend the person's driving privilege. If the person has an alcohol concentration of 0.08 or above or refuses a breath, urine or blood test, seize their Florida driver license if it is in their possession and attach it to the FLHSMV copy of the DUI citation. Within five days, forward the Florida license and a copy of it to FLHSMV for an administrative suspension hearing. If, before this citation, the driver license was valid, the driver is eligible to use the citation as a temporary driver license which will expire at midnight on the 10th day following the date of the suspension of their license. However, if their license is invalid at the time of this citation (suspended, etc.), then they cannot use this citation as a temporary driver license.

> LE1342.1. Describe how to complete a DUI citation

ARREST REPORT

Trials often take place many months after the defendant's arrest. It is essential that you write a clear and comprehensive report describing your observations and the results of your investigation for presentation to the prosecution. Doing so will allow you to recall details and present them through accurate and direct testimony in court.

The DUI report should establish the following elements for the arrest:

- There was reasonable suspicion for stopping or contacting the accused.
- The accused was the driver or in actual physical control of the vehicle, and there was probable cause to believe the accused was impaired.
- The officer followed lawful procedure regarding the rights of the accused.
- The officer followed lawful arrest procedures.
- Subsequent observation and interview of the accused provided additional evidence relevant to the alleged offense.
- The officer made a lawful request for the accused to submit to a breath, urine, or blood test, and for the results of the test.

> LE1342.2. Recognize the importance of preparing a clear and comprehensive DUI arrest report

> LE1342.3. List the elements of a clear and comprehensive DUI arrest report

Organize the DUI narrative in the report around the complete sequence of events from start to end. Begin at the first observation of the driver, continue through the arrest, and end with the incarceration or release of the person.

Chapter 14
Critical Incidents

UNIT 1 CRITICAL INCIDENT RESPONSE
- LESSON 1 Incident Command System and Response / 509
- LESSON 2 Natural Disasters / 511
- LESSON 3 Active Shooter / 513

UNIT 2 CHEMICAL AND HAZARDOUS MATERIALS
- LESSON 1 Hazardous Materials / 515
- LESSON 2 Methamphetamine and Chemical Suicide / 522

UNIT 3 EXPLOSIVE DEVICES
- LESSON 1 Types of Explosive Devices / 524
- LESSON 2 Responding to a Bomb Threat / 527
- LESSON 3 Searching for an Explosive Device / 530

UNIT 4 POST-CRITICAL INCIDENT CARE
- LESSON 1 Recovery After Disaster / 533

UNIT 1 CRITICAL INCIDENT RESPONSE
LESSON 1 Incident Command System and Response

◎ Lesson Goal

At the end of this lesson, you will understand the structure of the incident command system (ICS) as well as your role when responding to a critical incident.

Serving your community through law enforcement means that you must be ready to handle many situations. While every day as a law enforcement officer will offer unique challenges, sometimes you will be required to respond to events that are outside the scope of your typical duties.

Often classified as *critical incidents*, these are events that can put lives at risk and cause major damage to property and the environment. They can be natural or the result of human acts or error. Examples of natural critical incidents include hurricanes, tornadoes, floods, and wildfires. Human-made critical incidents include active shooter events, hazardous material spills, and bomb threats.

The effectiveness of your response can impact the public's confidence in law enforcement and can affect a community's ability to recover from a critical incident. Your community members will turn to you for support. When you display empathy, calmness, and professionalism, you are more likely to be successful in recovery efforts.

☑ LE1411.1. Describe the importance of an effective response to a critical incident

Public safety organizations often use the incident command system during a critical incident. The *incident command system (ICS)* is a standard, on-scene, all-hazards approach to manage and coordinate the operation of facilities, equipment, personnel, procedures, and communications under a common organizational structure. ICS helps manage resources effectively.

☑ LE1411.2. Describe the role and structure of the incident command system

Law enforcement and other public safety organizations use ICS to deal with many types of incidents. It has helped officers both locally and nationally manage situations, such as large vehicle crashes, hurricanes, wildfires, large social gatherings, and missing persons.

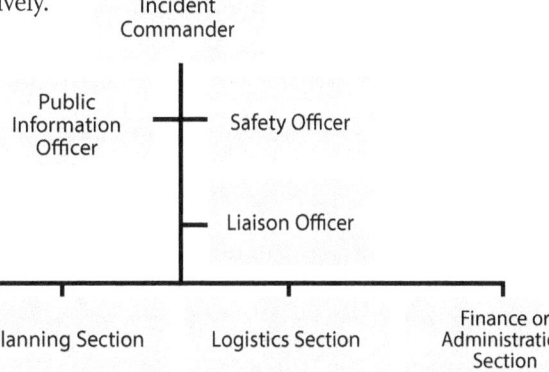

Figure 14-1 details the common structure of an incident command system. Note that ICS for different organizations might not include every aspect of this chart. Regardless, the basic structure of any ICS is similar.

Figure 14-1 Incident command system

☑ LE1411.3.
Describe an officer's role within the incident command system

When acting as part of the initial response to a critical incident, obtain the necessary information from dispatch and immediately do the following:

- Identify the type of incident or threat.
- Determine if the situation requires personal protective equipment (PPE).
- Establish an ICS.
- Set up a command post.
- Determine the resources needed, including the assistance of other agencies.
- Determine whether to shelter-in-place or evacuate (with evacuation routes and collection points). **Shelter-in-place** means taking immediate shelter in a readily accessible location or remaining inside a structure to prevent exposure to a dangerous situation that exists outside of the structure.

The ICS scope and structure can expand or contract based on the nature of the incident. Be prepared to transfer ICS command as needed.

You will get assignments and attend regular briefings for ongoing situations, such as hurricanes or wildfires, for which an ICS is already established. Personnel not at the scene or working in a command post depend on the responding officers to provide regular updates as events develop. Communicate in plain language since different agencies may use different radio codes. Most incidents require some type of debriefing or documentation when they are over. These will vary depending on the situation.

☑ LE1411.4.
Complete the two National Incident Management System online modules regarding incident command system (ICS)

The National Incident Management System (NIMS) provides ICS training on the Federal Emergency Management Agency (FEMA) website. It offers two courses: IS-100.C: Introduction to the Incident Command System, ICS 100; and IS-700.B: An Introduction to the National Incident Management System. You must complete the courses and pass the online exams. Print your certificates and give them to your instructor when you are finished.

UNIT 1 CRITICAL INCIDENT RESPONSE
LESSON 2 Natural Disasters

Lesson Goal

At the end of this lesson, you will know how to prepare your community and your personal life for a natural disaster as well as understand your role in the aftermath.

Think About This

Officer Ramos is preparing to help with evacuations for a hurricane that is heading toward Florida, but she is concerned about her own family's evacuation plan. How could Officer Ramos have prepared for this situation, so she would be ready to work her shift during the storm?

Florida is prone to many types of environmental disasters, particularly hurricanes, tornadoes, floods, and wildfires. As an officer, you must be ready to respond when a disaster strikes. Although an agency's response to natural disasters may vary with policies, certain law enforcement duties are relatively standard. You can expect to help with evacuations, traffic control, and directions, as well as provide security for shelters.

While your knowledge of your community is always valuable, it will be crucial during disasters. Officers who have established strong relationships with their community will have more knowledge of what the community needs before and after a disaster. For example, if you know that you have a large elderly population or many people who do not speak English, you can provide information about these needs to other assisting agencies.

☑ LE1412.1. Develop strong community relationships to aid in your response to natural disasters

Officers with strong community ties will also be more effective when delivering information about evacuations and safety procedures. Often, you will be responsible for relaying life-saving information, including information on family reunification, food banks, and shelters. If you have worked to build a bond with community members, there is a greater chance this information will persuade them to take appropriate precautions or be linked to the proper resources. A strong relationship with the community can potentially save many lives and help speed recovery after the disaster.

Before a disaster strikes, have an emergency plan in place for your family members and pets. You will be expected to work during all phases of the disaster. This will make it difficult for you to assist your family in their preparation or evacuation. Creating a plan for your family ahead of time will ease your anxiety and allow you to focus on your duties.

☑ LE1412.2. Describe the steps you should take in your personal life prior to a natural disaster

A few things to include in your family emergency plan include the following:

- a family meeting location
- at least one out-of-town contact

- a list of emergency management contacts for your county
- a method for your family to contact you once the disaster is over

Prepare disaster kits for both yourself and your family. The kits should contain the basic supplies needed for a 72-hour period. Your family's disaster kit should contain supplies such as a first aid kit, important paperwork, non-perishable food, water, toys for children, pet food, a flashlight, batteries, medications, and a radio. Your disaster kit should include many of the same items but also have an extra uniform and a change of clothes. Be sure to check the disaster kits every six months and replace any food, water, or medicines that might have expired.

☑ LE1412.3. Summarize the duties that an officer will perform in the aftermath of a natural disaster

Right after the disaster, your work will shift from evacuation to search and rescue and delivering supplies; providing security to shelters, distribution centers, and hospitals; and keeping the peace. While post-disaster recovery can often feel chaotic, your role is to help the community return to a sense of normalcy and order. Additionally, you will help provide support to those who may have lost everything.

As an officer, you will be one piece in the larger puzzle of disaster response and recovery. Your entire community, as well as outside emergency management agencies and first responders, will assist in recovery efforts. You will need to work alongside all of these individuals and agencies to ensure that your community recovers.

UNIT 1 CRITICAL INCIDENT RESPONSE
LESSON 3 Active Shooter

Lesson Goal

At the end of this lesson, you will know the motivations of an active shooter and the importance of following agency policies and procedures when responding.

Think About This

You are the first to arrive on the scene of an active shooter incident. What do you do?

The FBI defines an *active shooter* as an individual actively engaged in killing or attempting to kill people in a populated area. Occasionally, you might hear an active shooter also referred to as an "active threat." An active shooter's goal is mass murder, not traditional criminal acts, such as robbery or hostage taking.

Hundreds of active shooter attacks have occurred across the United States, and the threat of such violent incidents remains a primary concern for all law enforcement officers. As with many other types of critical incidents, agency policies and response protocols for addressing an active shooter event vary.

Certain traits are common to active shooters. They may experience hate, anger, and the feeling that they have been victimized by others, even if this is untrue. Some active shooters have had previous arrests for violent crimes, but others have had no interaction with law enforcement. This can make it difficult to identify the shooters before they act.

☑ LE1413.1.
Identify some of the characteristics and motivations of an active shooter

There are, however, certain factors common to active shooters, which may include the following:

- loss of significant relationships
- changes in financial status or loss of or termination from a job
- feelings of victimization
- major adverse changes to life circumstances
- feelings of perceived injustice

The majority of active shooters are often experiencing many of these indicators. However, these indicators alone do not mean that a person is likely to commit a shooting. It is also important to remember that there is not a single profile for a mass shooter.

Many active shooters show their desire to hurt others before carrying out a mass shooting. They may engage in certain behaviors that prompt people around them to realize they are thinking about carrying out mass violence. These behaviors may include showing their desire to hurt others through social media or journal writings, and making statements to other people.

☑ LE1413.2.
Describe your role in an active shooter incident

Current tactics focus on immediately locating the active shooter and ending the threat before helping the injured. If you respond to an active shooter situation, you should always be prepared to respond alone and not wait for backup. An active shooter incident is often a chaotic situation with large numbers of injured people, fleeing crowds, and the potential secondary hazards, such as improvised explosive devices. Follow your agency's policies and tactical training if you respond to an active shooter.

UNIT 2 CHEMICAL AND HAZARDOUS MATERIALS
LESSON 1 Hazardous Materials

Lesson Goal

At the end of this lesson, you will know how to respond to a hazardous materials incident while ensuring public and personal safety.

Think About This

You approach a commercial truck that has pulled over to the side of the highway. As you approach the truck, the driver hands you the paperwork explaining what the truck is carrying. Upon reading the driver's paperwork, you see the name of the substance but do not recognize it. What is your next step in this situation?

Law enforcement officers are sometimes required to assist in hazmat situations. As previously discussed in Chapter 12, a hazmat accident has the potential to cause enormous harm to a community. Traffic crashes are not the only incidents where you will potentially encounter hazmat situations. A few examples of other instances where you might encounter hazmat incidents include a factory explosion, a gas leak in a residential neighborhood, or a petroleum spill in a body of water.

In a hazmat incident the main objectives are to do the following:

- isolate the area without entering it
- keep people away from the scene
- ensure people are upwind and out of low-lying areas

☑ LE1421.1. List the main objectives of a hazardous materials response

Several laws, regulations, and standards list what an officer should do during a hazmat incident. The ***standard of care*** is the level of competency expected or required when performing this duty. Although public safety employees have this duty to act, as a responder, you should not try to do something beyond your level of training or the capability of your equipment when responding to an incident. Only a properly equipped and trained officer should approach any potential hazmat situation. Always use extreme caution.

☑ LE1421.2. Explain standard of care when responding to a hazardous materials incident

IDENTIFYING HAZARDOUS MATERIALS

To make accurate decisions, it is essential that you identify the type of hazardous material involved. Be careful to never put yourself at risk in the process. Prevent direct contamination by avoiding contact with the product and its gases, vapors, or smoke.

To identify the material, you may have to look at documents or shipping papers, or interview the transport driver or facility staff. Shipping company employees and vehicle drivers may be able to identify the product. If you cannot identify the material's specific name, make decisions as an awareness-level responder to minimize potential health hazards. Rely on agency policies and procedures to avoid risk to people and property.

☑ LE1421.3. Describe the primary methods to detect the presence of hazardous materials

Classes of Hazardous Materials

☑ LE1421.4. Identify the nine classes of hazardous materials

The U.S. Department of Transportation (USDOT) defines nine common classes of hazardous materials. This information can help you identify the type of hazardous material involved in a particular incident.

Classes of Hazardous Materials		
CLASS 1	explosives	*Explosives* are materials or devices designed to release energy very rapidly. Consider all explosives to be extreme hazards when they are involved in or near a fire. Some examples of explosive materials are dynamite, black powder, and small arms ammunition.
CLASS 2	gases	*Gases* are materials that are neither solid nor liquid at ordinary temperatures; they are contained under pressure. Gases may be flammable, non-flammable, poisonous, or corrosive. Some examples of potentially hazardous gases are acetylene, hydrogen, and anhydrous ammonia.
CLASS 3	flammable liquids and combustible liquids	These materials burn in the presence of an ignition source. Some examples are gasoline, diesel fuel, and acetone.
CLASS 4	flammable solid, spontaneously combustible, and dangerous when wet	These materials are neither liquid nor gas. They may burn in the presence of an ignition source, in the presence of heat or friction, ignite spontaneously, or when in contact with water. Some examples are magnesium, sulfur, and calcium carbide.
CLASS 5	oxidizers and organic peroxides	These materials may cause spontaneous combustion or increase the intensity of a fire. Examples include bromine or calcium hypochlorite (bleach).
CLASS 6	poison (toxic) and poison inhalation hazards	These materials include medical waste and biological hazards.
CLASS 7	radioactive substances	These materials include nuclear waste, radioactive medical materials, and x-ray equipment.
CLASS 8	corrosive substances	These materials include acids, solvents, or other materials that may cause irreversible damage to human tissues.
CLASS 9	miscellaneous dangerous goods	Not belonging to Classes 1–8, these materials are subject to USDOT regulations on transportation. Some examples are: • lithium ion batteries • dry ice • magnetized metals • auto-inflating devices, such as airbags • asbestos • molten sulfur, PCBs (polychlorinated biphenyls) • hazardous waste

Occupancy and Location

Occupancy refers to a structure and its use. Some examples are manufacturing facilities, storage facilities, retail establishments, and residences. Knowing the type of building you are entering will help you anticipate what hazardous materials may be there. If you do not know the type of building, assume that hazardous materials are inside. Location refers to an area and its use. Some examples are industrial parks, business districts, agricultural areas, and residential neighborhoods. Details such as traffic patterns, time of day, inhabitants, and type of location may affect how you respond to a potential hazard.

☑ LE1421.5. Describe how to identify hazardous materials

Container Shape and Size

The shape of the container involved in the hazmat incident can provide useful information about the type of hazard. The main types of containers include portable, fixed, and transportation containers. There is usually a direct relationship between the size of the container and the size of the affected geographical area. Therefore, the bigger the container, the bigger the area covered. Containers that store contents under pressure, such as propane or oxygen tanks, can have additional problems, like explosions and vapor releases.

Placards and Labels

Regulations govern the use of placards or labels on vehicles and facilities that store or transport hazardous materials. The USDOT requires most vehicles transporting hazardous materials to display placards that describe the class of hazardous materials on board. These placards are posted on all four sides of a vehicle, railcar, or other large container, and on the individual packages of the material. In special circumstances, the USDOT does not require placards.

Anything that holds two or more classes of hazardous materials should display a "DANGEROUS" placard and may use this placard instead of the specific placard for each class of material. This may not always be the case, however, as materials like explosives and toxic gases cannot use the "DANGEROUS" sign.

Other regulations, such as local ordinances, require commercial facilities to show other symbols that describe the hazardous materials on site. The U.S. Environmental Protection Agency requires all pesticides and some other chemical substances to show warning labels on the outside of the container to indicate harmful contents.

Remember that even if you do not see a placard, label, or other warning, hazardous materials may still be present.

Shipping Papers and Facility Documents

Commercial vehicle operators are required to carry documents that list the contents of their shipment. These documents are called shipping papers or shipping manifests.

They can help you identify the materials and associated hazards and take appropriate actions if exposure occurs.

Many places require facilities to keep documents that outline the type of hazardous materials stored or manufactured on site. One example of a facility document is the safety data sheet (SDS). These documents must be displayed in facilities where a hazardous substance is stored, manufactured, or used. Other facility documents include the employer's emergency response plan (ERP). An *emergency response plan (ERP)* is a written plan that describes what an organization will do during various major events. An agency ERP sets safe and uniform guidelines for response to incidents involving weapons of mass destruction or hazardous materials.

Colors and Markings

Colors of placards and labels also help identify a material's hazard classification. Company names and other unique markings may indicate the presence of hazardous materials. Familiarity with the users and suppliers of hazardous materials in the community can be helpful in a hazmat situation.

NFPA 704 Diamonds

The National Fire Protection Association (NFPA) has developed a standard facility and vehicle marking system called the 704 system. Placed on the outside of structures, storage facilities, or vehicles, this large symbol indicates that hazardous products are stored there. The diamond-shaped symbol is divided into four segments that indicate the following risks:

- blue—health hazards
- red—flammability hazards
- yellow—instability hazards
- white—special hazards (provides information on any special hazards of the material)

In each area, a number from zero to four indicates the material's relative hazard with zero indicating no hazard and four indicating the highest hazard.

Senses

Identifying a hazardous material through the five senses may place you at an unacceptable risk for exposure.

☑ LE1421.6. Distinguish between high-risk and low-risk senses

Sight and hearing are considered lower-risk senses when identifying hazardous materials. Use these senses from a safe distance and look for the following:

- pressure release
- smoke or fire
- liquids, gas leaks, or vapor cloud

- condensation on pipelines or containers
- chemical reactions
- mass casualties

Smell, touch, and taste are considered higher-risk senses when identifying hazardous materials. Never use them to identify a hazardous material.

USING THE *EMERGENCY RESPONSE GUIDEBOOK*

As previously discussed in Chapter 12, the *Emergency Response Guidebook (ERG)* can help you identify hazardous materials. When responding to hazmat situations, the orange color-coded pages are the most important part of the *ERG*. This section has three main topics for each substance identified.

Potential Hazards

Consult this topic first. It describes potential hazards that the material may display in terms of fire or explosion and health effects upon exposure.

☑ LE1421.7. Explain how to find hazmat information in the *ERG*

Public Safety

The Public Safety topic has three subsections: notification, protective clothing, and evacuation.

NOTIFICATION

The notification subsection lets you know the first thing to do when called to a scene. Some examples are activating an agency's ERP and making sure help is coming. Call the emergency contact number on the shipping papers or the emergency response telephone numbers listed inside the *ERG's* back cover for more information. Advise other responders of incident conditions, type and amount of materials, safe approach information, the *ERG* page to use, needed resources, and any actions taken.

PROTECTIVE CLOTHING

The protective clothing subsection tells you about protective clothing you may need. Protective clothing requires proper training to use. Most agencies do not furnish protective clothing to patrol officers.

EVACUATION

After isolating the immediate danger area, the next step is to evacuate or protect people in the downwind hazard area or within the radius of the incident. This distance can be very large, depending on the type of material and whether the material was spilled or involved in a fire, which may make the radius of the incident much wider than it would have been otherwise.

☑ LE1421.8. Explain how to secure a hazmat scene

The evacuation subsection also gives information about how far people should stay from a spill, known as the ***protective action distance***. Consult the Table of Initial Isolation and Protective Action Distances (green section) if the type of hazardous material is highlighted in the *ERG*.

Evacuate the area if the incident is going to last for an extended period or could potentially cause a fire or explosion. Because the evacuation process may be difficult (for example, due to dense population or the presence of a school or hospital) or expose people to greater hazards than remaining in the area would, rely on agency policies for guidance.

Fire creates the potential for an explosion. This includes vapor explosion from expanding boiling liquid. The *ERG* gives in-depth information about protective action distances. Recommendations depend on the spill's size, weather conditions, and time of day. Geographical conditions can also affect the distribution of hazardous materials.

Emergency Response

The Emergency Response topic has three subsections: fire, spill or leak, and first aid.

FIRE

The fire subsection provides guidelines to all levels of responders. Awareness-level responders must not attempt to extinguish a fire that involves hazardous materials. Normal fire extinguisher training is not sufficient to fight a fire that directly involves hazardous materials. You should attempt to fight such a fire only if you have proper training and protection. Operational-level personnel with the necessary protection and training can accomplish a defensive fire attack. Technician-level personnel must conduct an offensive fire attack.

SPILL OR LEAK

Personnel engaged in controlling spills and leaks must have proper protection and training. You do not have training in spill or leak control. Operational-level personnel can perform spill control if they avoid direct contact with the material and have proper protection. Operational-level responders can also activate remote shut-off. Technician-level responders can perform leak control.

FIRST AID

The first aid subsection outlines basic first aid for victims of exposure. Awareness-level responders may identify contaminated people who present a significant risk of secondary contamination, but should avoid direct contact with these people to prevent exposure. Encourage contaminated, conscious victims to move to an isolated area and await medical assistance from properly trained and protected personnel. Do not allow anyone or anything to leave the area without evaluation for decontamination by properly protected qualified personnel.

☑ LE1421.9. Describe OSHA requirements for terminating a hazmat incident

INCIDENT TERMINATION PROCEDURES

All awareness-level responders should follow agency policies and procedures to terminate their involvement in a hazmat incident. Occupational Safety and Health Administration (OSHA) regulations require a structured termination process. The three steps are on-scene debriefing, incident critique, and after-action analysis.

1. During the on-scene debriefing process, officers are advised of the materials to which they may have been exposed, signs and symptoms of overexposure, and who to contact if they notice signs or symptoms of exposure. If exposure exceeds the acceptable published limits, the agency will send the officer for medical evaluation.
2. During the incident critique phase, officers provide information on operational strengths and weaknesses.
3. In the after-action analysis, the agency's goal is to review any weaknesses and implement any additional or corrective training, as necessary.

UNIT 2 CHEMICAL AND HAZARDOUS MATERIALS
LESSON 2 Methamphetamine and Chemical Suicide

◎ Lesson Goal

At the end of this lesson, you will know how to respond to incidents involving methamphetamine and chemical suicide while ensuring public and officer safety.

Think About This

You respond to a local residence where a woman has passed out on her front lawn. When you approach the woman, you notice that her garage is open, and you see many bottles and what looks like something cooking on a fire. There is also a strong smell of rotten eggs. What should you do first to respond to this situation?

METHAMPHETAMINE LABORATORIES (METH LABS)

Meth labs are locations where methamphetamine is manufactured. A meth lab can be as small as a soda bottle or as large as a warehouse. A simple chemical process converts pseudoephedrine or ephedrine into methamphetamine.

☑ LE1422.1. Recognize some of the indicators of a meth lab

Dangerous chemicals used in the manufacturing process of methamphetamine can be found anywhere in a home, vehicle, vessel, shed, motel, or other location. The materials used are readily available items such as coffee filters, two-liter bottles, blenders, lithium batteries, red-tipped matches, cold tablets, camp stove fuels, drain cleaner, brake fluid, and bleach. The presence of a combination of these materials may indicate a meth lab.

Common methods used in making methamphetamine are the one-pot "Shake and Bake" method, the red phosphorous method, and the "Nazi" (anhydrous ammonia) method. Meth labs may produce strong chemical odors, similar to rotten eggs or cat urine. Areas surrounding meth labs often have dead vegetation. Be aware of the toxic nature of the discarded byproducts of the meth-manufacturing process.

SAFE RESPONSE

Meth labs are safety hazards. The ingredients used to produce meth are typically flammable, explosive chemicals when under pressure or heated. Mixing these chemicals can produce violent explosions or toxic gases. If you suspect a lab is present, do not inhale fumes, touch or taste the chemicals, or turn anything on or off. Meth labs can also be booby-trapped or planted with traps designed to cause injury when triggered. Use caution when coming into contact with any person exposed to a meth lab.

☑ LE1422.2. Describe how to respond to a meth lab

The decontamination process for a meth lab incident is the same as for any hazmat exposure. Evacuate the occupants and leave the premises immediately. Do not place anything in the patrol vehicle before decontamination or allow the removal of any items from the site. Establish a perimeter and follow agency policies and procedures for a meth lab response. Always use caution when encountering a meth lab or suspected meth lab. Remember that many meth labs are mobile and are found in vehicles. After the initial response, interview all involved people, document the incident, and identify any need for post-exposure medical evaluations.

CHEMICAL SUICIDE

Chemical suicide, also known as detergent suicide, is a method of committing suicide that involves mixing two or more easily acquired chemicals. Once mixed, these chemicals produce gases that quickly fill an enclosed area. Chemical suicide typically occurs in vehicles, closets, bathrooms, or other small, confined spaces where the concentration of gas can quickly accumulate to deadly levels.

There are several methods of chemical suicide. The most common method uses hydrogen sulfide and hydrogen cyanide. If you encounter a chemical suicide situation, follow the procedures for a hazmat response, including establishing a safe perimeter. Do not enter or let the public enter an area or vehicle, and do not rescue or resuscitate a person if the following indicators are present:

☑ LE1422.3. Recognize some indicators of a chemical suicide

- an unresponsive or sleeping person in a vehicle
- warning sign(s) taped to doors or windows
- unusual odors such as rotten eggs, sulfur, or burnt almonds
- a suicide note inside the vehicle or area
- pennies in the area tarnished with residue
- yellow-green or white residue on vehicle seats, dashboard, or windows
- household cleaning or pesticide containers
- buckets for mixing chemicals
- a vehicle's inside door handles removed
- tape or towels sealing a door or air vents
- a bag over the person's head

Symptoms of chemical suicide can be different depending on the amount of exposure. Mild exposure to such chemicals can irritate the eyes, nose, and throat. Moderate exposure can cause headaches, dizziness, nausea, vomiting, coughing, and difficulty breathing. High exposure symptoms include severe respiratory irritation, severe eye irritation, convulsions, coma, and death.

UNIT 3 EXPLOSIVE DEVICES
LESSON 1 Types of Explosive Devices

> ◎ **Lesson Goal**
>
> At the end of this lesson, you will know how to recognize types of explosive devices and take basic protective actions.

Many types of explosive devices exist. Agencies do not expect you to know and be able to identify all varieties of bombs, explosives, or military ordnance. Regardless of the type of explosive, always be careful and follow agency policies and procedures when dealing with a potential explosive device.

MILITARY ORDNANCE

Military devices can be easily acquired and are generally recognizable. They include hand grenades, landmines, and rocket launchers. You may encounter such devices when responding to a report of a found, abandoned, or suspicious military item. Military memorabilia or souvenirs accidentally discovered can be live or inert.

☑ LE1431.1. Describe how to respond to a potential military explosive

Always assume that such devices are live. Do not handle them. Clear the area and request assistance from a bomb squad for proper removal or disposal.

IMPROVISED EXPLOSIVE DEVICES

☑ LE1431.2. Describe methods of disguising IEDs

An *improvised explosive device (IED)* is a homemade bomb built and used in ways other than conventional military action. An IED is made from commercially available materials and can be disguised as almost anything. IEDs have been hidden in trash bins, backpacks, road signs, concealed under debris, and otherwise constructed to prevent discovery. Since these items may not be easily recognized, treat anything found under suspicious circumstances as a possible explosive device. Remember to consider the possibility that a door or entryway could have an IED attached.

Mail Bombs

Mail bombs are a special class of suspicious items. They could be delivered by the U.S. Postal Service, a commercial delivery service, or by hand.

☑ LE1431.3. Recognize indicators of mail bombs

Mail bombs can be difficult to detect. Some possible signs are envelopes or packages that:

- are rigid
- have too much postage
- have misspellings of common words
- are handwritten

- have poorly typed addresses
- have discoloration
- have protruding wires
- have strange odors

If you or others become suspicious of a mailed item, do not handle it. Isolate the item and evacuate the area.

Vehicle-Borne Improvised Explosive Devices

A motor vehicle used as a bomb is a ***vehicle-borne improvised explosive device (VBIED)***. VBIEDs can be very powerful and dangerous. They are capable of carrying extremely large amounts of explosives. It is very difficult to bring 7,000 pounds of explosives into a building, but a small rental truck carrying that amount could blow up in front of a building and cause mass destruction.

Indicators of a VBIED might include the following:

- a threat that specifically mentions explosives in a vehicle
- a vehicle that is parked suspiciously close to a building or in a restricted parking area without a proper decal or sticker
- a car that is unfamiliar to building occupants or seems to have a heavy load, indicated by riding low on its rear axle
- a vehicle that has a strange smell or leaks powder or liquid
- reports that a driver or passenger exited a vehicle and left hurriedly
- a bomb canine alerting officers that a vehicle is a threat

☑ LE1431.4.
Recognize indicators of a VBIED

If you suspect that a vehicle might contain explosives, note the description and size of the vehicle. Evacuate the area around the vehicle and establish a perimeter. Evacuation distance from a vehicle should be much greater than evacuation distance from a building because a VBIED is potentially very large, and pieces of the vehicle can act as shrapnel.

Incendiary Devices

Incendiary devices can start fires, destroy property, and harm people. Well known examples are Molotov cocktails, napalm, and firebombs. Rioters, arsonists, and criminals frequently use incendiary devices. These devices consist of a minimum of three components: an ignition source, a combustible filler material, and a container.

☑ LE1431.5.
Describe examples of incendiary devices and their manner of delivery

Common materials used in the manufacture of incendiary devices are roadway flares, gasoline or motor oil, and glass containers. These devices are very similar to explosive devices and can function in the same manner. They can be placed anywhere or thrown at a target. Respond to potential incendiary devices the same way you would respond to bomb situations and never touch, move, or disturb an incendiary device.

MEANS OF DETONATION

> LE1431.6. Identify different means of detonating an explosive device

A creative bomb maker can construct an explosive device to detonate through a number of methods. Some examples include tripwires, pressure switches, motion detectors, infrared beams, and remote triggers. A person can place a pressure switch under a rug, beneath a doormat, or in soil. They can wire a wall light switch into the bomb's triggering circuit so that it detonates by operating the switch. They can use a cell phone or a key fob to remotely detonate an explosive device.

UNIT 3 EXPLOSIVE DEVICES
LESSON 2 Responding to a Bomb Threat

Lesson Goal

At the end of this lesson, you will understand your role when responding to a bomb threat while ensuring public and officer safety.

Think About This

A bomb threat has been called into a local hardware store in your community. You arrive on the scene and begin to interview the person who took the call about the bomb threat. As you continue your interview, the owner of the store tells you that she noticed a large duffle bag at one of the cash registers. What should you do next?

INITIAL RESPONSE TO A BOMB THREAT

When responding to a bomb threat, get as much information as possible from dispatch. This initial information guides your actions upon arrival.

Information collected should include the following:

- the nature of the complaint
- the means of the threat
- the time the threat was received
- the alleged time of detonation
- a description of the device, if known
- the location of the device, if known
- who received the threat

☑ LE1432.1. Describe the information to collect in a bomb threat

If dispatch does not have all of the information listed above, gather as much missing information as possible from witnesses or the complainant.

Most threats come via telephone. Some, however, come by voice mail, a note left at the scene, social media, a mailed letter, a fax, or an email. Identify the time the complainant received the threat. If the threat contained a phrase such as "the bomb will go off one hour from now," the time of the call becomes very important. This allows you to estimate the possible time of detonation, the level of risk, and a deadline by which evacuations or searches must be completed.

A common policy or rule is to be out of a building at least 30 minutes before the alleged time of detonation and not return until the building has been cleared. If a threat includes information about a location of an explosive device, remember this information when approaching. This could change how you approach and allow you to stay as far away from the device as possible.

LOCATION

> ☑ LE1432.2. Identify the bomb's location

Street maps, building layouts, or someone familiar with the area can help provide additional, more detailed information related to the device's location, if known. This could help the bomb squad find the suspected device and predict possible damage caused by detonation. You must also determine and describe as best as you can where the item is in relation to both the layout of the building or area and any possible hazards. Such hazards could include fuel storage tanks, other stored chemicals, tanks of pressurized gas, steel rods, rolls of wire, or containers of bolts or nails. Be sure to inform the bomb squad of any additional hazards known.

USING RADIO AND TRANSMITTING EQUIPMENT

> ☑ LE1432.3. Identify how to use electronic equipment safely during a bomb threat

When approaching a possible bomb situation, decide whether to turn off radios and radio wave-transmitting devices. There is no universal agreement on whether to do this at or near a bomb threat scene. Agency policies will determine whether to use the radio. Avoiding radio use may stop the accidental triggering or detonation of a bomb designed to explode by radio waves. Notify dispatch and supervisors just before arrival if you plan to turn off radios or other equipment that emits radio waves.

APPROACHING THE SCENE SAFELY AND TACTICALLY

> ☑ LE1432.4. Describe how to safely approach the scene of a potentially explosive device

If you know the device's location, choose a route that leads to a stopping point a safe distance from the area. Never park too close to the incident or any suspicious item. Do not park in a manner that will block additional units. Follow your agency policies to determine a safe distance for evacuations when parking a patrol vehicle. If there is a compelling reason, you may need to move closer. The first officers on the scene often move closer to talk with representatives of the building, interview witnesses, and further assess the situation. Once you have parked, maintain a safe location and distance from the threat. Use natural or artificial structures for protective cover. Adjust your distance and location if new information indicates the initial stopping point is too close.

OBSERVATIONS DURING APPROACH

> ☑ LE1432.5. Describe what to observe when approaching the scene of a bomb threat

It is essential to follow a tactical approach when arriving at the site of a bomb threat. As you approach the scene, note landmarks and approximate safe distances so that you can give specific directions to other responding units. These may also serve as good evacuation gathering areas. When approaching the scene, look for secondary devices or suspicious packages and signs of hazardous materials. You might notice an unusual smell or irritation to your skin, eyes, or breathing passages. If this occurs, you should, if possible, move upwind and uphill from the hazard and seek medical attention.

If you approach the scene and see signs of an explosion, the situation has changed. Now, there may be additional safety issues such as broken gas lines, weakened building structures, debris, and fires. Immediately alert EMS, the fire department, and the bomb squad, and request additional backup. Remember to always review and follow your agency's policies and guidelines regarding bomb threats.

Increase the perimeter distance to secure the area. It has now become a possible crime scene. Be aware that items that may not initially appear important may be potential evidence.

ASSESSING THE CREDIBILITY OF THE THREAT

Locate the person who received the threat, even though that person may not be at the scene. The recipient is sometimes the most important witness, so interview them as soon as possible. If the recipient is present, do not allow them to leave the scene. Keep track of them for additional questioning by the bomb squad and investigators.

Interview the complainant and the owner or representative of the building or threatened area. Ask them to meet you away from the threatened area. Sources of additional information may include witnesses or key people, such as custodians or security personnel, with special knowledge about the area.

The owner or building representative may be able to answer some important questions. The information they provide can help you assess the situation and determine the answer to the following questions: Is the threat credible? What kind of risk is involved? What is the evacuation plan, and are there any problems with evacuating? How best can we all communicate? Are any building plans available? The owner or representative may also know the organization's or building's history of incidents or threats.

If there is video surveillance, view the footage as soon as possible. Exchange information with the owner or representative to help confirm and learn any additional information that may verify the threat's credibility.

Credibility will be the major issue in determining whether to search or evacuate. The owner or building representative must give permission to search or evacuate unless you find a device. In this case, the area has become a crime scene, and you will order a mandatory evacuation.

Ask questions about possible suspects (e.g., ex-employees, disgruntled employees, angry customers, expelled or suspended students, or employees who may be having domestic disputes) and find out who controls access to the building. Find and interview anyone who might know the caller's motivation.

If the threat takes physical form, such as a letter or note, collect that item as evidence. Identify and interview the person in possession of it. Secure, log, and protect all evidence.

Treat all threats and bomb situations as credible until proved otherwise. This assumption will help you decide what action to take next. You may recommend a search or evacuation, participate in a search, notify the bomb squad, fire department, or EMS, or move the public farther from the threat.

Finding a device, suspicious item, or other suspicious circumstances may indicate that the threat is credible. The amount of detail provided in the threat may also show that the threat is real and let you know the risk level involved.

> ☑ LE1432.6. Describe how to evaluate the credibility of a bomb threat

UNIT 3 EXPLOSIVE DEVICES
LESSON 3 Searching for an Explosive Device

Lesson Goal

At the end of this lesson, you will understand your role in the search for an explosive device.

SEARCH CONSIDERATIONS

☑ LE1433.1. Describe search considerations at the scene of a bomb threat

In a bomb threat situation, the decision to conduct a search depends on different factors:

- if permission is obtained to search a building or area
- the level of risk for those conducting the search
- the credibility and amount of detail provided in the threat
- additional threats or the possibility of secondary devices
- agency policies on searching for explosives

Always look for safe locations and protective cover to defend against an explosion. A general safe distance for the initial perimeter is 1,000 feet from the supposed location of the bomb. This is a minimum evacuation distance and applies to situations in which the type or amount of explosive is unknown. If there is no good protective cover available, or if the type and amount of the explosive requires it, substantially increase the evacuation distance. Upon arrival, direct everyone to move to a safe location. If circumstances allow, evacuate people upwind, or at least crosswind.

Permission to Search

In most cases, you must ask the owner or building representative for permission to search the property. The owner or building representative is usually cooperative regarding a search. In an emergency, if the owner or building representative cannot be located, you may conduct the search without consent.

Level of Risk for Searchers

Sometimes the risk level might be too high to conduct a search. The information received in a threat or warning may indicate that the device is booby-trapped. The bomber could also trigger the device remotely. If there is a booby-trap concern, only special units or bomb squads should conduct the search. If the bomb is supposed to detonate within a short time, postpone the search. Make sure everyone remains at a safe distance outside the building until after the alleged time of detonation. After that time passes, reevaluate the situation and determine if the search should resume. In some instances, an agency's procedure might require a waiting period before beginning a search.

Additional Threats or Secondary Devices

A *secondary explosive device* is a bomb placed at the scene of an ongoing emergency response that is intended to cause casualties among responders. Secondary explosive devices are designed to inflict additional injury, damage, and fear by exploding after a primary explosion or other major emergency response event has attracted large numbers of responders to the scene.

Typically, these devices are hidden or camouflaged. Bombers place the devices in ordinary objects such as vehicles, flashlights, backpacks, flowerpots, or garbage cans. These devices may detonate at a certain time, or radio-controlled devices or cell phones can cause detonation. During a search, always assume that there is a secondary device in the area.

CONDUCTING THE SEARCH

When planning a search, use resources, such as a person who has knowledge of the building layout, any existing search plan or search teams, and information contained in the threat or warning.

If no search plan exists, make a plan that will systematically cover all necessary areas and remove confusion. A chaotic search, done without knowledge of the building's layout, particularly in a large or complex building, might mean some areas are searched several times while others are completely missed. Searching systematically requires that you follow the search plan faithfully and that searchers use appropriate search methods and patterns. Recall from Chapter 9 that there are several systematic search patterns. Conduct the search thoroughly. Remember that explosives can be hidden anywhere.

☑ LE1433.2. Describe how to search the scene of a bomb threat

Unless you know the exact location of the device, conduct an exterior search of the building perimeter. Follow this by searching evacuation routes, evacuee collection points, staging areas, and command posts. These are ideal locations for a secondary device. If the building is next to a street, begin at the edge of the street.

After the exterior search, conduct an interior search. Look for any items that seem out of place, and search potential hiding spots. The most obvious areas to search are any mentioned in the threat. If you find no device in the suspected places, search the publicly accessible areas, including entryways and foyers, lobbies, waiting areas, restrooms, cleaning and storage closets, and elevator shafts, including the tops of elevators.

If the public area search yields nothing, determine whether to search the entire building. A building's interior search should go from bottom to top, beginning with the basement areas, including utility rooms and areas with heating, cooling, electrical power, and telephone equipment.

Be alert to the possibility of booby-trapped detonation devices. Watch where you step, and do not back up without first looking behind you. Before entering a doorway, visually inspect the doorway and the surrounding area. Watch for tripwires, look for lumps or bulges in the carpet and rugs, and step over floor mats. Do not rush into any room or space.

Divide and assign certain floors or rooms to different search teams. Each team should place tape across the doorway of a room or area when they have completely searched it. If using floor plans, check off rooms or areas as you search.

Pay attention to any vehicle parked unusually close to the building, abandoned luggage, gym bags, backpacks, buggies, strollers, or suspicious packages.

If you find nothing suspicious, be careful telling the property owner. Liability could be an issue if you offer such definitive statements as, "There are no explosives at this location," or "It is safe to go back inside."

RECOGNIZING A SUSPICIOUS ITEM

Many bombs do not appear to be bombs at all. Sometimes an explosive device is found simply because it is a suspicious item. A bomb may resemble almost anything.

LE1433.3.
Identify the elements of a potential explosive device

If you find an item that seems suspicious, ask someone if the item belongs there. Bombers may conceal explosives within some form of packaging. Never try to open or handle a suspected device or package. Sometimes officers will not see the device, and the information will come from interviewing someone who has seen it. The more details you can get, the better the bomb team can perform its job.

If you find a suspicious item, vacate the room or area immediately. Take a quick look at the device before leaving. Note any identifying features including type, color, shape, and size of the device as well as any names, labels, placards, chemical symbols, or signs indicating the type of explosive. Immediately notify anyone nearby, a building representative, and a commanding officer so that the evacuation process may begin.

UNIT 4 POST-CRITICAL INCIDENT CARE
LESSON 1 Recovery After Disaster

Lesson Goal

At the end of this lesson, you will understand the unique challenges of recovering after a critical incident.

As law enforcement officers, you will inevitably face situations that test not only your physical abilities but also your emotional resilience. Critical incidents—such as natural disasters, active threats, and mass casualty events—can expose officers to intense trauma. While your training will prepare you to respond effectively, it is equally important to understand the emotional toll that these events can take. You will respond to many critical incidents over the course of your career, and the constant exposure to these events can have a cumulative impact on your mental health. Recognizing and managing these challenges is crucial to coping with burnout, survivor's guilt, and public scrutiny during and after a critical incident; successfully managing these challenges will help you maintain your well-being, ensure good professional performance, and support the communities you serve.

BURNOUT

Critical incidents, especially those that require a prolonged recovery period like natural disasters, may cause burnout, which is a state of emotional, physical, and mental exhaustion caused by chronic workplace stress. For example, burnout may occur after a major hurricane when you work extra shifts to help with recovery while you and your family are displaced from your own home, dealing with storm damage, and trying to return to normalcy.

☑ LE1441.1. Describe how burnout can present during and after a critical incident

Law enforcement is especially susceptible to burnout due to the nature of the job. Chronic exposure to stressful situations, long hours, and trauma all create the conditions for exhaustion and disengagement. Recognizing the signs of burnout and seeking support is essential to building resilience; if left unaddressed, it can contribute to worsening mental health and negatively impact your personal health and well-being. The symptoms of burnout include the following:

- fatigue and stress
- irritability and impatience
- inability to cope with daily life
- changes to eating and sleep habits
- increased dependence on alcohol or other substances
- feelings of defeat and lack of a sense of accomplishment
- physical ailments, such as high blood pressure or a weakened immune system

While burnout directly impacts officers, it also affects the entire community in serious ways. When an officer experiences chronic stress, exhaustion, and emotional detachment, their ability to serve effectively is compromised. If citizens perceive officers as aggressive, indifferent, or ineffective, they may become less willing to cooperate with law enforcement. This distrust makes solving crimes and maintaining order more difficult, which will reflect poorly on the agency.

Another effect of officer burnout is an increase in officer turnover and inexperience. When experienced officers leave an agency, the agency may struggle to fill that position or may have to use time and resources to train a new recruit. The loss of trained officers and the lack of resources creates gaps in institutional knowledge, puts additional pressure on remaining officers, and increases the chance of burnout happening to others.

The consequences of burnout are far-reaching; it not only impacts an officer's personal and professional life, but it also affects an agency's ability to build and maintain trust with its community. Understanding how and when burnout is affecting you or a fellow officer, especially after a critical incident, will help you support a strong working relationship between law enforcement and the community it serves.

SURVIVOR'S GUILT

☑ LE1441.2. Explain how survivor's guilt may affect law enforcement officers

Alongside burnout, officers may suffer from survivor's guilt after experiencing a critical incident. Survivor's guilt occurs when an officer survives an incident—such as a shootout, ambush, or natural disaster—while a fellow officer, civilian, or suspect does not. This emotional burden can be overwhelming and can manifest in several ways. It can present as emotional detachment, impaired job performance, risky behavior, and guilt.

When a fellow officer falls in the line of duty or a civilian is caught in the crossfire, people who are left behind may struggle with overwhelming guilt. They may ask themselves "why them and not me" or agonize over what they could have done differently. This guilt can manifest in various ways, leading to self-doubt and emotional turmoil.

Officers who experience survivor's guilt may find themselves asking the following questions:

- Did I deserve to survive?
- Why was I spared while they were not?
- Did I do everything I could to prevent this?
- Am I still fit to wear the badge after this?
- How do I live with this guilt?

Ultimately, these questions point to a feeling that you did not do enough. For example, after a natural disaster, officers might wonder if they could have rescued more people or provided more aid. Even in situations where an officer did everything they could, the feeling of helplessness in the face of massive destruction can weigh heavily on them.

Survivor's guilt can be an intense and isolating experience. While the weight of losing a partner or an innocent civilian can lead to overwhelming self-doubt, grief, and emotional distress, there are ways to navigate through this difficult journey and find a path towards healing. Officers can cope with survivor's guilt by acknowledging their emotions and seeking support from peers and medical professionals.

PUBLIC SCRUTINY

There will likely be media coverage leading up to, during, and after a critical incident. Agencies often partner with local and regional news outlets to keep the public informed of expected dangerous storms, evacuation routes, and open shelters before major hurricanes. They also partner up afterward to keep people informed of the storm's impact such as power outages, road closures, and recovery resources. Most agencies have a public information officer or communications team that deals directly with the media and engages with the public on behalf of the agency through its social media accounts, press conferences, and public meetings.

☑ LE1441.3. Identify the impact of public scrutiny on mental health

It is easy for a person to get overwhelmed by the constant flow of information; however, officers can be directly impacted by members of the media or the general public interrupting a scene with questions or attempts to document an event by recording. Because the law enforcement profession is often in the spotlight due to high-profile stories in the media, officers deal with public perception that fluctuates between support and criticism. It can be demoralizing to work hard to serve your community only to be criticized for events that are beyond your control, such as the timing of recovery after a devastating storm or having your profession questioned based on the negative actions taken by a single officer who makes regional or national news.

While it is a good idea for you to be informed and to monitor the news, it is equally important to take care of your mental health in the process. Some actions you can take include the following:

- Limit your daily intake of the news. Checking the news in the morning and again after dinner will help you stay informed without overloading your day with information.
- Be selective about where you get information. Rather than viewing the news on social media sites, go directly to a news organization's site and view its content. Ideally, you should pick a handful of news outlets with varying perspectives and compare the content for overlap, which usually reflects the most accurate information about an event.
- Get off of social media or limit the time you spend on it. This action is especially important when people are reposting stories that cover traumatic events or that are unfairly critical of law enforcement. These posts can often spread misinformation, and it is possible that some posts originate from fake accounts or unreliable sources, which can distort the truth.
- Talk to friends and family offline if their social media comments and posts are inaccurate. It is easy to misunderstand each other online, so having face-to-face conversations about your job or the role of law enforcement in a community can give people a different perspective while helping you understand their points of view.

Being well-informed on current events can help you do your job more effectively, but it does not have to come at the expense of your mental health. Understanding how media, social media, and public opinion works will help you keep all of that information in perspective.

POST-CRITICAL INCIDENT RECOVERY

☑ LE1441.4. Describe the recovery process after experiencing a critical incident

Recovering from a critical incident is a complex and deeply personal process. Because law enforcement officers are subjected to repeat stress and trauma, they are at a higher risk of experiencing mental, physical, and emotional symptoms that directly and indirectly affect their lives. Understand that recovery is not a one-time event but a continuous process that includes building resilience, using agency resources, and seeking help from a licensed mental health professional.

Having resilience does not mean being unaffected by a critical incident; instead, it is the ability to process stress and trauma without becoming overwhelmed by it. You can build resilience by improving and maintaining your physical health, connecting with your support systems, and seeking professional help when you need it. Recall that most agencies provide recovery resources such as EAPs, peer support teams, and mental health services that are designed to offer stress management training, to connect officers with others who have experienced similar trauma, and to refer officers for confidential counseling or crisis intervention.

At times, help from a licensed mental health professional is needed to fully recover from the challenges officers face daily. A licensed mental health professional can provide a safe and confidential space to unpack complex emotions, make sense of negative memories, reduce feelings of shame and guilt, and learn positive coping strategies. It is crucial for you to care for your mental health and wellness due to the frequent exposure to high-pressure situations because it may impact not only your job performance but also your personal relationships, sleep, physical and mental health, and quality of life.

Needing mental health support is never a sign of weakness. It is a smart, professional way to ensure longevity in your career. With the right support, mindset, and commitment to self-care, it is possible to build resilience and have a fulfilling career in law enforcement.

Glossary

A

abandoned vehicle: a vehicle without a known driver or person responsible for the vehicle (Traffic Incidents)

abandonment: a situation involving a parent, legal custodian, or caregiver who, while being able, makes no significant contribution to a child's care and maintenance or has failed to establish or maintain a substantial and positive relationship with a child, or both (Crimes Against Persons)

absorption: the process by which alcohol enters the bloodstream (DUI Traffic Stops)

abuse of an elderly person or disabled adult: an offense in which the suspect knowingly or willfully inflicts intentional physical or psychological injury, commits an intentional act that could reasonably be expected to result in physical or psychological injury, or actively encourages another person to commit an act that results in or could reasonably be expected to result in physical or psychological injury to an elderly person or disabled adult (Crimes Against Persons)

accessory after the fact: a person who gives the principal (the person who commits the offense) any aid with the intent that the principal avoids or escapes detection, arrest, trial, or punishment (Legal)

acting within the scope of employment: the range of reasonable and foreseeable activities that an employee does while carrying out the employer's business (Legal)

active shooter: an individual actively engaged in killing or attempting to kill people in a populated area (Critical Incidents)

actual physical control: being physically in or on the vehicle and having the capability to operate the vehicle, regardless of whether the person is actually operating the vehicle at the time (DUI Traffic Stops)

actual possession: a controlled substance in the hands of or on the suspect, or in a container in the hands of or on the suspect, or so close as to be within ready reach and under the control of the suspect (Crimes Involving Property and Society)

acute stress: a type of stress that is often short-lived and occurs when a person experiences unexpected changes in their life (Introduction to Law Enforcement)

admissibility of evidence: the legal requirements that must be met before a jury can see or hear about evidence (Crime Scene Follow-Up Investigations)

affirmation: a solemn and formal declaration in place of an oath, usually taken to avoid the religious implications of an oath (Interviewing and Report Writing)

aggravated assault: an assault committed with a deadly weapon without intent to kill or with an intent to commit a felony (Crimes Against Persons)

aggravated battery: a battery that intentionally or knowingly causes great bodily harm, permanent disability, permanent disfigurement, or is committed with a deadly weapon (Crimes Against Persons)

aggravated child abuse: when a person either commits aggravated battery on a child; willfully tortures, maliciously punishes, or willfully and unlawfully cages a child; or knowingly or willfully abuses a child, causing great bodily harm, permanent disability, or permanent disfigurement (Crimes Against Persons)

algor mortis: the postmortem cooling of the body (Crimes Against Persons)

alphanumeric code: a communication system that combines letters and numbers that may include officer call signs or vehicle license plate numbers; for example, tag "RVB632" may be spoken as "Romeo Victor Bravo Six Three Two" (Fundamentals of Patrol)

Americans With Disabilities Act (ADA): a federal civil rights law that prohibits discrimination against people with disabilities in all areas of public life (Serving Your Community)

anti-lock braking system (ABS) scuff marks: patterns left by a vehicle with anti-lock brakes when a driver brakes hard (Traffic Crash Investigations)

area of collision (AOC): the location of the first harmful event, or the first damage-producing event in a traffic crash (Traffic Crash Investigations)

arrest: to deprive a person of their liberty by legal authority (Legal)

arrest warrant: a court order authorizing and requiring law enforcement to take the individual named on the warrant into custody to answer for charges specified in the warrant (Legal)

arrestee: a person who is under arrest or who has been arrested (Introduction to Law Enforcement)

assault: a criminal offense in which the offender intentionally and unlawfully threatened, either by word or act, to do violence to the victim; at the time, the offender appeared to have the ability to carry out the threat; and the victim had a well-founded fear that the violence was about to take place (Crimes Against Persons)

autism spectrum disorder (ASD): a type of developmental disorder that is diagnosed in early childhood and continues throughout adulthood and is characterized by language and social development delay and repetitive behaviors (Serving Your Community)

autonomous vehicle: a vehicle equipped with technology that senses the environment and allows the vehicle to move on the road without a person actively controlling or monitoring, such as a driverless, self-driving, or robotic car (Traffic Incidents)

B

bailiff: a court deputy who is generally a sworn law enforcement officer and responsible for security in the courtroom (Legal)

baiting: attacking with violence, provoking, or harassing an animal with one or more other animals to train it for fighting or to cause an animal to engage in fights with or among other animals; the use of live animals in the training of racing greyhounds (Crimes Involving Property and Society)

Baker Act: a Florida law that provides people who have a mental illness, or who may harm or neglect themselves or others, with an emergency service and temporary detention for psychiatric evaluation and voluntary or involuntary short-term inpatient treatment (Serving Your Community)

battery: a criminal offense in which a person actually and intentionally touches or strikes a victim against their will or intentionally causes bodily harm to the victim (Crimes Against Persons)

behavioral threat assessment and management (BTAM): a proactive, investigative process used to identify, assess, and manage the risk of targeted violence posed by an identified or identifiable person (Fundamentals of Patrol)

bias: the unfair treatment and attitude toward a group of people; classified as unethical behavior (Introduction to Law Enforcement)

bicycle path: any road or path open to bicycle travel; an open space or a barrier separates a bicycle path from motorized vehicular traffic and is often located either within the highway right-of-way or within an independent right-of-way (Traffic Incidents)

BOLO: a description of a vehicle or suspect; includes any other information that would help identify the suspect (Legal)

breach of duty: an unreasonable failure of the defendant to act in the duty they were obligated to perform (Legal)

breach of the peace or disorderly conduct: an act that corrupts public morals, outrages public sense of decency, affects the peace and quiet of the people who may witness it, or causes a brawl or a fight (Crimes Involving Property and Society)

bribery: to accept something for your benefit that influences your professional conduct or decision-making (Introduction to Law Enforcement)

burglary: the unlawful entry into any structure with the intent to commit a crime inside (Crimes Involving Property and Society)

burglary tools: anything used to gain entry during a burglary (Crimes Involving Property and Society)

C

canvass: an inquiry of all possible sources of information surrounding the incident or crime scene; happens most often when the suspect leaves the scene (Crimes Against Persons)

capias: a legal order for an arrest issued by the clerk of the court at the request of the state attorney's office (Legal)

caregiver: a parent, adult household member, or other person who is responsible for a child's welfare or who might have legal custody of a child; for a disabled adult or elderly person, a person who has been entrusted with or has assumed responsibility for the care of an elderly person or disabled adult and their property (Crimes Against Persons)

carjacking: robbing of a person of their vehicle to permanently or temporarily deprive the victim of their motor vehicle and take it for the subject's own or someone else's use by using force, violence, assault, or by placing the victim in fear during the course of the robbery (Crimes Against Persons)

***Carroll* doctrine:** the principle that an officer may conduct a mobile conveyance search without a warrant even if there may be time to obtain one if there is probable cause to believe that the vehicle contains contraband or evidence of criminal activity (Legal)

case law: the body of law that is formed by the decisions of the court system (Legal)

cause of death: the specific injury or disease that leads to death (Crimes Against Persons)

chain of command: the order of authority within an organization (Introduction to Law Enforcement)

chain of custody: the documentation of everyone who handled evidence as well as when, why, and what changes, if any, were made to the evidence (Crime Scene Follow-Up Investigations)

chemical suicide: a method of committing suicide by mixing two or more easily acquired chemicals; also known as "detergent suicide" (Critical Incidents)

child abuse: knowingly or willfully abusing a child younger than 18 by intentionally inflicting physical or mental injury, committing an intentional act that could reasonably be expected to result in physical or mental injury, or actively encouraging another person to commit an act that results in or could reasonably have been expected to result in physical or mental injury to a child (Crimes Against Persons)

child domestic battery: when a child commits an act of violence against a parent, sibling, or other family member living in the home (Crimes Against Persons)

child neglect: when a caregiver fails to provide food, nutrition, clothing, shelter, medicine, and medical services essential for the well-being of a child, regardless of age (Crimes Against Persons)

child pornography: any image depicting a minor engaging in sexual conduct or any image that has been created, altered, adapted, or modified by electronic, mechanical, or other means, to portray an identifiable minor engaged in sexual conduct; it may include children posing in a lewd and lascivious manner or performing a sexual act (Crimes Against Persons)

civil law: legal action that a person takes to resolve a non-criminal private dispute with another person (Legal)

civil liability: responsibility for a wrongful act or an omission that injures a person or property and most often involves negligence (Legal)

civil rights violation: an unlawful interference with the fundamental rights of another person (Legal)

civil standby: when an officer maintains the peace through officer presence while serving a court order or responding to a call for service (Fundamentals of Patrol)

clerk of the court: an elected official who is responsible for maintaining the court's files and official records and for issuing subpoenas (Legal)

clue: in a DUI investigation, a piece of evidence that suggests impairment; the behaviors observed during the performance of the standardized field sobriety tests (DUI Traffic Stops)

coercion: the use of bribes, threats of force, or intimidation to gain cooperation or compliance (Crimes Against Persons)

cognitive interviewing: an interviewing technique which tries to recreate the event, either physically or psychologically, to enhance memory recall (Interviewing and Report Writing)

color of law: when an officer acts or purports to act in the performance of official duties under any law, ordinance, or regulation (Legal)

communication: the exchange of verbal and non-verbal messages (Communication)

compassion fatigue: the emotional exhaustion that comes from caring for others in emotional distress on a long-term basis (Introduction to Law Enforcement)

compensatory damages: monetary awards designed to compensate for the actual property damage, harm, or injury that the plaintiff suffers (Legal)

complainant: a person who reports a crime or alleges that a crime has been committed (Introduction to Law Enforcement)

concealment: an object or group of objects that creates a visual barrier between an officer and a threat but may not stop a projectile (Fundamentals of Patrol)

confidential source: a person who provides information in confidence about a crime, either from a sense of civic duty or in the expectation of some personal benefit or advantage, and whose identity is normally not disclosed until required by law (Introduction to Law Enforcement)

conflict of interest: a situation, on or off duty, in which an officer is in a position to personally benefit from actions or decisions made in their official capacity (Introduction to Law Enforcement)

consensual encounter: when an officer has voluntary contact with a person and a reasonable person would feel free to leave, refuse to answer any questions, decline to identify themselves, and ask the officer to leave them alone (Legal)

consent: actively agreeing to do something or giving permission for something to happen; it is intelligent, knowing, and voluntary consent, and does not include submission by coercion (Crimes Against Persons)

constructive possession: when a controlled substance is in a place over which the suspect has control, or in which the suspect has concealed it (Crimes Involving Property and Society)

contact officer: the primary officer on a call (Fundamentals of Patrol)

contraband: anything that is illegal to produce, possess, or transport (Legal)

contributing traffic violation: a direct cause or contribution to the traffic crash itself, such as a vehicle running a red light and striking another vehicle (Traffic Crash Investigations)

corrections: the part of the legal system responsible for enforcing punishments and providing rehabilitation services as defined by the court system (Introduction to Law Enforcement)

court administrator: the person responsible for the day-to-day administration of a court system; responsibilities can include arranging facilities and scheduling and facilitating the interaction of the court system with other components of the criminal justice system (Legal)

court reporter: the person responsible for making a record of the proceedings (Legal)

court system: the part of the legal system responsible for the interpretation of laws (Introduction to Law Enforcement)

cover: anything that creates a bullet-resistant barrier between an officer and a threat (Fundamentals of Patrol)

cover officer: the backup officer who is strictly responsible for officer safety concerns at a scene (Fundamentals of Patrol)

crash privilege: the legal right of a driver to provide information during a civil investigation of a traffic crash that prohibits that information from becoming self-incriminating if the civil investigation becomes a criminal investigation (Traffic Crash Investigations)

credible threat: a verbal or non-verbal threat, or a combination of the two, that places someone in reasonable fear for their safety or the safety of their family and friends (Crimes Against Persons)

crime scene: the location that a crime occurred; an area that contains evidence from the crime committed; can be a location, a person, place, or object associated with criminal behaviors (Crime Scene Follow-Up Investigations)

crime scene log: a record that documents the name, rank, and agency of each person entering or leaving a crime scene, the date and time of the person's entry or exit, and the reason the person was at the scene; provides proof of security and validates the evidence collected at a crime scene (Crime Scene Follow-Up Investigations)

criminal gang: a formal or informal ongoing organization, association, or group that has as one of its primary activities the commission of criminal or delinquent acts, and that consists of three or more persons who have a common name or common identifying signs, colors, or symbols including, but not limited to, terrorist organizations, transnational organizations, and hate groups (Serving Your Community)

criminal intent: the conscious decision someone makes to deliberately engage in an unlawful act, or to harm someone else (Legal)

criminal justice: the governmental system that deals with the maintenance and enforcement of criminal laws and includes the structures, functions, and decision-making processes of the agencies that deal with the management and control of crime and criminal offenders (Introduction to Law Enforcement)

criminal law: law that identifies behaviors deemed unacceptable by society and sets punishments for those behaviors (Legal)

criminal liability: the liability that occurs if a person is found guilty of committing a crime and is sentenced to incarceration or other penalties (Legal)

criminal mischief: the willful and malicious damage of property belonging to another person (Crimes Involving Property and Society)

crisis: a time of intense difficulty, trouble, or danger, especially when the affected person feels unprepared and pressured to act or make a decision (Serving Your Community)

critical incidents: events that can put lives at risk and cause major damage to property and the environment; can be natural or the result of human error (Critical Incidents)

crosswalk: an area of a road within an intersection, distinctly marked on the surface to indicate a pedestrian crossing (Traffic Incidents)

cue: a reminder, prompt, or signal to do something, such as take law enforcement action or observe a vehicle more closely (DUI Traffic Stops)

culturally responsive: being open to learning about new cultures, being respectful of cultural differences, and recognizing the important role that culture plays in people's lives (Communication)

curtilage: the enclosed space of ground and outbuildings immediately surrounding a structure (Legal)

custody: when a person is deprived of freedom in a significant way (Interviewing and Report Writing)

cyberstalk: to communicate or cause to be communicated, directly or indirectly, words, images, or language by or through the use of electronic mail or electronic communication to a specific person, causing substantial emotional distress to that person and serving no legitimate purpose; to access the online accounts or internet-connected home electronic systems of another person without that person's permission, causing substantial emotional distress to that person and serving no legitimate purpose (Crimes Against Persons)

D

dating violence: violence between people who have or have had a continuing and significant relationship of a romantic or intimate nature (Crimes Against Persons)

deadly force: any force that is likely to cause great bodily harm or death under s. 776.06, F.S. (Legal)

debris: the loose material spread across the road due to a traffic crash (Traffic Crash Investigations)

deep corners: corners that cannot be visually cleared from a doorway and must be checked first upon entry (Fundamentals of Patrol)

defendant: a person formally accused of committing a crime or a civil wrong in a court proceeding (Introduction to Law Enforcement)

defense attorney: a member of the court system that represents the defendant's case (Legal)

delegation of authority: when a person with authority grants decision-making to another person (Introduction to Law Enforcement)

delusion: a false belief that is firmly held despite obvious proof or evidence to the contrary (Serving Your Community)

deposition: an official court proceeding in which the people involved, with the exception of the defendant, provide separate sworn testimonies regarding the facts of the case to one of the attorneys (defense or prosecutor) before the trial (Legal)

designations: wording printed on a Florida driver license that informs an officer of a person's health condition or public safety status; called informational alerts before 2017 (Traffic Incidents)

detoxification: the process of allowing the body to rid itself of a drug while managing the symptoms of withdrawal (Serving Your Community)

developmental disability: a disorder or syndrome that is attributable to intellectual disability, cerebral palsy, autism, spina bifida, Down syndrome, Phelan-McDermid syndrome, or Prader-Willi syndrome; a disability that manifests before the age of 18, constitutes a substantial handicap, and continues indefinitely (Serving Your Community)

direct evidence: evidence which proves a fact without an inference or presumption and which, if true, conclusively establishes that fact (Crime Scene Follow-Up Investigations)

direct liability: a liability which arises in cases where the officer committed an intentional or negligent tort in violation of the employing agency's orders or policies (Legal)

disabled adult: a person 18 or older who suffers from a condition of physical or mental incapacitation due to a developmental disability, organic brain damage, or mental illness, or who has one or more physical or mental limitations that restrict the person's ability to perform the normal activities of daily living (Serving Your Community)

disabled vehicle: a vehicle that is not drivable (Traffic Incidents)

discrimination: when people choose to act on their prejudices (Introduction to Law Enforcement)

disorderly intoxication: when an intoxicated person endangers the safety of another person or property, or when a person is intoxicated or drinks alcohol in a public place or public transportation, and causes a public disturbance (Crimes Involving Property and Society)

dispatchers: personnel who transmit calls, receive calls for assistance from officers, broadcast information about wanted and missing persons, check records, and perform many other tasks daily to assist patrol officers (Fundamentals of Patrol)

distinct and sustained nystagmus at maximum deviation: when the gaze of the eye has moved as far as it can go toward the shoulder, and no white is visible at the outside of the eye, and you observe the eye jerk when it is held at maximum deviation for a minimum of four seconds (DUI Traffic Stops)

distribution: the process by which the bloodstream carries alcohol to the body's tissues and organs (DUI Traffic Stops)

divided attention: the ability to concentrate on two or more tasks at the same time (DUI Traffic Stops)

documentary evidence: anything written or printed which is offered to prove or disprove facts pertaining to a case (Crime Scene Follow-Up Investigations)

domestic battery by strangulation: a felony battery that is battery against a family or household member or someone with whom the victim is in a dating relationship; the primary aggressor knowingly and intentionally impedes the victim's breathing or blood circulation against their will by applying pressure on the throat or neck, or by blocking the victim's nose or mouth (Crimes Against Persons)

domestic violence: any assault, aggravated assault, battery, aggravated battery, sexual assault, sexual battery, stalking, aggravated stalking, kidnapping, false imprisonment, or any criminal offense resulting in physical injury or death of one family or household member by another family or household member (Crimes Against Persons)

domestic violence protection order: a court order issued by a judge to protect someone against domestic violence (Legal)

driver: a person who is in physical control of a vehicle, or controlling or steering a vehicle in tow (Traffic Incidents)

driving under the influence (DUI): driving or in actual physical control of a vehicle while impaired by alcohol or certain chemical or controlled substances to the extent that the person's normal faculties are impaired (DUI Traffic Stops)

drug paraphernalia: equipment, products, and materials of any kind used or intended for use to plant, propagate, cultivate, grow, harvest, manufacture, compound, convert, produce, process, prepare, test, analyze, pack, repack, store, or contain, conceal, inject, ingest, inhale, or otherwise introduce a controlled substance into the human body (Crimes Involving Property and Society)

drug recognition expert (DRE): an expert specially trained to investigate incidents involving drug-impaired drivers (DUI Traffic Stops)

due process: the principle that laws must be applied fairly and equally to all people, including a person accused of a crime (Legal)

DUI detection process: the process of identifying and gathering evidence to determine whether a subject should be arrested for a DUI violation including three phases; Phase One: Vehicle in motion, Phase Two: Personal contact, and Phase Three: Pre-arrest screening (DUI Traffic Stops)

E

elderly person: a person 60 or older who experiences the infirmities of aging as manifested by advanced age or organic brain damage, or other physical, mental, or emotional dysfunctioning, to the extent that the ability of the person to provide adequately for the person's own care or protection is impaired (Serving Your Community)

elimination: a process by which the body expels alcohol through exhaled breath, sweat, tears, saliva, and urine (DUI Traffic Stops)

elimination prints: the physical evidence that allows a fingerprint analyst to distinguish between prints belonging to the victim or witness and possible suspects (Crime Scene Follow-Up Investigations)

emergency doctrine: a defense against liability that allows an officer to react instinctively to an unforeseen emergency without being held to the same legal standard of care as they would have if they had time to reflect upon the circumstances (Legal)

Emergency Response Guidebook (ERG): a resource that identifies hazardous materials, outlines basic actions for first responders, recommends areas of protective action, and gives responders an initial safety plan (Traffic Crash Investigations)

emergency response plan (ERP): a written plan that describes what an organization will do during various major events (Critical Incidents)

emotional intelligence: the ability to identify and cope with your emotions while also doing the same for the people around you (Introduction to Law Enforcement)

empathy: the ability to understand and care about the emotions of others (Communication)

endangered person: a missing child younger than 18; a missing adult younger than 26; a missing adult older than 26 and believed to be in danger or the victim of criminal activity; or a missing adult older than 18 who meets the criteria for a Silver Alert or Purple Alert; agency policies may also include persons with diminished, developmental, or intellectual capacity, regardless of age (Crimes Against Persons)

endorsement: a special authorization printed on a Florida driver license that permits a driver to operate certain types of vehicles, transport certain types of property, or transport a certain number of passengers (Traffic Incidents)

enhanced penalty: a sentence increased from one classification of offense to a more serious classification due to a prior conviction or the serious nature of the circumstances involved (Legal)

ethics: the standards of conduct based on the principles of right and wrong defined by society (Introduction to Law Enforcement)

evasive action: any action a driver takes to alter the speed or direction of a vehicle to avoid danger or hazard, such as applying the brakes, turning the steering wheel, or moving the vehicle out of the way (Traffic Crash Investigations)

evidence: anything that tends to prove or disprove the existence of a fact (Crime Scene Follow-Up Investigations)

ex parte **order**: a court order issued and signed by a judge that is initiated by one person in the absence of and without representation or notification of other parties (Legal)

exigent circumstances: certain emergencies, such as evidence destruction, an emergency scene, or fresh pursuit, that justifies a warrantless entry (Legal)

exotic animal: any animal that is not native to Florida (Fundamentals of Patrol)

explicit bias: self-awareness of one's dislike of certain groups of people that might be openly displayed in hateful and biased actions (Introduction to Law Enforcement)

exploitation of an elderly person or disabled adult: to knowingly obtain or use, attempt to obtain or use, or conspire with another to obtain or use an elderly person or disabled adult's funds, assets, or property with the intent to temporarily or permanently deprive the victim of the use, benefit, or possession of the funds, assets, or property, or to benefit someone other than the victim; abusing a special relationship with an elderly person or disabled adult that results in an unauthorized seizure or other qualifying social, financial, or physical hardship or neglect suffered by the elderly person or disabled adult (Crimes Against Persons)

explosives: materials or devices designed to release energy very rapidly (Critical Incidents)

extradition: the surrender of a fugitive to another state or nation that has jurisdiction (Fundamentals of Patrol)

eyewitness: a person who can identify another person by sight as someone involved in a criminal proceeding (Crime Scene Follow-Up Investigations)

F

false imprisonment: forcibly, by threat, or secretly confining, abducting, imprisoning, or restraining another person against their will without lawful authority; confining a child younger than 13 years of age against their will and without the consent of their parent or legal guardian (Crimes Against Persons)

family or household member: spouses, former spouses, people related by blood or marriage, people who are residing together as if a family, or who have resided together in the past as if a family, and people who are parents of a child in common regardless of whether they have been married; with the exception of people who have a child in common, the family or household members must be currently residing, or have in the past resided, together in the same single dwelling unit (Crimes Against Persons)

fatal funnels: narrow spaces that restrict movement; typically doorways, hallways, and windows (Fundamentals of Patrol)

fatal injury: an injury resulting in an individual's death within a 30-day period after the traffic crash accident (Traffic Crash Investigations)

felony: any criminal offense committed where the maximum penalty is death or incarceration in a state correctional facility for more than one year (Legal)

felony battery: an offense in which a person actually and intentionally touches or strikes a victim against their will, and causes significant injury, great bodily harm, permanent disability, or permanent disfigurement to the victim; also occurs when someone has a previous conviction for battery. Felony battery does not involve a conscious intent to cause great bodily harm; however, it does include the intent to touch or strike a victim against their will (Crimes Against Persons)

field contact: any person with whom an officer has contact while on patrol, such as concerned citizens, anonymous callers, confidential informants, and other law enforcement officers, who do not necessarily generate an incident report (Crime Scene Follow-Up Investigations)

field sketch: a rough drawing of the scene using simple symbols to indicate the details of the crash (Traffic Crash Investigations)

fight-flight-freeze response: the body's physiological response to a perceived or real threat, which involves the body preparing to fight, flee, or freeze (Introduction to Law Enforcement)

final rest: the point when all movement resulting from a traffic crash comes to a halt (Traffic Crash Investigations)

first harmful event: the first event during a traffic crash that caused injury or property damage; determines the jurisdiction, time, place, and type of crash (Traffic Crash Investigations)

Florida Crime Information Center (FCIC): a database, housed at the Florida Department of Law Enforcement, that provides statewide information on people and property, driver licenses and registration, wanted and missing people, stolen guns, vehicles, and other property, persons' status files and computerized criminal histories, and concealed weapon licenses (Fundamentals of Patrol)

Florida driver license: the license issued to Florida residents who have passed the Department of Highway Safety and Motor Vehicles tests, allowing them to legally drive in Florida (Traffic Incidents)

forfeiture: a civil proceeding in which a law enforcement agency asks the court to transfer ownership of the property from the defendant to the law enforcement agency (Legal)

forgery: falsely making, altering, forging, or counterfeiting a public record, certificate, legal document, bill of exchange, or promissory note, with the intent to injure or defraud someone (Crimes Involving Property and Society)

fraud: the intentional falsification of the truth to induce another person or other entity to part with something of value or to surrender their legal right to it (Crimes Involving Property and Society)

fresh pursuit: the immediate and continuous pursuit by officers of a suspect who is fleeing to avoid arrest (Legal)

fruits of a crime: the objects obtained by the defendant as a result of committing a crime (Crime Scene Follow-Up Investigations)

furrow mark: a type of trench dug by locked tires moving across a soft surface such as gravel, sand, grass, or dirt; it is shallow at the beginning of the skid and deepens with a piling of the surface material in front of the tire at the place where the vehicle finally rests (Traffic Crash Investigations)

G

gases: materials that are neither solid nor liquid at ordinary temperatures; flammable, non-flammable, poisonous, or corrosive materials in containers under pressure (Critical Incidents)

general intent: when a suspect intentionally commits an illegal act prohibited by law without considering the results of the illegal act (Legal)

gouge: a cut into the surface of the road where some part of the vehicle removed the road surface material (Traffic Crash Investigations)

grand theft: the theft of an item with a value of $750 or more, the theft of an item specified by statute regardless of its value, or the theft of an item with a value of $40 or more from a dwelling or from the unenclosed area of land surrounding a dwelling (Crimes Involving Property and Society)

gratuity: anything of value intended to benefit the giver more than the receiver (Introduction to Law Enforcement)

grid: a search pattern often used indoors and overlaps a series of lanes in a cross pattern, making the search more methodical and thorough (Crime Scene Follow-Up Investigations)

H

hallucination: a sensory experience in which a person can see, hear, smell, taste, or feel something that is not there (Serving Your Community)

hazardous material (hazmat): a substance or material that, when released, may cause harm, serious injury, or death to humans and animals, or harm the environment (Traffic Crash Investigations)

hearing impairment: any degree of hearing loss (Serving Your Community)

hearsay: an out of court statement offered for the truth of the matter asserted (Legal)

high-risk traffic stop: a traffic stop that an officer conducts when they reasonably believe that the vehicle was stolen or used in the commission of a felony, or that the occupant(s) of the vehicle has committed, or is committing a forcible felony or a crime of violence, may be armed and dangerous, may have an active violent felony warrant, or pose a higher risk to the officer or the public (Traffic Stops)

hit: an exact match in a database search (Fundamentals of Patrol)

home-invasion robbery: entering a victim's dwelling to commit robbery while the victim is present and aware that a robbery is taking place, and using force, violence, assault, or putting the victim in fear during the robbery (Crimes Against Persons)

homeless: when a person does not have a fixed, regular, and adequate nighttime residence (Serving Your Community)

homicide: the unlawful act of one human taking the life of another; types include murder, justifiable homicide, vehicular homicide, manslaughter, and DUI manslaughter (Crimes Against Persons)

horizontal gaze nystagmus (HGN): an involuntary jerking of the eyes as they move to the side (DUI Traffic Stops)

hostile work environment: a workplace that is difficult or uncomfortable for another person to work in because of a harasser's behavior (Introduction to Law Enforcement)

human trafficking: transporting, soliciting, recruiting, harboring, providing, enticing, maintaining, purchasing, patronizing, procuring, or obtaining another person for the purpose of exploitation of that person (Crimes Against Persons)

I

identity theft: the unlawful possession or use of a person's identifying information to commit acts of fraud, such as apply for credit or loans, acquire services, establish or take over accounts, and commit crimes (Crimes Involving Property and Society)

implicit bias: a bias or prejudice that is present but not consciously held or recognized. To simplify, implicit bias is when someone unconsciously makes judgments about others without being aware that they are making those judgments (Introduction to Law Enforcement)

implied consent: the fact that any person who accepts the privilege of driving a motor vehicle in Florida has consented to submit to testing for drug or alcohol impairment (DUI Traffic Stops)

impound: to tow a vehicle at the direction of law enforcement (Legal)

improvised explosive device (IED): a homemade bomb built and used in ways other than conventional military action (Critical Incidents)

incapacitating injury: a serious bodily injury other than fatal resulting in one or more of the following: severe laceration resulting in exposure of underlying tissues/muscles/organs or significant loss of blood; broken or distorted extremity (arm or leg); crush injuries; suspected skull, chest, or abdominal injury other than bruises or minor lacerations; significant burns (second- and third-degree burns over 10% or more of the body); unconsciousness when taken from the crash scene; paralysis (Traffic Crash Investigations)

incident command system (ICS): a standard, on-scene, all-hazards approach to manage and coordinate the operation of facilities, equipment, personnel, procedures, and communications under a common organizational structure (Critical Incidents)

indirect or circumstantial evidence: evidence that requires an inference or presumption to establish a fact (Crime Scene Follow-Up Investigations)

infant: a child a licensed physician would reasonably believe to be about 30 days old or younger (Crimes Against Persons)

injunction: a court order that requires a person to do or refrain from doing specific acts (Fundamentals of Patrol)

instrumentalities of the crime: the items used by the defendant to commit the crime (Crimes Against Persons)

insubordination: a violation that is often the result of failing to follow orders; it is often determined on an agency basis and may differ depending on the situation (Introduction to Law Enforcement)

intellectual disabilities: types of developmental disabilities that are lifelong conditions characterized by slow intellectual development (Serving Your Community)

interference with custody: to knowingly or recklessly take or entice, or aid, abet, hire, or otherwise procure someone else to take or entice, a minor or incompetent person from the custody of the parent, guardian, public agency, or any other lawful custodian, or when the parent, whether natural or adoptive, stepparent, legal guardian, or relative who has custody takes a minor or incompetent person with malicious intent to deprive the other person of their right to custody (Crimes Against Persons)

interrogation: questioning of a suspect initiated by law enforcement that is directly or indirectly intended to elicit an incriminating response (Interviewing and Report Writing)

intersection: the area within the connection of the lateral curbs or boundary lines of two or more roadways of two highways joined at approximately right angles or any other angle that may connect the two roads; the area where a highway includes two roadways 30 feet or more apart, every crossing of each roadway of the divided highway by an intersecting highway is a separate intersection (Traffic Incidents)

interview: a conversation with a person who has knowledge of an event or individual; not an arrest situation, and the person is free to leave (Interviewing and Report Writing)

investigative stop: a stop that may be made only if an officer has reasonable suspicion that the person stopped was committing, is committing, or is about to commit a law violation; also known as a *Terry* stop (Legal)

J

jargon: the vocabulary of a profession that has meaning only to the people who work in that particular field or profession (Interviewing and Report Writing)

joint possession: two or more suspects jointly possessing an article, exercising control over it (Crimes Involving Property and Society)

judge: the person who presides over the courtroom and decides questions of law (Legal)

jury: a group of citizens who determine questions of fact in a trial (Legal)

juvenile: any person younger than 18; sometimes referred to as a child or youth (Introduction to Law Enforcement)

K

kidnapping: to forcibly, secretly, or by threat confine, abduct, imprison, or restrain another person against their will without lawful authority and with the intent to hold the victim for ransom or reward, or as a shield or hostage, commit or help with the commission of a felony, inflict bodily harm upon or terrorize the victim or another person, or interfere with the performance of any government or political function (Crimes Against Persons)

L

lack of smooth pursuit: when the eye of an impaired driver jerks or bounces as the eye follows a smoothly moving stimulus (DUI Traffic Stops)

laned highway: a road divided into two or more clearly marked lanes for vehicular traffic (Traffic Incidents)

latent prints: a type of fingerprint that is invisible to the naked eye and is the most common evidence found at crime scenes; they result from body residues left behind when the friction ridges of the hands or feet make contact with a surface (Crime Scene Follow-Up Investigations)

lateral communication: communication across a level of the organization to employees on the same level within the chain of command (Introduction to Law Enforcement)

law enforcement: the part of the criminal justice system responsible for the enforcement of laws, maintaining civil order, and the protection of the constitutional rights of everyone within the United States (Introduction to Law Enforcement)

legal custody: a legal status created by a court, which appoints a custodian or guardian, whether an agency or an individual (for example, the Department of Children and Families, or a member of a child's extended family), the right to have physical custody of the child and the right and duty to protect, nurture, guide, and discipline the child, or the right to provide the child with food, shelter, education, and ordinary medical, dental, psychiatric, and psychological care (Crimes Against Persons)

lethality assessment: a tool that first responders use during a domestic violence call to predict the likelihood that a homicide will occur between intimate partners (Crimes Against Persons)

limited access facility: a road adjacent to private property to which the property owners have no right or easement to; however, the owners may have access to the light, air, or view over the property (Traffic Incidents)

live lineup: a procedure that displays a group of people to a victim or eyewitness so they can identify the perpetrator of a crime and eliminate any suspects (Crime Scene Follow-Up Investigations)

lividity: the color changes after death from the settling of blood due to gravity (Crimes Against Persons)

loitering or prowling: to linger or hang around in an area without any apparent purpose for being there in a place, at a time, or in a manner not usual for law-abiding people, and under circumstances that raise alarm or immediate concern for the safety of people or property in the vicinity (Crimes Involving Property and Society)

luring or enticing a child: when a legal adult intentionally lures or entices, or attempts to lure or entice, a child younger than 14 into or out of a structure, dwelling, or conveyance for other than a lawful purpose (Crimes Against Persons)

M

maliciously: wrongfully, intentionally, and without legal justification or excuse, and with the knowledge that injury or damage will or may be caused to another person or their property (Crimes Against Persons)

manner of death: the determination of how the injury or disease leads to death; five manners of death are natural, accidental, suicide, homicide, and undetermined (Crimes Against Persons)

Marchman Act: a law that provides people in need of substance abuse services access to emergency services and temporary protected custody for evaluation and treatment either on a voluntary or involuntary basis (Serving Your Community)

mental illness: an impairment of the mental or emotional processes that exercise the conscious control of one's actions or the ability to perceive or understand reality (Serving Your Community)

mental injury: as related to child abuse, injury to the intellectual or psychological health of a child (Crimes Against Persons)

mentally defective: a mental disease or disorder that renders a person temporarily or permanently incapable of judging their conduct (Crimes Against Persons)

mentally incapacitated: a person temporarily incapable of judging or controlling their own conduct due to the influence of a narcotic, anesthetic, or intoxicating substance administered without their consent or due to any other act committed upon them without their consent (Crimes Against Persons)

metabolism: the biological process by which the body breaks down alcohol for elimination (DUI Traffic Stops)

meth labs: locations where methamphetamine is manufactured (Critical Incidents)

minimal encouragers: brief statements that indicate that a person heard what the interviewee said and wants to hear more; can include non-verbal encouragers, such as nodding one's head (Interviewing and Report Writing)

mirroring: appropriately matching another person's speech patterns, gestures, body language, mannerisms, or posture (Interviewing and Report Writing)

misdemeanor: any criminal offense that is punishable by a term of imprisonment in a county correctional facility of up to one year (Legal)

missing adult: a person 18 or older whose temporary or permanent residence is in Florida, whose location has not been determined, and who is reported missing to a law enforcement agency (Crimes Against Persons)

missing child: a person younger than 18 whose temporary or permanent residence is in Florida, whose location has not been determined, and who is reported missing to a law enforcement agency (Crimes Against Persons)

modus operandi (MO): a Latin term meaning "the mode of operating" that refers to a distinct pattern of criminal behavior or procedure that is used to identify someone (Crime Scene Follow-Up Investigations)

motor vehicle: an automobile, motorcycle, truck, trailer, semitrailer, truck tractor and semitrailer combination, or any other vehicle operated on the roads, used to transport persons or property, and propelled by power other than muscular power; a recreational vehicle designed as temporary living quarters for recreational, camping, or travel use, that is self-motorized or mounted on or pulled by another motor vehicle; not a traction engine, road roller, personal delivery device, special mobile equipment, vehicle that runs only on a track, bicycle, swamp buggy, moped, or motorized scooter (Traffic Incidents)

N

narrative: a detailed account of an incident and events related to the incident (Interviewing and Report Writing)

National Crime Information Center (NCIC): a national database maintained by the Federal Bureau of Investigation that contains information from records of stolen, abandoned, and recovered property, and wanted and missing person files; contains the National Sex Offender Registry and files of people on supervised release, protection orders, foreign fugitives, immigration violators, and known or suspected terrorists or gang members (Fundamentals of Patrol)

neglect of an elderly person or disabled adult: an offense in which the suspect willfully fails to provide the care, supervision, and services necessary to maintain the physical or mental health of an elderly person or disabled adult or fails to make a reasonable effort to protect the victim from abuse, neglect, or exploitation by another person. The abuse may be repeated conduct or a single incident that resulted in a serious physical or psychological injury, or a substantial risk of death (Crimes Against Persons)

negligence: the failure to behave with the level of care that a reasonably prudent person would have exercised under the same circumstances (Legal)

no-approach tactic: used in traffic stops in which the officer calls the driver to the patrol vehicle instead of approaching the vehicle directly (Traffic Stops)

nolo contendere: a legal plea in which a person does not accept or deny responsibility for the charges but agrees to accept punishment (Introduction to Law Enforcement)

non-contributing traffic violation: a violation that has no direct bearing on the cause of the traffic crash, but is discovered during the investigation (Traffic Crash Investigations)

non-criminal violation: an offense for which the only penalty may be a fine, forfeiture, or other civil penalty, also known as a civil infraction (Legal)

non-incapacitating injury: a non-disabling injury, such as a laceration, scrape, or bruise (Traffic Crash Investigations)

non-traffic fatal injury: a fatality that is unrelated to the traffic crash accident, such as a heart attack, natural causes, suicide, or homicide (Traffic Crash Investigations)

non-traffic violation: a criminal offense discovered during the investigation of a traffic crash (Traffic Crash Investigations)

non-verbal communication: any message or signal sent from one person to another without the explicit use of language (Communication)

normal faculties: the ability to see, hear, walk, talk, judge distances, drive an automobile, make judgments, act in emergencies, and normally perform the mental and physical acts of daily life (DUI Traffic Stops)

notice to appear: a written order that may be issued by a law enforcement officer in lieu of a physical arrest requiring a person accused of violating the law to appear in court at a specified date and time (Legal)

numeric or 10-code: a communication system that uses the number "10" before other numbers that represent specific activities; for example, "10-15" often means prisoner in custody (Fundamentals of Patrol)

nystagmus: an involuntary jerking of the eyes (DUI Traffic Stops)

O

oath: a solemn and formal promise, often invoking God as a witness, to tell the truth regarding what one says or intends to do (Interviewing and Report Writing)

observation: the act of recognizing an occurrence using your senses by noticing people, things, or circumstances (Fundamentals of Patrol)

off the record: information not recorded in an official document during a court proceeding (Legal)

offender: a person convicted of a crime in a court of law (Introduction to Law Enforcement)

offense: a breach of law used to broadly describe criminal or non-criminal acts that are punishable under Florida law (Legal)

offset-angle position: a traffic stop position where the officer aligns the center of the patrol vehicle's hood with the taillight of the driver's vehicle, pointing the nose outward into the flow of traffic to provide a potential cover position for the officer if necessary (Traffic Stops)

omission: neglecting to perform what the law or duty requires (Legal)

onset of nystagmus prior to 45°: a clue that a driver has an alcohol concentration above 0.08; the point when the eye is first seen jerking prior to 45° (DUI Traffic Stops)

open house party: a social gathering at a residence that is legal unless minors at the party consume alcohol or drugs (Crimes Involving Property and Society)

ordinances: laws enacted by a municipal (city) or county government (Legal)

overdose: the accidental or intentional use of a dangerously large amount of a substance that can lead to death (Serving Your Community)

P

parole: the release of an inmate from a correctional institution before the conclusion of the inmate's court-imposed sentence (Introduction to Law Enforcement)

patent prints: fingerprints that are visible to the naked eye and are transferred from the friction ridges on fingers by a foreign substance like blood, paint, or dirt (Crime Scene Follow-Up Investigations)

pedestrian: a person on foot on a road, berm, shoulder, or sidewalk (Traffic Incidents)

perimeter: an area of containment surrounding the site of an incident (Fundamentals of Patrol)

perjury: the offense of lying in court after taking an oath (Introduction to Law Enforcement)

person of interest: someone involved in a criminal investigation who has not been arrested or formally accused of a crime (Introduction to Law Enforcement)

petit theft: a theft of property valued at less than $750 (Crimes Involving Property and Society)

phonetic-alphabet: a system of code that uses the letters of the English alphabet to identify letters in voice communication; for example, "A" = Alpha, "B" = Bravo (Fundamentals of Patrol)

photo array: a selection of photographs compiled to show to a victim or eyewitness in a non-suggestive manner for identifying a suspect (Crime Scene Follow-Up Investigations)

photo lineup: a procedure that displays an array of photographs to a victim or eyewitness so they can identify the perpetrator of a crime and eliminate suspects (Crime Scene Follow-Up Investigations)

physical injury: death, permanent or temporary disfigurement, or impairment of any bodily part (Crimes Against Persons)

physical or mobility impairment: a functional limitation that affects one or more of a person's limbs (Serving Your Community)

physical or real evidence: actual objects offered to prove or disprove facts about a case (Crime Scene Follow-Up Investigations)

physically helpless: unconscious, asleep, or for any other reason physically unable to communicate unwillingness to an act (Crimes Against Persons)

physically incapacitated: bodily impaired or handicapped and substantially limited in ability to resist or flee (Crimes Against Persons)

pickup order: a court order to take a juvenile into custody (Legal)

plain touch/feel doctrine: a rule that during a valid stop and frisk allows officers to seize an item they readily recognize as contraband even if it does not feel like a weapon (Legal)

plastic print: a molded or embedded fingerprint made by touching a surface that is impressionable, such as fresh paint, wax, bar of soap, or mud, that you can easily see (Crime Scene Follow-Up Investigations)

plus one rule: assumes that if you find one of something there is another. When you believe that you have removed all passengers from the suspect's vehicle, command any hidden passengers to make themselves known (Traffic Stops)

police legitimacy: when the community views law enforcement as fair, morally obligated to administer the law, and as a legitimate authority of power (Introduction to Law Enforcement)

polydrug use: using drugs from two or more drug categories at the same time (DUI Traffic Stops)

popped or damaged ignition: in a vehicle, popped open plastic housing around the steering column's base and exposed ignition wires pulled forward to start the car without a key; may indicate a stolen vehicle (Traffic Stops)

possession: having personal charge of or exercising the right of ownership, management, or control over the thing possessed (Crimes Involving Property and Society)

possible injury: any injury reported or claimed that is not a fatal injury, suspected serious injury, or suspected minor injury. Examples include momentary loss of consciousness, claim of injury, limping, or complaint of pain or nausea. A possible injury is reported by the individual or is indicated by their behavior, but no wound or injury is readily evident (Traffic Crash Investigations)

post-traumatic stress disorder (PTSD): a pattern of biological stress responses that may develop after a single stressful event or a series of stressful events (Introduction to Law Enforcement)

pre-existing damage: any damage existing on a vehicle before a crash (Traffic Crash Investigations)

prejudice: an unjustified and baseless attitude toward a person because of their membership in a social group (Introduction to Law Enforcement)

pretext stops: stops made by an officer on the basis of a traffic infraction, or if the vehicle shows evidence of an equipment violation, when there is not enough information for reasonable suspicion to make the stop but for the purpose of investigating other, more serious criminal activity (Legal)

principal in the first degree: a person who commits any criminal offense, whether felony or misdemeanor, that aids, abets, counsels, hires, or persuades an offense to be committed or attempted (Legal)

private road or driveway: a privately owned space that owners, including people who have permission from the owners, use for vehicular traffic (Traffic Incidents)

probable cause: a fair probability or reasonable grounds to believe that someone committed a crime, based on the totality of circumstances (Legal)

probable cause affidavit: a sworn, written statement by a law enforcement officer establishing certain facts and circumstances to justify an arrest; also called an arrest affidavit (Legal)

probation: a sentence placing a person under the supervision of a probation officer for a specified length of time instead of confinement (Introduction to Law Enforcement)

procedural due process: the procedures that must be followed to protect a person's rights during a criminal justice process (Legal)

procedural justice: an approach that focuses on carrying out justice in a fair and equitable manner (Introduction to Law Enforcement)

proof beyond a reasonable doubt: the standard used to determine if a criminal defendant is guilty and which holds that based on the facts of the case, there is no other reasonable explanation other than the defendant committed the crime (Legal)

prosecutor: a member of the court system who represents the government's case (Legal)

protection order: a court-issued order that is meant to protect a person, business, company, establishment, or entity and the general public from harm or harassment (Legal)

protective action distance: the distance that people should stay from a hazardous spill (Critical Incidents)

proximate cause: the legal phrase for the link between the breach of duty and the harm caused (damages) (Legal)

psychophysical test: a divided attention test that measures a person's ability to perform mental and physical tasks at the same time (DUI Traffic Stops)

public place: a place where the public has a right to be and to go (Crimes Involving Property and Society)

punitive damages: penalties intended to punish the defendant for their act and to warn others from doing the same act (Legal)

Q

qualified immunity: a defense which protects government officials from liability for civil damages insofar as their conduct does not violate clearly established statutory or constitutional rights of which a reasonable person would have known (Legal)

querying: gathering information by entering or running a search in a database for law enforcement purposes; sometimes called a vehicle check, records check, wants and warrants check (Fundamentals of Patrol)

quid pro quo: a Latin phrase meaning "something for something" (Introduction to Law Enforcement)

R

radio protocol: the customs and regulations for constructing and transmitting radio messages; also includes the proper use of codes and signals, which may be different among agencies and regions (Fundamentals of Patrol)

reaction time: the length of time between the point of perception and the beginning of the evasive action (Traffic Crash Investigations)

reasonable suspicion: the standard of justification needed to support an investigative stop where an officer can articulate, or put into words, the facts that support a suspicion of a law violation (Legal)

recklessness: a class of intent in criminal law that imposes criminal liability on defendants when they did not intend for a behavior to cause the resulting harm (Legal)

report: a written document that gives information about an event, situation, occurrence, or incident (Interviewing and Report Writing)

resilience: the capacity to effectively cope with stress, trauma, and other serious problems (Introduction to Law Enforcement)

resting nystagmus: an involuntary jerking of the eyes as a person looks straight ahead, usually indicating a pathological disorder or high doses of a dissociative anesthetic drug, such as PCP (DUI Traffic Stops)

restriction: the language printed on a Florida driver license limiting a driver from operating certain types of motor vehicles or requiring that they meet certain conditions when driving any motor vehicle (Traffic Incidents)

retail theft: individually, or conspiring with others, to take or carry away merchandise, property, money, or negotiable financial or legal documents; alter or remove a label or price tag; transfer merchandise from one container to another; or remove a shopping cart with the intent to deprive the merchant of the items or their full retail value (Crimes Involving Property and Society)

rigor mortis: the stiffening of body muscles after death (Crimes Against Persons)

risk protection order (RPO): a court order that temporarily restricts a person's access to firearms for up to one year in situations where they pose a significant danger to themselves or others by having a firearm or ammunition in their custody or control, or by purchasing, possessing, or receiving a firearm or any ammunition (Legal)

roadway: a portion of a highway used for vehicular travel that does not include the berm, shoulder, or sidewalk (Traffic Incidents)

robbery: taking money or other property from a person with the intent to either permanently or temporarily deprive the person of their money or other property by using force, violence, assault, or putting the person in fear (Crimes Against Persons)

roll call: a brief operational meeting that officers attend before starting a shift (Fundamentals of Patrol)

routine stress: stress that happens on a daily basis and is a normal part of life (Introduction to Law Enforcement)

rule of sequestration: a judge's order that forbids all witnesses from discussing any aspect of a case with anyone but the involved attorneys (Crime Scene Follow-Up Investigations)

S

scale or identifier: an object used to establish the size and original positions of evidence and draw attention to relevant objects at a crime scene; examples include a ruler, cards with rulers on them, a *Miranda* card, or a dollar bill (Crime Scene Follow-Up Investigations)

search: when an officer examines an area, person, or property for evidence in a place where a person has a reasonable expectation of privacy (Legal)

search warrant: a court order that authorizes law enforcement to conduct a search and seizure (Legal)

secondary explosive device: a bomb placed at the scene of an ongoing emergency response that is intended to cause casualties among responders (Critical Incidents)

secondary trauma: when someone is exposed to the trauma of others and experiences physical or mental impacts (Introduction to Law Enforcement)

seizure: when an officer affects a person's right to have or control their property, usually by physically taking it (Legal)

self-help repossession: the process where a creditor may take possession of the collateral after default without a court order, if the repossession can be done without breach of the peace (Fundamentals of Patrol)

self-stimulating behaviors: coping skills which may allow an overstimulated individual to calm down in a stressful environment or provide an under-stimulated individual with sensory stimulation (Serving Your Community)

sentence fragment: a group of words that lacks a subject, verb, or object (when one is needed) or fails to express a complete thought (Interviewing and Report Writing)

serious bodily injury: an injury to a person, including the driver, which consists of a physical condition that creates a substantial risk of death, serious personal disfigurement, or protracted loss or impairment of the function of a bodily member or organ (Traffic Crash Investigations)

sexting: a criminal offense in which a minor uses a computer or other electronic device, such as a cell phone, to transmit or distribute a nude photograph or video to another minor regardless of whether the minors consented to the act (Crimes Against Persons)

sexual activity: the oral, anal, or vaginal penetration by, or union with, the sexual organ of another or the anal or vaginal penetration of another by any other object; does not include an act done for bona fide medical purposes (Crimes Against Persons)

sexual battery: non-consensual oral, anal, or female genital penetration by, or union with, the sexual organ of another; anal or female genital penetration of another by any other object; does not include an act done for bona fide medical purposes (Crimes Against Persons)

sexual harassment: unwelcome sexual advances, requests for sexual favors, and other verbal or physical conduct of a sexual nature (Introduction to Law Enforcement)

shelter-in-place: the act of taking immediate shelter in a readily accessible location or remaining inside a structure to prevent exposure to a dangerous situation that exists outside of the structure (Critical Incidents)

showup: a one-on-one identification of a suspect in the field by a victim or witness orchestrated by a law enforcement officer a short time after the commission of an offense (Crime Scene Follow-Up Investigations)

sidewalk: the area pedestrians use between the curb or lateral line of a roadway and the adjacent property lines (Traffic Incidents)

sign language interpreter: a person who can both receive and express information and interpret it effectively, accurately, and impartially through sign language (Serving Your Community)

signals: a system of communication that uses the word "signal" before numbers for example, "signal 0" often means an armed person (Fundamentals of Patrol)

situational awareness: the ability to pay attention to what is going on around you; a state of mental responsiveness (Fundamentals of Patrol)

slang: informal, non-standard words often used by regional or specific groups (Interviewing and Report Writing)

sovereign citizen movement: a subculture of society that holds antigovernment beliefs and does not recognize federal, state, or local laws, regulations, or policies (Serving Your Community)

sovereign immunity: a legal concept derived from the common law idea that the king and his agents can do no wrong, which is applied to state and local government agencies and their employees to protect them from personal liability and from being named as defendants in a state civil lawsuit (Legal)

specific intent: the intent to commit a crime and the intent to deprive an owner of something permanently (Legal)

speech impairment: a physiological condition that causes a person to have difficulty in producing sound or understandable language (Serving Your Community)

spiral: a search pattern often used outside in which the searcher begins at a certain point and walks in increasingly larger circles to the outermost boundary of the search area (Crime Scene Follow-Up Investigations)

stalking: unwanted and repeated attention, contact, or harassment by a suspect toward a victim (Crimes Against Persons)

standard of care: the level of competency expected or required when an officer responds to a hazmat incident (Critical Incidents)

standardized field sobriety tests (SFSTs): three accurate and reliable tests to determine alcohol or drug impairment (DUI Traffic Stops)

state road: a highway the Department of Transportation designates as a state-maintained road (Traffic Incidents)

statement: a person's permanent record, oral or written, that explains an incident (Interviewing and Report Writing)

statutory law: written law enacted by Congress, state legislatures, or local governing authorities in response to a perceived need (Legal)

stereotyping: judging a group of people who are different from you based on your own or others' opinions or encounters (Introduction to Law Enforcement)

stigma: a set of negative and unfair beliefs that a society or group of people have about something (Introduction to Law Enforcement)

street or highway: the entire width between the boundary lines of a public space for vehicular traffic; the entire width between the boundary lines of privately owned space for vehicular traffic by the owner or those given permission by the owner; or any limited access road owned or controlled by a special district when a county or municipality exercises traffic control jurisdiction; an area not open to public vehicular traffic, such as a runway, taxiway, ramp, clear zone, or parking lot within the boundaries of an airport owned by the state, county, municipality, or political subdivision; a space used for vehicular traffic, on a controlled access basis, in a mobile home park recreation district, and open to the public (Traffic Incidents)

stress: the physical or emotional reaction to an event, situation or threat (real or perceived) (Introduction to Law Enforcement)

strip/line: a search pattern often used outside in which the search area is divided into lanes that are searched by one or more people in both directions until the entire area has been examined (Crime Scene Follow-Up Investigations)

subject: a known person accused or suspected of committing a crime; a subject may not have actually committed the crime (Introduction to Law Enforcement)

subpoena: a legal order for a person to appear before a court, imposing a penalty if the person does not comply (Legal)

substance abuse: the inappropriate use of a substance that negatively affects the mind and body, adversely impacting a person's social or occupational life and psychological or physical health (Serving Your Community)

substance use: the legal, or illegal, therapeutic, or recreational intake of a substance that can lead to substance abuse (Serving Your Community)

substantive due process: the fair and consistent enforcement of the law (Legal)

sudden unexpected infant death (SUID): a broad term that encompasses sudden infant death syndrome (SIDS), accidental infant suffocation and strangulation in bed, and other infant deaths from unknown causes (Crimes Against Persons)

suicidal ideation: when a person has thoughts about ending their own life (Introduction to Law Enforcement)

suicide by cop: an attempt by a suicidal person to intentionally provoke a deadly force response from a law enforcement officer (Serving Your Community)

suppression hearing: a hearing in which the defense files a motion to suppress or to exclude certain testimony or evidence from a trial, alleging that an officer's actions were improper and violated their client's rights (Legal)

surface mark: any mark created by a vehicle's tire at a crash scene (Traffic Crash Investigations)

suspect/detainee: a person believed to have committed a crime (Introduction to Law Enforcement)

suspicious activity: any activity that is abnormal for a specific time of day in a particular area (Fundamentals of Patrol)

sworn statement: written or oral facts that are stated under oath or penalty of perjury (Interviewing and Report Writing)

T

takedown area: a tactical area of advantage for the officer to handcuff and search the driver or passengers (Traffic Stops)

targeted violence: incidents of violence involving an identifiable person of concern (a perpetrator) who possesses the intent and capability to cause physical harm to an identifiable target (an intended victim); these incidents are goal-directed, premeditated, and predatory (Fundamentals of Patrol)

testimonial evidence: a witness statement that tends to prove or disprove facts about a case (Crime Scene Follow-Up Investigations)

textspeak: language that comes from text messages and digital communications, typically using abbreviations, acronyms, or initials, and usually not following standard grammar, spelling, or punctuation rules (Interviewing and Report Writing)

theft: knowingly obtaining, using, or trying to obtain or use property of another, doing it intentionally to either temporarily or permanently deprive the other person of their right to the property or any benefit from it, and taking the property for one's own use or to the use of any person not entitled to it (Crimes Involving Property and Society)

tort: a civil wrong in which the action or inaction of a person or entity violates the rights of another person or entity (Legal)

traffic crash: a collision involving one or more vehicles in motion causing property damage, personal injury, serious bodily injury, or death (Traffic Crash Investigations)

traffic flow: the general speed and direction of vehicle or pedestrian movement (Traffic Stops)

traffic stop: the lawful and temporary detention of a pedestrian or driver of a vehicle for the purpose of traffic enforcement (Traffic Stops)

transferred intent: a crime that is intended to harm one person and inadvertently causes another person to be hurt instead (Legal)

trauma-informed approach: a method of interviewing that acknowledges an interviewee's trauma and includes maintaining a demeanor that is reassuring, empathetic, and non-judgmental (Interviewing and Report Writing)

traumatic brain injury (TBI): structural and often occurs as the result of sudden injury that causes damage to the brain, frequently resulting from combat; some common signs and symptoms of TBI are loss of balance, slurred speech, disorientation, and irritability (Serving Your Community)

traumatic stress: when a person feels their personal safety or the safety of others is in danger, such as during major events like war, disasters, global pandemics, or incidents of assault (Introduction to Law Enforcement)

trespassing: willfully entering or remaining in a structure or conveyance, without being authorized, licensed, or invited, or after being told to leave by the owner or when a trespassing notice is posted, or having been authorized, licensed, or invited, and warned by the owner or lessee of the premises, or by a person authorized by the owner or lessee, to depart, and refusing to depart (Crimes Involving Property and Society)

tunnel vision: the narrowing of the field of view during a stressful event, such as a vehicle pursuit, foot chase, or armed confrontation; sometimes referred to as funnel vision (Fundamentals of Patrol)

U

unattended vehicle: a vehicle that the driver has left, the engine is still running, the key is still in the ignition, and the brake is not set (Traffic Incidents)

uniform traffic citation (UTC): the citation issued for traffic offenses described in chapters 316, 318, 320, and 322, F.S. (Traffic Incidents)

unknown-risk traffic stop: a type of traffic stop in which the potential risk of the situation is unknown at the time of the stop (Traffic Stops)

uttering: knowingly exhibiting or publishing a document or attempting to cash a check by claiming the check and the endorsement are real (Crimes Involving Property and Society)

V

vehicle: every device in, upon, or by which any person or property is or may be transported or drawn upon a highway, except personal delivery devices, mobile carriers, and devices used exclusively upon stationary rails or tracks (Traffic Incidents)

vehicle-borne improvised explosive device (VBIED): a motor vehicle used as a bomb (Critical Incidents)

verbal communication: what someone says with words (Communication)

vertical communication: the information that flows down through the supervision levels to the lowest levels of the organization (Introduction to Law Enforcement)

vertical gaze nystagmus (VGN): the involuntary jerking of the eyes as they move upward and are held at maximum deviation for a minimum or four seconds; a reliable indicator of a high dose of alcohol or the presence of certain drugs (DUI Traffic Stops)

vicarious liability: when a person or entity is held responsible for the negligent actions of another person, even though the first person or entity was not directly responsible for the injury (Legal)

victim: a person or entity that suffers an injury as a result of a crime (Introduction to Law Enforcement)

violation of probation (VOP): when an offender does not abide by all conditions ordered by the court (Legal)

violation of probation hearing: when an officer accuses an offender of violating their probation or community control and the offender contests the violation (Legal)

vision impairment: a loss or partial loss of sight that cannot be corrected by usual means, such as glasses (Serving Your Community)

voluntary examination: a decision made by a person to willingly seek a psychiatric evaluation for symptoms that may be due to a mental illness (Serving Your Community)

vulnerable adult: a person 18 or older whose ability to perform the activities of daily living or to provide for their own care or protection is impaired due to a mental, emotional, sensory, long-term physical, or developmental disability or dysfunction, brain damage, or the infirmities of aging (Serving Your Community)

W

wheel witness: someone who can place a driver in actual physical control of the vehicle at the time of the crash and who can provide a statement of observations of the crash and driver (DUI Traffic Stops)

withdrawal: the physical and mental symptoms that occur after chronic use of a drug is reduced or stopped (Serving Your Community)

witness: a person who has information about some element of the crime or about evidence or documents related to the crime and who may have heard statements or observed events before, during, or after the crime and may have information about a piece of evidence associated with the crime or knowledge of some document related to the crime (Introduction to Law Enforcement)

writ of replevin: a court order that allows the creditor to take possession of collateral after the borrower defaults (Fundamentals of Patrol)

Z

zone/quadrant: a search pattern often used for vehicles, or an area that is large, in which the area is divided into four different sections and searched using an alternative search pattern (grid, spiral, or strip/line) (Crime Scene Follow-Up Investigations)

Bibliography

Chapter 1   Introduction to Law Enforcement

American Psychological Association. (2018, April 19). Stigma. In *APA Dictionary of Psychology*. Retrieved August 11, 2023, from https://dictionary.apa.org/stigma

Braga, A. A., Brunson, R. K., & Drakulich, K. M. (2019, July). Race, Place, and Effective Policing. *Annual Review of Sociology*, *45*, 535–555. https://doi.org/10.1146/annurev-soc-073018-022541

Center for Justice Innovation. (2017, March 29). *Acknowledging and Managing Implicit Bias* [Video]. YouTube. https://youtu.be/toQCvWpyJXI?si=itSLJ6dwbG3i2169

Center for Justice Innovation. (2014, December 26). *Is Procedural Justice the Secret Ingredient? Tracey L. Meares at Community Justice 2014*. https://www.innovatingjustice.org/publications/procedural-justice-secret-ingredient-tracey-l-meares-community-justice-2014

Conroy, R. J. (2017, November). *Beyond Emotional Intelligence: A Correlational Study of Multifactor Measures of Performance and Law Enforcement Leadership Styles* (No. 10643144) [Doctoral dissertation, Dallas Baptist University]. ProQuest Dissertations Publishing. https://www.proquest.com/openview/920bf36262446dfa2b8493b153a36b2b/1?pq-origsite=gscholar&cbl=18750

Florida Department of Law Enforcement. *Professional Compliance (Disciplinary) Process*. https://www.fdle.state.fl.us/CJSTC/Professional-Compliance

Garner, B. A. (Ed.). (2008). *Black's Law Dictionary* (8th Ed.). Thomson West.

Harvard DCE Professional & Executive Development. (2025, February 24). *How to Improve Your Emotional Intelligence*. Harvard Division of Continuing Education. https://professional.dce.harvard.edu/blog/how-to-improve-your-emotional-intelligence/

Health Policy and Management – JHSPH. (2017, May 23). *Promoting Police Legitimacy and Procedural Justice* [Video]. YouTube. https://youtu.be/3FNHB5ExPZ8?si=KSgZ_wOcpE2t7VbC

Innocence Staff. (2019, November 18). *The Psychological Phenomena That Can Lead to Wrongful Convictions*. Innocence Project. https://innocenceproject.org/news/the-psychological-phenomena-that-can-lead-to-wrongful-convictions/

International Association of Chiefs of Police. (2021, January 1). *Law Enforcement Oath of Honor*. https://www.theiacp.org/sites/default/files/2021-01/246910_IACP_Oath_of_Honor_11x8.5_p1%20%281%29.pdf

International Association of Chiefs of Police. (n.d.) *Law Enforcement Code of Ethics*. https://web.archive.org/web/20240809182415/https://www.theiacp.org/resources/law-enforcement-code-of-ethics

Kahn, K. B., Steele, J. S., McMahon, J. M., & Stewart, G. (2017, April 1). How Suspect Race Affects Police Use of Force in an Interaction Over Time. *Law and Human Behavior*, *41*(2), 117–126. https://doi.org/10.1037/lhb0000218

Kunard, L., & Moe, C. (2015). *Procedural Justice for Law Enforcement: An Overview*. Office of Community Oriented Policing Services. https://portal.cops.usdoj.gov/resourcecenter/RIC/Publications/cops-p333-pub.pdf

Levi, M., Tyler, T., & Sacks, A. (2012, November). The Reasons for Compliance with Law. In R. Goodman, D. Jinks, & A. Woods (Eds.), *Understanding Social Action, Promoting Human Rights*, 70–93. https://doi.org/10.1093/acprof:oso/9780195371895.003.0004

Meares, T., Quattlebaum, M., & Tyler, T. (2018, January). *Principles of Procedurally Just Policing*. The Justice Collaboratory at Yale Law School. https://law.yale.edu/sites/default/files/area/center/justice/principles_of_procedurally_just_policing_report.pdf

Merriam-Webster. (n.d.-a). Implicit Bias. In *Merriam-Webster.com Dictionary*. Retrieved June 25, 2025, from https://www.merriam-webster.com/dictionary/implicit%20bias

Merriam-Webster. (n.d.-b). Stigma. In *Merriam-Webster.com Dictionary*. Retrieved June 25, 2025, from https://www.merriam-webster.com/dictionary/stigma

National Alliance on Mental Illness. (2016, December). *Public Policy Platform of the National Alliance on Mental Illness* (12th ed.). https://www.nami.org/getattachment/About-NAMI/Policy-Platform/Public-Policy-Platform-up-to-12-09-16.pdf

Office for Victims of Crime. (n.d.). *The Vicarious Trauma Toolkit*. U.S. Department of Justice. https://ovc.ojp.gov/program/vtt/introduction

Richardson, L. S. (2017, November 30). Implicit Racial Bias and Racial Anxiety: Implications for Stops and Frisks. *Ohio State Journal of Criminal Law, 15*, 74–88. https://ssrn.com/abstract=3080412

Staats, C., Capatosto, K., Tenney, L., & Mamo, S. (2017). *State of the Science: Implicit Bias Review*. The Ohio State University. https://offices.depaul.edu/academic-affairs/academic-diversity/Documents/State%20of%20Science%20Implicit%20Bias%20Review.pdf

Chapter 2 Communication

RSA. (2013, December 10). *Brené Brown on Empathy* [Video]. YouTube. https://youtu.be/1Evwgu369Jw?si=fYj60EXTRkIsyM-x

Zaki, J. (2015, September 25). *When Cops Choose Empathy*. The New Yorker. https://www.newyorker.com/tech/annals-of-technology/when-cops-choose-empathy

Chapter 3 Legal

Florida Supreme Court. (2019). *Florida Standard Jury Instructions*. https://supremecourt.flcourts.gov/Practice-Procedures/Jury-Instructions

Garner, B. A. (Ed.). (2008). *Black's Law Dictionary*. Thomson West.

National Institute of Justice. (2020, March 5). *Overview of Police Use of Force*. U.S. Department of Justice. https://nij.ojp.gov/topics/articles/overview-police-use-force

Chapter 4 Interviewing and Report Writing

Biggs, M. (2003, January 1). *Just the Facts: Investigative Report Writing* (2nd ed.). Prentice Hall.

Bollinger, P., & Winston, S. (2010, May 9). *Investigative Report Writing Manual for Law Enforcement and Security Personnel*. Police and Fire Publishing.

Hess, J. (2010). *Interviewing and Interrogation for Law Enforcement* (2nd ed.). Routledge. https://doi.org/10.4324/9781315721552

Holtz, L. E. (1997, January 1). *Investigative and Operational Report Writing* (4th ed.). Gould Publications.

Chapter 5 Fundamentals of Patrol

Goldstein, H. (1990). *Problem-Oriented Policing*. McGraw-Hill. https://popcenter.asu.edu/sites/default/files/2025-06/Goldstein_Book.pdf

Chapter 6 Serving Your Community

Brown, L. (n.d.). *Identity-First Language*. Autistic Self Advocacy Network. https://autisticadvocacy.org/about-asan/identity-first-language/?nowprocket=1

Taboas, A., Doepke, K., & Zimmerman, C. (2023). Preferences for Identity-First Versus Person-First Language in a US Sample of Autism Stakeholders. *Autism, 27*(2), 565–570. https://doi.org/10.1177/13623613221130845

Chapter 7 Crimes Against Persons

Center for the Advancement of Human Rights. (2025). Florida State University. https://cahr.fsu.edu/

Florida Council Against Sexual Violence. (2021). https://www.fcasv.org/

Florida Department of Children and Families. (2025). http://www.myflfamilies.com/

Krupinski, E., & Weikel, D. (1986, June 1). *Death from Child Abuse...and No One Heard*. Currier-Davis Pub.

U.S. Department of State. (2019, June). *Trafficking in Persons Report*. https://www.state.gov/wp-content/uploads/2019/06/2019-Trafficking-in-Persons-Report.pdf

Ward, Irene. (1994). *The Ten Commandments of Communicating With People With Disabilities* [Handout]. United Cerebral Palsy Association. https://www.disabilitytraining.com/pdf/tcd-wv.pdf

Chapter 11 Traffic Stops

Florida Statutes. (2011). *Florida Legal Guidelines in Florida Criminal Justice Sourcebook (2010–2011)*. Lexis Nexis Law Enforcement.

U.S. Department of Transportation, National Highway Traffic Safety Administration (NHTSA). (2025). https://www.nhtsa.gov/

Chapter 12 Traffic Crash Investigations

Division of Motorist Services. (2022, December). *Uniform Traffic Citation Procedures Manual*. Florida Department of Highway Safety & Motor Vehicles. https://www.flhsmv.gov/pdf/courts/utc/utccombinedmanual.pdf

Florida Department of Highway Safety & Motor Vehicles. (2015, March). *Instructions for Completing the Florida Uniform Traffic Crash Report Forms* [HSMV 90010S]. https://www.nhtsa.gov/sites/nhtsa.gov/files/documents/crashmanualcomplete2015.pdf

Florida Department of Highway Safety & Motor Vehicles. (n.d.). *Forms*. https://www.flhsmv.gov/resources/forms/

Florida Department of Highway Safety and Motor Vehicles. (2019, February 5). *Uniform Traffic Crash Report Manual* [HSMV 90010S]. https://www.flhsmv.gov/pdf/courts/crash/crashmanualcomplete.pdf

Martinez, L. (1994). Accident Investigation Manual for Patrol Officers (2nd ed.). http://www.tarorigin.com/art/Lmartinez/

Rivers, R.W. (1995). *Training and Reference Manual for Traffic Accident Investigation* (2nd ed.). Institute of Police Technology and Management, University of North Florida. https://archive.org/details/trainingreferenc0000rive/mode/2up

U.S. Department of Transportation. (2020). *Emergency Response Guidebook*. https://www.phmsa.dot.gov/sites/phmsa.dot.gov/files/2021-01/ERG2020-WEB.pdf

Chapter 13 DUI Traffic Stops

Cavenaugh, W. (2016, September 19). *DUI/DWI enforcement*. (6th ed.). LawTech Publishing.

The International Association of Chiefs of Police. (n.d.). *7 Drug Categories*. https://www.theiacp.org/7-drug-categories

National Highway Traffic Safety Administration (NHTSA). (n.d.). *Drug-Impaired Driving*. U.S. Department of Transportation. https://www.nhtsa.gov/risky-driving/drug-impaired-driving#:~:text=Overview,prescribed%20or%20over%20the%20counter.

National Institute on Drug Abuse. (2015). *Trends & Statistics*. U.S. Department of Health and Human Services. https://nida.nih.gov/research-topics/trends-statistics

Chapter 14 Critical Incidents

Federal Bureau of Investigation. (2013, September 16). *A Study of Active Shooter Incidents in the United Sates Between 2000 and 2013*. U.S. Department of Justice. https://www.fbi.gov/file-repository/active-shooter-study-2000-2013-1.pdf/view

Hylton, R. (2017). *Law Enforcement's Role in Responding to Disasters*. https://www.fema.gov/blog/2013-08-12/law-enforcements-role-responding-disasters

Occupational Safety and Health Administration. (n.d.). *Secondary Explosive Devices Guide*. U.S. Department of Labor. https://www.osha.gov/emergency-preparedness/guides/secondary

Schafer, J.A., & Varano, S.P. (2012, October 29). Policing Disasters: The Role of Police in Pre-Disaster Planning and Post-Disaster Response. In M. Deflem (Ed.). *Disasters, Hazards, and Law*: Sociology of Crime, Law, and Deviance, 17, 83–108. Emerald Group Publishing. https://doi.org/10.1108/S1521-6136(2012)0000017008

Schweit, K. W. (2013, May 7). *Addressing the Problem of the Active Shooter*. FBI Law Enforcement Bulletin. https://leb.fbi.gov/2013/may/addressing-the-problem-of-the-active-shooter

U.S. Department of Transportation. (2020). *Emergency Response Guidebook*. https://www.phmsa.dot.gov/sites/phmsa.dot.gov/files/2021-01/ERG2020-WEB.pdf

Statute and F.A.C. Index

This index is provided as a convenient reference for students who want more complete information. Students are not expected to memorize specific statutes or Florida Administrative Code numbers and names unless they appear in the textbook chapters.

Chapter 1 Introduction to Law Enforcement

Ch. 112, pt. VI, F.S., Law Enforcement and Correctional Officers

Ch. 777, F.S., Principal; Accessory; Attempt; Solicitation; Conspiracy

Ch. 837, F.S., Perjury

s. 92.525, F.S., Verification of documents; perjury by false written declaration, penalty

s. 112.313, F.S., Standards of conduct for public officers, employees of agencies, and local government attorneys

s. 112.532, F.S., Law enforcement officers' and correctional officers' rights

s. 815.06, F.S., Offenses against users of computers, computer systems, computer networks, and electronic devices

s. 838.015, F.S., Bribery

s. 838.016, F.S., Unlawful compensation or reward for official behavior

s. 839.20, F.S., Refusal to execute criminal process

s. 839.26, F.S., Misuse of confidential information

s. 914.14, F.S., Witnesses accepting bribes

s. 943.09, F.S., Criminal Justice Professionalism Program

s. 943.10, F.S., Definitions; ss. 943.085-943.255 (definition of a law enforcement officer)

s. 943.13, F.S., Officers minimum qualifications for employment or appointment

s. 943.135, F.S., Requirements for continued employment

s. 943.1397, F.S., Officer certification examinations; fee

s. 944.35, F.S., Authorized use of force; malicious battery and sexual misconduct prohibited; reporting required; penalties

s. 960.001, F.S., Guidelines for fair treatment of victims and witnesses in the criminal justice and juvenile justice systems

11B-27.0011, F.A.C., Moral Character

11B-27.00225, F.A.C., Controlled Substance Testing Procedures

11B-30.009, F.A.C., Applicant Conduct at Test Site and Notice of Protection of Program Privileges

11B-35.001, F.A.C., General Training Programs; Requirements and Specifications

11B-35.0024, F.A.C., Student Performance in Commission-approved High-Liability Basic Recruit Training Courses and High-Liability Instructor Training Courses

Chapter 3 Legal

Ch. 111, F.S., Public Officers: General Provisions

Ch. 790, F.S., Weapons and Firearms

Ch. 893, F.S., Drug Abuse Prevention and Control

Ch. 901, F.S., Arrests and Temporary Detentions

Ch. 933, F.S., Search and Inspection Warrants

s. 394.463, F.S., Involuntary examination

s. 768.28, F.S., Waiver of sovereign immunity in tort actions; recovery limits; civil liability for damages caused during a riot; limitation on attorney fees; statute of limitations; exclusions; indemnification; risk management programs

s. 775.08, F.S., Classes and definitions of offenses

s. 775.081, F.S., Classifications of felonies and misdemeanors

s. 775.082, F.S., Penalties; applicability of sentencing structures; mandatory minimum sentences for certain reoffenders previously released from prison

s. 775.083, F.S., Fines

s. 775.084, F.S., Violent career criminals; habitual felony offenders and habitual violent felony offenders; three-time violent felony offenders; definitions; procedure; enhanced penalties or mandatory minimum prison terms

s. 776.05, F.S., Law enforcement officers; use of force in making an arrest

s. 776.051, F.S., Use or threatened use of force in resisting arrest or making an arrest or in the execution of a legal duty; prohibition

s. 776.06, F.S., Deadly force by a law enforcement or correctional officer

s. 776.07, F.S., Use of force to prevent escape

s. 777.011, F.S., Principal in first degree

s. 777.03, F.S., Accessory after the fact

s. 777.04, F.S., Attempts, solicitation, and conspiracy

s. 790.015, F.S., Nonresidents; reciprocity

s. 790.06, F.S., License to carry concealed weapon or concealed firearm

s. 790.065, F.S., Sale and delivery of firearms

s. 790.25, F.S., Lawful ownership, possession, and use of firearms and other weapons

s. 870.01, F.S., Affrays and riots

s. 901.02, F.S., Issuance of arrest warrants

s. 901.15, F.S., When arrest by officer without warrant is lawful

s. 901.151, F.S., Stop and Frisk Law

s. 901.16, F.S., Method of arrest by officer by a warrant

s. 901.19, F.S., Right of officer to break into building

s. 901.25, F.S., Fresh pursuit; arrest outside jurisdiction

s. 901.211, F.S., Strip searches of persons arrested; body cavity search

s. 932.701, F.S., Short title; definitions (Florida Contraband Forfeiture Act)

s. 932.702, F.S., Unlawful to transport, conceal, or possess contraband articles or to acquire real or personal property with contraband proceeds; use of vessel, motor vehicle, aircraft, other personal property, or real property

s. 932.703, F.S., Forfeiture of contraband article; exceptions

s. 932.704, F.S., Forfeiture proceedings

s. 932.705, F.S., Law enforcement trust funds; Department of Highway Safety and Motor Vehicles deposits

s. 932.7055, F.S., Disposition of liens and forfeited property

s. 932.706, F.S., Forfeiture training requirements

s. 932.7061, F.S., Reporting seized property for forfeiture

s. 932.7062, F.S., Penalty for noncompliance with reporting requirements

s. 960.001, F.S., Guidelines for fair treatment of victims and witnesses in the criminal justice and juvenile justice systems

Fla. R. Crim. P. 3.125, Notice to appear

18 U.S.C. § 242, Deprivation of rights under color of law

18 U.S.C. § 926C, Carrying of concealed firearms by qualified retired law enforcement officers (Law Enforcement Officers Safety Act)

42 U.S.C. § 1983, Civil action for deprivation of rights

Chapter 4 Interviewing and Report Writing

s. 117.10, F.S., Law enforcement and correctional officers; administration of oaths

s. 943.0439, F.S., Interviews of victims, suspects, or defendants with autism or an autism spectrum disorder

s. 943.1718, F.S., Body cameras; policies and procedures

s. 985.101, F.S., Taking a child into custody

Chapter 5 Fundamentals of Patrol

Ch. 83, pt. II, F.S., Florida Residential Landlord and Tenant Act

s. 493.6101, F.S., Definitions

s. 509.141, F.S., Refusal of admission and ejection of undesirable guests; notice; procedure; penalties for refusal to leave

s. 513.13, F.S., Recreational vehicle parks; eviction; grounds; proceedings

s. 539.001, F.S., The Florida Pawnbroking Act

s. 559.917, F.S., Bond to release possessory lien claimed by motor vehicle repair shop

s. 679.601, F.S., Rights after default; judicial enforcement; consignor or buyer of accounts, chattel paper, payment intangibles, or promissory notes

s. 705.185, F.S., Disposal of personal property lost or abandoned on the premises of certain facilities

s. 713.78, F.S., Liens for recovering, towing, or storing vehicles and vessels

s. 812.014, F.S., Theft

s. 843.01, F.S., Resisting, obstructing, or opposing by offering or doing violence to legally authorized person, police canine, or police horse

s. 843.02, F.S., Resisting officer without violence to his or her person

s. 843.06, F.S., Neglect or refusal to aid peace officers

s. 856.011, F.S., Disorderly intoxication

s. 870.01, F.S., Affrays and riots

s. 870.02, F.S., Unlawful assemblies

s. 877.03, F.S., Breach of the peace; disorderly conduct

s. 901.18, F.S., Officer may summon assistance

s. 901.36, F.S., Prohibition against giving false name or false identification by person arrested or lawfully detained; penalties; court orders

s. 944.241, F.S., Incarcerated pregnant women

Chapter 6 Serving Your Community

Ch. 415, F.S., Adult Protective Services

Ch. 825, F.S., Abuse, Neglect, and Exploitation of Elderly Persons and Disabled Adults

s. 393.063, F.S., Definitions (developmental disability)

s. 394.455, F.S., Definitions (mental illness)

s. 394.463, F.S., Involuntary examination (the Baker Act)

s. 397.675, F.S., Criteria for involuntary admissions, including protective custody, emergency admission, and other involuntary assessment, involuntary treatment, and alternative involuntary assessment for minors, for purposes of assessment and stabilization, and for involuntary treatment (the Marchman Act)

s. 420.621, F.S., Definitions (homeless)

s. 817.535, F.S., Unlawful filing of false documents or records against real or personal property

s. 874.03, F.S., Definitions (criminal gang)

s. 943.0439, F.S., Interviews of victims, suspects, or defendants with autism or an autism spectrum disorder

s. 985.03, F.S., Definitions (child, juvenile, or youth)

Pub. L. No. 101-336, 104 Stat. 327 (codified as amended at 42 U.S.C. §§ 12101–12213 and scattered sections of 47 U.S.C.), Americans with Disabilities Act of 1990

24 C.F.R. § 578.3, Definitions

28 C.F.R. § 35.108, Definition of "disability"

Chapter 7 Crimes Against Persons

Art. I, § 16(b)–(e), Fla. Const., Marsy's Law

Ch. 39, F.S., Proceedings Relating to Children

Ch. 741, F.S., Marriage; Domestic Violence

Ch. 782, F.S., Homicide

Ch. 794, F.S., Sexual Battery

Ch. 800, F.S., Lewdness; Indecent Exposure

Ch. 825, F.S., Abuse, Neglect, and Exploitation of Elderly Persons and Disabled Adults

Ch. 827, F.S., Abuse of Children

s. 39.401, F.S., Taking a child alleged to be dependent into custody; law enforcement officers and authorized agents of the department

s. 119.07, F.S., Inspection and copying of records; photographing public records; fees; exemptions

s. 383.50, F.S., Treatment of surrendered infant

s. 415.1034, F.S., Mandatory reporting of abuse, neglect, or exploitation of vulnerable adults; mandatory reports of death

s. 415.1051, F.S., Protective services interventions when capacity to consent is lacking; nonemergencies; emergencies; orders; limitations

s. 741.28, F.S., Domestic violence; definitions

s. 741.29, F.S., Domestic violence; investigation of incidents; notice to victims of legal rights and remedies; reporting

s. 741.30, F.S., Domestic violence; injunction; powers and duties of court and clerk; petition; notice and hearing; temporary injunction; issuance of injunction; statewide verification system; enforcement; public records exemption

s. 741.31, F.S., Violation of an injunction for protection against domestic violence

s. 741.315, F.S., Recognition of foreign protection orders (out-of-state injunctions)

s. 784.011, F.S., Assault

s. 784.021, F.S., Aggravated assault

s. 784.03, F.S., Battery; felony battery

s. 784.041, F.S., Felony battery; domestic battery by strangulation

s. 784.045, F.S., Aggravated battery

s. 784.046, F.S., Action by victim of repeat violence, sexual violence, or dating violence for protective injunction; dating violence investigations, notice to victims, and reporting; pretrial release violations; public records exemption

s. 784.048, F.S., Stalking; definitions; penalties

s. 784.049, F.S., Sexual cyberharassment

s. 784.08, F.S., Assault or battery on persons 65 years of age or older; reclassification of offenses

s. 787.01, F.S., Kidnapping; kidnapping of child under age 13, aggravating circumstances

s. 787.02, F.S., False imprisonment; false imprisonment of child under age 13, aggravating circumstances

s. 787.025, F.S., Luring or enticing a child

s. 787.03, F.S., Interference with custody

s. 787.04, F.S., Removing minors from state or concealing minors contrary to state agency order or court order

s. 787.06, F.S., Human trafficking

s. 794.011, F.S., Sexual battery

s. 794.05, F.S., Unlawful sexual activity with certain minors

s. 794.052, F.S., Sexual battery; notification of victim's rights and services

s. 794.055, F.S., Access to services for victims of sexual battery

s. 800.03, F.S., Exposure of sexual organs

s. 800.04, F.S., Lewd or lascivious offenses committed upon or in the presence of persons less than 16 years of age

s. 810.14, F.S., Voyeurism prohibited; penalties

s. 812.13, F.S., Robbery

s. 812.131, F.S., Robbery by sudden snatching

s. 812.133, F.S., Carjacking

s. 812.135, F.S., Home-invasion robbery

s. 825.102, F.S., Abuse, aggravated abuse, and neglect of an elderly person or disabled adult; penalties

s. 825.1025, F.S., Lewd or lascivious offenses committed upon or in the presence of an elderly person or disabled person

s. 825.103, F.S., Exploitation of an elderly person or disabled adult; penalties

s. 825.1035, F.S., Injunction for protection against exploitation of a vulnerable adult

s. 827.04, F.S., Contributing to the delinquency or dependency of a child; penalty

s. 827.071, F.S., Sexual performance by a child; child pornography; penalties

s. 836.115, F.S., Cyberintimidation by publication

s. 847.002, F.S., Child pornography prosecutions

s. 847.0138, F.S., Transmission of material harmful to minors to a minor by electronic device or equipment prohibited; penalties

s. 847.0141, F.S., Sexting; prohibited acts; penalties

s. 901.15, F.S., When arrest by officer without warrant is lawful (warrantless arrest, no contact order and injunction violation)

s. 937.0401, F.S., Spectrum Alert

s. 985.031, F.S., Age limitation; exception

18 U.S.C. § 921(32), Definitions

Chapter 8 Crimes Involving Property and Society

Ch. 796, F.S., Prostitution

Ch. 812, F.S., Theft, Robbery, and Related Crimes

Ch. 893, F.S., Drug Abuse Prevention and Control

s. 267.13, F.S., Prohibited practices; penalties (archaeological site protection)

s. 509.151, F.S., Obtaining food or lodging with intent to defraud; penalty

s. 562. 11, F.S., Selling, giving, or serving alcoholic beverages to person under age 21; providing a proper name; misrepresenting or misstating age or age of another to induce licensee to serve alcoholic beverages to person under 21; penalties

s. 562.111, F.S., Possession of alcoholic beverages by persons under age 21 prohibited

s. 569.101, F.S., Selling, delivering, bartering, furnishing, or giving tobacco products to persons under 21 years of age; criminal penalties; defense

s. 569.11, F.S., Possession, misrepresenting age or military service to purchase, and purchase of tobacco products by persons under 21 years of age prohibited; penalties; jurisdiction; disposition of fines

s. 768.139, F.S., Rescue of vulnerable person or domestic animal from a motor vehicle; immunity from civil liability

s. 806.13, F.S., Criminal mischief; penalties; penalty for minor

s. 810.02, F.S., Burglary

s. 810.06, F.S., Possession of burglary tools

s. 810.08, F.S., Trespass in structure or conveyance

s. 810.09, F.S., Trespass on property other than structure or conveyance

s. 812.014, F.S., Theft

s. 812.0145, F.S., Theft from persons 65 years of age or older; reclassification of offenses

s. 812.015, F.S., Retail and farm theft; transit fare evasion; mandatory fine; alternative punishment; detention and arrest; exemption from liability for false arrest; resisting arrest; penalties

s. 812.019, F.S., Dealing in stolen property

s. 817.568, F.S., Criminal use of personal identification information

s. 817.61, F.S., Fraudulent use of credit cards

s. 828.12, F.S., Cruelty to animals

s. 828.122, F.S., Fighting or baiting animals; offenses; penalties

s. 828. 13, F.S., Confinement of animals without sufficient food, water, or exercise; abandonment of animals

s. 831.01, F.S., Forgery

s. 831.02, F.S., Uttering forged instruments

s. 831.09, F.S., Uttering forged bills, checks, drafts, or notes

s. 849.08, F.S., Gambling

s. 856.011, F.S., Disorderly intoxication

s. 856.015, F.S., Open house parties

s. 856.021, F.S., Loitering or prowling; penalty

s. 877.03, F.S., Breach of the peace; disorderly conduct

s. 893.02, F.S., Definitions

s. 893.03, F.S., Standards and schedules

s. 893.13, F.S., Prohibited acts; penalties

s. 893.135, F.S., Trafficking; mandatory sentences; suspension or reduction of sentences; conspiracy to engage in trafficking

s. 893.145, F.S., "Drug paraphernalia" defined

Chapter 9   Crime Scene Follow-Up Investigations

Ch. 90, F.S., Evidence Code

Ch. 119, F.S., Public Records

s. 90.616, F.S., Exclusion of witnesses

s. 92.70, F.S., Eyewitness identification

s. 893.03, F.S., Standards and schedules

s. 914.28, F.S., Confidential informants

s. 918.13, F.S., Tampering with or fabricating physical evidence

s. 943.1718, F.S., Body cameras: policies and procedures

Chapter 10   Traffic Incidents

Ch. 316, F.S., State Uniform Traffic Control

Ch. 318, F.S., Dispositions of Traffic Infractions

Ch. 320, F.S., Motor Vehicle Licenses

Ch. 322, F.S., Driver Licenses

s. 316.027, F.S., Crash involving death or personal injuries

s. 316.061, F.S., Crashes involving damage to vehicle or property

s. 316.172, F.S., Traffic to stop for school bus

s. 316.183, F.S., Unlawful speed

s. 316.187, F.S., Establishment of state speed zones

s. 316.189, F.S., Establishment of municipal and county speed zones

s. 316.1933, F.S., Blood test for impairment or intoxication in cases of death or serious bodily injury; right to use reasonable force

s. 316.1945, F.S., Stopping, standing, or parking prohibited in specified places

s. 316.1955, F.S., Enforcement of parking requirements for persons who have disabilities

s. 316.221, F.S., Taillamps

s. 316.520, F.S., Loads on vehicles

s. 316.605, F.S., Licensing of vehicles

s. 316.610, F.S., Safety of vehicle: inspection

s. 316.646, F.S., Security required; proof of security and display thereof

s. 316.650, F.S., Traffic citations

s. 318.14, F.S., Noncriminal traffic infractions; exception; procedures

s. 320.0605, F.S., Certificate of registration; possession required

s. 320.07, F.S., Expiration of registration

s. 320.0848, F.S., Persons who have disabilities; issuance of disabled parking permits; temporary permits; permits for certain providers of transportation services to persons who have disabilities

s. 320.131, F.S., Temporary tags

s. 322.03, F.S., Drivers must be licensed; penalties

s. 322.04, F.S., Persons exempt from obtaining driver license

s. 322.051, F.S., Identification cards

s. 322.15, F.S., License to be carried and exhibited on demand; fingerprint to be imprinted upon a citation

s. 322.16, F.S., License restrictions

s. 322.221, F.S., Department may require reexamination

s. 322.26, F.S., Mandatory revocation of license by department

s. 322.32, F.S., Unlawful use of license

s. 322.34, F.S., Driving while license suspended, revoked, canceled, or disqualified

s. 322.53, F.S., License required; exemptions

s. 713.78, F.S., Liens for recovering, towing, or storing vehicles and vessels

s. 775.21, F.S., The Florida Sexual Predators Act

s. 943.0435, F.S., Sexual offenders required to register with the department; penalty

Chapter 11 Traffic Stops

Ch. 316, F.S., State Uniform Traffic Control

Ch. 322, F.S., Driver Licenses

s. 316.221, F.S., Taillamps

s. 316.271, F.S., Horns and warning devices

s. 322.15, F.S., License to be carried and exhibited on demand; fingerprint to be imprinted upon a citation

s. 790.06, F.S., License to carry concealed weapon or concealed firearm

Chapter 12 Traffic Crash Investigations

Ch. 316, F.S., State Uniform Traffic Control

s. 316.027, F.S., Crash involving death or personal injuries

s. 316.061, F.S., Crashes involving damage to vehicle or property

s. 316.062, F.S., Duty to give information and render aid

s. 316.063, F.S., Duty upon damaging unattended vehicle or other property

s. 316.066, F.S., Written reports of crashes

s. 316.070, F.S., Exchange of information at scene of crash

s. 322.221, F.S., Department may require reexamination

Chapter 13 — DUI Traffic Stops

Ch. 893, F.S., Drug Abuse Prevention and Control

s. 316.193, F.S., Driving under the influence; penalties

s. 316.1932, F.S., Tests for alcohol, chemical substances, or controlled substances; implied consent; refusal

s. 316.1934, F.S., Presumption of impairment; testing methods

s. 316.1939, F.S., Refusal to submit to testing; penalties

s. 316.650, F.S., Traffic citations

s. 322.01, F.S., Definitions

s. 322.03, F.S., Drivers must be licensed; penalties

s. 322.2616, F.S., Suspension of license; persons under 21 years of age; right to review

s. 322.61, F.S., Disqualification from operating a commercial motor vehicle

s. 322.62, F.S., Driving under the influence; commercial motor vehicle operators

s. 322.63, F.S., Alcohol or drug testing; commercial motor vehicle operators

s. 322.64, F.S., Holder of commercial driver license; persons operating a commercial motor vehicle; driving with unlawful blood-alcohol level; refusal to submit to breath, urine, or blood test

s. 381.986, F.S., Medical use of marijuana

s. 877.111, F.S., Inhalation, ingestion, possession, sale, purchase, or transfer of harmful chemical substances; penalties

49 C.F.R. § 383.51, Disqualification of drivers

Chapter 14 — Critical Incidents

29 C.F.R. § 1910.120, Hazardous waste operations and emergency response

Court Case Index

This index is provided as a reference and convenience for students wishing for more complete information. Students are not expected to memorize case names unless they appear in the textbook.

Chapter 3 Legal

Arizona v. Gant, 556 U.S. 332, 129 S. Ct. 1710 (2009)
Carroll v. United States, 267 U.S. 132 (1925)
Chimel v. California, 395 U.S. 752 (1969)
Draper v. United States, 358 U.S. 307 (1959)
Georgia v. Randolph, 547 U.S. 103 (2006)
Graham v. Connor, 490 U.S. 386 (1989)
Harlow v. Fitzgerald, 457 U.S. 800, 818 (1982)
Hornblower v. State, 351 So. 2d 716 (Fla. 1977)
Illinois v. Gates, 462 U.S. 213, 232 (1983)
Illinois v. Wardlow, 528 U.S. 119, 124 (2000)
McDaniels v. State, No. 1D2023-0533, 2025 WL 2608688 (Fla. 1st DCA Sept. 10, 2025)
Minnesota v. Dickerson, 508 U.S. 366 (1993)
New York v. Belton, 453 U.S. 454 (1981)
Sawyer v. State, 842 So. 2d 310 (Fla. 5th DCA 2003)
Seibert v. State, 923 So. 2d 460 (Fla. 2006)
Steagald v. United States, 451 U.S. 204 (1981)
Tennessee v. Garner, 471 U.S. 1 (1985)
Terry v. Ohio, 392 U.S. 1 (1968)
Thornton v. United States, 541 U.S. 615 (2004)
United States v. Robinson, 414 U.S. 218 (1973)
United States v. Ross, 456 U.S. 798 (1982)
Whren v. United States, 517 U.S. 806 (1996)

Chapter 4 Interviewing and Report Writing

B.M.B. v. State, 927 So. 2d 219 (Fla. 2d DCA 2006)
Brewer v. Williams, 430 U.S. 387 (1977)
J.D.B v. North Carolina, 564 U.S. 261 (2011)
Lee v. State, 985 So. 2d 1210 (Fla. 1st DCA 2008)

Maryland v. Shatzer, 559 U.S. 98 (2010)
Miranda v. Arizona, 384 U.S. 436, 86 S. Ct. 1602 (1966)
Quarles v. State, 290 So. 3d 505 (Fla. 4th DCA 2020)
Ramirez v. State, 739 So. 2d 568 (Fla. 1999)
Rhode Island v. Innis, 446 U.S. 291 (1980)
Stansbury v. California, 511 U.S. 618 (1994)
State v. Roman, 983 So. 2d 731 (Fla. 3d DCA 2008)

Chapter 8   Crimes Involving Property and Society

Cresswell v. State, 564 So. 2d 480 (Fla. 1990)
Harris v. State, 954 So. 2d 1260 (Fla. 5th DCA 2007)
State v. Johnson, 561 So. 2d 1139 (Fla. 1990)
United States v. Sokolow, 490 U.S. 1 (1989)

Chapter 9   Crime Scene Follow-Up Investigations

Riley v. California, 573 U.S. 373 (2014)

Chapter 10   Traffic Incidents

Arizona v. Gant, 556 U.S. 332, 129 S. Ct. 1710 (2009)
New York v. Belton, 453 U.S. 454 (1981)

Chapter 13   DUI Traffic Stops

Berkemer v. McCarty, 468 U.S. 420 (1984)

Index

A

abandoned vehicles, 406
abandonment, concept of, 292–293
abbreviations, 126, 154, 458
absorption (alcohol and the human body), 476
abuse and neglect
    aggravated abuse, 292, 295
    of a child, 291–294
    of an elderly person, 295–298
    transport of victim to safe location, 279
Abuse Hotline, Florida, 294, 298, 309
abusive head trauma, 293
accessory after the fact, 73
active listening, 53, 58
active shooter, 513–514
active voice, 147–148
actual physical control of vehicle, 479–482
actual possession, 343
addiction, 234, 259, 342
administrative law, 64
administrative searches, 91
affidavit, 98, 114, 156–157, 219, 287, 481
affirmation, 127, 135, 137, 384
affray, 339
aggravated abuse, 292, 295
aggravated assault, 280
aggravated battery, 281, 292, 295
aggravated child abuse, 292, 301
aggravated stalking, 289–290
Aging Services Network, 304
alarms, 197, 206–207
alcohol abuse. *See* substance misuse
alcoholic beverages
    human body and alcohol, 476
    investigation of violations related to, 339–341
    possession of by person under, 340, 345
    selling or giving to a person under, 340, 345
algor mortis, 312
alien, 105
alphanumeric code system, 172

Alzheimer's disease, 225, 303–304
AMBER Alert, 303
Americans With Disabilities Act (ADA), 234–235
animals and pets
    complaints about, 195
    service animals, 128, 235
anti-lock braking system (ABS) scuff marks, 455
antisocial personality disorder, 247
anxiety disorders, 246–247
The ARC, 242
archaeological sites, protection of, 329
area of collision (AOC), 453
arrestees
    booking and processing, 218–219
    juveniles as, 218
    pregnant arrestees, 216
arrests
    definition and concept, 96
    documentation of, 219
    during traffic stops, 427–428
    first appearance hearing and, 114
    Fourth Amendment rights and, 67
    implied consent, 480–481, 503
    juvenile records of, 376
    laws of, 96–98
    legal justification levels and, 78–84
    physical custody, 214–215
    probable cause affidavit, 98, 156–157
    search incident to, 91–92
    use of force in, 101–102
    with a warrant, 96
    without a warrant (warrantless), 96–97, 283, 287, 323
assault and battery
    arrests for, 283
    enhancements, 282
    felony battery, 281
    victims' rights brochures, 278
assemblies/groups, 204–205
assumptions and false assumptions, 26
at-collision phase, 452
Attorney General, Florida Office of the, 64

Attorney's Office, U.S., 105
audio recording. *See* recordings
Autism Society of Florida, 244
autism spectrum disorder (ASD), 243–244
autonomous vehicle, 392

B

background investigations, 7
backup officers, 185, 422, 430–431, 434
bailiff, 113, 384
bails and fines, prohibition of excessive, 67
Baker Act (involuntary psychiatric examination), 253–255
basic recruit training program, 7
battery. *See* assault and battery
behavior
    community expectation of behavior of officers, 54
    core communication competencies, 58–60
    professional behavior, 47, 54, 416
    traffic stops and professional behavior, 415–416, 427
    unethical behavior, 21–24
    unprofessional behaviors, 54, 384
    use of radio and electronic devices, 171–173
behavioral threat assessment and management, 186–188
be on the lookout. *See* BOLO
bias
    explicit, 25
    implicit, 25, 60
bicycle path, 393
biking while under the influence, 479
Bill of Rights, U.S. Constitution, 66–68
bipolar disorder (BD), 246
blindness and vision impairments, 236–237
blood alcohol concentration (BAC), 480, 482
blood evidence, 359, 365
blood tests, 503
Blue Alerts, 181, 304
body cameras, 65, 136–137
BOLO, 80
bombs. *See* explosives, explosive devices, and bombs
bond hearing, 115
booking (intake) officer, 218–219
boundaries and personal space, 50
boundary disputes, 64, 200
breach of duty, 76, 104
breach of peace, disorderly conduct, 339

breath alcohol concentration (BrAC), 480–482, 502
breath test operator (BTO), 502
bribery, 21
building searches, 207–209
bullets, recovery of, 368
burglary, 327–328
burglary tools, possession of, 328
bystanders, assistance from, 410

C

calls for service
    approaching the scene and assessment of incident, 178–180
    crisis situations, 249–252
    dangers associated with and officer safety considerations, 168–169, 179–180
    high-priority calls and radio channels for emergency traffic, 173
    non-criminal calls, 189–190
    preserving life first, 273
    preserving scene for investigation, 274–275
cannabis, possession of, 343, 477
canvass, 318, 372
capias, 118, 371
capital felony, 70, 311
caregivers, 128, 226, 292–294, 341
carjacking, 317, 391
Carroll doctrine (mobile conveyance search), 87–88
case law, 64, 80–82, 88–89, 91–92, 99–101
causation or proximate cause, 76
CBRNE hazards, 442
cell phones, 198, 207, 368, 369, 531
Center for Autism and Related Disorders (CARD), 244
cerebral palsy, 240, 260
certification/certified officer, 7–9
chain of command and organizational structure, 14–15
changing hats rule, 469
charges, right to be informed of nature of, 67
chemical suicide, 523
child abduction response team (CART), 177, 305
child abuse or neglect
    DCF role in cases of, 294
    elements of crime, 291, 292
    interviews, 294
    investigations of, 291–294
    related to child to parent domestic battery, 287

reporting requirements, 294
transport of victim to safe location, 294
child custody issues
    A Child Is Missing organization, 305
    court orders related to, 287
    custody exchanges and civil standby, 202–203
    disputes about custody arrangements, 287, 299–300
Children and Families, Department of (DCF)
    abuse or neglect reporting requirements, 294
    autism, 244
    child abuse or neglect cases, role in, 294
    developmental disabilities, persons with, 241
    human trafficking victims, 345
    juveniles, arrest of, 218
    juvenile sexual offender victim, 309
    Marchman Act, 263
    prostitution, 345
    runaway children, 228
child to parent domestic violence, 287
chlorine, 167
circuit courts, 112
circumstantial (indirect) evidence, 349–350
civil disturbances, 202–203
civil infraction (non-criminal violation), 69–70
civil law, 64
civil liability, 103–107
civil processes, 119
Civil Rights Act (Title VII), 24
civil rights violations, 105–106
civil standby, 202–203
clerk of the court, 113
coercion, 79, 308–311
cognitive interviewing, 132
color of law, 105
combustible liquids, 516
command presence, 47
communication
    autism, people with, 244
    barriers to, 51–52
    conflict resolution, 52–53
    crisis situations communication with people in, 251
    definition and concept, 45
    developmental disabilities, people with, 240–241
    dispatch, communication with, 173, 418–419, 429–430
    effective communication, characteristics of, 45–47
    elderly people, communication with, 226
    homeless people, communication with, 232–233
    intellectual disabilities, persons with, 242
    juveniles, communication with, 228
    lateral communication, 15
    non-verbal communication and cues, 48–50
    privileged communication, 351
    suicide situations, 40–41, 255
    traffic stops, communication during, 415–416, 425–426
    vertical communication, 15
    veterans, communication with, 229–230
    vulnerable adults, communication with, 223–224
communications center (dispatch center), 171
community
    definition and concept, 54
    field contacts, 372
    negative perceptions of law enforcement in, 54
community control, 117
community-oriented policing
    community partnerships, 163–164
    definition and concept, 163
compassion fatigue, 42, 249
compensatory damages, 76–77
complainant, 12, 180, 189
computer evidence, 368
Computerized Criminal History (CCH), 175
concealed weapons. *See also* firearms/weapons
concealment, 166–167
confidential informants, 373
confidential information, 21–22, 294
conflict of interest, 22–23
conflict resolution, 52–53
consensual encounters/mere suspicion, 78–79
consent
    definition of, 308
    evictions, 200
    for access to a premise, 297
    implied, 90, 480–481, 503
    interviews, 131, 141
    of a parent or guardian, 90, 141
    searches, 89–90
constitutional law, 63
Constitution, Florida, 63
Constitution, U.S., 63, 66–68
constructive possession, 343

contact officer, 182, 434–435
contraband
    booking arrestees, 219
    controlled substances, 342–343, 409
    definition and concept, 93
    destruction of evidence, 88
    evidence, 86
    fleeing suspects and discard of, 86
    physical custody arrests and search for, 214–215
    plain touch/feel doctrine and seizure of, 81
    plain view and seizure of, 87
    protective search (frisk) of vehicle passenger compartment, 81
    search for, 92
    seizure and forfeiture of, 93
    vehicle inventory, 409
Contraband Forfeiture Act. *See* Florida Contraband Forfeiture Act
contributing traffic violation, 460
controlled substances
    chemical or toxicological evidence of, 369
    drug-impaired driving, 476–477, 479
    human trafficking, and, 311
    laws and regulations related to, 342, 343
    legal defense for possession of, 110
    positive test for and officer discipline, 8
conveyance, 87, 300, 326–327
correctional facilities
    booking and processing arrestees, 218–219
    juveniles in adult facilities, 218
    transporting arrestees to, 215–217
    types of, 11
corrosive substances, 516
counsel
    contact with suspect represented by, 141
    right to and request for during interrogations, 138, 140–141
    right to receive, 67–68
county courts, 111
county law enforcement agencies, 11
court administrator, 113
courtesy, 46
court proceedings and procedures
    bond hearing, 115
    deposition, 21, 92, 115–116, 123, 383, 385
    evidence use during, 116–117
    first appearance hearing, 114
    hearsay/hearsay testimony/hearsay evidence, 114
    objectionable questions, 385
    pretrial meeting, 116, 382
    rule of sequestration, 383–384
    sentencing hearing, 116–117
    speedy and public trial, right to, 67–68
    suppression hearings, 116
    testimony, preparing for and giving, 383–388
    trials, definition and concept, 116
    violation of probation hearing, 117
court reporter, 113, 115, 384
courts of appeal (circuit courts of appeals), U.S., 112
court system, 10, 106, 111–113
cover and concealment, 166–167
cover officer, 182, 434
crash privilege, 468–469
credible threat, 94, 289
crime scene
    chain of command, 357
    chain of custody, 370
    definition, 349
    documentation of, 358–360
    evidence-handling procedures, 361–370
    follow-up investigations, 372
    injured people, questioning of, 356–357
    photographs of, 358–360
    private property as, 354
    public property as, 354
    responding to, 352–353
    searching, 361–362
    search warrant requirements, 85–92
    securing and protecting, 353–354
    separation of people involved, 356
    sexual battery, 307
    statute of limitations, 124
crime scene log, 354
crimes/criminal offenses
    classification of, reclassification, 72, 282
    elements of, 71–72, 74
    intent and, 74–77
    people involved in, identification of, 72–73
    persons, crimes against, 280–301, 306–318
    property, crimes involving, 321–341
    torts compared to, 103–104
    traffic-related, 393, 479–482

vehicles involved in, 408, 469
white-collar crimes, 330–333
criminal gangs. *See* gangs/criminal gangs
criminal justice, 10
Criminal Justice Information Services (CJIS), 175
Criminal Justice Network (CJNet), 177
Criminal Justice Professionalism (CJP) Division, 6
Criminal Justice Standards and Training Commission (CJSTC), 6
criminal justice system, 10
criminal law, 63
criminal liability, 74–77, 103
criminal mischief, 325
crisis and crisis situations
    calls for service related to, 249–252
    communication and interaction with people in crisis, 251
    definition and concept, 250
    documentation of, 264–265
    interventions and referrals, 251–252
    interviews with people involved in, 255, 263
    officer safety and, 257
    transport of person in crisis, 264
crisis intervention team (CIT), 233, 251
cross-examination tactics, 385–388
crosswalk, 393
crowd control, 204–205, 340
culture
    community demographics, cultural sensitivity, and officer response, 55–56
    death notifications and, 193
    interviews and cultural sensitivity, 128
    non-verbal communication and, 50
curtilage, 92
custody
    definition and concept, 139
    information about, release of, 214–215
    interrogations, *Miranda* decision, and, 138–139
    juveniles, procedures for, 218
    physical custody arrests, 214–217
    protective custody, 228, 262–263, 297
cyberstalking, 289–290

D

damaged or popped ignition, 424
dangerous goods, miscellaneous, 516
databases
    access and restrictions, 175
    criminal history information sources, 175
    hit (exact match) confirmation process, 176
    information sources for officers, 174, 176–177
    misuse of information, 175, 177
    outstanding warrant checks, 181, 183
    suspect information, verification of through, 183–184
    traffic stops and checks of driver information, 427
dating violence, 278, 285
DAVID (Driver and Vehicle Information Database), 177
deadly force, 99–102, 110, 257
deafness, 237
death notifications, 193–194
deaths
    infant deaths or sudden unexpected infant deaths (SUID), 315
    investigations of, 312–315
    medical examiner notification, 313
    notifying next of kin, 193–194
    responding to a death, 313–315
    traffic crash involving, 470–471
deep corners, 208–209
defense attorney, 113
delegation of authority, 15
delinquent or dependent child, contributing to a child becoming a, 293
delusion, 246
dementia, 225, 260, 303–304
deposition, 115–116
depression, 28, 34, 38, 246
detention facilities. *See* corrections facilities/detention facilities
detoxification, 260
developmental and intellectual disabilities, 240–242
diabetes
    Americans with Disabilities Act and, 234
    characteristics of diabetic shock and coma, 260
    medical conditions that mimic impairment, 478
dining or lodging establishment, theft crimes from, 322
direct liability, 106
disabilities, people with. *See also* developmental and intellectual disabilities
    abuse or neglect of, 295–296
    ADA requirements and interaction with, 234–235
    physical impairments, 236–239

disabilities, people with *(continued)*
    service animals, 128, 235
    transporting an arrestee with disabilities, 216
disabled adult, 234, 295–298
disasters and emergencies
    environmental hazards and evacuations, 519–520
    incident command system (ICS), 509
    natural disasters, response to, 511–512
disciplinary action, 24, 175
discrimination
    definition and concept, 26
    discriminatory policing, avoidance of, 27
    sexual harassment, 23–24
disengagement (post-collision phase), 452
disorderly conduct. *See* breach of peace, disorderly conduct
disorderly intoxication, 339–340
dispatchers (public safety telecommunicators, PSTs), 171
distribution (alcohol and the human body), 476
district courts of appeal (DCA), 112
district courts, U.S, 112
divided attention, 488, 490–491
DNA evidence, 307, 350, 365
domestic terrorism, 268
domestic violence
    arrest for, 284, 286
    brochures about rights of victims, 278
    child to parent domestic battery, 287
    definition and concept, 284
    documentation of, 287–288
    false imprisonment and, 300
    human trafficking and, 311
    injunctions related to, 287
    interventions and referrals, 285–286
    privileged communications related to, 351
    transport of victim to safe location, 279, 286
double jeopardy, 67, 106
Driver and Vehicle Information Database. *See* DAVID
driver exchange of information, 459
driver licenses
    classes of, 398
    endorsements, restrictions, and designations, 396–398
    FCIC, 174
    format of, 395–398
    informational alerts, 396
    traffic citations related to, 400

driving under the influence. *See* DUI (driving under the influence)
driving under the influence of drugs, 476–477
drug abuse. *See* substance misuse
Drug Enforcement Administration (DEA), 342
drug offenses
    investigation of, 344
    laws related to, 342–343
    possession, 343
drug paraphernalia, 344
drug recognition expert, 504
drug treatment court programs, 260
due process, 67–68
DUI detection process. *See also* standardized field sobriety tests (SFSTs)
    field notes, 483–484
    psychophysical tests, 491
    visual cues, 486–488
DUI (driving under the influence)
    definition of, 479
    medical conditions that mimic impairment, 478
    portable breath test (PBT), 502
    report, 505
DUI offenses
    arrest reports, 505
    DUI manslaughter, 312
duty, 76, 104

E

Elder Affairs, Department of, 226, 304
elderly people
    aggravated abuse, 295
    Alzheimer's disease, 225, 303
    definition of, 225
    exploitation of, 296–297
    Silver Alert, 303–304
electronic evidence, 363, 368–369
electronic sources of information. *See* databases
elimination prints, 368
embezzlement, 323
emergencies. *See* disasters and emergencies
emergency doctrine, 110
emergency medical services (EMS), 171, 448
Emergency Response Guidebook (ERG), 442, 519–520
emergency response plan (ERP), 518
emotional intelligence, 5, 60

employment, off-duty, 22
encroachment, 452
endangered persons. *See* missing and endangered persons
enhanced penalties, 72
Environmental Protection Agency, 517
epileptic episode, 260
Equal Employment Opportunity Commission (EEOC), 24
equal protection under the law, 67, 105
equipment
    emergency notification, 420
    inspection and maintenance of, 164, 168
evacuations, 519–520
evasive action, 452
events/special events
    crowd control, 204–205, 340
evidence
    admissibility of, 350–351
    chain of custody, 370
    triangle of, 363
evidence types
    biological, 363, 365
    chemical or toxicological, 369–370
    contraband, 81
    direct evidence, 349
    documentary, 350, 370
    electronic, 363, 368–369
    fingerprints, 366–368
    hearsay, 114
    impression, 365
    money, 370
    perishable, 359
    physical or real, 350
    testimonial, 350
    trace, 363–364
exercise and wellness program, 169
exigent circumstances, 88–89, 354, 369
exotic animals, 195
ex parte order, 118
explicit bias, 25
exploitation of an elderly person or disabled adult, 296–297
explosive devices, 524–526
extremist groups, 268–270
eyewitness testimony, 349–350

F

false imprisonment, 300
family members, 315
fatal funnels, 208
fatal injury, 448
Federal Bureau of Investigation (FBI), 11, 105, 174
federal court system, 112–113
Federal Emergency Management Agency (FEMA), 510
federal law enforcement agencies, 11
felony battery, 281
felony offenses
    classification of, 69–70
    definition and concept, 69
    disciplinary penalty guidelines, 70
fentanyl, 167, 369–370
fiber analysis, 364
field contacts, 372–373
field notes, 123–125, 483–484, 500
field sketch, 458
field sobriety tests. *See* standardized field sobriety tests (SFSTs)
fields, searches of open, 92
fight-flight-freeze response, 34–35
final rest, 445, 454, 466
fingerprints
    as evidence, 366–368
    computerized criminal history (CCH), 175
firearms/weapons
    as evidence, 368
    legal possession of, 94–95
    risk protection orders, 95
    Second Amendment right, 67
    Terry stops and, 81–82
    traffic stops, 426
fires
    incendiary devices, 525
    vehicle fire, 196–197, 441
    wildfires, 509–511
first aid
    assistance from bystanders, 410
    civil liability related to failure to provide, 104
    well-being checks, 191
first appearance hearing, 114
first-degree felony, 70
first-degree misdemeanor, 69
first harmful event, 443

flammable liquids, 197, 516
flammable solids, 516
flashlight, 87, 164, 180, 207, 367, 444
Florida Administrative Code (F.A.C.), 64
Florida Comprehensive Drug Abuse Prevention and Control Act, 342
Florida Contraband Forfeiture Act, 93
Florida Crime Information Center/National Crime Information Center (FCIC/NCIC)
    access and restrictions, 175
    querying, 176
    sources of information for, 175
Florida Department of Law Enforcement (FDLE), 6, 174
Florida Evidence Code, 349, 351
Florida Highway Patrol (FHP), 303
Florida Residential Landlord and Tenant Act, 200
Florida Sexual Offender and Predator database, 177
Florida's Integrated Criminal History System. *See* FALCON
Florida Statutes
    how to read, 71–72
    training and certification requirements and standards, role in, 6–9
Florida Traffic Crash Report forms, 463
foot patrol, 165
foot pursuit, 212–213
force/use of force
    civil and criminal liability related to, 104
    deadly force, 99–102, 110, 257
    preventing escape of arrested person and use of, 102
    reasonableness test of the Fourth Amendment and, 99–101
    suicide by cop, 257
forcible felony, 228
forfeiture, 93
forgery, 330
found property, 143–144, 199
Fourteenth Amendment, U.S. Constitution, 67–68
fraud, 330–332
freedom of speech, press, peaceful assembly, and religion, 66
fresh pursuit, 88–89
fruits of a crime, 350
furrow mark, 456

G

gambling, 345
gangs/criminal gangs, 266–267, 345–346

gases, 516, 522–523
general intent, 75
glass/broken glass as evidence, 206, 323, 353, 363
good faith, acts done in, 110
good-faith exception doctrine, 351
gouge, 454
graffiti (tagging), 267
grammar and writing skills, 145–150
grand theft, 322
gratuity, 22–23
grid search pattern, 361–362
grounds searches, 211–212

H

hallucination, 246
handcuffs
    custody and use of, 139
    investigative (*Terry*) stop and use of, 82
    physical custody arrests, 214–216
    traffic stops and use of, 434–435
    use of on patrol, 183
handicapped parking, 405
hand signs (gang identifiers), 267
harassment, 23–24
hate crimes, 72
hazardous materials (hazmat)
    CBRNE, 442
    definition and identification of, 442
    fentanyl, 167, 369–370
    methamphetamine laboratories (meth labs), 522–523
    placards and labels, 517–518
    public safety and protective action distance, 519–520
    shipping papers and facility documents, 517–518
    traffic crash management, 442
head injuries, 230, 260
hearing and observation, 167
hearing impairments, 237–238, 416
hearsay, 114, 117, 350
highway or street, 392
Highway Safety and Motor Vehicles, Florida. *See also* driver licenses
    Department of (DHSMV) crash reports and forms, 459, 463–467
    Driver and Vehicle Information Database (DAVID), 177, 396
    identification cards issued by, 394
    uniform traffic citation (UTC), 401–402

hit-and-run crash, 469
holding facilities, county and municipal, 11
home-invasion robbery, 316–317
homeless people, 232–233
homicide
    death investigations as homicide investigations, 314
    vehicular homicide, 105, 312, 470–471
horizontal gaze nystagmus (HGN), 491–495
hostile work environment, 23–24
household member, 263, 281, 284, 292
HSMV 90010S (Long, Short, and Update forms), 463–467
HSMV 90011S (Driver Exchange of Information/Driver Report of Traffic Crash), 459
hull identification number (HIN), 176
human trafficking, 310–311, 345–346
hypervigilance, 36, 230

I

identifier (scale), 358
identity theft, 322, 332–333
ignition, popped or damaged (punched-out), 324, 424
impairment
    alcohol and drug, 479
    medical conditions that mimic, 478
    physical, 236–239
implicit bias, 25, 60
impounding a vehicle, 90, 408–409
impression evidence, 363, 365
improvised explosive devices (IEDs), 524–526
incapacitating injury, 447
incendiary devices, 525
incident command system (ICS), 509
incident reports. *See* reports/incident reports
incipient or impending skid, 455
independent administrator, 380–381
indirect or circumstantial evidence, 349–350
infants
    sudden infant death syndrome (SIDS), 315
    sudden unexpected infant death (SUID), 315
injunction
    arrest for violation of, 96–97, 287
    civil disturbances and, 202
    domestic violence and, 287
    InSite, 177
    protection against exploitation of a vulnerable adult, 298
    serving civil processes, 119

instrumentalities of a crime, 275
insubordination, 15
insurance. *See* vehicle insurance
intake (booking) officer, 218–219
intellectual disabilities. *See* developmental and intellectual disabilities
intent, 74–77
interpreters, 135, 193, 238, 416
interrogations, 138–141
intersection
    definitions related to traffic crashes, 393
    directing traffic, 410–411
    legal definition, 393
    traffic stops, 417
interviews
    deception signs, 134
    interviewee behavior and response, 133–135
    location of, 129–130
    Miranda warnings and, 138–141
    people with autism spectrum disorder, 128
    recording, 137
    sworn and written statements, 135–137
    techniques, 132
    trauma-informed approach, 133
    verbal and non-verbal cues, 48, 51
intoxication. *See* DUI (driving under the influence)
inventory searches, 90
investigations
    concept, 273–276
    flow chart of investigative process, 274
    follow-up investigations, 371
    information about, release of, 214–215
    preserving scene for, 273
investigative (*Terry*) stop, 80–82

J

jails, county, 11
jargon, 153–154, 159, 384
joint possession, 343
jurisdiction
    child custody-related court orders, 299–300
    definition and concept, 111
    fresh pursuit and, 88–89
    traffic crash management, 443
jury, 67–68, 116–117
justified under the law, acts, 110

juvenile assessment/detention center, 11
Juvenile Justice, Department of (DJJ), 218
juveniles/children/minors/youths
    arrest, booking, and processing, 218–219
    characteristics of and communication with, 227–228
    contributing to the delinquency or dependency of, 293
    definition of, 11
    interrogations of, 141
    offenders, 227–228
    sexual offenses involving, 308–309
    truant children, 311

K

kidnapping, 299–301

L

labor trafficking, 310–311
landlord and tenant disputes, 200–201
laned highway, 393
lascivious offenses. *See* lewd or lascivious offenses
latent prints, 366–367
lateral communication, 15
law enforcement agencies
    chain of command and organizational structure, 14–15
    county agencies, 11
    delegation of authority, 15
    local agencies, 10
Law Enforcement Code of Ethics, 19–20
Law Enforcement Oath of Honor, 19–20
Law Enforcement Officers Safety Act, 95
laws
    administrative law, 64
    case law, 64
    constitutional law, 63
    criminal law, 63
leading questions, 129
legal justification standards
    consensual encounters, 78–79
    probable cause, 83–84
    proof beyond a reasonable doubt, 84
    reasonable suspicion, 80–82
lewd or lascivious offenses
    elements of crimes, 307–308
    investigations of, 308

liability, 103–110
life felony, 70, 301
limited access facility, 393
line/strip search pattern, 361–362
lineup, 379–381
lip reading, 237
liquids, flammable and combustible, 516
listening, active, 58
lividity, 312–313
lodging or dining establishment, theft crimes from, 322
loitering, 338–339
lost property, 198
luring or enticing a child, 300

M

mail bombs, 524–525
major depressive disorder (MDD), 246
major life activities, 234, 240
manslaughter, 312
Marchman Act, 262–263
marijuana. *See* medical marijuana
Marsy's Law, 277
maximum deviation, 493–495
median, 465
medical marijuana, 342, 477
mental illness and psychiatric disorders
    anxiety disorders, 246–247
    Baker Act (involuntary psychiatric examination), 253–255
    calls for service related to, 247
    communication with people with, 248
    definition and concept, 245
    developmental disabilities, compared to, 245
    intelligence and, 245
    mood disorders, 246
    personality disorders, 247
    thought disorders, 246
mental injury, 291
metabolism (alcohol and body), 476
methamphetamine laboratories (meth labs), 522–523
military ordnance, 524
militias, 270
minimal encouragers, 132
minors. *See* juveniles/children/minors/youths
Miranda decision, 138

mirroring, 132
misdemeanor offenses
    animal cruelty, 334–337
    assault, 280–283
    criminal mischief, 325
    driving with suspended license, 394
    DUI, 479–482
    hit-and-run vehicle crash, 469
    issuing notices to appear for, 97
    petit theft, 322
    possession of drug paraphernalia, 344
    vehicle inventory, 409
    vice crimes, 345
    violation of archaeological sites, 329
    warrantless arrest, 96–97, 283
missing and endangered persons
    AMBER Alerts, 303
    Blue Alerts, 304
    definitions of, 302
    Missing Child Alert, 302–303
    Purple Alerts, 304
    Silver Alerts, 303–304
Missing Endangered Persons Information Clearinghouse (MEPIC), 303
mobile communication devices, 170
mobile conveyance search, 87–88
modus operandi, 374
mood disorders, 246
moral character of officers and recruits, 7–8
motorcycle, 392, 396, 398
motorcycle drivers, visual cues of DUI, 487–488
moving violations, 403
municipal (city) ordinance, 64
municipal law enforcement agencies, 10
murder. *See also* homicide

N

napalm, 525
narcissistic personality disorder, 247
narrative, 151–152, 155–159
National Center for Missing and Exploited Children (NCMEC), 305
National Crime Information Center (NCIC), 174
National Fire Protection Association (NFPA), 518
National Highway Traffic Safety Administration (NHTSA), 491

National Sex Offender Registry, 174
National Suicide Prevention Lifeline, 41, 258
natural disasters, 511–512
negligence, 75–77
neurological impairments, 234
nighttime crash scenes, 444
nolo contendere, 8–9, 116, 403
non-contributing traffic violation, 460
non-custodial transport, 264
non-incapacitating injury, 447
non-moving violations, 393, 403
non-traffic fatal injury, 448
non-traffic violation, 461
normal faculties, 479–480
notes and note taking
    abbreviations, 126, 153–154, 458
    DUI field notes, 483–484
    during interviews, 125–126
    evidence, notes as, 483
notice to appear (NTA), 97, 110
nystagmus, 491–495

O

oath, 135
Oath of Honor, 19–20
objectionable questions, 385
objective reasonableness standard, 100–101
observational skills and techniques, 166–167
obsessive compulsive disorder (OCD), 247
Occupational Safety and Health Administration (OSHA), 520–521
off-duty employment, 22
offenses, categories and classes of, 69–70
officer training program. *See* basic recruit training program
official position, misuse of, 22
offset-angle position, 421–422
off the record information, 116
omission, 104
One Leg Stand (OLS), 499–500
open-ended questions, 52, 129, 131
open house party, 340–341
ordinances, 64
organized crime operations, 345–346
overdose, 259, 369

P

panic attacks, 246–247
paper terrorism (sovereign citizen), 269
parked vehicles and traffic crash management, 469–470
parking violations, 405
Parkinson's disease, 260
parole, 11, 308
partial sight, 236
pat down, 81–82
patent prints, 366
pathway to violence, 187–188
patrols/patrolling. See also backup units/backup officers
    basics of, 163–177
    checking in and out, 170, 173
    safety and survival skills and procedures, 167–168
    suspicious activity, recognition of, 165
pawnbroker, stolen property in possession of a, 199
pedestrian, 392–393, 412, 417
pedophiles, 308
penalties/punishments/sentencing
    civil rights violations, 106
    criminal history and, 175
    cruel and unusual, prohibition of, 67–68
    enhanced sentencing, 72
    misdemeanor offenses, 69–70
    ordinance violations, 69–70
perception
    in procedural justice, 16–17
    of a person in crisis, 250
    of a victim, 133
    point of, 452
    reaction time, 452
    self-awareness, 57, 60
perimeter, 210–211, 353–354
perishable evidence, 359
perjury, 21
personal identification information, 156, 253, 294
personality disorders, 247
personal protective equipment (PPE), 167, 510
personal space and boundaries, 50
person authorized, 326–327
petit theft, 322
phonetic-alphabet system, 172
photo array, 379–381
photographs
    as evidence, 349, 357, 359
    booking and processing arrestees, 219
    crime scene management, 358–360
    photo array and lineup, 379–381
    stolen property, 199
    traffic crash scene, 456–457
photo lineup, 379–381
physical fitness program (CJSTC), 7
physical impairments, 236–239
physical injury, 291
pickup order, 118
plain touch/feel doctrine, 81
plastic prints, 366
plus one rule, 436
police departments, 10
polydrug use, 477
popped or damaged ignition, 424
pornography, 308
portable breath test (PBT), 502
possession
    of a person's identifying information, 332–333
    of burglary tools, 328
    of controlled substances, 110, 343
    of stolen property, 324
    of weapons and firearms, 94–95, 426
    writ of possession, 200
possible injury, 447
post-collision phase (disengagement), 452
post-traumatic stress disorder (PTSD), 36
precedent, 64
pre-collision phase, 452
pre-existing damage, 453
pregnant arrestees, 216
prejudice (bias)
    barrier to communication, 51
    bias-based policing, avoidance of, 26–27
    definition and concept, 26
    hate crimes and, 72
    in court testimony, 384
prescription drug misuse, 342
pretext stops, 82, 93
pretrial meeting, 116, 382
principal in the first degree, 73
prisons, federal and state, 11

privacy
    reasonable expectation of, 67, 85–86, 92
    right to, 78
private records, 376
proactive patrol, 163
probable cause
    definition of, 74
    development of, 83
    legal justification standards, 83
    search and seizure and, 85
probable cause affidavit (arrest affidavit), 98
probation, 11
procedural justice, 16–17
professionalism. *See* behavior
proof beyond a reasonable doubt, 84
property. *See also* stolen property
    abandoned property, search of, 92
    boundaries disputes, 200
    curtilage and open fields, 92
    inventory searches, 90–91
    lost property, 198
    recovered property, 199
    repossession of, 201
    search and seizure, prohibition of unreasonable, 67
    seizure and forfeiture of, 93
prosecutor, 113, 382–383
prostitution, 345
protective action distance, 519
protective custody, 228, 262–263, 297
prowling, 338–339
proximate cause, 76
psychiatric disorders. *See* mental illness and psychiatric disorders
psychophysical test, 491
PTSD. *See* post-traumatic stress disorder
public information officer (PIO), 215
public place, 339–340
public records, 170, 175, 369, 372, 376
public safety
    departments, 10
    telecommunicators (PSTs, dispatchers), 171
punitive damages, 77, 103

Q

quadrant search pattern, 361–362. *See also* zone/quadrant search pattern
qualified immunity, 109–110

questioned document evidence, 370
quid pro quo harassment, 23

R

Racketeer Influenced and Corrupt Organization (RICO) Act, 346
radio communications
    bomb situations and, 528
    conduct and procedures for, 171
    radio channels for emergency traffic, 173
rank structure, 14
reactive patrol, 163
reasonable doubt, proof beyond a, 84
reasonable expectation of privacy (REP), 86
reasonable manner, acts done in a, 110
reasonable suspicion, 80–82
recordings
    body cameras, 136–137
    of interviews, 136–137
    radio transmissions, 173
    reports, in preparing, 151
records, 113, 174–177, 277, 376, 463
recovery agent, 201
repeat violence, 278
reports
    crash reports and forms, 463–467
    incident reports, 371, 376
resisting an officer, 183
resting nystagmus, 492
retail theft, 323
rigor mortis, 312–313
riots, 204
risk protection order (RPO), 95, 118
roadblocks, 446
roadways, 392
robbery, 83–84, 316–318, 321, 327
roll call, 164
routine stress, 33–34
rule of sequestration, 383–384
runaway children, 228, 311

S

safety and survival skills
    approaching the scene and suspects and, 182–184
    cover and concealment, 166–167

directing traffic, 410–412
factors that compromise officer safety, 168–169
foot pursuit, 212–213
observational skills and techniques, 166–167
on patrol, 166–169
situational awareness, 168
traffic crash management, 444–446
traffic stops, 421–426, 432–436
safety data sheet (SDS), 518
scale (identifier), 358
schizophrenia, 246, 260
school buses and moving traffic violations, 404
schools
    trespassing on grounds of, 97, 326
    truant children, 311
scuff mark, 455
search and seizure and search warrants
    cellphones, 369
    civil liability related to, 104
    definition and concept, 85
    exceptions to search warrant requirements, 86–92
    execution of search warrants, 119–120
    exigent circumstances, 88–89, 354, 369
    probable cause and, 85–93
    prohibition of unreasonable, 67
    scope of searches, 92
    seizure and forfeiture, 93
    valid warrants, legal requirements for, 86
search types
    abandoned property, search of, 92
    administrative searches, 91
    consent searches, 89–90
    inventory searches, 90
    search incident to arrest, 91–92
    vehicle searches, 87–88, 91–92
seat belt, 364, 470
secondary explosive devices, 531
second-degree felony, 70
second-degree misdemeanor, 69–70
security checks, 192
seizure disorders, 244
self-awareness, 57, 60
self-de-escalation, 59
self-defense as justifiable use of force, 110
self-help repossession, 201
self-image, projection of positive, 47

self-incrimination, prohibition against compelling, 67–68
self-stimulating behaviors, 243
self-talk strategies, 57
sell/selling, 93, 94, 201, 324, 340, 345
senses and observation, 167
sentencing hearing, 116–117
service animals, 128, 235
sexting, 309
sexual abuse
    juvenile sex offenders, 309
    sexual performance or conduct of a child, 308
sexual assault
    as domestic violence, 284
    evidence, 286, 307
    privileged communications related to, 351
sexual battery
    as a felony, 306
    as domestic violence, 284
    brochures about rights of victims, 278
    definition and elements of, 306
    false imprisonment and kidnapping, 300–301
    initial response to, 307
    interviewing victims, 133
    medical examinations, 307
    of a child, 306, 308, 311
    reporting requirements, 307
Sexual Battery Victims' Access to Services Act, 307
sexual cyberharassment, 290
sexual harassment, 23–24
sexual offenses
    informational alerts on driver license of offenders, 397
    involving children, 308
    juvenile sex offenders, 309
    registry of offenders, 174
sexual organs, exposure of, 339
sexual predators, 308, 397
sexual violence, 278, 284, 300, 306–308
shelter-in-place, 510
showup, 378–379
signals communication, 172
sign language, 128, 237–238
sign language interpreter, 128, 238
Silver Alerts, 303–304
single-vehicle crash, 470
sirens and emergency lights, 178, 247, 420, 422, 431

situational awareness, 168
slang, 153–154, 159, 384
soil, 364–365
solids, flammable, 516
sovereign citizens, 268–270
sovereign immunity, 108
special events. *See* events/special events
specific intent, 75
speech impairment, 239
speed and moving traffic violations, 393, 403
spelling and capitalization of words, 148–149
spiral search pattern, 361–362
spontaneous statements, 139
stalking
    aggravated stalking, 289
    cyberstalking, 289–290
    definition and elements of, 289
    victim brochure, 278
standardized field sobriety tests (SFSTs)
    administering, 491
    horizontal gaze nystagmus (HGN), 491–495
    Miranda warnings and, 480
    One Leg Stand (OLS), 499–500
    Walk and Turn (WAT), 496–498
standard of care, 515
state court system, 111–112
state law enforcement agencies, 11
statements (record of person's account of an incident), 127
State Officer Certification Examination (SOCE), 7
state road, 393
statutory law, 63
stereotyping, 26
stigma, 42
stolen property
    database search on, 176–177
    dealing in (fencing), 324
    handling, 198–199
    possession of by a pawnbroker, 199
    stolen vehicles, 324
Stop and Frisk law, 82
stops. *See also* traffic stops
    investigative (*Terry*), 80–82
    legal justification levels and, 80
    pretext, 82, 93
    suspect information, gathering during, 80

strangulation, domestic battery by, 281
street or highway, 392
stress
    definition and concept, 33
    post-traumatic stress disorder (PTSD), 36
    stress management, 36–37, 536
strip/line search pattern, 361–362
stroke, 260
subpoena, 118
substance abuse. *See also* drug offenses
    compared to substance use, 259
    definition and concept, 259
    driver impairment as cause of crash, 471
    drug treatment court programs, 260
    illnesses and medical conditions that mimic, 260
    Marchman Act, 262–263
    substance abuse awareness, 38–39
    veterans and, 230
substance dependence, 259
substance misuse. *See also* substance abuse
substantial limitation, 234
sudden infant death syndrome (SIDS), 315
sudden unexpected infant death (SUID), 315
suicide situations
    communication and interaction with people at risk for suicide, 256–257
    indicators of suicide risk, 256
    National Suicide Prevention Lifeline, 41, 258
    stress and risk of, 34, 39
    suicide by cop, 257
supplemental (follow-up) reports, 144, 198
suppression hearings, 116
supremacy clause, U.S. Constitution, 63
Supreme Court, Florida, 112
Supreme Court of the United States, 113
surface mark, 455, 458
suspect
    approaching and contacting, 182–184
    definition and concept, 13
    description of, 377, 378
    fleeing, 88–89, 100–101, 212–213
    high-risk traffic stop, 429–431, 435–436
    identity of, developing and establishing, 355, 378–380
    information about, release of, 214
    information gathering about, 374–377

suspect *(continued)*
    interrogating, 139
    modus operandi, 374
    pat down, 81–82, 183, 435
    physical custody arrests, 214–215
    searching for and locating, 377
sworn statements, 135–137

T

takedown area, 432
takedown lights, 420, 431, 433
targeted violence, 186–188
tattoos, 124, 176, 267
TBI. *See* traumatic brain injury (TBI)
TDD (telecommunications device for the deaf), 238
teeth as evidence, 365
10-code system, 172
tenant and landlord disputes. *See also* landlord and tenant disputes
terrorism, 72, 268–269
Terry (investigative) stop, 80–82
testimony
    eyewitness testimony, 349–350
    hearsay, 114
    preparing for and giving, 383–385
    suppression hearings about, 116
texting, 154, 460
theft crimes
    dining or lodging establishment, theft crimes from, 322
    elements of, 321
    grand theft, 322
    investigation of, 321–324
    petit theft, 322
    retail theft, 323
    robbery compared to, 321
    stolen property in custody of a pawnbroker, 199
third-degree felony, 70
thought disorders, 246
threats, credible, 94, 289
tire marks, 455–456
tobacco products, 345
tornadoes, 511
torts, 103–104
totality of circumstances test, 83
touch and observation, 167

towing incidents and procedures, 406–407
toxic materials, 516
toxicological (chemical) evidence, 369–370
traffic control devices, 410, 412
traffic crashes and crash investigations
    assessing scene, 441–443
    completing report, 463–467
    crash management, 439–440
    enforcement action, 460–461
    evidence, 452–458
    information, obtaining, 449
    injuries, 447–448
    Miranda warnings, 469
    returning scene to normal, 462
    securing and preserving scene, 444–446
    unique circumstances, 468–471
traffic, directing, 410–412
traffic flow, 419
traffic stops
    high-risk traffic stop, 429
    traffic law, 392–393
    unknown-risk traffic stop, 417
traffic violations, 393
traffic warning devices and safety equipment, 445
transferred intent, 75
Transportation, Florida Department of (FDOT), 303
trash, search of, 92
trauma-informed approach, 133
traumatic brain injury (TBI), 230
trespassing, 326–327
trials. *See* court proceedings and procedures
tunnel vision, 168

U

unattended vehicles
    definition of, 406
    traffic crash management and, 469–470
unbiased policing, 25
uniform traffic citation (UTC), 401
urinating in public, 339
urine tests, 503
uttering a forged instrument, 330

V

vehicle-borne improvised explosive devices (VBIEDs), 525
vehicle identification number (VIN), 176, 400

vehicle incidents
    abandoned vehicles, 406–407
    fire, vehicle, 196–197, 441
    impounding a vehicle, 406, 409
    parking violations, 405
vehicle insurance, 400
vehicle licensing, 394–400
vehicle registration, 399–400
vehicles
    actual physical control, 479
    canine search of, 88
    definition of, 392
    FLHSMV records on, 177
    frisk of passenger compartment, 81
    impounding to tow yards, 409
    inventory searches, 90
    mobile conveyance search, 87–88
    search incident to arrest, 91–92
    trunk and trunk lid, observation of and touching, 423
vehicle weight limits, enforcement of, 398
vehicular homicide, 312
vertical communication, 15
vertical gaze nystagmus (VGN), 494
vessels, FLHSMV records on, 177
veterans, 229–231
vicarious liability, 107
vicarious trauma, 42
vice crimes, 345
victim
    definition and concept, 13
    interviews with, 133
victims' rights brochures, 277–278
video recording. *See* recordings
vision impairments, 236–237
vulnerable adult, 223–224

W

Walk and Turn (WAT), 496–498
warrantless arrest (probable cause arrest), 96–97
warrants. *See also* search and seizure and search warrants
    arrest warrant, 96
    outstanding warrant checks, 181
weapons. *See* firearms/weapons
well-being checks, 191
Wernicke syndrome, 260
wheel witness, 470, 501
white-collar crimes, 330–333
wildfires, 511
withdrawal, 261
witnesses
    definition and concept, 12
    interviews with, 128–129
    intimidation of, 346
    right to confront, 67
    traffic crash management and, 469–470
writ of replevin, 201
written statements, 135–136

Y

yaw mark, 456

Z

zone/quadrant search pattern, 361–362

www.ingramcontent.com/pod-product-compliance
Lightning Source LLC
LaVergne TN
LVHW061455100526
838390LV00004B/8